Principles and Practice of Resistance Training

Michael H. Stone, PhD
East Tennessee State University

Meg Stone, MS
East Tennessee State University

William A. Sands, PhD
United States Olympic Committee

Human Kinetics

Library of Congress Cataloging-in-Publication Data

Stone, Michael H., 1948-
    Principles and practice of resistance training / Michael H. Stone, Meg Stone, William A. Sands.
        p. cm.
    Includes bibliographical references and index.
    ISBN-13: 978-0-88011-706-7 (hard cover)
    ISBN-10: 0-88011-706-0 (hard cover)
1. Weight training.   2. Weight training--Physiological aspects.   3. Isometric exercise.
4. Isometric exercise--Physiological aspects.   I. Stone, Meg, 1952-   II. Sands, Bill,
1953-   III. Title.
    GV546.S73 2007
    613.7'13--dc22   2006036334

ISBN: 978-0-88011-706-7

Acquisitions Editor: Michael S. Bahrke, PhD; **Developmental Editor:** Renee Thomas Pyrtel; **Managing Editor:** Lee Alexander; **Assistant Editor:** Jillian Evans; **Copyeditor:** Joyce Sexton; **Proofreader:** Erin Cler; **Indexer:** Gerry Lynn Shipe; **Permission Manager:** Dalene Reeder; **Graphic Designer:** Nancy Rasmus; **Graphic Artist:** Kathleen Boudreau-Fuoss; **Photo Manager:** Laura Fitch; **Cover Designer:** Keith Blomberg; **Photographer (interior):** Michael H. Stone; photos on pages 13, 61, 155, and 239 © Getty Images/Stockbyte; **Art Manager:** Kelly Hendren; **Illustrator:** Tammy Page; **Printer:** Total Printing Systems

Printed in the United States of America   10   9   8   7

The paper in this book is certified under a sustainable forestry program.

Human Kinetics
Web site: www.HumanKinetics.com

United States: Human Kinetics, P.O. Box 5076, Champaign, IL 61825-5076
800-747-4457
email: info@hkusa.com

Canada: Human Kinetics, 475 Devonshire Road Unit 100, Windsor, ON N8Y 2L5
800-465-7301 (in Canada only)
email: info@hkcanada.com

Europe: Human Kinetics, 107 Bradford Road, Stanningley, Leeds LS28 6 AT, United Kingdom
+44 (0) 113 255 5665
email: hk@hkeurope.com

Australia: Human Kinetics, 57A Price Avenue, Lower Mitcham, South Australia 5062
08 8372 0999
e-mail: info@hkaustralia.com

New Zealand: Human Kinetics, P.O. Box 80, Mitcham Shopping Centre, South Australia 5062
0800 222 062
e-mail: info@hknewzealand.com

CONTENTS

PREFACE

Collectively the authors have spent more than 100 years dealing with various aspects of strength training and sport conditioning. These 100-plus years have included coaching and teaching as well as conducting considerable research. From a coaching standpoint, all three authors have coached national- and international-level athletes, including Olympians. As coaches we have attempted to use methods and techniques based on sound scientific concepts. From a research standpoint we have investigated strength and conditioning issues ranging from their impact on health parameters to the design of training programs for elite strength-power athletes. Moreover, as researchers, our primary focus has been as sport scientists. As sport scientists we have attempted to investigate physiological, psychological, and biomechanical parameters associated with improved sport performance. As a result of these experiences we believe that we have developed some unique insights concerning adaptations to strength and conditioning and particularly the development of training and monitoring programs. In *Principles and Practice of Resistance Training*, we have presented the material in a manner that challenges the postgraduate but remains coach friendly. The material includes objective, research-based information as well as empirical observation. In cases in which key questions have not been satisfactorily answered, we have offered speculative explanations based on the best available information and data. This approach is meant to stimulate additional observation and research that will eventually offer a clearer understanding and resolution of the problems and issues involved.

The first chapter of *Principles and Practice of Resistance Training* deals with principles of training. This discussion was placed first in the book in order to give the reader a good understanding of principles necessary for understanding sport science, detail the construction of the training process, and provide basic terminology and definitions that pertain to topics covered in the following discussions (parts I-IV). The second six chapters of the book (parts I and II, chapters 2-7) are devoted to basic and applied science, offering the reader appropriate background material and a strong scientific basis for practical application. Part III (chapters 8-11) concerns adaptations to various types of training programs and covers testing, monitoring, and evaluation of these adaptations. Of particular note in part III is observation of the important nature of appropriate monitoring of training programs and how monitoring can result in feedback allowing the coach and athlete to adjust programs so that goals are more effectively and efficiently achieved. Chapters 12 through 14 (part IV) deal with exercise selection, training principles, and theory, and, most important, how to create and develop an effective program. To a great extent each chapter was written in a "stand-alone" manner so that readers may dip in and out of the material as needed.

Although issues such as health-related adaptations to resistance training are dealt with briefly, our primary reason for developing and writing this book was to make contributions to coaching and sport science. In our opinion, these are the most important contributions that a sport scientist can make:

- Provide coaches and athletes with sound theoretical and practical information that can be used in planning and adapting training programs. A scientific background gives the coach and athlete tools that can aid in making choices concerning the monitoring and planning of training.

- Assist coaches and athletes in developing a reasonable knowledge base for interaction with sport scientists. This textbook will also aid sport scientists in understanding aspects of sport and coaching sport that are not normally dealt with in academic programs.

- Inspire sport scientists to greater creativity and productivity.

- Inspire potential sport scientists to consider an experience not easily procured in the normal academic pathways.

We sincerely hope that this book will become one avenue by which readers (as well as the authors) can begin to fulfill these contributions.

ACKNOWLEDGMENTS

While many people contributed to this textbook, we owe a special thanks to our students, colleagues, and the athletes we have coached. The following are among those who made a very special contribution.

The athletes: Carla Garret, Becky Levi, Mike Davis, Donnie Robbins, Jim Kramer, Stuart Yule, Neil Potts, Bruce Robb

The coaches: Kyle Pierce, Paul Fleschler, Robert Morris, John Coffee, Steve Plisk, Dan Wathen, Ken Allen, Greg Marsden

The students and scientists: Jon Carlock, Brian Schilling, Andy Fry, Ron Byrd, Dave Collins, Jay T. Kearney, Harold O'Bryant, Ross Sanders, Travis Triplett, Robert Newton, John Garhammer, Hiroshi Hasagawa, Karen Daigle, Robyn Mason, Greg Haff, Mike Ramsey, Barry Shultz, Keith Henschen, Hester Henderson, Jeni McNeal, Steve Johnson, Mel Siff, Monem Jemni, Lowell Weil, Ron Kipp, Phil Cheetham, Larry Nassar

CHAPTER 1

Introduction

Definitions, Objectives, Tasks, and Principles of Training

Resistance training is a general term that includes different modes and methods of regular exercise. The mode of training can include both machines and free weights. Resistance training comprises training processes that can have the following goals:

- Injury prevention and rehabilitation
- General fitness training
- Cosmetic training (bodybuilding)
- Training for competitive sport

This textbook deals primarily with resistance training for competitive sport. Within this context resistance training includes the strength sports of weightlifting and powerlifting, in which resistance exercise used in training becomes the competition tool, and bodybuilding, in which resistance exercise training is used to create an idealized physique. Additionally, resistance training has become an integral part of training in other sports such as American football, track and field, or tennis. While these sports depend on specific talents and characteristics, such as strength, explosiveness, power, endurance capabilities, and agility, ideally these sports also depend on a training process that develops and maximizes such talents. Resistance training is a primary ingredient in that process—in many sports perhaps the most important ingredient. Therefore, designing a training process becomes paramount. In this chapter we present definitions, terminology, and concepts necessary for the development of the training process and provide a basis for understanding the more detailed and comprehensive information presented in later sections of this text.

Resistance training is multifaceted. Although several models of training have been proposed (Banister 1982, 1991; Banister et al. 1986; Bondarchuk 1988; Calvert et al. 1976; Hugh Morton 1991; Lutz 1990; Morton, Fitz-Clarke, and Banister 1990; Ozolin 1970; Tabachnik and Mekhrikadze 1986; Taranov, Mironenko, and Sergejev 1995), many sports are currently searching for the ideal model of training. A model is a guide, a means of making the real world more manageable and easier to think about. Modeling is extremely important in science, including scientific approaches to training (Estes 1957; Shultz and Sands 1995). This chapter identifies definitions, objectives, tasks, and principles that interact to form a model of training.

Defining Training

Training is the process of preparing an athlete physically, technically, tactically, psychologically, and theoretically for the highest levels of performance (Harre 1982). This contrasts sharply with exercise, which engages people in activities that are not designed to achieve the *highest* levels of performance. Of course, the highest levels of performance are relative. Each individual athlete has a genetic limit or ceiling that cannot legitimately be overcome. What training attempts to do is take athletes as close as possible to their genetic limits of performance by the safest, quickest, and most ethical means possible (Hoberman 1992; Pope, Katz, and Champoux 1988; Yesalis 1993).

Training Objectives

The objectives of training are largely exploitive, but not in a negative sense. Training involves the exploitation of known principles of physics, physiology, psychology, and other areas of performance in order to reach a higher level of capability. The coach and athlete seek to exploit principles of training and performance so that the athlete can achieve as much as possible within the constraints of his or her talents and preparation. The highest possible performance of each athlete is relative to the athlete's unique characteristics and abilities. It is also relative to the age or career status of the athlete, or both. A novice athlete's highest level of performance is considerably lower than the same athlete's after 5 to 10 years of training.

A second component of the objectives of training is optimization (Banister 1982, 1991; Banister and Calvert 1980; Calvert et al. 1976). Optimization of training seeks to achieve an ideal performance capability rather than simply increasing or decreasing some characteristic (Olbrecht 2000). Training loads should be optimized. Increasing training loads does not always result in increased performance (Olbrecht 2000). All other things being equal, an athlete who trains 30 h per week is likely to improve more than an athlete who trains 5 h per week. However, an athlete can also train too much, training more but benefiting less. Thus, there are limits to training loads. If an athlete trains too little, he or she may fail because an opponent worked harder. If an athlete trains too much, he or she may fail because of overtraining, which is often expressed as injury or burnout. Therefore, training is a "Goldilocks" problem (Sands 1991a). The athlete must train neither too hard, nor too little, but to just the right extent.

The concept of training optimization can be broadened to include many dimensions and contexts. For example, the optimal training load for a novice is likely to be quite different from the optimal training load for an elite performer. By optimizing the training load with regard to age, sex, current fitness level, talents, environment, and so forth, the athlete should be able to progress more efficiently and effectively. The objective of identification and implementation of optimum training loads applies particularly to junior athletes who are not mature physically or mentally.

A special objective of training includes the identification of talent and the training of junior athletes (Bloom 1985; Bompa 1985, 1990b; Drabik 1996; Matsudo 1996; O'Brien 1993; Sands 1993). Talent identification and junior athlete training are usually linked by simple temporal order, but they are also linked by the fact that all athletes must develop from lower levels to higher and more refined levels.

It is assumed that identifying talented athletes reduces the time, effort, and cost of athlete development. Presumably an athlete's abilities will be better applied, with the result that the athlete will be directed into sports that are more likely to match his or her particular gifts (Bompa 1985; Drabik 1996; Sands 1993). Many characteristics of athletes are highly heritable and thus can be detected with reasonable precision (Masood 1996).

Special attention should be directed to talent identification as it applies to junior athletes. Junior athletes grow and mature at different rates. Talent identification is a process more than an outcome. Junior athletes require constant monitoring of progress and opportunities to demonstrate newly acquired abilities. Talent identification should be sensitive to the specific context of the athletes being assessed. Training demands and activities should be age appropriate in nature and developmental in focus (Greenspan 1983; Hoberman 1992; Hodge and Tod 1993; Preising 1989; Press 1992). When studying and working with junior athletes, scientists and practitioners must take care not to simply transplant ideas and processes developed for adults.

The objectives of training are wide and variable. Objectives vary relative to the goals of the athlete, coach, training program, and sport system. Identification of objectives for each athlete should be undertaken prior to initiating training, and periodically thereafter to ensure that the training program remains focused on these objectives.

The Main Tasks of Training

Ideally, training sets itself various tasks that lead directly to the achievement of high levels of performance and the objectives of training just outlined. These tasks include the development of personality, fitness, technique, knowledge, healthy lifestyle, and sport-specific tactics. The specific means of accomplishing these tasks should be age, experience, and talent appropriate so that each training program is individualized for each athlete to the extent that each athlete is encouraged to achieve his or her maximum performance.

Personality Development

The first task of training is the development of the personality of the athlete. The athlete's personality, more specifically his or her character, is developed by and through training. Resistance training should attempt to teach discipline, courage, tenacity, and other qualities by and through the training and sport experience. The long and difficult hours of training and conditioning help athletes experience hardship, set goals, work under duress, and ultimately reap the benefits of their efforts. Training experience serves athletes not only in sport, but also throughout their adult lives. Although these ideas may seem somewhat trite in the modern world of athletics, they still form the essence of a strong foundation for the development of the athlete's character. Relatively recent developments in amateur sport have served notice that attention must be directed to personality development in the hope that resistance and sport training build "character rather than characters." Considerable discussion has emerged in recent years regarding the relative worth of sport for young people and whether sport has lost its moral high ground to money, contracts, endorsements, agents, television, and so forth (Editors 1985; Hill 1996; Hoberman 1992; Miracle and Rees 1994; Murphy 1991; Simon 1991; Telander and Sullivan 1989; Yesalis, Courson, and Wright 1993). Resistance training should acknowledge and embrace the powerful influence that coaches and sport training programs have on developing young people, and should continue to encourage the sound development of strong Americans through sport.

Coaches and other leaders in sport training should always keep the overall healthy development of the athlete in mind when weighing training and competition decisions. Because training is a fragile process, it is incumbent on all participants to plan for all contingencies in the development of the young athlete.

Sport-Specific Fitness

The second task of training is the development of general and sport-specific fitness. General fitness in this context does not mean that fitness can be generalized; rather it means that the athlete will train in a more or less multilateral fashion, particularly in the early stages. Multilateral development means that early training focuses on developing basic biomotor abilities that form the foundation for all sports. In conjunction with general training, the athlete will also perform specific training that more clearly reflects the actual nature of sport-specific performances. A deeper discussion of the various areas involved in sport training follows. However, it is important to understand initially that there are several constraints to fitness and that these constraints help define and direct training.

Sport-specific fitness is vitally important to all levels of performance. Training effects from particular training tasks bring about quite specific adaptations to the athlete's body. One proposed model (see figure 1.1) of fitness has as its vertices skill, strength, endurance, speed, and flexibility (Siff and Verkhoshansky 1993). The connections between the vertices involve a number of hyphenated terms reflecting a blending of fitness characteristics. Some of these terms are speed-strength, flexibility-strength, strength-endurance, and speed-endurance. The point of the hyphenated terms is to provide a simple means of describing the dominant form of fitness or effort that is required in a given activity. For example, weightlifting requires strength-speed, which means that the athlete must be strong but also must be able to move fairly heavy resistance at high speeds. The strength-speed requirement is due to the biomechanical constraints of the lifts, in which a large amount of force is needed to move a relatively heavy object (body mass + the weight) during a brief lifting movement from the floor.

The fact that no athlete can be maximally fit in all dimensions of fitness at the same time indicates that there are serious constraints on choosing the optimal tasks and the optimal timing of presentation of tasks for training (Todd and Hoover 1979). Because athletes cannot be maximally fit in all fitness dimensions simultaneously, sport training must involve intelligent selection of priorities.

Neuromuscular Fitness

The largest component of resistance exercise fitness is neuromuscular fitness. This term was selected to emphasize the important role of skill, strength, speed, and flexibility in resistance training. All of these characteristics are dependent on energy supply, but in a typical well-nourished athlete, energy supply is usually not the dominant problem. The strength and power athlete who is quick, supple, strong, and explosive, and who can perform the desired skills, usually has the higher probability of winning. All of these factors are highly specific and highly dependent on the interaction of the nervous and muscular systems (Sale and MacDougall 1981). Neuromuscular fitness is also highly specific to the context in which the training and performance occur.

The principle of specificity is one of the most well-understood and thoroughly investigated areas of neuromuscular fitness training (Morrissey, Harman, and Johnson 1995; Sale and MacDougall 1981). The principle of specificity is summarized by the acronym SAID, which stands for specific adaptations to imposed demands. Specificity of training,

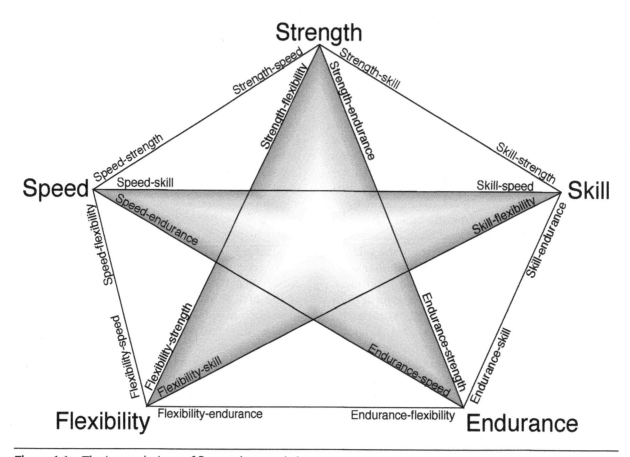

Figure 1.1   The inter-relations of fitness characteristics.

Reprinted from M.C. Siff and Y.V. Verkhoshansky, 1993, *Supertraining* (Johannesburg, South Africa: University of the Witwatersrand, School of Mechanical Engineering).

the SAID principle, refers to the idea that the body's neuromuscular system will adapt to the demands made of it, no more and no less. The specificity of adaptation is surprisingly narrow. For example, training a specific joint movement such as knee extension is highly specific to type of tension, position in the range of motion, speed, and body position:

1.   Type of tension:

   • Concentric—shortening of the muscle. In concentric tension the muscle is able to produce enough force that the tension in the muscle overcomes the resistance and the muscle shortens. When an athlete trains concentrically, the newly acquired strength or power fitness does not generalize well to other types of tension.

   • Eccentric—lengthening of the muscle. Eccentric tension is commonly seen in landings from a jump and in lowering a weight. During eccentric tension the athlete's muscle is producing force, but the force is not great enough to raise the resistance against gravity or to shorten the muscle. As such, the muscle lengthens while still producing tension.

   • Static or isometric—no change in muscle length. Static tension (i.e., isometric tension) refers to the situation in which a muscle is maintaining a constant length and producing just enough force to hold the resistance still, neither raising nor lowering it.

   • Stretch–shortening cycle (e.g., in a rebound-type jump)—a special class of neuromuscular activity involving eccentric tension followed by concentric tension. The eccentric tension lengthens a muscle and the muscle's connective tissue; then the reverse movement is performed via concentric tension and recoil of the elasticity of the muscle. Athletes are familiar with the stretch–shortening cycle as the type of movement they do when they perform a quick rebound or "ricochet" into a jump. The term "plyometrics" is commonly and mistakenly used synonymously with the term "stretch–shortening cycle." Plyometrics is a type of exercise for training that uses the stretch–shortening cycle. The stretch–shortening cycle is the mechanism that permits plyometric-type exercises.

- Isokinetic—constant-velocity movement (Rasch and Morehouse 1957). True isokinetic movements are performed at a constant speed, regardless of the range of motion or the resistance being moved. Usually, isokinetic movements require special machines. Currently no true isokinetic device is sold commercially.

2. Position in the range of motion or angle specificity, particularly in isometric training: When neuromuscular training occurs in some specific range of motion of a joint, the adaptations that result from that training are specific to the range of motion in which the training occurred (Campney and Wehr 1965; Graves et al. 1989; Oda and Moritani 1994).

3. Speed of the movement: Movement speed tends to generalize slightly to lower speeds rather than to higher speeds (Moffroid and Whipple 1970). This idea simply means that if you want to acquire adaptations that function at high speeds, you must train at high speeds.

4. Body position: Training in one body position does not transfer well to other body positions (Sale and MacDougall 1981). Interestingly, even body position can be highly constraining on the magnitude of adaptations that take place. For example, if an athlete trains some movement while standing, the resulting adaptations will largely vanish if the athlete tries similar movements while lying down.

The main tasks of training should be understood and appreciated. Moreover, the role of resistance training in the overall preparation of sports should be clearly understood prior to sport-specific training. To maximally achieve the tasks of training, one should be familiar with a number of training principles that have been established, as discussed in the following sections.

Principles of Training

Training is a complex process, guided by principles that serve to unify the training effort and catego-

rize the various tasks into an easily understood structure. Within each principle are more specifically focused concepts (subprinciples) that serve to assist in the implementation of the tenets of each principle.

Principle of Increasing Load Demands

The basic assumption of the principle of increasing load demands is that the coach must plan and implement ever-increasing demands (Harre 1982). Improvement can occur only when training loads are above average and the athlete must dip into adaptational reserves (i.e., the athlete is stressed and the body must respond by adapting to the new stress) (Verkhoshansky 1985). Pursuing and achieving higher athletic performance are inseparably linked with the development of new and more difficult training tasks. The results of the adaptation will be somewhat delayed depending on a myriad of factors. The delay of training results as manifested in enhanced fitness is called the "long-term lag of the training effect" (LLTE) (Verkhoshansky 1985). The LLTE merely indicates that the results of training tasks are not seen for a period of time after the training tasks have been imposed. The LLTE indicates that training is an investment and not a purchase.

You can increase load demands by increasing volume (how much you do) and intensity (how hard you do it or how hard the task is). Increasing volume and intensity is difficult to generalize to individuals and to different sports. This difficulty arises in measurement and implementation. Mileage and speed are particularly useful as volume and intensity measures in track and field, while sets, repetitions, and weight serve as indicators for weightlifters; there is no simple corresponding training unit that fits all sports equally well. Moreover, if two athletes perform the same skills or training tasks, and one athlete performs the tasks quite easily while the other struggles due to lack of experience, there is an automatic disparity of effort because the novice must try harder. Intensity and volume measurement in some sports is challenging due to the lack of a common measurement unit. One can count the takedowns, gymnastics skills, exercises, or sport drills (i.e., volume), and difficulty ratings can be substitutes for the intensity measures found in other sports that are measured and timed. Whatever is used to measure volume and intensity, both must increase in reciprocal fashion in order to bring an athlete into a new level of adaptation that leads to enhanced fitness.

Training load (volume and intensity) can be increased by any or all of the following:

1. Increase demands on coordination by making coordination demands more difficult—for example, perform a skill under slightly different conditions.

2. Increase number of competitions.

3. Increase number of competitions against superior opponents.

4. Decrease external equipment, such as stiffer springboards in diving or stiffer poles in pole-vaulting.

5. Increase duration of training or sets and repetitions during training.

6. Increase task difficulty of training, or shorten training duration while requiring the same amount of training load.

7. Decrease rest time between training tasks.

Training demands should not be increased at random. The increase in demands should be purposeful and planned. Training analyses have shown that among advanced athletes, a gradual and linear increase in training demands may not work as well as sudden (but planned and reasonable) "jumps" in training load. It is vitally important that the increased training demand produce a significant disturbance in the psychological and physical resources of the athlete. Moreover, we should note that the increases in training demand and adaptation to training do not occur simultaneously. There is a lag between implementation of the higher training demand and adaptation to the new load demand (i.e., LLTE) (Siff and Verkhoshansky 1993; Verhoshansky 1985b; Verkhoshansky, U. 1981; Verkhoshansky, Y.V. 1977, 1981, 1985).

Because one cannot express magnitudes of increasing loads in common units for all sports and all athletes, it is almost impossible to make generally valid statements about how much one should increase training loads. It has been shown that slight increases in load demands tend not to lead to enhanced performance over the long term. The increase in training demands must be sudden, substantial, and systematic. Some guidelines for the implementation of increasing load demands are the following (Harre 1982):

1. The athlete must participate in the demands of training consciously. The idea of just putting in the numbers is not appropriate. The athlete should consciously and conscientiously participate in each training task.

2. The increase in training demands should be directed from the overall goals and objectives of the training program. If you cannot determine how a training task fits into the overall scheme of training toward a specific goal, you should reassess the training task, substitute a different task, or simply abandon the task.

3. The increase in training loads should be reasonably large. The increase should force the athlete to focus a considerable portion of his or her adaptive reserves on meeting the training demand.

4. Training demands should be increased in a coordinated fashion with all other training demands. All of the various training demands cannot be increased at once. However, a balance must be struck. Overemphasis on one training task at the expense of other necessary training tasks invites failure due to a lack of variety of training stimuli.

Principle of Continuous Load Demands

The principle of continuous load demands simply indicates that athletes should avoid long interruptions to training (Harre 1982). There are well-documented declines in performance capabilities following long layoffs (Fleck 1994; Graves et al. 1988; Verhoshansky 1985a, 1985b). When fitness is increased, the athlete in a way acquires a "new" body. In other words, a former homeostatic level of functioning has been elevated by a new level of fitness. This idea of an increased level of homeostasis is summarized by the idea of nonequilibrium homeostasis. Nonequilibrium homeostasis has also been described as a homeodynamic state in which the increase in fitness can be maintained or enhanced only by *continued* high training demands (Siff and Verkhoshansky 1993). The term "homeodynamic" is somewhat paradoxical, but summarizes the idea that training involves a change in fitness and then a relative stabilization of that change.

There is a heterochronicity (variable timing and duration) of adaptation in the various elements of fitness (Verkhoshansky 1985). Interruptions to training also tend to influence different aspects of fitness at different rates (Harre 1982). For example, following a period of two months' cessation of strength training, a 5% to 6% decrease in the strength of the extensors and a 15% to 20% decrease in the strength of the flexors were observed (Harre 1982). The longer an athlete has trained, generally the more stable his or her performances. Thus, long interruptions to training appear to negatively influence experienced athletes less than novice athletes. However, sudden cessation of training results in serious disturbances to the athlete both physically and mentally (Gilbert 1980; Johnson and Verschoth 1991). The following are some guidelines for continuous load demands (Harre 1982):

1. Avoid interruptions to training as much as possible.

2. Plan training for noncritical periods that takes advantage of the existing environment and focuses training toward future development.

3. Interruptions to training do not include recovery periods. *Recovery periods are absolutely essential to long-term development.* Recovery periods should be planned regarding timing and content so that athletes have the best opportunity for full recovery and return to training rested and refreshed.

4. Interruptions due to injury are the most serious and often the most difficult to surmount. The coach should consult with the sports medicine physician on the training tasks (if any) that can be continued and that do not further jeopardize the injury.

Principle of the Cyclic Arrangement of Load Demands

The "principle of the cyclic arrangement of load demands" consists of two concepts working simultaneously: (1) cycling and (2) stages (Harre 1982, p. 78). Cycles of training are organized so that work is punctuated with rest and so that athletes progress through a program that systematically varies the training tasks and load. The overall cycle that each athlete goes through consists of repeating three stages: (a) acquisition of athletic form, (b) stabilization of athletic form, and (c) temporary loss of athletic form (Harre 1982). Practical experience has shown that athletes do not continue to improve in a progressive linear manner. Athletes require work periods that cause fatigue, and then these work periods are followed by rest and adaptation (LLTE). Training load is cycled by increasing load demands followed by decreasing demands. The second concept, stages, is again based on practical experience. Athletes simply cannot work on all of the demands of training and competition at the same time. The demands are too numerous, and available time is too limited. Taken together, these two concepts are united under the modern training approach called periodization.

The concept of periodization has been around at least since the 1920s (Nilsson 1987), and there are at least a dozen models of periodization. Caution should be exercised in their use due to the tendency to infer too much from individual models (Francis and Patterson 1992; Siff 1996a, 1996b; Siff and Verkhoshansky 1993; Verkhoshansky, U. 1981; Verkhoshansky 1977, 1985; Viru 1988, 1990, 1995). Further, most of the models have been tested only cursorily, if at all. Table 1.1 presents a list of several models.

Planning With Periodization

The most common method of developing a periodization plan is to divide a competitive season into three levels of cycles: (a) macrocycles—several months in duration up to a year or slightly more; (b) mesocycles—from approximately two to approximately eight weeks in duration; and (c) microcycles—usually 7 to 14 days in duration. The three levels of training organization permit a "divide and conquer" approach to the assignment of training tasks in a definite pattern for a definite period. Unfortunately, various authors have taken considerable liberty in using terms to describe varying durations, contents, and objectives of training within this context. The three levels of training duration are placed within an overall structure of the training year that consists of a preparatory period, a competitive period, and a transition or rest period. An athlete requires approximately 22 to 25 weeks to reach peak performance (Verkhoshansky 1985) before a type of fatigue or exhaustion occurs that is poorly understood (Poliquin 1991). Experience has shown that performance generally declines within these time constraints, but the mechanisms of the decline are unknown. This idea of a limited time for adaptation leads to the concept of multiple periodization, which simply means that the training year is usually divided into two, rarely more, phases consisting of preparatory, competitive, and transition periods (Bompa 1990a, 1990b, 1993; Siff and Verkhoshansky 1993; Verkhoshansky 1985). Perhaps unfortunately, many modern training programs force athletes to attempt to peak too often.

The preparatory period is usually divided into general and specific phases. The general preparatory phase is used for broad or multilateral training (Bompa 1990b). The training tasks are aimed at improving the athlete's overall strength, flexibility, stamina, coordination, and so forth. The specific preparatory phase more closely resembles the sport and sport-specific tasks. Training tasks during the specific preparatory phase are aimed at improving

Table 1.1 **Examples of Periodization Models**

Model	Comments
Matveyev	Volume and intensity are reciprocal.
Conjugate sequence system	Different training tasks are specifically linked to optimize results.
Concentrated loading	Part of the conjugate (overlapping) sequence system, but also a model unto itself. Period of very high loads followed by relative rest.
High-performance Matveyev	Volume and intensity are reciprocal, but are maintained at much higher loads.
Francis	Intensity remains constantly high; volume oscillates.
Varying intensity	Volume remains constant while intensity oscillates.
Oscillatory	Volume and intensity are increased and decreased together in a wavelike pattern.
Bondarchuk	Specialized training immediately and throughout the training program.
Sleamaker	Primarily for endurance athletes.
Clustering	Primarily for relative strength development.
Incremental	Volume and intensity are gradually increased. Primarily used by team sports.
Instinctive	No formal plan except to proceed based on the "feelings" of the coach, athlete, or both at the moment of training.
Professional competitive	Contest-to-contest training with little time for anything but travel to a new competition site and immediate preparation for the subsequent competition.

sport-specific tasks and fitness such as jumping, flexibility, and strength in extreme ranges of motion, and applying any newly acquired fitness to solving specific sport tasks. The preparatory period should be relatively longer for inexperienced athletes in order to allow for sufficient development of basic fitness. However, in elite athletes the preparatory period may be relatively short due to frequent competitions and the necessity of elite athletes to remain close to top condition throughout the training year (Francis and Patterson 1992; Siff 1996b; Siff and Verkhoshansky 1993; Zatsiorsky 1995).

The competitive period involves the majority of competitions during the particular season or macrocycle. The fitness of the athlete should be relatively stable during this period, and training focuses on maximizing and stabilizing performance. The preparatory period is linked to the competitive period in that a well-executed preparatory period, with sufficient duration to achieve a high level of fitness at a reasonable pace, allows the athlete to demonstrate more stable performances during the competitive period (Harre 1982; Siff and Verkhoshansky 1993; Verkhoshansky 1985). The idea of performance stability is particularly important for athletes in resistance training, and may differ somewhat from sport to sport. For example, the tactical approach of a pole-vaulter is quite different from that of a diver. The pole-vaulter may often face performances that he or she has never equaled. This is seen in

personal best records. The pole-vaulter may try previously unachieved heights in many competitions throughout a season. The diver should face this type of scenario only in the protected environment of training. The diver must perform what he or she has performed (i.e., dives) hundreds or thousands of times before, but must perform dives precisely in the decisive moment of competition. No byes or failed attempts are allowed in diving. Therefore, the diver seeks to stabilize performance at a level that is consistent with his or her skills, while the pole-vaulter must assault and achieve new levels of performance during a competition and can use more than one attempt.

The transition or rest period involves one to four, rarely more, weeks of reduced training load to facilitate recovery from the rigors of previous training both physically and mentally (Bompa 1990a, 1990b; Harre 1982, 1986; Siff and Verkhoshansky 1993). During the transition period the athlete should attempt to maintain fitness while allowing injuries to heal, develop new goals for the next competitive season, evaluate the previous competitive season, and basically ensure that the next competitive season begins with a renewed vigor and commitment.

Types of Periods

There are a number of different types of periods of training depending on training goals, time of the season, and capabilities of the athlete. Macrocycles are usually described based on commonsense understanding of the nature of the competitions within the macrocycle. For example, there may be an Olympic preparation type of macrocycle due to the modification of competition schedules to fit properly with the Olympic Games. There may also be a Pan American, national championship, or other type of macrocycle depending on the most important goal of the macrocycle. The second level, mesocycles, can be categorized by the objectives of the mesocycle. Mesocycle-level objectives are relatively similar across macrocycles, which aids in the consistency of their defining characteristics. Mesocycles thus become similar to interchangeable planning "parts" that can be used and reused in different macrocycles. Table 1.2 shows a list of mesocycle types and corresponding tasks (Harre 1982).

The mesocycles listed in table 1.2 can be linked to form an annual plan (Bompa 1990b), or a specific macrocycle (Harre 1982, 1990; Matveyev 1977).

An example of such linkage is shown in table 1.3 (Harre 1982).

Microcycles are periods of training lasting from 7 to 14 days. Microcycles are the smallest basic unit of training planning that has strictly applied objectives. The training lesson is a smaller training unit, but the goals of any particular training lesson can be modified based on current circumstances. However, the objectives of the microcycle remain intact so that subsequent training lessons are adapted to reach the objectives set for the microcycle (Verkhoshansky 1985). Various types of microcycles are shown in table 1.4 (Kurz 1991).

As described earlier, the cyclic arrangement of load demands refers to periodization, which is composed of two concepts used simultaneously. The first concept is that of *cycling* the training load by alternating between work and rest. The second concept is that of *periods* of training with specific, distinct, and linked goals. The importance of these periodization concepts lies in the organized and

Table 1.2 Mesocycle Classifications

Type (name)	Typical durations	Main tasks
General	Almost any duration	General education and training, primarily general preparatory phase; develops basic fitness.
Basic sport specific	~6 weeks	Improving the functional level of performance in specific skills and fitness; develops specific fitness.
Preparatory	~6 weeks	Training focused on competitive preparedness; submaximum to maximum loads to directly enhance fitness and skills for competitive mesocycles.
Immediate preparatory	~2 weeks	Training focused on recovery and peaking for a competition; tapering or testing.
Stabilization	~4 weeks	Perfecting technique and fitness; eliminating technique and fitness errors while stabilizing acquired skills and fitness. Stabilization is the most important.
Build up	~3 weeks	Further buildup of training loads to enhance foundational skills or fitness during a long preparatory period; more general training and conditioning than specific; active recovery from earlier specific and high-load training.
Precompetitive	~6 weeks	Development of the optimum expression of all skill and fitness factors for a specific competition or series of competitions; specific training with individualized loads; focused on bringing all fitness and skill characteristics to their peak.
Competitive build up	~3 weeks	Focused on restoring fitness during a long period of competitions.
Competitive	~2-6 weeks	Special emphasis on a specific competition that occurs during the mesocycle.
Recovery	~1-4 weeks	Specific focus on recovery and rehabilitation. May follow a series of competitions or serve between important competitions such as World Cups.

Table 1.3 **Example of Mesocycle Linkage**

Type	Duration (approximate)	Comments
1. General	8 weeks	Start enhancing general fitness and skills.
2. Basic sport specific	6 weeks	Enhance sport-specific fitness and skills.
3. Recovery	2 weeks	Active recovery (i.e., rest).
4. Basic sport specific	4 weeks	Return to general fitness training and skills.
5. Stabilization	4 weeks	Stabilize the general and specific sport skills.
6. Preparatory	6 weeks	Increase loads to maximize fitness and skills.
7. Precompetitive	4 weeks	Prepare for competitions.
8. Competitive build up	3 weeks	Recover and taper for first competitive series.
9. Competitive	3 weeks	Compete at qualifying contests.
10. Precompetitive	2 weeks	Prepare for next series of competitions.
11. Competitive	6 weeks	Compete at major competitions.
12. Recovery	2-4 weeks	Rest and rehabilitate for next season or macrocycle.

Table 1.4 **Microcycle Classifications**

Type	Comments
General preparatory	Main type of microcycle, used mostly at the beginning of the preparatory period. Focused on developing general fitness and skills.
Special preparatory	Greater proportions of specific exercises, used at the end of the preparatory period. Focused on developing sport-specific fitness and skills.
SUBTYPES OF GENERAL AND SPECIAL MICROCYCLES	
Preparatory build up	Gradual increase in training load across the microcycle.
Shock	Sudden and severe increase in training load to shock the athlete, increase fatigue, and force LLTE (long-term lag of training effect).
Competition/Camp	Mimics the load that will be faced in a competitive setting lasting several days, resulting in either tapering or high psychological and physiological concentrated loading.
SUBTYPES OF THE INTRODUCTORY MICROCYCLE	
Tapering	Decrease in training load to enhance recovery and later peak performance.
Competitive simulation	Increase in training load to "teach" the athlete about the types and magnitudes of stress that will be faced during an upcoming competition.
Competitive	Immediate training preparation, travel, site preparation for a contest, warm-up routines, and the competition.
Recovery	Used after a series of shock microcycles and following a competition or a series of competitions. The primary goal is to rest, recuperate, heal, and prepare for the next training or competition.

systematic fashion in which training loads can be applied. The concepts of periodization are well established; however, individual adaptation capabilities and laboratory tests of the various specific models of periodization are largely unknown. The fact that the proposed models are dramatically different indicates that periodization is not well understood. Considerable scientific work remains to be performed on the concepts involved in periodization.

Principle of Awareness

The "principle of awareness" simply implies that the athlete should undertake all training consciously and intelligently (Harre 1982, p. 87). The athlete should not participate in a training program without being intimately familiar with its goals and tasks. The athlete who is aware of the purposes of the training program can be the most impressive source of feedback on the effectiveness of the program. Coaches who do not inform and explain all aspects of the planned training to their athletes lose considerable information on how well the training is going. The athlete should always be involved in the preparation and development of the training program, should have homework, and should be given responsibility for carrying out appropriate tasks. Involving the athlete in all aspects of the training program means that the athlete becomes a more informed participant, and also serves as a sort of apprenticeship in the training of athletes.

Principle of Planning and Systems

Training is not a random process. Modeling the training of athletes based on scientific principles can be extremely useful in establishing intelligent plans for future athletes (Harre 1982). The training setting is a type of laboratory that demands the same scrutiny and record keeping required in any scientific setting. Training management and evaluation require a structured format that allows easy interpretation of all aspects of the training process.

Coaches should always be guided by the overall training plan and objectives when making individual training decisions. Each part of the plan should come logically from what has preceded. Training plans should always be defined in terms of the critical tasks that must be accomplished in the long-term development of the athlete. Periodization models of training are attempts to establish a sort of cookbook of logical approaches to systematically enhance performance. The coach who has a large repertoire of these models at his or her disposal will be able to bring a wider variety of planning skills to the training and performance of each athlete, thus responding better to individual needs. Training systems can be implemented and monitored for their effectiveness while the coach learns along with the athlete as long-term training unfolds. The ability of the coach to plan effectively can be as important as the specific "people skills" that make up much of the art of coaching.

Principle of Presentation

The principle of presentation refers to the vividness, richness, and precision of communication between coach and athlete (Harre 1982). The basic premise is that coaches should invest considerable time and resources in developing a rich and diverse repertoire of presentation skills and technologies so that athletes can experience the skills to be learned by the most clear and precise means available. This is particularly important in appearance sports in which body shapes, spatial orientation, and difficult maneuvers must be performed under competitive stress and threat of injury. Kinesthetic feedback from the movement, visual feedback (via mirrors, film, and videotape), clear language, computer simulators, spotting belts, and other means can aid the coach in communicating the demands of the skills to the athlete. The coach should develop a large repertoire of skills and technologies for skill presentation based on the understanding that different athletes respond to different styles and types of presentation (Cratty 1971; Jones 1988; Reeve and Mainor 1983; Sands 1991b).

Principle of Individualization

Individualization is perhaps *the* central principle of modern athletic training (Bompa 1990b). Individualization is not simply correcting specific technique errors, but also serves as the means to high-performance development of each athlete. Coaches often apply unscientific training programs to athletes based simply on testimony or rumors regarding what champion athletes have done. Of course, imposing difficult or unsound training programs on an athlete cannot result in high performance. However, individualization is not as necessary when athletes are all at roughly the same level and stage of training. The factors that must be addressed with regard to the individualization of training are shown in table 1.5.

Principle of Variety

There is a saying in athletic training: "Any idiot can train an idiot for a year" (Mel Siff, personal communication 1997). The idea behind this statement is that in the initial adaptations to almost any conditioning or training program, an athlete's performance will improve. Improvements in early training are largely neural. The athlete simply learns how to perform better. The long-term improvement of the athlete relies on considerable investment of effort in a variety of training approaches that lead paradoxically to a narrower and narrower focus on sport-specific fitness and skills (Bompa 1990b; Garhammer and Takano 1992; Poliquin 1988; Viru 1988, 1995). A constantly applied training load leads rapidly to stagnation of the athlete and little further improvement. This is one of the basic reasons

Table 1.5   **Individualization Factors**

Factor	Comments
Age and maturity	Numerous training and performance approaches are appropriate for a physically mature adult but not a child. Children are immature both physically and mentally, and all training plans must take age and maturity into account. Merely scaling a training program down for children usually does not meet the specific needs of the growing and immature child.
Training age	The training age of an athlete refers to the number of years the athlete has engaged in serious training. Some training tasks are suitable only for experienced athletes. This is particularly important in acrobatic sports, in which experience must be achieved in a long list of skills before safe performance of difficult skills can be accomplished.
Work capacity	Athletes vary considerably in their durability. Moreover, athletes often vary in their ability to tolerate training loads, injury, frustration, and so forth. These factors must be addressed individually to achieve maximum performance from each athlete.
Fitness and preparation	A highly trained and fit athlete can tolerate higher loads than an athlete who is less fit. An ill athlete will not tolerate high training loads for long periods. The type of illness and the physiological reserves of the athlete interact to determine how much training an athlete can withstand and still be able to progress. Excessive training loads and inappropriate training loads applied to an unprepared or underprepared athlete will result in poor adaptation at best, and disaster at worst.
Body type	The anthropometric characteristics of the athlete interact with training and performance. A short athlete will not play basketball well against taller opponents. An excessively tall person will find it difficult to be a great diver due to the difficulty of moving a large body through compact and quickly changing body positions. Although there is generally little one can do about body type, counseling an athlete toward sports that are more suitable for the athlete's size and shape may help the athlete reach success.

for the principle of increasing load demands described earlier. Because athletes adapt to training demands within a few days or weeks, it is important that the training demands vary enough to cause the athlete to face each demand anew. This forces the athlete to adapt, which leads to LLTE and enhanced fitness. Failure to change training demands for long periods results in boredom, poor performance, and little fitness enhancement. However, as with most concepts in this chapter, the principle of variety is an optimization problem. Many adaptations to a new training demand are completed within the first two weeks of the new demand. However, many other adaptations require up to six weeks to become fully manifested (Olbrecht 2000).

CHAPTER SUMMARY

The principles of training discussed in this chapter should serve as guidelines for the development of training models that can be modified to fit a particular training program. The principles of training also form a sort of gauntlet to test training decisions. Failure to pass the gauntlet of these principles should result in reevaluation of the training program. Although abiding by these principles is not a guarantee of success, working within the guidelines should provide a framework within which a coach's creativity and personality can greatly influence the ultimate success of the athlete. Few great artists develop without understanding the nature of their medium (e.g., canvas, clay, stone) and their skills within the medium. Coaches must fully understand the nature of training and the athletes who will participate in the training if they are to maximize their effectiveness.

PART 1

Basics of Muscle Contraction and Mechanics

Part I of this text focuses on the underlying mechanisms and principles associated with neuromuscular physiology and the more applied science of biomechanics. Chapter 2 deals with the structure of the somatic nervous system, skeletal muscle, and the underlying mechanisms of its function (contraction and force production). Chapter 3 deals with force production, motor control, and the interaction of the skeletal and neuromuscular systems in creating movement.

An understanding of these principles is necessary to prepare the reader for the more practical discussions found in parts III and IV of this text. The coach and sport scientist must develop an understanding of basic science. This understanding of basic science creates a higher potential to formulate a sound training process that is more likely to produce the desired short- and long-term adaptations. This part of the book, along with part II, lays a strong foundation aiding in that development.

CHAPTER 2

Neuromuscular Physiology

With the exception of thinking, all human activity requires bodily movement. Animals, including humans, depend on movement for survival. Humans and some animals are often engaged in movement simply for enjoyment; and among humans, movement often takes the form of physical competition and sport. The basic organ system allowing movement to take place is the somatic neuromuscular system. Skeletal muscle is made up of approximately 75% water, 20% protein, and 5% other substances such as minerals, carbohydrate, and phosphagens. Humans contain 640 muscles, which have varying size and shape. Muscles cross skeletal joints and are attached to levers (bones) at two or more points; contraction of the muscles moves the lever ends closer together, creating movement and locomotion. This chapter deals with the components of skeletal muscle, its innervation, and function.

Defining Muscle

The basic function of muscle is to generate force. Secondarily, muscles can provide some shape and form to the organism. Anatomically and functionally, muscle can be divided into two types, smooth and striated. Striated or striped muscle can be further divided into skeletal muscle and cardiac (heart) muscle. Regardless of the type, all muscles share the following basic properties (Gowitzke and Milner 1988):

- Conductivity: A muscle has the ability to conduct an action potential.
- Irritability: When stimulated, the muscle will react.
- Contractility: A muscle can shorten or produce tension between its ends.
- Relaxation: A muscle can return to resting properties after contraction.
- Distensibility: A muscle can be stretched by a force outside of the muscle itself. The muscle is not injured as long as it is not stretched past its physiological limits.
- Elasticity: The muscle will resist elongation and will return to its original position after passive or active elongation. Elasticity is the opposite of distensibility.

Smooth muscle and striated muscle can easily be differentiated from each other in a variety of ways, including appearance. For example, smooth muscle is uni-nucleated and contains sarcomeres (the functional units of muscle) that are arranged at oblique angles to each other; under a light microscope smooth muscle appears to be relatively featureless as a result of the orientation of its sarcomeres. On the other hand, striated muscle contains protein arrays called myofibrils that are parallel to each other and thus form striations or stripes. Cardiac muscle can be easily identified as distinct from skeletal muscle by appearance and differences in function, such as an intrinsic ability to contract. (We will not go into detail on smooth and cardiac muscle because though interesting, such discussion is not within the scope of this book.)

Muscle Structure and Function

Skeletal muscle is found in many sizes and various shapes. The small muscles of the eye may contain only a few hundred cells, while the vastus lateralis may contain hundreds of thousands of muscle cells. The shape of muscle is dependent on its general architecture, which in turn helps to define the muscle's function. Some muscles, such as the gluteal muscles, are quite thick; some, such as the sartorius, are long and relatively slender; and others, such as the extensors of the fingers, have very long tendons. These differences in muscle shape and architecture permit skeletal muscle to function effectively over a relatively wide range of tasks.

For example, thicker muscles with a large cross-sectional area can produce great amounts of force; longer muscles can contract over a greater distance and develop higher velocities of shortening; muscles with long tendons can form pulley arrangements that allow large external movement (e.g., grasping by the fingers) with relatively small movement of the muscles and tendons. Some long slender muscles such as the sartorius and biceps femoris are divided by transverse fibrous bands that form distinct sections or compartments (McComas 1996). Although fibers were previously believed to run the length of these muscles, because of these compartments the longest possible human muscle fiber is about 12 cm (4.7 in.) in length (McComas 1996). The individual compartments can have different fiber type distributions and different cross-sectional areas (English and Ledbetter 1982). Each compartment has a separate innervation; however, individual motor neurons often innervate muscle fibers in adjacent compartments. But the functional outcomes of compartmentalization are not completely understood. One possible consequence of compartmentalization is that it could ensure that contraction occurs relatively synchronously and rapidly along the muscle belly. However, it is also possible to recruit compartments separately (English 1984).

Muscle fibers can be arranged into two basic structural patterns, *fusiform* and *pinnate* (also spelled *pennate*). Most human muscles are fusiform, with the fibers largely arranged in parallel arrays along the muscle's longitudinal axis. In many of the larger muscles the fibers are inserted obliquely into the tendon, and this arrangement resembles a feather (i.e., pinnation). The fibers in a pinnate muscle are typically shorter than those of a fusiform muscle. The arrangement of pinnate muscle fibers can be single or double, as in muscles of the forearm, or multipinnate, as in the gluteus maximus or deltoid (figure 2.1).

The fibers of a pinnated muscle pull on the tendon at an angle, and the amount of force actually exerted on the tendon can be calculated using the cosine of the angle of insertion. At rest, the angle of pinnation in most human muscles is about 10° or less and does not appear to have a marked effect on most functional properties such as force production (Roy and Edgerton 1992; Wickiewicz et al. 1983, 1984). However, during muscle contraction the angle of pinnation can vary and may change some functional parameters, at least in some muscles (Fukunaga et al. 1997; Otten 1988). It is possible that during muscle contraction the angle of pinnation increases enough to decrease speed of contraction and increase force production. It is also possible that hypertrophy, which adds sarcomeres in parallel and can alter the angle of pinnation, can alter functional properties (Binkhorst and van't Hof 1973; Tihanyi, Apor, and Fekete 1982).

Pinnation offers a force advantage over fusiform fibers because with pinnation there are more fibers

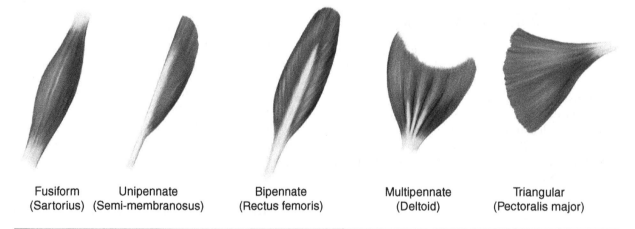

Fusiform   Unipennate   Bipennate   Multipennate   Triangular
(Sartorius)   (Semi-membranosus)   (Rectus femoris)   (Deltoid)   (Pectoralis major)

Figure 2.1 Variations in muscle fiber arrangements.

Reprinted, by permission, from W. Whiting and S. Rugg, 2005, *Dynatomy* (Champaign, IL: Human Kinetics).

in a muscle of a given volume; thus the effective cross section of the pinnated muscle is larger. Pinnation also permits more sarcomeres to be arranged in parallel (at the expense of those in series), resulting in enhanced force production (Gans and Gaunt 1991; Roy and Edgerton 1992; Sacks and Roy 1982). Additionally, the central tendon moves a greater distance in comparison to the shortening length of the muscle fibers, allowing the fibers to operate over the optimum portion of their length–tension curves (Gans and Gaunt 1991; McComas 1996).

About 85% of the mass of a muscle is made up of muscle fibers; the remaining 15% is mostly connective tissue. Muscle is organized and largely shaped by the connective tissue, which is composed of a ground substance, collagen, and reticular and elastin fibers of varying proportions. In muscle, the connective tissue is largely responsible for transmitting forces, for example the transmission of forces from the muscle to the bone by the tendon. The connective tissues' elasticity and distensibility help to ensure that the tension developed by the muscle is smoothly transmitted and that a muscle will return to its original shape after being stretched. Thus, the connective tissue of a muscle provides a framework for the concept of series and parallel elastic components within a muscle. When a muscle is passively stretched or when it actively contracts, the resulting initial tension is largely caused by the elastic properties of the connective tissue. During a contraction, the muscle cannot actively develop

force or perform work against a resistance until the elastic components are stretched out and the muscle tension and resistance (load) are in equilibrium.

There are three levels of muscle tissue organization: epimysium, endomysium, and perimysium. These three levels are a consequence of differing sizes and orientations of connective tissue fibers, particularly collagen (figure 2.2). The outside surface of a muscle is covered by a relatively thick and very tough connective tissue, the epimysium, which separates it from surrounding muscles. Arteries and veins run through the endomysium. The collagen fibers of the epimysium are woven into particularly tight bundles that are wavy in appearance. These collagen bundles are connected to the perimysium. The perimysium divides the muscle into bundles typically containing about 100 to 150 muscle fibers, which form a fasciculus or fascicle. However, muscles that function in producing small or very fine movements have smaller fascicles containing relatively few fibers and a larger proportion of connective tissue (Gowitzke and Milner 1988). The muscle fibers take on a polygonal cross-sectional shape that allows a greater number of fibers to fit into a fascicle (McComas 1996). Typically the interstitial spaces between fibers are about 1 μm. The perimysium also forms connective tissue tunnels, the intramuscular septa, which run through the muscle belly and provide a pathway for larger arterioles, venules, and nerves. The perimysium contains many large collagen bundles that encircle the outer surface of

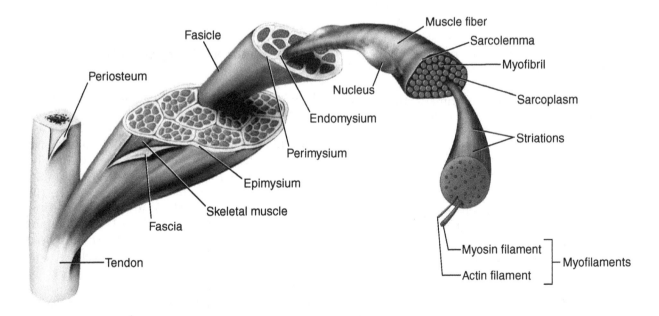

Figure 2.2 Organization of skeletal muscle.

Reprinted, by permission, from W. Whiting and S. Rugg, 2005, *Dynatomy* (Champaign, IL: Human Kinetics).

the muscle fibers lying on the outside of a fascicle. Some of the collagen bundles encircle the fascicles in a cross pattern, adding stability to the structure of the fascicle. Underneath the thicker perimysial sheets of connective tissue is a much looser network of collagen fibers that run in various directions and connect with the endomysium. The endomysium, which is made up of collagen fibers 60 to 120 nm in diameter, surrounds each muscle fiber, again adding more stability. Capillaries run between individual muscle fibers and lie within and are stabilized by the endomysium. Many of the endomysial fibers connect with the perimysium and likely connect to the basement membrane, which lies on the outside of the muscle cell sarcolemma (McComas 1996).

Muscle Connective Tissue Interface

Muscle fibers narrow considerably as they approach the tendon of origin. At the end of the fiber the sarcolemma consists of extensive folds that interdigitate with the folds of the connective tissue surrounding the fibers. The extensive folding and interdigitation ensure that muscle force is distributed over a large area, which reduces surface stresses (McComas 1996). Additionally, the fibers interact with the various layers of the basement membrane at an oblique angle, reducing shearing stress (Tidball 1983). The myofibrils do not connect directly with the sarcolemma of the muscle fiber; the actin filaments are attached to connecting proteins, such as vinculin, talin, paxilin, and tensin, lying within the basement membrane that is attached to the outer surface of the sarcolemma (McComas 1996).

The basement membrane, consisting of three layers, lies between the endomysium and the sarcolemma. The basement membrane is composed of a glycoprotein complex and has structural, trophic, and enzymatic functions. The primary functions of the basement membrane are as follows (McComas 1996):

- Regulates the neuromuscular junction (NMJ)
  - Stimulates the development of synaptic folds and the incorporation of acetylcholine receptors into the sarcolemma
  - Guides regenerating axons to the site of the original NMJ
  - Provides signal for the development of specialized motor end-plate structures
- Terminates the synaptic transmission (the basement membrane contains acetylcholinesterase [AChE])

- Attaches the muscle fiber to the endomysium
- Attaches the NMJ
- Provides scaffolding for muscle cell regeneration

Muscle Fibers

Although muscles can have differing morphology, all muscles are made up of individual cells or *muscle fibers*. Muscle fibers are elongated and tapered at either end. A typical muscle fiber is about 50 µm in diameter (range: 10 to 150 µm), and some fibers within a muscle may run the entire length of the muscle or compartment (Feinstein et al. 1955; McComas 1996). Thus, some fibers appear to be quite long, up to 20 cm (7.9 in.) (Roy and Edgerton 1992). However, the exact nature of a functional versus an anatomical muscle fiber is controversial (Roy and Edgerton 1992). On the basis of the presence of connective tissue intercepts along the length of presumed functional fibers and using a variety of mammalian muscles, Richmond and Armstrong (1988) and Gordon and colleagues (1989) have found fibers typically to be about 2 cm (0.8 in.) in length. Previous studies (Alexander and Vernon 1975; Sacks and Roy 1982; Spector et al. 1980), suggesting that fibers may be quite long, did not use specific techniques for identifying connective tissue intercepts (Roy and Edgerton 1992). Thus, typical mammalian muscle fibers are likely to be in the range of 1 to 3 cm (0.4-1.2 in.) in length.

Sarcoplasm and Organelles

Skeletal muscle cells contain a semifluid cytoplasm made up of water, salts, proteins, and various other substances known as sarcoplasm. Suspended in the sarcoplasm are various organelles including nuclei, mitochondria, cytoskeletal and cytotubular systems, glycogen granules, and lipid vacuoles. Generally, the proteins of a muscle cell can be grouped into four categories: (1) granules and organelle, (2) stroma and sarcolemmal, (3) myofibrillar, and (4) sarcoplasmic (Gowitzke and Milner 1988; McComas 1996). Sarcoplasmic proteins occupy the spaces between myofibrils and include myoglobin and glycolytic enzymes.

Muscle fibers contain various organelles of specific function, including those dealing with replication and energy production. Many muscle cell organelles have a distinct nomenclature distinguishing them from the organelles of other cells.

The cell membrane, or sarcolemma, which contains the sarcoplasm, is a fluid mosaic, approximately 7.5 nm thick, primarily made up of lipids and proteins. As with other cell membranes, its two major functions are to enclose the cell contents and to regulate the passage of various materials into and out of the cell. Ultrastructural and biochemical analyses indicate that the sarcolemma is largely composed of a bilayer of phospholipids arranged perpendicularly to the longitudinal axis of the fiber (figure 2.3). The hydrophilic lipid heads form the inner and outer surface of membrane, with the hydrophobic tails forming the interior of the membrane. The heads are primarily composed of choline, phosphate, and glycerol; the tails consist of fatty acid chains (McComas 1996). Cholesterol is found between the phospholipid molecules and adds structural stability and stiffness to the membrane.

The sarcolemma has a relatively irregular surface due to several convolutions and infolding of the membrane. In the area of the synapse with the motor end plate of the α-motor neuron, there are many convolutions due to the junctional folds. Type II (fast) fibers generally have more extensive junctional folds than do type I (slow) fibers. At other sites along the surface are folds that are present during rest but that stretch out and disappear during contraction or passive stretching (McComas 1996). There are also cavities, forming pockets, termed caveolae, that are connected to the outer surface by narrow necks. In smooth muscle the caveolae may have a similar function to the T-tubules in skeletal muscle. Although the exact function of the caveolae in skeletal muscle is uncertain, they may act as surface reserves when the membrane is stretched (Dulhunty and Franzini-Armstrong 1975). Additionally, there are different types of proteins embedded in the lipid bilayer.

Intrinsic and extrinsic proteins are contained in the lipid bilayer (figure 2.3). Intrinsic proteins completely penetrate the bilayer; extrinsic proteins are attached only at the inner or outer surface of the sarcolemma and are easily removed by chemical means (McComas 1996). Many proteins are glycosylated and have sugar residues extending

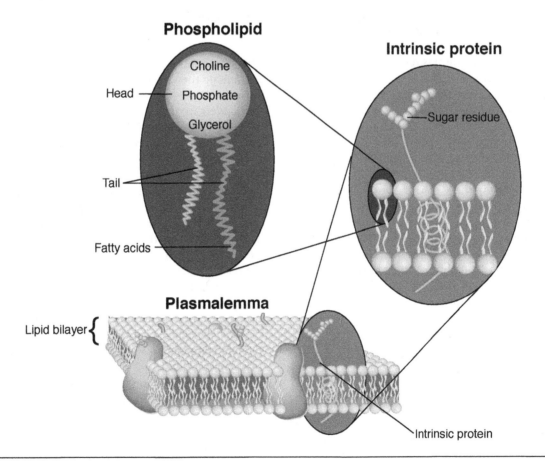

Figure 2.3 Basic structure of the sarcolemma.

Adapted from B.R. MacIntosh, P.F. Gardiner, and A.J. McComas, 2006, *Skeletal muscle*, 2nd ed. (Champaign, IL: Human Kinetics), 12.

up to the basement membrane. The sugar residues apparently function to trap various molecules in the extracellular fluid and direct them toward the protein in the membrane (McComas 1996). The intrinsic and extrinsic proteins include the following (McComas 1996):

- Transport proteins, which include the proteins active in electrolyte movement, such as the sodium-potassium pump, ion channels, and neurotransmitter receptors (acetylcholine)

- Adenyl cyclase, which is responsible for catalyzing the reaction forming cyclic adenosine monophosphate (AMP)

- Regulatory proteins, such as G proteins, which bind guanosine triphosphate (GTP) and are involved in the activation of adenyl cyclase

- Various kinases, which activate proteins by phosphorylation

- Various hormone receptors

- Integrins, which link the basement membrane and the endomysium to the sarcolemma and cytoskeletal structures

While the lipid portion is relatively fluid at body temperatures, the proteins are more stable and restricted in movement as a result of being attached to intra- or extracellular structures through binding proteins (see the section "Muscle Connective Tissue Interface").

The cytoskeletal system consists of a protein network that strengthens and stabilizes various structures within the cell (McComas 1996). The cytoskeleton proteins, such as dystrophin, actin, and spectrin, support the sarcolemma and prevent tearing during contraction. Desmin, synemin, and vimentin encase the myofibrils near the Z-discs and bind the myofibrils together. The cytoskeleton also supports and positions other organelles such as the nuclei and mitochondria.

Cytotubular Systems

The tubular system of skeletal muscle fibers can be divided into two parts, the sarcoplasmic reticulum and the transverse tubular system (T-tubules). The sarcoplasmic reticulum (SR) is a longitudinal network of tubules analogous to the smooth endoplasmic reticulum in other cells. These tubules parallel the myofibrils and surround them. The SR consists of a longitudinal portion that contains a Ca^{++}-ATPase (adenosine triphosphatase) pump and

a saclike terminal cisterna (figure 2.4a). The longitudinal portion of the SR is interconnected with the rest of the SR throughout the cell by side channels; thus a giant tubular network is formed (McComas 1996). Upon contraction, the longitudinal portion becomes shorter and wider. The SR acts as a reservoir for Ca^{++}; under normal resting conditions the concentration of Ca^{++} inside the SR is about 10,000 times higher than in the surrounding sarcoplasm (Billeter and Hoppler 1992). Calcium ions are released through ryanodine (RYR) channels into the sarcoplasm as a result of depolarization, which is essential for activation of muscle contraction (Wagenknecht et al. 1989). Upon resegregation of Ca^{++} into the SR, muscle relaxation takes place.

The T-tubules lie perpendicular to the axis of the muscle fiber. The T-tubules contain intercellular fluid and invaginate the sarcolemma at regular intervals, forming relatively narrow channels encircling the myofibrils at the junction of the A and I bands of the sarcomere. The T-tubules traverse the SR at dilated portions called terminal cisternae. The point where the T-tubules interrupt the SR forms a structure made up of three elements termed the *triad*. By electron microscopy the T-tubule and the SR appear to be connected by large protein complexes termed junctional feet (Eisenberg 1983). The junctional feet appear to be part of the proteins making up the RYR channel in the SR and are likely connected to dihydropyridine (DHP) channels embedded in the T-tubules (Wagenknecht et al. 1989). The function of the T-tubule is to transfer the action potential from the sarcolemma to the inside of the cell and the SR (figure 2.4b). It has been speculated that an action potential stimulus in the T-tubule causes a change in the conformation of the DHP channels, which in turn causes the junctional feet to change conformation. The junctional feet are embedded in the membranes of the SR next to calcium channel proteins, which act as a gate. Under normal conditions the calcium channel gates are closed, keeping the Ca^{++} segregated in the SR. When the junctional feet change conformation, the calcium channel gates open and Ca^{++} moves into the sarcoplasm along a concentration gradient, allowing the concentration of Ca^{++} in the sarcoplasm to rise approximately 100-fold (Billeter and Hoppler 1992). The increase in sarcoplasmic Ca^{++} concentration triggers events in regulatory proteins leading to muscle contraction.

Mitochondria

The mitochondria are typically oblong structures approximately 1.5 μm in length. Because of the

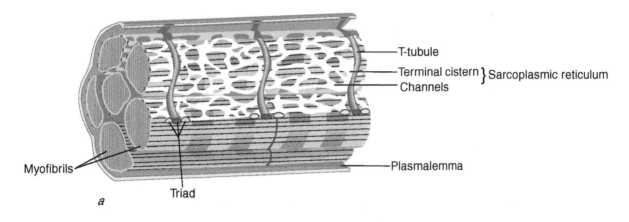

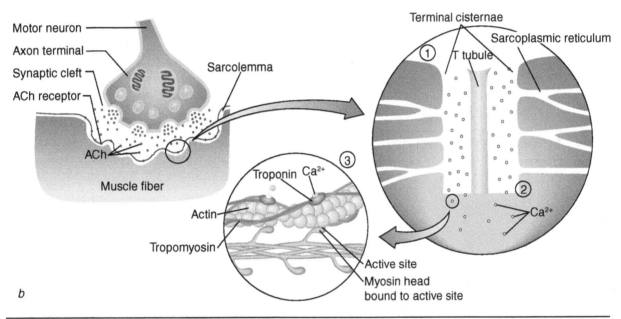

Figure 2.4 (a) The sarcoplasmic reticulum and (b) the T-tubules. In step 1, action potential moves across the sarcolemma and down the T-tubules. In step 2, the action potential is transferred from the T-tubule to the SR, causing the release of calcium. In step 3, Ca^{2+} interacts with troponin C, triggering muscle contraction.

myofibrils and other organelles, muscle cells are rather tightly packed and the mitochondria (sarcosomes) are typically shorter than those of other types of cells. Mitochondria are located in areas where energy supply is a primary requisite, near the myofibrils, for example. Mitochondria contain double membranes with the inner membrane folded into cristae, resulting in a large inner membrane surface area (figure 2.5). The area within the cristae is referred to as the matrix or matrix space. The outer membrane contains many different types of embedded proteins, most of which function as transport molecules (McComas 1996). The transport proteins allow molecules of 10 kilodaltons (kD) or less to pass freely into the intermembrane space. The inner membrane also contains transport proteins that control the movement of various substances from the intermembrane into and out of the matrix space.

The matrix space contains enzymes for the Krebs cycle, β-oxidation, and the formation of acetyl coenzyme A (CoA) from pyruvate. The 15 molecules associated with cellular respiration are located on the inner membrane (McComas 1996). The outer portions of the inner membrane contain the enzymes necessary for lipid synthesis. A unique aspect of mitochondria is that they also contain DNA (deoxyribonucleic acid) that is specific to the mitochondria and apparently derived directly from the female (you can thank your mother for your mitochondrial DNA).

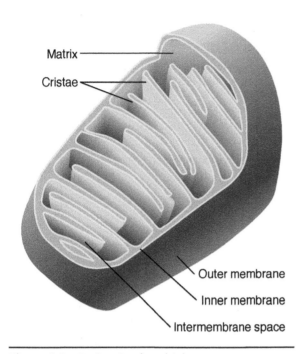

Matrix

Cristae

Outer membrane

Inner membrane

Intermembrane space

Figure 2.5 Basic mitochondrial structure.

Adapted, by permission, from B.R. MacIntosh, P.F. Gardiner, and A.J. McComas, 2006, *Skeletal muscle,* 2nd ed. (Champaign, IL: Human Kinetics), 19.

Mitochondrial DNA apparently functions in the replication of organelles and in the production of various transport and enzymatic proteins contained in the mitochondria.

Nuclei

Muscle cells are multinucleated, and human nuclei contain 23 pairs of chromosomes with many thousands of genes per chromosome. The nuclei are contained within a double-layered membrane and normally are dispersed near the inner surface of the sarcolemma. There is a particularly high density of nuclei near the motor end plate. The muscle cell nucleus contains chromosomes that impart instructions for protein synthesis in the sarcoplasm (see protein synthesis in the section on hypertrophy and hyperplasia in chapter 10).

Under a light microscope, muscle cell nuclei are indistinguishable from the nuclei of satellite cells. Satellite cells are attached to the sarcolemma (basement membrane) by a double membrane that separates the satellite cell from the sarcoplasm of the muscle fiber (McComas 1996). Satellite cells make up about 1% of the nuclei in adult human

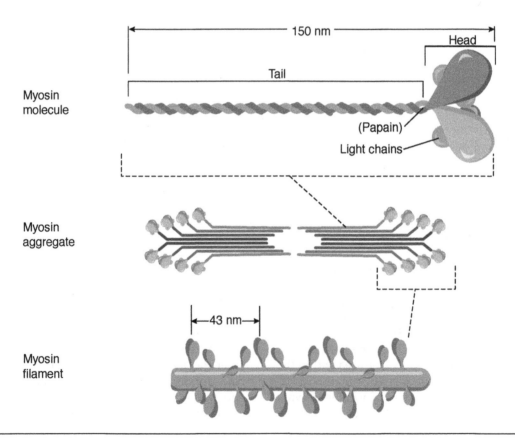

Figure 2.6 Myosin and myosin filament structure.

Adapted, by permission, from B.R. MacIntosh, P.F. Gardiner, and A.J. McComas, 2006, *Skeletal muscle,* 2nd ed. (Champaign, IL: Human Kinetics), 154.

muscle and are particularly important in regenerating muscle tissue subsequent to disease or injury (McComas 1996). Satellite cells may be important in the process of hyperplasia, which may result from heavy weight training.

The Sarcomere

Sarcomeres, as mentioned previously, are the functional unit of muscle. They are constructed of various elements containing a variety of different proteins, which are discussed next.

Protein arrays, or myofibrils, are primarily made up of the contractile proteins actin and myosin along with smaller amounts of regulatory and structural proteins. Approximately 80% of the myofibrillar protein is actin and myosin (Gowitzke and Milner 1988). Myosin makes up about 60% to 70% of the myofibrils, has a relatively high viscosity, and weighs about 500 kD, while actin makes up about 20% to 25% of the myofibrils and is a low-viscosity protein weighing about 75 kD. Myosin molecules, which are about 150 nm long, consist of two heavy chains with long tails wrapped in an alpha-helix connected to two pear-shaped heads (figure 2.6).

Treatment with the enzyme trypsin breaks up myosin molecules into two subunits, heavy meromyosin (HMM) and light meromyosin (LMM). Treatment of HMM with the enzyme papain results in a linear fragment (HMM-S_2) and a globular fragment (HMM-S_1) containing two myosin heads. The HMM-S_1 fragment contains the myosin heavy chains (MHC), which are responsible for ATPase activity; and the associated "heads" are the force-generating sites in muscle. Because the MHC are the primary determinant of ATPase activity, they are also primarily responsible for the speed of shortening (Reiser et al. 1985; Ennion et al. 1995). In the neck region of the molecule, each of the heads is bound to two molecules of light myosin (MLC) weighing 20 kD that influence the ATPase activity of the globular heads, perhaps by regulating the speed of the power stroke during contraction (Lowey, Waller, and Trybus 1993). It is isoforms of MHC and MLC that are the primary determinants of human skeletal muscle fiber type classification (Baldwin 1984; Billeter et al. 1981; Gardiner 2001; Staron 1997). Essentially, there are two isoforms of the MHC, fast and slow, and at least four isoforms of MLC (see table 2.1). Myosin ATPase activity can be ordered with regard to fiber type as follows: IIB > IIX > IIA > IIC > I. Some controversy exists over the exact type of MHC present in human muscle; data suggest that human and primate muscle contains

Table 2.1 Relation of MHC and MLC to Fiber Type

Fiber type	MHC	MLC
IIB	2 FM (HCIIb)	2 F_2, 2 F_3
IIA	2 FM (HCIIa)	1 F_1, 2 F_2, 1 F_3
IIC	1 FM (HCIIa), 1 SM	2 F_1, 2 F_2
I	2 SM	2 S_1, 2 S_2

FM = fast heavy myosin chain*; S_1 = slow light myosin chain type 1; SM = slow heavy myosin chain; S_2 = slow light myosin chain type 2; F_1 = fast light myosin chain type 1; F_2 = fast light myosin chain type 2; F_3 = fast light myosin chain type 3.

Myosin ATPase activity: IIB > IIX > IIA > IIC > I.

Based on Billeter et al. 1981; Baldwin 1984; Pette and Staron 1990; Pette and Staron 2000; Sant'Ana Pereira et al. 1996; Staron 1997.

only IIX MHCs rather than IIB. The relative shortening velocity (unloaded) would be I < IIA < IIX < IIAB < IIB. Types IIB and IIAB are found in small mammals (see Gardiner 2001 for discussion).

The heads of the myosin appear to consist of three globular proteins of 20 kD, 25 kD, and 50 kD. The MLC are attached to the 20 kD protein (figure 2.7). The 50 kD protein is the portion of

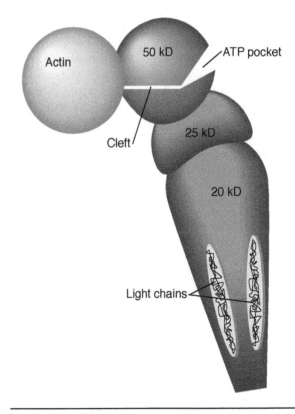

Figure 2.7 Structure of the myosin head.

Adapted, by permission, from B.R. MacIntosh, P.F. Gardiner, and A.J. McComas, 2006, *Skeletal muscle*, 2nd ed. (Champaign, IL: Human Kinetics), 157.

the head that appears to actually attach to actin in forming the cross-bridge. There appears to be a variable-sized pocket or cleft in the 50 kD protein. Adenosine triphosphate (ATP) controls the size of the pocket and the strength of the attachment to actin (Rayment et al. 1993).

Myosin filaments consist of an overlapping array of 200 to 400 myosin molecules, with the heads projecting outward and the LMM portion overlapping in parallel to form the spine of the filament. The heads of the myosin constitute the cross-bridges of the sarcomere. The molecules of myosin are oppositely oriented along each half of the myosin filament with the LMM tails directed toward the center. The $HMM\text{-}S_1$ and the $HMM\text{-}S_2$ and the $HMM\text{-}S_2$ are attached by flexible joints to the LMM. These joints allow the cross-bridges to have a relatively large range of movement (Huxley 1969).

Actin exists in a globular form (G-actin) and a filamentous form (F-actin) (figure 2.8). G-actin is made up of a single peptide chain. F-actin consists of two G-actin polymers wrapped around each other, creating a double helix with a 360 Å period, and forms the thin filaments of the sarcomere. Each actin filament contains about 350 G-actin molecules. In solution, actin and myosin bind, forming actinomyosin, strands of which will contract in the presence of ATP (McComas 1996).

The primary regulatory proteins are tropomyosin and troponin. Tropomyosin is a rod-shaped molecule weighing about 70 kD, which is bound to the actin filaments and consists of α and β chains wrapped around each other in an alpha-helix. The ratio of α and β chains is different in type I and type II skeletal muscle and may play a role in the speed of contraction (Pette and Staron 1990). In human muscle, tropomyosin spans seven G-actin residues of the thin filament and is attached to a second regulatory protein, troponin. Troponin is actually a complex of three globular-shaped proteins, each with a specific function (Billeter and Hoppler 1992). Troponin T binds the troponin complex to tropomyosin; troponin C binds calcium; and troponin I sterically inhibits the interaction of actin and myosin. One tropomyosin molecule plus its attached troponin complex is a regulatory unit. An actin filament (thin filament) contains 52 regulatory units and consists of about 360 G-actin molecules (Billeter and Hoppler 1992; Payne and Rudnick 1989). The binding of calcium to troponin C causes a change in conformation of the regulatory unit, which in turn causes actin to activate myosin ATPase and results in contraction (Ebashi and Endo 1968).

Under a light microscope the myofibrils of a sarcomere can be seen to lie in a parallel orientation (figure 2.9). Each sarcomere is bound by a Z-disc. At rest, each thick filament (myosin) extends the length of the A band, and the thin filaments (actin) pass from each I band into the A band as far as the H zone. The H zone is less dense than other areas of the A band because it contains only myosin filaments. The I band is the least dense portion of the sarcomere because it contains no myosin filaments. The H zone is not homogeneous; it shows considerable variation in density. The denser M region runs through the center of the H zone. The M region is made up of very thin filaments (M-filaments) approximately 5 nm in diameter that are connected to the myosin filaments as well as to each other. The proteins making up the M-filaments are not completely known but include M-protein, myomesin, and creatine kinase. These proteins form a complex latticework that gives structural stability to the three-dimensional aspects of the sarcomere (figure 2.10).

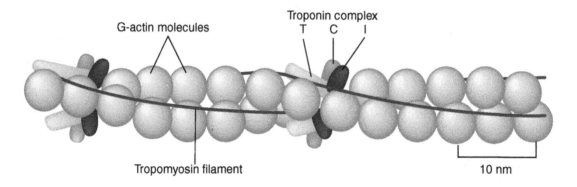

Figure 2.8 Structure of the actin myofilament and regulatory proteins. G-actin (globular actin) polymers combine to form F-actin (filamentous actin). Two F-actins wrap around each other in an alpha-helix to form an actin myofilament. Regulatory units containing troponin and tropomyosin are embedded in the actin myofilament.

Adapted, by permission, from B.R. MacIntosh, P.F. Gardiner, and A.J. McComas, 2006, *Skeletal muscle*, 2nd ed. (Champaign, IL: Human Kinetics), 159.

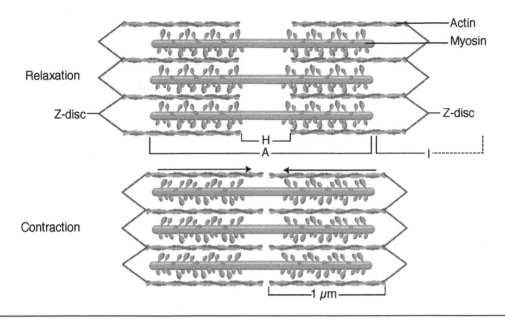

Figure 2.9 Basic sarcomere structure.

Adapted, by permission, from B.R. MacIntosh, P.F. Gardiner, and A.J. McComas, 2006, *Skeletal muscle,* 2nd ed. (Champaign, IL: Human Kinetics), 154.

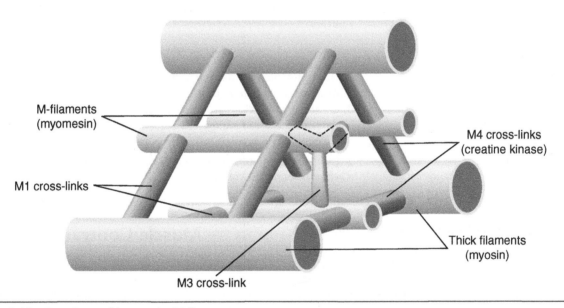

Figure 2.10 Proteins making up the M-line.

Adapted, by permission, from B.R. MacIntosh, P.F. Gardiner, and A.J. McComas, 2006, *Skeletal muscle,* 2nd ed. (Champaign, IL: Human Kinetics), 15.

The relationship of the actin and myosin filaments to fiber banding can be clearly observed in electron micrographs of cross sections through various portions of the sarcomere (Gowitzke and Milner 1988; McComas 1996). A cross section of the denser portion of the A band shows that each myosin filament is surrounded by a hexagonal array of actin filaments. The actin filaments also contain two regulatory proteins, tropomyosin and troponin, as well as the structural protein nebulin.

A secondary array of filaments composed of titin stabilizes myosin filaments along a longitudinal axis. Titin is a large protein (3000 kD) that runs the length of the myosin filaments and also attaches them to the Z-discs (Trinick 1991). Titin appears to function in stabilizing and maintaining myosin positioning in the center of the sarcomere during both contraction and relaxation. Nebulin may act in a similar manner in the stabilization of actin. Both titin and nebulin likely contribute to the

Table 2.2 **Elements of the Sarcomere**

Element	Associated protein	Function
Thick filament	Myosin	1. Interacts with actin 2. Myosin ATPase activity (MHC)
	Titin	1. Associated with elastic properties 2. Stabilizes the thick filaments longitudinally 3. May offer some control of myosin molecule number per filament
Thin filament	Actin	1. Interacts with myosin
	Nebulin	1. Longitudinal stabilization of thin filaments (?) 2. May control the number of G-actin monomers linked together in a thin filament
	Tropomyosin	1. Transfers the conformational change of the troponin-tropomyosin complex to actin
	Troponin	1. Binds calcium 2. Inhibits or stimulates actin and myosin interaction
Z-disc	α-Actinin	1. Holds the thin filaments in place and in register; connects actin to the Z-disc; type I fibers contain more α-actinin
	Desmin Vimentin Synemin Dystrophin Spectrin	1. Connect to cytoskeletal proteins in the sarcolemma and basement membrane. The basement membrane in turn attaches to the endomysium
M-line	M-protein Myomesin Creatine kinase	1. Holds the thick filaments in a proper array 2. Attaches and anchors titin 3. Creatine kinase also catalyzes the reaction ADP + PCr → ATP + Cr, which provides rapid energy
C-stripes	C-, X-, H-protein	1. Probably hold thick filaments in proper array 2. Controls the number of myosin molecules in the thick filaments at a relatively constant value

Adapted from Pette and Staron 1990; Billeter and Hoppler 1992; McComas 1996.

elastic properties of muscle (McComas 1996; Trinick 1991). Differences in protein species, particularly titin, may contribute to differences in strength, power (McBride et al. 2003), and running economy (Kyrolainen et al. 2003) and may be related to training status.

The Z-disc is primarily composed of the proteins α-actinin, desmin, vimentin, synemin, dystrophin, and spectrin. Actin myofilaments appear to be connected on both sides of the Z-discs by α-actinin (McComas 1996). Desmin, vimentin, and synemin appear to form a structural scaffolding (intermediate filaments) that is wrapped around the actin myofibrils and the Z-disc. Together these proteins serve to hold the actin myofibrils in position. Additionally, the proteins forming the Z-discs are connected to the cytoskeletal proteins in the sarcolemma and basement membrane and ultimately to the endomysium surrounding the muscle fiber (see table 2.2).

Muscle Contraction

Muscular contraction is the basis for human movement. At the simplest level, contraction involves the interaction of myosin and actin and the sliding of the thin filaments past the thick filament (Huxley 1958; Huxley and Hanson 1954; Huxley and Niedergerke 1954). Although the molecular basis of muscle contraction has been studied for more than 50 years, the details are still unclear.

The initiation of a voluntary muscle contraction begins in the central nervous system. Briefly, an action potential (AP) arrives at the motor end plate; the AP is transferred to the sarcolemma by the neurotransmitter acetylcholine (ACh). The AP moves along the sarcolemma and down the T-tubules into the interior of the fiber (Gage and Isenberg 1969). At the terminal cisternae the AP is transferred to the SR, likely by way of the DHP calcium channels or by a chemical messenger such as inositol triphosphate (Nosek et al. 1990). Upon depolarization, the junctional feet of the SR change conformation, releasing calcium into the sarcoplasm through RYR calcium channels. The 100-fold increase raises the probability of Ca^{++} binding with troponin C.

The attachment of the myosin head to actin and subsequent contraction is quite complex and may occur as follows (McComas 1996; Rayment et al. 1993):

1. Under resting conditions there is no interaction between actin and myosin, as this interaction is blocked or inhibited by the regulatory unit that covers binding sites on the actin (steric block model).

2. The binding of four Ca^{++} to troponin C results in a conformational change in the regulatory unit and activation of the myosin heads (figure 2.11). This allows a strong bond to form between actin and myosin in the absence of ATP.

3. After the strong bond is formed, ATP enters the cleft of the 50 kD portion of the head. The adenine ring is left protruding out of the cleft. The entry of ATP opens the cleft, creating a weak binding situation.

4. As the cleft widens, the ATP completely enters the cleft, causing the head to detach from actin and move 5 to 11 nm farther down the actin filament. Adenosine triphosphate is

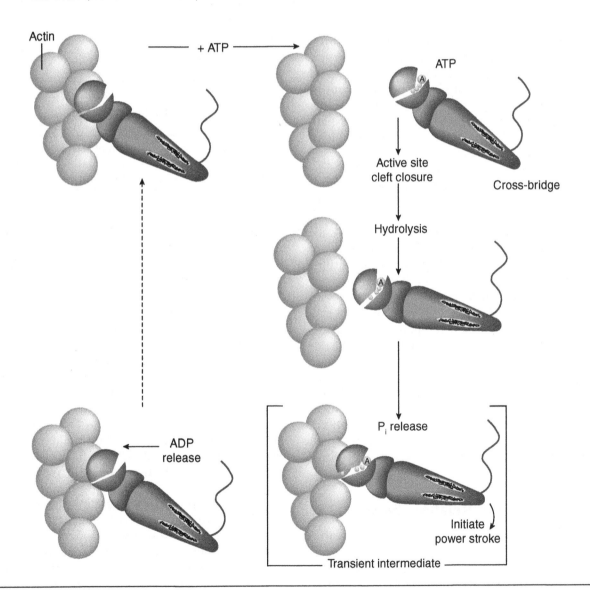

Figure 2.11 Myosin head activation.

Adapted, by permission, from B.R. MacIntosh, P.F. Gardiner, and A.J. McComas, 2006, *Skeletal muscle*, 2nd ed. (Champaign, IL: Human Kinetics), 160.

hydrolyzed with the end products remaining in the cleft, forming a transient intermediate complex.

5. The lower part of the 50 kD portion re-forms a weak bond with actin. The reattachment closes the cleft, expelling inorganic phosphate (P_i) and adenosine diphosphate (ADP).

6. The removal of P_i and ADP opens the cleft and simultaneously causes the lower part of the head to swivel, resulting in the power stroke, producing approximately 3 to 4 pN of force and moving between 5 and 11 nm (Finer, Simmons, and Spudich 1994; Rayment et al. 1993).

7. The process starts over.

Thus, each cycle of the cross-bridge requires the hydrolysis of one ATP molecule. In order for the cross-bridge to continue to generate force, ATP must be replenished; if a specific power output is to be maintained, ATP must be regenerated at the same rate as it is being used. This can create an accumulation of breakdown products, including ADP, P_i, and H^+, which can interfere with cross-bridge performance. Under dynamic conditions the amount of ATP hydrolyzed is proportional to the heat liberated and work accomplished (Fenn effect; Fenn 1923).

Termination of a voluntary contraction is initiated at the motor end plate. When an AP is no longer arriving at the terminal, acetylcholinesterase (AChE), which is present in the synaptic cleft, reduces the concentration of ACh in the NMJ. Reduction of the ACh concentration reduces the number of activated ACh receptors in the sarcolemma, stopping the AP stimulation of calcium release by the SR. The SR pumps Ca^{++} out of the sarcoplasm, reducing the sarcoplasmic concentration and reducing the availability of Ca^{++} for binding with troponin C. The regulatory units change conformation back to their resting configuration, reducing the probability of strong interactions between actin and myosin. The muscle returns to resting conditions.

Length–Tension Relationships

The number of cross-bridges formed relates to the degree of myosin activation resulting from changes in Ca^{++} concentration in the sarcoplasm, and also to the degree of overlap of actin and myosin filaments. Length-clamp experiments have demonstrated that sarcomeres (and muscles) have optimum lengths

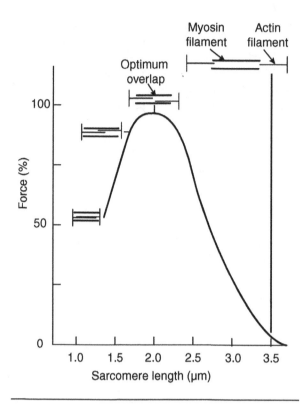

Figure 2.12 Force as a function of sarcomere length.

Adapted, by permission, from K.A.P. Edman and C. Reggiani, 1987, "The sarcomere length-tension relation determined in short segments of intact muscle fibres of the frog," *Journal of Physiology* 385: 709-732.

at which maximum force can be produced (Edman and Reggiani 1987; Gordon, Huxley, and Julian 1966). The change in isometric force capabilities appears to be related to the number of cross-bridges formed at varying lengths of the sarcomere (figure 2.12). The optimum sarcomere length appears to be approximately 2.0 µm (Edman and Reggiani 1987). At very long lengths (>2.0 µm), few cross-bridges are formed because the filaments are too far apart. It appears that at very short lengths (<2.0 µm), few cross-bridges are formed because the actin filaments (I-filaments) pass into the opposite half of the sarcomere; and it is possible that cross-bridges interact with the opposite actin filament, in effect pulling against one another and reducing force generated. Isolated whole muscle shows similar length–tension relationships.

In an isolated muscle preparation (figure 2.13) in which both ends are fixed, electrical stimulation results in an isometric contraction (muscle gains tension but does not change length). A short stimulation period (0.2 ms) produces an isometric twitch (figure 2.14a). Various aspects of the isometric twitch can be used for physiological or biomechanical comparison. These aspects (variables)

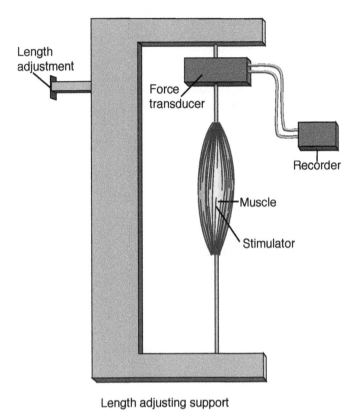

Figure 2.13 Isolated muscle preparation for length–tension investigations.

include total tension, developed force, time to peak tension, time to relaxation, and rate of force development. These variables can be used to compare muscles with different myosin capabilities or the same muscle from animals that have been treated or trained differently (Stone and Lipner 1978).

The total tension produced by a muscle is a function of the resting tension and the developed force. Resting tension is largely a function of the elastic properties of the muscle, and the developed force is a function of the contractile apparatus. Changes in resting length of the muscle produce different degrees of developed force and total tension as a result of isometric contractions (figure 2.14b). Increasing the frequency of stimulation leads to tetany (figure 2.15). Tetany likely results from the inability of the Ca++ pump of the SR to keep up with the increasing calcium concentration in the sarcoplasm.

Force–Velocity Relationships

"Isotonic" means having same tone or force. Isotonic contractions can occur only in isolated muscle preparations and are of two types. If upon

stimulation a muscle contracts (shortens) and lifts a load such that external work (W = f × d) is performed, the contraction is termed a concentric contraction. Loads larger than the maximum isometric capabilities of a muscle cause the muscle to lengthen, even though it is attempting to contract, producing a negative velocity; this type of contraction is termed an eccentric contraction. It may be argued that the terms isometric and eccentric contraction are inappropriate since a true contraction (i.e., shortening) is not occurring. Thus, the term "muscle action" may be used instead of "contraction" (Knuttgen and Kraemer 1987). During concentric muscle actions, as the load increases, the velocity of shortening decreases. However, during eccentric muscle actions, as the load increases, so does velocity to a point. These relationships are shown in figure 2.16. Note the following in terms of maximum force production:

concentric < isometric < eccentric

The difference between concentric and isometric force production may be explained by the number of cross-bridges formed at any moment in time. As the muscle (sarcomere) begins to move, it is difficult for the cross-bridges to attach to a moving filament and thus fewer attachments are formed. Thus, there is a relationship between velocity of shortening and the number of cross-bridges formed and therefore the force generated (Huijing 1992). The additional force generated by the stretching of the elastic elements of muscle explains the higher maximum forces produced by eccentric muscle actions (Huijing 1992). Vmax (figure 2.16) represents the fastest possible cross-bridge cycling rate of a muscle and correlates well with the maximum hydrolysis rate of ATP (Barany 1967; Edman et al. 1988; Pette and Staron 1990).

Although the speed and force of shortening appear to be strongly related to myosin ATPase, other contractile attributes such as time to peak tension are not as strongly correlated (Pette and Staron 1990). Power is the product of force and velocity; note that in isolated muscle, maximum power occurs at about 30% of maximum velocity or maximum isometric force (figure 2.17).

For intact whole muscles, the peak internal tension or external force produced is a function of the interaction of numerous sarcomere lengths and the mechanical attributes of the bone lever system. However, the force–velocity characteristics of intact muscle are similar to those of isolated muscle (see chapter 3, "Biomechanics of Resistance Training").

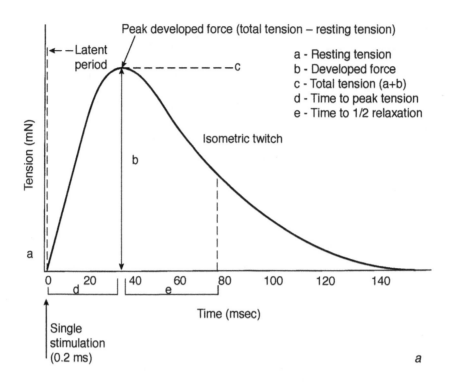

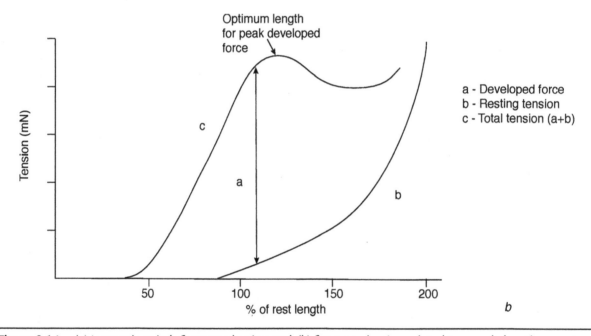

Figure 2.14 *(a)* Isometric twitch force production and *(b)* force production related to muscle length.
(b) Adapted from *Organ physiology: Structure and function of the nervous system*, 10th ed, A.C. Guyton, pg. 73. Copyright 1976 with permission from Elsevier.

Somatic Nervous System Structure and Function

Simplistically, the nervous system is a mass of nerve cells and supporting connective tissue. The nervous system can be assessed according to its anatomical characteristics or by its functional characteristics.

From an anatomical perspective, the central nervous system (CNS) consists of the brain and spinal cord, and the peripheral nervous system (PNS) consists of the peripheral nerves. From a functional perspective, the function of the CNS is either autonomic or somatic. The autonomic nervous system is responsible for nonvoluntary actions involved

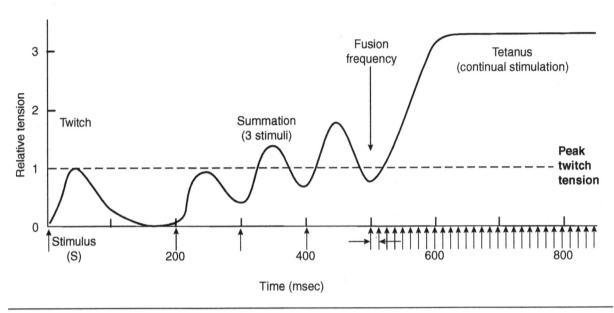

Figure 2.15 Force production in relation to increased stimulation frequency.

Adapted from A.J. Vander, J.H. Sherman, and D.S. Luciano, 1980, *Human physiology: The mechanisms of body function,* 3rd ed. (New York: McGraw-Hill Companies), 228. With permission of The McGraw-Hill Companies.

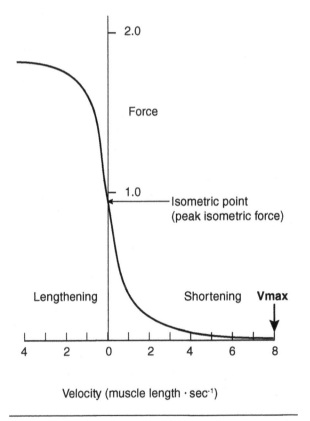

Figure 2.16 Force–velocity relation during concentric-isometric-eccentric muscle actions in isolated muscle.

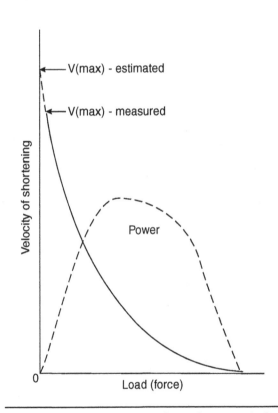

Figure 2.17 Power as a product of concentric force and velocity.

in "housekeeping" and maintenance of homeostasis, such as peristalsis and regulation of heart rate and blood pressure. The somatic system works in an integrative fashion with the muscular system, forming the neuromuscular system.

The CNS contains neurons and glial cells. Glial cells are specialized nerve cells that do not conduct impulses and have no direct role in impulse transmission. These cells provide a structural matrix and metabolic support for neurons in controlling the passage of substances from capillaries into the neuronal environment (McComas 1996).

The smallest functional unit of the nervous system is a neuron. Functionally, neurons are either sensory (afferents) or motor (efferents). Sensory neurons transmit information from sensory receptors to the CNS. Motor neurons transmit information from the CNS to effector cells. The basic anatomy of the neuron is shown in figure 2.18. The anatomical nervous system is made up of billions of neurons, which can have different sizes and shapes. Information is transmitted by way of changes in the electrical potential of the cell.

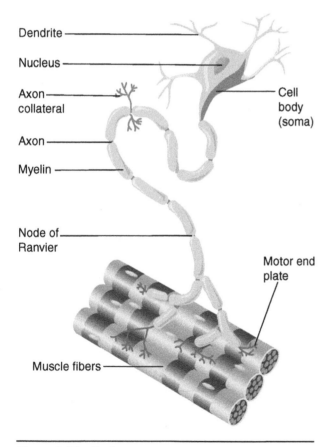

Figure 2.18   Basic neuron anatomy.

Adapted, by permission, from J. Hoffman, 2006, *Physiological aspects of sport training and performance* (Champaign, IL: Human Kinetics), 8.

At rest, neurons (and muscle cells) have a negative charge on the inside compared to the outside that is referred to as the resting membrane potential (RMP). The RMP results from an excess of anions (negative ions) trapped inside and an excess of cations (positive ions) on the outside of the cell. The RMP is set up by the selective permeability of the plasma membrane. The excess positive and negative ions accumulate along a narrow band on either side of the plasma membrane, resulting in an RMP that essentially straddles the plasma membrane. The RMP is disturbed by changes in the number of anions or cations on the outside or inside.

Two basic mechanisms create RMPs: (1) active transport of ions across the plasma membrane and (2) diffusion of ions through the membrane as a result of a concentration gradient. Under resting conditions the RMP is largely a function of $[Na^+]$ and $[K^+]$. Na^+ is found in relatively high concentrations outside the cell (142 mEq/L), and K^+ is found in relatively high concentrations inside the cell (140 mEq/L). These Na^+/K^+ concentrations are largely maintained by an ATP-dependent electrogenic pump (Dean 1941) found in the plasma membrane (figure 2.19). The inside is typically −70 to −85 mV compared to the outside. The reason is that the neuron's plasma membrane is 50 to 100 times more permeable to K^+ compared to Na^+ and allows K^+ to "leak" out of the intracellular fluid into the extracellular fluid, resulting in more cations on the outside of the cell (Caldwell 1968).

Chloride ions (CL^-) readily diffuse through the plasma membrane and are not dependent on a pump. Thus, $[CL^-]$ is determined by electrical potential; CL^- is repelled by the negative inside of the cell, resulting in a high concentration (103 mEq/L) on the outside of the cell. Therefore, the role of CL^- in the development of the RMP is passive. However, the rapid movement of CL^- can affect the duration and magnitude of the AP. Other ions are affected in the same way as Na^+, K^+, and CL^-. For example, Ca^{++} ions behave in much the same way as Na^+ ions. However, the concentrations and the permeabilities of the plasma membrane to these ions are small, so there is little net effect on the RMP. The most important role for these additional ions, particularly calcium and magnesium, is in their effect on the membrane permeability of other ions.

Action Potential

The AP, a wave of depolarization that occurs along the surface of excitable tissue, is the result of a sequence of changes in the membrane potential lasting a fraction of a second. Depolarization of a

Figure 2.18 labels: Dendrite, Nucleus, Axon collateral, Axon, Myelin, Node of Ranvier, Muscle fibers, Cell body (soma), Motor end plate

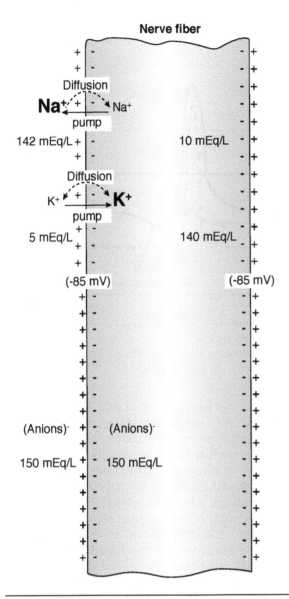

Nerve fiber

Diffusion

Na Na⁺
pump

142 mEq/L   10 mEq/L

Diffusion

K⁺   **K⁺**
pump

5 mEq/L   140 mEq/L

(-85 mV)   (-85 mV)

(Anions)⁻   (Anions)⁻

150 mEq/L   150 mEq/L

Figure 2.19 Example of an ionic dynamic equilibrium across cell membranes.

Adapted from *Organ physiology: Structure and function of the nervous system*, 10th ed., A.C. Guyton, pg. 8. Copyright 1976, with permission from Elsevier.

membrane is followed by a rapid return to RMP values. The AP is associated with rapid changes in membrane permeability for Na⁺ and K⁺. Rapid changes in membrane permeability for various ions are associated with the opening and closing of ionic gates or channels that, along with electrogenic pumps, control the movement of specific ions into and out of the cell (Barchi 1988; Catterall 1988; Kamb, Iverson, and Tanouye 1987; McComas 1996). Various stimuli, including extreme temperature changes and chemical, mechanical, and electrical stimuli, are capable of producing an AP.

The AP occurs in two stages, depolarization and repolarization (Guyton 1976). These two stages are influenced by a sequence of changes in permeability to Na⁺ and K⁺ (figure 2.20):

1. As a result of a stimulus, the permeability of the membrane for Na⁺ suddenly increases, and many Na⁺ rush to the inside of the fiber because of the initial concentration gradient between the outside and inside of the cell. The net effect is that enough cations enter the cell to make the inside positive compared to the outside, resulting in a *reversal potential* and depolarization of the cell.

2. Immediately after the reversal potential takes place, the permeability of the membrane for Na⁺ returns to the resting state; simultaneously there is an increase in the permeability to K⁺. The change in permeability allows large amounts of K⁺ to diffuse out of the cell, returning the membrane potential back to its negative resting state.

3. Once the resting electrical potential is reached, the membrane permeability for K⁺ is returned to the resting state. As resting permeabilities are reached, the electrogenic pump re-establishes the resting concentrations of the cell.

An AP occurs at one spot on an excitable membrane and subsequently excites adjacent portions of the membrane, causing AP propagation. Propagation occurs as a result of completion of a local circuit of current flow (Guyton 1976). There is no single direction of propagation; the AP can travel in all directions away from the initial site of the AP. Once the AP is initiated, the wave of depolarization travels over the entire surface of the membrane (this is an example of the all-or-none principle). In physiological situations, with intact nervous systems, direction of propagation is determined by anatomy, and the AP typically moves from the soma down the axon. Additionally, the strength of the AP can be influenced by changes in the extra- and intracellular physiological environment (e.g., ionic concentrations, pH). The AP lasts for about the same time period at each point on the membrane. Repolarization occurs at the point that was initially depolarized and then spreads progressively behind the AP. Thus repolarization is propagated in the same direction as depolarization but is about 0.002 s behind.

In order for a neuron to carry an AP, an increase of 10 to 15 mV in the RMP must be reached; this represents a threshold value of activation (figure 2.20). In a neuron this value is initiated by increased Na⁺ permeability; however, if the influx of Na⁺ is small and the threshold value is not reached, no AP

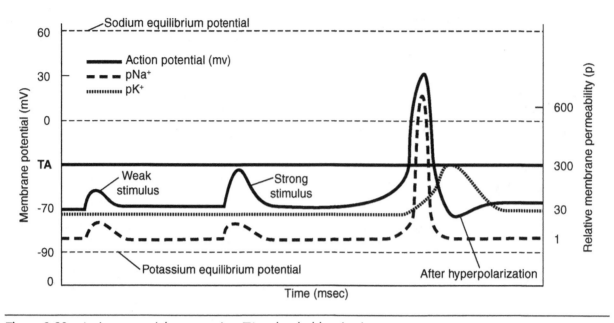

Figure 2.20 Action potential propagation. TA = threshold activation.

Adapted from A.C. Guyton, 1976, *Organ physiology: Structure and function of the nervous system* (Philadelphia, PA: W.B. Saunders), 58.

will be propagated. In intact animals, the threshold value may be reached through an increased frequency of impulses arriving from the same neuron (temporal summation) or when a large number of separate neurons activate the effector cell (spatial summation).

Neurons often transmit a series of APs; however, a second AP cannot occur as long as the membrane is depolarized from the preceding AP. No matter how strong the stimulus, an AP cannot be propagated during the absolute refractory period, which lasts about 0.0025 s in a myelinated fiber. Thus the maximum number of impulses possible is about $2500 \cdot s^{-1}$.

Neuron Structure and Function

Muscle contraction in an intact animal is initiated in the motor cortex of the cerebrum. The muscle is sent information for contraction, in the form of a series of AP, by large cells lying in the ventral gray matter of the spinal cord or a corresponding area of the brainstem (McComas 1996). These large cells are motor neurons. Figure 2.18 shows the basic structure of a typical α-motor neuron, which consists of a soma (cell body); short projections from the cell body known as dendrites; and a long projection, the axon, with terminal endings that release neurotransmitters. The cell bodies of motor neurons are arranged in longitudinal columns within the spinal cord. Typically the cells within a column innervate the same muscle (McComas 1996; Romanes 1941,

1951). Motor neurons are of two types: γ, which innervate intrafusal muscle fibers (muscle spindle), and α, which innervate extrafusal muscle fibers.

Under normal intact conditions, the dendrites and soma receive information from other neurons and transmit information down the axon to the terminal endings, where the release of a neurotransmitter can transfer information across a synapse to an effector cell. The effector cell may be another neuron or a muscle fiber. The transmitter substance released by a neuron depends on its location and function; for example, in the brain the transmitter may be ACh, norepinephrine, serotonin, or γ-aminobutyric acid. Peripheral α- and γ-motor neurons that innervate muscle cells release ACh.

The soma of an α-motor neuron has a diameter of about 70 μm and is much larger than the soma of a γ-motor neuron. The soma contains a single large nucleus with a prominent nucleolus. Various organelles are found in the soma, including Nissl bodies (tightly packed endoplasmic reticulum), mitochondria, and a complex cytoskeleton system. The soma typically has several dendrites radiating in various directions. The dendrites show considerable arborization and extend for relatively long distances into the gray matter of the spinal cord, which allows them to receive information from a variety of other neurons (McComas 1996).

The axon arises from the axon hillock, a conical projection of the soma, and may extend only a few centimeters or more than a meter, depending on the location and tissue innervated. The axon forms a cylinder that extends into the muscle. The axonal cylinder is bound by a plasma membrane that has properties similar to those of the sarcolemma of muscle. A long axon of a large α-motor neuron may have as much as 100 times more cytoplasm than its soma. The axonal cylinder contains arrays of cytotubules and neurofilaments that run its entire length; these function as support structures and in axonal transport.

All neurons have a lipid covering around the axonal cylinder as the result of a myelin sheath formed by Schwann cells (Geren 1954). However, neurons can be classed as myelinated or unmyelinated depending on the thickness of the sheath, which in turn is related to the number of layers of *sphingomyelin*. Unmyelinated fibers have a single wrapping of myelin; somatic motor neurons have multiple layers of myelin and are classed as myelinated. Myelin is an excellent insulatory material, increasing the capacitance of the sheathed section of axon and preventing the flow of ions. In myelinated neurons, the sheath is about as thick as the axon cylinder (Guyton 1976). In adults the myelin sheath is interrupted approximately once every 1000 μm along the axon by a node of Ranvier. The node is a small area of noninsulation where ions can easily flow between the extracellular fluid and the inner surface of the plasma membrane of the axon (figure 2.18). Because of the relative ease of the flow of ions in the node, an AP can jump from node to node (i.e., saltatory conduction). Saltatory conduction has several advantages over typical local circuit conduction. First, saltatory conduction increases the velocity of AP propagation; in typical α-motor neurons, propagation velocity is about 40 to 120 m · s⁻¹ (Guyton 1976; McComas 1996). Second, only

the nodes depolarize during saltatory conduction; thus fewer ions are transported and less energy is involved in reestablishing the RMP.

The diameter of the axon also influences neural transmission. Generally, the greater the axon diameter, the faster the velocity of conductance. In unmyelinated fibers, such as those associated with many sensory functions, the velocity of conduction increases with the square root of the diameter of the axon; in myelinated axons, the velocity increases linearly (approximately) with the change in diameter (Guyton 1976). The axon of a motor neuron branches out as it approaches the muscle and may innervate as many as several hundred muscle fibers. The synapse between the terminal ending of an axonal branch and a muscle cell is a specialized area termed the *neuromuscular junction*.

Neuromuscular Junction Structure and Function

The interface between a motor neuron and a muscle cell is the neuromuscular junction (NMJ). As the motor axon enters a muscle it loses its myelin sheath and divides into branches or axonal twigs (Guyton 1976; Hubbard 1973; McComas 1996). The twigs lie in grooves in the sarcolemma and form a circular area on the surface of the muscle cell (figure 2.21). This circular area is covered by a Schwann cell cap that electrically isolates the area. At the ends of the axonal twigs are small irregular expansions, the terminal boutons, which correspond to the area of neurotransmitter release. The axon terminals contain numerous small spheres, about 55 nm across, with membranous linings. These are synaptic vesicles containing ACh; they are manufactured in the soma and then transported to the terminal

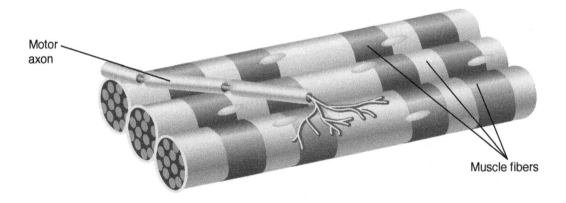

Figure 2.21 Axonal branching at the neuromuscular junction.

Adapted, by permission, from B.R. MacIntosh, P.F. Gardiner, and A.J. McComas, 2006, *Skeletal muscle*, 2nd ed. (Champaign, IL: Human Kinetics), 33.

boutons, or they are formed by invagination and pinching of the axonal plasma membrane of the terminal ending (Heuser and Reese 1973).

Some evidence indicates that ACh is formed by the acetylation of choline in the axon terminal and that it enters the vesicle as a result of an H^+ gradient that attracts the ACh into the vesicles (Anderson, King, and Parsons 1982). Each vesicle contains about 10,000 molecules of ACh (Kuffler and Yoshikami 1975). The terminal endings also contain a large concentration of mitochondria that likely provide energy for the synthesis of new transmitter.

The motor end plate is the area of muscle lying directly under the Schwann cell cap, including the sarcolemma and a mound of sarcoplasm known as the sole plate. Within the sole plate is a high concentration of muscle nuclei, mitochondria, ribosomes, and pinocytic vesicles (McComas 1996). The terminal ending of the axon is separated from the sarcolemma by a synaptic cleft of about 70 nm, although folding and invaginations of the sarcolemma into the sole plate may create secondary synaptic clefts as deep as 1 μm and may greatly increase the surface area of the synaptic cleft that can combine with ACh. The sarcolemma lining the motor end plate is thicker than other parts of the cell, largely due to an increased number of acetylcholine receptors (AChR) in the outer membrane. The invaginations increase the number of AChRs as well as the amount of AChE available for interaction with ACh. The AChRs are not permanent fixtures within the sarcolemma but are continually renewed and replaced, a process controlled by the myonuclei within the sole plate (Fambrough 1979; McComas 1996; Usdin and Fischbach 1986).

Acetylcholine is the neurotransmitter that acts to transfer the AP from the neuron across the NMJ to the muscle cell. When an AP arrives at the terminal endings of an axon, the depolarization resulting from the opening of Na^+ triggers Ca^{++} channel activation. Ca^{++} enters the axon terminals along a concentration gradient. The activation of Ca^{++} channels causes the ACh-containing vesicles to attach to the sarcolemma near the Ca^{++} channels. The vesicles fuse with the sarcolemma and release their ACh into the NMJ by the process of exocytosis (Bennett, Callakos, and Scheller 1992). Two molecules of ACh then attach to an AChR on the sarcolemma, causing a channel in the center of the receptor to open. This channel allows Na^+ and K^+ to move according to concentration and electrical gradients, thus producing an *end plate potential* (EPP). A single AP causes the release of 25 to 45

quanta (vesicles) in human muscle (Engel et al. 1990; Slater et al. 1992). If a sufficient quanta of ACh are released and the EPP is large enough, an AP will be propagated.

The enzyme AChE is found in the basement membrane of the sarcolemma and is positioned between the site of ACh release and the receptors (McComas 1996). Although AChE is continuously activated, ACh can reach the receptors because there are more molecules of transmitter released than there are molecules of enzyme present in the basement membrane. After opening the AChR channels, the ACh detaches and diffuses toward the basement membrane, where the transmitter is deactivated by hydrolysis and transmission is eventually terminated. The products of hydrolysis, choline and acetic acid, are taken up by the axon terminals, converted into ACh, and repackaged into vesicles.

The Motor Unit

The motor unit (MU) consists of the motor neuron and all of the muscle cells it innervates (Sherrington 1929). When an AP is propagated in a motor neuron, all of the muscle fibers innervated by that motor neuron are stimulated to contract; thus the muscle and nerve fibers act as a unit (this is known as the all-or-none principle). The CNS plans and initiates movement in terms of MUs, rather than muscle cells; thus the MU is the functional unit of the neuromuscular system. In this section we consider the large α MUs of the somatic nervous system innervating skeletal muscle extrafusal fibers.

Within a muscle the distribution of fibers generally covers a relatively broad area, with adjacent fibers being from different MUs. A single α-motor neuron in relation to the number of muscle fibers innervated is termed the innervation ratio. The innervation ratio changes according to the functional characteristics of the muscle. For example, in a muscle able to function in fine motor control, such as the intraocular muscles of the eye, the innervation ratio ranges from 1:5 to 1:100; in muscles that are able to produce large amounts of force, and in which fine movements are not an issue, the innervation ratio may be as large as 1:2000 (Gowitzke and Milner 1988; McComas 1996). Although there can be considerable variation, the number of MUs per muscle can vary from about 100, as in the first lumbrical, to about 3000 in the vastus lateralis. There can also be considerable variation of MU size within a muscle (McComas 1996).

It is important to note that MUs display considerable plasticity of phenotypic expression and are not static structures (Pette and Staron 1990). Motor units appear to adapt to a variety of neural, hormonal, and metabolic stimuli resulting from functional demands and neuromuscular activity patterns. Their dynamic nature makes it difficult to classify them as distinct and separate entities. This difficulty in classification is exacerbated by the possibility of local factors modulating gene expression in different fibers within MUs and along the length of single fibers (Pette and Staron 1990). Nevertheless, classification schemes are important tools for the sport scientist because these schemes allow for the delineation of specific muscle fiber populations with similar functional properties.

Motor units can be separated and identified according to their contractile characteristics (Burke 1981; Burke, Levine, and Zajac 1971). Based on contractile properties, three types of MUs have been characterized:

1. Fast-twitch fatigue sensitive (FF): These are large MUs found primarily in pale muscle; they produce the fastest time to peak force, highest force, and greatest speed and power of contraction. However, FF also fatigue at the fastest rate during sustained tetanic contractions.

2. Fast-twitch fatigue resistant (FR): These are large MUs found in "mixed" muscle; they produce intermediate time, force, speed, power, and endurance capabilities.

3. Slow-twitch (S): These are relatively small MUs found in red muscle; they produce the slowest time to peak force and lowest force, speed, and power; however, they have the greatest endurance capabilities.

Although this classification system (Burke 1981) works well in small animals, classifying human MUs in this manner is difficult due to differences in muscle size and the invasive nature of the methods necessary for classification (Noth 1992b).

The muscle fibers that make up an α MU generally have a relatively homogeneous biochemical consistency from fiber to fiber (Pette and Staron 1990, 2000). This finding has allowed for the development of classification schemes based on histochemical identification. Two basic histochemical schemes are currently used:

1. Myosin ATPase and metabolic (enzymatic) properties (Barnard, Edgerton, and Peter 1970; Peter et al. 1972). This nomenclature uses a classification system based on myosin ATPase activity and also uses the activities of specific metabolic enzymes. This system identifies three types of MUs whose properties have been related to the contractile characteristics displayed by the FF, FR, and S motor units (Burke 1981; Burke, Levine, and Zajac 1971):

a. Fast-twitch glycolytic (FG). This MU type has contractile properties similar to those of the FF and displays a high glycogenolytic enzymatic activity profile.

b. Fast-twitch oxidative glycolytic (FOG). This MU type has contractile properties similar to those of the FR and has both a high oxidative and a high glycolytic enzyme activity profile.

c. Slow-twitch oxidative (SO). This MU type has contractile properties similar to those of the S and has a high oxidative enzyme activity profile.

2. Myofibrillar ATPase. It has been demonstrated that slow and fast myosins have different alkaline and acidic stability (Seidel 1967), and this observation has allowed the development of refined methods for myosin ATPase histochemical delineation (Brooke and Kaiser 1970; Gardiner 2001; Pette and Staron 1990; Staron and Hikida 1992). Using this system, a continuum of MU types based on myosin ATPase has been identified that relates to the content of MHC (table 2.1). While it is tempting to relate the myosin ATPase system to the metabolic-based system, evidence indicates that the two systems are not completely compatible (Pette and Staron 2000; Sant'Ana Pereira et al. 1996). In normal animal limb muscles there is general agreement that the IIB, IIA, and I MUs correspond to the FF, FR, and S MUs described by Burke and colleagues (1971). However, MU types in some of the smaller muscles, such as those in the hand and foot, do not seem to correlate well (Brooks, Fahey, and White 1996; McComas 1996). Additionally, metabolic attributes do correlate with the general classification of type I and type II, with type I fibers being metabolically and enzymatically suited for aerobic endurance activities and type II MUs being suited for anaerobic power-type activities. Furthermore, contractile properties, particularly speed of shortening and power outputs, do correlate well with myosin ATPase activities. Thus a continuum of maximum contractile speed and power output can be assumed to exist: IIB > IIX > IIA > IIC > I (McComas 1996; Pette and Staron 1990; Staron and Hikida 1992). Recent evidence indicates that the IIB fiber type exists in small animals (e.g., rats),

but not in humans, where the faster fiber type is the IIX (Gardiner 2001).

The characteristic contractile and metabolic properties of MUs are shown in table 2.3.

A sample of muscle tissue for muscle fiber typing in humans is usually obtained using a muscle biopsy technique (Bergstrom 1962). This technique, in appropriate muscles, has allowed for the intra- and intermuscular comparison of human tissue and allowed insights into the functional capabilities of human muscle. For example, it has been shown that fiber type generally correlates well with athletic performance. Strength-power athletes have a predominance of type II fibers, and aerobic endurance athletes have a predominance of type I fibers. The degree to which physical activity effects changes in MU type is unknown and is subject to controversy. However,

changes in muscle fiber type and MHC can occur as a result of specific conditions. Fast-to-slow transitions can occur as a result of increased neuromuscular activity, mechanical loading, and hypothyroidism. Slow-to-fast transitions can occur with reduced neuromuscular activity, mechanical unloading, and hyperthyroidism (Pette and Staron 2000).

Voluntary Movement

Voluntary muscle contraction and directed movement are planned and organized by the CNS (Noth 1992a). An understanding of the hierarchy of the somatic-somatosensory system is crucial for understanding the organization and patterning of MU activation in carrying out coordinated movement (figure 2.22). Here we briefly describe the process of voluntary movement.

Table 2.3a Motor Unit Properties—Contractile

Properties	MOTOR UNIT TYPE		
	FF, FG	FR, FOG	S, SO
Twitch time	Fast	Fast	Slow
Contraction force	High	Intermediate	Low
Contraction speed	High	Intermediate	Low
Contraction power	High	Intermediate	Low
Fatigue sensitivity	High	Moderate	Low
Relaxation time	Fast	Fast	Slow

Based on Burke 1981; McComas 1996; Pette and Staron 1992.

Table 2.3b Motor Unit Properties—Metabolic and Physiologic

Properties	MOTOR UNIT TYPE		
	FF, FG	FR, FOG	S, SO
Relative size	Large	Large	Small
Glycogen content	No major differences		
Triglyceride content	Low	Moderate to high	High
Mitochondrial density	Low	Moderate to high	High
Capillary density	Low	High	High
Myoglobin content	Low	Moderate to high	High
Ca^{++}-sequestering ability (SR)	Fast	Fast	Low
CPK concentration	High	High	Low
Glycogenolytic enzyme activity	High	High	Low
Oxidative enzyme activity	Low	High	High
Motoneuron	α_1	α_1	α_2
NMJ	Large, complex	Large, complex	Small, simple
Activation threshold	High	High	Low

Based on Burke 1981; McComas 1996; Pette and Staron 1992.

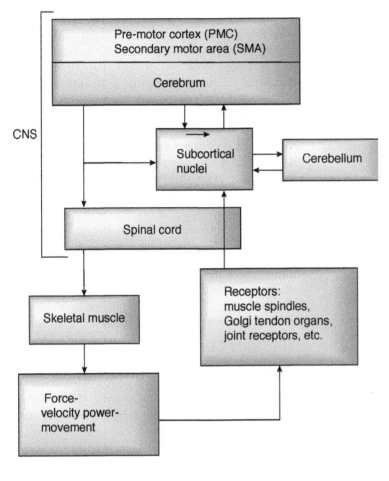

Figure 2.22 Hierarchy of the somatic-somatosensory nervous system.

Adapted from J. Noth, 1992, Cortical and peripheral control. In *Strength and power in sport*, edited by P.V. Komi (London: Blackwell Scientific), 9-20.

Motor programming takes place in the premotor cortex (PMC) and the secondary motor area (SMA). The PMC relays information from cortical and subcortical nuclei to the primary motor cortex. The transfer of sensory information from subcortical areas to the primary motor cortex (MI) is crucial for coordinated movement to occur. The PMC also appears to function in the preparation for movements, postural control, visual guidance of movement, and rapid corrections during movement in response to sensory cues (Noth 1992a). The function of the SMA is not clear, but appears to be involved with the initiation of movements and internal guidance (Wise and Strick 1984).

The MI lies in the central gyrus and extends into the central sulcus of the cerebrum (Noth 1992a). It is the terminal focus of subcortical sensory input. The primary outflow is along the corticospinal tract, which originates in the large Betz cells of the MI. The primary function of the MI is to select appropriate MUs within specific muscles that result in a specific movement pattern. It appears that there are multiple discrete and separate nuclei within the MI that are task related; that is, the motor cortex organizes the MUs according to muscle synergies rather than isolated muscles (Noth 1992a; Sato and Tanji 1989).

The cerebellum contains about 50% of the neurons in the brain (Noth 1992a). The neuronal matrix of the cerebellum is uniform, in contrast to most areas in the brain, which suggests that the internal functioning in all areas of the cerebellum is similar. The primary function of the cerebellum is in motor learning. All voluntary actions as well as reflexes require input from the cerebellum in the learning process. The cerebellum receives information from a variety of sensory pathways and uses this information in the refinement of the motor learning process. The cerebellum appears to be responsible for adaptation of movement to changes in internal or external restraint; this is associated with high-precision movement (Noth 1992a). Unlike the cerebellum, the basal ganglia do not appear to receive direct sensory input. The basal ganglia appear to be involved in the release of motor programs and in the preparation of axial and proximal limb muscles for the initiation of goal-oriented movements; additionally, the basal ganglia appear to be important in selecting behaviorally relevant internal and external cues (Kimura 1990; Noth 1992a).

Motor neurons are located in the spinal cord (SC), as well as in the brainstem; the SC is the lowest portion of the CNS hierarchy. The major function of the SC is the integration of descending motor commands with peripheral sensory input. The SC also processes sensory information and transmits it to supraspinal areas. A third important function is the generation of spinal reflexes. Some evidence suggests that coordinated voluntary movement depends on a series of spinal reflexes and feedback loops (Soechting and Flanders 1991).

Motor Unit Recruitment

The neuromuscular system can increase the contraction force of a muscle through two basic

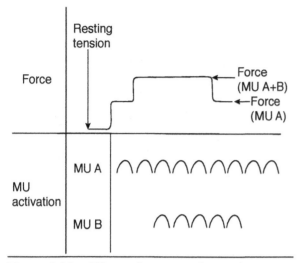

Figure 2.23 Effects of motor unit recruitment on force production.

mechanisms: recruitment (increasing the number of MUs activated) and rate coding. Recruitment can increase the muscular force production in an additive fashion (figure 2.23). Our present understanding of the pattern of recruitment is based largely on the size principle (Hannerz 1974; Henneman et al. 1974). Generally, the smaller the neuron's soma, the lower the threshold of activation. Thus smaller

MUs are usually recruited before the larger ones as the force or intensity (power output) of muscle contraction increases (Brooks, Fahey, and White 1996; Hannerz 1974; Henneman et al. 1974). This relationship, shown in figure 2.24, means that generally the order of recruitment is S > FR > FF. It also suggests that the FF and FR MUs will be recruited less frequently in daily tasks that do not require high contraction forces or intensities. Recruitment of larger MUs as greater force or power output is necessary is in keeping with the contractile and metabolic characteristics of the larger fibers (i.e., type II).

Rate coding deals with the frequency of activation of MUs; thus, as the frequency of activation increases, so does force. This holds true for single fibers, MUs, and whole muscles (figure 2.15). We should note that dependence on recruitment or rate coding varies from muscle to muscle (McComas 1996). Chapter 3 contains a detailed discussion of the effects of recruitment and rate coding on force production.

Proprioception and Kinestheses

Proprioception is the ability to sense the body in space; it also deals with the ability to perceive the

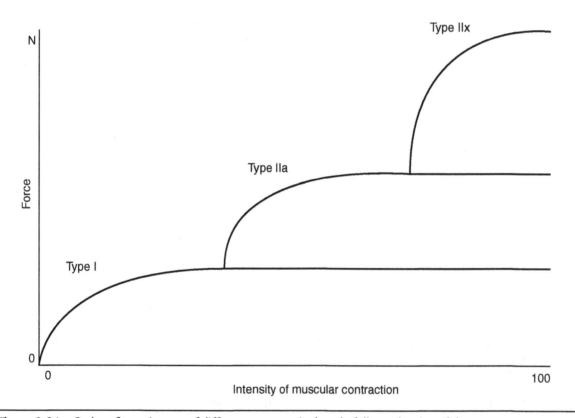

Figure 2.24 Order of recruitment of different motor units largely follows the size of the neuron.

Adapted from E.H. Henneman et al., 1974, "Rank order of motoneurons within a pool, law of combination," *Journal of Neurophysiology* 37: 1338-1349.

relationship of body parts to each other. Kinesthesia is often used interchangeably with proprioception or used to mean the finely tuned ability to make skilled movements.

Sherrington (1906) noted that proprioceptors are those end organs that are stimulated by the body itself. These are the somatosensory organs, located so as to gather information concerning various aspects of position and movement such as joint angle, muscle length–tension–speed characteristics, and contact with surfaces. The nervous system can use this information to modify subsequent muscle actions. Much of this information can be used in negative feedback loops (reflexes), allowing motor activity to become self-regulating.

Two proprioceptors that have a major impact on muscle functional characteristics are the muscle spindle and the Golgi tendon organ. The muscle spindle is a fluid-filled fusiform-shaped capsule 2 to 20 nm long that encloses 5 to 12 specialized intrafusal muscle fibers (Gowitzke and Milner 1988). The primary functions of the muscle spindle have to do with length–velocity characteristics of muscle contraction (Grill and Hallet 1995; McComas 1996; Noth 1992a) and can be summarized as follows:

- The servo-assist characteristics of muscle spindle operation allow the brain to cause voluntary muscle contraction with less energy expenditure.

- The muscle spindle allows the muscle to contract at appropriate force outputs when the resistance encountered changes during or between successive contractions.

- Failure in the muscle contraction force due to fatigue can be partially compensated for by a stretch reflex.

- Appropriate use of the stretch reflex can aid in producing concentric muscle force (stretch–shortening cycle).

The muscle spindles are embedded in the skeletal muscle fibers (extrafusal fibers) and act in parallel with them. The capsule contains two types of intrafusal fibers based on the number and distribution of their nuclei. Typically there are two to four nuclear bag fibers; in this type of fiber, most of the nuclei are located in the middle. The bag fibers are thicker and longer than the nuclear chain fibers. There are 8 to 12 nuclear chain fibers, which have nuclei distributed fairly evenly along their length. The bag fibers are innervated by γ_1-motor neurons, and the nuclear chain fibers by γ_2-motor neurons (McComas 1996). Group Ia sensory neurons inner-

vate the central portions of both the bag and chain fibers, while group II sensory neurons innervate one end, typically opposite the motor neurons, of both fibers. The characteristics of the intrafusal fibers are given in table 2.4.

Activation of the group Ia fibers by forceful or rapid stretching of the extrafusal fiber can elicit a myotatic or stretch reflex, producing a more forceful concentric contraction following the stretch. The stretch reflex causes facilitation of the agonist and inhibition of the antagonist. A very slow or static stretch can activate the group II fibers, which will result in facilitation of the antagonist and inhibition of the agonist (figure 2.25, *a & b*). The static reflex can be used to facilitate stretching programs (Hutton 1992). During contraction of the extrafusal fibers, it is imperative that the intrafusal fibers maintain appropriate lengths, or their ability to sense changes in length–velocity parameters will be compromised. Cocontraction of intra- and extrafusal fibers is accomplished by simultaneous activation of both α- and γ-motor neurons (Noth 1992a).

The Golgi tendon organs (GTO) are oblong capsules located primarily within the musculotendinous junction; they act in series with the extrafusal fibers and apparently respond to changes in tension. The GTO contains a single Ib sensory fiber with connections in the SC. As evidenced in some animal studies (Eccles, Eccles, and Lundberg 1957; Granit, Kellerth, and Szumski 1966; Green and Kellerth 1967) using both dynamic and isometric contractions, the GTO appears to function to protect the muscle and tendon from excessive forces. When muscle contraction produces a force that may damage the tissue, the GTO causes a reflex similar to that of the muscle spindle group II fibers, resulting in agonist inhibition and antagonist facilitation. Theoretically, adaptations to strength-power training could result in deinhibition of the GTO. However, recent reexamination of the data concerning

Table 2.4 **Characteristics of the Intrafusal Fibers of the Muscle Spindle**

Characteristic	Nuclear bag	Nuclear chain
Number per capsule	2-4	8-12
Diameter (µm)	20-25	10-12
Motoneuron	γ_1	γ_2
Sensory axon	Ia, II	Ia, II
Sensory response	Dynamic	Static

Adapted, by permission, from B.R. MacIntosh, P.F. Gardiner, and A.J. McComas, 2006, *Skeletal muscle*, 2nd ed. (Champaign, IL: Human Kinetics).

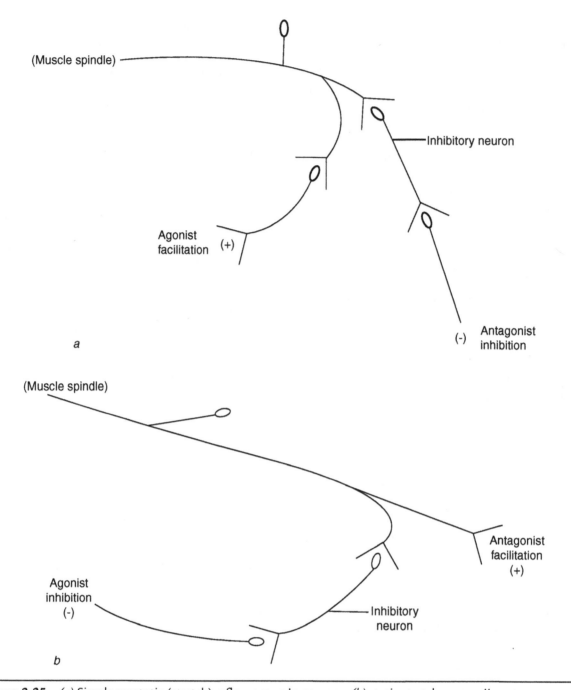

Figure 2.25 *(a)* Simple myotatic (stretch) reflex—group Ia neurons; *(b)* static stretch—group II neurons.

the potential functions of the GTO suggests that activation may have variable effects depending on several factors, including the type of task, the forces encountered, the type of contraction, the muscle(s) activated, and input from higher centers (Chalmers 2002; Duysens, Clarac, and Cruse 2000).

CHAPTER SUMMARY

This chapter concerns basic muscle and nerve physiology and the function of the neuromuscular system. The ability as well as the capacity of the neuromuscular system to function governs physical aspects of behavior and influences psychological aspects of behavior. The action potential is the mechanism of information transfer among neurons and between neurons and muscles. Initiation and propagation of action potentials depend on cellular electrical properties and the interaction and exchange of electrolytes, particularly Na^+ and K^+. The neuron is the functional unit of the nervous system, and its interaction with muscle creates the neuromuscular system.

The sarcomere is the smallest unit containing the necessary contractile and regulatory components, making it the functional unit of the muscular system. Muscle fibers contain thousands of sarcomeres, and muscles contain many fibers. Motor units are made up of a motor neuron and its innervated muscle fibers and represent the functional unit of the neuromuscular system. Motor neurons can have different contractile and metabolic profiles, and their patterns of activation are compatible with these profiles. Activation of motor units by task-specific nuclei in the cortex results in task-specific voluntary movements. Information on how these systems operate is fundamental to development of the knowledge necessary to plan and design reasonable and efficient training programs.

CHAPTER 3

Biomechanics of Resistance Training

Biological mechanics (biomechanics) deals with the application of physical laws to biological motion. In humans, biomechanics concerns the interaction of the skeletal and neuromuscular systems in creating movement (Harman 1994a, 1994b). Muscles transmit force, by way of tendons, to the bones, allowing joint segments to accelerate and produce a velocity and direction of movement. Transmission of force allows humans to walk, run, jump, or lift and thus provides the mechanism of motion for activities ranging from the performance of a simple daily task to the performance of skills by an elite athlete. The transmission of muscle force and realization of movement are governed by certain physical laws and principles of biomechanics. In order to gain a reasonable understanding of how movement is produced, one must understand these fundamental principles and laws; this will allow the formation of a biomechanical perspective in the study and understanding of human motion. With a sound understanding of mechanical principles and laws, this biomechanical perspective will enhance one's ability to produce safe and effective training programs.

In chapter 2 we discussed the basic functions of the neuromuscular system; in the present chapter we expand on that discussion. Biomechanical considerations can be applied at two different levels: microanatomical, which concerns the cellular level, and the macroanatomical level. At the microanatomical level, we can consider the architectural arrangements of sarcomeres and how these arrangements affect function. Macroanatomical considerations can be divided into two parts: (1) whole-muscle mechanical aspects and (2) the mechanical aspects of the intact neuromusculoskeletal system. The chapter also addresses strength, work, and power. It is difficult to completely separate micro- and macroanatomical considerations, so at times the discussions of these levels overlap.

Microanatomical and Force-Producing Characteristics: Sarcomere

The specific tension or specific force is the maximum amount of isometric force a sarcomere or muscle can generate. Sarcomeres are able to produce a specific tension of about 23 newtons · cm^{-2} of muscle tissue (Brooks, Fahey, and White 1996; Edgerton et al. 1986). Sarcomeres transmit forces serially by way of titin to the Z-disc, then to the next sarcomere, and eventually to the tendon of the muscle. Forces are also transmitted laterally to the endomysial connective tissue (Street 1983). Lateral transmission occurs at several levels: from myofibril to myofibril by intermediate filaments that connect adjacent M-lines and Z-discs; from the myofibrils to the sarcolemma and basement membrane by costomeres and the dystrophin complex; and from the muscle fiber to the endomysium.

Longitudinal transmission of force builds some redundancy into the muscle structure. If all or part of a serial sarcomere is damaged or inactive, longitudinal force can be transmitted by the intermediate filaments laterally to adjacent myofibrils or to connective tissue (Patel and Lieber 1997). This finding provides a basis for the lack of complete correlation between muscle injury and function (Friden, Sjostrom, and Ekblom 1981; Lieber, McKee-Woodburn, and Friden 1991). It may also partially explain the ability of muscle to transmit forces along a tapering fiber (the ends of which would have fewer sarcomeres in parallel) to the tendon (Patel and Lieber 1997; Roy and Edgerton 1992).

Muscle contraction is a product of the interaction of actin and myosin and the formation of cross-bridges that generate force and displacement. The magnitude of force generation is dependent on the environmental conditions (e.g., pH, [Ca^{++}]) and length–tension characteristics of the sarcomere. As a result of these conditions, active muscle force is related to the number of cross-bridges formed (Huxley 1957; Zahalak 1986). However, the arrangement of cross-bridges, either in parallel or in series, has additional effects on force and velocity characteristics of muscle contraction (Huijing 1992). Cross-bridges arranged in series within a sarcomere (figure 3.1) must act together if force and displacement are to be equally transmitted on both sides of the sarcomere. In terms of force generated, the force produced by a half sarcomere in series is equal to the force of the whole unit (both halves). In order for balanced force to be transmitted to the Z-disc at both ends, an equal number of cross-bridges must be formed in the two halves of the sarcomere.

The shortening of half a sarcomere is equal to the shortening resulting from any single cross-bridge cycle multiplied by the number of cycles. Therefore, displacement in one half must be added to that in the other half in order to obtain the displacement of the entire sarcomere.

However, if we consider the parallel arrangement, the force produced by each half sarcomere can act independently, producing a total force equal to the sum of the forces of each half sarcomere (Huijing 1992). Whole sarcomeres arranged in series or parallel produce force in a manner similar to that of a single sarcomere (Edgerton et al. 1986; Huijing 1992).

Figure 3.1, a and b, represents two theoretical muscles composed of only four sarcomeres. Based on mathematical modeling, these two arrangements would result in different contractile characteristics at maximum stimulation (Edgerton et al. 1986; Huijing 1992; Jones and Round 1990; Spector et al. 1980) as shown in table 3.1. While force, displacement, and velocity are unequal, equivalent work and power potentials are present.

The energy costs for work and power during maximum activation are also equivalent. This is so because the series arrangement is more energy efficient in terms of displacement; however, this is offset by the efficiency of force production of the parallel arrangement of sarcomeres (table 3.1).

Another energy cost consideration deals with the sarcomere arrangements when they are activated so that equal force is produced. In this case, all sarcomeres would be active in the series arrangement, but only one sarcomere would be active in the parallel arrangement. Equal force production requires more ATP per unit of force for the series compared to the parallel arrangement, but would result in a greater displacement and power output (Edgerton et al. 1986).

The design of a muscle (sarcomere arrangement) can have a marked effect on various aspects of power production. The velocity at which peak power occurs and the range over which power production occurs for sarcomeres in series are about twice the values for the parallel arrangement (Edgerton et al. 1986). If these theoretical muscles had a common insertion, then the power–velocity differences could be relatively large, with the longer muscle able to supply power through a much greater range of velocities compared to the shorter muscle. The longer muscle would also be able to maintain near-peak or peak power over a greater range of velocities. This wider range of peak power would result from the ability of the longer muscle to take over as the shorter muscle's peak power began to drop at higher velocities (figure 3.2).

Macroanatomical Considerations: Muscle

Evidence suggests that the function of a whole muscle generally conforms to the force–length and force–velocity relationships predicted by the sarcomere models (Huijing 1992). Considering the advantages of the parallel sarcomere arrangement in producing force, strong correlations should be found between the cross-sectional area of a muscle and force production. An accurate estimate of the physiological cross-sectional area (PCSA) is necessary to test this relationship. The PCSA is not exactly the same as the anatomical cross section typically measured by noninvasive techniques such as magnetic resonance imaging (MRI) (Conley et al. 1997), but is supposed to equal the sum of the largest cross-sectional areas of the individual fibers (Patel and Lieber 1997). Under in situ conditions in which whole muscles can be tested in isolation and then removed for examination of fiber diameter and length, the PCSA can be estimated as follows (Herzog 1996; Patel and Lieber 1997; Roy and Edgerton 1992):

$$PCSA = \frac{\text{muscle mass (wet)} \times \text{cosine } v}{p \text{ (g/cm}^2) \times \text{fiber length (cm)}}$$

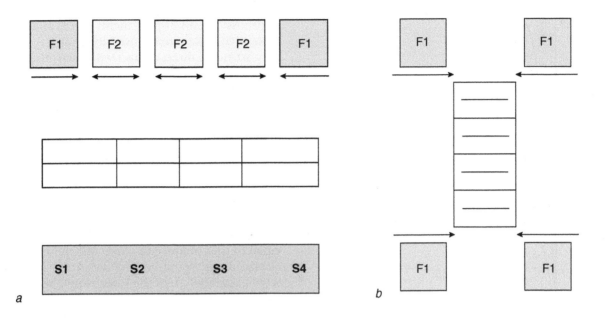

Figure 3.1 *(a)* Four sarcomeres in series. Force (F2) is canceled as the sarcomeres pull against each other; thus the sarcomere force = F1 + F1. *(b)* Four sarcomeres in parallel. Sarcomeres act independently so that total force = the sum of F1 for each sarcomere.

Based on Edgerton et al. 1986 and Huijing 1992.

where p equals muscle density (mammalian p = 1.056 g × cm³) and υ is the angle of pinnation at rest. Fiber length is calculated as the average fiber length within the muscle.

Using this method of determining PCSA, predictions of specific muscle tension for a variety of muscles are strongly correlated to actual measurements (Patel and Lieber 1997; Powell et al. 1984; Roy and Edgerton 1992; Spector et al. 1980), except for the soleus muscle, which contains almost 100% type I fibers (Powell et al. 1984). However, problems with changes in the angle of pinnation during contraction and with the actual measurement of fiber length reduce the accuracy of estimation of the PCSA (see chapter 2, "Neuromuscular Physiology").

In many situations, invasive techniques are not possible (humans typically do not like having muscles removed, as they are difficult to get back into the same place!). Under in vivo conditions the PCSA can be estimated with fair accuracy using the following equation (Fukunaga et al. 1996; Roy and Edgerton 1992):

$$PCSA = \frac{muscle\ volume}{fiber\ length}$$

where muscle volume is estimated by MRI or other noninvasive techniques, and estimates of fiber

Table 3.1 Contractile Properties of Two Theoretical Muscles With Different Sarcomere Arrangements

Properties	SARCOMERE ARRANGEMENT	
	Series	Parallel
Contraction time	1	1
Specific tension	1/4	1
Maximum displacement		1/4
Maximum velocity	1	1/4
Maximum work	1	1
Maximum power	1	1
Maximum power per kilogram muscle	1	1
ATP/unit force	1	1/4
ATP/unit displacement	1/4	1
ATP/unit work	1	1
ATP/power	1	1

Adapted from R.R. Roy and V.R. Edgerton, 1992, Skeletal muscle architecture and performance. In *Strength and power in sport*, edited by P.V. Komi (London: Blackwell Scientific), 115-129.

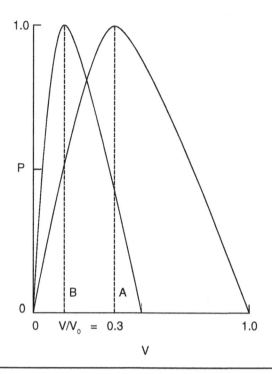

Figure 3.2 The theoretical power output of two muscles of different lengths but with the same number of sarcomeres (see figure 3.1, *a* & *b*). Note that the longer muscle (figure 3.1*a*) produces power over a wider range of velocities; also note that as one muscle begins to decrease power output, the other can take over.

Reprinted, by permission, from V.R. Edgerton et al., 1986, Morphological basis of skeletal muscle power output. In *Human muscle power,* edited by N.L. Jones, N. McCartney, and A.J. McComas (Champaign, IL: Human Kinetics), 45.

length are made based on data from previously dissected muscles (Cutts and Seedhom 1993; Roy and Edgerton 1992).

Although these methods of calculating PCSA are estimations, findings from both the in situ and in vivo techniques indicate that the parallel arrangement of sarcomeres is advantageous in producing force. Hypertrophy (increased cross-sectional area) of muscle through resistance training is accomplished as sarcomeres are added in parallel, which can bring about increases in maximum strength. As with the sarcomere arrangement models (table 3.1 and figure 3.2), evidence indicates that muscle displacement, Vmax, and the range of power output are related to the muscle fiber length or the number of sarcomeres in series (Bodine et al. 1982; Edgerton, Roy, and Gregor 1986). Sarcomeres are added in series as a result of growth or chronic stretching, while immobilization in a shortened position, such as casting a broken limb, can remove sarcomeres in series.

As evidenced by animal models, the spatial arrangement of motor units may also affect force transmission and displacement. Fibers of a motor unit (MU) appear to be spatially arranged so that they are not in direct contact with each other; they can form staggered (overlapping) arrays, and the area covered can extend nearly the entire length of a muscle (Bodine et al. 1987; Ounjian et al. 1991; Roy and Edgerton 1992). The mechanical characteristics of a muscle would be affected by the interaction of MU recruitment and the complex spatial arrangement of the MUs. If two MUs containing the same number of fibers were recruited simultaneously, the functional outcome would differ if the fibers were arranged in series or parallel. If the fibers were in series, the force produced by both units would be equal to that produced by one MU; however, the displacement would be additive. If the two MUs were in parallel, then the force would be additive but not the displacement (Roy and Edgerton 1992). If the MUs were serially arranged and were not recruited at the same time, it is possible that the nonactivated MUs would unload the active unit (Clamann and Schelhorn 1988). Due to the infinite possibilities for MU arrangement, simply knowing the recruitment order and its force capabilities is insufficient to enable one to accurately predict the mechanical characteristics of intact muscle contraction (Roy and Edgerton 1992).

While it is clear that differences in muscle architecture can result in force, velocity, and power differences during muscular contraction (Wickiewicz et al. 1983, 1984), intrinsic (biochemical) properties also contribute to these differences. Studies in which architectural differences have been minimized or obviated indicate that the intrinsic properties (e.g., fiber type) of muscle are more important in accounting for differences in velocity and power (Fitts and Widrick 1997; Spector et al. 1980).

Studies of isolated bundles of human muscle fibers and single fibers indicate that there are differences in maximum isometric twitch force, tetanic force, rate of force development, and power output among MUs. Although peak power is reached at about 30% of Vmax, human muscle fiber bundles containing homogeneous MU types (II vs. I) show strikingly different power curves (figure 3.3). Differences in specific tension and isometric twitch tension are small but indicate that type IIx > type IIa >> type I (Fitts and Widrick 1997; Powell et al. 1984). However, differences among MU types in the force–velocity curve and power production are larger (figure 3.4, *a* & *b*). Single-fiber analyses of human muscle (Fitts and Widrick 1997) indicate that Vmax and peak power production show dif-

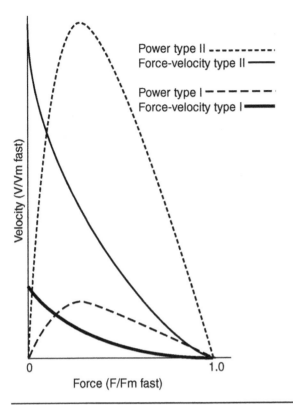

Figure 3.3 Muscle fiber type has a profound effect on force, velocity and power characteristics. The figure shows the force-velocity curves and power curves of two different muscles containing different fiber types. Velocities have been normalized by maximum concentric velocity for Type II fibers (Vm). Force has been normalized by the maximum Type II force output (Fm).

Reprinted, by permission, from J.A. Faulker, D.R. Claflin, and K.K. McCully, 1986, Power output of fast and slow fibers from human skeletal muscles. In *Human muscle power*, edited by N.L. Jones, N. McCartney, and A.J. Comas (Champaign, IL: Human Kinetics), 84.

ferences that are large and statistically significant: IIx > IIa >>> I. However, with the exception of a few muscles such as the soleus, most muscles are made up of various combinations of different MUs; thus, it is important to understand how these different MUs function in combination. In a muscle composed of 50% type II and 50% type I, peak power is about 55% of that of a muscle composed of all type II fibers. Furthermore, the power output in this mixed muscle is almost completely a function of the type II fibers (Faulkner, Claflin, and McCully 1986). This suggests that athletes with higher percentages of type II fibers in the muscles used in performance would have an advantage in strength-power activities.

Table 3.2 shows the approximate percentages of type II fibers in the vastus lateralis of various athletes and untrained subjects (Alway, Grumbt,

and Gonyea 1989; Burke et al. 1977; Edstrom and Ekblom 1972; Holloszy and Coyle 1984; Komi et al. 1977a; Miller et al. 1993; Saltin et al. 1977; Simoneau and Bouchard 1989; Tesch and Larsson 1982; Tesch, Thorsson, and Essen-Gustavsson 1989; Thorstensson et al. 1977). Generally endurance athletes possess more type I fibers, and strength-power athletes more type II fibers. Slight differences in mean percentage of fiber type are found between men and women (Miller et al. 1993; Simoneau and Bouchard 1989). Although fiber type is genetically determined to a large degree (Komi et al. 1976, 1977b), both strength and aerobic endurance training can result in substantial alterations in metabolic and contractile properties (Adams et al. 1993; Fitts and Widrick 1997; Schantz and Dhoot 1987; Staron et al. 1989).

In previous sections we established that force-length and force–velocity characteristics related to movement are dependent on architectural and intrinsic properties. During in vivo movements, these characteristics are also dependent on the recruitment patterns of MUs (intramuscular recruitment) and whole muscles (intermuscular recruitment). Although there may be exceptions (Grimby and Hannerz 1977; Nardone, Romano, and Schieppati 1989), MUs are recruited according to size (Bawa 2002; Henneman, Somjen, and Carpenter 1965a, 1965b); this has implications for metabolic and mechanical outcomes of performance. Typically, larger, more powerful MUs would be recruited during high-force or high-power anaerobically supported movements (see chapter 2, "Neuromuscular Physiology"). However, there is evidence for MU task specificity, which depends on the type of action and movement pattern the muscle is undertaking, force production, the rate of force development, and the velocity necessary to complete a movement (Fleckstein et al. 1992; Desmedt and Godaux 1979, 1981; Morrow and Miller 2003; Nakazawa et al. 1993; Sale 1992). For example, when the biceps brachii is contracting during elbow flexion, MUs in the lateral portion of the long head are preferentially activated; however, during supination of the forearm, MUs in the medial portion are activated. During elbow flexion, MUs in the biceps and the brachialis have different thresholds of activation depending on contraction type (eccentric vs. concentric) or the speed of movement (Tax et al. 1989; Sale 1992).

A great deal of evidence exists for task specificity among whole muscles (Loeb 1985; Sale 1992; Tax et al. 1990; Yamashita 1988). Activation–coactivation–relaxation patterns are specific for the type, velocity,

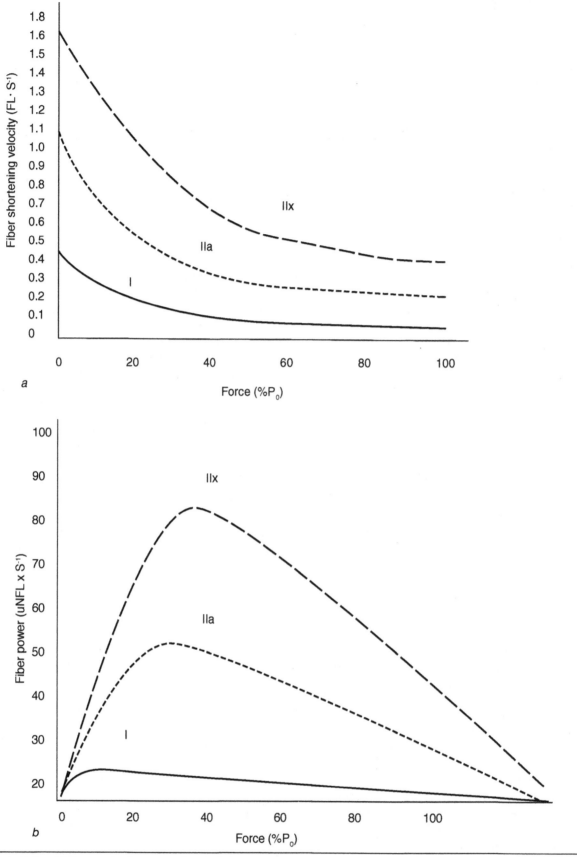

Figure 3.4 (*a*) Force-velocity curves for single human gastrocnemius fibers of different types. (*b*) Power curves for single fibers of the human gastrocnemius.

Adapted from R.H. Fitts and J.J. Widrick, 1997, Muscle mechanics: Adaptations with exercise training. In *Exercise and sport sciences reviews* (Baltimore, MD: Williams and Wilkins), 427-473.

Table 3.2 Approximate Average Percent Type II Fiber Content of the Vastus Lateralis: Elite or National-Level Athletes

Group	Men	Women
Sedentary	52	47
Cross-country skiers	35	35
Distance runners (>5 km)	20	40
Distance cyclists	40	NA
Alpine skiers	40	40
Bodybuilders	55	50
Powerlifters	57	50
Weightlifters	60	NA
Sprinters	70	60

Based on Alway et al. 1989; Burke et al. 1977; Edstrom and Ekblom 1972; Holloszy and Coyle 1984; Komi et al. 1977a; Miller et al. 1993; Saltin et al. 1977; Simoneau and Bouchard 1989; Tesch and Larsson 1982; Tesch et al. 1989; Thorstensson et al. 1977.

and power requirements of an activity (Sale 1992). An important issue is how different muscles with different combinations of MU types may be recruited and used in physical activity. As an example, consider the function of the gastrocnemius and soleus, which share a common insertion. In mammals, the gastrocnemius contains more type II fibers and the soleus contains a very high proportion of type I fibers, and there are corresponding differences in power production (Roy and Edgerton 1992; Spector et al. 1980). In the cat, different speeds of walking and running cause preferential recruitment of the soleus or medial gastrocnemius; substantial recruitment of the gastrocnemius was seen to occur only at higher speeds (Roy and Edgerton 1992). Similar observations have been made for humans during cycling at different speeds (Duchateau, LeBozec, and Hainaut 1986) and during hopping (Moritani, Oddsson, and Thorstensson 1990). In addition, selective activation of these two muscles has been observed as a function of position, contraction type, and speed (Nardone and Schieppati 1988).

It is apparent that the recruitment of MUs and muscles can have profound effects on mechanical characteristics of movement. Furthermore, there is evidence that strength and skill training can alter recruitment patterns in a specific manner, such that mechanical outcomes improve performance (Aagaard 2003; Bernardi et al. 1996; Sale 1992; Schmidtbleicher and Gollhofer 1982).

The muscle–tendon–bone interface allows humans to move. This is accomplished as muscles pull against bones, rotate them about joints, and transmit force through various tissues, including skin, to the external environment (Harman 1994a). Although muscles attempt to contract (i.e., shorten), the resulting forces are manifested in the environment as either pulling (shortening) or pushing forces against external objects.

The previous chapter presented a detailed discussion of muscle. The major muscles of the human body are shown in figure 3.5, *a* and *b*. A brief discussion of the skeletal system is presented here. The human body typically contains 206 bones (figure 3.6, *a* & *b*); this number can vary somewhat due to individual differences. The skeleton functions in providing support, protection of major organs, and leverage. The axial skeleton consists of bones making up the head, spinal column, and chest; the appendicular skeleton consists of the bones of the arms, shoulder girdle, pelvis, and legs.

Joints are the point at which bones form junctions or articulations. Joints allow rotation of bones and movement of the skeleton. The degree to which joints allow movement depends on the type of joint (see table 3.3).

Articulating bones of synovial joints are covered in hyaline cartilage at the ends, which are surrounded by a capsule containing synovial fluid. Synovial fluid lubricates and provides nutrients to the joint area. Bones are "tied" together by connective tissue (ligaments), and there may be supporting cartilage such as the meniscus of the knee joint. The rotational characteristics of joints depend on the number of available axes, which allows us to categorize joints into three types: uniaxial joints (e.g., elbow), biaxial joints (e.g., ankle and wrist), and multiaxial joints (e.g., shoulder, hip, and knee).

Muscles are typically attached to bones by fibrous connective tissue (tendons) at the origin and insertion of a muscle. The tendons are continuous with both the muscle sheaths and the connective tissue surrounding a bone. Fibers from the tendon also penetrate into the bone, increasing the strength of the bone–tendon interface (Harman 1994a, 1994b).

Anatomically, muscles that surround joints can be divided into three basic categories. Agonists are the muscles primarily responsible for causing joint rotation. Antagonists are responsible for deceleration of movement and providing protection for joint structures against potentially destructive forces during rapid movements; they also assist in providing joint stability. Synergists act as secondary movers or stabilizing muscles. Anatomically, a particular muscle or muscle group may act in

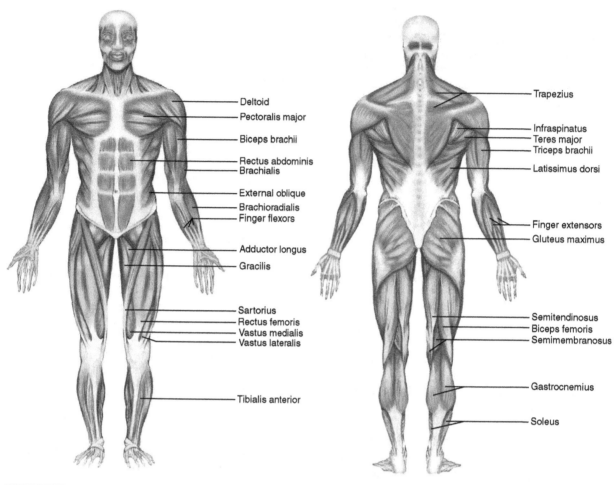

Figure 3.5 Front and rear views of an adult human male, skeletal muscle.

Reprinted, by permission, from National Strength and Conditioning Association, 2000, *Essentials of strength training and conditioning,* 2nd ed. (Champaign, IL: Human Kinetics), 29.

◇ Applications to Resistance Training

Resistance can be encountered from a number of sources including gravity, inertia, friction, elastic properties, and fluid (Harman 1994b). While these sources are actively encountered in a number of daily and sport activities, they can also be used to provide resistance for resistance training. Resistance training is the purposeful use of resistance equipment in order to reach a desired goal. These goals include changing body shape (e.g., bodybuilding), general fitness, athletic competition (e.g., weightlifting, powerlifting), training for other sports, and rehabilitation. Various modes and devices for resistance training take advantage of one or more sources of resistance. The degree to which these modes of training affect various parameters of in vivo neuromusculoskeletal characteristics directly affects the desired outcome. Not all modes of training produce the same adaptations. Chapter 12 presents detailed comparisons of various modes of training.

different roles; for example, the hamstrings act as antagonist during rapid extension of the knee but as agonist during flexion at the knee. Although the ratio of agonist to antagonist strength (muscle balance) changes depending on the measurement conditions (e.g., mode, speed, contraction type), some evidence suggests that it may be related to both performance and injury (Wathen 1992).

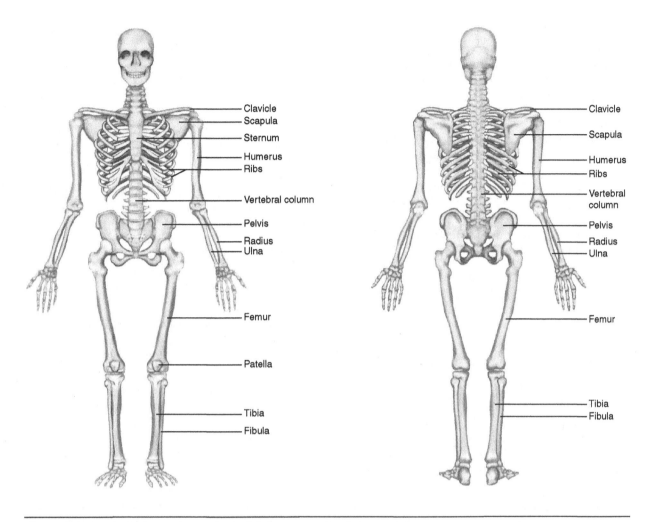

Figure 3.6   Front and rear views of an adult human male, skeleton.

Reprinted, by permission, from National Strength and Conditioning Association, 2000, *Essentials of strength training and conditioning,* 2nd ed. (Champaign, IL: Human Kinetics), 27.

Table 3.3   **Skeletal Joint Types**

Joint type	Example	Relative movement
Fibrous	Sutures of the skull	Limited
Cartilaginous	Vertebral discs	Moderate
Synovial	Knee	Large

However, we should note that the anatomical terms agonist and antagonist are somewhat artificial, in that the role of a muscle may change during multijoint movements and with the velocity of contraction (Zajac and Gordon 1989). Thus, with the possible exception of actions in some uniarticular muscles, muscle actions may be more correctly viewed in terms of dynamic optimization, in which the role of a muscle is defined not simply by its anatomical location and force production but through model-ing techniques that include the task the muscle's actions are attempting to achieve (Zajac 2002; Zajac and Gordon 1989). Furthermore, muscles should be viewed functionally, as prime movers and synergists rather than as agonists and antagonists, especially during multijoint movements.

Mechanics are governed by three basic laws of motion described by Isaac Newton (Barham 1978):

First law: inertia. An object at rest remains at rest until acted upon by an outside force. Once an object is moving, it will continue to move in a straight line at a uniform speed unless acted on by an external force.

Second law: acceleration. When an object is acted upon by an outside force, the resulting acceleration is proportional to the mass of the object and takes place in the direction of the force (F = MA).

Third law: reaction. For every action there is an equal but opposite reaction. When a force is applied to an object, the object pushes back in the opposite direction with a force equaling that of the source.

These laws govern the mechanical outcomes of exerting force and therefore weight training exercises. They can be restated and modified in terms of both linear and angular movement.

From a functional standpoint the skeleton is a system of levers. A lever is a device for transmitting force in the process of performing work. For an understanding of leverage, a number of definitions are pertinent (Harman 1994a):

Lever: a semirigid or ridged mass (bone) that, subjected to a force having a line of action not passing through its axis of rotation (pivot), exerts force on any object resisting its tendency to rotate.

Fulcrum: the pivot point (axis) of a lever.

Moment arm (force arm, torque arm, lever arm): the perpendicular distance from the line of action of the force to the fulcrum.

Line of action: an infinitely long line passing through the point of force application, which is oriented in the same direction as the force application.

Torque (moment): the tendency of a force to cause rotation about a specified fulcrum (axis); torque = force × moment arm length.

Strength: the ability to produce external force by muscle contraction.

Muscle force: force generated by muscle activation that tends to pull the two ends of a muscle together.

Resistive force: force generated external to the lever system (e.g., gravity, inertia, friction), acting in opposition to muscle force.

Force arm: the distance from the point of force application to the fulcrum.

Resistance arm: distance from the fulcrum to the center of mass of the resistance.

Mechanical advantage: the ratio of the moment arm through which an applied force acts (force arm) to the moment arm through which a resistive force acts (resistance arm); for equilibrium to exist between the applied and resistive torques,

$$F \times MA_F = R \times MA_R = 1.0$$

where F = muscle force, MA_F = the muscle force moment arm, R = resistance force, and MA_R = resistance moment arm.

A mechanical advantage of <1.0 requires a great deal of muscle force to overcome a relatively small resistance. A mechanical advantage >1.0 results in a relatively small muscle force required to overcome a resistance. A lever with a greater resistance arm than force arm (RA > FA) emphasizes speed at the expense of strength; the opposite (FA > RA) favors strength over speed of movement. Similarly, a mechanical advantage of <1.0 typically indicates speed production at the expense of muscle force, and a mechanical advantage >1.0 favors muscle force at the expense of movement speed.

Levers can be classified according to the relationship of the FA, RA, and placement of the fulcrum:

First class: Muscle force and resistive force act on opposite sides of the fulcrum. An example of a first-class lever is an extension of the elbow by the triceps (figure 3.7).

Second class: Muscle force and resistive force act on the same side of the fulcrum. A second-class lever always has FA > RA; thus force is emphasized over movement speed. An example of a second-class lever is lifting the heel while moving onto the ball of the foot (figure 3.8).

Third class: Muscle force and resistive force act on the same side of the fulcrum. A third-class lever always has RA > FA; thus movement speed is emphasized over strength. An example of a third-class lever is flexion at the elbow (figure 3.9).

Most major limb movements are accomplished with the muscles acting on third-class levers; thus internal muscle force must be larger than the external force produced by the resistance. These large internal forces may be a reason for the susceptibility to injury of muscles and tendons associated with third-class levers (Harman 1994a). Mechanical advantage is an important concept in that it allows an understanding of the force and torque requirements of actual movements. However, mechanical advantage changes continuously during human movement (Gowitzke and Milner 1988; Harman 1994a, 1994b):

1. During flexion and extension at the knee, the joint does not act as a true hinge because the axis of rotation changes during the movement. This changing axis in turn affects the distance (moment arm) through which the muscles act.

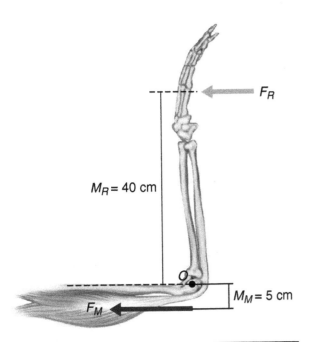

$M_R = 40$ cm

$M_M = 5$ cm

Figure 3.7 Example of a first-class lever: extension at the elbow, where F_M = muscle force, F_R = resistive force, M_M = the moment arm of the muscle force, and M_R = moment arm of the resistive force. Mechanical advantage (MA) = F_M / F_R. MA typically is poor in first-class levers (in this example it would be less than 1.0). Note that F_M and F_R are on opposite sides of the fulcrum. Note that as M_M is much smaller than M_R, F_M must be much larger than F_R in order for extension to occur (i.e., a large muscle force is required to overcome a relatively small resistance). However, velocity would be augmented by the long lever (M_M).

Reprinted, by permission, from National Strength and Conditioning Association, 2000, *Essentials of strength training and conditioning*, 2nd ed. (Champaign, IL: Human Kinetics), 31.

2. During extension at the knee, the patella acts to prevent the quadriceps tendon from moving close to the axis of rotation, therefore minimizing changes in mechanical advantage. During knee (or elbow) flexion, in which there is no sesamoid bone to maintain tendon distance from the axis of rotation, the torque produced will be lower at the extremes of the joint range because the tendon moves very close to the axis.

3. During weight training exercise, the resistance arm varies directly with the horizontal distance from the weight to the axis of rotation. Thus, large differences in mechanical advantage can occur with changes in lifting technique that move the weight being lifted farther from or closer to the joint (figure 3.10).

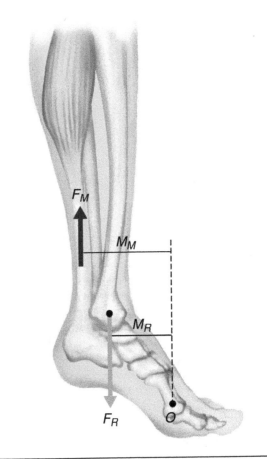

F_M

M_M

M_R

F_R

Figure 3.8 The ankle, an example of a second-class lever, where F_M = muscle force, F_R = resistive force, M_M = the moment arm of the muscle force, and M_R = moment arm of the resistive force. Mechanical advantage (MA) = F_M / F_R. Plantar flexion (raising the body) on the ball of the foot (fulcrum) produces $M_M > M_R$ and $F_M < F_R$ and a relatively large mechanical advantage.

Reprinted, by permission, from National Strength and Conditioning Association, 2000, *Essentials of strength training and conditioning*, 2nd ed. (Champaign, IL: Human Kinetics), 31.

Intra- and interindividual structural differences can contribute to differences in mechanical advantage. For example, a tendon insertion closer to or farther away from the axis of rotation can favor strength or speed. Mechanical advantage is gained if the tendon is inserted farther away; then the longer muscle force arm results in a higher joint torque, producing higher external forces. On the other hand, mechanical advantage is lost if the tendon is closer; the resistance arm is longer and more internal force is required to overcome a given resistance. However, there is a speed advantage with longer resistance arms.

The angular speed and displacement are directly related to the length of the resistance arm. For a

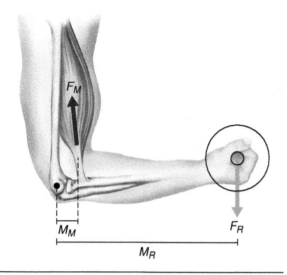

Figure 3.9 The biceps, an example of a third-class lever. F_M = muscle force; F_R = resistive force; M_M = the moment arm of the muscle force; M_R = moment arm of the resistive force. Mechanical advantage (MA) = F_M / F_R. Because M_M is smaller than M_R, Fm must be greater than F_R, producing a relatively small MA.

Reprinted, by permission, from National Strength and Conditioning Association, 2000, *Essentials of strength training and conditioning*, 2nd ed. (Champaign, IL: Human Kinetics), 31.

given length of muscle shortening, the longer resistance arm produces a higher angular velocity and displacement than a shorter resistance arm. Thus to produce a given angular velocity, a muscle with a long force arm must contract at a higher speed than one with a short force arm. Because of the inverse relationship of force and velocity during shortening, the muscle's force-producing capabilities are reduced at higher speeds of contraction. However, the speed advantage of longer resistance arms can be lost as the resistance to be overcome increases, requiring greater levels of strength.

Resistance training can change the angle of pinnation of a muscle as a result of hypertrophy. Changes in the angle of pinnation may improve the force-producing capabilities of a muscle, although this may occur at the expense of contraction speed (see chapter 2, "Neuromuscular Physiology"). Speculation suggests that if hypertrophy were great enough, it might also change the angle of insertion of the tendon, again affecting maximum force capabilities.

It is apparent that subtle changes in structure, whether resulting from heredity or training, can bring about marked changes in function. For example, powerlifters would likely benefit from tendon insertions farther away from the joint, while sprinters might benefit from the opposite.

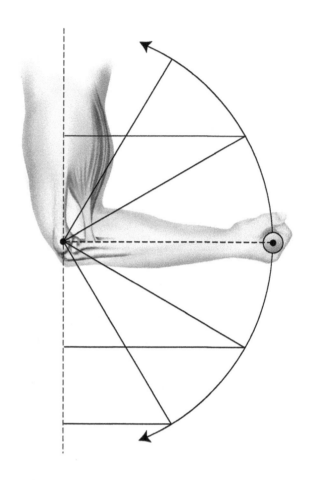

Figure 3.10 In this example, as the load is lifted, the moment arm (and therefore the resistive force) changes with the horizontal distance from the fulcrum (elbow joint). The longer the lever, the greater the internal muscle force necessary to overcome the load. Conversely, the longer the lever, the smaller the external force production (i.e., the sticking range).

Reprinted, by permission, from National Strength and Conditioning Association, 2000, *Essentials of strength training and conditioning*, 2nd ed. (Champaign, IL: Human Kinetics), 33.

Strength, Work, and Power

Strength can be defined as the ability to produce external force (Siff 2001; Stone 1993). The magnitude of force production can range from zero to maximum. Force exerted on an external object having a mass results in that object's acceleration (F = MA) and a velocity of movement. Thus force production can occur at zero velocity (isometric) or result in a variety of contraction velocities. Furthermore, depending on the muscles and body segments involved, the summation of forces imparts a direction to movement.

In vivo strength production is influenced by a variety of factors, which include force–velocity and force–length (joint angle) characteristics, fiber type, contraction type, neural activation, and cross section. Strength can be measured isometrically or dynamically. Dynamic measurements can be carried out with eccentric, concentric, or plyometric muscle actions. Typical maximum strength measures performed isometrically or with the 1-repetition maximum (1RM) method can have limited usefulness in predicting or monitoring performance in more dynamic activities (Stone 1993; Wilson and Murphy 1996). Measurement of force magnitude and related characteristics, such as rate of force development and time to peak tension, broadens the scope of both dynamic and isometric strength measurements and increases their usefulness in monitoring performance (Hakkinen, Alen, and Komi 1984; Stone 1993). (See chapter 8, "Testing, Measurement, and Evaluation," and chapters 1, "Definitions, Objectives, Tasks, and Principles of Training," and 12, "Modes of Resistance Training.")

When strength is exerted and movement occurs, work (measured in joules) is performed. Work is the product of force and the distance an object is moved:

$$W = F \times d$$

where W = work, F = force, and d = displacement. If the force is not in the same direction as displacement, then

$$W = F\cos \upsilon \times d$$

where Fcos υ = the component of the angle between the line of force and the line of displacement. This indicates that efficiency is increased if the lines of force and displacement are the same. Work is directly related to energy use; the more work performed, the more kilocalories used.

Kinetic energy is the energy of motion and can be quantified as follows:

$$KE = 1/2\ mv^2$$

where KE = kinetic energy, m = mass, and v = velocity. The greater the kinetic energy of a body, the more difficult it is to stop it. The more kinetic energy a mass has, the more force and work required to decelerate the object.

The rate at which work is accomplished is termed power (measured in watts). Quantitatively power can be expressed as follows:

$$P = \frac{f \times d}{time}$$

where P = power and f × d = work. This equation can be rearranged as

$$P = force \times velocity$$

Thus power is the product of external force (strength) and the velocity of an object in the direction of force exertion. Power is proportional to the rate of energy used. The higher the work rate, the more rapidly energy is used. Athletes able to accomplish work at faster rates have an advantage. Power (the rate of work) is arguably the most important factor in athletics, separating winners from losers in most strength-power sports.

These work and power equations relate to an object moving from one place to another. Work and power are also necessary to start movement or to change the velocity of movement. Because the human body is made up of a system of levers rotating about axes, rotational or angular characteristics of movement must be considered. Angular displacement is the angle through which an object rotates (SI unit = radian = 57.3°); angular velocity is the object's rotational speed in radians/time (rad × s⁻¹). Torque can be expressed as newtons × meters (N × m). Rotational work and power then are expressed as

$$work = torque \times angular\ displacement$$

$$power = \frac{torque \times angular\ displacement}{time}$$

or

$$power = torque \times angular\ velocity$$

An understanding of the concepts of work and power can obviate common misunderstandings of these terms. For example, the term powerlifting denotes a sport in which performance involves very high forces but low speeds and relatively low power outputs compared to many other sports, including weightlifting (Garhammer 1989). Nor is it correct necessarily to associate low speeds with low power outputs or high speeds with high power outputs; it should be remembered that power is a function of both force and speed. The critical issue is the ability to exert force that results in acceleration, velocity, and power characteristic of a sport's performance requirements.

Muscle Actions: Contraction Types

There are three basic contraction types:

Concentric: Muscle gains tension and shortens (contraction force > resistive force).

Isometric: Muscle gains tension but does not appreciably change length (contraction force = resistive force).

Eccentric: Muscle gains tension but is forced to lengthen (contraction force < resistive force).

External and internal muscle force changes with joint angle as a result of the length–tension properties and contraction type. The term strength curve refers to a graph of the maximum resultant moment exerted about an axis (maximum external force) versus joint angle (Hay 1992). Measurements for a variety of joints and motions show that there are three characteristic strength curves: ascending, descending, and ascending-descending (figure 3.11). These curves can be measured using dynamic or isometric muscle actions (Asmussen, Hansen, and Lammert 1965; Harman 1994a, 1994b; Hay 1992). In keeping with force–velocity–length relationships, typical intact human strength curves show that there is a hierarchy of force production such that eccentric > isometric > concentric (figure 3.12). Isokinetic strength curves have also been measured and generally conform to the characteristic shape of strength curves measured with freely moving weights; however, due to inherent problems with isokinetic dynamometers, these data should be interpreted with caution (Chow, Darling, and Hay 1997; Hay 1992; Osternig 1986). Thus the ability to exert external force over a range of motion is dependent on a number of interacting factors.

A fourth type of muscle action is also possible: stretch–shortening cycle (SSC) muscle action (plyometric). An eccentric muscle action immediately precedes a concentric action—the point of crossover between eccentric and concentric is termed the amortization phase and is actually a brief isometric action. It may also be possible (depending on the change in angle) that in very brief plyometric movements no substantial eccentric action occurs, but instead an isometric action is followed by a concentric action. The important factor is that the subsequent concentric action is enhanced. The exact mechanism of enhancement is unclear but could include the following:

1. Reutilization of stored elastic energy

2. A myototic reflex

3. Muscle–tendon interactions allowing the muscle to remain closer to its optimal length and also shorten at a more favorable velocity for force production

4. Optimization of the muscle activation pattern

5. Eliciting a greater preforce at initiation of the concentric phase (Bobbert 2001; Cronin, McNaira, and Marshall 2000; Finni, Ikegewa, and Komi 2001)

The SSC is commonly used during such activities as walking, running, and jumping.

Strength-to-Mass Ratio

According to Newton's second law, force is a product of mass and acceleration. Thus

$$\text{acceleration} = \frac{\text{force}}{\text{mass}}$$

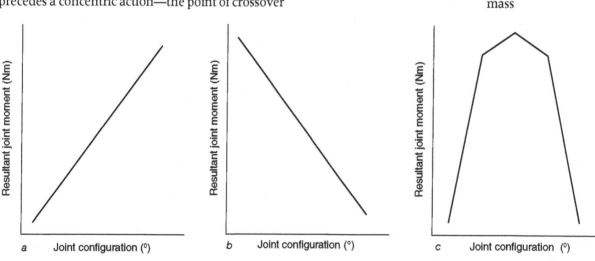

Figure 3.11 The three general forms of human strength curves: *(a)* ascending, *(b)* descending, and *(c)* ascending-descending.

Reprinted, by permission, from V. Zatsiorsky and W. Kraemer, 2006, *Science and Practice of Strength Training*, 2nd ed. (Champaign, IL: Human Kinetics), 40.

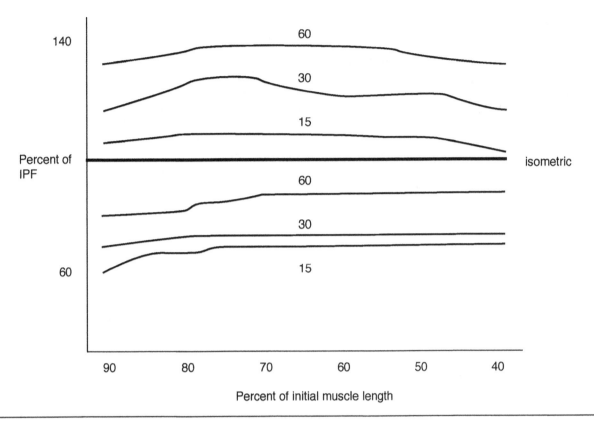

Figure 3.12 Maximum-effort concentric and eccentric contractions (elbow flexion) demonstrate a hierarchy of force production such that eccentric > isometric > concentric even when muscles are intact and under voluntary control. IPF=isometric peak force.

Based on P.O. Åstrand and K. Rodahl, 1970, *Textbook of work physiology* (New York: McGraw-Hill Companies).

In sports in which the athlete must propel the body or a body segment, the strength-to-mass ratio is critical, as this ratio is directly related to the athlete's ability to accelerate the body (Harman 1994a). Training programs for these athletes must be designed to effectively improve the strength-to-mass ratio. If body mass goes up and strength does not increase in proportion, then performance suffers. In sports with body weight classifications such as powerlifting, weightlifting, and wrestling, competitors often have the same body mass; thus, the strongest competitor has an advantage.

Large athletes typically have a lower strength-to-mass ratio than smaller athletes (Harman 1994a; Kauhanen, Garhammer, and Hakkinen 2000; Kauhanen, Komi, and Hakkinen 2002). This results from muscle force capabilities that are proportional to the cross-sectional area, which is related to the square of linear body dimensions. However, muscle mass is proportional to its volume, which is related to the cube of linear body dimensions. Thus, as body size increases, the body mass increases at a faster rate than strength. Given constant body proportions, smaller athletes are stronger on a per kilogram of body mass basis than larger athletes (i.e., have a larger strength-to-mass ratio).

While larger athletes lift more weight, comparisons between athletes of different sizes may provide an index as to which athlete is actually the better performer. Simply dividing weight lifted by body mass biases the results toward the smaller competitor, because it does not take into account the expected decrease in the strength-to-mass ratio with increasing body size. Dividing the weight lifted by body mass$^{2/3}$ is an attempt to obviate differences in size but apparently biases results toward middle-sized athletes (Hester et al. 1990; Hunter et al. 1990). A number of different models have been developed that (to an extent) obviate body mass differences for both powerlifting and weightlifting (Hester et al. 1990; Hunter et al. 1990; Siff 1988; Sinclair 1985; Stone et al. 2005). These formulas are often used to determine the "best lifter" in competitions.

CHAPTER SUMMARY

Resistance training is used by both athletes and nonathletes for a variety of reasons ranging from body-building to rehabilitation. Knowledge of biomechanical factors and how they can influence training adaptations allows the practitioner to design more productive training programs.

This chapter includes discussions of micro- and macroanatomical considerations affecting external force production (strength). Strength production is subject to the contractile characteristics of muscle (i.e., force–length–velocity considerations), muscle architecture, fiber type, and neural factors. When a muscle contracts, work is performed; the rate of work performance is termed power. Power is likely the characteristic that most influences winning or losing in most athletic events. Understanding the biomechanical factors involved in strength and power production lays the foundation for the mechanical aspects of specificity of exercise and training. This understanding leads to more productive training programs.

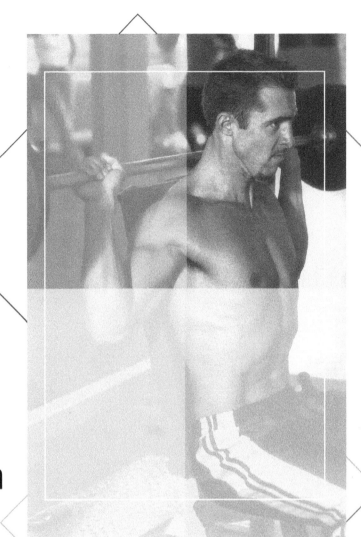

PART II

Bioenergetics and Metabolism

As in part I, this section of the book deals with the principles of basic and applied science. This section presents discussions of various physiological systems, nutrients, and ergogenic aids that potentially interact to affect metabolism and metabolic processes. These discussions address how movement is powered by use of biological energy systems (chapter 4) and how hormones and the neuroendocrine system are involved in resting homeostasis, exercise, and training (chapter 5). Chapters 6 and 7 present information on the effects of nutrition and ergogenic aids and the ways in which these factors may act to alter metabolism positively or negatively. As with part I, this part of the book lays a strong foundation to aid in the development of the basic scientific knowledge necessary for the creation of sound training programs.

CHAPTER 4

Bioenergetics and Metabolic Factors

Understanding energy use and production in biological systems forms the metabolic basis for the concept of specificity of exercise and training. Understanding how energy is produced for various exercises, and how energy production can be modified by specific types of training, makes it possible to design more efficient and productive training programs.

Energy can be defined as the ability or capacity to perform work. We can conceptualize energy as either potential (stored) or kinetic (performing work). Various forms of energy exist: nuclear, electromagnetic, mechanical, and chemical. Metabolic processes are biochemical in nature, and the transformation of energy is necessary for every activity accomplished by living systems. Bioenergetics deals with the flow of energy in living systems and how carbohydrates, fats, and protein from food are converted into usable chemical energy. Metabolic potential energy can be considered to be the energy stored in the chemical bonds of various molecules (i.e., fats, carbohydrates, proteins). The realization of kinetic energy for movement requires the transformation of chemical energy into mechanical energy. This transformation process is accomplished by the destruction of chemical bonds and subsequent release of energy for muscle contraction.

The breakdown or destruction of large molecules (food and energy substrates) into smaller molecules associated with the release of energy is termed *catabolism*. Larger molecules are constructed from smaller molecules using the energy released by the catabolic process. This synthetic or building-up process is termed *anabolism*. An example of catabolism is the breakdown of proteins into amino acids; the synthesis of proteins from amino acids is an anabolic function. Exergonic reactions release energy and are typically catabolic. Energy-requiring reactions are endergonic, and in living systems include anabolic reactions and the muscle contraction process. Metabolism describes the summation of all of the exergonic-catabolic and endergonic-anabolic reactions occurring in a biological system. Note in figure 4.1, which illustrates the basic concept of metabolism, that energy derived from exergonic-catabolic reactions cannot be used directly by endergonic-catabolic reactions. The energy used to drive endergonic-anabolic reactions is transferred by an intermediate molecule, *adenosine triphosphate (ATP)*. Adenosine triphosphate allows the coupling or energy transfer from exergonic to endergonic reactions to occur. Because it is an energy conveyor, ATP is of primary importance in muscle contraction (endergonic reaction) and therefore human movement.

Adenosine Triphosphate

Adenosine triphosphate is constructed from the nitrogen-containing base adenine, the sugar ribose (five carbons), and three phosphate groups (figure 4.2). The hydrolysis, or removal, of one phosphate yields adenosine diphosphate (ADP); the hydrolysis of a second phosphate yields adenosine monophosphate (AMP). Each time a phosphate group is removed, some usable energy as well as heat is released (Brooks, Fahey, and White 1996; Cain and Davis 1962; Lehninger 2000; McGilvery 1975). Under normal conditions, the terminal phosphate group is cleaved (hydrolyzed) enzymatically to drive various endergonic reactions. Potentially, this enzymatic process could markedly decrease ATP concentrations, limiting muscular activity. Because ATP stores in muscle are small and because muscular contraction requires a constant ATP supply,

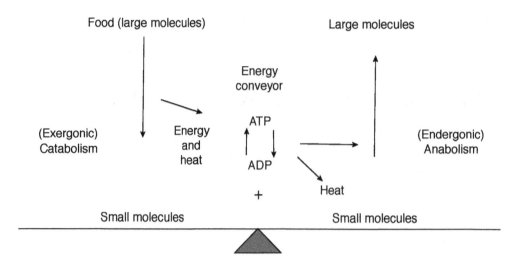

Figure 4.1   Overview of metabolism.

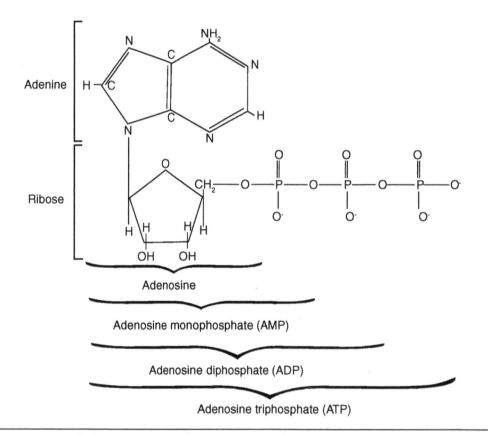

Figure 4.2   Structures of adenosine triphosphate, diphosphate, and monophosphate (ATP, ADP, and AMP).

Reprinted, by permission, from NSCA, 1994, *Essentials of strength and conditioning,* edited by T. Baechle (Champaign, IL: Human Kinetics), 68.

an important consideration is the replenishment of ATP. Muscular contraction and energy (ATP) use can occur at a variety of rates dependent on the intensity of muscular contraction; therefore replenishment of ATP must be available at rates matching the intensity of muscular contraction if activity is to be maintained. Matching ATP demand with supply is accomplished through energy systems that have different rates and capacities of ATP production.

The Bioenergetic Systems

Three basic energy systems operate simultaneously to replenish ATP. Of the three food groups, only carbohydrates can be used for energy production without the direct use of oxygen. Thus, one should not underestimate the importance of carbohydrates for high-intensity exercise depending on anaerobic mechanisms. All systems are continually active; the extent to which any one of these energy systems is used depends primarily on the intensity of physical activity and secondarily on the duration (Dudley and Murray 1982). These are the three systems:

Phosphagen system (ATP-PCr system and the myokinase reaction)

Glycolytic system (fast and slow)

Oxidative system

The Phosphagen System

The phosphagen system primarily provides energy for short-term high-intensity activities such as weight training exercise and sprinting, and it is active at the initiation of all exercise regardless of intensity (Brooks, Fahey, and White 1996). The primary reactions of the phosphagen system involve the phosphagens ATP and *creatine phosphate (PCr)* and two enzymes, *myosin ATPase* and *creatine kinase (CK)*. During muscle contraction, myosin ATPase catalyzes the hydrolysis of ATP, producing ADP and inorganic phosphate (P_i). Creatine kinase catalyzes the reaction in which PCr donates its phosphate group to ADP, re-forming ATP. These reactions provide energy at a high rate:

$$1. \quad ATP \xrightarrow{\text{myosin ATPase}} ADP + P_i + energy + heat$$

$$2. \quad ADP + PCr \xrightarrow{CK} ATP + Cr$$

Adenosine triphosphate and PCr (phosphagens) are stored within muscle in very small quantities. Approximately 5 to 6 mmol of ATP and 16 to 18 mmol of PCr are stored per kilogram of muscle (Cain and Davis 1962; Hultsmann 1979). Because of the relatively small muscular stores of phosphagens, this system cannot supply energy for continuous long-duration events (Cerretelli, Rennie, and Pendergast 1980). Although phosphagens alone cannot support exercise for long periods (<15 s), ATP can be delivered very quickly. Typically, type II muscle fibers contain higher concentrations of phosphagens than type I fibers (Essen 1978).

Another reaction associated with the phosphagen system that is important in high-intensity work is the myokinase (or adenylate kinase) reaction (Brooks, Fahey, and White 1996; Lehninger 2000):

$$2\ ADP \xrightarrow{\text{myokinase}} ATP + AMP$$

This reaction is important not only because of its rapid ATP production, but also because AMP is a potent stimulant for glycolysis (Brooks, Fahey, and White 1996; Lehninger 2000). The ATP-PCr system is active at the initiation of all exercise. Phosphagens, along with the myokinase reaction, are especially important in high-intensity exercise such as weight training or sprinting (Boobis, Williams, and Wooten 1983; Thorstensson 1976).

Regulation of ATP concentration is dependent on negative feedback. The activity of the enzyme CK is the primary regulator of the breakdown of PCr. An increase in the cellular concentration of ADP stimulates CK activity, while increases in ATP concentration inhibit its activity (Powers and Howley 1997). Initiation of exercise increases ADP concentrations as a result of ATP hydrolysis; the change in ADP concentration stimulates CK to catalyze the formation of ATP from the breakdown of PCr. Creatine kinase activity remains high if exercise is continued at high intensities. If exercise is terminated or the intensity falls low enough that glycolysis or the aerobic system can match energy consumption rates, then the cellular concentration of ATP will increase. The resulting increase in ATP concentration will reduce the activity of CK, allowing the concentrations of PCr to increase.

The Glycolytic System

Glycolysis is a process by which glucose can be catabolized to produce energy. Glucose can be derived from two sources—glucose in the blood and from the breakdown of muscle glycogen. Glycolysis is catalyzed by a series of nine enzymes found in the cytoplasm (figure 4.3). Depending on exercise intensity, glycolysis can proceed at either a fast (anaerobic) or a slow (aerobic) rate. In the past, the terms anaerobic and aerobic glycolysis were used as a result of the final fate of pyruvate, as described in the next paragraph. However, the terms *fast* and *slow* better describe the processes, because the glycolytic pathway itself does not depend on oxygen and because energy production occurs at a rapid rate during fast compared to slow glycolysis (Brooks, Fahey, and White 1996).

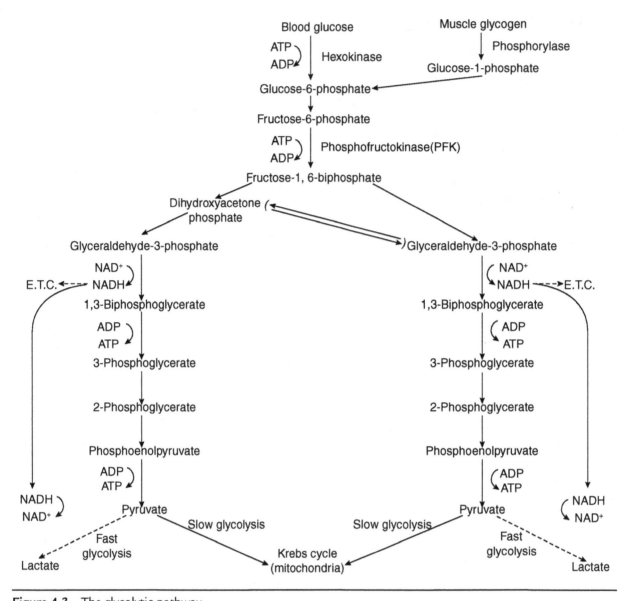

Figure 4.3   The glycolytic pathway.

Adapted from J.H. Wilmore and D.L. Costill, 2004, *Physiology of sport and exercise*, 3rd ed. (Champaign, IL: Human Kinetics), 125.

Fast Glycolysis

During fast glycolysis, pyruvate is converted into lactate, providing a relatively rapid production of ATP. During slow glycolysis, pyruvate is transported into the mitochondria, reduced to acetyl, and used in the oxidative system. The fast glycolytic process can use either blood glucose or muscle glycogen, although muscle glycogen appears to be the preferred pathway (Brooks, Fahey, and White 1996). Fast glycolysis is particularly important for moderately high- to high-intensity exercise (Brooks, Fahey, and White 1996; Powers and Howley 1997).

The end product of fast glycolysis is lactic acid, which can be associated with fatigue. Lactic acid and the production of NADH + H⁺ increase [H⁺] and decrease pH. During very intense exercise, intracellular muscle pH may fall below 6.5, and the rise in [H⁺] decreases the rate of glycolysis and glycogenolysis through enzymatic inhibition (Brooks, Fahey, and White 1996; Butler, Waddel, and Poole 1967; Plisk 1991). Increased [H⁺] directly inhibits muscle contraction, possibly by displacing Ca⁺⁺ at the troponin-tropomyosin complex or interfering with cross-bridge formation (Fabiato and Fabiato 1978; Fuchs, Reddy, and Briggs 1970; Hermansen and Vaage 1977; Nakamura and Schwartz 1972;

Tesch 1980). Additionally, the change in [H+] stimulates pain receptors also associated with the manifestation of fatigue (Plisk 1991; Tesch 1980).

Lactic acid is converted to its salt, lactate, by buffering systems found in the muscle and blood (Brooks 1986; Brooks, Fahey, and White 1996). Lactate is not directly associated with fatigue production; it can act as an energy substrate and is an important gluconeogenic precursor during long-term exercise and recovery (Brooks 1986; Mazzeo et al. 1986; Plisk 1991).

Lactate Accumulation Lactate accumulation in the blood is related to lactic acid production and clearance and exercise intensity. The amount of lactate in the blood postexercise is related to the degree of disturbance of resting homeostasis as a result of exercise. Removal of lactate from the blood reflects the ability to return to homeostasis and is associated with recoverability. Typically, postexercise lactate concentrations return to baseline within an hour; light aerobic exercise (<70% $\dot{V}O_2$max) may facilitate removal (Gollnick, Bayly, and Hodgson 1986).

Because of the high energy demands of type II muscle fibers, it is not surprising that these fibers contain higher concentrations or activities (or both) of glycolytic enzymes, as well as enzymes of the phosphagen system (Barnard et al. 1971; Burke and Edgerton 1975; Opie and Newsholme 1967). Fast-twitch fibers (type II) can also contain different *isozyme* patterns than slow-twitch fibers (type I). For example, LDH_M (muscle type) is found in higher concentrations in type II fibers, whereas LDH_H (heart type) is found in higher concentrations in the heart muscle and slow-twitch fibers (Barnard et al. 1971; Burke and Edgerton 1975; Mazzeo et al. 1986; York, Oscai, and Penny 1974). Because of these differences in muscle fiber types, type II fibers have a greater rate and capacity of production of lactic acid compared to type I fibers. The maximum rate of lactic acid production is approximately 0.5 mmol · g^{-1} of wet muscle in type II muscle fibers and approximately 0.25 mmol · g^{-1} in type I muscle fibers (Meyer and Terjung 1979). Differences in enzyme activity and other differences (such as capillarization) also allow type I fibers and heart muscle to take up lactate and convert it to pyruvate, which can then be oxidized in the Krebs cycle (Brooks 1986; Plisk 1991).

There can be several reasons for the production of lactic acid besides lack of oxygen or insufficient oxygen. For example, during aerobic exercise, if glycolysis is accelerated as a result of increased exercise intensity, the aerobic system may be momentarily unable to keep up with the sarcoplasmic production of NADH+. Therefore, some lactic acid may be produced until the aerobic system "gears up" and can accommodate the increase in NADH+. Furthermore, a finding of a constant blood lactate concentration does not necessarily mean that no lactic acid is being produced; it may mean that production and removal are equal (Brooks 1986; Brooks, Fahey, and White 1996). Several factors can influence the accumulation of blood lactate. Acceleration in the rate of glycogenolysis as a result of increased catecholamine concentrations, an increase in the recruitment of type II muscle fibers, and a rate of lactate production that is greater than clearance will affect increases in blood lactate accumulation (Brooks, Fahey, and White 1996; Plisk 1991). These factors tend to increase with increasing intensity of exercise.

The state of training can also affect blood lactate accumulation (Gollnick and Bayly 1986). Aerobically trained subjects can maintain lower blood lactate concentrations at submaximal absolute power outputs than untrained subjects (Plisk 1991). This is due largely to increased mitochondrial activity (Gollnick et al. 1972, 1973), increased muscle capillary density (Sjogaard 1984), lower catecholamine concentrations, and perhaps a shift in isozyme patterns such as from LDH_M to LDH_H as a result of training (Sjodin et al. 1976). Anaerobically trained athletes can also produce lower lactate concentrations at submaximal power outputs during weight training exercise than untrained subjects (Pierce et al. 1987, 1993; Stone et al. 1987)—an observation consistent with posttraining lactate responses after short-term anaerobic interval training (Roberts, Billeter, and Howald 1982). The reason anaerobic training results in lower lactate concentrations at submaximal exercise intensities is not clear but may in part relate to changes in the lactate threshold (Marcinik et al. 1991; Stone et al. 1991a).

At maximum exercise intensities, anaerobically trained athletes accumulate higher lactate concentrations than untrained or aerobically trained athletes (Jacobs 1986; Parkhouse et al. 1983; Stone et al. 1987). As a result of anaerobic training, the ability to accumulate high concentrations of lactate at maximum exercise intensities may be related to increases in anaerobic enzyme activities, changes in isozyme patterns, and increased lactic acid-buffering capabilities, allowing more work to be accomplished or attainment of higher maximum exercise intensities (Bell and Wenger 1986; Parkhouse et al. 1983; Stone et al. 1987). Very intense exercise of sufficient duration can elicit blood lactate concentrations of over 20 mmol · L^{-1} (Hermansen and Stenvold 1972; Jacobs 1986). The highest blood lactate concentrations have been reported as a result of repeated high-intensity exercises with short rest periods (Hermansen and Stenvold 1972; Kraemer et al. 1987).

Low glycogen stores can also affect lactate production (Gollnick and Bayly 1986). Low-carbohydrate diets and previous exercise can diminish glycogen stores, resulting in lower blood lactate concentrations during exercise (Asmussen et al. 1974). Overwork leading to an overtrained state may also produce low exercise lactate concentrations as a result of chronic glycogen depletion (Stone et al. 1991b).

Postexercise Lactic Acid and Lactate Removal
Short-term high-intensity exercises of less than 8 min yield similar high blood lactate concentrations (Gollnick and Bayly 1986). The highest blood lactates typically occur after multiple bouts of high-intensity intermittent exercise (Hermansen and Stenvold 1972). Peak blood lactate concentrations typically occur approximately 5 to 7 min postexercise (Gollnick and Bayly 1986), although peak blood lactate concentrations during intermittent high-intensity exercise may occur before the last bout.

However, peak muscle lactate concentrations can occur within 2 min of the initiation of intense exercise (Hermansen and Vaage 1977; Jacobs, Kaiser, and Tesch 1981; Karlsson 1971; Sahlin et al. 1976; Sahlin 1978). It is the muscle lactic acid concentrations that may in some way be a limiting factor for exercise and not the blood lactate concentration. The postexercise lag time in peak blood lactate concentration results from a cellular transport mechanism for lactate (Juel 1988), the monocarboxylate transporters. Although diffusion contributes to lactate uptake and removal, entry into and out of the cell is facilitated by monocarboxylate transport proteins (MCT) (Billat et al. 2003). There are several species found in different tissues. MCT1 is responsible for enhanced uptake, and MCT4 is responsible for facilitated removal of cellular lactate against a concentration gradient. It is believed that endurance training enhances the expression of MCT1 and that anaerobic training enhances the expression of MCT4 (Billat et al. 2003).

Although blood lactate has not been directly associated with fatigue (Bangsbo et al. 1992), very high concentrations of the lactate ion may be associated with reduced muscle force output (Hogan et al. 1995); and its removal does, to an extent, reflect recovery ability (Plisk 1991). Lactate clearance

postexercise is a first-order exponential function that operates independently of initial concentration (Freund and Gendry 1978). Typically, blood lactate concentrations return to baseline within an hour (Gollnick and Bayly 1986). Clearance rate can be affected by the type of recovery and the trained state. Active postexercise recovery relative exercise intensities of 50% to 70% of $\dot{V}O_2$max appear to be optimal for increasing lactate clearance rates in endurance-trained subjects (Freund and Gendry 1978; Gollnick and Bayly 1986; Hirvonen et al. 1987; Plisk 1991). Both aerobically trained (Gollnick and Bayly 1986; Plisk 1991) and anaerobically trained athletes (McMillan et al. 1993; Pierce et al. 1987, 1993; Warren et al. 1992) show enhanced lactate recovery rates. However, faster lactate postexercise clearance does not necessarily produce enhanced subsequent performance for all types of activities. For example, Bond and colleagues (1991) found that faster clearance as a result of active recovery did not affect isokinetic measures of maximum strength and fatigue profiles; this finding also agrees with the authors' observations of cycling and advanced and elite weightlifters and powerlifters compared to aerobically trained athletes. These observations indicate that other factors such as increases in intracellular PO_4^{+4}, Ca^{++}, or K^+ efflux may be more important in producing fatigue than lactate (Nielsen et al. 2004; Westerblad, Allen, and Lannegren 2002).

Lactate Threshold and Onset of Blood Lactate
Evidence (Coyle et al. 1984; Davis et al. 1979; Kindermann, Simon, and Juel 1979; Komi et al. 1981) suggests that there are specific breakpoints in the lactate accumulation curve as exercise intensity increases (figure 4.4). The exercise intensity or relative intensity at which blood lactate begins an abrupt increase above the baseline level has been termed the lactate threshold or LT (Yoshida 1984). The LT reflects the increasing reliance on anaerobic mechanisms as exercise intensity increases. The LT typically begins at 50% to 60% of $\dot{V}O_2$max in untrained subjects and at about 70% to 80% in trained subjects (Cerretelli et al. 1975; Farrel et al. 1979). A second increase in the rate of lactate accumulation has been noted at higher relative intensities of exercise. This second point of inflection, which has been termed the onset of blood lactate (OBLA), generally occurs when the concentration of blood lactate is near 4 mM (Hill 1924; Sjodin and Jacobs 1981; Tanaka et al. 1983). It has been suggested that the breaks in the lactate accumulation curve are somewhat similar to the points at which intermediate and large motor units

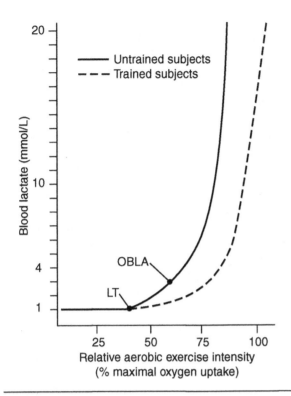

Figure 4.4 Lactate threshold (LT) and onset of blood lactate (OBLA).

Reprinted, by permission, from National Strength and Conditioning Association, 2000, *Essentials of strength training and conditioning*, 2nd ed. (Champaign, IL: Human Kinetics), 79.

are recruited during increasing exercise intensities (Jones and Ehrsam 1982). The muscle cells associated with large motor units are typically type II fibers and are metabolically suited for anaerobic metabolism and lactic acid production.

Some studies suggest that training at intensities near or above the LT or OBLA will push the LT and OBLA to the right, resulting in a later occurrence of lactate accumulation at higher exercise intensity. This shift probably occurs as a result of several possible mechanisms: (1) changes in hormone release, particularly reduced catecholamine concentrations; (2) reduction in the use of type II fibers at a given relative intensity, or (3) increased clearance capabilities. Regardless of the mechanism, this shift in LT or OBLA allows the athlete to perform at higher percentages of $\dot{V}O_2$max without as much lactate production or accumulation in the blood (Brooks, Fahey, and White 1996; Davis et al. 1979).

Furthermore, endurance performance can vary greatly among individuals even when $\dot{V}O_2$max values are equal. Endurance, especially at high percentages of $\dot{V}O_2$max, may be more closely related to lactate production and removal, glycogen utilization, and running economy than to $\dot{V}O_2$max. High-volume weight training has been shown to

increase high-intensity work time without similar changes in $\dot{V}O_2$max (Hickson, Rosenkoetter, and Brown 1980; Hickson et al. 1988; Stone et al. 1983). It has been speculated that some types of weight training may in some manner modify the factors mentioned, allowing greater endurance (Stone et al. 1983). Both cross-sectional (McMillan et al. 1993; Stone et al. 1987) and longitudinal training studies (Pierce et al. 1987, 1993; Stone and Fry 1997) suggest that weight training reduces serum lactate at submaximal loading. Marcinik and colleagues (1991) have provided evidence indicating that resistance training can beneficially alter the LT and increase endurance on a cycle ergometer, a finding suggesting that there can be a transfer of metabolic training effect from one mode to another.

Slow Glycolysis

Slow glycolysis can also use blood glucose or muscle glycogen as an energy source. Aerobic glycolysis or slow glycolysis occurs when the activity of the mitochondria is sufficient to accept the two NADH produced by glycolysis (Pasteur effect; Krebs 1972; McGilvery 1975) (figure 4.3). An additional six ATP can be formed as a result of the entrance of the two NADH into the electron transport system. During slow glycolysis, pyruvate can enter the mitochondrial matrix via a localized carrier mechanism on the outer membrane (Brooks, Fahey, and White 1996; Chappell 1968). In this manner pyruvate can be made available for oxidation.

Glycolytic Energy Yield If glycolysis begins with glucose, then the following equations summarize glycolysis.

Fast glycolysis:

$$\text{glucose} + 2\ P_i + 2\ \text{ADP} \rightarrow$$
$$2\ \text{lactate} + 2\ \text{ATP} + H_2O$$

Slow glycolysis:

$$\text{glucose} + 2\ P_i + 2\ \text{ADP} + 2\ \text{NAD}^+ \rightarrow$$
$$2\ \text{pyruvate} + 2\ \text{ATP} + 2\ \text{NADH} + 2\ H_2O$$

Thus, the net ADP production of glycolysis beginning with one molecule of glucose is two ATP. If, however, glycogen is broken down via the enzyme phosphorylase, forming G-6-P, then three ATP are produced (figure 4.3). This is so because the phosphorylation step that uses an ATP (via hexokinase) is bypassed and one ATP is spared. In comparing fast versus slow glycolysis and the fate of the two sarcoplasmically produced $NADH_2$, one can argue that the net ATP production for slow glycolysis can be as much as eight ATP when the process starts with glucose. Note that in skeletal muscle as opposed to the heart, the protons carried by $NADH_2$ can be transferred to FAD in the shuttle system of the mitochondria, thus reducing the net ATP production.

Control of Glycolysis   Glycolysis is stimulated by ammonia, P_i, ADP, and pH and is strongly stimulated by AMP (Brooks, Fahey, and White 1996; Sugden and Newsholme 1975). It is inhibited by markedly lowered pH, ATP, PCr, citrate, and free fatty acids (FFA) (Brooks, Fahey, and White 1996; Hermansen 1981; Lehninger 2000). The primary control of glycolysis is accomplished through the phosphorylation of glucose (G-6-P) by hexokinase (Brooks, Fahey, and White 1996; Krebs 1972; Lehninger 2000). The rate of glycogen catabolism by phosphorylase also must be considered (Brooks, Fahey, and White 1996; Pike and Brown 1975; Richter, Galbo, and Christensen 1981). The rate-limiting step is as follows:

$$\text{F-6-P} \xrightarrow{\text{PFK}} \text{F-1-6DiP}$$

Thus, the activity of phosphofructokinase (PFK) is of particular importance in the regulation of glycolytic rate. Phosphofructokinase is strongly stimulated by AMP. Therefore, activation of the phosphagen system and production of AMP through the myokinase reaction stimulate glycolysis to contribute to energy production during high-intensity exercise (Brooks, Fahey, and White 1996; Tesch, Colliander, and Kaiser 1986). Ammonia produced during high-intensity exercise as a result of AMP deamination or amino acid deamination can also stimulate PFK (Sugden and Newsholme 1975). Stimulation of PFK by ammonia may partially offset the effects of decreasing pH, as a result of an increase in [H$^+$] with increasing exercise intensity; otherwise this increased proton content can inhibit several glycolytic enzymes including PFK and phosphorylase. However, both phosphorylase and PFK are almost completely inhibited at pH values at or below 6.3 (Hermansen and Stenvold 1972).

The Oxidative (Aerobic) System

The oxidative energy system can use proteins, fats, or carbohydrates as a substrate. Of the ATP produced at rest, about 70% is derived from fats and about 30% comes from the oxidation of carbohydrates. During low-intensity exercise the contribution of fats (and protein) can increase with duration; however, as the intensity of exercise increases, substrate preference shifts toward carbohydrates because

they are a more efficient fuel (Brooks, Fahey, and White 1996; Powers and Howley 1997).

We will first consider carbohydrate oxidation, which begins with the initial catabolism of glucose during glycolysis. When the activity of the mitochondria is high, pyruvate can be decarboxylated (lose a CO_2), forming acetyl, then combine with coenzyme A (CoA) and enter the Krebs cycle (figure 4.5). The $NADH_2$ produced during glycolysis, and during other degradative processes such as the oxidation of fats, can enter the mitochondria via specific shuttle systems (Brooks, Fahey, and White 1996; Chappell 1968; Klingerberg 1970). The $NADH_2$ can then be processed through the electron transport system (ETS) and used in ADP rephosphorylation (oxidative phosphorylation). The complete oxidation of glucose produces approximately 38 ATP (see figure 4.5). This value is an approximation because one of the shuttle systems necessary to move $NADH^+$ across the mitochondrial membrane (and other factors) requires energy. It is also an approximation because the reactions themselves do not always proceed with the same efficiency depending on metabolic conditions such as changes in pH (Lehninger 2000).

Triglycerides are stored in fat cells and to a small extent in muscle. Hormone-sensitive lipase breaks down triglycerides into the energy substrates FFA and glycerol. Free fatty acids and glycerol produced by triglyceride catabolism in fat cells can be released into the blood and be taken up by muscle and used for energy (Boger et al. 1992; Hermansen 1981; Jacobs 1981; Lambert et al. 1991). Muscle also contains small amounts of an intramuscular hormone-sensitive lipase and can produce an intramuscular source of FFA and glycerol. Glycerol can be converted to glycerol-3-phosphate and enter glycolysis. In the cytoplasm (sarcoplasm) of cells, FFA are attached to CoA. The FFA-acyl CoA molecule enters the mitochondria via a carnitine carrier system (Brooks, Fahey, and White 1996; Chappell 1968; Hultsmann 1979; Jones et al. 1980). Free fatty acid undergoes β-oxidation, resulting in acetyl CoA (which can enter the Krebs cycle) and H$^+$, which are carried to the ETS by nicotinic adenine dinucleotide (NAD) and flavin adenine dinucleotide (FAD) (see figure 4.5). This is especially important in slow-twitch fibers, which generally contain high concentrations of oxidative enzymes (Brooks, Fahey, and White 1996; Dufaux, Assmann, and Hollman 1982).

Proteins are constructed from amino acids, which are nitrogen-containing molecules. Proteins can be broken down into constituent amino acids by

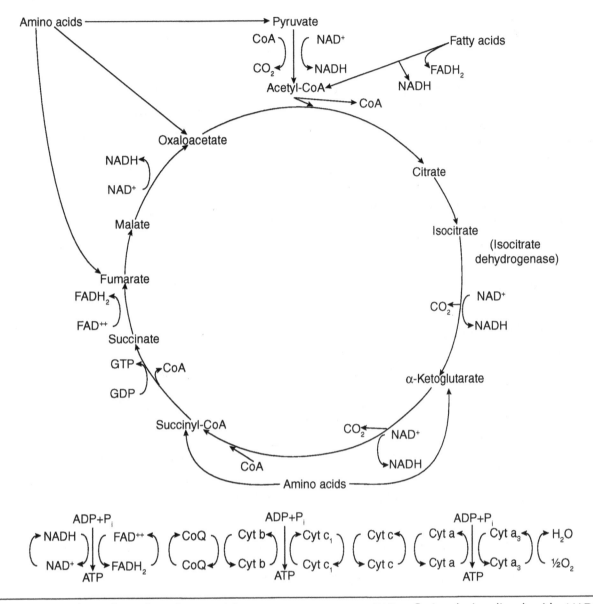

Figure 4.5 The Krebs cycle and proton/electron transport system. FAD = flavin adenine dinucleotide; NAD = nicotinic adenine dinucleotide; GTP = guanosine triphosphate; GDP = guanosine diphosphate; CoQ = coenzyme Q; CYT = cytochrome.

various catabolic processes. Skeletal muscle provides the primary reserve of amino acids. Through transamination and deamination reactions, amino acids can be converted to their carbon skeletons, which in turn can be converted into glucose (gluconeogenesis) (Brooks, Fahey, and White 1996; Lehninger 2000). Most carbon skeletons and amino acid residues appear as pyruvate or Krebs cycle intermediates (Brooks, Fahey, and White 1996; Hultsmann 1979). The nitrogenous waste produced by amino acid degradation is eliminated primarily through urea formation and excretion, along with

the release of small amounts of ammonia (Brooks, Fahey, and White 1996; Meyer and Terjung 1979; Triplett et al. 1990). The elimination of many nitrogenous waste products, especially ammonia, is important because they are toxic and also possibly act as fatigue products (Brooks, Fahey, and White 1996; Triplett et al. 1990). Evidence suggests that during long-term exercise (>90 min), if no additional substrate such as carbohydrate is ingested, there can be an increased use of protein; perhaps as much as 15% to 20% of the energy consumed may be derived from protein (Green et al. 1979;

Young and Torun 1981). (See chapter 6, "Nutrition and Metabolic Factors.")

ATP Production of the Oxidative Systems

During aerobic conditions, starting with glucose, two ATP are produced in the cytoplasm (three ATP when starting with glycogen) for each glucose molecule. Additionally, two cytoplasmic $NADH^+$ can be shuttled into the mitochondria. Within the mitochondria, H^+ (therefore electrons) is introduced to the ETS by either $NADH_2$ or $FADH_2$. The oxidative phosphorylation potential (P:O) is three ATP for $NADH_2$ and two ATP for $FADH_2$ (Lehninger 2000; McGilvery 1975). Slow glycolysis and subsequent oxidation can produce as many as 38 ATP, depending on efficiency. The complete oxidation of glucose and the associated energy conversions are shown in table 4.1.

Control of Oxidation

Regulation of the Krebs cycle is partially controlled by reactions producing $NADH_2^+$ or $FADH_2^+$. The ratio of oxidized to reduced coenzymes is controlled by the availability of ADP and P_i for oxidative phosphorylation in the ETS. If the coenzymes FAD^+ and NAD^+ are not available to accept electrons (H^+ in biological systems), the rate at which the Krebs cycle proceeds is reduced. Additionally, when guanine triphosphate (GTP) accumulates, the increase in succinyl CoA inhibits the initial reaction: oxaloacetate + acetyl CoA → citrate + CoA. The rate-limiting step in the cycle is isocitrate → α-ketoglutarate. The rate-limiting reaction is catalyzed by isocitrate dehydrogenase. This enzyme is stimulated by ADP and generally inhibited by ATP.

Control of the ETS is relatively simple: It is stimulated by ADP and inhibited by ATP (Brooks, Fahey, and White 1996; Lehninger 2000).

Hormonal Control of Energy Metabolism

The mobilization and release of substrates required for the energy systems are to a large extent the result of hormonal actions. Chapter 5, which deals with the neuroendocrine aspects of exercise, covers in detail the actions these hormones exert on physiological and metabolic functions related to aerobic or anaerobic exercise.

The initiation of substrate mobilization for use in energy production is a function of hormones such as epinephrine. For example, specific epinephrine receptors on muscle cell membranes initiate a series of actions known as the cascade effect. This effect is illustrated in figure 4.6 (Brooks, Fahey, and White 1996; Lehninger 2000). This series of events is responsible for the mobilization and release of FFA by fat cells, the release of glucose by the liver, and the intramuscular breakdown of triglycerides and glycogen for use in energy production.

Fuel Efficiency

We can consider the efficiency of glycolysis and the oxidative system in different ways. One method of estimating energy production efficiency is to consider calories extracted relative to calories stored in a molecule, as in the following example (Brooks, Fahey, and White 1996; Lehninger 2000; Stone and O'Bryant 1987):

Table 4.1 **The Oxidative ATP Yield of Glucose**

Location	Reaction	Coenzyme	Theoretical ATP yield
Cytoplasm	Glucose → pyruvate	2 NAD	2
Cytoplasm	Glucose → pyruvate	2 NAD	6
Mitochondria	Pyruvate → acetyl CoA	2 NAD	6
Mitochondria	Isocitrate → α-ketoglutarate	2 NAD	6
Mitochondria	α-ketoglutarate → succinyl CoA	2 NAD	6
Mitochondria	Succinyl CoA → succinate	2 GDP	2*
Mitochondria	Succinate → fumarate	2 FAD	4
Mitochondria	Malate → oxaloacetate	2 NAD	6
			Total = 38

*Substrate-level transformations.

Data from National Strength and Conditioning Association, 1994, *Essentials of strength training and conditioning* (Champaign, IL: Human Kinetics), 67-85.

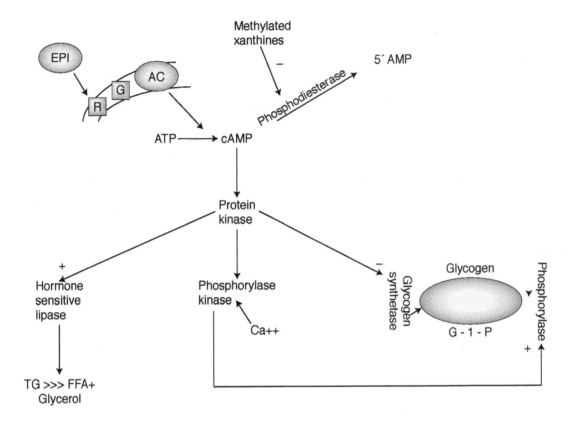

Figure 4.6 The cascade effect. A hormone such as epinephrine attaches to a receptor protein (R) in the cell membrane. The hormone–receptor interaction changes the conformation of a regulatory protein (G), which in turn activates an enzyme (such as adenyl cyclase) or a calcium channel. The activated enzyme then initiates a cascade of events. This example deals with the second messenger cyclic adenosine monophosphate (cAMP), which affects alterations in energy substrate mobilization. EPI = hormones; AC = adenyl cyclase.

Based on Powers and Howley 1997; Guyton and Hall 2000; MacIntosh, Gardiner, and McComas 2006.

ATP = 7.3 kcal · mol⁻¹; glucose = 686 kcal · mol⁻¹; stearate = 2100 kcal · mol⁻¹

1. Fast glycolysis = 2 ATP (14.6 kcal)
2. Slow glycolysis = 38 ATP (277 kcal)
3. Oxidation of stearate = 148 ATP (1080 kcal)

Using this information, we can calculate a ratio of calories extracted to calories stored as follows:

$$1.\ \text{Fast glycolysis} = \frac{14.6}{686} = 2\%$$

$$2.\ \text{Oxidation of carbohydrates} = \frac{277}{686} = 40\%$$

$$3.\ \text{Oxidation of stearate} = \frac{1080}{2100} = 51\%$$

With use of this method, it appears that anaerobic metabolism is not as efficient as the aerobic system and that fat metabolism is somewhat more efficient than glucose metabolism. However, this does not consider the total rate of ATP production or free energy production in biological systems. Free energy is that energy free to perform work (Brooks, Fahey, and White 1996; Lehninger 2000). The energy change (ΔH) from glucose to lactate is approximately −47 kcal · mol⁻¹. The potential energy available (ΔG) for ATP is approximately −7.3 kcal · mol⁻¹. The negative sign indicates energy given up during exergonic reactions, which is available to perform work. In living systems the ΔH for the biological release of ATP is approximately −11 kcal · mol⁻¹. Thus, the efficiency of fast glycolysis and the total oxidation of glucose can be calculated as follows:

Fast glycolysis

$$\text{efficiency} = \frac{2(-11)}{47} = 47\%$$

Complete oxidation of glucose

$$\text{efficiency} = \frac{38(-11)}{686} = 61\%$$

Using this reasoning, anaerobic glycolysis is only somewhat less efficient than the oxidative system. Another method of assessing efficiency is to examine the relation of lactate accumulation to constant decreases in $\dot{V}O_2$ during increasing work rates. Using this method, Gladden and Welch (1978) have presented data suggesting that ATP synthesized by anaerobic pathways is not much less efficient than aerobically synthesized ATP; this agrees with the ΔH changes just discussed. However, when work produced was compared with energy expended, anaerobic efficiency (high-intensity exercise) was less than aerobic efficiency (steady-state light work) (Brooks, Fahey, and White 1996; Gladden and Welch 1978). This result may have been obtained because high-intensity exercise results in decreased muscle efficiency or because metabolism is not directly related to an increase in external work, or both (Gladden and Welch 1978). Regardless of the mechanisms, as exercise moves toward maximum intensity it becomes less efficient. Changes in the cellular environment also affect efficiency. For example, decreased pH and increased [H^+], alterations in inter-intracellular K^+, and alterations in PO_3^{+4} and Ca^{++} can interfere with excitation–contraction coupling and enzyme activity, which can change system efficiency. It should also be noted that fiber type influences efficiency; for example, type I motor units (MUs) appear to be more fuel efficient because of tighter coupling in the ETS.

Respiratory Exchange Ratio

Another important consideration in determining bioenergetic efficiency is the respiratory quotient (RQ). The RQ is the ratio between CO_2 produced and O_2 used during the oxidation of food (i.e., protein, carbohydrate, or fat). Respiratory quotient and kilocalories per mole of a substrate can be measured with a bomb calorimeter (Kleiber 1950). In exercise situations, a respiratory exchange ratio (RER) can be obtained through measurement of expired CO_2 and oxygen uptake (Brooks, Fahey, and White 1996; Powers and Howley 1997). The term RER is used because of a small amount of additional energy expended in the digestion of protein that is not completely accounted for by the RQ, and also because of the effect of hyper- or hypoventilation and the buffering systems, which can cause a disproportionate change in gaseous exchange. The effect of buffering systems is especially important at high intensities of exercise in which excess CO_2 can be blown off, resulting in an inflated exchange ratio that is not completely indicative of the oxidation of food. Thus the RQ is a better measure of cellular respiration, whereas the RER is a measure of exchange at the lungs. Using calorimetry and the RER, caloric equivalents have been determined (table 4.2).

This method assumes that protein is not a major energy source—an assumption that may not be correct in the case of long-term exercise (Brooks, Fahey, and White 1996). (See also chapter 6, "Nutrition and Metabolic Factors.")

If we consider the RER values, carbohydrates are the most efficient fuel, producing about 6% more energy per unit of O_2 used than is produced by fats and about 10% more than is produced by proteins. Thus, carbohydrates are the preferred fuel (Brooks, Fahey, and White 1996). The RER value can serve during exercise to qualitatively determine the primary energy substrate (food) being used for energy and to estimate the relative intensity of exercise. The RER value can decrease during light exercise but can rapidly increase as exercise intensity increases (figure 4.7). The decreased RER during low-intensity exercise indicates a greater reliance on fats (and perhaps proteins during exercise lasting longer than 90 min). At an exercise intensity about 65% of $\dot{V}O_2$max, total fat oxidation reaches its peak, about 50% of the total energy requirements—the rest being primarily supplied by carbohydrates (Romijn et al. 1992). This increased use of fats during long-term low-intensity exercise is due to two factors: (1) the mobilization of FFA caused by release of specific hormones, especially growth hormone (Brooks, Fahey, and White 1996; Powers and Howley 1997; Terjung 1979); and (2) a momentary faster acceleration of the ETS compared to glycolysis

Table 4.2 **Caloric Equivalents**

Food	CALORIMETRY		BIOLOGICAL	
	(kcal · g⁻¹)	(kcal · g⁻¹)	RER	kcal · L O₂⁻¹
Protein	5.7	4.2	0.8	4.5
Fat	9.5	9.5	0.7	4.7
Carbohydrate	4.2	4.2	1.0	5.0

Data from National Strength and Conditioning Association, 1994, *Essentials of strength training and conditioning* (Champaign, IL: Human Kinetics).

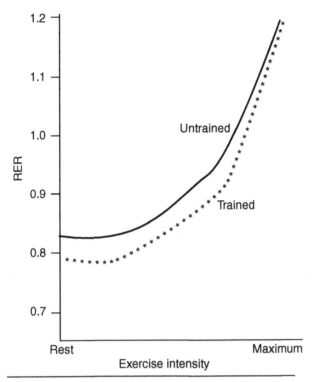

Figure 4.7 Respiratory exchange ratio (RER) values for trained and untrained subjects at rest and during different levels of exercise.

STONE, M.H. and O'BRYANT, H.S., WEIGHT TRAINING: A SCIENTIFIC APPROACH, ©1987, pp. 30. Reprinted by permission of Pearson Education, Inc., Upper Saddle River, NJ.

so that the capacity for oxidation exceeds the supply of pyruvate. Additionally, FFA inhibits PFK, the rate-limiting enzyme for glycolysis.

As the exercise intensity increases, the need for a fast supply of energy increases and ADP concentrations increase. As ADP concentrations increase with exercise intensity, those processes that rephosphorylate the most ADP with the least O_2 use are favored (Brooks, Fahey, and White 1996). Therefore, as a result of increasing exercise intensity, there is an increase in the use of fast glycolysis. Some data from animal studies and reviews of the literature indicate that increasing blood lactate concentrations may inhibit FFA mobilization (Gollnick and Hermansen 1975; Issekutz et al. 1965; Jones et al. 1980), which would further depress the oxidative processes. Findings regarding this effect are largely based on sodium lactate infusion into resting dogs (Issekutz et al. 1965; Miller et al. 1964), and these studies do not take into account the complete physiological environment created by exercising muscle. More recent evidence suggests that increasing lactate concentrations in exercising humans may not necessarily inhibit FFA mobilization or limit their use as an energy substrate (Boger et al. 1992;

McMillan et al. 1993; Stone and Fry 1997). The lack of FFA mobilization inhibition is likely a result of hormonal influences (McMillan et al. 1993; Stone and Fry 1997).

It is possible for the RER values to exceed 1.0, the maximum obtainable value in nonbiological bomb calorimeter reactions. This occurs because fast glycolysis produces protons, which increases blood and tissue [H^+], lowering pH. This process can overcome the blood buffering systems (Brooks, Fahey, and White 1996). For example,

$$\text{buffering reaction: } CO_2 + H_2O \leftrightarrow H_2CO_3$$
$$\leftrightarrow HCO_3^- + H^+$$

$$\text{increasing exercise intensity} = \uparrow H^+$$

The production of protons pushes this reaction to the left, causing additional CO_2 to be released. The excess CO_2 is removed through the lungs during exhalation, which raises the RER values above 1.0 (Brooks, Fahey, and White 1996; Parkhouse et al. 1983). The importance of RER values above 1.0 (as high as 1.45) is in estimations of heavy and maximal efforts (Brooks, Fahey, and White 1996).

Aerobically trained subjects typically have lower RER values during exercise than untrained subjects, except at maximum or near-maximum efforts. Lower RER values occur as a result of aerobic training because of metabolic adaptations that allow trained people to use FFA more efficiently. These adaptations may include an enhancement of oxidative enzymes and a predominance of specific isozymes (Brooks, Fahey, and White 1996; York, Oscai, and Penny 1974). For example, LDH_H (catalyzes lactate to pyruvate) concentration is enhanced in aerobically trained people. The importance of increased FFA use in trained people is that it spares glycogen, an important consideration in endurance activities. The sparing of glycogen is particularly important to the central nervous system, which relies primarily on carbohydrates for energy (Brooks, Fahey, and White 1996).

It is not unusual to observe low RERs after anaerobic exercise. A decreased recovery RER has been observed in weight trainers (Melby et al. 1993) and weightlifters (McMillan et al. 1993) after weight training exercise; this effect can persist for several hours. The mobilization and use of fats postexercise are likely related to glycogen depletion and hormonal effects. This suggests that fats can be used in the recovery process from anaerobic exercise and may have implications for body composition effects (see chapter 10, "Physical and Physiological Adaptations to Resistance Training").

Energy Production Power (Rate) and Capacity

Of importance to the sport scientist as well as the coach and athlete is how these energy systems are used in a practical setting. The bioenergetic systems differ in their ability to supply energy for various intensities and durations of exercise (table 4.3). Conley and colleagues (1993), using cycle ergometry, and Harman (personal communication), using a treadmill, have shown that power (intensity) at $\dot{V}O_2$max is only about 25% to 35% of peak power. Therefore exercise that is aerobic, even at 100% of $\dot{V}O_2$max, should not be classified as high-intensity exercise. A maximum rate of energy demand requires a maximum rate of energy production, resulting in the predominant use of the phosphagen system in maximum-intensity exercise. High-intensity exercise can be supported by fast glycolysis, while long-term aerobic exercise is supported by the oxidative system because of its high capacity for ATP production. Because of the time required to gear up the other systems, the ATP-PCr system is also used to a small extent at the initiation of most exercises (Brooks, Fahey, and White 1996).

The preceding discussions suggest that the prominent energy system used during exercise is primarily a function of the intensity of exercise. Thus, typical weight training or sprinting is supported primarily through anaerobic systems, while typical endurance training is supported largely by oxidative mechanisms. The primary energy system will shift between these two extremes depending on intensity and duration. However, in no case does any exercise or even resting condition rely completely on one system or another. During physical activity, anaerobic and oxidative systems always contribute to a greater or lesser extent, primarily depending on intensity and secondarily on duration (Brooks, Fahey, and White 1996). This consideration is a basis of interval training (see later section, "The Metabolic Cost of Exercise").

Time is also a factor in the use of bioenergetic systems. Athletic events range from a snatch or shot put (1-2 s) to marathons (more than 2 h). While a maximum sustained effort is possible for very short periods (<10 s), longer events require pacing, resulting in a best-effort performance. The relationships between time, relative intensity, and energy systems are shown in table 4.4 (Brooks, Fahey, and White 1996; Edington and Edgerton 1976; Hermansen 1981; Robergs et al. 1991; Tesch 1980; Thorstensson 1976).

Table 4.3 Rates and Capacities of the Bioenergetic Systems

System	Rate of ATP production	Capacity of ATP production
Phosphagens	1	5
Fast glycogenolysis	2	4
Slow glycolysis	3	3
Oxidation of carbohydrate	4	2
Oxidation of fats and protein	5	1

1 = highest, 5 = lowest.

Reprinted, by permission, from National Strength and Conditioning Association, 2000, *Essentials of strength training and conditioning*, 2nd ed. (Champaign, IL: Human Kinetics), 83.

Table 4.4 Time and Intensity Considerations for Energy Production

Primary energy system	Event duration	Relative intensity
Phosphagens	0-6 s	Maximum
Phosphagens + fast glycolysis	6-30 s	High
Fast glycolysis	30 s to 2 min	Moderately high
Fast glycolysis + oxidative system	2-3 min	Moderate
Oxidative system	>3 min	Low

Adapted, by permission, from National Strength and Conditioning Association, 2000, *Essentials of strength training and conditioning*, 2nd ed. (Champaign, IL: Human Kinetics), 83.

Substrate Depletion and Repletion: Recovery

Energy substrates can be selectively depleted during exercise of varying intensities and durations. Substrate depletion is partially responsible for fatigue, particularly in terms of phosphagens and glycogen (Gollnick and Bayly 1986; Hermansen 1981; Hultman and Sjoholm 1986; Jacobs, Kaiser, and Tesch 1981; Lambert and Flynn 2002). Depletion of other substrates such as amino acids and fatty acids typically does not occur to the extent that performance is limited. Consequently the depletion and repletion of phosphagens and glycogen have received considerable attention from exercise and sport scientists.

Exercise Depletion and Postexercise Recovery of ATP-PCr

Although the exact mechanism is unclear (Bridges et al. 1991), fatigue during exercise can be at least partially related to the decrease in phosphagens (Gollnick and Bayly 1986; Hultman and Sjoholm 1986). Phosphagen muscle concentrations are more rapidly depleted as a result of high-intensity anaerobic exercise than by aerobic exercise. Even as the result of very intense exercise, muscle ATP concentrations do not decrease markedly (Henry 1957), typically to no more than about 60% of initial values (Jacobs 1986). However, PCr can decrease more markedly (50-70%) during the first moments (5-30 s) of high-intensity exercise and to near zero concentrations as a result of maximum effort or very intense exercise to exhaustion (Hirvonen et al. 1987; Jacobs et al. 1983; Karlsson 1971; McCartney et al. 1986). It should also be noted that muscle actions producing external work (dynamic) use more metabolic energy and typically deplete phosphagens to a greater extent than do isometric muscle actions (Bridges et al. 1991).

The intramuscular ATP concentration is largely spared during exercise as a consequence of PCr depletion and because of the contribution of additional ATP from the myokinase reaction and from other energy sources such as glycogen or FFA. Postexercise phosphagen repletion can occur in a relatively short time. Complete resynthesis of ATP appears to occur within 3 to 5 min (Harris et al. 1976; Hultman and Sjoholm 1986) and complete PCr resynthesis can occur within 8 min (Harris et al. 1976), although very high-intensity exercise results in a slower PCr repletion rate (up to 15 min), which is likely related to increased [H+] (McCann, Mole, and Caton 1995). Repletion of phosphagens is largely accomplished as a result of aerobic metabolism (Harris et al. 1976), although fast glycolysis can contribute to recovery after high-intensity exercise (Cerretelli et al. 1975; diPrampero, Peeters, and Margaria 1973).

The effects of training on the concentrations of phosphagens are not well studied or understood. A small amount of ATP may be lost during high-intensity exercise as a result of the conversion of AMP to inosine monophosphate (IMP). Although most of the IMP is reaminated to AMP, a small amount is subsequently dephosphorylated, producing hypoxanthine and uric acid. However, high-intensity training results in adaptations that minimize this loss. Aerobic training may increase resting concentrations of phosphagens (Ericksson,

Gollnick, and Saltin 1973; Karlsson et al. 1972) and decrease their rate of depletion at a given submaximal power output (Constable et al. 1987; Karlsson et al. 1972), but not at a relative submaximal power output (Constable et al. 1987).

Although indications of increased resting concentrations of phosphagens have been noted (Roberts, Billeter, and Howald 1982), short-term (eight weeks) studies of sprint training have not shown alterations in resting concentrations of phosphagens (Boobis, Williams, and Wooten 1983; Thorstensson, Sjodin, and Karlsson 1975). However, total phosphagen content can be larger after sprint training due to increases in muscle mass (Thorstensson, Sjodin, and Karlsson 1975). Weight training has been shown to increase the resting concentrations of phosphagens in the triceps brachii after five weeks of training (MacDougall et al. 1977). The increases in phosphagen concentration may have occurred due to selective hypertrophy of type II fibers, which can contain a higher phosphagen concentration than type I fibers (MacDougall 1986).

Exercise Depletion and Postexercise Recovery of Glycogen

Limited stores of glycogen are available for exercise. Approximately 300 to 400 g of glycogen is stored in the muscle, and about 70 to 100 g is stored in the liver (Newsholme 1986; Sherman and Wimer 1991). Resting concentrations of liver and muscle glycogen can be influenced by training and dietary manipulations (Friedman, Neufer, and Dohm 1991; Sherman and Wimer 1991). See chapter 6, "Nutrition and Metabolic Factors," for further discussion. Considerable information suggests that anaerobic training, including sprinting and weight training (Boobis, Williams, and Wooten 1983; MacDougall et al. 1977), as well as aerobic training (Gollnick et al. 1972, 1973), can increase resting muscle glycogen concentrations.

The rate of glycogen depletion is related to exercise intensity (Sherman and Wimer 1991). Muscle glycogen is a more important energy source during moderate- and high-intensity exercise. Liver glycogen appears to be more important during low-intensity exercise, and its contribution to metabolic processes increases with duration of exercise. Increases in relative exercise intensity of 50%, 75%, and 100% of $\dot{V}O_2$max lead to increases in the rate of muscle glycogenolysis of 0.7, 1.4, and 3.4 mmol $\cdot$ kg^{-1} $\cdot$ min^{-1}, respectively (Saltin and Karlsson 1971). At relative intensities of exercise above 60% of $\dot{V}O_2$max, muscle glycogen becomes an increasingly important energy substrate, and the entire glycogen content of some muscle cells can become depleted during exercise (Saltin and Gollnick 1983). Blood glucose concentrations are maintained at very low exercise intensities (<50% $\dot{V}O_2$max) as a result of low muscle glucose uptake (Ahlborg and Felig 1967); as exercise duration increases, glucose concentrations fall after 90 min but rarely fall below 2.8 mmol · L^{-1}. Long-term exercise (>90 min) at higher intensities (>50% $\dot{V}O_2$max) may result in substantially decreased blood glucose concentrations as a consequence of liver glycogen depletion (Ahlborg and Felig 1982). Hypoglycemic reactions may occur in some individuals, with exercise-induced blood glucose values below 2.5 mmol · L^{-1} (Ahlborg and Felig 1982; Coyle et al. 1983). A decline in blood glucose to 2.5 to 3.0 mmol · L^{-1} results from liver carbohydrate decline and causes decreased carbohydrate oxidation and eventual exhaustion (Coggan and Coyle 1987; Coyle et al. 1983; Sherman and Wimer 1991).

Very high-intensity intermittent exercise such as weight training can cause substantial muscle glycogen depletion (20-50%) with relatively few sets (low total workloads) (Lambert et al. 1991; MacDougall et al. 1988; Robergs et al. 1991; Tesch 1980). Although phosphagens may be the primary limiting factor during resistance exercise performed with a few repetitions or few sets (MacDougall et al. 1988), muscle glycogen may become a limiting factor for resistance training with many total sets and larger total amounts of work (Lambert et al. 1991). It is also important to note that this type of exercise could cause selective muscle fiber glycogen depletion (greater depletion in type II fibers), which could also limit performance (Lambert et al. 1991). As with other types of dynamic exercise, the rate of muscle glycogenolysis during resistance exercise is intensity dependent. The rate of muscle glycogenolysis during six sets of six repetitions of leg extensions at 70% 1RM was double that of six sets at 35% of 1RM (0.46 ± 0.05 mmol · kg^{-1} · s^{-1} vs. 0.21 ± 0.03 mmol · kg^{-1} · s^{-1}). However, it appears that equal amounts of total work produced equal amounts of glycogen depletion regardless of relative exercise intensity (Lambert et al. 1991). These findings for the rate of muscle glycogenolysis during resistance training exercise are similar to those observed during electrical stimulation of the vastus lateralis (Spriet, Lindinger, and McKelvie 1989) and maximal intermittent isokinetic cycling (McCartney et al. 1986; Spriet, Lindinger, and McKelvie 1989).

Repletion of muscle glycogen during recovery is related to postexercise carbohydrate ingestion.

Reviews of the literature suggest that repletion appears to be optimal if 0.7 to 3.0 g of carbohydrate · kg^{-1} is ingested every 2 h postexercise (Friedman, Neufer, and Dohm 1991; Sherman and Wimer 1991). This level of carbohydrate consumption can maximize muscle glycogen repletion at 5 to 6 µmol · g wet muscle mass^{-1} · h^{-1} during the first 4 to 6 h postexercise. Muscle glycogen can be completely replenished within 24 h provided sufficient carbohydrate is ingested (Friedman, Neufer, and Dohm 1991; Sherman and Wimer 1991). (See also chapter 6, "Nutrition and Metabolic Factors.") However, if the exercise has a large eccentric component, the rate of muscle glycogen replenishment can be reduced (Costill et al. 1990; Doyle et al. 1993; Widrick et al. 1992). The rate of replenishment is linear over the first 6 to 48 h postexercise and not different from replenishment after concentric exercise (Widrick et al. 1992; Doyle et al. 1993). After the first 6 to 48 h, the rate of replenishment may be reduced up to 10 days depending on the trained state and carbohydrate intake (Doyle et al. 1993). The reduced glycogen resynthesis may be related to impaired glycogen synthetase activity, insulin action, or glucose uptake, possibly as a result of muscle damage (Doyle et al. 1993). The reduced glycogen replenishment may be partially offset by a large intake of carbohydrates (at least 1.5 g · kg body mass^{-1} · h^{-1}) with feedings beginning immediately after exercise and occurring every 2 h. This type of carbohydrate feeding raises insulin and glucose to higher and more consistent blood concentrations, enhancing glycogen resynthesis.

Bioenergetic Limiting Factors

Limiting factors for maximal performance (Brooks, Fahey, and White 1996; Brouha and Radford 1960; Eriksson, Gollnick, and Saltin 1973; Hermansen 1981; Hultsmann 1979; Jacobs 1981; Powers and Howley 1997) must be considered in the accumulation of fatigue from exercise and training. Table 4.5 provides examples of the various possible limiting factors based on depletion of energy source or substrate and increases in muscle [H^+].

Glycogen can become a limiting factor for both long-term low-intensity exercise supported primarily by aerobic metabolism and repeated very high-intensity exercise primarily supported by anaerobic mechanisms. Of importance to weight training, sprinting, and other primarily anaerobic activities is the possible effect of lactic acid and increased tissue [H^+] in both indirectly and directly limiting contractile force (Hermansen 1981).

Table 4.5 **Examples of Bioenergetic/Metabolic Limiting Factors**

Type of exercise	ATP-PCr	Muscle glycogen	Liver glycogen	Fat stores	[H⁺]
Light (marathon)	1	5	4-5	2-3	1
Moderate (1500 m)	1-2	3	2	1-2	2-3
Moderately high (400 m)	3	3	1	1	4-5
Maximum (discus)	2-3	1	1	1	1
*Repeated (very intense)	4-5	4-5	1-2	1-2	4-5

*Example: sets of 10 repetitions in the power snatch with 60% of maximum.

[H⁺] (hydrogen ion content) also reflects the changes in other ions such as K^+, Ca^{++}, and PO_4^{-3} that are related to fatigue.

1 = lowest; 5 = greatest.

Adapted, by permission, from National Strength and Conditioning Association, 2000, *Essentials of strength training and conditioning*, 2nd ed. (Champaign, IL: Human Kinetics), 85.

The Metabolic Cost of Exercise

Oxygen uptake is a measure of an organism's ability to function aerobically. The volume of oxygen uptake per minute ($\dot{V}O_2$) depends on a central (cardiac output) and a peripheral (a-$\bar{v}O_2$ diff) factor. A rearrangement of the Fick equation describes this relationship:

$$\dot{V}O_2 = C.O. \times a\text{-}\bar{v}O_2 \text{ diff}$$

Therefore, maximum oxygen consumption ($\dot{V}O_2$max) depends on the maximum attainable values for the central and peripheral factors.

During submaximal exercise of a constant power output, $\dot{V}O_2$ increases for the first few minutes until a steady state of $\dot{V}O_2$ is reached (Åstrand and Rodahl 1970; Hill 1924). During this steady state, oxygen demand equals oxygen consumption (figure 4.8). However, during the initial phase (3-5 min) of aerobic steady-state exercise, some of the energy cost must be supported anaerobically (Åstrand and Rodahl 1970; Brooks, Fahey, and White 1996). This anaerobic metabolic contribution to the total energy cost of exercise is termed the *oxygen deficit* (Hill 1924; Brooks, Fahey, and White 1996). At the termination of exercise, $\dot{V}O_2$ remains above resting levels for a period of time depending on the intensity and duration of the exercise (see figures 4.8 and 4.9). This postexercise $\dot{V}O_2$ (above resting) has been termed the O_2 debt (Hill 1924) or the excess postexercise oxygen consumption (EPOC), or simply recovery oxygen (Brooks, Fahey, and White 1996; Burleson et al. 1998).

If the intensity of work is above the $\dot{V}O_2$max one is capable of producing, then much of the work must be supported by anaerobic mechanisms. This occurrence is described in figure 4.9. In general, as the contribution of anaerobic mechanisms supporting the exercise increases, the exercise time

decreases (Hadmann 1957; Wells, Balke, and Van Fossan 1957; Whipp, Scard, and Wasserman 1970; Brooks, Fahey, and White 1996; Powers and Howley 1997). Measurement of the anaerobic contribution to both steady-state and high-intensity exercise can be accomplished through evaluation of the oxygen deficit (Medbo et al. 1988; Olsen et al. 1994; Tabata et al. 1997).

The contributions of anaerobic and aerobic mechanisms to maximal sustained efforts on a cycle ergometer are shown in table 4.6 (Vandewalle, Peres, and Monod 1987; Withers et al. 1991). During maximal sustained efforts on a cycle ergometer, contributions from anaerobic mechanisms are primary for about 30 to 60 s; thereafter aerobic metabolism becomes the primary energy-supplying mechanism. Thus, maximal sustained efforts to complete exhaustion may depend greatly on aerobic metabolism. The contribution of anaerobic mechanisms to this type of exercise represents the anaerobic capacity (Medbo and Burgers 1991; Vandewalle, Peres, and Monod 1987).

Power output decreases as the contribution of energy from aerobic mechanisms increases. On a cycle ergometer, the power output that can be briefly sustained at $\dot{V}O_2$max is typically less than 35% of the peak power output. Thus, exercise primarily supported by aerobic metabolism must proceed at low exercise intensities relative to maximum power output capabilities. Enhancement of either anaerobic or aerobic capacity can increase endurance and the total amount of work accomplished during sustained maximal efforts to exhaustion (Vandewalle, Peres, and Monod 1987). Different types of training may enhance either anaerobic or aerobic capacity (Medbo and Burgers 1991). The simultaneous enhancement of aerobic power, anaerobic power, and anaerobic capacity is possible through manipulation of the exercise-to-rest

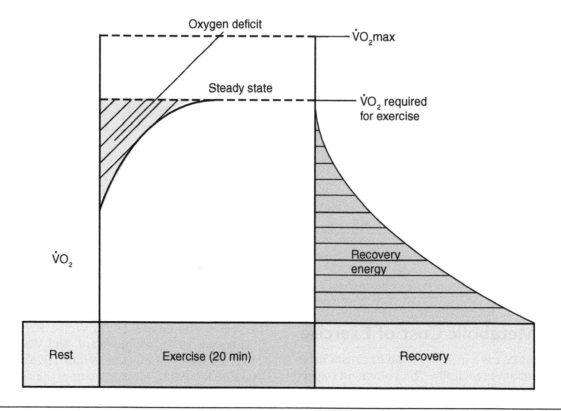

Figure 4.8 Representation of low-intensity steady-state exercise. In this example $\dot{V}O_2$max is 5 L · min^{-1} and the exercise is being performed at 4 L · min^{-1}.

Reprinted, by permission, from National Strength and Conditioning Association, 1994, *Essentials of strength training and conditioning* (Champaign, IL: Human Kinetics), 77.

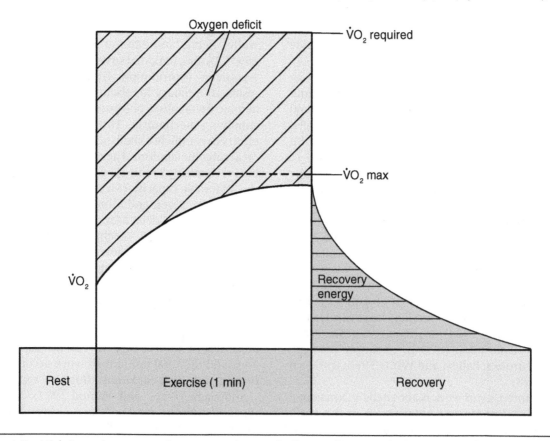

Figure 4.9 High-intensity non-steady-state exercise metabolism. In this example the exercise is being performed at 75% of maximum power output, approximately twice the power at maximum $\dot{V}O_2$. In this case the required $\dot{V}O_2$ is considerably above the maximum $\dot{V}O_2$. Thus the oxygen deficit is sustained throughout the exercise and is quite large.

Reprinted, by permission, from National Strength and Conditioning Association, 1994, *Essentials of strength training and conditioning* (Champaign, IL: Human Kinetics), 77.

Table 4.6 Contribution of Anaerobic and Aerobic Mechanisms to Maximal Sustained Efforts

Contribution %	EFFORT DURATION			
	0-5 s	30 s	60 s	90 s
Anaerobic	96	75	50	35
Aerobic	4	25	50	65
Power (% max)	100	55	35	31

Adapted from H. Vandewalle, G. Peres, and H. Monod, 1987, "Standard anaerobic exercise tests," *Sports Medicine* 4: 268-289; R.T. Withers et al., 1991, "Muscle metabolism during 30, 60, and 90 s of maximal cycling on an airbraked ergometer," *European Journal of Applied Physiology* 63: 354-362.

intervals (Medbo and Burgers 1990; Tabata et al. 1996; Tabata et al. 1997).

Few sports or other physical activities require maximum sustained-effort exercise to exhaustion or near exhaustion. Most sport and training activities (such as football, interval jumping and sprinting, weight training) produce metabolic profiles that are very similar to those for a series of high-intensity constant or near-constant-effort exercise bouts interspersed with rest periods. In this type of exercise, the exercise intensity (power output) that must be met during each exercise bout is much greater than the maximal power output that can be sustained using aerobic energy sources.

Enhancing aerobic power through aerobic training while simultaneously compromising (or neglecting) anaerobic power and capacity training is of relatively little benefit to strength-power athletes (Koziris et al. 1996). See the section "Energy Production Power (Rate) and Capacity."

One method of training that allows appropriate metabolic systems to be stressed is interval training. Interval training is based on the concept that, compared to continuous exercise, more work can be performed at higher exercise intensities with the same or less fatigue (Brooks, Fahey, and White 1996). The theoretical metabolic profile for exercise-to-rest intervals stressing aerobic metabolism, fast glycolysis, and the immediate system can be based on the knowledge of which energy system predominates during exercise and time of substrate recovery. The examples in table 4.7 represent reasonable exercise-to-rest intervals based on exercise relative to maximum attainable power and substrate (phosphagen) recovery times (Stone and Conley 1992).

On the other hand, we should note that the dynamics of many sports do not lend themselves to a strict application of exercise-to-rest intervals. Perhaps a more usable method from a practical point of view would be training using intensity–time profiles. Using this method, the intensities and durations of athletic events are duplicated in training (Plisk and Gambetta 1997). This method allows for an interval type of training that simulates the intensities and exercise and rest intervals in an actual contest situation. For American football, for example, the number of plays, distance covered, and relative intensity of play can be approximated for each position and then duplicated in training programs, thus more readily ensuring that the athlete will possess sufficient conditioning to play the game.

Choosing appropriate exercise intensities, exercise durations, and rest intervals enables one to train the appropriate energy systems. Note that exercise-to-rest intervals may change as physiological adaptations are made across a training program or as a result of changes in long-range programming of training (e.g., periodization).

Recovery Oxygen Consumption: Recovery Energy

Coaches and athletes have often underestimated the energy cost of resistance training. Many also believe that resistance training has little or no effect on body fat. Such misconceptions may arise from the commonly held beliefs that the caloric cost of typical aerobic exercise is substantially higher and that only aerobic exercise can burn fat. However, these beliefs may not be correct.

Table 4.7 Example of Proposed Exercise-to-Rest Intervals

Percent maximum power	Primary system stressed	Typical exercise time	Exercise:rest
90-100	Phosphagens	5-10 s	1:12-1:20
75-90	Fast glycolysis	15-30 s	1:3-1:5
30-75	Fast glycolysis + aerobic metabolism	60-180 s	1:3-1:4
20-35	Aerobic metabolism	>180 s	1:1-1:3

Adapted, by permission, from National Strength and Conditioning Association, 2000, *Essentials of strength training and conditioning*, 2nd ed. (Champaign, IL: Human Kinetics), 88.

Postexercise recovery energy consumption is an important consideration for a number of reasons, including its possible effect on body mass and body composition and its effect on subsequent exercise. The energy cost of exercise is not simply confined to the time of the exercise itself, but may persist for some period after exercise is ended. The effects of steady-state exercise on recovery energy consumption and total energy consumed have been well studied (Bahr et al. 1987; Bahr and Sejersted 1991; Brehm and Gutin 1986; Elliot, Goldberg, and Kuel 1992; Scholl, Bullough, and Melby 1993; Sedlock, Fissinger, and Melby 1989). These studies indicate that training intensity has a somewhat greater effect on recovery energy consumption than does the duration of exercise (Melby 1993). Increasing the duration of low-intensity exercise (<60% $\dot{V}O_2$max) results in linear increases in total recovery energy (Bahr 1987; Bahr and Sejersted 1991; Melby 1993); increasing the intensity of exercise appears to produce an exponential effect (Bahr and Sejersted 1991; Melby 1993). Higher intensities of exercise appear to disturb homeostasis to a greater degree than low-intensity exercise, resulting in greater postexercise energy consumption. This suggests that non-steady-state anaerobic exercise, such as weight training or sprinting, would require more energy and longer durations for recovery.

Although fast glycolysis can contribute to recovery from high-intensity exercise, most of the recovery process from all types of exercise is accomplished through aerobic metabolism. One important method of describing recovery energy consumption is through measurement of the *recovery oxygen consumption* (ROC) and converting it to a caloric value. The ROC is the amount of O_2 uptake above baseline used to restore the body to the pre-exercise condition (Stainsby and Barclay 1970). Early experiments suggested that the ROC was moderately or strongly related to the O_2 deficit and largely due to the resynthesis of glycogen from lactate (80%) or the further oxidation of lactate (20%) via pyruvate and the Krebs-ETS pathway (Hill 1924). However, Margaria and colleagues (1933) observed that the initial portion of the ROC occurred without any drop in blood lactate and that a small ROC could be incurred (2-3 L) without any significant change in blood lactate. They speculated that the ROC is made up of two phases: the alactic phase and the lactic acid phase. The alactic phase was believed to represent O_2 consumption used for the restoration of ATP-PCr stores and for reloading myoglobin and hemoglobin. The lactic acid ROC was believed to be the O_2 used in reconverting lactate to glycogen. This is now known to be not completely accurate.

Only small to moderate relationships have been established between the O_2 deficit and the ROC (Berg 1947; Henry 1957). Although the O_2 deficit can influence the total ROC consumed, the two are not equal. Furthermore, infusion of radioactive labeled lactate into rat muscle showed that 75% of the labeled carbon appeared as CO_2 (Brooks, Brauner, and Cassens 1973). This finding suggests that the major portion of lactate accumulated could be used to produce energy aerobically during recovery. Furthermore, blood lactate can be substantially reduced at 10 min postexercise with no glycogen resynthesis occurring (Weltman and Katch 1977). Thus, only a small amount of lactate may be resynthesized to glycogen.

Increases in physiologic functioning during exercise that persist into recovery may account for significant and perhaps major portions of the ROC. Increased temperature stimulates metabolism and elevates O_2 consumption (Brooks et al. 1971). Increased respiratory muscle and heart function as a result of exercise requires an increased rate of energy supply (Karlsson 1971). Using only these criteria (increased temperature and cardiorespiratory function) to account for ROC, it appears that the theoretical maximum O_2 debt should not exceed 3 to 5 L (Brooks et al. 1971; Brooks, Brauner, and Cassens 1973; Welch and Stainsby 1967). However, after steady-state exercise (>1 h), total recovery oxygen values as high as 18 L have been reported (Margaria, Edwards, and Dill 1933), and higher values (over 19 L) have been reported for weight training lasting 30 to 90 min (Burleson et al. 1998; Melby et al. 1993). These large total oxygen consumptions may be wholly or partially accounted for by a variety of factors including resynthesis of phosphagens, resynthesis of glycogen from lactate (<20%), increased temperature, additional cardiorespiratory work, resaturation of tissue water, oxygen resaturation of venous and skeletal muscle blood, oxygen resaturation of myoglobin, redistribution of ions within various body compartments, the effects of Ca^{++} on mitochondrial respiration, residual effects of hormone release and accumulation, and tissue repair and remodeling (Brooks et al. 1971; Brooks, Brauner, and Cassens 1973; Brooks, Fahey, and White 1996; Welch et al. 1970).

Recovery From Submaximal Exercise

The ROC as a result of 2 to 3 min of submaximal work can be larger than the ROC of longer exercise periods at equal intensities (Whipp, Scard, and Wasserman 1970). This suggests that part of the ROC may be accounted for during steady-state aerobic work. Support for this suggestion comes from the observation that lactate removal (a measure of recovery) is increased by light to moderate aerobic exercise (50-70% of $\dot{V}O_2$max) during recovery (Gollnick and Hermansen 1975; Plisk 1991).

Recovery From Intermittent Anaerobic Training

Intermittent non-steady-state work can allow accomplishment of a larger total workload or work rate; this is a basis for the concept of interval training (Plisk 1991). Stopping intermittently for rest periods also produces an increased total ROC and an increased total caloric consumption as compared to nonintermittent exercise. This increased caloric cost can occur because several bouts can be performed at the same or a higher relative intensity compared to continuous exercise, creating more total work.

Evidence indicates that weight training exercise can disturb homeostasis sufficiently to produce moderate to large ROCs, depending on the volume of exercise (Burleson et al. 1998; Elliot, Goldberg, and Kuel 1992; Melby, Tincknell, and Schmidt 1992; Melby et al. 1993; Murphy and Schwarzkopf 1992). Furthermore, weight training can produce larger ROCs than typical aerobic exercise (Burleson et al. 1998; Elliot, Goldberg, and Kuel 1992; Scholl, Bullough, and Melby 1993)—a factor that may be important in a variety of health and performance parameters.

The use of resistance training in body mass and body composition management is controversial (Melby et al. 1993; Stone et al. 1991a). Although weight training exercise can elevate recovery energy consumption beyond that with typical aerobic exercises, this level may not be high enough to alter body mass or composition. For example, in the study by Burleson and colleagues (1998), approximately 95 kcal (19 L of O_2) was used in 30 min of recovery from circuit weight training exercise. This value is unlikely to make a marked impact on body mass or composition even if training takes place several times per week. However, the training protocol used (Burleson et al. 1998) resulted in neither a high relative weight training intensity (≤60% of 1RM) nor a large volume of work (volume load <6000 kg [13,200 lb]). Weight training according to a protocol similar to that used by strength-power athletes, lasting 60 to 90 min and producing volume loads of 15,000 to 40,000 kg (33,000-88,200 lb) per session, results in much greater total energy consumptions such

that complete recovery might not be achieved even at 15 h postexercise (Melby 1993). Thus, volume of weight training exercise (and other concurrent training modes) may be a critical factor influencing recovery. Furthermore, the accumulative effect of high-volume weight training on athletes who train several times per week can be sufficient to effect changes in body mass and composition, especially if training consists of multiple sessions per day.

Indeed, a review of the literature indicates that weight training can increase lean body mass as well as effect changes in percentage fat and losses in total fat (Stone et al. 1991a). The use of FFA as a fuel source is enhanced postexercise as a result of weight training (McMillan et al. 1993; Melby et al. 1993; Scholl, Bullough, and Melby 1993). The increased use of FFA after weight training exercise may be related to decreased muscle glycogen content and the residual effects of hormones (McMillan et al. 1993; Melby et al. 1993). Therefore, body mass and composition can be affected by both energy consumption and the enhanced use of FFA during recovery. See chapter 10, "Physical and Physiological Adaptations to Resistance Training."

During large parts of a season or macrocycle, the training frequency of most high-level athletes exceeds three sessions per week, and many athletes use multiple training sessions per day. Among strength-power athletes, the number of weight training sessions per week may exceed eight during a preparation phase (see chapter 13, "The Concept of Periodization"). Training at this level makes recovery an extremely important issue (Stone et al. 1991b).

The sport of weightlifting can serve as an example. It is not uncommon for elite weightlifters to train twice a day, four to six days per week, and lift 30,000 to 70,000 kg (66,100-154,300 lb) per week (Stone and Fry 1997). During a preparation phase of weightlifting, volume loads of over 90,000 kg (198,400 lb) per week can be associated with energy expenditures as high as 600 to 1000 kcal per hour and over 3000 kcal per week (Laritcheva et al. 1978; Scala et al. 1987; Stone and Fry 1997). As competition approaches, the energy cost usually decreases as volume of training decreases. Much of the energy expenditure resulting from weight training and weightlifting takes place during recovery (Byrd et al. 1996; Burleson et al. 1998; Melby et al. 1993; Schuenke, Mikat, and McBride 2002). Furthermore, the magnitude of energy expenditure during recovery appears to be dependent on the volume of training (Melby 1993), and complete recovery may take as many as 38 h (Schuenke, Mikat, and McBride 2002). Therefore, as a result of a high-volume training session, with large muscle mass exercises, it is probable that a sizable portion of the energy cost, if not most, occurs during recovery.

Adequate energy intake is necessary to maintain body mass and support the extra energy requirements associated with training. Considering the relatively large total energy expenditure that can occur during weightlifting training, caloric intake (food) can be quite high, especially among the larger weight classes. The relatively high energy cost of weightlifting training, coupled with an increased mobilization and use of fats during recovery (Hunter et al. 2000; McMillan et al. 1993; Stone and Fry 1997), helps to explain the relatively low percentage body fat found among elite weightlifters and other strength-power athletes. (See chapter 6, "Nutrition and Metabolic Factors," and chapter 10, "Physical and Physiological Adaptations to Resistance Training.")

It is possible that the acute effects of recovery from previous exercise could interfere with subsequent exercise performance, even several hours or days later, reducing training adaptations. Although it is known that fatigue can alter various aspects of muscular force production (Stone et al. 1988), no studies have specifically addressed the physiologic or metabolic effects of a weight training session on subsequent weight training or other anaerobic exercise sessions. However, the volume of exercise likely plays a role in recovery and therefore subsequent exercise (Behm et al. 2002; Melby 1993). Additionally, a weight training session may affect various strength-related components differently. For example, unpublished data from our laboratory indicate that maximum strength (as measured by 1RM) and explosiveness (measured by a vertical jump) are less affected than strength-endurance by a high-volume training session performed 4 h earlier.

Studies have addressed the effects of weight training on subsequent aerobic exercise. Crawford and colleagues (1991) suggest that strength training has minor effects on subsequent aerobic (treadmill) exercise. However, in that study, only a few sets of one exercise were used, resulting in a low training volume. Baily and colleagues (1996) used a routine consisting of nine upper and lower body exercises with a much larger training volume than used by Crawford and colleagues (1991). Baily and colleagues found that weight training exercise can alter the typical rate-pressure product response and the heart rate–$\dot{V}O_2$ relationship. These two studies, while not definitive, suggest that the volume of

weight training exercise influences the physiological sequelae related to recovery. For various reasons, during a daily training routine many athletes first complete a strength training session and then move to a different type of conditioning exercise such as a running session, or vice versa. Often only a few minutes separate these training sessions. Unfortunately information is lacking with regard to the metabolic efficacy of this type of training routine.

It is logical to believe that insufficient recovery time between training sessions may alter physiological responses and decrease the ability to perform in a subsequent exercise session. The reduction in subsequent exercise performance may reduce the expected training adaptations to the given exercise. Furthermore, insufficient recovery could predispose an athlete to overtraining (Stone et al. 1991b). Although evidence indicates that prior exercise can have an effect on subsequent exercise, guidelines and timelines for recovery are not known. Thus, coaches and athletes should be circumspect in planning sufficient time for adequate recovery from exercise, especially from resistance training.

Metabolic Specificity of Training

Appropriate exercise intensities and durations and appropriate rest intervals can permit the selection of energy systems during exercise and result in specific adaptations for different athletic events (Brooks, Fahey, and White 1996; Koziris et al. 1996). Interval training is the basis for weight training and typically forms the foundation for the training programs of most anaerobic sports such as sprinting and football. Although weight training and other forms of anaerobic interval training can increase aerobic power to a small extent (4-9%) over the short term (McCarthy et al. 1995; Stone et al. 1987), major effects have to do with anaerobic factors. Weight training, sprint training, and other forms of anaerobic training can potentially increase stores of phosphagens and glycogen, enhance the myokinase reaction (Brooks et al. 1971; MacDougall et al. 1977), result in preferential hypertrophy of type II fibers (Gollnick and Saltin 1982; Houston and Thompson 1977), and generally enhance anaerobic metabolism (Abernethy, Thayer, and Taylor 1990; Brooks, Fahey, and White 1996; Campos et al. 2002), leading to improved performance.

Oxidative metabolism is important in recovery from heavy anaerobic exercise (e.g., weight training, sprint training) (Brooks, Fahey, and White 1996); however, care must be taken in prescribing aerobic training for anaerobic sports. Although not all studies agree (McCarthy et al. 1995), there is evidence that aerobic training, even at low volumes, may reduce anaerobic performance capabilities, particularly high-power and speed performance (Hakkinen et al. 2003).

Aerobic training has been shown to reduce anaerobic energy production capabilities in rats (Vihko, Salmons, and Rontumaki 1978). Additionally, several studies suggest that combined anaerobic and aerobic training can reduce the gain in muscle girth (Bell et al. 1991; Craig et al. 1991), maximum strength (Bell et al. 1991; Buskirk and Taylor 1957; Craig et al. 1991; Hickson 1980), and especially speed- and power-related performance (Dudley and Djamil 1985; Hakkinen et al. 2003; Hennessy and Watson 1994; Kraemer et al. 1995). Although the mechanism(s) is unclear (Stone et al. 1991a), reductions in performance gains resulting from combined training may be partially related to changes in muscle fiber types and testosterone and cortisol concentrations (Kraemer et al. 1995). Although aerobic training appears to compromise gains in strength and power as a result of resistance training, it does not appear that the opposite holds true. Several studies and reviews suggest that anaerobic training, including strength training, can improve low-intensity exercise endurance (Bastiaans et al. 2001; Hickson, Rosenkoetter, and Brown 1980; Hickson et al. 1988; Stone et al. 1983, 1991a).

Suggestions that aerobic training should be added to the training of anaerobic athletes to enhance recovery (Plisk 1991)—because recovery primarily relies on aerobic mechanisms—are not uncommon. However, the extent to which increased aerobic power can influence recovery is not clear. While several studies showed an association between $\dot{V}O_2$max and recovery parameters such as lactate removal, replenishment of PCr, or postexercise oxygen consumption (Hoffman 1997; Short and Sedlock 1997; Tomlin and Wenger 2001), many have not (Bell et al. 1997; Cooke, Petersen, and Quinney 1997). However, Hoffman (1997) indicates that recoverability increases with aerobic fitness only to a point, after which there is no additional benefit. Thus, there may be an upper limit for $\dot{V}O_2$max above which there is no effect on recovery parameters (Hoffman suggests approximately 45 ml $\cdot$ kg^{-1} $\cdot$ min^{-1} for men). As training with a primary anaerobic component can have substantial effects on both anaerobic and aerobic metabolism (Linossier et al. 1997; Nummela, Mero, and Rusko 1996) and can result in increases in $\dot{V}O_2$max, stores of PCr and glycogen, and both anaerobic and aerobic enzyme activity (Dawson et al. 1998; Harmer et al. 2000; MacDougall et al. 1998; Rodas et al. 2000), there may be little need for additional aerobic training from a recovery standpoint.

In this context, we note that specific anaerobic training programs can stimulate increases in aerobic power and enhance markers of recovery (McMillan et al. 1993; Stone et al. 1987, 1991b; Stone 1997; Tabata et al. 1996; Tabata et al. 1997; Warren et al. 1992). Cross-sectional (McMillan et al. 1993) and longitudinal (Pierce et al. 1987, 1993; Stone 1997) studies suggest that weight training, particularly high-volume weight training, can enhance markers of recovery including a faster return to baseline values for heart rate, lactate, ammonia, and various hormones. Thus, extensive aerobic training to enhance recovery from anaerobic events is not necessary and may be counterproductive for most strength-power sports (Koziris et al. 1996).

CHAPTER SUMMARY

This chapter has presented the underlying biochemical basis for the concept of specificity of exercise and training. Physical activity requires the use of muscle contractions, which demand energy. Energy is derived from the hydrolysis of the energy conveyor ATP. The higher the intensity of muscular contraction, the faster energy (ATP) is consumed. There are three basic energy systems available to replace ATP. These energy systems operate with different rates and capacities for ATP production, allowing energy consumption to be matched by energy production. Depletion of energy stores is related to fatigue; recovery can replete energy stores and potentially restore normal function. Adaptations to training can be enhanced by an understanding of how energy production can be modified by specific training programs. Fundamentally, exercise selection and energy system selection are functions of exercise intensity, duration, and recovery intervals, which are important considerations in the development of productive training programs.

CHAPTER 5

Neuroendocrine Factors

The neuroendocrine system, in addition to having morphogenic and normal homeostatic effects, is involved in exercise-induced homeostatic adjustments as well as chronic adaptations to training. Homeostasis is the equilibrium and constancy of the internal environment. Provision of a mechanism for homeostatic control and regulation of functions involved in the internal environment (e.g., cardiovascular, renal, and metabolic systems) requires systems that are able to sense information, organize a response, and deliver the response to the appropriate tissues. Both the nervous system and the endocrine system are structured to provide a homeostatic control mechanism. These two systems operate together; the term neuroendocrine system reflects this interdependence (Powers and Howley 1997). Thus, maintenance of homeostasis is the primary function of the neuroendocrine system. Additionally, the neuroendocrine system functions in promoting adaptations in various tissues as a response to a changing external environment (e.g., training).

Regulation of homeostasis is accomplished through initiation of tissue responses and adaptations as a result of endocrine function and the release of a hormone directly into the circulation, or by neural function and the release of a neurotransmitter. The functional unit of the endocrine system is the secretory cell of the endocrine gland. Endocrine glands are ductless glands that manufacture, store, and secrete hormones. Hormones are chemical messengers that are released in very small amounts and have effects on specific target tissues. Hormones can also be produced and act within a cell (autocrine function); or a hormone can be released from one cell but act in another cell without entering the circulation (paracrine function). Neurons synthesize, store, and release neurotransmitters, which act to relay messages (action potentials; see chapter 2) from neuron to neuron or from a neuron to an effector tissue. Some neurotransmitters can also act as hormones. Thus, the substances (hormones and neurotransmitters) released by the endocrine and nervous systems have "neurohormonal" properties and integrative functions.

Neurotransmitter Release

This section contains a brief description and an example of how the autonomic nervous system functions to provide a relatively fast-acting feedback loop in the control of homeostasis. In particular, the sympathetic nervous system is an important regulator of the activities of organs such as the heart, tissues such as the peripheral vasculature, and metabolic processes. A major group of neurotransmitters having hormone activity are the catecholamines. The primary catecholamines are epinephrine (EPI) and norepinephrine (NEPI), which are secreted by the majority of postganglionic sympathetic fibers and have profound effects on a number of tissues. Dopamine is a third naturally occurring catecholamine found predominately in the basal ganglia.

Norepinephrine is the primary catecholamine released by the neuron (80% NEPI and 20% EPI), while EPI is the primary catecholamine released by the adrenal medulla (Mayer 1980). In the process of neural catecholamine synthesis, the amino acid phenylalanine is converted to NEPI in four enzymatic steps (figure 5.1). A small amount of NEPI is converted to EPI by an additional step. Upon release, catecholamines can bind to several types of receptors, causing various effects in different

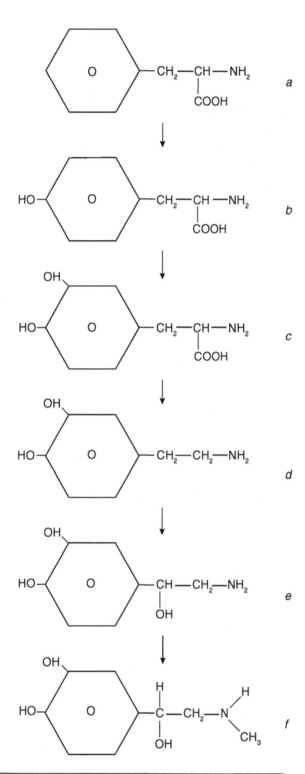

Figure 5.1 Synthesis of catecholamines from phenylalanine. *(a)* phenylalanine; *(b)* tyrosine; *(c)* DOPA; *(d)* dopamine; *(e)* norepinephrine; *(f)* epinephrine.

tissues (O'Dowd et al. 1989) (table 5.1). The release of catecholamines by the sympathetic nervous system and subsequent physiologic actions occur quite rapidly compared to effects of the endocrine system.

Catecholamines are stored in synaptic vesicles, and release occurs by exocytosis (Krnjevic 1974; Mayer 1980). Synaptic transmission is terminated by

- synaptic concentration dilution by diffusion out of the synapse;
- the synaptic enzyme catechol-O-methyl-transferase (COMT); or
- reuptake, which is the primary terminator of transmission.

Additionally, intra- and intercellular (among various tissues) turnover and metabolic transformation of catecholamines result from breakdown by both COMT and mitochondrial monamine oxidase (MAO) (Mayer 1980).

Hormone Release

Endocrine glands are stimulated by chemical substances (e.g., releasing factors or neurotransmitters). Stimulation subsequently leads to the secretion of a hormone, a process that has several characteristics:

- Secretion occurs in very small amounts; many, if not all, endocrine glands release their hormones in a pulsatile fashion.
- The hormone has no effect on its secretory gland; it affects target tissue only.
- The target tissues may be discrete or ubiquitous.
- Hormones may trigger changes in the rate of biochemical reactions, which can persist even after the hormone has returned to baseline concentrations.

The target tissues' response to the hormone depends on factors that influence receptor–hormone interaction and the blood concentration of the hormone. These factors are as follows:

- Blood concentration. Blood concentration is related to the amount of hormone released, clearance rate, and plasma volume changes. Clearance is a function of metabolic inactivation and excretion. Hormone inactivation can take place at or near the receptor, or more typically in the liver or kidneys.

Table 5.1   **Action and Distribution of Catecholamine Receptors in Human Tissues**

Membrane receptor type	Tissue	Response	Bound enzyme	Mediator
Alpha$_1$	Most vascular smooth muscle	Contraction	Phospholipase C	Ca^{++}/IP$_3$
	Radial muscle, iris	Contraction		
	Pilomotor smooth muscle	Contraction, hair erection		
	Heart	Positive inotropic		
Alpha$_2$	Postsynaptic CNS adrenoreceptors	Multiple?	Adenyl cyclase	cAMP
	Adrenergic and cholinergic terminals	Presynaptic inhibition of neurotransmitter release; generally blocks action of β_1 and β_2 receptors		
	Platelets	Aggregation		
	Some vascular smooth muscle	Contraction		
	Fat cells	Inhibition of lipolysis		
Beta$_1$	Heart	Positive inotropic and chronotropic	Adenyl cyclase	cAMP
Beta$_2$	Respiratory, uterine, and vascular smooth muscle	Relaxation	Adenyl cyclase	cAMP
	Skeletal muscle	Increased K$^+$ uptake		
	Liver, skeletal muscle	Activates glycogenolysis		
	Fat cells, skeletal muscle	Activates lipolysis*		
	Skeletal muscle	Increased contraction force		
	Pancreas	Enhanced insulin release		

*Possibly beta$_3$ receptors.

Columns 1 and 2: Adapted, by permission, from B.B. Hoffman, 1992, Adrenoceptor-activating drugs. In *Basic and clinical pharmacology*, 5th ed., edited by B.G. Katzung (Englewood Cliffs, NJ: Appleton & Lange), 114. With permission from The McGraw-Hill Companies.

Excretion is usually through the kidneys. Plasma volume shifts can change the concentration of hormones independent of secretion or clearance rates. The plasma volume change and loss of water from the blood compartment resulting from exercise can cause substantial increases in hormone concentration. Regardless of the mechanism (secretion, clearance, plasma volume), changes in the concentration of a hormone will influence receptor–hormone interaction. The following three factors are important aspects of hormone release.

• Free versus bound transport proteins. Several hormones, including steroid hormones, insulin, growth hormone, and thyroxin, are transported bound to proteins in the blood. Binding transport proteins protect the hormone from being attacked by hydrolytic enzymes and can act as a storage depot. However, for a hormone to interact with its receptor and exert its biological activity, it must be in the free form. The amount of free hormone depends on the binding affinity of the protein for the hormone, the quantity of the protein present, and the binding capacity (Keizer and Rogol 1990). Changes in the binding affinity, capacity, or binding protein concentration will change the ratio of free to bound hormone. Additionally, some binding proteins may have biological functions beyond transport of hormones (Kraemer 1992b).

• The health of the target tissue. Unhealthy target tissue can alter the production and excretion of a hormone. For example, the response of the testes to luteinizing hormone can be exaggerated as a result of a testicular tumor, producing testosterone concentrations several times higher than normal.

• The number and activity of hormone receptors. In order for a hormone to stimulate its target tissue it must bind to a receptor. Although some cross-reactivity occurs within a family of hormones, hormone–receptor interaction is specific and behaves in a lock-and-key fashion. Receptors are large proteins found embedded in the cell membrane or bound to the nuclear membrane of a cell. Some receptors contain allosteric binding sites, which interact with hormone cofactors, altering the receptor affinity and therefore the cellular response (Kraemer 1992b). Receptors may transmit a signal directly to the nucleus or stimulate a membrane-bound regulatory protein, resulting in an enzyme-activated cascade effect (see chapter 4, "Bioenergetics and Metabolic Factors"). Receptor affinity for a hormone may change with alterations in chronic hormone concentration. Desensitization of a receptor (decreased receptor and tissue response) can occur as a result of exposure of the receptor to the hormone. For example, after a peak level is reached (e.g., increased cellular cyclic adenosine monophosphate [cAMP] concentrations, Na^+ flux), there is a gradually diminished response over seconds or minutes (Bourne and Roberts 1992). Desensitization is reversible upon removal of the hormone for a few minutes. Chronic saturation of the receptors will result in downregulation, in which the number of receptors decreases. However, chronic exposure to a low concentration of hormone can result in upregulation, or an increased number of receptors. Up- or downregulation can markedly alter a tissue's responsiveness to hormonal stimulation.

Hormone Mechanisms of Action

Hormones can stimulate target tissues and modify cellular activity by at least three different mechanisms (Bourne and Roberts 1992). Our current understandings of these mechanisms encompass alteration of membrane transport and second messenger formation.

Membrane transport can be altered because some hormones, such as insulin, affect target tissues by activating carrier molecules in or near the cell membrane (Becker and Roth 1990; Powers and Howley 1997). Activation of these carrier molecules can increase the movement of various substances into and out of the cell.

The formation of a second messenger is a mechanism that transmits the hormonal signal (hormone–receptor interaction) into the cell. Peptide and polypeptide hormones cannot easily cross cell membranes because of their lipid insolubility. These hormones bind to the intrinsic and extrinsic protein receptors embedded in the cell membrane and eventually result in the formation of a second messenger. Formation of second messengers occurs indirectly as a result of the hormone signal, causing conformational changes in a series of membrane-bound proteins (Bourne and Roberts 1992; Freissmuth, Casey, and Gilman 1989).

hormone → receptor → regulatory protein (G-protein) → effector element

Activation of the effector element (enzyme or a calcium channel) creates a second messenger and results in a cascade effect. G-proteins, which are embedded in the cell membrane and can contain alpha, beta, and gamma subunits, are regulatory proteins that can regulate the activity of enzymes or calcium channels important for second messenger production. Based on current knowledge, two primary second messenger systems can be activated: cAMP and Ca^{++}/IP_3 (figure 5.2, *a* & *b*). G-protein activation of the enzyme adenyl cyclase results in cAMP formation; in the Ca^{++}/IP_3 system, the G-protein simultaneously activates inositol triphosphate (IP_3) formation and opens Ca^{++} channels. The cAMP and Ca^{++}/IP_3 systems are complementary in some cells but have opposite effects in other tissues (Bourne and Roberts 1992). For example, liver glycogenolysis is complementary, but contraction and relaxation of smooth muscle can require different second messengers. A third type of second messenger, cyclic guanosine monophosphate (cGMP), has been established in only a few tissues (Bourne and Roberts 1992).

The formation of the second messenger and subsequent cascade of events involve a series of reversible phosphorylation steps (Bourne and Roberts 1992). Phosphorylation is an important regulatory event starting with the receptors, then moving to the subsequent activation of protein kinases and eventually to the substrates that the kinases act on in the cascade effect. Phosphorylation results in the formation of a covalent bond and produces two important functions, amplification and flexible regulation. Amplification requires a phosphate group attachment to a specific amino acid residue; this attachment creates a molecular memory that

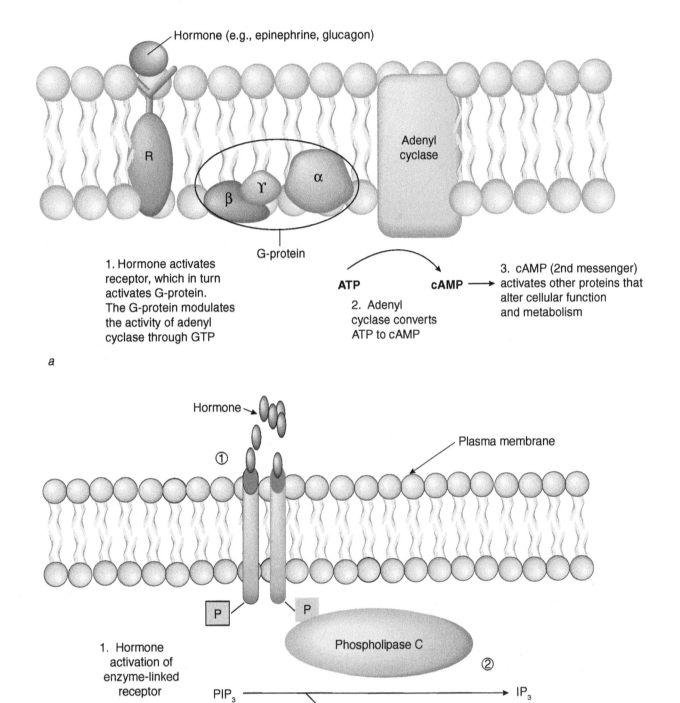

Figure 5.2 *(a)* Cyclic AMP second messenger system (see chapter 4, "Bioenergetics and Metabolic Factors"). *(b)* IP$_3$/calcium second messenger system. DAG = diacylglycerol; PIP$_3$ = phosphatidylinositol 4,5 bisphosphate; IP$_3$ = inositol triphosphate. *(c)* Mechanism of action for steroid hormones.

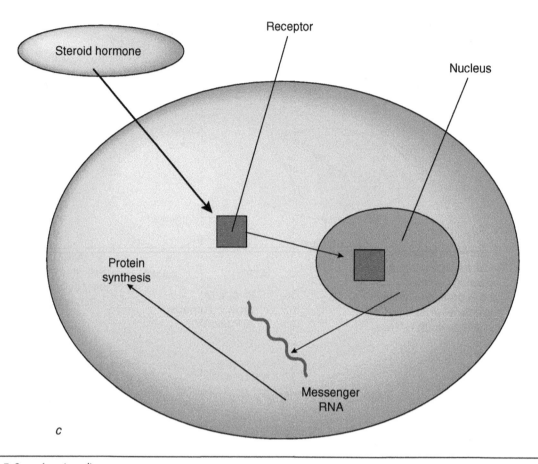

Figure 5.2c   *(continued)*

the pathway has been activated. Detachment of the phosphate group erases the memory. However, the molecular memory can persist even after complete removal of the hormone and allosteric ligand because dissociation of the covalent bonds and removal of the phosphate group require more time. Flexible regulation provides a mechanism whereby a second messenger system can produce different effects in different cells. This can occur as a result of the presence or absence of specific kinases or substrates in a particular cell.

Several hormones are lipid soluble, which allows them to move through the cell membrane and interact with a cytosolic or nuclear receptor (figure 5.2c). These "gene-activating" hormones include steroids, vitamin D, and thyroxin. The receptors for these hormones are cytosolic and, upon binding the hormone–receptor complex, move into the nucleus; exceptions are estrogens and thyroxin, which have receptors already located inside the nucleus. Hormone–receptor interaction produces a protein–hormone complex (activated receptor) that is able to bind to specific DNA sequences called *enhancers*. DNA binding and

activation of the enhancer result in transcription of specific genes (gene derepression) and eventually the synthesis of a specific enzyme. The enzyme then initiates the characteristic cellular response to the hormonal signal.

Unlike the second messenger systems with their relatively rapid response, gene-activating hormones, which result in protein synthesis, require 0.5 h or more to produce their effects (Bourne and Roberts 1992; Powers and Howley 1997). Furthermore, the effects of hormones can persist for several hours or even days after the hormone has returned to baseline blood concentrations. There are likely two reasons for the long-lasting effects: The receptors have a very high affinity for the hormone, producing a slow dissociation, and turnover of the synthesized enzymes is relatively slow.

Hormone Action and Regulation

Hormones have many different biological actions (table 5.2). This section deals with the endocrine

Table 5.2 Endocrine Glands, Hormones, and Primary Functions

Endocrine gland	Hormone	Target tissue	Functions
Pituitary anterior	Growth hormone (hGH)	Ubiquitous	Promote growth and development of all tissues; promote protein synthesis and a positive nitrogen balance; mobilize free fatty acids; indirectly decrease use of carbohydrates as a fuel
	Luteinizing hormone (LH)	Gonads	Promote secretion of estradiol; promote release of ovum; promote secretion of testosterone
	Follicle-stimulating hormone (FSH)		Promote follicle growth and secretion of estradiol; promote growth and maintenance of the germinal epithelium of the testes; promote sperm production
	Prolactin	Breast	Breast development and milk secretion
	Adrenocorticotropic hormone (ACTH)	Adrenal cortex	Control secretion of cortisol
	Thyroid-stimulating hormone (TSH)	Thyroid gland	Control secretion of T_3 and T_4
Pituitary posterior	Antidiuretic hormone (ADH)	Kidneys	Aid in controlling body water; cause vasoconstriction
Kidneys	Renin	Adrenal cortex	Aid in blood pressure control
	Erythropoietin	Bone marrow	Erythrocyte production
Adrenal gland medulla	Epinephrine (80%) (EPI)	Ubiquitous	Mobilize glycogen and FFA release; increase skeletal muscle blood flow; positive inotropic and chronotropic cardiac effects; increase VO_2
	Norepinephrine (20%) (NEPI)	Ubiquitous	Similar to EPI; vasoconstriction
Adrenal gland cortex	Mineralocorticoids (aldosterone)	Kidneys	Increase Na^+ retention and K^+ excretion
	Glucocorticoids (cortisol)	Ubiquitous	Fuel substrate metabolism; anti-inflammatory actions
	Estrogens, androgens	Primary and secondary sex tissues, muscle	Aid in development of male and female sex characteristics; increase muscle mass
Pancreas	Insulin (islets, β cells)	Ubiquitous	Increase substrate entry into cell
	Glucagon (islets, α cells)	Ubiquitous	Increase blood glucose, fat mobilization, protein catabolism, gluconeogenesis
	Somatostatin (islets, D cells)	Islets of Langerhans, GI tract	Depress insulin and glucagon secretion
Parathyroid	Parathormone	Bone, blood	Increase plasma calcium
Thyroid	Triiothyronine (T_3)	Ubiquitous	Increase metabolic rate; mobilization of fuels; inotropism and chronotropism
Gonads, testes	Testosterone (interstitial cells)	Sex organs, connective tissue, muscle	Protein synthesis; primary and secondary sex characteristics; promote sperm production; promote muscle and connective tissue growth
Thyroid, gonads, ovaries	Estrogens	Sex organs, fat tissue	Primary and secondary sex characteristics; increase fat storage; menstrual cycle regulation

Based on Lefkowitz and Caron 1988; Hoffman 1992; Powers and Howley 1997.

glands and hormones that have marked effects on muscle physiology, function, and performance.

Catecholamines (Sympathomimetic Amines)

Catecholamines, secreted by the adrenal medulla, are fast-response hormones involved in the homeostatic regulation of various central and peripheral functions, including cardiovascular response, bronchial airway tone, psychomotor activity, carbohydrate and fatty acid metabolism, and appetite (Weiner 1980; Viru 1992). Stimulation of the sympathetic nervous system is mediated primarily by NEPI; the stress response can simultaneously activate the adrenal medulla, resulting in increases in both NEPI and EPI in the circulation (Weiner 1980). The output of the adrenal medulla is about 20% NEPI and 80% EPI. While there are some similarities between the actions of NEPI and EPI at some sites, there may be quantitative and qualitative differences depending on the type of adrenergic receptor activated (table 5.1) or the ratio of α to β activation (Kjer 1992; Powers and Howley 1997; Weiner 1980). For example, compared to NEPI, EPI has equivalent or greater effects on α receptors, equal effects on β_1 receptors, and much greater effects on β_2 receptors (Weiner 1980; Powers and Howley 1997). Here we discuss the primary effects of EPI and NEPI.

Catecholamines are powerful cardiac stimulants, with both inotropic and chronotropic effects mediated by β_1 receptors on the sinoatrial (SA) node and conducting tissues (Weiner 1980). Heart rate is accelerated through an increase in the slow depolarization of the SA nodes during diastole (Weiner 1980). Ventricular extrasystoles (premature ventricular contractions, PVCs), tachycardia, and fibrillation can be caused by endogenous release of catecholamines, particularly EPI, in a sensitized heart (Dresel, MacCannel, and Nickerson 1960; Weiner 1980). Increased blood pressure (BP) is a myocardial sensitizing factor for catecholamine-induced arrhythmias; thus factors such as exercise that simultaneously raise catecholamines and BP may induce arrhythmias among susceptible individuals (Benfy and Varma 1967; Weiner 1980). Epinephrine can also cause a decreased T wave amplitude, and large doses can cause S-T segment depression on the electrocardiogram (EKG) (Weiner 1980).

Catecholamines partly mediate the vasopressor response; the exact result depends on the ratio of α to β receptors stimulated in the various vascular beds (Shepard 1982; Weiner 1980). Therefore, catecholamine response to stress, including exercise, is important (along with other integrative systems) in elevating BP and heart rate as well as in regulating appropriate blood flow and blood redistribution responses (Rowell 1974; Von Euler 1974). Changes in catecholamine serum concentrations or receptor sensitivity as a result of training or overtraining could produce abnormal BP responses or problems in blood distribution.

Catecholamines have profound effects on metabolism, especially in influencing the rate of carbohydrate oxidation and fatty acid metabolism. Insulin secretion is inhibited by α receptor stimulation (Porte and Robertson 1973; Himms-Hagen 1967; Weiner 1980). Glycogenolysis and gluconeogenesis are stimulated via β_2 receptors and mediated by cAMP (Porte and Robertson 1973; Shepard 1982; Weiner 1980). However, Clark and colleagues (1983) presented evidence suggesting that hepatic glycogenolysis is mediated by α_1 receptors and that it causes an increase in the cytosolic [Ca^{++}], activating phosphorylase kinase (which activates phosphorylase). Furthermore, catecholamines may activate phosphofructokinase (PFK) by both α and β receptor stimulation (Clark et al. 1983).

Catecholamines increase the concentration of free fatty acids in the blood by β_2-stimulated activation of cAMP and the subsequent activation of hormone-sensitive lipase. During aerobic exercise, and perhaps after resistance exercise, this is an important mechanism (along with growth hormone) in supplying fatty acid substrate to the working muscle.

Catecholamine infusion also increases plasma cholesterol and low-density lipoprotein cholesterol (LDL-C) (Weiner 1980), suggesting that chronically raised catecholamine concentrations could influence atherosclerotic events. Training can alter both the responses and chronic elevations of hormones, including catecholamines, reducing the potential negative effects.

Catecholamines regulate CNS energy metabolism through β_2-adrenergic mechanisms, and NEPI may be responsible for the stimulation of accelerated energy requirements in specific areas of the CNS, such as the motor cortex, activated during exercise (Bryan 1990; Scheurink, Stephens, and Gaykema 1990).

The effects of exercise on catecholamines are readily apparent. Increases in NEPI occur even at relative intensities less than 50% $\dot{V}O_2$max (Bloom et al. 1976; Hartley et al. 1972). Serum EPI is not increased appreciably during light exercise unless it is accompanied by emotional stress (Shepard 1982). However, during heavier exercise (>60% $\dot{V}O_2$max), EPI can increase sharply (Bloom et al. 1976; Hartley et al. 1972); and both NEPI and EPI can increase up to 15-fold during anaerobic exercise (Kindermann et al. 1982, 1987; McMillan et al. 1993). Some studies have indicated that NEPI and EPI show differential responses to exercise, suggesting a partial separation of the sympathetic nervous system and the adrenal medulla (McMillan et al. 1993). Although catecholamine responses to exercise may be more related to the absolute intensity than to relative intensity, appropriate training may reduce exercise serum catecholamine concentrations at a given exercise intensity, thus potentially reducing any physiological consequences resulting from higher catecholamine concentrations (McMillan et al. 1993; Powers and Howley 1997; Tharp 1975).

During exercise, the rise in catecholamines would support cardiovascular adjustments and is partly responsible for glycogenolysis associated with supplying glucose to fuel the increased metabolic rate. Thus, glycogen concentrations would diminish. However, the effect of catecholamines (and perhaps other hormones) is not limited to the working muscles. Bonen (1985) has demonstrated decreased glycogen concentrations in nonexercised muscles and suggests that this is a catecholamine-mediated effect. Chronically depleted glycogen stores may be related to aspects of overtraining (see chapter 13, "The Concept of Periodization").

Cortisol

Cortisol is a steroid hormone secreted by the zona reticularis and zona fasciculata of the adrenal cortex. Its production and secretion are stimulated by adrenocorticotropic hormone (ACTH), which is released by the anterior pituitary and regulated by hypothalamic-pituitary feedback mechanisms (Jones and Gillham 1988). Cortisol, a primary stress hormone, is involved in fuel substrate mobilization, gluconeogenesis, and immune system suppression and generally has catabolic effects (Munck, Guyne, and Holbrook 1984). These effects are mediated by gene derepression and RNA synthesis (Shutz et al. 1979). The primary functions of cortisol are discussed here.

Cortisol suppresses the primary immune responses, including inhibition of the synthesis of interferon, lymphokine, and interleukins 1 and 2, and depresses the activity of natural killer cells (Munck, Guyne, and Holbrook 1984). Cortisol also has anti-inflammatory properties including suppression of histamine production. Immune system suppression prevents an "overshoot phenomenon" and the resulting damage in response to stress (Munck, Guyne, and Holbrook 1984). It is possible that long-term stress, which chronically elevates plasma cortisol, could be related to the appearance of immune diseases, cancers, or both (Spiegel and Giese-Davis 2003).

- Cortisol stimulates gluconeogenesis by mobilizing fat and protein (Shepard 1982). Additionally, cortisol can reduce the rate of muscle glucose uptake and increase adipocyte lipolysis along with the synthesis of adipolytic lipase (Shepard 1982).

- Cortisol is a catabolic hormone, and its administration may cause considerable muscle wasting as well as a reduction of bone matrix and increased calcium loss (Kraemer 1992a, 1992b; Shepard 1982). Cortisol also has antianabolic effects and antagonizes testosterone production (Doerr and Pirke 1976; Kraemer 1992a, 1992b; Wilkerson, Swain, and Howard 1988).

- Cortisol may also facilitate EPI release (an activator of cAMP). Additionally, cortisol can affect fluid balance by increasing sodium retention and concomitant potassium excretion (Shepard 1982).

- Changes in cortisol concentration may have important effects on behavior. For example, Addison's disease (decreased cortisol) produces apathy, depression, and irritability; however, Cushing's disease (increased cortisol) produces euphoria, insomnia, and restlessness (Haynes and Murad 1980). These behavioral effects could be due to a receptor-mediated response or to changes in the brain's electrolyte balance (Haynes and Murad 1980). One can ascertain the importance of cortisol by observing adrenalectomized animals. These animals do not respond well to any form of stress, especially exercise, and work capacity is diminished. They become diseased more rapidly and generally do not complete a normal life span without exogenous cortisol supplementation (Haynes and Murad 1980; Shepard 1982).

Generally, aerobic exercise (<60% $\dot{V}O_2$max) produces no change or slight decreases in serum cortisol concentrations (Bloom et al. 1976; Galbo et al. 1977; Tabata, Atomi, and Miyashita 1984) unless the exercise is of long duration (>45 min) (Brisson, Volle, and Tanaka 1977). The increase in cortisol with long-term low-intensity exercise may be partly in response to decreased blood glucose concentrations (Tabata, Atomi, and Miyashita 1984). Aerobic exercise above 60% $\dot{V}O_2$max and anaerobic exercise can produce marked increases in cortisol concentrations (Kindermann et al. 1982). High-volume resistance training exercise can result in marked increases in cortisol (Kraemer 1992a, 1992b), especially with large muscle mass exercises (McMillan et al. 1993; Pierce et al. 1987). Cortisol concentrations may be elevated for more than an hour postexercise (McMillan et al. 1993; Sutton, Farrel, and Haber 1990), and the responses are sometimes greater in the afternoon (Hakkinen and Pakarinen 1991). As with catecholamines, emotional state may modify the cortisol response (Mason et al. 1973). Severe anxiety before physical exercise (Sutton and Casey 1975) or psychological stress (Hodges, Jones, and Stockman 1962) may raise plasma concentrations of ACTH or cortisol, or both, to levels as high as those found in Cushing's disease, suggesting that maximum stimulation of the adrenocortical system can be attained.

In animals, physical training can produce adrenal enlargement and increased serum cortisol concentrations during the first few weeks of adaptation (Shepard 1982); as training continues, concentrations can return to normal or become slightly below normal, suggesting an adaptation to the stress (Shepard 1982; Tharp 1975). This same adaptive response appears to function in humans as a result of both aerobic (Jovy et al. 1965; Shepard 1982; Tharp 1975) and resistance training (McMillan 1993; Pierce et al. 1987; Stone and Fry 1997). Severe (high volume or intensity) training can result in adrenal exhaustion in animals (Vernikos-Daniellis and Heybach 1980) and is likely related to some aspects of overtraining in humans (see chapter 13, "The Concept of Periodization"). As with many hormonal alterations occurring with training, resting concentrations and response to exercise appear to be related to changes in training volume and intensity (Fry and Kraemer 1997, unpublished data; Stone, Borkowski, and Smith 2003).

Testosterone

Testosterone is a primary androgenic-anabolic hormone. It is a member of a family of steroid hormones termed *androgens;* these are primarily produced and secreted by the Leydig (interstitial) cells in the testes, although small amounts are produced by the adrenal cortex and ovaries (Stone

1993). The mechanism of action of testosterone is through gene derepression (Florini 1985; Mainwaring 1979). In males, testosterone production is mediated primarily by the gonadotropin luteinizing hormone (LH), which is secreted from the anterior pituitary. Luteinizing hormone stimulates testosterone production via cAMP (Dufaux and Katt 1978). Some of the testosterone produced is converted, within the testes and peripherally, to dihydrotestosterone (DHT), estrone, and estradiol (E_2). These testicular metabolites are also active in the hypothalamic-hypophyseal negative feedback regulating LH and follicle-stimulating hormone (FSH) release (figure 5.3a). The negative feedback system in the female human is similar to that of the male (figure 5.3b). Neural stimulation of the testes also contributes to androgen release (Robaire and Bayly 1989). In sex-related tissues, DHT is biologically more active than testosterone (Brooks 1984; Stone 1993). The primary functions of testosterone are as follows:

- Testosterone is largely responsible for the development of male primary and secondary sex characteristics (androgenic) and has profound protein anabolic properties affecting nearly every tissue and organ system, including the central and peripheral nervous systems (Arnold 1984; Kraemer 1992c; Sar and Stumpf 1977; Stone 1993). Androgens, especially testosterone, may act by binding with or inducing changes in glucocorticoid cytoplasmic receptors, inhibiting the catabolic effects of cortisol and enhancing anabolic effects (Meyer and Rosen 1975).

- Testosterone likely promotes a greater glycogenolytic profile in type II muscle fibers compared to type I muscle fibers and promotes glycogen synthesis by stimulating the production of glycogen synthetase (Adolphsson 1973; Allenberg et al. 1983; Kraemer 1992c).

- Testosterone and its derivatives have also been related to various behavioral phenomena, including aggression (Stone 1993).

- Testosterone has been associated with muscle cross-sectional area, the magnitude and rate of force production, and power production (Bosco, Tihanyi, and Viru 1996; Hakkinen and Pakarinen 1993; Storer et al. 2003). The decline in testosterone with aging may be associated with the decline in neuromuscular performance capacity, especially in women (Hakkinen and Pakarinen 1993).

Light aerobic exercise (<60% $\dot{V}O_2$max) has little effect on serum testosterone concentrations (Wilkerson, Horvath, and Gutin 1980), although long-term light exercise may produce decreases (Dessypris, Kuoppasalmi, and Aldercreutz 1976) or increases (Galbo et al. 1977). Decreases in testosterone as a result of prolonged low-intensity exercise could be due to a reduced production, cortisol antagonism or a decrease in sex steroid hormone-binding globulin (SHBG), or a decreased testosterone-to-SHBG ratio, which would expose more free testosterone to hydrolytic enzymes (Kuoppasalmi et al. 1981).

Both aerobic exercise (Jezova et al. 1985; Wilkerson, Horvath, and Gutin 1980) and anaerobic exercise (Jensen et al. 1991; Kindermann et al. 1982; Kraemer et al. 1990, 1992; McMurray,

Eubank, and Hackney 1995; Schwab et al. 1993; Weiss, Cureton, and Thompson 1983) generally produce increases in testosterone approximately in proportion to the relative intensity, volume of the exercise, and the size of the muscle mass exercised. The primary mechanism of exercise-induced increases in testosterone is unclear, but may result from catecholamine stimulation of β_2 receptors in the testis (Eik-Nes 1969; Jezova and Vigas 1981; Jezova et al. 1985) and not via enhanced LH secretion by the pituitary (Galbo, Hammer, and Peterson 1977; Jezova and Vigas 1981), or a reduced clearance rate due to decreased splanchnic blood flow (Terjung 1979; Cumming et al. 1989), or both. However, as the duration of endurance exercise increases, testosterone concentrations tend to decrease (Galbo et al.

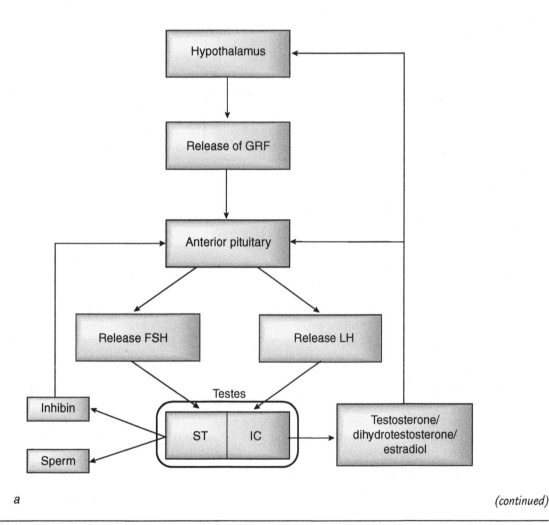

a

(continued)

Figure 5.3 *(a)* Feedback system for male reproductive hormones. GRF = gonadotropin releasing factor; FSH = follicle-stimulating hormone; LH = luteinizing hormone; ST = seminiferous tubules; IC = interstitial cells. *(b)* Feedback for female reproductive hormones. CL = corpus luteum; F = follicle; G = granulosa before conversion to CL.

Based on S.K. Powers and E.T. Howley, 1997, *Exercise physiology*, 3rd ed. (Dubuque, IA: Brown and Benchmark), 76.

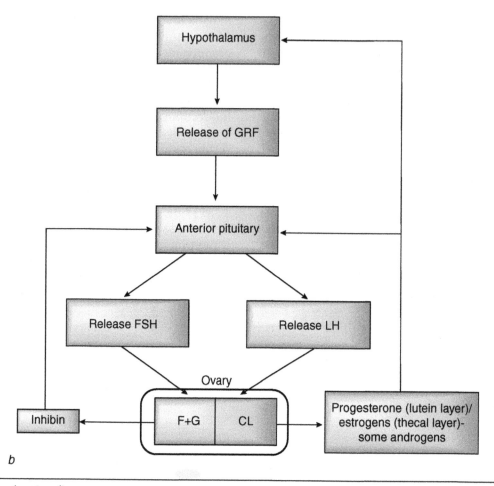

b

Figure 5.3 *(continued)*

Based on S.K. Powers and E.T. Howley, 1997, *Exercise physiology*, 3rd ed. (Dubuque, IA: Brown and Benchmark), 76.

1977), sometimes to levels below baseline resting concentrations (Kindermann et al. 1982).

Training studies have produced conflicting results in the measurement of resting serum or plasma testosterone concentrations. In animals, prolonged endurance training has produced serum testosterone decreases (Dohm and Louis 1978; Guezennec, Ferre, and Serrurier 1982). In humans, aerobic training has produced no change (Fellmann et al. 1985), as well as both lowered (Frey et al. 1983; Young and Ismail 1978) and increased (Young and Ismail 1978) resting testosterone concentrations. Resistance training has also produced a variety of effects: for example, no change or a decrease in sedentary and moderately trained young men (Ostrowski et al. 1997; Stromme, Meen, and Aakvaag 1974) and middle-aged men (Niklas et al. 1995) and increased resting testosterone concentrations in boys (Tsolakis et al. 2000), young men (Staron et al. 1994), middle-aged sedentary men (Johnson et al. 1983), and young women (Marx et al. 2001).

However, among well-trained weightlifters, short-term (one to four weeks) very high-volume (increased volume load) resistance training programs can decrease resting testosterone concentrations (Busso et al. 1992; Hakkinen et al. 1987, 1988a). Although perturbations due to changes in volume can be observed, long-term training in weightlifters has little effect on resting testosterone (Hakkinen et al. 1987). However, lowering the volume of training among weightlifters (e.g., tapering) has resulted in increased resting testosterone concentrations (Busso et al. 1992). Among younger weightlifters (14-20 years), both short-term and long-term weightlifting training can result in increased resting testosterone concentrations and increased testosterone response to exercise (Fry et al. 1994; Kraemer et al. 1992; Stone and Fry 1997).

As Fry and Kraemer (1997) point out, the changes in hormonal concentrations during long-term training can be quite subtle. While small alterations in resting total testosterone occur, marked alterations in associated parameters can include increased free testosterone, free testosterone:cortisol, and total testosterone:cortisol (Hakkinen et al. 1988a; Fry et al. 1994; Hakkinen et al. 1985, 1987, 1988b; Stone and Fry 1997). Increased total hormone turnover and altered receptor activity (Alen et al. 1988) can also be observed. The difference in adaptation among training programs may result from differences in trained state, age, general health, and fitness levels of the subjects (Kraemer et al. 1992; Young and Ismail 1978). It may also result from the type and intensity of exercise (weight training [anaerobic] versus jogging [aerobic] [Blessing et al. 1986; Johnson et al. 1983; Stone, Byrd, and Johnson 1984]) or the size of the muscle mass engaged (Kraemer 1992a; Kraemer et al. 1992). It does appear that there is a negative relationship between large or abrupt increases in training volume and resting testosterone concentrations and other related parameters.

The potential to gain muscle mass and perhaps strength as a result of resistance training may also be associated with testosterone and related factors such as the testosterone-to-cortisol ratio (T:C) (Hakkinen et al. 1989; Staron et al. 1994), particularly in women (Hakkinen et al. 1989, 1990; Hakkinen, Pakarinen, and Kallinen 1992).

The T:C has been related to the general anabolic or catabolic state (Aldercreutz et al. 1986) and lean body mass (LBM), as well as to measures of maximum strength-power performance (Hakkinen et al. 1985; Koziris et al. 1992). These relationships may partially explain and characterize the importance of the balance between androgenic-anabolic activity (testosterone) and catabolic activity (cortisol) during prolonged strength training (Alen and Hakkinen 1987; Stone et al. 1991).

Exercise appears to have little effect on the T:C, with baseline and resting values being similar to the postexercise values (Fry et al. 1994; Stone and Fry 1997). Stressful (high volume) weight training has been shown to cause reductions in testosterone and the T:C and T:SHBG ratios with a simultaneous increase in LH (Hakkinen et al. 1985). During periods of "normal" or reduced training, cortisol and LH concentrations decreased. The stressful training resulted in a fall in strength performance.

Long-term strength training may or may not increase the resting and exercise response values for the T:C (Fry and Kraemer 1997; Fry et al. 1994; Stone and Fry 1997). However, changes (sometimes subtle) in the T:C and related ratios accompanying training programs have resulted in significant correlations with strength performance (Alen et al.

1988; Busso et al. 1992; Fry et al. 2000; Hakkinen et al. 1987; Hakkinen and Pakarinen 1991; Koziris et al. 1992). As with other endocrine parameters, training volume and intensity appear to have a strong influence on alterations of these ratios and their relation to performance. For example, figure 5.4 (unpublished data) shows the T:C ratio among national-level American weightlifters over a 12-week period; note that the changes in the T:C tend to be inversely related to the alterations in training volume (volume load). As a result, these ratios (T:C and T:SHBG) may be sensitive indices of training stress and overall stress. Thus, changes among individual T:C or the T:SHBG may be an index for the overworked or overtrained state (Alen and Hakkinen 1987; Hakkinen et al. 1987). Additionally the T:C may be an indicator of "preparedness" in relation to physical performance. For example, if the T:C is high, then an athlete has a greater potential to perform well than if the T:C is low. A training taper may increase the T:C sometimes beyond baseline (i.e., supercompensation effect), thus potentially augmenting preparedness (figure 5.4).

Estrogens

Estrogens are a family of steroid hormones that are primarily produced and secreted in the ovaries (figure 5.3b), although several other tissues including the placenta, adrenal cortex, liver, fat, and skeletal muscle can also form estrogens. Small amounts of estrogens are also produced in the testis (Murad and Haynes 1980; Bunt 1990). The mechanism of action is by gene derepression. Estrogens are formed as a result of the aromatization of the A ring of either androstenedione or testosterone, a reaction catalyzed by the enzyme *aromatase*. The primary estrogens are estrone, estriol, and E_2, the latter having the greatest potency.

During the menstrual cycle, production of estrogens by the ovaries is regulated by cyclical LH and FSH production of the pituitary. During the follicular phase (days 1-13), LH stimulates androgen production by the follicle; during the ovulatory phase (day 14) there is a large surge in FSH that subsequently influences the conversion of androgens to estrogens by the corpus luteum in the luteal phase (days 15-28). Thus, the menstrual cycle is characterized by two phases and double peaks in estrogen concentrations over an average of 28 days (figure 5.5). Because of the cyclic fluctuation in estrogens and other hormones, as well as normal individual variation, it is difficult to ascertain the estrogen status of a woman at any one point in time (Bunt 1990). Estrogens stimulate primary and

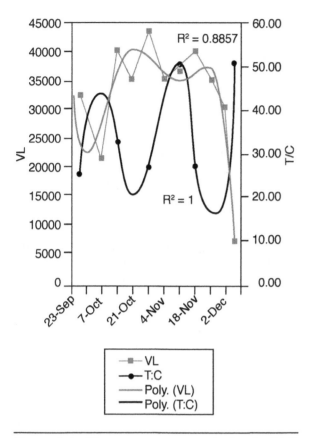

Figure 5.4 The testosterone-to-cortisol ratio (T:C) versus volume load (VL) over 12 weeks in four male weightlifters. Generally, volume and the T:C are inversely related. The T:C was higher than baseline values following a taper, possibly indicating a super-compensation effect.

secondary female characteristics and fat accretion and have marked metabolic effects (Ellis et al. 1994). Here we discuss the primary effects of the estrogens (Bunt 1990; Murad and Haynes 1980; Powers and Howley 1997).

- Estrogens are responsible for the feminizing effects in girls at puberty, which includes directly stimulating the growth and development of the primary and secondary sex tissues.

- Estrogens cause retention of salts, water, and nitrogen and thus have weak protein anabolic properties. Estrogens also promote bone mineral incorporation and increased bone strength.

- Estrogens can modify blood lipid profiles, resulting in lower total cholesterol and higher HDL_2 cholesterol and triglyceride concentrations. Additionally, normal physi-

ological concentrations of estrogens appear to produce beneficial effects on glucose tolerance.

- The metabolic effects of estrogens include increased lipolysis in muscle and fat tissue and decreased rates of gluconeogenesis and glycogenolysis. Estrogen effects on gluconeogenesis are partially related to its stimulation of an increased insulin-to-glucagon ratio (I:G).

Assessing the effects of exercise or training on estrogen concentrations is difficult. However, the general pattern of response of estradiol (also progesterone and gonadotropins) appears to be small increases in concentration as the intensity of exercise rises, which can occur independently of menstrual cycle phase (Jurkowski et al. 1978; Powers and Howley 1997). The increased estradiol is likely a result of plasma volume shifts and changes in clearance rather than increased production (Bunt 1986; Terjung 1979).

Findings on short-term aerobic training effects have been equivocal at best (Bunt 1990; Powers and Howley 1997). Long-term resistance training does not seem to markedly affect resting E_2 concentrations in women (Stoessel et al. 1991); however, other studies of women involved in high-volume training programs such as distance running and gymnastics have noted lower E_2 concentrations, which have been associated with athletic amenorrhea (Highet 1989; Keizer and Rogol 1990). Athletic amenorrhea (absent menses) can be associated with aberrant blood lipid profiles and bone mineral loss (Highet 1989; Keizer and Rogol 1990; Lamon-Fava et al. 1989; Powers and Howley 1997).

Among males, increased E_2 production has been noted concomitant to testosterone reductions as a result of aerobic training (Frey, Doerr, and Srivastava 1983), and decreases in E_2 concentrations were observed among middle-aged sedentary males after a short-term weight training program (Blessing et al. 1986). Some evidence indicates that increased E_2 or an increased E_2-to-testosterone ratio increases the risk for cardiovascular disease in males (Phillips 1977).

Women have been shown to use less carbohydrate and more fat as a fuel substrate during aerobic exercise compared to men (Tarnopolsky et al. 1990), an effect consistent with the properties of E_2. Estrogen supplementation may augment this effect (Bunt 1990; Ellis et al. 1994) and can also increase endurance as measured by treadmill time in both male and female animals (Kendrick et al. 1987). Estrogen supplementation has been used in post-

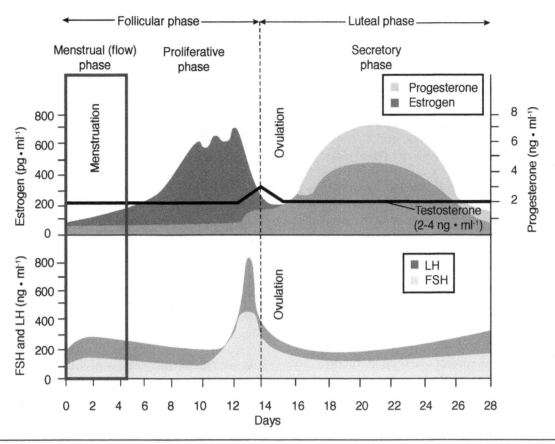

Figure 5.5 The normal menstrual cycle. Note that testosterone is essentially at a constant concentration except near ovulation.

Adapted, by permission, from J.H. Wilmore and D.L. Costill, 2004, *Physiology of sport and exercise* (Champaign, IL: Human Kinetics), 584.

menopausal women to reduce bone mineral loss, with varying degrees of success (Bunt 1990); additionally, supplementation of both E_2 and progesterone may be related to strength increases in women (Heikkinen et al. 1997). These effects suggest that estrogens may be a potential ergogenic aid.

Growth Hormone (Somatotropin)

Growth hormone (GH) is a polypeptide released in a pulsatile fashion by the anterior pituitary in response to a variety of stimuli including emotional stress, fasting, sleeping, certain amino acids, certain drugs, and exercise (Stone 1995). Its release is activated by a growth hormone-releasing factor (GH-RF) secreted by the hypothalamus. Growth hormone interacts with insulin-like growth factors (IGF), which are the primary effector hormone for protein synthesis; and these two hormones regulate each other's secretion in a feedback system, possibly including GH-RF and the stimulation of somatostatin (SRIF) in the hypothalamus (Kraemer 1992b; Laron 1983).

Growth hormone functions to stimulate anabolism in nearly all tissues (Kraemer 1992b; Laron 1983). This is primarily accomplished through insulin-like growth factors (IGF_1) or somatomedin C (Borst et al. 2001; Florini 1987; Laron 1983). Long-term exposure to relatively high concentrations of GH can result in acromegaly, a condition in which all tissues show substantial enlargement and deformity and sometimes giantism. The primary effects of GH are discussed here.

- Growth hormone promotes a positive nitrogen balance and growth in all tissues (Florini 1987). Testosterone may enhance the pulsatile release of GH (Link et al. 1986), and these two hormones work synergistically in promoting muscle growth (Scow and Hagan 1965). Additionally, there is evidence that IGF_1 may be active in promoting skeletal muscle satellite cell proliferation (Dodson, Allen, and Hossner 1985).

- Growth hormone also stimulates lipolysis through hormone-sensitive lipase via cAMP. Growth hormone is antagonistic to insulin.

- Growth hormone increases (often after several minutes) as much as 20- to 40-fold in response to both aerobic and anaerobic exercise; the final serum concentration appears to be related to both duration and intensity of the exercise and to the size of the muscle mass involved (Kindermann et al. 1982; Kraemer 1992a; Shepard 1982; Vanhelder, Radomski, and Goode 1984). The concentrations may increase to a greater extent as a result of intermittent anaerobic exercise compared to other forms (Fry and Kraemer 1997; Vanhelder, Radomski, and Goode 1984). Multiple training sessions per day do not appear to alter the GH response to exercise (Hakkinen et al. 1988a). Growth hormone may remain elevated for 30 min or longer postexercise (Fry et al. 1990; Kraemer et al. 1990; McMillan et al. 1993). The trained state of the subject markedly influences the exercise and postexercise serum concentrations of GH, with well-trained aerobic and anaerobic (weightlifters) subjects showing muted responses to standardized exercise and a faster recovery (McMillan et al. 1993; Shepard 1982; Terjung 1979).

Insulin

Insulin is a peptide hormone synthesized and released by the cells of the *islets of Langerhans* in the pancreas. The production and release of insulin are controlled by a complex interplay of nutrients, gastrointestinal hormones, and various other hormonal and neural stimulus-inhibitory factors (Kraemer 1992b; Larner 1980; Renold et al. 1978). Glucose appears to be the only physiological stimulus for both synthesis and secretion (Larner 1980). However, this effect is mediated by gastrointestinal hormones, especially gastric inhibitory peptide, which is similar in structure to glucagon (Renold et al. 1978). Both EPI and NEPI can inhibit insulin secretion by α-adrenergic mediation, although selective β_2 activation can stimulate secretion (Larner 1980). The following are the primary functions of insulin (Kraemer 1992b; Larner 1980; Manchester 1972):

- Insulin increases cell membrane permeability to glucose, amino acids, and free fatty acids and promotes the storage of energy substrates.

- Insulin is an anabolic hormone, has anti-catabolic properties, and generally promotes growth.

- The underlying mechanisms of insulin action may include insulin–cell membrane receptor-mediated increases in cGMP, activation of IGF receptors, a decreased activity of adenylate cyclase, activation of phosphodiesterase, a decreased activation of cAMP, an increased activity of glycogen synthetase, increased polyribosome formation, and activation of membrane-bound lipoprotein lipase (Hepp 1977; Kraemer 1992b; Larner 1980; Manchester 1972).

- Insulin is antagonistic to glucagon and GH (Larner 1980).

Aerobic exercise lasting less than 5 min has little effect on resting serum insulin concentrations (Lamb 1984). Long-term aerobic exercise produces decreases in serum insulin up to 50% (Wirth et al. 1981a). This fall in insulin concentration is believed to be due to a decreased secretion by the pancreas as a result of α-adrenergic stimulation (Jarholt and Holst 1979) and increased uptake by the working muscles. Short-term (<2 min) anaerobic exercise has produced substantial increases in serum insulin concentrations, the mechanisms being unknown (Kindermann et al. 1982). However, intermittent anaerobic exercise (30 min of weight training) produces decreases in insulin similar to those observed with aerobic exercise, even though glucose is elevated (McMillan et al. 1993). The postexercise decrease in insulin may persist for several hours or until a meal is eaten (McMillan et al. 1993).

Long-term aerobically trained (Lamb 1984; Wirth et al. 1981a) and weight-trained (McMillan et al. 1993) subjects have lower insulin concentrations at rest and during exercise. Although short-term training studies using animals agree with the observation of reduced insulin concentrations in trained humans (Wirth et al. 1981b), short-term training in sedentary human subjects does not always produce similar responses (Gyntelberg et al. 1977), suggesting that the trained response may require a considerable time period to develop. The alterations in insulin concentration resulting from exercise may be partially related to the catecholamine responses in trained and untrained subjects (Hartley et al. 1972).

Both aerobic (Bjorntorp 1981; Lamb 1984) and anaerobic training (McMillan et al. 1993; Miller, Sherman, and Ivy 1984; Yki-Jarvinen and Koivisto 1983; Yki-Jarvinen et al. 1984) may increase insulin sensitivity and glucose tolerance. Several factors may be responsible for these observations, including an increased number of insulin receptors, an increased muscle mass, and a decrease in the ratio of body fat to LBM (Miller, Sherman, and Ivy 1984; Yki-Jarvinen and Koivisto 1983).

Glucagon

Glucagon is a peptide hormone secreted from the α cells in the islets of Langerhans of the pancreas. Glucagon functions in energy substrate control. The primary regulation of glucagon appears to occur through stimulation or inhibition by nutrients. A rise in serum glucose causes a reduction in serum glucagon, and vice versa (Kjer 1992; Larner 1980). In animals, fatty acids and ketones inhibit glucagon secretion and glucose metabolism (Larner 1980). Gastric inhibitory peptide (GIP) and secretin are released as a result of gastrointestinal and hormonal signals. GIP may stimulate secretion, while secretin may decrease glucagon secretion (Larner 1980; Unger and Orci 1976). Glucagon is also stimulated by sympathetic nerve stimulation and sympathomimetic amines (Larner 1980). Glucagon has several primary effects (Larner 1980; Sutton, Farrel, and Haber 1990; Unger and Orci 1976), as discussed next.

Glucagon is antagonistic to the actions of insulin and serves to mobilize energy substrates (i.e., glucose and fatty acids). Glucagon's effects are mediated by cAMP, and its metabolic effects in the liver and adipose tissue are essentially the same as those of EPI.

Both animal studies and human studies (Luyckx et al. 1981; Kjer 1992) show that serum glucagon concentration increases with prolonged (>1 h) aerobic work. Animal studies suggest that a catecholamine response causes the rise in glucagon during prolonged exercise (Terjung 1979); however, in humans, decreased blood glucose concentrations appear to be the more important factor (Lamb 1984; Terjung 1979). Short-term anaerobic work produces no change (Weicker et al. 1981) or a delayed postexercise increase (Galbo and Gollnick 1984); weight training also produces a delayed postexercise increase in glucagon concentration (McMillan et al. 1993; Vanhelder, Radomski, and Goode 1985).

Both aerobically trained and resistance-trained subjects display muted glucagon responses to exercise at both absolute and relative intensities (Gyntelberg et al. 1977; McMillan et al. 1993; Winder et al. 1979). The training adaptations may occur in response to training-induced reductions in serum catecholamines. However, adrenergic receptor blockade does not alter the typical glucagon response to exercise (Terjung 1979). Training does not appear to cause major alterations in the serum glucose response to exercise (Lamb 1984). Therefore, the muted exercise response posttraining may be unrelated to either serum catecholamine or glucose concentrations, and the exact mechanism remains unclear (McMillan et al. 1993).

Hormone Function During Resistance Training

The basic response of a hormone to exercise, including resistance exercise, is an increased concentration, which is dependent on intensity, duration, and size of muscle mass. Indeed, many hormones, such as catecholamines, clearly display an exercise intensity threshold after which hormonal concentrations exhibit a sharp increase. The only major exception is insulin, which typically shows a decline in concentration with exercise. Training generally results in a muted response to an absolute submaximal intensity of exercise and a shorter time to return to baseline values (Kjer 1992; McMillan et al. 1993; Pierce et al. 1987). With the possible exception of growth hormone, well trained subjects compared to lesser trained subjects produce the same or higher hormonal responses to a relative intensity (Kjer 1992). Furthermore, responses to maximum efforts are almost always higher in trained subjects (Kjer 1992; McMillan 1993). These training adaptations appear to alter the acute physiological response to a given submaximal level of exercise in a manner indicating reduced physiological and perhaps psychological stress.

Although there is considerable overlap at times, hormone function can be divided into (1) substrate control and mobilization and (2) anabolic and catabolic actions.

Hormones affecting substrate control and mobilization during resistance exercise include catecholamines, cortisol, insulin, glucagon, GH, and thyroxin (table 5.3). Ratios of hormones having antagonistic effects are often better indicators of the control of metabolic actions than individual hormones. For example, the insulin-to-glucagon ratio (I:G) may be a better indicator of blood glucose control than either hormone alone (Williams 1981; McMillan et al. 1993). During resistance training exercise there can be substantial increases in serum concentrations of lactate and glucose (McMillan et al. 1993; Vanhelder, Radomski, and Goode 1984).

Table 5.3 **Effects of Hormones on Metabolic Functions**

Process	Hormone (+)	Hormone (−)
Cellular glucose uptake	Insulin	Glucagon
Blood glucose	Glucagon Catecholamines Cortisol	Insulin
Glycolysis	Catecholamines	Glucagon Growth hormone
Muscle glycogenolysis	Catecholamines	Insulin Growth hormone
Liver glycogenolysis	Catecholamines Glucagon	Insulin
Liver gluconeogenesis	Catecholamines Glucagon Cortisol	Insulin
Glycogen synthesis	Insulin Testosterone	Catecholamines Glucagon
Lipolysis	Cortisol Catecholamines Growth hormone Glucagon Thyroxin	Insulin
Triglyceride synthesis	Insulin	Catecholamines

Based on Lefkowitz and Caron 1988; Hoffman 1992; Powers and Howley 1997.

These metabolic responses result from the mechanism of energy production (fast glycolysis) and the mobilization of glucose through glycogenolysis. There is little doubt that the neuroendocrine system is operating to aid in driving these responses (Kjer 1992). Hormonal responses involved in supporting the metabolic alterations during resistance exercise would likely include catecholamines, glucagon, thyroxin, and perhaps cortisol as it potentiates the release of EPI.

Postexercise, responses include mobilization of free fatty acids (FFA) and glycogen replenishment. Growth hormone, catecholamines, and cortisol all likely have an effect on mobilizing FFA, which partially supports recovery (McMillan et al. 1993; Melby et al. 1993). Maintenance of blood glucose homeostasis postexercise requires reductions in the I:G (Friedman, Neufer, and Dohm 1991; Wolfe et al. 1986). Replenishment of glycogen postexercise is partially a function of insulin. Insulin (and exercise) increases the uptake of glucose and stimulates glycogen and fat storage. The concentration of insulin during and after exercise is enhanced by both carbohydrate and protein ingestion; higher concentrations of insulin stimulate a faster rate of glycogen repletion (Zawadski, Yaspelkis, and Ivy 1992). Additionally, testosterone may affect glycogen synthesis and restoration postexercise in that it increases the production of glycogen synthetase.

Hormones that act in restructuring and remodeling muscle and connective tissue include the anabolic hormones, testosterone, GH, IGF_1, and insulin, and perhaps to a small extent estrogens in women and the catabolic hormone cortisol. Remodeling of connective and muscle tissue includes the repair and hypertrophy process, which entails a very complex interplay of nutrients, the immune system, and the neuroendocrine system.

Because muscle cross-sectional area is related to performance (i.e., strength, power), an important question regarding hormonal responses and adaptations to resistance exercise concerns the extent to which these hormones affect tissue remodeling and hypertrophy. It is commonly believed that higher repetitions per set (8-15), short rest periods (≤ 1 min) between sets, and multiple sets per exercise stimulate muscle hypertrophy to a greater extent than other methods of training. Short-term studies have shown that the method of training using high repetitions and short rest periods produces greater increases in several anabolic hormones, especially GH and testosterone (Gotshalk et al. 1997; Kraemer et al. 1990, 1987; Smilios et al. 2003). Higher repetitions engage fast glycolysis to a greater extent than do lower repetitions, and the resulting lactate production may influence hormonal (particularly human GH) responses (Luger et al. 1992; Vanhelder, Radomski, and Goode 1985). Data also indicate that increased volume created by multiple sets can produce greater hormonal responses than a single set (Craig and Yang 1994; Mulligan et al. 1997). Evidence suggests that among untrained and moderately trained men, over a short term, multiple-set training with higher repetitions per set (8-12) may stimulate hypertrophy to a greater extent than lower repetitions or very high repetitions per set (Stone and O'Bryant 1987). Furthermore, Kraemer (1992a) presents a reasonable argument that the interaction of resistance training exercise (muscle damage) and changes in hormone concentrations may stimulate protein synthesis and tissue remodeling.

However, several observations suggest that the link between hormone responses to exercise and tissue remodeling is not particularly strong:

• Many and perhaps all of the hormonal responses observed as a result of resistance exercise can also occur as a result of aerobic exercise, particularly aerobic exercise near $\dot{V}O_2$max; however, aerobic exercise is not known to be a particularly potent stimulus for tissue hypertrophy (Stone 1992). It should be pointed out, however, that the adaptive interactions between the hormonal responses and the stimuli offered by different types of exercise may differ and therefore that the hypertrophy response or adaptation will differ.

• Small muscle mass exercises such as biceps curls do not result in marked hormonal responses compared to large muscle mass exercises (Kraemer et al. 1992); indeed, hormonal responses may be quite small. However, training with these small muscle mass exercises still produces substantial hypertrophy in the trained muscles.

• Bodybuilders tend to train with short rest periods "to get a better pump," and use higher repetitions per set in the belief that this may augment the hypertrophy response (Tesch 1992). Part of the reason for the use of short rest periods has to do with the potential for short rest periods to augment hormonal responses to resistance exercise (Kraemer 1992a); this in turn is believed to augment hypertrophy. However, there is no convincing evidence that, within a commonly trained muscle, the average cell size in advanced bodybuilders is significantly larger than that of advanced powerlifters or weightlifters who do not consistently train with short rest periods or high repetitions per set (Fry et al. 2003; Stone et al. 1996; Tesch 1992). Nor is there convincing evidence that short rest periods actually increase the hypertrophic response. For example, using moderately trained young males, Nimmons (1995) compared the hypertrophy adaptation of thigh muscles over nine weeks of training with short (30 s) and long (3 min) rest periods; no difference was noted in the average gain in thigh

circumference or the cross-sectional area (measured using magnetic resonance imaging [MRI]) of the thigh or of any individual thigh muscle. Assuming that the hormonal responses to the short rest periods were greater in the 30 s group, these results suggest that the hypertrophic adaptations were not augmented by hormonal responses.

• Since there is substantial evidence that hormonal responses may be involved with metabolic responses to exercise (Kjer 1992), it is possible that there will be little or no effect on the hypertrophic mechanisms resulting from hormone responses to exercise. Basically this means that if a molecule of a specific hormone interacts with a receptor that functions in a metabolic activity, it cannot simultaneously activate receptors involved in tissue remodeling. Thus, some of the hormone molecules released as a result of exercise will be "tied up" modulating metabolic reactions. However, it is possible that there are different species of hormone, some having greater or smaller anabolic properties and responding to different stimuli (i.e., high vs. low intensity).

• Studies of exercise-induced hormonal responses and hypertrophy are equivocal. Findings noted by McCall and colleagues (1999) and Hickson and colleagues (1994) do not indicate a strong relationship between hormonal responses and hypertrophic adaptation. On the other hand, Ahtianen and colleagues (2003) found that both resting and exercise responses were strongly correlated with strength and hypertrophy gains.

Until more data are available, we must conclude that hormonal responses to exercise likely have relatively minor influences on muscle or connective tissue hypertrophy. This suggests that the critical factor in gaining a marked hypertrophy adaptation may not be the hormonal response to exercise but rather other factors such as the immune system response and especially paracrine and autocrine responses (White and Esser 1989; Yamada et al. 1989). Although hormonal responses to exercise may not be the critical factor related to alterations in size and function, it must be pointed out that these responses may not be inconsequential. Thus, training routines that maximize the hormonal responses may play a positive role in tissue remodeling. Maximization of the training session could include several elements:

• Volume. Although some short-term studies have not substantiated a volume effect (Ostrowski et al. 1997), most studies indicate that greater volumes of work (which typically result in larger hormonal responses; Gotshalk et al. 1997) generally augment the hypertrophy gains afforded by resistance training (Fleck and Kraemer 1987; MacDougall 1986; Rhea et al. 2003; Stone and O'Bryant 1987; Williams et al. 2002). These larger volumes of work are generally accomplished using relatively high repetitions per set (6-12) and multiple sets (Stone et al. 1996, 1998).

• Size of the muscle mass exercised. Large muscle mass exercises stimulate greater hormonal responses than smaller muscle mass exercises (Kraemer 1992a; Kraemer et al. 1992).

• Power output. Maintaining higher power outputs during the exercise, independent of repetitions per set, may enhance the production of testosterone; higher repetitions per set may enhance the accumulation of GH (Bosco et al. 2000), perhaps as a result of a greater lactate accumulation (Gray, Telford, and Weidermann 1993).

Figure 5.6 offers a sequential model of events for the interaction of factors involved in tissue hypertrophy as a result of resistance exercise.

Chronic hormonal alterations may also play an important role in the development of tissue hypertrophy, as well as in gains in strength and power. Chronic hormonal adaptations may have a greater effect on tissue hypertrophy. A chronic elevation of the resting concentrations of an anabolic hormone, or the decrease of a catabolic hormone, would allow a greater opportunity for chronic exposure of the receptors involved in protein synthesis and muscle remodeling to occur. This chronic hormonal alteration, coupled with periodic muscle damage stimuli resulting from resistance training exercise, could enhance the possibility of a hypertrophic adaptation. Support for this contention comes from two areas. First, studies have shown that chronically increased androgen concentrations can alter muscle size and function (Storer et al. 2003). (See chapter 7, "Ergogenic Aids.") Second, as previously noted, studies using both men and women have related subtle chronic alterations in resting hormone concentrations to changes in muscle size and strength (Aizawa et al. 2003), particularly for testosterone and the T:C (Fry et al. 2000; Hakkinen et al. 1989; Staron et al. 1994).

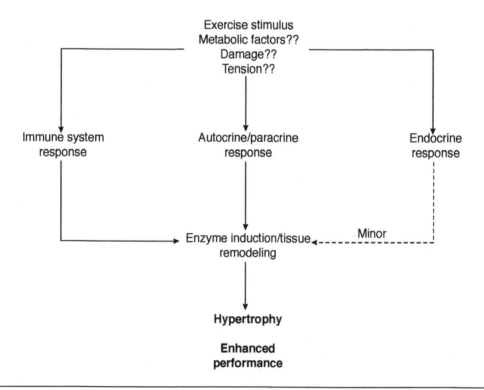

Figure 5.6 Theoretical effect of the endocrine, immune, and paracrine or autocrine response on tissue remodeling and performance alterations as a result of training.

CHAPTER SUMMARY

Homeostasis largely depends on the regulatory constraints imposed by the neuroendocrine system. The neuroendocrine system acts by releasing neurotransmitters and hormones that can interact with specific receptors. Activation of specific receptors brings about a specific response, altering metabolism.

Hormones are released by endocrine glands and have a variety of effects ranging from mobilization or storage of fuel sources to anabolic and catabolic actions. Exercise typically causes concentrations of hormones (except insulin) to increase; the increase is generally dependent on intensity. Training typically mutes this response at absolute submaximal exercise intensities. At maximum efforts, the hormone response is typically higher in trained subjects as a result of their ability to exercise at higher intensities.

Training can result in marked adaptations in physiology and performance. These effects may reflect the manner in which the neuroendocrine system functions (i.e., muted hormonal responses), or they may result from adaptations mediated by the neuroendocrine system (i.e., muscle hypertrophy). The physiological effects and adaptations resulting from neuroendocrine function during exercise or from training should be viewed as a complex interplay of a variety of neural and hormonal factors, and not simply the effects of isolated hormones or neurotransmitters.

CHAPTER 6

Nutrition and Metabolic Factors

Currently sport nutrition is one of the most studied areas of sport science; many long-held beliefs and concepts concerning good nutrition are being challenged, particularly for athletes. Since the late 1970s, studies of vitamin, mineral, fat, carbohydrate, and particularly protein needs for exercise and training have brought about a reevaluation of the nutritional needs and a restructuring of diets for athletes.

Recent information from studies dealing with carbohydrate and protein intake, creatine supplementation, and their interaction with exercise and training suggests that the diets of many athletes may be inadequate to support training and performance at high levels. For example, both carbohydrate and creatine can be thought of as ergogenic aids as they can affect increases in performance. Carbohydrate ingestion contributes to both liver and muscle glycogen and generally creates a more anabolic environment; these factors can affect both aerobic and anaerobic activities. Only a few years ago, most nutritionists and sport scientists suggested that the recommended dietary allowance (RDA) for protein was completely sufficient for athletes. Currently most sport scientists recommend that both endurance and strength-power athletes include higher levels of protein in their diets than nonathletes. Creatine supplementation can enlarge creatine phosphate stores and likely enhance the recovery process—factors that can have a large impact on high-intensity exercise performance. Vitamins and minerals are also receiving renewed interest and emphasis as to their importance during heavy athletic training schedules, as well as for long-term health. On the other hand, poor nutrition can contribute to various nonbeneficial adaptations to training (and health), including poor recovery and likely overtraining.

What athletes eat, how they eat, when they eat, and how much they eat can have substantial effects on health and performance. The purpose of this chapter is to review various nutritional and dietary aspects, especially those that influence athletic performance.

Energy Expenditure and Energy Intake

Energy can be defined as the ability or capacity to perform work and is typically measured in kilocalories (kcal). A kilocalorie is the energy required to raise the temperature of one kilogram of water by one degree Celsius. The rate of expenditure and total energy cost are related to several physical, physiological, and performance factors. The intensity and duration of exercise can have marked effects on energy expenditure. As exercise intensity increases, the rate of energy expenditure also increases; and the more total work accomplished, the more total calories used. Furthermore, energy expenditure resulting from exercise is directly or indirectly influenced by body mass and composition and the efficiency of substrate mobilization.

Exercise energy expenditure also has effects on postexercise energy consumption and recovery parameters (Burelson et al. 1997). The accumulative effects of energy expenditure as a result of training appear to be related to several training adaptations, including altered body mass and composition, serum lipids, and cardiovascular function, as well as sport performance (Stone et al. 1991a). Considering these relationships and effects, reasonable estimates of energy consumption rates and *energy cost* (total energy used) for various activities are valuable in the planning of training programs.

Typical rates of energy consumption for various activities are shown in table 6.1. As noted in the table, some activities have a wide range of energy expenditures. This range in expenditure values results from various determining variables such as differences in body mass, exercise intensity, and intermittent activity, as well as practical aspects of sports (e.g., linemen vs. backs).

From a health perspective, some studies and reviews suggest that reducing risk for degenerative disease, particularly cardiovascular disease, is associated with increased rates of energy expenditure and energy cost (Stone et al. 1991a). Furthermore, reduced health risk may be related to intensity and volume thresholds (Morris 1987). The suggested intensity threshold is approximately 7.5 kcal · min⁻¹, and the volume threshold begins at 500 kcal · week⁻¹ and increases up to 2000 extra kcal · week⁻¹. Training programs costing more than 2000 extra kcal · week⁻¹ may improve performance but are unlikely to further affect health parameters. Considering the energy expenditures associated with various physical activities and sport training (tables 6.1 and 6.2), it becomes apparent that several different activities, including weight training, can meet the intensity and volume threshold requirements

provided that the activity is performed in a vigorous manner and the volume of training is high. It has also been suggested that there is an asymptotic graded relationship between health parameters, particularly cardiovascular disease risk, and energy expenditure (Blair 1993, Blair et al. 1989). Thus, to a point, the greater the total energy expenditure, the greater the potential protective effect of the increased energy cost.

The energy cost of training for sport is typically much greater than that necessary (or practiced) to provide for good health. The training of athletes may occur several times per week and often more than once per day. For example, among many elite weightlifters and throwers, it is not uncommon to train two to three times per day, four to six days per week, during a preparatory phase. During these training sessions a considerable amount of work can be performed, and the accumulative training effect can produce a large energy cost. In order to reduce the potential for nonbeneficial adaptations such as overstress or overwork (Stone et al. 1991b) and loss of body mass or lean body mass (LBM), adequate calories must be consumed to balance the energy expenditure. Typical caloric expenditures and consumptions are shown in table 6.2; again it is important to note that some sports can have a rather wide range of energy expenditures and consumptions. As with the rates of energy expenditure, these wide ranges are due to differences including body mass, intensities, and volumes of exercise and training. For example, a superheavy weightlifter (150⁺ kg or 331⁺ lb) expends considerably more energy performing the same training routine at the same absolute or relative intensities

Table 6.1 Energy Cost of Various Physical Activities

Activity	Energy cost (kcal · min⁻¹)
Lying supine	1
Sitting	1-1.5
Standing still	1-1.5
Basketball (mean values for a game)	3-15
Cycling (4 km · h⁻¹)	7-8
Football (during activity)	6-15
Jogging (160 m · min⁻¹)	7-9
Sprinting (maximum running)	18-22
Volleyball (mean values for a game)	3-7
Weight training (mean values)	9-10
Circuit priority	5-10
Small muscle mass exercises	3-7
Large muscle mass exercises	6-18
Combination (emphasizing large muscle mass exercise)	9-10

Based on AAHPERD 1971; Hunter et al. 1988; Nicolette 1993; Scala et al. 1987; Wilmore 1994.

Table 6.2 Caloric Expenditure and Consumption of Sport Activities

Activity	Expenditure (kcal · kg⁻¹ · day⁻¹)	Consumption (kcal · day⁻¹)
Untrained	<40	2000-3000
Marathon	50-80	2500-6000
Basketball	55-70	5000-6000
Sprinting	55-65	4300-6000
Judo	55-65	3000-6200
Throwing (field events)	60-65	6000-8500
Weightlifting	55-75	3000-10,000

Note: Values are based on males; women's values are typically 10% to 25% less.

Based on McMillan et al. 1993; Scala et al. 1987; Wilmore and Costill 1994.

than a smaller athlete, and would require a greater energy intake.

A number of additional factors can influence the rate of energy expenditure and energy cost, such as the size of the muscle mass involved and the length of rest periods between sets. The use of large muscle mass exercises or short rest periods would increase the energy expenditure of a training session. Total energy cost resulting from exercise is also influenced by the postexercise energy expenditure.

Typically, energy expenditure is influenced by four primary factors:

Basal metabolic rate (BMR)

The thermic effect of food (TEF)

The thermic effect of physical activity (TEA)— energy used during exercise

Adaptive thermogenesis (AT)

The BMR is measured in the laboratory in a fasted rested state in which the subject is isolated, recumbent, and free from medications and stress (Manore and Thompson 2000). The BMR represents the energy necessary to maintain homeostasis at rest. The BMR accounts for 60% to 80% of the total energy expenditure among healthy sedentary adults (Manore and Thompson 2000). The BMR measurement is often inconvenient in that it requires an overnight stay in a laboratory, so typically the resting metabolic rate (RMR) is measured instead. The RMR measurement requires that the subject (usually fasted) rest for a short specified time period before metabolism is measured. The BMR and RMR usually agree within 10%. Among athletes, the RMR accounts for a smaller percentage of daily energy expenditure (20-45%) than among sedentary subjects (Rontoyannis, Skoulis, and Pavlou 1989; Thompson, Manore, and Skinner 1993). A number of factors may modify the RMR. These potential modifying factors include age, sex, body mass, LBM, trained state, and heredity.

The thermic effect of food (TEF) is the extra energy above the RMR used that results from food consumption during the day, including digestion, absorption, transport, metabolism, and storage. The TEF can account for approximately 6% to 10% of the total energy expenditure per day. Women are usually on the lower end of the TEF with expenditures of about 6% to 7% above the RMR (Manore and Thompson 2000). Measurement of the TEF requires the use of a metabolic chamber. Although the TEF concerns the cumulative effect of eating throughout the day, most researchers measure the thermic effect of a meal (TEM), as this is less difficult and time-consuming. The TEM can last for several hours after a meal and is influenced by the meal composition. The TEM of carbohydrate is approximately 5% to 10%, of fat is 3% to 5%, and of protein is 20% to 30% (Flatt 1992). Additionally, both acute and chronic exercise as well as sex differences may influence the TEF and TEM.

The thermic effect of activity (TEA) represents the energy expenditure above the RMR that is required by physical activity. This extra energy includes the cost of daily living, planned exercise, and also involuntary muscle actions such as shivering. The TEA is the most variable of the extra energy-consuming factors and may represent as little as 10% of total energy expenditure in sedentary individuals and as much as 50% to 60% in athletes (Manore and Thompson 2000).

Adaptive thermogenesis (AT) results from a number of factors that modify the three primary thermic effects (RMR, TEF, and TEA). These factors include growth, pregnancy, environmental temperature, altitude, medication, drug use (e.g., alcohol, methylated xanthines, smoking), and physical and emotional stress (Manore and Thompson 2000).

Caloric Density and Nutrient Density

As a result of differences in molecular structure, the amount of energy metabolically liberated from food (protein, carbohydrate, or fat) differs for a given mass of food depending on the type of food eaten. Protein and carbohydrate yield about 4 kcal · g^{-1}, and fat about 9 kcal · g^{-1}. The caloric value of food is termed the *physiological fuel value (PFV)* and actually represents averages of different molecules for each food type. Using these values one can calculate the energy intake for a diet by adding up the grams of protein, carbohydrate, or fat ingested and then multiplying the grams by the PFV. If the total caloric value of the diet is known, then percentages of the total calories eaten can be ascertained for each food type. For example, if a 100 kg (220 lb) athlete has a daily intake of 120 g protein, 700 g carbohydrate, and 150 g fat, then the total calories taken in are as follows:

protein = 120 g × 4 kcal · g^{-1} = 480 kcal

carbohydrate = 700 g × 4 kcal · g^{-1} = 2800 kcal

fat = 150 g × 9 kcal · g^{-1} = 1350 kcal

total kcal = 4630 kcal

These are the percentages of each food type (as calories):

$$protein = 480 / 4630 = 10.4\%$$
$$carbohydrate = 2800 / 4630 = 60.5\%$$
$$fat = 1350 / 4630 = 29.2\%$$

In certain cases an athlete may adjust a specific caloric intake so that each food type reflects a specific percentage; for example, a 110 kg (243 lb) athlete eating 6000 kcal · day^{-1} needs to adjust the diet for 20% protein, 55% carbohydrate, and 25% fat:

$$protein = 6000 \text{ kcal} \times 0.2 \times 1 \text{ g} / 4 \text{ kcal} = 300 \text{ g}$$
$$carbohydrate = 6000 \times 0.55 \times 1 \text{ g} / 4 \text{ kcal} = 825 \text{ g}$$
$$fat = 6000 \times 0.25 \times 1 \text{ g} / 9 \text{ kcal} = 167 \text{ g}$$

Using these simple formulas, athletes can adjust their diet to fit their needs.

Nutrient density refers to the amount of macro- and micronutrient(s) present in a food per calorie. Meat and many vegetables are nutrient dense as they contain high concentrations of energy as well as vitamins and minerals, while many packaged and processed foods containing mostly sugar, salt, and preservatives are not dense in nutrients. While nutrient density is not usually a problem for large athletes consuming large amounts of food, smaller athletes eating low-calorie diets must pay attention to the micronutrient (vitamins and minerals) content.

Measurement of Energy Expenditure

The most common method of assessing energy consumption is indirect calorimetry (Montoye et al. 1996). This method measures oxygen consumption ($\dot{V}O_2$) and carbon dioxide release. Indirect calorimetry can be accomplished in a metabolic chamber or through use of a mouthpiece whereby expired gases are collected and analyzed during a specific time period (see chapter 4, "Bioenergetics and Metabolic Factors"). The ratio of oxygen consumed ($\dot{V}O_2$) to carbon dioxide released ($\dot{V}CO_2$) is the respiratory ratio. At the cellular level this ratio is termed nonprotein *respiratory quotient (RQ)*. The nonprotein RQ represents the ratio of the oxidation of carbohydrate compared to lipid.

However, the nonprotein RQ cannot be directly measured in humans at the cellular level; therefore the respiratory exchange ratio (RER) is used. The

RER is a measure of the gas exchange at the mouth and is a reasonable estimate of the RQ under steady-state conditions. The RER depends on the substrate being oxidized; pure fat has a value of 0.7, protein of 0.8, and carbohydrate of 1.0. As humans eat a mixed diet (protein, carbohydrate, and fat), the RER typically ranges from 0.80 to 0.72 at rest. The RER reflects the primary energy substrate being oxidized. Under normal conditions, the oxidation of protein (from ketoacids) is small, and the RER largely reflects the oxidation of fat and protein. For example, enhanced fat metabolism is reflected in the RER among trained athletes (RER = 0.72-0.77), and during fasting and starvation (i.e., weight loss) the RER can approach 0.7. Increased RER can occur with high-carbohydrate meals, and the RER can reach 1.0 (or more) as exercise intensity increases. Thus, the RER value can be affected by the foods eaten, maintenance of body mass, and exercise.

Energy consumption is measured by oxygen uptake; in general, 1.0 L of oxygen consumed is equal to 4.8 kcal at an RER of 0.82. As the RER increases, for example with the intensity of exercise, the caloric value of a liter of oxygen also increases. This method has been used to estimate the caloric cost of various types of physical activity (table 6.1).

Recovery Energy Expenditure

A factor people often overlook when considering exercise energy expenditures is the postexercise or recovery energy expenditure (see chapter 4, "Bioenergetics and Metabolic Factors"). Several studies have demonstrated the effects of aerobic steady-state exercise on recovery energy consumption (Bahr et al. 1987, 1991; Brehm and Gutin 1986; Scholl, Bullough, and Melby 1993; Sedlock, Fisinger, and Melby 1989). These studies generally indicate that exercise intensity (power output) can have a greater effect on energy expenditure postexercise than does duration. Higher intensities of exercise disturb homeostasis to a greater degree than lower intensities, resulting in the use of more energy for recovery (Burleson et al. 1997; Kindermann et al. 1982). This observation indicates that because of the high intensities involved, anaerobic exercise such as weight training could require more recovery energy and possibly a longer duration for recovery compared to aerobic exercise. Several studies dealing with weight training postexercise energy expenditure suggest that this does occur (Burhus et al. 1992; Burleson et al. 1997; Elliot, Goldberg, and Kuehl 1992; Scholl, Bullough, and Melby 1993).

While typical low-volume recreational weight training may not produce a large enough post-exercise energy consumption to markedly affect body composition or substantially increase total energy consumption, this may not be the case among athletes. For example, evidence indicates that after weight training, exercise energy consumption is related to the volume of exercise performed and that considerable energy may be required for recovery from high volumes (Melby et al. 1993). Furthermore, the accumulative effect of daily weight training among strength-power athletes who train at high levels may produce a substantial recovery energy requirement and expenditure. Postexercise energy expenditure is a factor not generally considered in calculations of exercise energy expenditure and is not generally included in table 6.1. Thus, the requirements for energy expenditure and consumption (intake) may be substantially higher for some athletes than can be ascertained from estimated expenditure, and may be important factors in producing the large range of energy consumption noted in some sports (table 6.2) and among some individual athletes.

Types of Weight Training and Energy Expenditure

Priority weight training is a method in which the most important exercises, relative to goal accomplishment (importance for the sport), are placed first in the training session. Less important exercises are performed after the more important ones. Typically this means that large muscle mass exercises precede small muscle mass exercises. With priority training, the person performs all of the sets and repetitions for each exercise before moving to the next and takes sufficient rest between sets to ensure that the appropriate number of repetitions per set is completed.

In circuit weight training, typically upper and lower body exercises are alternated with each set, and short (<1 min) rest periods are used. The short rest periods are used to stimulate metabolism and increase energy expenditure. Compared to priority training programs, circuit training typically emphasizes smaller muscle mass exercises. Because of the use of small muscle mass exercises and short rest periods, the training intensity (average mass lifted) is usually considerably lower than that of priority training.

The energy expenditure during circuit training can result in fairly high energy expenditures provided that large muscle mass exercises are used. However, priority training (table 6.1) emphasizing large muscle mass exercises can produce similar caloric expenditures, even with relatively long interset rest intervals, due to the heavier loading (Scala et al. 1987).

As with aerobic training, weight training energy expenditure is related to energy (food) intake (Campbell et al. 1994); thus when the volume load of training is increased, caloric intake should increase concomitantly. Considering the energy expenditures possible as a result of high-level (heavy loading) training, and the possibility of prolonged recovery, it is not unreasonable to expect the strength and conditioning coach and athlete to think carefully about the selection of exercises, the length of training sessions, the volume and intensity of exercise, and the number of training sessions per day.

Protein

For many years, athletes, coaches, and sport scientists have had an interest in the role of protein in the diet and the usefulness of protein supplementation. Some aspects of dietary protein for athletes in training are presently unclear. Many athletes and coaches, on the basis of personal experience, believe that the intake of protein above the RDA or DRI is necessary for optimal or maximal performance or gain in LBM. Even scientists often disagree on the exact protein requirements for athletes, especially for those athletes in very high-intensity or high-volume training. Much of the confusion stems from the inadequacies in the experimental design of many scientific studies, particularly the use of short-term and poorly designed training programs. A lack of understanding of all aspects of protein metabolism also contributes to the problem. This section briefly reviews the current knowledge concerning major features of protein metabolism and the effects of training on protein requirements.

Protein Metabolism and Function

Approximately 9% to 16% of the total caloric intake of the typical adult American diet consists of protein (Hamilton, Whitley, and Sizer 1985; NHANES III 1988-2004; Pike and Brown 1984); many athletes, particularly strength-power athletes, ingest 15% to 25% of their total caloric intake as protein (Ivy and Portman 2004; Tarnopolsky et al. 1992, Tarnopolsky 2000). Proteins are relatively complex molecules that can have enzymatic or structural functions and are important in a variety

Recommended Dietary Intakes (Dietary Reference Intakes)

Before considering intakes of micro- and macronutrients, we need to discuss the current recommendations for these nutrients. In 2002, a joint Canada-U.S. expert report was released that provided a comprehensive set of reference values for nutrient intakes for healthy U.S. and Canadian individuals and populations. The report, "Dietary Reference Intakes (DRIs) for Energy, Carbohydrate, Fiber, Fat, Fatty Acids, Cholesterol, Protein and Amino Acids," was released by the U.S. Food and Nutrition Board, Institute of Medicine of the National Academies, in collaboration with Health Canada (Lupton 2005).

This report provides a critical review of the evidence relating macronutrient intake to reduction of risk for chronic diseases and to amounts needed for maintaining health. The authors of the report establish a set of reference values to expand and replace previously published U.S. Recommended Dietary Allowances (RDAs) and Canadian Recommended Nutrient Intakes (RNIs). However, the report does not address nutrition for high-level sport participation. Use (from the report) of the dietary reference intake (DRI) encompasses the following concepts:

DRI Terminology

The DRIs for macronutrients are composed of a set of reference values, defined as follows:

- *Acceptable macronutrient distribution range (AMDR):* a range of dietary intakes (as a percent of energy intake) for a particular energy source that is associated with reduced risk of chronic disease while providing adequate intakes of essential nutrients.

- *Recommended dietary allowance (RDA):* the average daily dietary nutrient intake level sufficient to meet the nutrient requirement of nearly all (97-98%) healthy individuals in a particular life stage and biological sex group.

- *Adequate intake (AI):* the recommended average daily intake level based on observed or experimentally determined approximations or estimates of nutrient intake by a group (or groups) of apparently healthy people that are assumed to be adequate, used when an RDA cannot be determined.

- *Tolerable upper intake level (UL):* the highest average daily nutrient intake level that is likely to pose no risk of adverse health effects to almost all individuals in the general population. As intake increases above the UL, the potential risk of adverse effects may increase.

- *Estimated average requirement (EAR):* the average daily nutrient intake level estimated to meet the requirement of half the healthy individuals in a particular life stage and gender group.

- *Estimated energy requirement (EER):* the average dietary energy intake that is predicted to maintain energy balance in a healthy adult of a defined age, gender, weight, height, and level of physical activity, consistent with good health.

of biosynthetic and bioenergetic actions related to body growth, maintenance and repair, and energy production. Under normal resting conditions the energy derived from protein is about 1% to 2% of the total energy required; however, because energy requirements are a priority function, substantial protein can be used as an energy source if dietary carbohydrate and fat become inadequate (Horton 1982). An important function of the skeletal muscle is to serve as a reservoir for protein that can be catabolized for energy when dietary intake is low, as in starvation (Sparge 1979).

Muscle protein is in a constant state of turnover. The amount of protein contained in muscle is largely determined by the balance between protein anabolism and catabolism (Booth, Nicholson, and Watson 1982). If excess dietary protein is ingested, it can be oxidized for energy or converted to fat (Hamilton, Whitley, and Sizer 1985; Tarnopolsky, MacDougall, and Atkinson 1988; Tarnopolsky et al. 1992). Thus, eating an excessive amount of protein can increase body fat (the same is true of carbohydrate).

Composition of Protein

The basic units of protein structure are *amino acids,* all of which contain nitrogen. The nitrogen is necessary for the formation of peptide bonds, which link amino acids together. Proteins are essentially long chains of amino acids linked together by peptide bonds. Additional (secondary, tertiary, and quaternary) protein structure can be created by hydrogen and covalent bonding.

Because amino acids are the basic structural unit, protein requirements are related to amino acid requirements. Free amino acids are normally found only in small quantities in the food we eat. Food proteins contain mixtures of amino acids, and digestion must occur before the amino acids can be released for absorption.

The biological value (BV) of a protein is a measure of the absorption and utilization of a protein. The higher the BV of a protein, the more nitrogen absorbed, used, and retained. As a result, proteins with the highest BV typically promote greater levels of tissue remodeling and muscle gains. Protein synthesis in humans requires approximately 22 distinct amino acids, nine of which are *essential amino acids* (EAA) in adults. Essential amino acids are those amino acids that cannot be synthesized but must be obtained in the diet (table 6.3). The nonessential amino acids can be synthesized from other substances, such as carbohydrate, provided that an adequate nitrogen source (such as other amino acids) is available. Dietary proteins that contain very low amounts of one or more EAA are termed *incomplete proteins*. Incomplete proteins are generally of plant origin and include nuts, grains, legumes, and seeds. However, the quantity of protein available in some plant products, particularly

beans, is relatively high and can partially offset the lower BV. Dietary proteins that contain all of the EAA needed for the synthesis of human tissue have a high BV and are known as *complete proteins*. Complete proteins are typically found in animal sources and products such as red meat, dairy products, eggs, fish, and fowl.

The catabolism and turnover (breakdown and replacement) of protein result in the deamination of amino acids and consequently the excretion of nitrogen. Stored protein is remodeled by a continuous process of catabolism and synthesis. In adult humans with adequate diets, daily remodeling amounts to about 3% to 4% of whole-body protein (De Feo 1996) and likely a greater percentage among athletes during hard training. Compared to carbohydrate or lipid turnover, the breakdown and replacement of protein are less efficient, accounting for 10% to 25% of the RMR (De Feo 1996; Reeds, Fuller, and Nicholson 1985). Protein turnover can be studied by two primary methods: (1) the labeled amino acid infusion method and (2) measurement of nitrogen balance.

The labeled amino acid infusion method is based on isotope dilution and subsequent precursor–product reactions. This method can be used to follow the kinetics of whole-body protein, mixed proteins of specific tissues, and single proteins (Bier 1989; De Feo and Haymond 1994). The method is used to calculate the rate of release of a specific amino acid from a specific endogenous protein. A specific radiolabeled amino acid (RLAA) is intravenously infused, and blood samples are collected at set time intervals to determine the dilution of the RLAA by the endogenous amino acid. The ratio RLAA to endogenous amino acid is defined as specific activity (SA). The changes in rate of release of the amino acid from the endogenous protein can be calculated as follows:

$$RA\ (\mu mol \cdot min^{-1}) = \frac{i}{plasma\ amino\ acid\ SA}$$

where i is the RLAA infusion rate in decays per minute (dpm) and SA is the specific activity of the amino acid (dpm × μmol). Leucine is the amino acid most commonly used in the estimation of whole-body protein turnover (De Feo 1996). Leucine is typically chosen because it is an EAA, it is easily oxidized, and it is completely oxidized in skeletal muscle. A major advantage of this method over other methods such as nitrogen balance studies is that it allows a more direct determination of the mechanisms by which changes in substrate, hormones, or other stimuli can affect protein metabolism (De Feo 1996).

Table 6.3 **The Amino Acids**

Nonessential	Essential
Glycine	Leucine
Alanine	Isoleucine
Aspartic acid	Valine
Glutamic acid	Threonine
Serine	Lysine
Cystine	Methionine
Tyrosine	Phenylalanine
Arginine	Tryptophan
Proline	Histidine*
Hydroxyproline	
Asparagine	
Glutamine	

*Some adults can synthesize histidine. For most adults and for infants, histidine is an essential amino acid.

Adapted from M.H. Stone and H.S. O'Bryant, 1987, *Weight training: A scientific approach* (Minneapolis: Burgess).

Measurement of nitrogen balance provides an estimate of nitrogen intake versus loss and provides a reasonable estimate of protein balance. A negative nitrogen balance occurs when nitrogen loss is larger than intake, indicating a loss of body protein. A positive nitrogen balance occurs when intake is greater than loss, indicating a state of protein anabolism. The formula for nitrogen balance is as follows:

$$Bn = I - (U + F + S + SW)$$

where Bn is the nitrogen balance; I is nitrogen intake; U, F, S, and SW are nitrogen lost in urine, feces, skin, and sweat, respectively.

Nitrogen balance is affected by a number of factors including the physiological state and health of the subject, energy intake, and the essential and nonessential amino acid intake.

Very low dietary intake of an EAA reduces the rate of protein synthesis and impairs the use of other amino acids for protein synthesis. If protein synthesis is reduced sufficiently, catabolic effects begin to predominate, resulting in an increased excretion of nitrogen. A negative nitrogen balance can occur if the proportions of EAA in the diet are unbalanced and overall protein intake is not sufficient to offset the negative nitrogen balance. Increased protein catabolism and a negative nitrogen balance can occur even if only one EAA is limited as a result of dietary inadequacy (Pike and Brown 1984).

Two incomplete proteins that are each limiting due to deficiencies in different EAA can provide a complete-protein diet when both are supplied together, a practice referred to as *mutual supplementation*. In order for vegetarians to obtain sufficient complete protein for good health it is necessary to eat foods containing complementary proteins, which together will supply all of the necessary EAA. The following are typical combinations of foods that can provide complementary protein combinations:

Soybeans and rice

Peas and wheat

Beans and corn

Lentils and wheat or rice

Cereals and legumes

Whole grains and sunflower seeds

Peanuts and wheat (bread)

The timing of meals *may* be important for optimal protein synthesis. Some evidence suggests that mutual supplementation can be less effective if all of the EAA are not ingested within 2 h (Alfin-Slater 1973). Although this idea has been challenged, it is possible that eating two meals containing incomplete proteins widely separated in time may not result in the most efficient mutual supplementation. Additionally, exercise immediately after meals tends to reduce absorption of amino acids and other nutrients. Therefore, considering the relatively high protein requirements for athletes during heavy training, the timing of protein (i.e., amino acid) intake should be considered.

Protein quality is an important factor in establishing the daily intake requirement for protein. While many food products are claimed to have high protein content, the quality may be poor due to deficiencies in one or more EAA. Dietary variety can increase the potential for intake of high-quality protein foods and increases the probability of meeting the requirements for protein as well as other nutrients.

Digestion of Protein

Digestion begins with mastication (chewing) and the mechanical breakdown of food particles. Upon swallowing, hydrochloric acid and pepsin released from the stomach wall act to further break down smaller particles in the stomach. No amino acids are absorbed in the stomach of an adult. Various inactive digestive enzymes are released from the pancreas, such as trypsin, chymotrypsin, and carboxypeptidase, and travel to the small intestine. These enzymes are activated in the small intestine and catalyze the hydrolysis of specific peptide bonds between amino acids, producing small peptides and individual amino acids. Individual amino acids can be absorbed by the mucosal cells but are more typically absorbed as di- or tripeptides. During the absorption process, these small peptides are broken down into amino acids and released into the blood. In healthy humans, almost 100% of the amino acids entering the small intestine are absorbed; only 3% to 5% enter the large intestine (Pike and Brown 1984).

Absorption in the small intestine is rapid and depends on specific active transport systems. Amino acids (AAs) can be classified by chemical structure and function; AAs differ largely according to their side chains (R-group). There are 6 structurally related groups of amino acids based on similarities in the R-groups (aliphatic, aromatic, ether or thioether substitutes, acid or amide functional groups, basic functional groups, and odd groups). Each structurally related amino acid has its own transport system, which facilitates absorption along the length of the small intestine (Hamilton, Whitley, and Sizer 1985; Pike and Brown 1984). Amino acids of the same structural group compete for transport sites, and absorption occurs on a first-come, first-served basis (Bleich et al. 1971). For example, lysine, arginine, cystine, and ornithine share the same transport sites; an excessive amount of one of these amino acids can impair the absorption of the other three. Thus, ingesting a food or amino acid or protein supplement containing an excess of one or more amino acids potentially results in a reduced absorption of other amino acids.

Because of the manner in which amino acids are absorbed, protein obtained from typical food appears to have more optimal amino acid combinations and ratios for digestion and absorption than free-form amino acids and some types of protein supplements. The time involved in the digestive process allows for gradual absorption of amino acids and peptides. As a result of the mechanism and timing for digestion and absorption, a steady, but not overwhelming, supply of amino acids can be made available. It is possible that large amounts of predigested protein and free amino acids, as found in some supplements, can overwhelm available transport systems, reducing total amino acid absorption.

Nearly all of the proteins that enter the stomach and small intestine are digested and absorbed. Enzymes or peptide hormones taken orally are largely inactivated or rendered ineffective because they are also subject to digestion. Glandular substances and other protein-containing substances that are claimed to be anabolic steroid substitutes are likely ineffective because they are broken down by digestive processes before entering the blood. After absorption from the small intestine, amino acids are released into the portal circulation and then travel to the liver. Amino acids can be released by the liver into the blood, and from there taken up by various tissues depending on specific needs.

Protein Metabolism and Control

The U.S. RDA for protein is $0.8 \text{ g} \cdot \text{kg}^{-1} \cdot \text{day}^{-1}$ (National Academy of Sciences 1989). A margin of safety is included in this RDA in an attempt to account and control for individual differences in protein metabolism, normal nitrogen loss, and degree of physical activity. According to RDA standards, due to the safety margin there is no need for additional protein in the diet for any reason among healthy humans. Interestingly, some countries have slightly higher values for protein intake; for example, Germany uses $0.83 \text{ g} \cdot \text{kg}^{-1} \cdot \text{day}^{-1}$. Indeed,

several factors may reduce the effectiveness of and call into question the standards for the RDA and therefore the DRI among very physically active groups such as elite athletes.

It has been assumed that the RDA is largely unaffected by caloric consumption. However, caloric intake must be adequate, or total protein requirements can increase (Tarnopolsky 2000). Typically, as energy requirements increase with the demands of physical training, food consumption and caloric intake also increase in order to meet the demands. In order to maintain normal nitrogen balance, protein intake would have to increase in proportion to the greater caloric consumption. However, this increased protein intake does not always occur. For example, when an athlete changes from one phase of training to another, two to four weeks may be necessary to readjust energy and protein intake and output; longer adjustment periods are likely required if body mass is gained or lost (Åstrand and Rodahl 1970; Pike and Brown 1984). An important possibility to be noted here is that changes in the volume or intensity of training that are not accompanied by appropriate changes in diet (e.g., changes in calories, protein) could result in nonbeneficial alterations in body mass, body composition, and protein status (body protein content), at least for the adjustment period.

Proteins are degraded in the liver and skeletal muscle into their constituent amino acids. Eventually, all amino acids undergo reactions that result in donation of their amine groups ($--NH_2$) to α-ketoglutarate to form glutamic acid. Mammalian liver cells are responsible for the final degradation and disposal of amino acid nitrogen, which are linked to the deamination of glutamic acid and the subsequent production of ammonia. Ammonia (NH_3^+) is a highly toxic substance and must be removed or buffered rapidly. Most of the ammonia produced is converted to urea by the ornithine-arginine pathway (urea cycle). Urea is a nontoxic substance that can be excreted in the urine. Exercise can markedly raise ammonia and urea concentrations as a result of increased protein catabolism and degradation.

Protein metabolism can be affected by various hormones (De Feo 1996; Goldberg 1980; Tischler 1981). Testosterone, insulin, insulin-like growth factors, and growth hormone are anabolic hormones that can directly enhance protein synthesis or inhibit catabolism. Additionally, epinephrine has a net anabolic effect on protein metabolism by decreasing the rate of degradation (De Feo 1996). Cortisol has catabolic properties that enhance protein catabolism, and it antagonizes testosterone. Glucagon and thyroid hormones also have net catabolic effects due to their metabolic actions. These hormones have wide-reaching metabolic and physiological effects. They influence not only protein metabolism, but also carbohydrate and lipid metabolism, water and electrolyte balance, behavior, growth, and numerous other physiologic functions related to protein status. Changes in resting and postexercise hormone concentrations resulting from exercise and training can affect protein metabolism, both synthesis and degradation.

Effects of Exercise and Training on Protein Synthesis

Generally, during exercise, protein synthesis is depressed, and degradation of noncontractile muscle proteins and degradation in the liver are unchanged or increased depending on exercise intensity and duration (Dohm et al. 1985; Graham, Rush, and MacLean 1995; Mero et al. 1997). The degradation of contractile proteins is generally reduced during exercise (Graham, Rush, and MacLean 1995). The net effect, especially as a result of aerobic exercise, is that amino acids are made available for catabolic processes. During recovery, protein catabolism returns toward baseline and protein synthesis can increase (Dohm et al. 1985).

Observations of 3-methylhistidine excretion support the concept of accelerated protein degradation resulting from exercise. This amino acid is formed primarily as a result of contractile protein (actin and myosin) degradation and is not reused in the synthesis of new protein (Booth, Nicholson, and Watson 1982; Graham, Rush, and MacLean 1995). Thus, changes in 3-methylhistidine excretion can be associated with the degree of contractile protein degradation occurring during and after exercise. Both animal (Bylund-Fellenius et al. 1984; Dohm et al. 1982, 1987) and human (Rennie et al. 1981) studies indicate that 3-methylhistidine released from muscle is decreased during aerobic and anaerobic exercise, including weight training (Dohm et al. 1982; Evans et al. 1986; Pivarnik, Hickson, and Wolinsky 1989); however, its release is greatly increased postexercise, suggesting that contractile protein catabolism does take place. The exact nature of protein catabolism resulting from exercise is not clear and likely depends on a number of factors, including the volume, intensity, and type of exercise. Some caution must be used in the interpretation of data using 3-methylhistidine, as a few extramuscular sites contain contractile protein

(gut and skin) that could contribute substantially (up to 25%) to the 3-methylhistidine excretion in humans (Afting et al. 1981).

Training (both aerobic and anaerobic) increases the need for dietary protein intake (Lemon 1991; Lemon and Nagle 1981; Rozenek and Stone 1984). However, the primary use of the additional protein may vary depending on the type of exercise and training regimen. Aerobic training results primarily in an increased oxidation of amino acids (protein) for energy; anaerobic training, particularly weight training, primarily results in an increase in amino acid use in tissue repair and hypertrophy (Mero et al. 1997; Lemon 1995; Tarnopolsky et al. 1991; Tarnopolsky 2000).

Studies based on both isotope dilution and nitrogen balance have shown that aerobic (Friedman and Lemon 1985; Gontzea, Sutzscu, and Dumitrache 1974, 1975) and anaerobic training (Lemon et al. 1992; Mero et al. 1997; Tarnopolsky, MacDougall, and Atkinson 1988), including weightlifting (Celajowa and Homa 1970; Laritcheva et al. 1978), can result in an increased requirement for protein. A negative nitrogen balance, depending upon its degree and duration, can result in losses in LBM that could include hormones, structural and enzymatic proteins, antibodies, and other necessary proteins. These nonbeneficial effects could cause an increased potential for injury, disease, reduced performance capabilities, and overtraining (Mero 1997; Stone et al. 1991b).

Related to the observation of a negative nitrogen balance with training are studies and reviews suggesting that high-volume aerobic training and perhaps anaerobic training (Pitkanen et al. 2003) increase the need for specific amino acids. Approximately six amino acids can be oxidized by skeletal muscle: alanine, aspartic acid, glutamic acid, and particularly the branched chain amino acids (BCAA) leucine, isoleucine, and valine (Babij, Matthews, and Rennie 1983; Dohm et al. 1985; Evans et al. 1983; Hood and Terjung 1990). Branched chain amino acids can donate nitrogen to pyruvate, which can be formed from glucose or amino acids (Galim, Hruska, and Bier 1980). Pyruvate and BCAAs combine as follows:

$$\text{pyruvate} + \text{BCAA} \rightarrow \text{alanine} + \alpha\text{-ketoacid}$$

Alanine is a nontoxic carrier that can transport amino groups to the liver for *gluconeogenesis*, a process by which lactate, glycerol, and amino acids are converted into glucose. Aerobic exercise can greatly accelerate this process, especially in the absence of exogenous carbohydrate intake (Felig and Wahren 1971). The oxidation of the resulting α-ketoacid can provide additional fuel to meet the metabolic demands of the liver and muscle. Both liver and muscle can catabolize substantial amounts of protein and release amino acids (Dohm et al. 1977, 1978; Lemon and Mullin 1980; Young and Munroe 1978). The alterations in protein metabolism resulting from exercise can be physiologically significant in at least three ways (Dohm et al. 1985):

- Amino acid conversion to Krebs cycle intermediates can increase the rate of oxidation of acetyl coenzyme A (CoA) generated from glucose and fatty acid oxidation.
- Increased conversion of amino acids to glucose can help prevent hypoglycemia.
- Oxidation of specific amino acids can provide additional energy for muscular contraction.

The net effect is related to accelerated gluconeogenesis, and the faster gluconeogenesis proceeds, the more protein catabolized.

An important factor influencing the rate of protein oxidation is the initial muscle glycogen concentration (Lemon and Mullin 1980). Reliance on protein and protein degradation is higher if skeletal muscle glycogen concentrations are low. Ten percent or more of the total energy demands can be derived from protein during aerobic exercise if muscle glycogen is inadequate (Lemon and Mullin 1980). The probability of LBM loss is increased when high training loads are coupled with inadequate diets; this scenario increases the likelihood of overtraining (Stone et al. 1991b). Consequently dietary protein should represent approximately 15% of the calories consumed by both endurance and strength-power athletes in hard training, especially during high-volume phases, or among physical laborers performing very hard work (Tarnopolsky et al. 1992; Tarnopolsky 2000). Carbohydrate should represent about 55% to 60% of the dietary calories to ensure adequate glycogen concentrations in muscle and liver, thus reducing potential protein catabolic effects (Rozenek and Stone 1984; Stone et al. 1991b).

Loss of body mass and adverse alterations in body composition as a result of chronic overwork may also be related to psychological changes, such as loss of appetite (Ayers et al. 1985; Stone et al. 1991b; Yates, Leechy, and Shisslak 1983). These changes are likely to lead to a loss of performance, especially in activities requiring a high degree of strength or power.

Protein Intake

Although the exact amount is still somewhat controversial, there is a great deal of evidence that athletes require protein intakes above the RDA, especially during periods of high-volume training (Brooks 1987; Butterfield 1987; Dohm et al. 1978; Lemon 1987, 1995, 1996; Lemon, Berardi, and Noreen 2002; Rozenek and Stone 1984; Wilmore and Freund 1984; Wolfe 1987). The actual requirement for protein is dependent on several factors including exercise type, volume and intensity of training, length of training period, carbohydrate intake, environmental factors, the timing of intake, quality of protein ingested, and perhaps gender (Lemon 1987; Lemon, Berardi, and Noreen 2002). Both aerobic and anaerobic training increase the protein requirements (Lemon 1987; Tarnopolsky et al. 1992; Tarnopolsky 2000), although the exact mechanisms and reasons for the increased requirement appear to be different (Lemon 1995, 1996; Mero et al. 1997). Among endurance athletes, the increased requirement appears to be partially associated with tissue repair but is primarily associated with the increased use of amino acids, particularly BCAAs, as fuel during exercise. On the other hand, for strength-power athletes the increased protein appears to be used for tissue repair, tissue remodeling, and maintenance of a positive nitrogen balance so that the hypertrophic adaptation to training is maximized (Lemon 1987; Tarnopolsky 2000).

The protein requirement for endurance athletes appears to be between 1.2 and 1.4 g · kg^{-1} · day^{-1} (Fielding and Parkington 2002; Lemon 1995, 1996). Much of the requirement beyond the RDA is likely due to the increased oxidation of amino acids, particularly BCAAs (Friedman and Lemon 1985; Lemon 1987, 1995, 1996). Branched chain amino acid supplementation could theoretically prolong endurance performance (Bloomstrand, Celsing, and Newsholme 1988). This may occur for two reasons. First, BCAAs can influence metabolic changes, which could prolong endurance; for example, the exogenous source of BCAAs may reduce protein catabolism and promote the use of free fatty acids as an energy source, thus sparing glycogen (Dioguardi 1997). The second reason is the relationship between BCAAs and the brain's uptake of tryptophan. Tryptophan, an aromatic amino acid, has been associated with feelings of sleepiness, lethargy, and fatigue, resulting from its conversion to the neurotransmitter serotonin. Tryptophan has also been implicated in fatigue caused by exercise and in the etiology of the overtrained state (Acworth et al. 1986; Liberman, Corkin, and Spring

1983; Newsholme 1990; Newsholme, Acworth, and Bloomstrand 1985). Tryptophan and the BCAAs compete with each other for entry through the blood-brain barrier (Newsholme et al. 1985; Newsholme 1990; Yokogoshi et al. 1987).

Serum and brain concentrations of tryptophan appear to be highly correlated in animals (Acworth et al. 1986; Yokogoshi et al. 1987) and humans (Davis 1995). During exercise, in trained and untrained rats, as blood concentrations of BCAA decrease because of amino acid catabolism, the relative concentration of tryptophan increases (Acworth et al. 1986), which in turn can increase the concentration of tryptophan in the brain. In animals, increasing the brain tryptophan concentrations can increase concentration of the neurotransmitter serotonin (Davis 1995); the increased serotonin can result in feelings of fatigue, which in turn *may potentially* result in reduced performance (Newsholme 1990; Newsholme, Acworth, and Bloomstrand 1985). Experimental evidence from animals has confirmed the increased concentrations of serotonin in the brain as a result of endurance exercise (Acworth et al. 1986; Davis 1995). While some evidence suggests that alterations in serotonin can affect aerobic endurance performance in both rats and humans (Davis and Baily 1997), it is not convincing. Additionally, alterations in training volume that increase feelings of fatigue were not associated with changes in tryptophan-to-BCAA ratios among humans (Lehmann et al. 1996; Tanaka et al. 1997). Nor have convincing data been generated in humans indicating that alterations in serotonin would result in the same type of fatigue as is associated with anaerobic activities or with overwork (Gastmann and Lehmann 1998).

In rats, BCAA supplementation has produced mixed results, with one study showing increased endurance (Calders et al. 1997) and the other showing no effect (Verger et al. 1994). In humans, supplementation with BCAAs has produced increases (Bloomstrand et al. 1991; Mitchell et al. 1991), decreases (Petruzzello et al. 1992; Vandewalle et al. 1991), and no effect (Bloomstrand et al. 1995; van Hall et al. 1995) on endurance performance. Decreased performance may be associated with increased ammonia concentrations that have been shown to occur with BCAA supplementation (Dioguardi 1997; MacLean, Graham, and Saltin 1996; Wagenmakers et al. 1991). Performance decreases may also be due to the decrease in Krebs cycle intermediates as a result of increase in the BCAA amino transferase reaction, which requires additional Krebs cycle intermediates (Wagenmakers et al.

1991). Increased ammonia concentrations have also been associated with decreased endurance performance in animals (Alborn, Davis, and Baily 1992). Furthermore, carbohydrate ingestion can attenuate or markedly reduce the reliance on BCAA oxidation during exercise (Davis 1995; Wagenmakers et al. 1991). Obviously, additional study is needed to elucidate the role of amino acid supplementation as it relates to fatigue and overwork.

Lemon (1995, 1996), Tarnopolsky and colleagues (1992), and Fielding and Parkington (2002) suggest that the protein requirement for strength-power athletes is approximately 1.4 to 1.8 g $\cdot$ kg^{-1} $\cdot$ day^{-1}. Indeed, some evidence suggests that dietary increases in protein may enhance increases in strength and muscle mass among strength athletes, even though initial values for dietary protein intake are above the RDA. For example, increasing the protein intake among elite Romanian weightlifters from 225% to 438% of the RDA (approximately 3.5 to 4.0 g $\cdot$ kg^{-1} $\cdot$ day^{-1}) was associated with gains in strength of 5% and gains in muscle mass of 6% (Dragon, Vasilu, and Georgescu 1985); however, the potential influence of androgen use among these athletes is an unknown factor. Fern and colleagues (1991) found that over four weeks of supplementation combined with weight training, gains in body mass and LBM were greater among subjects ingesting 3.3 versus 1.3 g $\cdot$ kg^{-1} $\cdot$ day^{-1} of protein. These studies provide evidence of the potential for protein supplementation combined with resistance training to enhance muscle and performance gains.

On the other hand, untrained subjects engaging in weight training and increasing dietary supplementation of protein to 3.67 times the RDA did not show alterations in body composition compared to controls (Weideman et al. 1990). Moderately trained subjects increasing *both* protein and caloric intake along with performing a weight training program have shown enhanced increases in body mass, LBM, and measures of strength performance compared to controls (Nimmons et al. 1995). However, during periods of very heavy training, among advanced athletes the protein requirement for gaining strength or LBM may be higher (2.0-2.2 g $\cdot$ kg^{-1} $\cdot$ day^{-1}) (Ivy and Portman 2004). Some athletes may routinely lose weight (make weight for sports with weight classes) by using hypocaloric diets; an increased protein intake may be necessary in order to partially offset the accompanying negative nitrogen balance and loss of lean tissue (Walberg et al. 1988). (See "Nutritional Supplements" section in chapter 7, "Ergogenic Aids.")

Amino acid supplementation has been believed to produce a wide variety of effects, including increased LBM. Although supplementation with amino acids was popular among some strength athletes and bodybuilders during the 1990s (Grunwald and Baily 1993; Philen et al. 1992), there is little evidence of its efficacy. For example, amino acid supplementation in elite junior weightlifters for one week (Fry, Kraemer, and Stone 1991) and one month (Fry et al. 1993) had no effect on a variety of physical, physiological, and performance measures (see chapter 7, "Ergogenic Aids"). It is possible, however, that the total amount of protein supplemented (Fry, Kraemer, and Stone 1991; Fry et al. 1993) was not sufficient to promote recovery and growth.

Even when adequate energy is being supplied through the diet, initiation of training or increasing the training volume or intensity can lead to a decreased or negative nitrogen balance (Gontzea, Sutzscu, and Dumitrache 1974, 1975; Lemon 1987). As training proceeds, nitrogen balance returns toward positive values; this can be partially explained by changes in exercise intensity. Protein use during exercise is related to the intensity and relative intensity (percentage of maximum) of exercise and training (Butterfield 1987; Lemon 1987). As training proceeds and adaptation takes place, the relative intensity may decrease and reduce dependence upon protein (Lemon 1987). Increases in training volume or intensity can be accompanied by a reduction in testosterone or an increase in cortisol concentrations, resulting in a reduction of the "anabolic state" of the organism (Hakkinen et al. 1985). Among well-trained cyclists, eight weeks of substantially increased training volume caused significant reductions in resting testosterone concentrations (Hackney et al. 1989). However, protein supplementation reduced the fall in testosterone and increased growth hormone concentrations. Carbohydrate supplementation had no effect on testosterone or growth hormone (Hackney et al. 1989). During periods of increased volume or intensity of training, when short-term negative nitrogen balances are likely to occur, protein intakes as high as $2 \text{ g} \cdot \text{kg}^{-1} \cdot \text{day}^{-1}$ may not be sufficient to maintain a positive nitrogen balance (Butterfield 1987). It is also possible that too little protein, especially when associated with a hypocaloric diet, can potentiate or worsen overtraining symptoms.

Another factor associated with protein intake concerns the timing of protein ingestion. Several reviews (Fielding and Parkington 2002; Mosoni and Mirand 2003; Volek 2003) indicate that ingesting protein during and immediately after exercise (particularly strength exercise) may stimulate tissue repair and protein accretion, especially if substantial amounts of EAA, as in whey protein, are ingested (Borsheim et al. 2002; Tipton et al. 2002). Thus recovery and adaptation may be enhanced by ingestion of a protein (and carbohydrate) drink (see chapter 7, "Ergogenic Aids").

Regardless of the conditions, it is becoming apparent that the protein intake for athletes should be higher than the RDA, especially during high-volume training. This realization was evidenced recently in the joint position stand published by the American College of Sports Medicine, American Dietary Association, and Dieticians of Canada (2000). The authors of this statement on protein consumption recommend 1.2 to $1.4 \text{ g} \cdot \text{kg}^{-1} \cdot \text{day}^{-1}$ for endurance athletes and 1.6 to $1.7 \text{ g} \cdot \text{kg}^{-1} \cdot \text{day}^{-1}$ for strength athletes. Protein intake should represent approximately 15% of the caloric intake, assuming that caloric intake increases in proportion to the energy requirement of training. If there is a marked decrease in caloric intake, the percentage of protein should be raised above 15% (Walberg et al. 1988).

Carbohydrate

Carbohydrate is a compound composed of carbon, hydrogen, and oxygen in the ratio of approximately 1:2:1, with at least three carbon atoms. Carbohydrate can be classified into three primary groups (Pike and Brown 1984):

1. *Monosaccharides:* simple sugars typically composed of three to seven carbon atoms. Biologically important monosaccharides are glucose and fructose.

2. *Oligosaccharides:* carbohydrates made up of 2 to 10 monosaccharides chemically bonded together. For example, sucrose (table sugar) is a disaccharide composed of a glucose and a fructose molecule.

3. *Polysaccharides:* carbohydrates that contain more than 10 monosaccharide units bonded together in linear or complex branching chains. *Homopolysaccharides* (a type of polysaccharide) contain only one type of monosaccharide.

Glycogen is an important example of a homopolysaccharide containing only glucose units arranged in a highly branched structure. Glycogen is the only important homopolysaccharide in animal metabolism. Plant starch is a mixture of two glucose homopolysaccharides: amylose (a linear polymer) and amylopectin (a branched polymer). These two substances are the most common polysaccharides in the American diet. *Heteropolysaccharides* contain two or more different monosaccharides in their structures. Examples include *mucopolysaccharides,* which make up part of the structure of the ground substance of connective tissue.

From a bioenergetic energy production standpoint, carbohydrate is the preferred metabolic fuel. Of the three macronutrients (carbohydrate, protein, and fat), carbohydrate is the only one that can be metabolized for energy production without the direct involvement of oxygen. Thus, the importance of carbohydrate and its relation to anaerobic metabolism cannot be underestimated. Furthermore, carbohydrate can be oxidized and used in long-term exercise.

Carbohydrate is especially important in the performance of long-lasting aerobic activities and in activities that involve high volumes of repeated anaerobic bouts (Haff et al. 1998). Carbohydrate can be synthesized from amino acids and thus is required only to a small extent for growth; however, the addition of carbohydrate to the diet can accelerate growth. Carbohydrate is found in almost all food items except pure fats. Low-carbohydrate diets (below 30% by kilocalories) are often associated with symptoms of fatigue, and adaptation to these diets is difficult at best (Brooks, Fahey, and White 1996; Pike and Brown 1984; Stone et al. 1991b).

In addition to energy supply, carbohydrate contributes to a variety of physiological functions including the following (Brooks, Fahey, and White 1996; Pike and Brown 1984):

- Avoiding ketone formation (ketones result from excessive fat metabolism)
- Reducing the loss of cations
- Formation of the cell coat
- Formation of the ground substance of cartilage and bone
- Formation of heparin and naturally occurring anticoagulant

Both liver and muscle glycogen act as stores of carbohydrate. Of the total caloric intake in the typical American diet, about 45% to 52% consists of carbohydrate. Small amounts of excess dietary carbohydrate may be converted to body fat; however, the majority may be used preferentially for energy production, thereby sparing fat (Horton et al. 1995). Thus, ingesting large amounts of carbohydrate without adequate exercise may promote obesity.

Digestion of Carbohydrate

Monosaccharides, most oligosaccharides, and starches are completely digestible. Nondigestible plant polysaccharides include pectin, hemicellulose, and cellulose. Other plant polysaccharides such as galactogens, inulin, and raffinose are partially digestible.

Digestion of complex carbohydrate begins with mastication. In the mouth, the enzyme *salivary amylase* catalyzes the breakdown of starch to *maltose* (disaccharide containing two glucose units); this stage of digestion occurs only if there is sufficient time between chewing and swallowing. The optimal stomach pH range for amylase activity is 6.6 to 6.8; the enzyme is active until the pH is further decreased by stomach acid secretion. Although some additional digestion of carbohydrate can occur in the stomach as a result of acid hydrolysis, most digestion occurs after the stomach contents move into the duodenum of the small intestine, into which more amylase is secreted by the pancreas. Pancreatic amylase further digests carbohydrate, producing maltose, *maltotriose,* and a mixture of *dextrins.* Enzymes on the surface of the intestinal wall are responsible for the final hydrolysis of these molecules into glucose (Pike and Brown 1984).

Disaccharides (either from the digestion of starch or from ingestion) are broken down into their constituent monosaccharides through the action of specific *disaccharidases* in the intestinal mucosa. For example, sucrase breaks down sucrose, and lactase breaks down lactose. A disaccharidase deficiency results in incomplete hydrolysis of a disaccharide before absorption (Dalqvist 1962; Pike and Brown 1984). One of these disaccharidases, lactase, catalyzes the breakdown of lactose into glucose and galactose prior to absorption. Lactase deficiency is a relatively common condition that results in lactose intolerance. Lactose remains unabsorbed in the digestive tract and is fermented in the large intestine, causing flatulence, abdominal bloating, and sometimes cramps (Dalqvist 1962; Pike and Brown 1984). Although the severity of symptoms can vary, people with lactose intolerance usually must abstain from or greatly reduce their intake of foods containing lactose, such as milk and some milk products.

Absorption of the digestive products occurs primarily in the duodenum of the small intestine. Monosaccharides are absorbed and appear in the blood within a few minutes (<20 min). More complex carbohydrates such as starches are typically absorbed and appear in the blood within 30 to 60 min after the initiation of mastication (Pike and Brown 1984).

Galactose and glucose are absorbed by a selective Na^+-dependent active transport system. Because of the degree of selectivity in the active transport system, galactose and glucose are absorbed faster than other hexoses that are absorbed by a diffusion process (Pike and Brown 1984). Fructose, which is absorbed by facilitated diffusion, enters faster than mannose, xylose, or arabinose. After absorption, monosaccharides enter the blood and can be taken up by the liver or other tissues. Most of the absorbed fructose is transported to the liver where it is converted into glucose, which is released into the blood or stored as glycogen.

Carbohydrate Metabolism and Control

Glucose uptake by muscle cells is regulated by a family of proteins termed *glucose transporters* or *GLUTs* (Banks et al. 1992; Barnard and Youngren 1992; Friedman, Neufer, and Dohm 1991; Houmard et al. 1991; Slentz et al. 1992). Under normal basal conditions, glucose transport is regulated by GLUT-1, which is located along plasma membranes and capillary endothelial cells. Glucose transporter-4 is a more important GLUT in skeletal muscle because of its greater transport efficiency. It is normally stored in an intracellular pool. Insulin stimulation or exercise results in a translocation of GLUT-4 from the intracellular pool to the plasma membrane and the T-tubules. This translocation results in an acceleration of glucose uptake. Once the glucose has entered the cell, it may be used for energy or stored depending upon the needs of the cell. Storage and breakdown of carbohydrate are important considerations for an understanding of how muscles maintain and supply adequate energy substrate for contraction. Although not consistent across different muscles (Borghouts et al. 2000), concentrations of GLUT-4 tend to be greater in type I muscle fibers (Gaster et al. 2002). However, GLUT-4 concentration is greatly influenced by the level of physical activity (Daugaard and Richter 2001).

Glycogen is stored in muscle and the liver bound to two enzymes (Friedman, Neufer, and Dohm 1991), glycogen synthetase (glycogen buildup) and phosphorylase (glycogen breakdown). Two additional enzymes (isozymes) important in glucose and glycogen regulation are hexokinase (in muscle, liver, and other cells) and glucokinase (only in the liver). These two isozymes are responsible for phosphorylating the sixth carbon of glucose, as follows:

$$\text{ATP} + \text{glucose} \xrightarrow{\text{hexokinase or glucokinase}} \text{ADP} + \text{glucose-6-phosphate}$$

In most cells, including liver and muscle, conversion of glucose into glycogen requires this reaction, which is also necessary as a first step in the entry of glucose into glycolysis.

Glucokinase becomes more active as blood glucose concentrations increase, so that the liver can take up more glucose and convert it to glycogen. The increased activity of glucokinase results from the induction effect of insulin, which causes increases in synthesis and concentration of glucokinase. Insulin can increase its blood concentration in response to increasing blood glucose concentrations. As blood glucose concentrations decrease, the activity of glucokinase decreases and less glycogen will be stored in the liver (Brooks, Fahey, and White 1996).

Hormones have profound effects on carbohydrate storage and catabolism (see chapter 5, "Neuroendocrine Factors"). Blood glucose concentrations can be increased by catecholamines, cortisol, glucagon, and indirectly by growth hormone. Blood glucose concentration can be decreased by insulin. Glycogen synthesis and storage in liver and muscle are enhanced by insulin and testosterone. Glycogen stores are mobilized by catecholamines and glucagon. As with protein and fat, the regulation of carbohydrate as an energy substrate depends on neural and endocrine mechanisms that can be modified by a number of factors including nutritional status, physical exercise, and training (Brooks 1987; Brooks, Fahey, and White 1996).

In particular, the responses of the two hormones insulin and cortisol to carbohydrate ingestion can have considerable influence on the responses and adaptations to resistance training. Both aerobic (Sutton, Farrell, and Harber 1990) and resistance exercise (McMillan et al. 1993) can result in decreased postexercise insulin concentrations. Reduced insulin concentrations enhance the mobilization of free fatty acids from fat cells and allow the liver to catabolize glycogen and release glucose into the blood, facilitating energy substrate availability for the exercising muscle (Sutton, Farrell, and Harber 1990). Although a reduced insulin concentration would normally lower resting cellular glucose uptake, exercise itself enhances glucose uptake in the working muscle. Both aerobic- and resistance-trained athletes may have an increased insulin sensitivity at rest and during exercise; thus less hormone is required to control substrate availability (McMillan et al. 1993; Sutton, Farrell, and Harber 1990).

Insulin acts to enhance glycogen storage by inducing glycogen synthetase and promoting energy substrate uptake. Insulin is also an anabolic hormone, promoting amino acid uptake and protein synthesis. Increasing insulin concentrations during or especially after exercise can enhance the recovery of glycogen and may promote a more anabolic environment conducive to increasing muscle mass (i.e., hypertrophy). Therefore, ingesting carbohydrate during and immediately after exercise provides glucose (substrate) and a stimulus for enhanced glycogen recovery and protein anabolism. The intake of carbohydrate and small amounts of protein appears to enhance these effects (insulin related), as well as stimulating increases in growth hormone (Chandler et al. 1994; Fahey et al. 1993). Care should be taken to limit fat consumption during a time interval associated with increased insulin concentrations, as this would enhance fat deposition (Conley and Stone 1996).

Cortisol is a glucocorticoid produced and secreted by the adrenal cortex (see chapter 5, "Neuroendocrine Factors"). The basic functions of cortisol are (Conley and Stone 1996; De Feo 1996) (1) maintenance of blood glucose concentrations, (2) reduction of inflammation by inhibiting the shift of water away from the blood into the tissues, (3) conversion of amino acids to carbohydrate, (4) induction of proteolytic enzymes, (5) inhibition of protein synthesis and increasing general protein degradation, and (6) antagonism to testosterone. While cortisol is essential in aiding in the resistance to stressors, its secretion may also elicit physiological responses that are counterproductive to the normal adaptations to training, particularly resistance training—for example, the general catabolic effects of cortisol. The primary metabolic effect of cortisol appears to be gluconeogenesis, which requires protein degradation. Muscle atrophy and loss of strength have been associated with chronically elevated cortisol concentrations (Florini 1987).

Exercise-induced muscle damage can result from various types of exercise, particularly from eccentric muscle actions (Newman et al. 1983). Resistance exercise can have a large eccentric component and can cause considerable muscle damage. An efficient immune function appears to be critical to tissue repair postexercise and likely influences the hypertrophy effect of resistance training (Ryan 1977; Smith 1992; White and Esser 1989; Yamada et al. 1989). However, elevated cortisol concentrations resulting from heavy exercise or overtraining suppress immune system function, increasing tissue repair time and perhaps interfering with tissue hypertrophy. Evidence suggests that carbohydrate ingestion can inhibit the secretion of cortisol (Mitchell et al. 1990); this inhibition may act to promote a more anabolic environment. Over time, this environment may stimulate enhanced adaptations to resistance training (Conley and Stone 1996).

Carbohydrate Intake

The importance of carbohydrate in the diets of athletes was recognized as early as 1901 (Williams 1976). In 1939, diets high in carbohydrate content were found to enhance the ability to perform prolonged heavy work (Christensen and Hansen 1939). Several studies and reviews have documented a strong relationship between a high carbohydrate intake, preexercise muscle glycogen concentrations, and work performance or endurance (Bergstrom and Hultman 1966; Conley and Stone 1996; Karlsson and Saltin 1971; O'Keefe et al. 1987; Snyder et al. 1983). Additionally, muscle glycogen concentrations may be related to muscle strength, short-term high-intensity (anaerobic) exercise, and the ability to repeat or sustain high-intensity exercise (Conley and Stone 1996; Forsberg, Tesch, and Karlsson 1978; Haff et al. 1998, 2003; Jacobs, Kaiser, and Tesch 1982; Lambert et al. 1991).

Because of the relationship of dietary carbohydrate to muscle and liver glycogen stores (Conley and Stone 1996; Simonses et al. 1991) and to the protein-sparing effect of high concentrations of muscle glycogen (Lemon 1987), dietary carbohydrate is an important factor to consider in physical training. In some cases, carbohydrate-poor diets or training programs that chronically deplete glycogen stores may be a strong contributor to overtraining and reduced performance (Stone et al. 1991b). Most dietary intake should probably consist of complex carbohydrates rather than simple sugars (Pike and Brown 1984); an exception may be during and immediately after exercise, as simple sugars tend to be absorbed faster and can have a greater effect on insulin release. Daily intake of carbohydrate should range from 6 to 11 g · kg body mass^{-1}. Carbohydrate intake beyond this range does not appear to provide additional benefit. The proportion of calories derived from carbohydrate should be approximately 55% to 60% for athletes in hard training, especially during high-volume periods, who are eating sufficient calories (Conley and Stone 1996; Strauzenberg et al. 1979).

Aerobic work can be prolonged, and the amount of work during a given period of time can be increased, through manipulation of the carbohydrate intake (Conley and Stone 1996). Some evidence (Jenkins, Palmer, and Spillman 1993; Maughn and Poole 1981), but not all (Lamb et al. 1990), indicates that carbohydrate intake beneficially affects intermittent anaerobic exercise (e.g., resistance training). The amount, timing, and form of carbohydrate ingestion and its effects on resistance exercise and training have not been well studied. The earliest investigation (Lambert et al. 1991) concerning carbohydrate ingestion and resistance exercise examined the effects of a carbohydrate beverage on multiple bouts of leg extensions. Using a double-blind crossover technique, the study showed that a glucose polymer ($1 \text{ g} \cdot \text{kg}^{-1}$) ingested immediately before exercise and $0.17 \text{ g} \cdot \text{kg}^{-1}$ after every five sets produced more total sets ($p = 0.067$) and repetitions ($p = 0.056$) than a placebo drink (Lambert et al. 1991). Haff and colleagues (2001) found that carbohydrate supplementation increased the total amount of work performed during 16 sets of 10 repetitions on a semi-isokinetic device at $120° \cdot \text{s}^{-1}$.

However, other researchers have not noted an ergogenic effect during resistance exercise. Conley and colleagues (1995), using a double-blind crossover protocol, gave subjects $0.3 \text{ g} \cdot \text{kg}^{-1}$ of carbohydrate immediately prior to exercise and $0.15 \text{ g} \cdot \text{kg}^{-1}$ after each completed set of squats. This protocol resulted in no difference in the work accomplished from squats (sets of 10 repetitions at 65% of 1RM) performed to failure. In a study by Vincent and colleagues (1993), subjects drank 100 g of carbohydrate immediately before a free weight training session and then exercised on an isokinetic device (Biodex, $75° \cdot \text{s}^{-1}$ legs and $90° \cdot \text{s}^{-1}$ arms) after the session. Biodex measurements of force, power, and work output indicated no advantage as a result of carbohydrate ingestion. It should be noted that those studies showing an ergogenic effect from carbohydrate ingestion lasted more than 55 min and involved much greater total workloads; those not showing an effect lasted a much shorter time period. These data indicate that during resistance exercise occurring over relatively long periods of time or requiring relatively greater total workloads, carbohydrate supplementation may be effective as an ergogenic aid (Haff et al. 2003). This observation suggests that carbohydrate supplementation may be beneficial in other high-intensity activities that last more than 55 min, such as rugby and American football.

It is not uncommon for athletes, especially advanced and elite athletes, to use multiple training sessions during a day. It is possible that carbohydrate ingestion might influence the outcome of a second or third training session provided that enough is ingested (Haff et al. 1998).

Protein and carbohydrate supplementation combined, especially when used pre- and post-exercise, may provide a more anabolic environment and promote glycogen resynthesis and tissue remodeling to a greater degree than either protein or carbohydrate supplementation alone (Volek 2003). The use of this combination is discussed in detail in chapter 7, "Ergogenic Aids."

Fat

The physiological functions for fat are quite diverse, ranging from their use as physiological structures to its use in energy production. Fat provides the largest energy store readily available for biological work. In a typical Western diet, approximately 35% to 45% of the daily caloric intake consists of fat (Hawley 2000). Fat (lipid) is relatively insoluble in water but can be extracted from biological materials via organic solvents such as ether or acetone. Depending on the temperature, fat can exist as either a solid or liquid. Fat is involved in a variety of metabolic processes and has been associated with disease states including cardiovascular disease and some types of cancer. The functions of fat include the following (Hawley 2000; Pike and Brown 1984):

- Energy source
- Lipid-soluble vitamin transport
- Structural components of cell membranes
- Structural components of the myelin sheath of nerve cells
- Production of cholesterol and associated steroid synthesis

Fat is present in all human cells. The primary storage of fat is in adipose cells and in lipid vacuoles found in muscle fibers (Hawley 2000). Fats can be classified into three groups: simple fats, compound fats, and derived fats.

Simple fats are fatty acids and triglycerides. Fatty acids (FA) are the simplest lipids, consisting of monocarboxylic acids with long-chain hydrocarbon side groups. Fatty acids can be unsaturated or saturated. Unsaturated FAs can be mono- or polyunsaturated. Monounsaturated FAs contain only one double bond between carbon atoms, while polyunsaturated FAs contain two or more. Saturated FAs contain only single bonds between carbon atoms. Most commonly eaten foods contain mostly straight-chain saturated or unsaturated FAs with an even number of carbon atoms. Linoleic, oleic, palmitic, and stearic FAs account for 90% or more of the FAs in the typical American diet. Linoleic, linolenic, and arachidonic FAs are synthesized only in very small amounts by humans and are termed essential fatty acids (EFAs). For good health, these EFAs must be consumed in the diet.

Triglycerides consist of the three-carbon molecule, glycerol, and three FAs. One FA is attached to each of the three glycerol carbons. Triglycerides are the primary storage form of fat and make up about 95% of the fat found in food (Hawley 2000); thus, most fat is ingested as triglycerides. At room temperature, triglycerides containing long-chain FAs (eight or more carbons) are typically solid (e.g., lard); those having short chains or containing unsaturated FAs are typically liquid (e.g., corn oil). There are notable exceptions, such as coconut oil, which contains saturated FAs.

Compound fats consist of lipids combined with a different moiety. Compound lipids include lipoproteins, glycolipids, and phospholipids. Lipoproteins are transporters for different types of lipids in the blood. Glycolipids contain carbohydrate and make up various structures in the cell membrane and myelin sheath. *Phospholipids* have a structure similar to that of triglycerides, with a three-carbon phosphatidic acid core (PCA). The PCA contains only two FAs with a phosphate group attached to the third carbon. Phospholipids differ largely in the type of compound attached to the phosphate group. Phospholipids are components of cell and subcellular membranes. Phospholipids have a fat-soluble (FA end) and a water-soluble portion (glycerol and organic base portion); as a result they can function as liaisons between fat- and water-soluble materials that must pass through a membrane. Typically, because of their important structural and transport roles, phospholipids are rarely used for energy production.

Derived fats are lipids that are created or derived from other lipids or from precursor molecules. Derived fats include alcohols, sterols, steroids, and hydrocarbons. These fats serve a variety of functions involved in provision of cell membrane integrity, synthesis of vitamin D, and synthesis of cholesterol. Cholesterol (a sterol) is the most familiar derived fat and is synthesized from acetate in all animal tissue. Typically, cholesterol is found in its free form or bound to FAs, forming cholesterol esters. Cholesterol is the precursor for cholic acid (a bile acid), vitamin D, and steroid hormones.

Digestion of Fat

Fat digestion is initiated with mastication; while no hydrolysis of triglycerides occurs in the mouth, the presence of triglycerides and other fats results in the release of lingual lipase from the serous glands at the base of the tongue. Lingual lipase is active in the stomach; optimal fat hydrolysis occurs at a pH range of 4.5 to 5.4 (Hamosh and Scow 1975). Ten percent or less of the triglyceride entering the stomach is digested there. As fat enters the duodenum, gastric emptying is slowed, likely due to the release of the hormone enterogastrone. As a result of the slowed gastric emptying, the rate of fat entrance into the duodenum is associated with the ability of pancreatic lipases to hydrolyze fats. Glycerol ester hydrolase is the primary lipase acting to reduce triglycerides to FAs, glycerol, and monoglycerides. Cholesterol esterase breaks down cholesterol esters into cholesterol and FAs. The breakdown of triglycerides depends on the presence of bile salts released from the gallbladder. The bile salts, along with cholesterol and FAs, act as a detergent and aid in the emulsification of triglyceride particles.

The resulting products of fat hydrolysis aggregate in particles termed *micelles*. The micelles interact with the mucosal wall cells of the intestine, and in this manner fat is transported into the intestinal wall. The fate of the absorbed FA depends on chain length. Short- and medium-chain FAs are absorbed through the mucosal cells into the portal vein and transported directly to the liver. Long-chain FAs and glycerol are resynthesized into triglycerides, bound to proteins and other fats, forming *chylomicrons* and a small amount of very low-density lipoproteins (VLDL). The chylomicrons and VLDL are taken up by the lymphatic system and enter the blood by way of the thoracic duct. Among all the lipoproteins, chylomicrons contain the greatest percentage of triglycerides (85%).

Fat Transport and Cellular Uptake

After entering the blood, chylomicrons and VLDL can be broken down by various tissues. The remnants of these particles can be taken up by the liver and converted into other lipids or bile salts. Specific fats and protein–fat complexes are manufactured in the liver and released into the blood (e.g., lipoproteins). Lipoproteins are molecules that contain various combinations of triglycerides, phospholipids, and cholesterol surrounded by phosphatidylcholine and a protein coat. The protein coat partly serves to increase the water solubility of the lipoprotein and also to protect the lipoprotein from being hydrolyzed during blood transport (Leon 1985). The lipoprotein coat contains one or more specific proteins, each class of which imparts different properties to different lipoproteins.

In order to be taken up by cells, circulating triglycerides must first be broken down into glycerol and FAs. The process is catalyzed by the enzyme lipoprotein lipase, which is bound to capillary endothelial cells (Brown, Kovanen, and Goldstein 1981). Fatty acids and glycerol are converted back to triglycerides and stored in the fat cells, a process that occurs on a smaller scale in muscle and other tissues (Dufaux, Assmann, and Hollman 1982). Thus, there are three "storage pools" of fats (triglycerides) available for use as an energy substrate: circulating triglycerides (chylomicrons), adipose tissue, and intramuscular stores. In the well-trained endurance athlete, this would amount to about 5000 to 10,000 g (11-22 lb) of adipose tissue and about 350 g of intramuscular stores (Hawley 2000).

To release fats into the circulation, hormone-sensitive lipase (HSL), present in adipose tissue, reduces triglycerides to glycerol and free fatty acids. Fatty acid mobilization is enhanced by fasting and by exercise-stimulated release of mobilizing hormones, including glucagon and catecholamines. The reaction controlled by HSL is the rate-limiting step for lipolysis (Hollet and Auditore 1967). Once the free fatty acids are released into the circulation, they can be taken up by other tissues and be used for energy, be stored as triglycerides, or become incorporated into a cellular structure such as a membrane. Muscle contains an isozyme of HSL that catalyzes the breakdown of stored triglycerides for use as an energy substrate in the mitochondria (Dufaux 1982).

The liver releases VLDL, some low-density lipoproteins (LDL), and high-density lipoproteins (HDL) into the circulation. As these lipoproteins pass through the tissues, lipoprotein lipase removes most of the triglycerides, by breakdown to FAs and glycerol, which can be taken up by the tissues. After cell entry, the FAs can re-form triglycerides or be used for energy. Removal of triglycerides from VLDL leaves a "remnant" in the circulation termed the intermediate-density lipoprotein (IDL). Most of the IDL is degraded in the liver, and the cholesterol is removed and converted into bile salts. Some of the IDL has more triglyceride removed, resulting

in the formation of LDL (Dufaux, Assmann, and Hollman 1982).

Low-density lipoprotein is a primary carrier of cholesterol that can bind to receptors in many tissues, including liver, muscle, and arterial walls (Dufaux, Assmann, and Hollman 1982). Cholesterol can be deposited into the cells of various tissues in this manner. Once deposited, cholesterol can be used to form various membrane structures or in the production of vitamin D or steroid hormones. However, uncontrolled and excessive binding of cholesterol to arterial wall receptors appears to be a primary step in the formation of atherosclerosis (Dufaux, Assmann, and Hollman 1982; Goldstein, Kita, and Brown 1983). As a result of some diseases or the ingestion of excessive amounts of dietary saturated fat, liver cholesterol concentrations can increase. The rise in liver cholesterol can result in a decrease in the number of receptors for IDL and LDL (Goldstein, Kita, and Brown 1983). This decrease in receptor number, as a consequence of increased liver cholesterol concentrations, leads to a greater conversion of IDL into LDL and a greater potential for atherosclerosis.

High-density lipoprotein can remove cholesterol from arterial walls and accept cholesterol from VLDL. The transfer of cholesterol to HDL is accomplished via a reaction catalyzed by lecithin cholesterol acetyl transferase (LCAT). High-density lipoprotein is degraded in the liver via a reaction catalyzed by hepatic lipase. Hepatic lipase activity is negatively correlated with serum HDL concentrations (Wood and Stefanic 1990).

As a result of the underlying mechanisms controlling lipoprotein synthesis and degradation, these blood lipids are associated with cardiovascular disease (CVD). High total cholesterol, LDL cholesterol, VLDL, and triglycerides are associated with increased risk for CVD. High HDL cholesterol concentrations, low ratio of LDL to HDL cholesterol, and low total cholesterol-to-HDL cholesterol ratio are associated with lower risk (National Cholesterol Education Program—ATP III 2001; Shahar et al. 2003). Potential risks for CVD in relation to blood lipids are shown in table 6.4. Reductions in total cholesterol, ratio of total cholesterol to HDL, and ratio of LDL to HDL cholesterol have been associated with a reduced incidence and mortality from CVD.

Dietary intervention can beneficially alter blood lipids. Diets high in saturated and trans fatty acids tend to raise total and LDL cholesterol. When carbohydrate is used to replace saturated fat in a low-fat diet, LDL and HDL tend to decrease equally,

Table 6.4 **Relative Risk for CVD Based on Blood Lipoproteins and Triglyceride Concentrations (mg · dl⁻¹)**

Particle	Relative risk
LOW-DENSITY LIPOPROTEIN CHOLESTEROL	
<100	Optimal (no relative risk)
100-129	Near to above optimal
130-159	Borderline high
160-189	High
>190	Very high
TOTAL CHOLESTEROL	
<200	Desirable (low risk)
200-239	Borderline high
>240	High
HIGH-DENSITY LIPOPROTEIN CHOLESTEROL	
<40	High
41-59	Moderate
>60	Low
TRIGLYCERIDES	
<150	Normal (low risk)
150-199	Borderline high
200-499	High
>500	Very high

The ratio of total cholesterol to HDL cholesterol should be under 4.5, and the ratio of LDL to HDL should be under 5.

Adapted from American Medical Association, 2001, "National Cholesterol Education Program, expert panel on detection, evaluation and treatment of high blood cholesterol in adults (Adult Treatment Panel III)," *Journal of the American Medical Association* 16(285): 2486-2497; and E. Shahar et al., 2003, "Plasma lipid profile and incident ischemic stroke: The Atherosclerosis risk in community (ARIC) study," *Stroke* 34: 623-631.

and triglycerides tend to increase unless foods low on the glycemic index are used (Sacks and Katan 2002). Indeed, among sedentary adults, a very high-carbohydrate diet (>57.4% of energy intake in males and >59.1% in females) has been associated with low-serum HDL cholesterol and high-serum triglyceride (Yang et al. 2003). While evidence indicates that both aerobic and resistance training (Stone et al. 1991a) can decrease triglycerides and increase HDL cholesterol, typical low-volume exercise protocols have little effect on total and LDL cholesterol unless there is a loss of body mass, or total fat intake is reduced, or both (Durstine et al. 2002).

However, some evidence suggests that having a low total cholesterol, prior to any drug treatment, is not always associated with lower mortality (Capurso 1992; Casiglia et al. 2003; Neaton et al. 1992) and may in fact predict a higher mortality in elderly persons (Casiglia et al. 2003). These reviews suggest that a total cholesterol of <160 mg may be related to a variety of noncardiovascular diseases including liver and pancreatic cancer, digestive diseases, and behavior disorders such as alcoholism and suicide (Capurso 1992; Casiglia et al. 2003; Neaton et al. 1992). Although a cause-and-effect relation between a low total cholesterol and higher mortality is unclear, caution should be taken in reducing baseline total cholesterol to very low concentrations.

Fat Metabolism

Fat metabolism is profoundly affected by the endocrine system. In general, fat synthesis is enhanced by insulin, and lipolysis (fat breakdown) is enhanced by growth hormone, thyroxin, catecholamines, and cortisol (Hawley 2000; McMillan et al. 1993). One of the most important aspects of fat metabolism involves the mobilization and use of FAs for energy during and after exercise.

Mobilization of free fatty acids is an important fuel source during aerobic exercises (Hawley 2000) and can be a postexercise consequence of anaerobic exercise, including resistance exercise (McMillan et al. 1993; Petitt, Arngrimsson, and Cureton 2003). Fatty acids are oxidized by the process of β-oxidation, which takes place in the mitochondria. β-Oxidation comprises four separate reactions in which the acyl CoA derived from the FA is degraded to acetyl CoA, which then enters the Krebs cycle. Fatty acid oxidation rate is dependent on the rate of entry of acetyl CoA derived from pyruvate and on chain length. Medium-chain fatty acids are oxidized more rapidly and more completely than long-chain fatty acids (Hawley 2000; Rassmussen and Wolfe 1999).

Various nutritional strategies have been proposed to enhance the mobilization and oxidation of fat during and after exercise. These strategies, although similar in mechanism, have different goals; one is to raise the rate of fat oxidation and spare glycogen during long-term exercise, and the other is to promote fat loss.

Sparing glycogen to prolong endurance could (in theory) occur by use of methylated xanthines such as caffeine (Hawley 2000), the efficacy of which is questionable (see chapter 7, "Ergogenic Aids"), or by fat supplementation. Fat supplementation has included preexercise feeding and the ingestion of long- and medium-chain triglycerides during exercise; these types of supplementations or interventions can enhance the rate of fat oxidation (reviewed by Hawley 2000). However, in general, these interventions did not enhance performance and in some cases decreased performance (Hawley 2000; Wee, Williams, and Garcia-Roves 1999).

Another dietary strategy used to enhance the oxidation of fat (and perhaps spare carbohydrate) involves long-term adaptation to a high-fat diet. Adaptation to a high-fat, low-carbohydrate diet appears to increase the relative contribution of FAs as an energy source to the total energy required for an exercise by about 40% (Hawley 2000). However, the dietary adaptation does not appear to alter the rate of muscle glycogen use or to improve moderate-intensity exercise endurance (Kiens and Helge 2000). Although theoretically a long-term high-fat, low-carbohydrate diet might benefit ultraendurance performance, the potential health risks (and few experimental confirmations of benefits) associated with the diet preclude recommending this approach.

Other strategies to improve long-term endurance include a type of "carbohydrate loading" in which a high-fat, low-carbohydrate diet (followed for about five days) is used to deplete muscle glycogen and increase the oxidative rate of fat. On the sixth day, a high-carbohydrate diet can restore muscle glycogen. During 2 h of moderate-intensity exercise (cycling at 70% of $\dot{V}O_2max$), muscle glycogen use was lower as a result of fat adaptation; however, performance times did not differ substantially from those with high-carbohydrate diets (Burke et al. 2002; Burke and Hawley 2003).

Of interest is the use of a relatively high-fat, high-protein, and low-carbohydrate diet to promote body fat loss among bodybuilders. The underlying concept is that fat oxidation is enhanced (Hawley 2000) and any excess carbohydrate is not stored as fat, so body fat is decreased; the additional protein along with training will help maintain LBM (Walberg et al. 1988). While this type of diet may work acutely for bodybuilders, long-term use *may* result in prolonged fatigue, ketosis, decreased calcium concentrations, and adverse blood lipid profiles (Bray 2003; Kennedy, Bowman, and Spence 2001).

Promotion of fat loss by nutritional supplements is quite popular. Fatty acid oxidation is related to exercise-induced body fat loss; thus both aerobic and anaerobic exercise should be useful in body fat loss. Both endurance and resistance training can produce significant body fat and percent fat losses in relatively short-term periods (months) provided that volume and intensity of exercise are sufficient (Gippini et al. 2002; Hickson, Roesenkoetter, and Brown 1980; Hunter et al. 2002). Increasing the rate of FA mobilization (e.g., with methylated xanthines, ephedra) or increasing the rate of FA entry into the mitochondria (with L-carnitine) could theoretically increase the loss of fat. However, the efficacy of these ergogenic aids is questionable at best, and some supplements, such as ephedra, are potentially dangerous (see chapter 7, "Ergogenic Aids").

Vitamins and Minerals

Vitamins are organic compounds that are essential in very small amounts for normal metabolic functioning. An important aspect of vitamins is that humans cannot synthesize them (except for vitamin D) and thus they must be ingested in the diet. Vitamins can be classified according to solubility: Fat-soluble vitamins are A, D, E, and K, and water-soluble vitamins are B complex and C.

Vitamins have various functions. Most water-soluble vitamins act as coenzymes, which are organic molecules loosely bound to enzymes that are necessary for full activation of the enzyme. Fat-soluble vitamins typically have antioxidant properties or possess hormonelike properties. Vitamins are largely active in reactions directly or indirectly involved in muscle contraction and energy expenditure, but also are involved in hemoglobin synthesis, immune function, and bone metabolism (table 6.5).

Minerals are inorganic salt ions that act as cofactors or as a part of mineralized structures such as teeth or bone (table 6.5). A cofactor has the same function as a coenzyme. Based on dietary requirements, minerals can be classified as macrominerals (sodium, potassium, calcium, phosphorus, and magnesium) or trace elements (iron, zinc, copper, chromium, and selenium). The daily allowance for macrominerals is greater than $100 \text{ mg} \cdot \text{day}^{-1}$ and for trace elements is less than $20 \text{ mg} \cdot \text{day}^{-1}$ (Fogelholm 2000). Vitamins and minerals are important for optimal and maximal performance.

Vitamins and minerals are obviously essential micronutrients. It is commonly believed that all of these essential micronutrients for healthy humans can be obtained in a "well-balanced" daily diet. However, many coaches recommend that athletes take vitamin and mineral supplements, believing them to be beneficial for recovery and adaptation and for good performance (Ronsen, Sundgot-Borgen, and Maehlum 1999).

There is little consistent evidence (Brubacher 1989; Fogelholm 2000) that a large intake of micronutrients makes a large impact on performance; and

Table 6.5   Functions of Selected Vitamins and Minerals

Nutrient	Energy metabolism	Nervous system and muscle function	Hemoglobin synthesis	Immune system function	Antioxidant function	Bone structure and metabolism	Blood clotting
WATER SOLUBLE							
Thiamin (B1)	X	X					
Riboflavin	X	X					
Niacin	X	X					
Pyridoxine (B6)	X	X	X	X			
Cobalamin (B12)		X	X				
Pantothenic acid	X						
Folic acid		X	X				
Biotin	X						
Ascorbic acid (vitamin C)				X	X	X	
FAT SOLUBLE							
Retinol (vitamin A)				X	X		
Calciferol (vitamin D)						X	
α-Tocopherol (vitamin E)				X	X		
Vitamin K							X
MINERALS							
Macro							
Calcium		X				X	
Potassium		X					
Magnesium	X	X		X		X	
Sodium		X					
Phosphorus							
Trace							
Iron	X		X		X		
Zinc	X				X		
Copper	X			X	X		
Chromium	X						
Selenium					X		

Adapted from M. Fogelholm, 2000, Vitamin, mineral and antioxidant needs of athletes. In *Clinical sports nutrition*, edited by L. Burke and V. Deakin (Rossville, NSW: McGraw-Hill Australia), 312-340. With permission of The McGraw-Hill Australia.

some micronutrients, such as fat-soluble vitamins, in large amounts may be detrimental (McMillan, Keith, and Stone 1988). Although a few studies have shown that micronutrient supplementation can beneficially affect performance (Dibbern 1981; Strauzenberg et al. 1979), most have not (Fogelholm 2000).

Vitamin and mineral supplements may be useful if the RDA or the athlete's personal requirements are not being met by his or her diet (Short and Short 1983). It is known that deficiencies in vitamins and minerals result in performance decrements (Strauzenberg et al. 1979). Athletes ingesting enough calories and eating a nutritionally sound diet should ingest adequate amounts of vitamins and minerals without supplementation. However, athletes do not always eat a "balanced" diet, and many athletes regularly have to "make weight." Both of these factors are reasons to assume that dietary intake of vitamins and minerals may not be sufficient. For example, Guillard and colleagues (1989) evaluated the blood concentrations of fifty-five 20-year-old male athletes from various sports and 20 sedentary controls. Both groups had lower than normal concentrations of vitamins B1, B6, and E. However, the frequency, and in many cases the severity, of the deficiency was greater in the athletes than in the controls. A one-month supplementation with the deficient vitamins markedly improved the micronutrient status of the controls but did not completely restore status among the athletes. Furthermore, caloric restriction and making weight can negatively alter the micronutrient status (Fogelholm et al. 1993; Fogelholm 2000).

For athletes, one possible exception to simply meeting the micronutrient RDA (and DRI) is the potential of antioxidants to influence performance outcomes. Exercise can result in an increased production of free radicals and other forms of reactive oxygen species (ROS). Theoretically these radicals and ROS may represent a mechanism in exercise-induced disturbances in a muscle's redox status that could result in fatigue or cellular injury (Powers and Hamilton 1999; Takanami et al. 2000). Enzymatic and nonenzymatic antioxidants work together in reducing the harmful effects of ROS at the cellular level. Antioxidant enzymes include superoxide dismutase, glutathione peroxidase, and catalase. The important nonenzymatic antioxidants include vitamins C and E and beta-carotene. Several animal studies (Asha Devi, Prathima, and Subramanyam 2003; Hargreaves et al. 2002; Hauer et al. 2003; Scott et al. 2001) have demonstrated improved endurance performance with antioxidant supplementation; limited evidence directly or indirectly supports improved human endurance or strength performance (Avery et al. 2003; Groussard et al. 2003; Powers and Hamilton 1999; Rokitski et al. 1994).

It is possible that training could alter the micronutrient status (tissue concentrations of vitamins and minerals) even if the RDA is being met. For many micronutrients, nutritional status is not easy to establish. Lack of certainty concerning individual dietary needs and inaccuracies in dietary assessment preclude the use of dietary intake assessments as the sole criteria of status. Furthermore, serum and plasma concentrations of micronutrients are relatively insensitive to marginal micronutrient deficiency, and additional body compartments or tissues must be identified that would better represent micronutrient status. Fogelholm (2000) argues that ideally the status should be assessed by use of a combination of clinical, anthropometric, dietary, and biochemical markers. Thus, accurately assessing micronutrient status is difficult at best.

The requirements for some vitamins, particularly vitamins B1, B2, and niacin, are approximately proportionate to the metabolic demand; thus requirements may increase with the demands of physical activity and the accumulative effects of training (Bobb, Pringle, and Ryan 1969; van der Beck 1991). Assuming that extra food intake with adequate micronutrients will be sufficient to compensate for the increased metabolic demand with increased physical activity may not be valid. It is possible that high-volume training or very intense training could alter micronutrient status to such an extent that performance is impaired. It is also possible that altered status as a result of the accumulation of stressors could contribute to overtraining. Unfortunately there are very few data concerning the micronutrient intake or status of athletes during intense or high-volume training, particularly for elite athletes.

Although there is little evidence that alterations in single nutrients lead to decreased performance, at least over the short term (Fogelholm 2000), there is evidence that marginal deficiencies of multiple micronutrients can (at times) negatively affect performance (Fogelholm 2000). A summary of Soviet research on nutrition (Dibbern 1981) suggests that stressful situations, such as altered environment, sport activities, and military tasks, decreased micronutrient status and increased the need for vitamins and minerals, particularly water-soluble vitamins and vitamins A and E. Zelessky (1977) indicated that multivitamin supplementation enhances the performance and "general well-being" of athletes with a low work tolerance. Van der Beck and colleagues (1991) found that combined depletion of thiamin, riboflavin, and B6 affected a measure of status, erythrocyte transketolase activation coefficient (E-TKAC), and aerobic power.

Subnormal resting serum concentrations of minerals have also been noted among athletes. Strauzenberg and colleagues (1979) reported low potassium and magnesium concentrations among female athletes participating in a variety of sports. Even relatively mild iron deficiency can have a negative effect on endurance performance (Deakin 2000). Anemia and low iron and ferritin concentrations have been reported among male and particularly female endurance athletes (Clement and Admundsun 1982; Deakin 2000). Ferritin is a protein that binds iron and is stored in the liver, spleen, and bones (Pike and Brown 1984). Thus ferritin represents a storage form of iron. It should be noted that a vegetarian diet can produce alterations in ferritin status, especially when associated with physical training. Female distance runners consuming less than 100 g (3.5 oz) of red meat per week had significantly lower resting serum ferritin concentrations and iron-binding capacity than a control group eating substantial amounts of red meat (Snyder, Dvorak, and Roepke 1989). As the vegetables eaten contained substantial amounts of iron, this observation (Snyder, Dvorak, and Roepke 1989) suggests that the form of dietary iron intake can affect iron status.

Among endurance athletes, iron deficiency could be associated with decreased aerobic power ($\dot{V}O_2$max), which could reduce performance. If the decreased aerobic power is associated with a decreased hemoglobin concentration, then performance may suffer substantially (Davies, Maguire, and Brooks 1982; Davies et al. 1984). Iron supplementation can partially or completely reestablish status; supplementation can return aerobic power back to normal faster than it can performance. Iron uptake can increase during periods of deficiency; however, low iron values may not be very responsive to diet and may necessitate supplementation in some athletes (Risser et al. 1988). Additionally, some research suggests that athletes may absorb less than half the dietary iron compared to anemic sedentary individuals (Ehn, Carlwark, and Hoglund 1980). Poor iron absorption and the potential for increased hemolysis due to vigorous physical activity could contribute to anemia.

Calcium and phosphorus are primary constituents of bone and teeth. Bone acts as a reservoir for both minerals, and in response to changes in blood concentrations (and endocrine influence) can store or release minerals (particularly calcium), thus increasing or decreasing calcium concentrations. Both calcium and phosphorus have high rates of turnover and must be continuously replaced through diet or in some cases supplementation.

Osteoporosis is a condition resulting from loss of bone mass. Osteoporosis, if left unchecked, leads to considerable structural weakness of the affected bone. There are two types of osteoporosis. Type 1 osteoporosis typically occurs in people 50 to 60 years old, is eight times more prevalent in women than in men, and is associated with distal radius and vertebral fractures. Type 2 osteoporosis is twice as prevalent in women compared to men; is associated with hip, pelvic, and distal humerus fractures, and usually occurs after age 70 (Johnston and Slemeda 1987; Kenny et al. 2003). Among women, osteoporosis is likely associated with menopause and the subsequent reduction in estrogen; this may explain the greater prevalence of osteoporosis among women. However, postmenopausal estrogen replacement therapy may slow the rate of bone loss, although it will not result in bone replacement (Lindsay 1987). Dietary calcium is important in preventing the development of osteoporosis (Moyad 2003). The RDA for calcium is 800 mg · day^{-1} for children 4 to 8 years, 1300 mg · day^{-1} for those 9 to 18 years, 1000 mg · day^{-1} for adults 19 to 50 years, and 1200 mg · day^{-1} for adults over 50 years (Dietary Reference Intakes 1997). However, the actual requirements for pre- and postmenopausal women may be as much as 1500 mg · day^{-1}. Some women may ingest less than the RDA in their diet (Heaney 1987; Moyad 2003); thus, increasing dietary calcium (and increasing weight-bearing exercise) may reduce the potential for developing osteoporosis.

Osteoporosis may be prevented or reversed by physical training, especially when associated with diets high in calcium or calcium supplementation. Studies (Conroy et al. 1993; Lane et al. 1988; Shibata et al. 2003) and reviews (Seguin and Nelson 2003; Stone 1990; Stone and Karatzeferi 2002) of the literature indicate that physical training, especially weight-bearing and weight training exercises, can increase the density and tensile strength of connective tissue, including bone. It is also likely that diet and exercise can better reduce the potential for developing osteoporosis compared to either intervention alone.

However, long-term high volumes of some types of training, such as distance running, may actually reduce bone density; thus some caution must be observed in the planning of training programs. For example, both male (Hetland, Haarbo, and Christiansen 1993) and female distance runners (Suominen 1993) can show reduced bone mineral density and bone mineral content compared to sedentary controls or lower-mileage athletes. Female athletes who become amenorrheic are especially susceptible to training-induced reductions in bone density and bone mineral content (Drinkwater et al. 1984; Lindsay 1987; Suominen 1993). Because of the susceptibility of female athletes, especially distance runners, to the development of low bone density and osteoporosis, increased dietary calcium and perhaps calcium and vitamin D supplementation, along with resistance training, may be of benefit.

Practical Nutritional Considerations for Athletes

Several aspects of nutrition beyond the norm are commonly encountered by athletes. The types and amounts of food eaten are important, but *when* foods are eaten may be just as important. For example, pre- and postevent meals can be of considerable benefit if the appropriate amount, type, and timing of ingestion are taken into account. Athletes (particularly in body weight category sports) are constantly faced with "making weight," and all athletes must pay special attention to fluid balance in order to avoid dehydration and its consequences.

Pre- and Postevent Meals

Athletes can derive both physiological and psychological benefits from a precompetition meal. Under certain conditions, protein intake shortly before training may enhance tissue remodeling and hypertrophy (Volek 2003); protein taken in as a large meal several hours before competition may not have profound physiological benefits but may be psychologically satisfying. A pretraining or precompetition meal high in fat may reduce performance by slowing gastric emptying.

The amount of carbohydrate taken in before an event is an important consideration because of the relationship of carbohydrate to performance. However, some data suggest that consuming relatively large amounts of glucose or sucrose 30 to 60 min before exercise can lead to a rebound depression of blood glucose as a result of an insulin spike in susceptible individuals (Foster, Costill, and Fink 1979). Other studies indicate that a rebound effect will not occur with the ingestion of simple sugars and that glucose ingestion 30 to 60 min preevent can make more glucose available to the muscle during exercise (Gleeson, Maugn, and Greenhaff 1986; Hargreaves et al. 1987). Large amounts of carbohydrate (and protein) ingested as preevent meals typically should be in the form of a drink, especially immediately before or during exercise, as considerable discomfort can occur from the ingestion of a large amount of carbohydrate in the form of food.

During prolonged aerobic exercise (Lamb and Brodowicz 1986) and repeated bouts of anaerobic exercise (Lambert et al. 1991), especially in hot environments, drinks containing glucose or glucose polymers may reduce cardiovascular and thermoregulatory disturbances better than water alone. The "strength" of the solutions should be 4% to 20% carbohydrate, and the drink should be consumed every 15 to 20 min, especially during the final stages of long-term endurance events when blood glucose may be decreasing. However, solutions above 6% may be unsuitable for some types of endurance events as a result of gastric upset or delayed gastric emptying. Although increasing the concentration of carbohydrate in solution will increase absorption, this effect is offset by a decreased gastric emptying. Carbohydrate solutions greater than 20% should not be used because they slow gastric emptying to the point that increased absorption will not compensate for the higher concentrations. Fructose should be avoided during exercise, as it has been associated with gastric upset.

Postevent meals should consist of high carbohydrate content to aid in glycogen restoration. One can maximize glycogen recovery by consuming 1 to 3 g carbohydrate per kilogram of body mass within 2 h and continuing every 2 h following exercise (Friedman, Neufer, and Dohm 1991; Sherman and Wimer 1991). Some evidence indicates that simple carbohydrates ingested during the first 6 h postexercise result in greater glycogen repletion than do complex carbohydrates (Kiens et al. 1990). Additionally, some evidence indicates that glucose more readily promotes muscle glycogen storage and that fructose may more adequately restore liver glycogen (Friedman, Neufer, and Dohm 1991). Although not all studies agree, the addition of protein may enhance glycogen repletion as well as contribute to tissue repair and remodeling, particularly when ingested as an immediate pretraining or recovery drink (Ivy 2001; Volek 2003).

Depressed Appetite

Loss of appetite often accompanies fatigued states and overwork or overtraining. Loss of appetite can result in too little energy and underconsumption of other nutrients (Jaquier 1987). The resulting loss of food energy and nutrients could compound or potentiate overreaching and overtraining, leading to poor performance. For example, alterations were noted in food intake among 16 junior weightlifters during a one-week camp (Stone et al. 1989, 1991b). Many of the athletes reported depressed appetites. Although the percentage of caloric intake for carbohydrate increased slightly, total calories were reduced by approximately 350 kcal as a result of a lower fat intake and simply eating less. Intake of B vitamins decreased over the week. Potentially this trend of fewer calories and lower vitamin intake, if continued, may eventually have contributed to an overtrained state. Therefore one factor that may help to avoid overtraining is adequate nutrition.

Water and Electrolytes

Water is the most plentiful component in the human body (Herbert 1983). Water makes up about 60% of a male's body weight and about 50% of a female's body weight. Of the total body water, about 55% is intracellular, 39% is intercellular, and about 6% is found in the plasma and lymph. Intracellular water functions in providing form and structural support and providing a medium for various biochemical reactions. Extracellular water serves as a means of transport and exchange of biological materials such as nutrients and metabolic by-products like gases, and as a medium for heat exchange. Even small changes in intra- or extracellular water content can result in large functional changes, since biological reactions, thermoregulation, and electrolyte balance are dependent on adequate water.

Dehydration can result in a variety of performance and health problems, even death. Dehydration resulting in the loss of as little as 1% to 2% of body mass, even for short periods of time (i.e., hours), can adversely affect a variety of mental and physiological functions. Mild dehydration (1-2%) can result in loss of performance, including cardiovascular function and performance (Maughn 2003; Saltin and Stenberg 1964), intermittent cycling performance (Walsh et al. 1994), perhaps muscle strength (Schoffstall et al. 2001), and memory processing and cognitive function (Wilson and Morley 2003). Indeed, prolonged mild dehydrated states have been associated with central nervous system damage (Wilson and Morley 2003). Of particular importance is the relationship between hydration state and thermoregulation; dehydration can promote feelings of fatigue, heat exhaustion, and heatstroke. Thus, any level of dehydration prior to and during exercise should be avoided.

During exercise, sweating rates can be affected by a number of factors, including temperature, humidity, and the type of clothing worn. It is not uncommon to lose 2% to 3% of body mass, mostly water, during a typical exercise session, especially in hot environments. When fluid replacement is inadequate, losses of up to 8% of body mass have been reported during very long-term exercise, such

as marathon running, or repeated high-intensity exercise such as fall football training (Bowers and Fox 1992; Roy and Irwin 1983). Of note is the observation that thirst often lags behind the need for water (Engell et al. 1987). Thus, fluid should be ingested even though thirst may not yet be recognized by the athlete. Typically 450 to 600 ml (15-20 fl oz) every 30 min should be adequate fluid replacement for long-term exercise, as well as prolonged intermittent high-intensity exercise such as football training.

Hydration of athletes, especially at altitude and in hot environments, is a must (Oppliger and Bartok 2002). While blood measures of hydration are the most accurate, they are invasive and quite expensive. Urinary specific gravity measured by refractometry is relatively easy and is a reasonably accurate indicator of hydration state. Weighing the athlete before and after practice is also valuable for determining rehydration; a pint (at least) per pound of body weight lost should be replaced.

Electrolytes are minerals that have a positive or negative charge, are associated with membrane potentials, and are soluble in body fluids (Herbert 1983). Substantial loss of electrolytes can interfere with a variety of physiological functions, including active and passive transport systems and fluid balance, and can indirectly affect thermoregulation as well as various metabolic functions. Of the electrolytes potentially lost during exercise, largely through sweat, the most important are sodium, potassium, and chloride (Maughn 2000). Sodium and potassium are cations (positive charge), and chloride is an anion (negative charge). Most electrolytes, including these three, are easily obtained in the diet.

Both sodium and potassium are related to blood pressure maintenance and to the development of hypertension. A high sodium intake may increase blood pressure; however, if the potassium intake is ≥40% of the sodium intake, blood pressure may decrease. The sodium:potassium ratio is a primary factor in reducing hypertension, particularly among sodium-sensitive individuals (Geleijnse, Kok, and Grobbee 2003; Kaplan 1986). A serum sodium: potassium ratio of 0.6 is generally recommended as helpful in reducing the incidence of hypertension.

Electrolytes are usually available in sport drinks, most of which also contain carbohydrate. These sport drinks, used to prevent dehydration, counter losses of electrolytes as a result of sweating and enhance recovery, particularly of glycogen. While electrolytes and some vitamins may be lost in sweat during exercise, losses are not typically large or significant, especially among acclimatized athletes (Herbert 1983). Although the content of sweat is variable, sweat is always hypotonic compared to fluid compartments; thus the net effect of sweating is an increase in osmolality of the plasma (Maughn 2000). Thus, the replacement of electrolytes may be unnecessary. However, although scientists' attitudes were initially skeptical, sport drinks likely offer benefits to athletes, at least under certain conditions. Most sport drinks contain low amounts of sodium (10-25 mmol · L^{-1}), partly to replace lost sodium and partly because of the expectation that sodium may enhance intestinal absorption of fluid (Burke and Read 1993). Additionally, during exercise lasting more than 4 h, such as ultramarathons, low plasma sodium concentrations can result (hyponatremia), especially if low-sodium drinks (water or cola) are ingested along the way (Maughn 2000). Training in hot environments may also result in low sodium concentrations, especially in nonacclimatized or partially acclimatized athletes; this condition usually takes three to five days to develop (McCance 1936; Sohar and Adar 1962), and it is possible that chronic ingestion of a sport drink could offset its development.

Weight Gain

It is not unusual to find body mass values of 100 to 160 kg (220-353 lb) in sports such as American football, rugby, and throwing events and in the heavier classes for boxing, judo, powerlifting, and weightlifting. Considerable thought and planning are required for an athlete to achieve these large body masses such that LBM gains are optimized and fat gains are minimized, resulting in a greater potential for superior performance. The planning includes not only physical training but also optimal nutritional strategies. For those athletes contemplating increases in body mass, the following issues should be considered.

Although the goal of gaining weight is to maximize the increase in LBM and minimize fat gains, well-trained athletes will almost always gain some fat (Forbes 1983, 1985; Forsberg, Tesch, and Karlsson 1978), and substantial gains in body mass are almost always accompanied by an increased body fat percentage (Forbes 1985).

Although not all studies agree (Dich et al. 2000), some data suggest that even in diets with the same number of calories (isocaloric), people can gain greater amounts of body fat with a diet that contains relatively more fat calories, especially if they stay with it for a long time (months) (Boissonneault,

Elson, and Pariza 1986; Donato and Hegsted 1985; Tsai and Gong 1987). Part of the reason for the greater gain in body fat with a greater dietary fat content may relate to the type of fat ingested. Some evidence indicates that monounsaturated fat may produce less fat gain because of their higher thermic effect compared to that of saturated fats, even in isocaloric diets (Piers et al. 2002). So it would be prudent when one is gaining body mass to keep the fat content under 30% of total calories and to ingest a relatively greater amount of unsaturated fats (70-80% of total fat intake). Keeping the fat content low may be difficult, particularly when the athlete is consuming substantial calories (>5000 kcal · day^{-1}). Additionally, individual differences can affect dietary outcomes. Some evidence indicates that individuals eating different amounts of macronutrients can maintain similar total and percent body fats even with similar energy expenditures (Whitley et al. 1998). Thus, meals should be planned carefully; if difficulty arises (such as large gains in fat), a nutritionist should be consulted.

Special weight gain products purchased over the counter are usually not warranted. Some of these products contain relatively large amounts of fat (>30%) and should be avoided. People can add extra energy to the diet by ingesting extra food; however, this often leads to increased and uncomfortable feelings of fullness, especially if the extra food is eaten in one sitting. If work, school, training schedules, cost, or simply individual preferences preclude the ingestion of extra food, then a supplement is useful. A relatively inexpensive source of protein and carbohydrate (and additional calories) is skim milk. Skim milk can be flavored to taste or mixed with other food and can be used in liquid or powder form. However, among advanced elite athletes, supplementation may be useful in order to promote positive adaptations to hard training (see chapter 7, "Ergogenic Aids").

It is best to increase body mass using a planned diet and specific physical training, particularly weight training, which can enhance gains in LBM. Gains in body mass should be made relatively slowly, at approximately 0.5 to 1.0 kg · week^{-1} (1-2 lb), as this lower rate of body mass gain has been observed to reduce body fat gains (Birrer 1984). Prolonged weight gain (less than six months) during which large amounts of weight are gained should occur at an even slower rate. During long-term weight gain, the rate of body mass increase should be about 0.25 to 0.5 kg · week^{-1} (0.5-1.0 lb) to ensure that fat gain is minimized.

Body mass gains and alterations in body composition should be monitored closely, every one to two weeks, by skinfolds or hydrostatic weighing. If the percentage of body fat increases markedly, then the training and diet program should be altered. The authors' observation suggests that high-level athletes (American football players, throwers, and weightlifters) already training with high volumes and intensities typically gain 1% to 3% in body fat for each 10 kg (22 lb) of body mass gained.

Upon retirement, large athletes should be encouraged to lose body mass. Reductions in body mass and fat content can reduce the potential for heart and other degenerative diseases. In the college and professional setting, it would not be unreasonable to make nutritional and training counseling available through the appropriate specialists.

Weight and Fat Loss

Weight loss (or making weight) is not uncommon among sports with stringent body weight limitations (body weight classes) such as boxing, judo, lightweight crew, wrestling, and weightlifting. It is essential to take care in both maintaining and losing body mass; otherwise performance can suffer. Even in sports without body weight classes, such as gymnastics, achieving and maintaining low body weight and body fat are necessary in order to be competitive. Achieving body mass and body fat goals often requires considerable body mass reduction. Athletes (and their coaches) contemplating a reduction in body mass should consider the following issues.

Untrained individuals and beginning athletes can lose body fat (and sometimes body mass) while increasing LBM as a result of caloric restriction and training (Stone et al. 1983). However, it is unlikely that athletes already possessing a low body fat and low percent fat can lose substantial body mass and not lose some LBM as well, especially if caloric restriction is used to enhance body mass loss (Ballor et al. 1988; Walberg et al. 1988). The loss of LBM due to caloric restriction can be reduced through training, particularly resistance training (Ballor et al. 1988), and through use of a high-protein diet during the caloric-restricted period (Walberg et al. 1988). The use of fad diets such as total liquid diets should be discouraged.

The ideal weight for performance is not necessarily the lowest body mass an athlete can maintain. Semistarved or dehydrated athletes do not perform well. Caloric restriction can potentiate depleted energy stores, fatigue, and overtraining (Stone et al. 1991b). Among children and adolescents, some

evidence suggests that caloric restriction can reduce adult stature (Smith 1976).

The *maximum* rate of acceptable loss of body mass appears to be about 1% per week. For most athletes this would be approximately 0.5 to 1.0 kg · week^{-1} (1-2 lb) and would equal a caloric deficit of about 500 to 1000 kcal · day^{-1} (Fogelholm et al. 1993). Slower rates of body mass loss are typically more desirable, resulting from a caloric deficit of about 100 to 400 kcal · day^{-1}. Faster rates can potentiate marked loss of LBM, glycogen stores, dehydration, and loss of vitamin and mineral intake and can increase the potential for overtraining (Fogelholm et al. 1993; Walberg-Rankin 2000). Caloric restriction and loss of body mass carried out over more than four weeks, or a total body mass loss of more than 5%, may also alter the micronutrient status of the athlete such that performance could be adversely affected (Fogelholm 1993). It is important to realize that the weight loss needs of very small or very large athletes have not been adequately addressed in the literature.

Body fat may also be too low. A low body fat content in males has been associated with lowered testosterone concentrations and increased incidence of injury (Strauss, Lanese, and Malarky 1985; Vorobyev 1978). The incidence of impact injury and perhaps overuse injury may also be increased as a result of low body fat (Nindl et al. 1996; Wang et al. 2003). Body fat in males should typically not drop below 6% and in females not below 10%.

People can accomplish rapid reductions in body mass with fluid restriction (short-term). The practitioners believe that these rapid reductions enhance performance because much of the LBM acquired at heavier body masses is retained. Although this method of rapid weight loss is widely practiced, it may be accompanied by the following potentially nonbeneficial effects (Walberg-Rankin 2000):

Reduced strength (probably least affected unless weight loss is very rapid) and power

Decreased low- and high-intensity endurance

Lowered plasma volumes

Reduced cardiac function

Impairment of thermal regulation

Decreased renal function

Decreased glycogen concentrations

Loss of electrolytes

Rehydration often takes more than 5 h. Although the practice of dehydration-rehydration is common among weight class sports, the potential positive effects of dehydration-rehydration during subsequent competition may be negated. Observation suggests that the effect of dehydration is often quite negative (Vorobyev 1978; authors' observation), especially with losses of more than 2% body mass. Furthermore, the cumulative effects of repeated bouts of rapid dehydration may also be negative (Vorobyev 1978). Rehydration by artificial means, such as intravenous infusion of fluid, can be dangerous and should be avoided. When making weight it would be prudent to avoid foods that cause water retention (salty foods) and high-fiber foods.

CHAPTER SUMMARY

During the last 25 years, great strides have taken place in nutrition and especially sport nutrition. Several factors have brought nutrition and nutritionists to the forefront of sport management and have made nutrition an integral part of planning programs for sports. These factors include the realization that the RDA values for some nutrients, particularly protein, can be inadequate for the demands of many sports; the understanding that recovery drinks can actually enhance recovery; and the implementation of superior methods of gaining and losing weight. Indeed, some universities now offer specialty degrees in sport nutrition. As more interest develops and more research takes place in the future, it is likely that nutrition for sport will play an even greater role in sport success.

CHAPTER 7

Ergogenic Aids

Ergogenic (from Greek) means "work creating." Therefore, ergogenic aids have the common characteristic of enhancing work (i.e., performance). The concept of ergogenic aids or performance enhancers is not new, and ergogenic aids have long been used in daily work endeavors or in stressful situations such as fighting. For example, for several centuries some South American Indians have chewed coca leaves to help sustain hard work, and Viking berserkers ate mushrooms containing muscarine before battle.

We would argue that being competitive is part of the basic nature of humankind. This competitive nature is quite obvious in sport. Athletes make an effort to outperform their opponents or may actually compete with themselves in attempting to create personal records. As a result of a competitive spirit, humans have developed an array of tools to enhance performance. These tools can be referred to as ergogenic aids. The use of ergogenic aids in sport also has a very long history, at least as far back as the ancient Olympics (Antonio and Stout 2001; Burks 1981; Catlin and Murray 1996; Grivetti and Applegate 1997). Ergogenic aids can be classed into environmental, psychological, mechanical, pharmaceutical, and nutritional aids to sport performance. Currently, the use of ergogenic aids (or potential ergogenic aids) is commonplace in sport.

In this chapter, we very briefly discuss a few examples of each class of ergogenic aid; it is not our purpose to provide an in-depth discussion of the potential usefulness of every potential ergogenic aid. Detailed information, particularly concerning potential nutritional and pharmaceutical ergogenic aids, appears in several reviews of the literature (Antonio and Stout 2001; Bohn, Khodace, and Schwenk 2003; Corrigan 2002; Kreider 1999; Silver 2001; Stone 1993, 1995; Thien and Landry 1995; Wagenmakers 1999; Williams 1984, 1996, 2000). Our intention here is to provide discussion challenging the reader to consider whether or not the use of ergogenic aids and the testing for ergogenic aids follow ethical and practical lines of reasoning.

Environmental Ergogenic Aids

Although the environment is not typically thought of as an ergogenic aid, certain manipulations of the environment may have a positive or negative effect on sport performance.

One way of manipulating the environment is to alter the playing field or surface to enhance the performance of athletes (or negate an opponent's strengths). Examples would include mowing the grass on a football field to enhance a team's running game, allowing the grass to grow longer in order to slow down a good running team, and slanting the foul line on a softball field so that bunts have a greater potential to roll foul (or fair).

One might also alter the atmospheric conditions to enhance the performance of athletes. Examples might be opening or closing large doors in a stadium to alter air flow (wind speed and direction) during a discus competition so that athletes on the home team have a favorable wind and the opponents do not (M. Ritchie-Stone, personal communication).

Another method of manipulation is altering equipment to take advantage of changing environmental conditions in order to enhance the performance of athletes. Examples might include changing the wax on skis to fit the ice or snow conditions and using altitude tents or rooms to simulate live-high–train-low conditions (Saunders et al. 2003; Wilber et al. 2003).

For strength-power athletes, the use of specialized shoes and better surfaces on lifting platforms for strength training and weightlifting competition could enhance performance and provide for greater athlete safety.

Psychological Ergogenic Aids

While physical training can raise the state of physiological preparedness to optimal or maximal levels, it should be rather obvious that the mind (psychological factors) can have a profound influence on performance. Indeed, the achievement of the "ideal performance state" is a goal for most athletes (Williams 1993). This state of mind can include several characteristics:

- Being in the "zone"—a disorientation of time and space
- A sense of personal control
- A sense that the physical demands are effortless
- Increased ability to concentrate on the task at hand
- Automatic motor control—not having to think about or analyze movement during a performance
- Not fearing failure

These characteristics, while generally thought of as associated with competition, can also be advantageous for training. Although achieving these characteristics can be an intrinsic process, external aids may assist the athlete. Such aids might include the following:

- Proper motivational techniques used by a coach (McClelland et al. 1953; Whitmore 1992)
- Proper use of positive and negative reinforcement (Martens 1975)
- Arousal techniques (Hanin 1989)
- Proper use of relaxation techniques
- Mental imagery (Sinclair and Sinclair 1994; Wilkes and Summers 1984)

These techniques can be considered potential ergogenic aids in that they may help a specific athlete achieve levels of training or performance that are not typical. In this respect the sport psychologist may be considered an ergogenic aid as he or she assists in developing these techniques and

potentially enhancing performance. A more complete description of psychological factors and their influence on training and performance appears in chapter 11, "Psychological Aspects of Resistance Training."

Mechanical Ergogenic Aids

A variety of mechanical aids to sport performance have been developed over the years. These can be *roughly* divided into those devices that enhance the outcome of training (i.e., physical and physiological adaptation) and those that might enhance performance in competition.

Training devices can include weights, weighted vests, resistance training machines, electrical stimulation to enhance muscle growth, chains and elastic bands, and heart rate monitors.

Chains and elastic bands can alter the normal pattern of resistance afforded by free weights (and perhaps machines) by adding or reducing resistance at specific points within a range of motion. For example, elastic bands suspended from the top of a power rack can reduce the resistance below the sticking region during a squat. As the bar (lifter) ascends through the sticking region, resistance increases as the movement nears the end of the range of motion; because more external force can be exerted toward the end of the range of motion, the added resistance may train this range more effectively than traditional squats. Chains have also been used to add resistance through a range of motion; however, the effectiveness of this type of training is still unknown (Ebben et al. 2002).

Recently, vibration training has been used to enhance neuromuscular training especially among strength-power athletes. Vibration activates muscle afferents, modulates hormone release (Gosselink et al. 2004), and can result in increased reflexive activity and increased blood flow, which may alter subsequent muscle activity (Bosco, Cardinale, and Tsarpela 1999; Delecluse, Roelants, and Verschueren 2003; Rittweger, Beller, and Felsenberg 2000). Acute vibration (single application) has been shown to enhance maximum strength and explosive strength (jumping performance) among untrained males and females (Bosco et al. 2000; Torvinen et al. 2002; Warman, Humphries, and Purton 2002). Furthermore, acute vibration has been shown to increase serum testosterone and growth hormone concentrations and decrease cortisol concentrations postvibration (Bosco et al. 2000). Vibration training alone using whole-body vibration (vibration plates) may (Delecluse, Roelants, and Verschueren 2003;

Roelants et al. 2004) or may not (De Ruiter et al. 2003) increase maximum strength or measures of explosive strength and power among untrained subjects. When whole-body vibration is coupled with strength training, it may (Delecluse, Roelants, and Verschueren 2003) or may not (Roelants et al. 2004) enhance strength to a greater degree than strength training alone among untrained subjects.

The potential beneficial effects of vibration exercise and training may be enhanced through the use of appropriate frequencies and amplitudes of vibration, as well as through appropriate timing of the vibratory treatment (Cardinale and Lim 2003; Cardinale and Pope 2003; Warman, Humphries, and Purton 2002). Thus, vibration is a potentially useful tool for enhancing neuromuscular performance among athletes, particularly strength-power athletes (Cardinale and Pope 2003). Some caution should be used in the long-term application of vibration, as damage to soft tissue is a possibility (Cardinale and Pope 2003).

Performance devices might include Klap skates, speed suits, and padding. Several banned mechanical ergogenic aids also come to mind, such as corked bats in baseball, lengthened hammer wires, and heated blades on bobsleds.

Varieties of mechanical aids have been used in competition; these include items such as platforms and special shoes (e.g., weightlifting shoes). For example, supersuits and bench press shirts can substantially increase the amount of weight lifted in the squat and bench press.

Essentially, these mechanical ergogenic devices are products of technological advances, enterprising coaches and athletes, and good engineering.

Pharmaceuticals (Drugs) and Nutritional Supplements

Drugs and nutritional supplements are being considered under the same topical heading because it is not always easy to define exactly how to categorize a product or substance. For this discussion one should consider the following definitions:

A drug is a substance that alters a physiological or biochemical process.

A nutritional supplement is a component of a normal physiological or biochemical process.

However, these simple definitions leave considerable room for debate and controversy (especially from a legal standpoint); thus more detailed defini-

tions are necessary and can be used. According to the Food and Drug Administration (FDA), a drug is any article (not including devices) intended for use in the diagnosis, cure, mitigation, treatment, or prevention of a disease, or any article (other than food) intended to affect the structure and function of the body. The FDA mandates a premarket evaluation for a drug before it can be sold. This evaluation includes clinical studies of the drug's effectiveness, potential interactions with other substances, safety, and appropriate dosage (Antonio and Stout 2001). The FDA does not mandate premarket evaluation for supplements. As defined by the Office of Dietary Supplements at the National Institutes of Health (NIH), a dietary supplement is a product (except tobacco) intended to supplement the diet that contains one or more of a number of dietary ingredients (a vitamin, mineral, amino acid, herb or other botanical, a dietary substance intended to supplement the diet by increasing the total dietary intake, or a combination of any of these ingredients); a dietary supplement also is intended for ingestion in the form of a liquid, capsule, powder, softgel, or gelcap and is not represented as a conventional food or as the sole item of a meal or the diet (Antonio and Stout 2001; Dietary Supplement Health and Education Act [DSHEA] 1994).

Drugs

Using these definitions, the discussion will begin with drugs. We consider two categories: drugs that potentially enhance protein synthesis, and stimulants. Primary examples are discussed for each category. These categories were chosen as they represent commonly used ergogenic aids.

Androgens

Protein synthesis enhancers include both drugs that potentially stimulate protein synthesis directly and those that have anticatabolic properties. Perhaps the best-known drugs within this category are androgens. *Androgen* (from Greek) means "male creating." Androgens are steroid hormones, and the primary androgen is *testosterone*. Testosterone is produced in relatively large amounts by the testes of males and in very small amounts by the adrenal gland. In females, small amounts are produced by the ovaries and adrenal glands. Androgens' primary functions involve growth and maintenance of the primary and secondary sex characteristics of males; androgens also have anabolic and anticatabolic functions (see chapter 5, "Neuroendocrine Factors"). The normal pathway for testosterone production is shown in figure 7.1. Anabolic steroids (AS) are synthetic derivatives of testosterone and have been widely used in medicine and sports, particularly strength-power sports and bodybuilding (Kicman and Gower 2003; Silver 2001; Stone 1993). Although attempts have been made at separating the anabolic effects from androgenic effects, there has been little success; indeed, review of the literature indicates that a weak androgen is also a weak anabolic agent (Stone 1993).

Androgens are potent ergogenic aids (Kuhn 2002; Silver 2001; Stone 1993) that promote protein synthesis (Hartgens and Kuipers 2004) and anticatabolic effects (Hickson et al. 1990), especially during recovery after weight training exercise. Greater muscle hypertrophy and possibly increased incorporation of satellite cells can also occur with androgen administration, even among already well-trained athletes (Kadi et al. 1999). Enhanced glycogen repletion (Ustunel, Akkoyunlu, and Demir 2003), higher androgen:cortisol ratios, lower lactate concentrations, and lower subjective feelings of fatigue (Rozenek et al. 1990) also potentially contribute to enhanced recovery and adaptation. Androgens can beneficially alter body composition, lowering fat content and raising lean body mass, especially when coupled with heavy resistance training (Bhasin 2003a, 2003b; Stone 1993). From a performance standpoint, androgens can have profound effects on strength and power production (Alen, Hakkinen, and Komi 1984; Bhasin et al. 1996, 2001), can increase strength-power performance in a dose-dependent manner (Bhasin et al. 2001; Storer et al. 2003), and generally increase work tolerance (Tamaki et al. 2001). Furthermore, androgens may have profound effects on aggressive behavior and sport training drive leading to superior sport performance (Salvadora et al. 1999; Stone 1993). Considering the potential effects of androgen administration, it is not hard to understand the temptation for athletes to use these drugs as ergogenic aids.

In recent years prohormones have become increasingly popular as potential ergogenic aids. These prohormones include dehydroepiandrosterone (DHEA), androstenedione, norandrostenedione, and pregnenolone, which can be sold as food supplements (DSHEA 1994) (which is stretching the definition). Although they are weak androgens, these products are marketed on the basis that they are precursors for the production of testosterone (see figure 7.1). Despite considerable press coverage (e.g., on Mark McGwire), to date these prohormones have been shown to have little effect as an ergogenic aid (Brown et al. 1999; Earnest et al. 2000; King et al. 1999), and in normal males they may actually raise estrogen concentrations (King et al. 1999).

Androgens, particularly high doses or long-term administration, may be associated with a number of potential nonbeneficial health effects including masculinization among women, certain types of cancer, cardiovascular disease, and liver disease (Kieman and Gower 2003; Silver 2001; Stone 1993; Wu 1997). Most of the potential nonbeneficial effects are related to ingestion of 17-alpha-alkylated steroids, which are typically oral preparations (Kopera 1993; Stone 1993). Furthermore, as

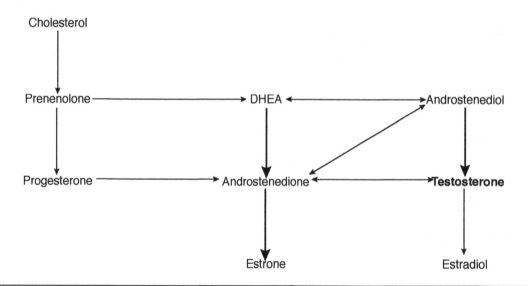

Figure 7.1 The biochemical production of testosterone.

with most drugs, untoward effects increase with dosage. Although these side effects are possible, the degree to which they actually occur in users or past users may not be as great as once believed, particularly when doses are low (Evans 2004; Street, Antonio, and Cudlipp 1996).

Growth Hormone

Growth hormone or somatotropin is a polypeptide hormone secreted in a pulsatile manner by the anterior pituitary gland. Growth hormone has various functions including stimulation of protein synthesis and mobilization of fatty acids for energy. The influence of growth hormone on protein synthesis is largely mediated by insulin-like growth factor 1 (IGF_1) (see chapter 5, "Neuroendocrine Factors").

Athletes and coaches believe that human growth hormone (hGH) administration in combination with resistance training can enhance muscle growth and maximum strength beyond levels achieved with training alone. Because of this belief and the extreme difficulty of accurately and reliably measuring exogenous hGH (Kneiss et al. 2003; Sonksen 2001), its illicit use in sport has increased over the last decade.

Acute administration of hGH can stimulate increased amino acid uptake and protein synthesis in animals and human adults (Fryberg, Gelfeld, and Barrett 1991). Human GH treatment can enhance muscle mass and strength among hGH-deficient human adults (Cuneo et al. 1991). Some (Rudman et al. 1990; Svensson et al. 2003) but not all studies (Lange et al. 2002) have shown that prolonged hGH treatment can increase lean body mass and strength in elderly men and women. Replacement therapy among adults with adult-onset hGH deficiency leads to strength increases that may not be fully normalized, resulting in relatively large but weak skeletal muscle (Svensson et al. 2003). Additionally, growth hormone administration may alter the myosin heavy chain profile, resulting in an increase in the amount of MHC 2X isoform (Lange et al. 2002).

However, it should be noted that there are few data to indicate an ergogenic effect in adults with a normally functioning pituitary. Furthermore, animal studies (Bigland and Jehring 1952) have demonstrated that while growth hormone administration could increase muscle cross-sectional area in young rats, the muscles of these animals showed less isometric strength per gram than those in nontreated animals. In old rats, growth hormone administration and treadmill exercise produced an increased muscle cross-sectional area, and the maximum tetanic strength of the triceps surae muscle

was increased by 23% in 2.5 months. While these data indicate that hGH could have an ergogenic effect, closer scrutiny suggests that use in young athletes may not produce the same effects as in elderly persons.

Acromegaly produces gigantism and apparently large musculature. However, the strength of human acromegliacs is not increased in proportion to their size (Lombardo, Hickson, and Lamb 1991; Nagulesparen et al. 1976), which agrees with the earlier animal observations of Bigland and Jehring (1952). Such individuals have a greatly increased connective tissue development that accounts for much of their large size (Nagulesparen et al. 1976). Among young men, hGH administration in conjunction with resistance training led to an increased lean body mass and a significant decrease in fat mass after six weeks; however, functional alterations were not reported (Crist et al. 1988). Administration of hGH produced significant increases in whole-body protein synthesis and lean body mass among young men who performed resistance training for 12 weeks (Yarasheski et al. 1992). However, there were no increases in muscle mass or strength, a finding consistent with the increased connective tissue seen among individuals with acromegaly. Presently, there are few data to support the use of hGH as an ergogenic aid in young athletes (Frisch 1999).

Potential adverse effects of hGH administration include excessive bone and connective tissue growth, enlargement of organs, cardiomyopathy, reduction in insulin sensitivity, and insulin resistance (Frisch 1999; Lombardo, Hickson, and Lamb 1991).

Administration of large amounts of amino acids (e.g., arginine and lysine) has been used to raise hGH "naturally" as a result of increased pulsatile secretion (Besset et al. 1982; Isidori, Lo Monaco, and Cappa 1981). These data have prompted athletes to attempt to increase hGH using amino acids as a nutritional supplement. However, neither acute nor long-term ingestion of amino acids (weeks) has demonstrated an effect on resting or postexercise concentrations of hGH among weight trainers (Lambert et al. 1993; Walberg-Rankin et al. 1994) or strength-power athletes in hard training (Fogelholm et al. 1993; Fry et al. 1993; Gater et al. 1992). Thus, there is little reason to believe that amino acid supplementation would markedly raise growth hormone among athletes.

Stimulants

Stimulants are substances that can increase alertness and arousal and reduce fatigue. Stimulants include sympathomimetics such as epinephrine and methoxamine, as well as central nervous system stimulants such as amphetamines and caffeine. Stimulants such as caffeine, ephedra alkaloids, and pseudoephedrine are commonly used by the nonsport populace, but ephedra and most related compounds are currently banned by many sport governing bodies (including the International Olympic Committee/World Anti-Doping Agency [IOC/WADA]). While most stimulants are relatively easy to detect and are no longer used widely by athletes, two stimulants (caffeine and pseudoephedrine) deserve discussion.

Caffeine and the related compounds theophylline and theobromine are methyl xanthines found naturally in coffee, tea, and chocolate. A derivative of theophylline (aminophylline) is commonly used to treat the symptoms of asthma. Caffeine is likely the most commonly used drug in the world (Paluska 2003). As an athletic ergogenic aid, caffeine is probably best known as potentially enhancing long-term endurance performance by inhibiting glycogen depletion and enhancing the use of free fatty acids for energy by inhibiting the inactivation of cyclic adenosine monophosphate (Conway, Orr, and Stannard 2003; Ryu et al. 2001). However, caffeine is also a central nervous system stimulant. Caffeine can cross the blood-brain barrier and antagonize the effects of adenosine by interfering with the attachment of adenosine to its receptor (Paluska 2003; Spriet and Gibala 2004). Through antagonism of the effects of adenosine in the brain, concentrations of stimulatory neurotransmitters remain elevated (El Yacoubi, Costenin, and Vaugeois 2003). Thus, low-dose caffeine ingestion during training or competition may allow the intensity (power output) of exercise to remain higher than would otherwise be possible (Spriet and Gibala 2004). Maintenance of higher intensities during training may increase the adaptive response.

Pseudoephedrine (PSE) is a sympathomimetic with peripheral effects similar to those of epinephrine and central effects somewhat similar to those of amphetamine, but less intense. Pseudoephedrine and similar drugs such as ephedra alkaloids are potential ergogenic aids and are commonly used by athletes and recreational trainers (Bohn, Khodace, and Schwenk 2003).

Oral preparations of PSE are used as a decongestant and are commonly found in over-the-counter medicines. While PSE potentially has ergogenic properties as a stimulant, its efficacy as an ergogenic aid, when taken in doses for medical purposes, is questionable (DeMeersman, Getty, and Schaefer 1987; Swain et al. 1997). However, over-the-counter preparations do contain enough PSE to raise urinary concentrations to levels above 12 mcg · ml^{-1} (the former IOC/WADA cutoff for doping) for at least 16 h (Chester et al. 2004). In the past, athletes testing positive for PSE (with doses consistent with medical use) received a warning or lighter punishments from the appropriate sport governing body.

Interestingly, both caffeine and PSE were removed from the IOC/WADA banned list effective January 1, 2004. The reasoning dealt with the ubiquitous nature of caffeine and the common use of PSE as a decongestant. One must wonder if the underlying reason for removing these agents from the banned list was that medals have been taken away as a result of athletes' testing positive for low doses of substances that may not be ergogenic aids (e.g., the 2000 Olympic women's gymnastics competition).

Nutritional Supplements

While much of the topic of nutritional supplements is covered in chapter 6, "Nutrition and Metabolic Factors," one area of primary importance is addressed here: recovery and adaptation and supplements that potentially enhance this process.

Creatine (Cr) is an amino acid derivative synthesized primarily in the liver, kidneys, and pancreas at an average rate of 1 to 2 g · day^{-1} (Loike, Somes, and Silverstein 1986; Walker 1979). The total Cr stored in the body (free and phosphorylated form) is about 120 g for a 70 kg (154 lb) person (Balsom, Soderlund, and Ekblom 1994). Approximately 95% of the total Cr pool is stored in skeletal muscle. Approximately 60% to 66% of the Cr in skeletal muscle is in the form of phosphocreatine (PCr). Elimination of Cr at a rate of 1 to 2 g · day^{-1} (approximately 1.6% of the total Cr pool per day) occurs in the kidneys through irreversible conversion of Cr and excretion of creatinine. Approximately half of the daily need of Cr is obtained from dietary intake, primarily from meat and fish. Endogenous synthesis of Cr from the amino acids glycine, arginine, and methionine contributes to the remaining daily need of Cr (Kreider 1999).

Creatine is part of the phosphagen system and functions to rapidly rephosphorylate ADP. As a result of short-term anaerobic exercise, particularly explosive exercises, the energy supplied to rephosphorylate ADP to ATP is primarily determined by the amount of PCr stored in the muscle. Performance is likely to deteriorate as PCr is depleted due to the inability to restore ATP at a rate matching muscle contraction intensity (Balsom, Soderlund, and Ekblom 1994). Because the availability of PCr can markedly affect the amount of energy generated by muscle during brief periods of high-intensity exercise, increasing muscle Cr content through supplementation could increase the availability of PCr. Increased PCr stores, in turn, would allow a higher rate of resynthesis of ATP postexercise (Balsom, Soderlund, and Ekblom 1994). Although not all studies agree (Delecluse, Roelants, and Verschueren 2003; Finn et al. 2001; Wilder et al. 2002), most studies and reviews indicate that Cr supplementation can increase muscle Cr content; enhance explosive exercise and repeated explosive exercise performance (Ekerson et al. 2004; Haff et al. 2000; Kirksey et al. 1999; Koak 2003; Rawson and Volek 2003; Schedel, Terrier, and Schutz 2000); and promote greater gains in strength, power, and fat-free mass during training (Rawson and Volek 2003; Stone et al. 1999). Improved explosive performance as a result of training and supplementation is more likely to be positively effected when the supplementation period lasts at least five days (Eckerson et al. 2004).

Some data indicate that males may derive a greater ergogenic effect from Cr supplementation than females (Ayoama, Hiruma, and Sasaki 2003), and that gains in strength and power are proportional to the Cr uptake by the muscle (Kilduff et al. 2003). The latter finding, suggesting that individuals already having high concentrations of muscle Cr may not benefit from Cr supplementation, may explain why Cr supplementation produces somewhat variable ergogenic results. Additionally, some data indicate that supplementation effects may be more pronounced in large muscle mass exercises compared to small muscle mass exercises (Urbanski, Vincent, and Yaspelkis 1999).

Creatine supplementation typically takes two forms, loading and maintenance. Creatine loading involves increasing dietary availability of Cr in an attempt to rapidly increase muscle concentrations of total Cr and PCr. This typically involves ingesting $0.3 \text{ g} \cdot \text{kg}^{-1} \cdot \text{day}^{-1}$ for five to seven days, followed by the maintenance period ($0.03 \text{ g} \cdot \text{kg}^{-1} \cdot \text{day}^{-1}$) for several weeks to maintain saturated stores. The loading phase is necessary only when very rapid muscle tissue saturation is needed; otherwise, saturation will occur with the maintenance dose, although this may take several weeks.

While anecdotal evidence and speculation have suggested that Cr may be related to nonbeneficial health effects such as heat illness, muscle cramps, kidney disease, and liver disease (Juhn 2000),

to date only one objective report has indicated significant adverse effects as a result of Cr supplementation. Schroeder and colleagues (2001) found evidence that Cr supplementation was related to abnormal anterior compartment pressures at rest and after aerobic exercise. However, subsequent research indicated that compartment pressure alterations are transient and do not induce symptoms of compartment syndrome (Hile et al. 2006). Indeed, the majority of studies and reviews in both animals and humans have not shown any evidence of heat illness, muscle cramps, muscle injury, heart disease, kidney disease, liver disease, or abnormal hematological indices as a result of Cr supplementation lasting several days to several years (Farquhar and Zambraski 2002; Kreider et al. 2003; Mendes and Tirapegui 2002; Poortmans and Francaux 2000; Robinson et al. 2000; Schilling et al. 2001; Taes et al. 2003a, 2003b). Some evidence suggests that Cr supplementation may, in fact, reduce the incidence of heat illness, muscle injury, and muscle cramps (Greenwood et al. 2003; Schilling et al. 2001); enhance glucose tolerance (Derave et al. 2003); enhance glycogen storage (van Loon et al. 2004); improve brain performance (Rae et al. 2003); and play a role in protection against neurological and cardiovascular or atherosclerotic disease (Taes et al. 2003a; Wyss and Schulze 2002).

One side effect that may occur with Cr supplementation is water retention (Demant and Rhodes 1999; Kutz and Gunter 2003). Body mass gains due to water retention range from 1% to 3% and appear to be largely dependent on the dose and individual characteristics of the athlete, with most of the water retention occurring within the first few weeks of supplementation (Brilla et al. 2003; Demant and Rhodes 1999; Kutz and Gunter 2003; Powers et al. 2003; Saab et al. 2002). Exactly how the water retention is compartmentalized (intra- vs. extracellular) is not completely clear (Brilla et al. 2003; Powers et al. 2003; Saab et al. 2002); however, the influx of water into the cell may stimulate or otherwise be associated with increased protein synthesis (Brilla et al. 2003; Haussinger and Lang 1991; Haussinger et al. 1993). Considering these data, it is not surprising that Cr has become one of the most popular nutritional supplements among athletes in recent times (Schilling et al. 2001).

Recovery-adaptation nutrition supplementation is one of the most important areas for research dealing with ergogenic aids. The importance of recovery relates not only to returning the athlete to the preexercise state (recovery), but also to making positive physical, physiological, and performance improvements (adaptation) to the training program. Evidence indicates that nutrition can play an important role in the recovery-adaptation process. This concept concerns not only what nutrients are important to recovery-adaptation but also the type and timing of nutrient intake (Lemon, Berardi, and Noreen 2002). Ivy and Portman (2004) indicate that there are three important phases to consider in promoting adaptation to strength training: the energy phase, the anabolic phase, and the growth phase.

• The energy supply phase involves the use of energy during a training session. A primary objective of the physiological machinery involved in training is to release and supply sufficient energy to drive the training session. During exercise, cortisol, catecholamine, and nutrient uptake by muscle rises and insulin concentrations and energy stores decrease. As insulin is a strong anabolic regulator in muscle, maintaining higher concentrations during (and after) exercise would provide a more anabolic environment. Appropriate supplementation can reduce the decrease in blood insulin concentration and can increase nutrient (carbohydrate, amino acids, and vitamins) supply to the muscle. Supplying carbohydrate and protein before and during this phase can potentially reduce the decrease in glycogen stores and promote faster resynthesis of glycogen (Conley and Stone 1996; Haff et al. 2003; Zawadzki, Yaspelkis, and Ivy 1992), may blunt the catabolic response (e.g., the rise in cortisol), may limit subsequent immunosuppression (Gleeson, Lancaster, and Bishop 2001; Lancaster et al. 2003), can increase the intensity with which the training session proceeds (i.e., less fatigue) (Conley and Stone 1996; Haff et al. 2003), and can prepare the neuromuscular system for enhanced recovery and adaptation. The addition of antioxidants (vitamins C and E) during this period may help limit muscle damage (Rokitzki et al. 1994).

• The anabolic phase is a 30 to 45 min period immediately following the end of a training session during which nutrient uptake by muscle is still elevated and synthetic reactions, including those involving glycogen and protein, are initiated. While protein synthesis is partly dependent on hormonal influence, especially insulin, it is also very sensitive and responsive to changes in blood amino acid concentrations (Biolo et al. 1995; Biolo et al. 1997; Fafournoux, Bruhat, and Jousse 2000; Rasmussen et al. 2000; Van Loon et al. 2000a, 2000b; Volek 2004). During the anabolic phase, muscle nutrient uptake (resulting from the effects

of exercise) is still elevated; however, at the end of this 45 min window, nutrient uptake begins to decrease, muscles actually become insulin resistant, and anabolic activity decreases (Ivy 2001; Ivy et al. 1988; Levenhagen et al. 2002). Supplementation of carbohydrate, protein, and antioxidants during this phase can stimulate glycogen resynthesis and protein accretion (i.e., tissue repair and hypertrophy), and may limit further immunosuppression (Ivy and Portman 2004).

• The growth phase has the longest time frame, extending from the end of the anabolic phase until the next training session. It is during this phase that the majority of adaptations in the neuromuscular system occur. Ivy and Portman (2004) identify two subphases within the growth phase that can be characterized by the rate of anabolic activity. (1) The rapid growth segment is a period of high anabolic activity lasting up to 4 h beyond the anabolic phase, provided that it is properly primed by supplementation during the anabolic phase. (2) The sustained or slow growth segment is a relatively long period of slower anabolic activity and is primarily influenced by the nonsupplemental diet; the provision of adequate protein becomes a primary factor (Forslund et al. 1998, 1999). During this period a positive nitrogen balance and muscle growth can be stimulated as long as nutrient intake is sufficient (see chapter 6, "Nutrition and Metabolic Factors"). Adequate protein intake is necessary (Ivy and Portman 2004; Volek 2004). For example, among bodybuilders and strength trainers, Fern and colleagues (1991) found that $3.3 \text{ g} \cdot \text{kg}^{-1} \cdot \text{day}^{-1}$ of protein produced greater gains in muscle mass than $1.3 \text{ g} \cdot \text{kg}^{-1} \cdot \text{day}^{-1}$, indicating that large amounts of protein stimulated lean body mass growth. However, the authors noted that at the higher intake (3.3 g), a significant amount was oxidized and not used to promote growth. Tarnopolsky (1999) found that $1.4 \text{ g} \cdot \text{kg}^{-1} \cdot \text{day}^{-1}$ produced greater gains in lean body mass compared to $0.9 \text{ g} \cdot \text{kg}^{-1} \cdot \text{day}^{-1}$, but additional gain did not occur when the intake was increased to $2.4 \text{ g} \cdot \text{kg}^{-1} \cdot \text{day}^{-1}$. Furthermore, some evidence (Lemon 2000) suggests that at least 1.6 to $1.8 \text{ g} \cdot \text{kg}^{-1} \cdot \text{day}^{-1}$ of protein is needed to promote a positive nitrogen balance (i.e., positive protein accretion). Additionally, Forslund and colleagues (1999) have shown that during a 24 h period, macronutrient intake containing $2.5 \text{ g} \cdot \text{kg}^{-1} \cdot \text{day}^{-1}$ not only promoted a positive nitrogen balance, but also resulted in a negative fat balance (promoted fat loss).

Supplementation and timing are critical to properly stimulating each phase. Furthermore, evidence indicates that supplementation should usually be in liquid rather than solid form (Dangin et al. 2001). Liquid meals are generally more easily digested and have a fast absorption profile; thus liquids can be more easily used to fit into the proper timing sequence. For the energy supply phase, the following forms of supplementation are appropriate:

- Carbohydrate—high glycemic index (glucose, sucrose, maltodextrins)

- Whey protein (contains large amounts of essential amino acids)

- Vitamin C (30-120 mg) and vitamin E (20-60 IU)—antioxidants may limit muscle damage and immunosuppression

- Sodium (100-250 IU), potassium (60-120 mg), and magnesium—can be added to improve taste and set the stage for faster recovery

Carbohydrate should be mixed with protein in a ratio of 4 or 5 to 1, for example 25 g of glucose and 6 g of whey protein mixed with 500 ml (17 fl oz) of water. The exact amount depends on body mass and, to an extent, taste. The fluid also aids in reducing the dehydrating effects of exercise.

Some authors (Ivy and Portman 2004) recommend adding 1 g of leucine, as it can be a strong stimulator of insulin release and protein synthesis. About 30% to 50% of the supplement drink should be ingested immediately before the training session, and small portions should be consumed during the workout. Care should be taken not to ingest too much at one time so that comfort during the strength training session is compromised.

For the anabolic phase, the following supplementation can be used:

- Carbohydrate—high glycemic index (glucose, sucrose, maltodextrins)

- Whey protein (contains large amounts of essential amino acids)

- Creatine ($0.3 \text{ g} \cdot \text{kg}^{-1}$)—can be added as nutrient uptake is increased during this phase

- Leucine—1 g

- Glutamine (Ivy and Portman 2004)—1 to 2 g may limit immunosuppression

- Vitamins C (60-120 mg) and E (80-400 IU)

Carbohydrate and whey protein can be mixed (500 ml [17 fl oz] of water) in a 4:1 ratio, for example, 50 g of glucose and 12 g of whey protein. The fluid can aid in postexercise hydration.

The rapid growth subphase can benefit from the following supplementation and diet. Carbohydrate (high glycemic index, 2-4 g), whey protein (10-20 g), and casein (1-3 g) mixed in 500 ml of water can aid in maintaining increased insulin sensitivity and the anabolic environment (Ivy and Portman 2004). This mixture should be taken approximately 2 to 4 h postexercise. A small amount of carbohydrate is necessary to promote insulin release; however, large amounts of carbohydrate (used for energy production during exercise and recovery) or protein ingested during the growth phase may be converted to fat. Various types of protein have fast or slow digestion and absorption rates, which can affect their ability to sustain anabolic effects (Boirie et al. 1997; Dangin et al. 2001; Fruhbeck 1998). Whey protein is fast and casein slow; addition of casein during the rapid phase may make it possible to sustain enhanced protein synthesis for longer periods (Ivy and Portman 2004). The athlete can also include leucine (2-3 g) and glutamine (1 g).

The slow growth subphase lasts the longest, and it is during this phase that the bulk of calories are consumed in the diet. As a result of the length of the phase and the intake of a relatively large number of calories, this phase has the greatest influence on muscle growth (Ivy and Portman 2004). Although insulin concentrations decline, it is still possible to sustain a reasonable level of protein synthesis and positive nitrogen balance with an appropriate diet and supplements between meals.

Meals during normal training should address caloric concerns and contain approximately 15% protein, 40% to 50% carbohydrate, and 25% to 35% fat (mostly unsaturated). During relatively long periods (more than two weeks) of high-volume training, caloric content (plus 100-200 kcal) and carbohydrate content may be adjusted upward (>45%).

If strength gain is a primary goal, meals should contain approximately 20% to 25% protein, 45% to 50% carbohydrate, and 25% to 35% fat (mostly unsaturated). Calories should be increased (plus 50 kcal) to ensure a positive nitrogen balance. If gains in body mass and lean body mass (with limited fat gains) are the goal, then the total caloric consumption should be increased by 100 to 200 $\text{kcal} \cdot \text{day}^{-1}$.

If fat loss with limited loss of lean body mass is a goal, meals containing 25% protein, 40% to 45% carbohydrate, and 25% to 30% fat (mostly monounsaturated) should be considered. Calories should be decreased (minus 100-200 $\text{kcal} \cdot \text{day}^{-1}$).

Snacks between meals should have a high-protein, low-carbohydrate, very low-fat content. Whey protein plus a small amount of casein mixed in diluted sport drinks is reasonable. These types of supplemental meals do not produce large alterations in insulin; chronic elevation of insulin coupled with high-carbohydrate or high-fat diets can lead to increased fat storage, elevated cholesterol, and metabolic diseases. Furthermore, eating a number of small meals provides a small bolus of protein that may promote protein synthesis better than one or two large ingestions of protein.

These recommendations are one end of the nutritional supplementation continuum. There are likely individual differences that must be worked out to provide optimal nutrition for sport. However, with use of reasonable dietary strategies it is possible that adaptations to training programs can be greatly enhanced.

Ongoing Issues in the Ergogenics Debate

There is little doubt that athletes use and will continue to use ergogenic aids. Coaches and athletes should address four important questions before deciding on the use of ergogenic aids:

1. Which items really are ergogenic?
2. Which items are potentially ergogenic?
3. Which items are worthless?
4. Which items are banned by sport governing bodies or are simply illegal, and what are the ethical ramifications that accompany this question?

For the coach and athlete, these can be difficult questions. Better education in sport science could help coaches and athletes better understand the potential efficacy of items touted as ergogenic aids. It is through sport science that definitive answers to the first three questions can most often be (eventually) determined. While numerous promises or quasi-promises, labeled as "cutting-edge research," have been made over the years, most have not resulted in furthering sport performance. Unfortunately, the coach or athlete is not always knowledgeable enough to distinguish between reasonable scientific information and fads, gimmicks, and just plain misleading information. Coaches and athletes are bombarded by publicity about many dietary supplements, few of which actually work. Numerous gadgets are touted as miraculous in their ability to improve performance and almost never live up to their billing. This problem can be compounded at times by the relative slowness of

science and scientific methodology and by sport scientists themselves. Sport scientists seldom speak in a language that nonscientists can completely understand. All of this, combined with the recent apparent increase in sport "guruism," leaves the coach and athlete wondering which way to turn. Therefore, it is reasonable to expect coaches and athletes to begin

- learning the language of science (and sport scientists should learn sport language) and learning to evaluate research,
- accumulating sufficient knowledge to critically evaluate claims by manufacturers of potential ergogenic aids, and
- working in partnership with sport scientists in order to evaluate potential ergogenic aids as well as to move the sport ahead.

As for the fourth question, knowing which ergogenic aids are banned by governing bodies is relatively simple. For example, the World Anti-Doping Agency (WADA) and its national counterparts, such as the United States Anti-Doping Agency (USADA), publish banned drug lists; these can easily be found on appropriate Web sites (WADA's, for example, is www.wada-ama.org/en/prohibitedlist.ch2).

However, the ethics surrounding the use of ergogenic aids are not so simple. This discussion does not pretend to be an exhaustive examination of all the ethical ramifications associated with using ergogenic aids; rather the aim is to point out that there are shades of gray. Here we outline several of the more important issues.

Health Issues

In high-level sport, the expectation of the competitors and their supporters is to win. In some countries, second place is termed the *first loser*. Several factors drive competition, coaches, and athletes. First are factors intrinsic to the nature of sport competition; good athletes like to compete, are motivated to win, and generally hate to lose. There are also extrinsic factors that can add pressure, including social, monetary, and even political ramifications of winning or losing (consider the 1980 and 1984 Olympics). Consequently, because of these intrinsic and extrinsic pressures, the elite athlete is expected to be a winner.

In this context it is not difficult to understand why athletes would use ergogenic aids. However, many types of ergogenic aids are banned by various supporting agencies. Reasons given for the bans range from health considerations to the feeling that it is just plain cheating to use ergogenic aids to create an uneven playing field. While these concepts seem simple, they may not be. As an example, we can consider doping. The IOC/WADA policy stand on doping includes statements suggesting that some drugs are banned (at least in part) as a precaution against damaging the athletes' health. However, sport, particularly at high levels, can be an inherently dangerous and unhealthy undertaking. If health is a factor, why are certain sports with high injury rates and high rates of traumatic injury, such as boxing, not banned as well? Being overweight and overfat is potentially responsible for various metabolic and degenerative diseases, including cardiovascular disease and some types of cancer (Hubbard et al. 2004; Jeffreys et al. 2003). However, to perform well at certain sporting activities it is necessary to be very large (e.g., NCAA and NFL linemen, superheavy weightlifters, and athletes in some throwing events); yet these activities are not banned, nor are weight- or fat-level restrictions placed on the participants. Nor is there typically an effort on the part of most governing bodies to help large athletes reduce body mass after retirement.

As yet, no studies are available that compare the harmful effects of sport participation with the effects of using ergogenic aids. However, there is information indicating that the harmful effects of ergogenic aids, particularly androgens, have been overstated (Street, Antonio, and Cudlipp 1996). This is not to suggest that ergogenic aids cannot cause harm, but rather to place them in a more appropriate context. It could be argued with some logic that ergogenic aids such as androgens might offer some protection against injury due to their anabolic properties. Indeed, the misinformation concerning androgens and many other ergogenic aids has been so persuasive, pervasive, and prevalent that one might expect to walk into gyms and health clubs and observe dead people lying on the floor. The fear of harmful effects as a result of androgen use and the exaggerated media attention, along with the fear of being found positive on a drug test, have often precluded its beneficial use for valid medical reasons, such as injury rehabilitation (Beiner et al. 1999).

The point is, one might argue that being fit for sport is often quite different from being fit for health. So is a reevaluation of the relationship of health and sport perhaps necessary and reasonable?

Playing to the Whistle

Lying, when one is not under extreme duress, is universally considered dishonest and unethical, as is being intentionally misleading. Yet, many sports

foster this behavior, and this is accepted and even expected as part of the game. For example, in track and field, if a shot-putter knowingly fouls, but the throw is deemed good and legal by the judge, should the shot-putter tell the judge and lose the throw? What is the correct and ethical choice? In 40 years of involvement with athletics (track and field) and particularly weightlifting, the authors have only once observed an athlete tell the judge he had fouled. One may argue that it is up to the individual and his or her conscience or that it is simply part of the game (i.e., "playing to the whistle"). But if this practice is acceptable, then is it acceptable to sneak a light shot or discus into the competition provided the judge does not know? While in the first example it would be difficult for a sportsman (including the authors) to advocate telling the judge, the type of behavior that is accepted is seemingly at odds with the concept of good sportsmanship and fair play—the same principles that are invoked to substantiate drug testing. Is trying to beat the doping control simply playing to the whistle?

Perhaps the most disturbing issue is the attitude and behavior of international and national governing bodies such as the IOC and IAAF (International Association of Athletics Federations) toward the use of ergogenic aids. It is our opinion that to anyone who is around a sport long enough, it becomes apparent that many athletes from many different countries intentionally use a variety of banned ergogenic aids, including androgens, and get away with it. Unfortunately, many governing bodies indicate that if athletes only train hard, eat right, get plenty of sleep, and so on they can be winners, all the while knowing that their "clean" athletes are less likely to win against athletes who are taking androgens and other ergogenic aids and also training hard, eating right, and getting plenty of sleep. Most high-level athletes believe (correctly) that it would be fairly difficult (not impossible) to win against those using ergogenic aids.

To say that this situation is disheartening is an understatement. For coaches, this really hits home when they are asked by athletes if winning is possible without taking ergogenic aids, particularly androgens. It is interesting that international and national governing bodies (NGB) speak strongly of ethics and morals in the context of "doping" and in describing those who "cheat" but apparently see nothing wrong with using misleading statements.

Men's weightlifting can serve as an example. Within weightlifting circles, it has been suspected for some time that weightlifters in certain countries, particularly in eastern Europe, regularly use small doses of androgens in training. Canada, Great Britain, Finland, Sweden, Norway, and the United States have about 7000 active weightlifters; they do not typically win medals in most international competitions, including the world championships and the Olympics. It is unlikely that eastern Europeans are genetically superior, nor is it likely that eastern Europeans have discovered a vastly superior training program and have been hiding it for 25 years. What is interesting is that weightlifting in Canada, Great Britain, Finland, Sweden, Norway, and the United States has had strict doping control procedures in place for about 25 years. Weightlifting's finances (mostly derived through the NGB), as with other sports, are usually directly related to how well the athletes perform and how many medals they produce in major events (e.g., world championships and Olympics). Thus, governing bodies expect medals to be won knowing that it is extremely unlikely that their athletes can compete on an equal basis. Imagine what these countries' weightlifting budgets look like and the impact this has on the sport. This problem is not isolated to weightlifting.

What Is an Ergogenic Aid and What Isn't?

"My ergogenic aid is okay, but yours is not." There is still a great deal of argument over what constitutes an ergogenic aid, both among sport scientists and among sport administrators. Extremes exist: Basically there are three different arguments or concepts that reflect on the ethics surrounding the use of ergogenic aids:

1. Some sport officials have argued that almost anything that is not directly shown to be a "naturally" occurring nutrient should be banned; this would encompass vitamins and artificially packaged or refined substances including sport drinks.

2. On the other extreme are those who would allow any method of potentially increasing performance to be used. While this stance is clear-cut, the first is not, as it requires definitions of what constitutes an ergogenic aid.

3. While most sporting authorities and sport scientists are not exactly at either extreme, they tend to choose one side over the other. Obviously proponents in any of these three groups will not agree on a clear-cut definition for the use of ergogenic aids. It is with

the act of trying to define what an ergogenic aid is and when such aids can be used that difficulty begins.

For example, androstenedione, DHEA, and a few related compounds (prohormones) can be legally sold without a physician's prescription in the United States and several other countries. Whether they work or not as ergogenic aids is open to question (King et al. 1999). The IOC and its associated governing bodies ban these compounds as they are related to androgens (which are ergogenic). As of this writing (2005), baseball, the NHL, and a few other governing bodies for professional sports that have not banned prohormones in the past are considering making them banned substances largely as a result of pressure from the U.S. Congress. In 1998, Randy Barnes, the world record holder in the shot put, was banned for life for taking androstenedione; Mark McGwire, who admitted taking androstenedione, broke a long-standing home run record. According to the media, Randy Barnes was a disgraced cheater and Mark McGuire was a hero. Which characterization was correct?

The IOC/WADA policy on doping basically states that the use of an "expedient substance or method" in order to gain a performance advantage is against the rules. The use of birth control pills to regulate the menstrual period during training and competition is not banned, yet clearly places women in an unnatural state and is quite expedient. The argument in support of this practice is that the hormones supplied by the birth control pills basically represent replacement therapy (Reis, Frick, and Schmidtbleicher 1995). Increased training volume or intensity has been shown to decrease the testosterone concentrations in males and has been associated with symptoms of overtraining and overstress (Hakkinen et al. 1987; Stone et al. 1991). However, the use of exogenous testosterone in males, even as replacement therapy, is banned. Could one not interpret this information to indicate that ergogenic hormone therapy is acceptable for women but not for men?

Altitude training may be a viable ergogenic aid for endurance athletes, particularly if the competition is at altitude. Indeed, recent evidence strongly supports the concept of living high–training low for improved performance at or near sea level (Levine and Stray-Gundersen 1997; Saunders et al. 2003; Wilber et al. 2003). Unless one already lives at altitude, taking advantage of this type of ergogenic aid requires considerable monetary support. The athlete either must have considerable personal finances or must be sponsored (usually through the

NGB). If athletes (or their NGB) do not have the necessary resources, then they are not likely to be able to take advantage of the potential ergogenic effects of altitude and simulated altitude, placing them at a disadvantage to those athletes who do have resources.

Erythropoietin (EPO) is a hormone produced by the kidneys that when taken exogenously stimulates red blood cell production and can mimic some of the effects of altitude. Interestingly, EPO is banned by all amateur sporting bodies, but altitude or simulated altitude training is not. Athletes perceived to be taking EPO, especially if they happen to win, have been criticized ("Brown Misses Out" 1998), often by competitors who regularly spend a considerable amount of money and time training or living at altitude. One wonders why one ergogenic aid is acceptable but others are not.

Testing Issues

The prevailing attitude about testing can be expressed as "This testing procedure works and even if it doesn't, it still works." In any discussion of ergogenic aids and doping, one must consider the tests and the testing procedures themselves. Science and science-based testing procedures are founded on probabilities, not absolutes. There is always a degree of error in the tests and testing procedures.

We Never Make Mistakes?

Because there is always a degree of error, there will always be false positives and false negatives. Unfortunately, to date the IOC and its subsidiaries have released little or no data on their testing procedures dealing with athletes. Most of the published data on testing, particularly with AS, have been obtained with very small numbers of untrained nonathletes. So the exact degree of error is unknown to scientists not directly involved in sport drug testing. For the sake of argument, one might assume that the chance of a false positive is 0.0015% (Dehennin and Scholler 1990). This seems quite small; however, if 10,000 athletes were to be tested in a year, one might expect as many as 15 false positive tests (at least on the A sample). In reality this means that, potentially, 15 athletes will be accused of being cheaters, have their character and reputations dragged through the mud by the media, and have little or no recourse. Furthermore, as of 1996 the degree of agreement among six IOC laboratories was not acceptable (Catlin et al. 1996). This means that the degree of error was not consistent between laboratories and the chance of a false positive or false negative test may have been greater in some laboratories, exacerbating the problem. The authors could find no evidence in the scientific literature indicating that this problem is now corrected (U.K. Sports Council 2003), although it can be assumed that by now the problem has been corrected.

Unnatural or Natural?

Certain drugs such as cocaine are not found naturally occurring (as far as we know) in humans. Thus, detection of these substances is relatively easy. Many hormones, when used as ergogenic aids, are quite difficult to detect; growth hormone is an example. Androgens are male hormones that have anabolic properties; testosterone is the most powerful of the naturally occurring androgens. The term *anabolic steroid* is typically (but incorrectly) applied to synthetic androgens. The AS are similar to testosterone in chemical structure and function. Some of these AS have been recently shown to occur naturally (i.e., nandrolone); thus cutoff limits for drug testing must be established.

The sporting world, particularly track and field, has been shocked by the number of positive doping tests for nandrolone. Included in these positive tests were a number of superstars of track and field, including Linford Christie and Merlene Ottey. Nandrolone is typically injected in an oil base and is the primary anabolic agent that athletes who are subject to drug testing have avoided because it is easily detected even months after injection (Kintz, Crimele, and Ludes 1999). Only in the last two to three years has nandrolone been shown conclusively to be a naturally occurring steroid, with the IOC adopting a doping positive cutoff of 2 ng · ml^{-1} (Dehennin, Bonnaire, and Plou 1999; Kintz, Crimele, and Ludes 1999). It is quite interesting that many of the positive tests produced concentrations of only 8 to 12 ng · ml^{-1} (U.K. Sports Council 2003). This suggests several possibilities. One is that the tests are becoming more sensitive (i.e., the IOC position) and the athletes really were taking a banned substance. Another is that the test does not work and is producing false positives, or other outside variables such as exercise elevated the urinary concentrations of nandrolone metabolites (i.e., the position of some athletes, coaches, and scientists) (Kohler and Lambert 2002). A third possibility is that the athletes were taking (legally purchased) over-the-counter food supplements that contained a substance such as androstenedione, which produces nandrolone or its metabolites, unbeknownst to them (i.e., the position of some athletes, coaches, and scientists) (Kohler and Lambert 2002; Pepin, Vayssette, and Gaillard 2001; U.K. Sports Council 2003).

The stature and number of athletes testing positive have raised questions about the validity of the tests, questions that have reached national government levels ("Demands Grow for Drug Test Review" 1999; "Call for Fail Safe Drug Tests" 1999). To date the IOC/WADA has released little information on the testing program that would allow independent verification of their testing procedures.

Several additional problems arise from the testing of androgens, testosterone (T) among them. Because T is produced in relatively large amounts naturally, simply finding an amount that is somewhat over the average limits cannot be considered positive. Furthermore, it is apparent that some athletes have higher naturally occurring T concentrations than others (so much for a level playing field). Currently the test for the use of exogenous T is the testosterone-to-epitestosterone ratio. In normal untrained adult humans, the ratio of production is approximately 1:1. This ratio can be disturbed slightly by alcohol ingestion (especially in women), aging (Karila et al. 1996; Starka et al. 1996), possibly physical activity, and possibly sexual activity. The established ratio (currently) for testing positive is 6:1. The use of this ratio in drug testing is greatly complicated because there is evidence that at least 1 in 2000 (0.0005%) men are deficient in the enzyme(s) necessary for the production of epitestosterone (Eichner 1997), which can mean their T:E ratio will be higher than 6:1.

The likelihood of finding athletes with high T:E ratios is illustrated by the Swedish antidoping program. As reported in 1996, 28 athletes out of 8946 samples (0.003%) produced T:E ratios higher than 6; only one of these 28 samples was conclusively considered to be the result of exogenous T use (Garle et al. 1996). This study not only points out the difficulty of determining whether exogenous T was used, but also suggests that the actual incidence of naturally occurring high T:E ratios may be as high as 0.003% in male and female athletes. Detection of exogenous T use can be further complicated if the athlete simultaneously uses exogenous epitestosterone (Dehennin and Peres 1996). Because it is difficult to determine the difference between natural and synthetic T using the T:E ratio, alternate or additional methods are being considered, such as the use of a testosterone-to-luteinizing hormone ratio (Perry et al. 1997). Another alternative is the use of carbon isotope ratios. There are differences between the ratio of carbon isotopes

used to construct T synthetically and the ratio found in naturally occurring T. However, currently, the isotope ratio method of determining these differences is not any more accurate than the T:E ratio. Furthermore, the carbon isotope ratio $(C12:C13)$ may be affected by the types of foods eaten (Shackleton et al. 1997).

Is Fair Play in the Eye of the Beholder?

Over 40 years, the authors have had the opportunity to discuss drug testing, at length, with coaches, athletes, sport scientists, sport administrators, and drug testing staff involved in a number of different sports. Drug testing is supposed to be a tool used to enforce fair play. The zealousness with which some of the doping control staff, particularly those directly involved in drug testing, pursue cheaters, is surprising. Stories that have been related to the authors and have been told by more than one athlete—that testers said, "We believe you're cheating and we're going to catch you"—would seem to reduce the supposed objectivity of scientific testing and call into question the use of appropriate procedures. It is interesting that some athletes believe they are tested more than others. When one chooses to become an athlete, it is unfortunate that with drug testing come several problems, such as anxiety and inconvenience. Athletes become anxious because of a well-founded fear that a positive test will end their career. It is inconvenient to have to travel to a testing site. In other situations the tester may show up at an athlete's house unannounced at 5 a.m. (yes, this has happened), or athletes are detained several hours after the end of a contest because they are unable to produce enough urine; and most importantly, they have to give up their legal and civil rights.

In the United States, for example, the question of civil and legal rights has been raised in several lawsuits framed around the Fourth and Fourteenth Amendments to the U.S. Constitution (e.g., *Treasury Employees v. Von Raab*, 1989; *Larry v. Lockney*, 2000; *Veronia v. Acton*, 1995; *Board of Education v. Earles*, 2002). The Fourth Amendment deals with protection from illegal and unreasonable search and seizure. The Fourteenth Amendment (section 1) deals with the legal and civil rights of a U.S. citizen and the due process of law. United States courts (including the Supreme Court) have ruled that drug testing, including urine sampling, constitutes a search (*Veronia v. Acton*, 1995). However, those in favor of testing argue that certain conditions warrant searches for the good of the whole (e.g., airlines, sports). The basic tenet of random or total participant drug testing is that someone may be guilty; however, the argument against drug testing is that many athletes (or other individuals) are searched without probable cause and are subjected to the possibility of a "false" positive (Yamaguchi, Johnston, and O'Malley 2003). As the courts have (narrowly) usually ruled in favor of sport drug testing, the argument is that one must waive civil rights in order to participate. Additionally, there is some question about the degree to which drug testing limits or curtails (if at all) the use of illicit drugs (Yamaguchi, Johnston, and O'Malley 2003), adding to the controversy.

In the process of drug testing, two samples of urine are collected and stored. If a positive test occurs for the A sample, the NGB and the media are notified, as is the athlete. The athlete or his or her representative can observe testing of the B sample. Typically the media frenzy starts as the athlete is labeled "the disgraced cheater" or something along those lines; then the media drags up every old story on that particular substance and everyone who has ever been caught taking it. The athlete has a right to arbitration, which basically is a trial. The term "trial" is used to suggest the feelings of anyone (on either side) who has gone through an arbitration; often lawyers are present for both sides, and a panel of "arbitrators" serves as the judge and jury.

In many sports there are two trials. First is the trial within the athlete's own governing body or doping control group (e.g., USADA); then there can be a trial within the international body. This system can place the athlete and his or her NGB in adversarial roles. In track and field, for example, the International Association of Athletics Federation (IAAF) is the international governing body. First the athlete must go through arbitration within his or her NGB (U.K. Athletics or USADA, for example). The results of this trial are then forwarded on to the IAAF. Rarely, if ever, does the IAAF accept an NGB arbitration verdict that the athlete was innocent of doping (e.g., Dennis Mitchell and Dougie Walker). The stated position of the IAAF is that the athlete is guilty until proven innocent and that the reason for the presence of the substance does not matter ("Athlete Guilty" 1999). Thus, the second trial begins with the IAAF; rarely, if ever, do the athletes prove themselves not guilty to the IAAF (e.g., Dennis Mitchell and Dougie Walker). The athlete is also able to present his or her case to the Court of Arbitration for Sport in Belgium, a process that is new as of this writing. A number of potential rea-

sons can be given for a positive test, which should be taken into consideration. These reasons include individual differences in metabolism, unknowingly taking a legal supplement that contains a banned substance, and sabotage. None of these reasons are sufficient in the eyes of the IOC/WADA or other international governing bodies such as the IAAF.

The end product of this process is that the athlete's reputation is damaged; considerable amounts of time, money, and effort are spent; and often a lawsuit results, taking more time, effort, and money. Often (e.g., in the case of Diane Modahl) the athlete wins the lawsuit and the NGB loses a great deal of money, though the IAAF and IOC so far have been protected. Even when a national court finds in favor of an athlete (e.g., Butch Reynolds), the IOC/IAAF and other organizations do not meet their obligations openly or fairly but instead have threatened to punish or otherwise sanction the entire federation the offending athlete is a member of. Yet this process is supposed to protect the athlete.

Final Thoughts

Although many other problems could be pointed out, we believe that the preceding discussion indicates a problem with the antidoping process. Pointing out these problems is not a blanket indictment of doping control but rather an attempt to call attention to deficiencies.

We have little doubt that ergogenic aids will continue to be used (consider the controversy in track and field surrounding the 2004 Olympic trials and Olympics and the recent Balco case). We have little doubt that banned substances will be used until adequate testing methods can be devised. We also strongly believe that the vast majority of athletes would not use banned substances if they believed that the playing field was level. We are also equally convinced that the current testing methods do not work as well as they should. We do not advocate the use of banned substances; however, we also cannot condone the use of inadequate testing methods and processes that place innocent athletes in jeopardy. The following suggestions are worth consideration:

- The IOC/WADA testing procedures should be reviewed by independent agencies (U.K. Sports Council 2003). University laboratories (singly or in combination) could be set up for this type of review. The IOC should release data on athletic testing (especially for testosterone and nandrolone) to independent agencies for evaluation and validation.

- IOC/WADA should rethink and revise their rules on inadvertent doping (e.g., many nandrolone positive tests).

- Until adequate tests can be devised for testosterone, consideration should be given to removing testosterone from the banned list.

It is obvious that doping control is not a sound process at present. But, as Sweeney (2004) suggested, just wait until genetic manipulation is possible!

CHAPTER SUMMARY

The use of ergogenic aids has been surrounded by considerable controversy. Ergogenic aids consist of several different types, including environmental, psychological, mechanical, and pharmaceutical aids and nutritional supplements. The use of ergogenic aids in sport has a very long history, at least as far back as the ancient Greek Olympics. Ergogenic aids are widely used by athletes; the more commonly used ergogenic aids include stimulants, protein-building drugs, and nutritional supplements. The problem and controversy arise with the ethics and particularly the legality of the use of these aids. Equally problematic and controversial has been the use of drug testing in order to limit the use of ergogenic aids.

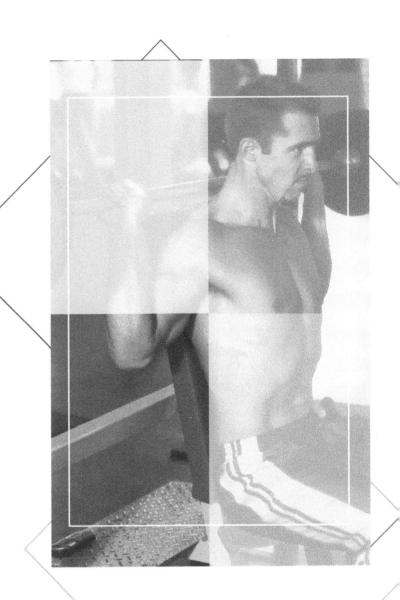

PART III

Adaptations and Benefits of Resistance Training

The product of the training process is adaptation (chapters 10 and 11). The adaptation may be associated with biomechanical, physical, physiological, or psychological characteristics and may eventually alter performance positively or negatively. One of the most important and often overlooked parts of the training process is monitoring and evaluating specific characteristics associated with a sport and the potential adaptations in these characteristics (chapters 8 and 9). The monitoring and evaluation of these characteristics and potential adaptations require that valid and reliable testing procedures be carried out (chapter 8). If appropriate monitoring is integrated into the training process, the potential for producing positive rather than negative adaptations is greatly increased. Part III of the book deals with how to monitor the athlete and with the importance of testing and monitoring the athlete within the training context.

CHAPTER 8

Testing, Measurement, and Evaluation

Before discussing the adaptations and benefits of resistance training, and before considering training principles and theory in part IV, we need to address the importance and necessity of testing and providing adequate measurement and evaluation. Gauging adaptation or tracking progress without these tools is impossible.

Testing, in the sport or sport science context, deals with detailed examination of the characteristics and properties of an athlete or of equipment related to sport. Testing can be biomechanical, physiological, psychological, or performance oriented. Measurement deals with quantifying (assigning numbers) to the properties and characteristics being tested. Evaluation is the decision made about the significance or quality of the sport or the sport-related characteristic or property based on the measurements made. Evaluation must be based on a careful consideration of the significance of the measurement. Often in sport the evaluation has to do with the degree of change in a specific measure, which can reflect either a positive or a negative adaptation to training. Adequate evaluation is possible only if the testing and measurements have been appropriately carried out.

Because testing and evaluation largely fall into the realm of sport science, anyone involved in testing must have some understanding of sport science. Stone and colleagues (2004) have presented definitions related to sport science and sport scientists. Consider the following basic terminology:

• Biology is the interdisciplinary study of life.

• Exercise science is the study of biological responses and adaptations to exercise and training. Exercise science depends on various disciplines including biomechanics, physiology, and psychology and sociology. There are various specialties within exercise science, including geriatrics, adult fitness and wellness, ergonomics, and pediatric exercise. Presently, exercise science is primarily concerned with health, health-related performance, and underlying mechanisms. Although there can be carryover to sport, the carryover is mostly indirect.

• Sport science is concerned with the enhancement of sport performance through the application of scientific methods and principles. There are several basic sport science functions. As with exercise science, sport science has an educational role. However, unlike exercise science, sport science involves tightly integrated and regular sport testing and feedback, as well as practical and applied research. Although health and mechanistic factors are addressed indirectly, the major concern of sport science is physical performance.

Thus, conceptually:

Exercise scientists use exercise and training to understand human biology.

Sport scientists use human biology to understand exercise and training.

Therefore, a major purpose of sport science is to bridge the gap between science and sport.

This chapter is divided into two major portions. The first part is a general discussion of measurement and measurement techniques. The second part is a more specific discussion of the measurement and evaluation of strength and strength-related parameters such as rate of force development and power. The next chapter, chapter 9, provides a detailed discussion of how performance and the training process can be successfully tracked and monitored.

Principles of Testing, Measurement, and Evaluation

One of the most important aspects of sport science and coaching is the ability to make accurate measurements (Hopkins 2000), for two primary reasons. The first is the need to accurately assess the characteristics or value of something, leading to answers to certain kinds of questions, for example: How much did it weigh? How large is an object? How much time elapsed? How long is it? The second reason is the need to differentiate and objectively evaluate potential differences. This evaluation process can allow determination of the winner in a race or throwing contest, or it can allow a coach to determine if a training program is accomplishing the desired goals.

There are two primary areas, in a sporting context, requiring accurate measurement and evaluation: service and research. *Service* deals with providing the coach and athlete with information pertaining to the athlete's current training state. Thus, the service tests should provide information concerning either positive or negative adaptation to training programs. Service measurements include biomechanical (technique), physiological, and psychological measurements. The measurements should fit sport and athlete requirements (specificity of measurement), should be easily interpreted by the coach and athlete, and typically should be rapidly returned to the coach and athlete. Rapid return is quite important, as the coach needs to be able to make any necessary loading changes before nonbeneficial adaptations occur. This means that any data analysis must also be rapid.

The frequency of measurements depends on factors such as the availability of the athletes, the sophistication and intricacy of measurements, and the amount of time taken for return. Athletes in residence, as at colleges or at Olympic training centers, can typically be tested more often and on a more regular basis; but for many sports the

athletes may be spread out over a large geographical area, and in such cases regular camps must be organized so that testing can be carried out. If testing results cannot be returned rapidly (usually within zero to three days), then the coach cannot make potential alterations in training load in time to make a difference in the outcome of the training program. However, certain tests, such as technique analysis using videography, are time-consuming and may take weeks for return, especially if large numbers of athletes are involved. Certain types of invasive tests, such as blood draws and hormone analyses, can take several days to weeks to analyze. The potential time lag between testing and data return should be communicated to the coach and athlete before the testing session. Less involved, easily administered, rapid-return tests can be administered more often.

Research is a search for truth and clarity. In the sport context, research deals with the efforts of sport scientists and coaches to push the sport ahead. Sport science research should be applied research, with the goal of improved performance as the primary outcome. Often research is necessary to understand the types of service tests that are best suited for a particular sport. Frequently the service program and research investigations can be carried out simultaneously. Whether one is dealing with service or research, appropriate experimental designs are a necessity.

Service and Research Testing Design

Choosing an appropriate design depends on several factors: the nature of the question or topic; the mode of investigation; methods of investigation; ideological stance; political stance; subject availability; and funding, facilities, and instrumentation. Many of these characteristics that influence the design of a research project have been discussed in detail by Hopkins (2000):

• *The nature of the question or topic.* A research or service project begins with the identification of a specific question or problem to be solved, for example: What are the performance needs or characteristics of a specific sport? Does a nutritional supplement actually work? What are the most efficient measurement tools for a particular sport? The

Physical characteristics - performance - biomechanical/physiology - psychology/sociological

Figure 8.1   The testing-research continuum.

nature of potential topics forms a continuum that extends from purely physical topics at one end to social topics at the other end (figure 8.1).

• *The scope of an investigation.* The scope of the research design must also be considered. For example, is the investigation dealing with a single case or with a sample population? Single case studies investigate "what happens here." Population sample studies allow greater generalization by determining what happens in general.

• *The mode of investigation.* The mode of investigation can be observation or intervention. In an observational investigation, the investigators do not influence the outcome in any way. Observational investigation characterizes most sport service projects. In an intervention or experimental investigation, responses or adaptations can be characterized as a result of an intervention conducted by the investigators.

• *Methods of investigation.* An investigation can be qualitative or quantitative. Using qualitative methods, the investigator gathers information or themes from texts, conversations, or loosely structured interviews, then attempts to relate a coherent story. With use of quantitative methods, data are gathered with a measurement instrument, such as a timing gate, a force plate, or a structured questionnaire. The data are then quantified and analyzed to uncover the relationships between variables derived from the data.

• *Ideological stance.* A researcher can take an objective or a subjective stance. Most researchers assume that they can obtain and share data concerning objects or conditions, then identify and solve problems related to those objects and conditions without disagreement about the nature of meaning or reality. Other investigators place more importance on the subjective aspects of meaning and truth. "This dimension helps characterize some of the so-called research paradigms, from the objectivity of positivism (the dominant paradigm) through the enigmatic ambivalence of poststructuralism to the subjectivity of interpretivism and grounded theory" (Hopkins 2000). Thus much of qualitative research is derived from postmodernist theory, which holds that all truth is filtered.

• *Political stance.* Investigations can be neutral or partisan. Most researchers try to present all sides of an issue impartially. However, some adopt (or purposefully choose) a partisan or adversarial stance by overtly (or covertly) selecting specific data and biasing arguments toward a particular point

of view (invariably their own). This type of value-laden subjective research is the basis for the critical or radical paradigm in social sciences. However, this dimension of design is sometimes also seen in the physical and biological sciences. While there is always room for different opinions based on sound science, a good teacher, scientist, or coach will not present two arguments as equal when they are really not. The object of science is not a debate; science is a search for truth and clarity.

• *Subject availability.* If an investigator wishes to study 12-year-old female gymnasts and none are available, the project topic should be changed. Additionally, it may be that the population sample is nearby but that due to work, school, or training schedules they cannot be consistently available for testing; then a longitudinal project may be unreasonable.

• *Funding, facilities, and instrumentation.* Obviously if funding (which is almost always a problem), facilities, or instrumentation is not available, the project must be designed to take advantage of those elements that are available.

Types of Experimental Designs

The choice of experimental design largely depends on the nature of the topic, as already discussed, and the availability of subjects and funding. There are basically three types of experimental designs: cross-sectional, time lag, and longitudinal (figure 8.2). With cross-sectional designs, data are gathered on a sample population essentially at one time point.

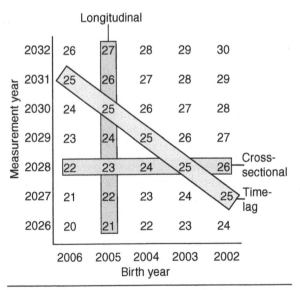

Figure 8.2 Three types of research design: cross-sectional, time lag, and longitudinal.

With reference to figure 8.2 as an example, if a study involved the body composition of 22- to 26-year-old male sprinters, one method would be to measure the body composition on all available 22- to 26-year-olds at the same time (in this case, in the year 2028). An advantage to this design is that time (and likely money) is saved in that comparisons across ages can be made without the need to pursue the study for several years. The disadvantage is that the comparison can be made at only one time period (2028), and sprinters may change over time.

In a time lag design, one defined group (in figure 8.2, 25-year-olds) is measured over an extended time period—in the example, over a five-year period, as it takes five years for 20-year-olds to reach the age of 24 years. An advantage to this design is that changes in 24-year-olds can be studied from year to year. However, each sample is different, and it takes several years to gather the data.

A longitudinal study is basically a series of measurements performed on the same population over a defined time period. In the example, the 21-year-olds measured initially in 2026 were measured each year over the next six years. An advantage of this design is that the same sample population is followed over time, so measurements more likely reflect maturation as well as environmental aspects. The disadvantage is again the amount of time necessary.

Tools for Measurement

Regardless of whether a project is research, service, or a combination of the two, the tools used to measure the variables of interest must be valid and reliable. *Validity* refers to whether or not the instrument is actually measuring what it is supposed to be measuring. There are basically three different types of measurement validity:

- Internal validity refers to how well the tool measures the variable in question (e.g., strength, power, speed, endurance).

- External validity concerns the ability of the tool to predict changes in a population other than the one being studied, for example, when investigators measure strength in one group and then generalize to another group.

- Prediction validity refers to the ability to predict one variable from another, for example, when investigators measure strength to predict the vertical jump.

Measurements must also be reliable. *Reliability* refers to the degree of consistency of measurement; that is, how much error is in the measurement? Sport scientists and coaches must be concerned with test-retest reliability. Test-retest reliability has to do with the degree to which an instrument can produce the same measurements at different times under the same conditions. Methods of establishing reliability include intraclass correlation (ICC), coefficient of variation (CV), and the standard error of the mean (SEM). (For more detail on these methods, see Hopkins 2000.)

Calculating reliability is a must; otherwise comparison between groups or longitudinal alterations in performance cannot be established. If the measurement instrument is not reliable, then any data gathered with that instrument cannot be trusted, as it will not be possible to know with any degree of certainty whether potential differences in performance or physiology, for example, are real or are a result of measurement error.

Investigators in sport, however, can have problems dealing with small differences in measurement owing to the error of measurement being larger than the actual differences. Often changes in physiology are smaller than can be detected by laboratory measures. At the elite performance level (world championships and Olympics), the difference between first and fourth place is often less than 1% to 1.5%, and underlying physiological mechanisms explaining those differences may not be detected with current instrumentation.

Those involved in testing must ask a number of questions to ensure adequate validity and reliability:

1. Is the measurement device appropriate for the population? Are age, sex, skill level, and so on taken into consideration? If the test is too difficult or otherwise not suitable for a particular group, then its validity and reliability will be questionable.

2. Is the measurement relevant to sport or activity requirements? If a test does not reflect specificity and cannot be shown to be associated with sport performance, then other more specific tests should be found. The most efficient test or tests for some sports may not be known; in this case, studies should be undertaken to establish what tests are relevant for a particular sport before long-term testing or monitoring of athletes takes place.

3. Has prior experience of the athletes (familiarization) been considered? As with most

activities, some period of practice time before testing may be necessary so that the subjects can become familiar with the tests. Otherwise, early testing results may be simply reflecting a learning process.

4. How aware is the investigator of the testing environment? The testing environment should be controlled as closely as possible so that the athletes will have the best possible chance of performing well; and if tests are repeated later on, the environment should be the same as in the first testing period. The environment includes not only temperature and humidity but also factors such as measurement precision of investigators, time of day, day of the week (similar short-term training status, degree of fatigue), extraneous noise, appropriate lighting, and clothing.

5. Are the instruments properly calibrated? Instrument calibration is a must in providing reasonable reliability and validity. Lack of appropriate instrument calibration can be a major source of error. The investigator must know how to calibrate all instruments and have them calibrated well in advance of the testing.

6. Have bias been removed (subjectivity vs. objectivity)? In order to remove as much subjectivity as possible, the testing instrument must allow all of the subjects to have an equal chance of performing well. Furthermore, investigators must be objective in their selection of an appropriate measurement instrument and in their interpretation of the data.

7. Has a "floor or ceiling effect" been inadvertently set up? If the test is too easy and all subjects perform well (ceiling), or if the test is too difficult and all subjects perform poorly (floor), then differentiation among subjects (or groups) will not be possible.

8. What is the optimal order of testing? When several tests are administered in the same testing period, it is important that a given test not be fatiguing to the extent that it greatly alters the results on subsequent tests. For example, if a 1RM squat, a countermovement vertical jump (VJ), and a static vertical jump (SJ) are to be administered on the same day, an appropriate order might be VJ, SJ, 1RM squat; because the 1RM squat is the most fatiguing, performing it first may affect performance on the other two tests. Also, with the order VJ, SJ, 1RM squat, the jumps may serve as additional warm-up for the squat. Consistency of testing order is also quite important; as a result of fatigue or potentiation, both validity and reliability can be greatly affected if the order of testing changes from one testing period to another.

If these factors are not addressed and controlled for, then testing data cannot be trusted.

Statistical Analysis

Any item with properties or a characteristic that can have different values is termed a variable. Variables are manipulated or studied in experiments by researchers. An independent variable is an item that is manipulated by the investigator; the dependent variable is a variable that is dependent on the manipulative process and is the item being studied. As variables can be quantified (assigned a value), they can be discrete or continuous. Discrete variables have a defined or noncontinuous value; for example, parents can have one, three, or six children but not 2.34654 children. Variables are continuous when the scale used for quantification is uninterrupted and not made up of discrete values—for example, the range of times possible for the finish of a 100 m sprint. Variables have a frequency of distribution; a normal frequency of distribution (a bell-shaped curve) is shown in figure 8.3.

In order to differentiate and evaluate, appropriate statistical methods are necessary; indeed, differentiation and evaluation really begin with proper statistical applications. Simple statistics include the mean or average of a distribution, the median or middle data value in a distribution, and the mode or data value most often observed. These measures of central tendency allow the investigator to make some judgment as to how much a specific data point may vary from a more typical "central" value (mean, median, or mode). In a normal distribution, the mean, median, and mode will be the same value (figure 8.3). Because there is a distribution or frequency of observational occurrence, there will be variation around the mean of the distribution.

It is possible (and often the norm) for data to be skewed. Figure 8.4 shows two examples of skewed data. The curve in figure 8.4a represents a positive skew (tail to the right), and the curve in figure 8.4b represents a negative skew (tail to the left). Note that in skewed distribution curves, the measures of central tendency are not the same as with the

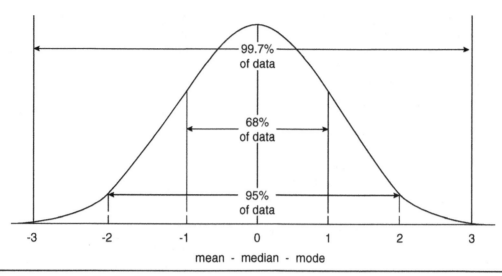

Figure 8.3   Frequency of distribution curve.

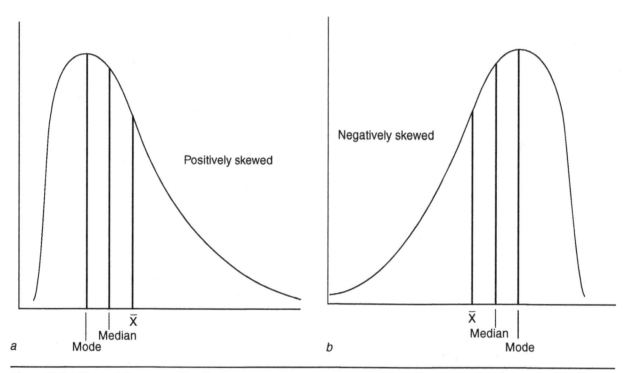

Figure 8.4   Skewed frequency distribution curves.

normal distribution. Figure 8.5 presents an example of a skewed curve; these data, in histogram form, show the frequency (percentage) of occurrence for the ages of all registered female gymnasts in 1991 (Sands 1991).

A simple method of characterizing the variability of a distribution is to use the range, or the scores from the minimum value to the maximum value. A deviation is a measure of variation and is equal to the value of a variable (x) minus its mean (x – mean$_x$). The standard deviation (SD) is a summated measure of the difference of each observation from the mean (Hopkins 2000).

The standard deviation can be calculated from the *variance*.

$$\text{variance} = \frac{\sum \left(\text{mean}_1 - \text{mean}_2\right)^{-2}}{n - 1}$$

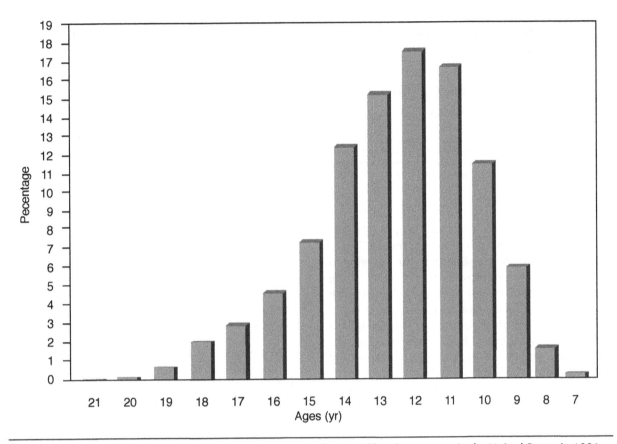

Figure 8.5 Example of a skewed distribution curve: ages distribution of female gymnasts in the United States in 1991.

The square root of the variance produces the standard deviation. Compared to the range, the standard deviation is a better measure of the variation of a variable as it allows some degree of judgment about how far a measure of a specific variable is from the mean. One standard deviation (right and left side of the mean) includes 67% of the observations in the sample; 1.96 SDs (about 2 SDs) encompass 95% of the observations; and 3 SDs account for 99.7% of the observations. So, a data point lying 3 SDs away from the mean would typically represent a rare observation. Thus, the standard deviation provides limits from which probabilities can be calculated.

Comparison of the deviation of variables is an important process in determination of the degree of association of two (or more) variables. Covariance is a measure of the degree to which the deviations of two variables match. Covariance can be described by the following equation:

$$\text{covariance of variables a and b} = \text{sum}\ [(a - \text{mean}_a)\ (b - \text{mean}_b)]$$

When the association is greatest, high positive deviations in variable a are matched by high positive

deviations in variable b, or high negatives by high negatives. A correlation is a measure of the covariance of standardized variables (subtract the mean and divide by the standard deviation). A correlation can have a value of 1.0, indicating a perfectly matched order of the two variables, when the calculated covariance is as high as the greatest possible covariance. A value of –1.0 is perfect negative covariation, in this case matching the highest positive values of one variable with the highest negative values of the second variable. A correlation of 0 indicates a random or no relationship (by order) between the two variables. Thus, a correlation is a mathematical representation of the degree of relationship (strength) between two (or more) variables. Cohen (1988) and Hopkins (2000) have assigned magnitudes of strength to correlation coefficients (table 8.1).

From a practical standpoint, correlations can be used to indicate what factors contribute to a specific measured variable—for example, to determine the factors that potentially contribute to successful sport performance or what factors might be appropriate for tests in a talent ID program. Figure 8.6, *a* and *b*, shows visual representations of strong and weak correlations as scatter plots.

Table 8.1 **Relative Strength of Correlations**

Trivial	0.0	Very strong	0.7
Small	0.1	Nearly perfect	0.9
Moderate	0.3	Perfect	1.0
Strong	0.5		

Adapted from J. Cohen, 1988, *Statistical power analysis for the behavioral sciences*, 2nd ed. (Hillsdale, NJ: Lawrence Erlbaum Associates); and W.G. Hopkins, 2000, *A new view of statistics*. Internet Society for Sport Science. www. sportsci. org/resource/stats/.

Often the value of a correlation is presented as the coefficient of determination (r^2). The coefficient of determination is the square of the correlation coefficient. The r^2 represents the percent of the variance shared by two or more variables. Because a correlation is bidirectional, a correlation could indicate the percent of variance in the dependent variable that is explained by the independent variable, or the percent of the shared variance of the independent variable accounted for by the dependent variable. A correlation cannot predict cause and effect; therefore the coach or sport scientist must attempt to determine the nature and direction of the cause based on data or logical assumptions that are external to the correlation, but that are supported by the correlation. Therefore, a correlation can be a first step toward the determination of cause and effect and is a useful tool in hypothesis-generating research.

One of the most important aspects of research or service monitoring programs for sport is determining if two sample distributions are actually different; for example, the frequency distributions in figure 8.7 could represent the same variable collected on two different sample populations at the same time, or two different distributions of the same variable on the same group collected at different times. The question is, how do we really know if athletes are different? Additionally, when one is gathering data for research or monitoring, it is unlikely that an entire population can be measured. However, it is possible to measure a sample population and generalize to a larger population. To generalize in this manner requires a large enough sample population and the use of inferential statistics.

Inferential statistics rely on the concept of probabilities, that is, calculation of the probability that one group or frequency distribution is actually different from another. If the probability that groups are different is high, then the ability to confidently generalize or infer from the results

of a study is also high. Typical tests of probability include effect size (practical significance). The effect size (EF) can be calculated as follows (Rhea 2004):

$$mean_1 - mean_2 / \text{highest SD} = EF$$

The higher the effect size, the greater the probability that the two sample distribution means are actually different. Several tests can be used to calculate a probability:

t-tests

ANOVA (analysis of variance)

ANCOVA (analysis of covariance)

G×T (repeated measures) factorial ANOVA

MANOVA (multivariate analysis of variance)

Meta-analysis (a method of "quantifying" the results of multiple studies)

In essence these tests calculate the probability that the difference in the means of two frequency distributions reaches a statistical difference. A statistical difference basically means that there is a very good chance that the means of the two distributions really are different. To determine the statistical difference, a probability value (p value) is determined. For example, a p value of 0.05 (p = 0.05), or 1.96 SDs, means that there is only a 5% chance that the means of two sample populations are not really different.

While these statistical techniques are used to study long-term adaptations to sport, other techniques may be more useful in sport monitoring programs. Some of these techniques are the following:

Single-subject designs

Trend analyses

Autocorrelation (cyclical trends)

Frequency analysis (patterns in data) (not based on probabilities)

Statistical process control

For example, trend analyses can be used to give the coach and athlete a clearer picture of the direction of training adaptations. Figure 8.8, *a* and *b*, describes the potential relationship of volume of work (volume load) and the testosterone-to-cortisol ratio (T:C) among six female weightlifters preparing for the American championships in 2002. A sixth-order polynomial trend line was generated for each variable. The data suggest an inverse relationship between the T:C and the volume load (an estimate

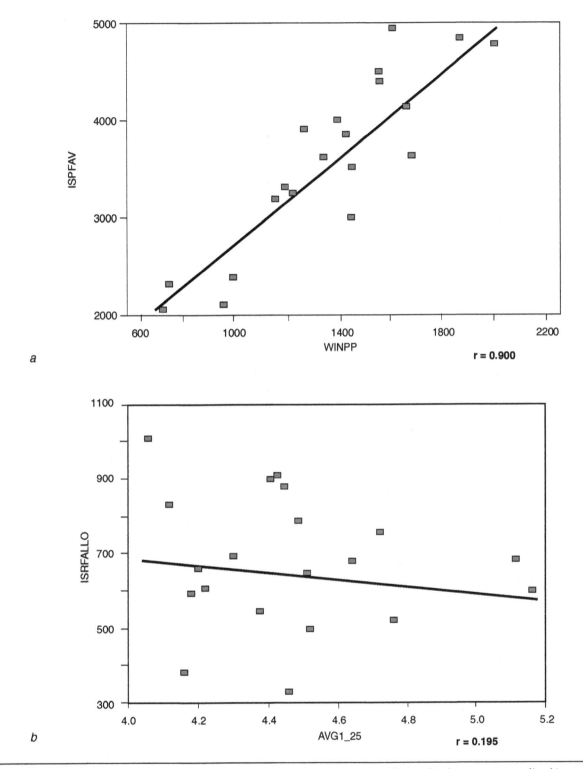

Figure 8.6 *(a)* Example of a scatter plot for a very strong correlation: the relationship between normalized isometric peak force (midthigh pull) and Wingate peak power (n = 20). *(b)* Example of a scatter plot for a weak correlation: the relationship between normalized isometric rate of force development (midthigh pull) and cycling sprint times for 25 m (n = 20).

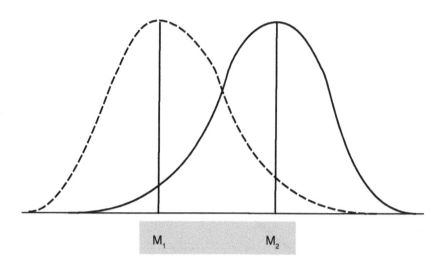

Figure 8.7   Different distributions.

of work), but the same relationship was not noted for the T:C and training intensity (average load). Individual data were also generated, allowing the coach to understand the general trend of adaptation both for the group and for each individual. These data can be rapidly returned to the coach, who can then make necessary adjustments in training programs.

Another example of a very useful statistical method for monitoring sports is statistical process control (SPC) (Shewart 1986). In essence this method allows the coach or sport scientist to automatically monitor data for outliers. The potential outliers have been previously identified by the coach or sport scientist through the setting of tolerance limits. Figure 8.9 depicts the basis of SPC. Essentially, a frequency distribution curve is laid on its side, and over time, outliers are identified using previously set tolerance limits. The tolerance limits are determined from previous experience and through literature search. This process can be computerized, and the computer can be programmed to detect outliers, greatly speeding up the procedure. Once extremes are identified, information can be returned rapidly to the coach and athlete.

Practical Aspects of Testing, Measurement, and Evaluation

Sport performance requires varying degrees of force application. For sports in which performance demands are achieved through high levels of force production, obviously maximum strength and

strength training are an integral part of the overall training program. However, even in those sports in which great endurance is a primary consideration, the ability to generate relatively high levels of force may be more important than many coaches and athletes believe (Bastiaans et al. 2001; Bosco 1982; Paavolainen et al. 1999). Furthermore, force production characteristics, including the rate at which force is produced and related variables such as power production, can be as important as, or even more important than, the maximum level of force production. There is evidence that strength training can enhance these force production characteristics. Thus, appropriate strength and conditioning protocols, properly integrated into overall training programs, can enhance sport performance beyond that with typical sport training alone. This section deals with the measurement and evaluation of strength and related characteristics. We present terminology for force production characteristics and briefly discuss their potential importance to sport; outline measurement of force production characteristics; and provide a description and evaluation of tests concerned with enhancement of force production characteristics.

Terminology

Coaches, athletes, medical professionals, and sport scientists often disagree on the use of terminology, especially when that terminology is employed in both scientific and athletic settings. The terms "strength," "power," and "endurance" fall into this category. Indeed, many coaches and athletes have used "strength" to mean "powers of resistance" or "toughness." It is not uncommon for track athletes

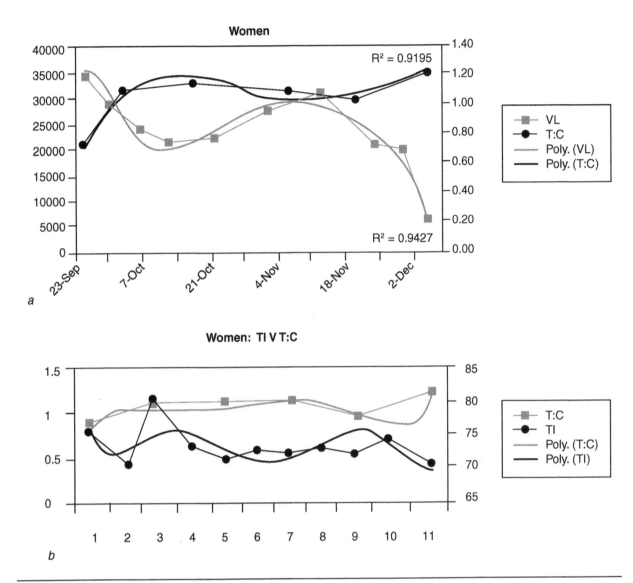

Figure 8.8 Resting hormones. *(a)* The testosterone-to-cortisol ratio (T:C) versus volume load. *(b)* The T:C versus training intensity.

to use "strength" to denote endurance or strength-endurance. On the other hand, throwers, American football players, or weightlifters may use "strength" to denote the ability to lift heavy weights or to denote very powerful movements. Such differences in definition and interpretation of terminology can lead to confusion among both sport scientists and coaches. These examples point out the need for a concise set of definitions between the two groups.

Strength

In the scientific literature, several definitions of strength have been used over the years. For example, Steindler (1935) defined strength as the "maximum display of power." However, as pointed

out by Atha (1981), this definition is again unclear as it simply substitutes one unexplained term (power) for another (strength). Those who presented later definitions began to consider strength and force as linked; for example, Muller (1970, p. 449) suggested that strength should be defined as the "maximum force that can be exerted against an immovable resistance by a single contraction," the idea being that isometric contraction resulted in maximum activation of the contractile elements. However, Muller's (1970) definition implies that all strength is a maximum isometric effort. Many scientists and practitioners have disagreed with this definition, pointing out that force production can have a dynamic aspect and that strength is an important factor in dynamic activities. For example,

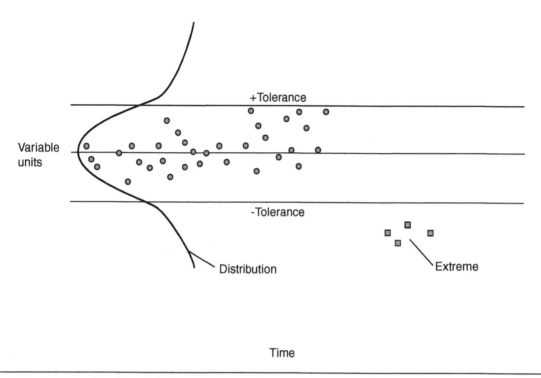

Figure 8.9 An example of statistical process control. Data points outside the tolerance limits are flagged as extreme.

Adapted from W.A. Shewart, 1986, *Statistical method from the viewpoint of quality control* (New York: Dover).

we have known for some time that force production is related to performance in terms of muscular endurance and speed of movement (McCloy 1934; Nelson and Fahrney 1965; Nelson and Jordan 1969). Furthermore, force is particularly important to power production (Berger and Henderson 1966). Researchers have noted that measures of maximum strength including 1RMs are strongly associated with maximum power production (Moss et al. 1997; Robinson et al. 1995; Stone et al. 2002). Thus, a definition of strength as a maximal isometric contraction may be simplistic, and does not take into account strength under all conditions. Perhaps a better way to begin to understand the concept of strength is to consider it an ability. These observations and arguments lead us to the following definition (Siff 2001; Stone 1993):

> strength = the ability of the neuromuscular system to produce force against an external resistance

With this definition, force is essentially the result of a strength display; thus force and strength can be equated. Furthermore, use of this definition removes the earlier specific limitation of isometric conditions but does require the further use of a set of descriptive limitations (i.e., a given set of conditions that govern the strength display). For example, force is a vector quantity and has a magnitude and direction; additionally we can describe force in static or dynamic terms. Therefore, strength has a magnitude ranging from 0% to 100% (maximum), has a direction that results from the manner in which a specific group of muscles is activated, and results in a speed of movement ranging from 0% to 100%.

In a sport context, Zatsiorsky (1995) suggests that three different levels of maximum strength are possible. It is important that the conditions in which these types of maximum strength are generated be carefully defined. Absolute maximum strength (AMS) refers to the greatest amount of strength that a muscle or one or more groups of muscles are capable of producing, and can be determined isometrically or dynamically. Superimposing an electrical stimulation on a maximal voluntary contraction, thus augmenting motor unit recruitment, can produce AMS (Westing, Seger, and Thorstensson 1990). Maximum voluntary strength (MVS) is the maximum amount of strength that can be produced voluntarily without electrical augmentation. The difference between MVS, under a defined set of conditions, and the AMS can be referred to as a strength deficit (Zatsiorsky 1995). Although there can be limitations due to electrode placement, pain, motivation, specific muscle mass, and so on, differences in MVS and AMS may be as high as 20% among untrained subjects during eccentric contractions (Westing, Seger, and Thorstensson 1990). Smaller differences have been noted for isometric and concentric muscle actions (Westing, Seger, and Thorstensson 1990), and an even smaller strength deficit occurs among highly strength-trained athletes for both eccentric and concentric conditions.

A measure of AMS is normally achieved with single-joint movements and isolated muscles; as Siff (2001) points out, achieving a true AMS for the various muscles involved in complex multijoint movements commonly used by athletes would be difficult if not dangerous. Measurement of AMS in isolated muscle would likely not relate well to the complex use of muscles during multijoint movements (Stone et al. 2003a; Zajac and Gordon 1989). Currently the AMS is not a viable measurement for use in sport settings.

Maximum voluntary strength refers to the peak force resulting from a maximal voluntary effort and can be measured either isometrically or dynamically. It is important to note that the MVS can be affected by emotional states (e.g., arousal). Considering emotional states, Zatsiorsky (1995) suggests that within a sporting context, MVS can be further subdivided into competitive maximum strength (Cmax) and training maximum strength (Tmax). This division is based on the observation that under a given set of conditions, the training maximum (1RM) is typically less than the competitive maximum because of differences in motivation and arousal. It is difficult to achieve the same level of arousal and neural excitation in training that can be achieved during competition. Thus the Tmax is essentially equivalent to the maximum load that can be lifted, or the maximum force produced, without substantial emotional excitement. As an example, the difference between Tmax and Cmax among elite weightlifters has been noted to be as much as 12[+]%, with heavier classes typically producing greater differences than lighter classes (Zatsiorsky 1995). Although among advanced and elite athletes both Cmax and Tmax are relatively stable for weeks and months, neither is particularly stable among beginners or novices. Furthermore, among novices and particularly beginners, the differences between Tmax and Cmax may be quite small. Realization of the differences in strength levels can have impor-

tant implications for measurement as well as for prescribing training loads.

One can argue the importance of strength (force) by considering Newton's second law of motion, which describes the characteristics of force:

$$F = MA + W$$

where

M is the mass of an object,

A is the acceleration opposing gravity created by application of force, and

W is the weight of the mass due to the effect of gravity.

Thus, increasing the level of acceleration requires a greater force production; and because acceleration eventually results in some velocity, greater forces will produce higher velocities. Therefore achieving high velocities is dependent on high force production (i.e., strength). Furthermore, power production is also dependent on force production and is related to maximum strength levels (see "Power (P) and Its Components" section).

An example of the importance of force (strength) production (and time interval) can be derived from the forces needed to sprint at an elite level. It can be argued that the limiting factor in upright sprinting results from vertical forces (Mann 1994; Weyand et al. 2000). The foot contact time of the world's best sprinters is approximately 0.087 s, and the vertical velocity of the center of mass during sprinting averaged 0.49 m · s^{-1} up and 0.49 m · s^{-1} down during alternating ground reaction phases (Mann 1994). Using a body mass of 79.5 kg (175 lb) for a male sprinter, the peak vertical force can be calculated using Newton's second law:

vertical force (Fv) = mass × change in vertical velocity / ground time

Fv = 79.5 (0.98) / 0.087 = 91.4 kg (9.8 m · s^{-1} · s^{-1}) = 896 N

total vertical force (Ft) = Fv + W (body weight) =

Ft = 896 N + 779 N = 1675 N = 375 lb (171 kg)

Thus an elite male sprinter would produce a force of about 1675 N on one leg (approximate knee angle of 135° to 140°). From this example we can ascertain that elite sprinters not only have to be quite strong but also have to be quite explosive in producing this force very rapidly (within 0.087

Influence of Rate of Force Development on Performance

Another factor influencing performance is the amount of time over which maximum force is exerted. Andersen and Aagaard (2005) compared maximum isometric voluntary strength (MIVS) and maximum voluntary rate of force development (MVRFD) during a leg extension with the rate of force developed during an electrically evoked twitch (EERFD). The EERFD represents the intrinsic properties of the muscle. At contraction times <40 ms, MVRFD was moderately correlated with EERFD and to a lesser extent with MIVS. However, at a contraction time of 50 ms, MVRFD was moderately correlated with MIVS, and the relationship strengthened as the contraction increased. From 90 ms to 250 ms, MIVS explained 52% to 91% of the variance. This observation indicates that the intrinsic properties of the muscle may be more related to explosiveness in activities lasting less than 40 ms, and that the role of maximum strength may be more important as the time duration of the contraction increases. This observation also highlights the necessity of performing strength (force) measurements at different time intervals, as well as the importance of rate of force development.

s). In some sports (perhaps most sports), one may argue that rate of force development is as important as, or more important than, maximum force production (i.e., maximum strength). Thus, rate of force development is an important characteristic to measure.

Rate of Force Development

Rate of force development (RFD) is change in force divided by change in time and is directly related to the rate of increase in muscle activation by the nervous system (Komi and Viitasalo 1976; Sale 1992). Although force is directly responsible for the acceleration of an object, one may argue that the faster a given force is attained, the more rapid the corresponding acceleration of a mass. Thus, RFD can be associated with the ability to accelerate objects (Schmidtbleicher 1992). Therefore, attaining a high average or peak RFD (explosive strength) is associated with high acceleration capabilities. Rate of force development can be measured during both isometric and dynamic movements.

Power (P) and Its Components

Power production may be the most important characteristic in sport; thus its measurement becomes a priority. However, before a discussion of evidence for this statement, it is important to examine power and its components.

Speed is a scalar quantity and is the magnitude component for the vector termed velocity. Velocity has both a magnitude (speed) and a direction. Force is defined as any action that causes or tends to cause a change of motion of an object and is described by Newton's second law. Work is an expression of force acting on an object through a distance and is independent of time or velocity. Work (in linear systems) can be expressed by the equation

$$W = F(\cos \upsilon)\,s$$

where

F is the applied force,

υ is the angle of force application, and

s is the displacement of the object due to the force application.

Not all work is linear. In angular movement, such as the rotation of segments about a joint, work can be described as

$$W = Fr\,\upsilon$$

where

F is the applied force,

r is the radius, and

υ is the angular displacement (radians).

Work can be measured with a number of different ergometers, for example a cycle ergometer in which displacement is a result of the rotation of a flywheel. In typical strength measurements using a barbell, external concentric work can be estimated using the product of the weight of the bar and the vertical displacement. However, a more accurate description of the amount of work performed in lifting a barbell (or sporting movements) would require a detailed analysis of joint torques (force), segment displacements, and efficiency of movement.

Power is essentially a work rate and may be described by the derived equations:

$$P = W / T = F \times V$$

Power can be calculated as an average over a large range of displacement or as an instantaneous value occurring at a specific brief moment during the displacement of an object. Peak power (PP) is the highest instantaneous power value found over a range of displacement under a given set of conditions (e.g., state of training, type of exercise, training or competition, etc.). Maximum power (MP) is the highest peak power output one is capable of generating during optimal conditions. Schmidtbleicher (1985, 1992) has presented a theoretical framework indicating that maximum strength is the basic quality that affects power output. He further suggests that maximum strength affects power in a hierarchical manner, with diminishing influence as the external load decreases to a point at which other factors such as RFD may become more important. However, the exact relationship between power and maximum strength is still not completely clear (Stone 1993; Stone et al. 2003a&b).

Power output (or work rate) is likely the most important factor in separating sport performances (i.e., who wins and who loses). Thus, as a training goal, the appropriate development of power can be paramount. While average power output may be more associated with performance in endurance events, for maximum-effort single-movement activities such as jumping, sprinting, and weightlifting movements, PP is typically strongly related to success (Garhammer 1993; Kauhanen, Garhammer, and Hakkinen 2000; McBride et al. 1999; Thomas, Fiataron, and Fielding 1994).

Specificity Factors and Measurement of Performance Variables

Specificity of exercise and training is among the most important considerations when one is designing a training program and selecting appropriate equipment for strength-power testing (and training), especially if performance enhancement is a primary goal. Specificity includes both bioenergetic aspects and mechanics of training (Stone and O'Bryant 1987; Wilmore and Costill 1994). The discussion here concerns mechanical specificity.

The term specificity does not mean that two variables are identical; rather specificity deals with the degree of association between or among exercise variables. Thus, when the association between variables is large, a relatively large degree of specificity can be inferred. The term "transfer-of-training effect" can be used to describe the degree

of performance adaptation that can result from a training exercise and is strongly related to specificity. Mechanical specificity refers to the kinetic and kinematic associations between a training exercise and a physical performance. This includes consideration of the movement characteristics necessary for optimal transfer. These characteristics include the following (Siff 2001; Stone 1993; Stone, Plisk, and Collins 2002):

- Movement patterns
  - Complexity of the movement
  - Body position factors
  - Range of movement and accentuated regions of force production
  - Types of muscle actions (e.g., concentric, eccentric, stretch–shortening cycle)
- Force magnitude (average and peak force)
- Rate of force development (average and peak)
- Acceleration and velocity parameters
- Ballistic versus nonballistic movements

Substantial evidence from reviews of the literature supports the idea that an appropriate overload within the context of specificity enhances the probability of transfer (Behm 1995; Plisk and Stone 2003; Sale 1992; Schmidt 1991; Stone, Plisk, and Collins 2002). This means that in order to enhance the potential for measuring strength-power gains (or any other performance variable), the exercises used in testing should be the same or as similar as possible with respect to the transfer characteristics listed. The more mechanically dissimilar the test becomes, the lower the potential for observing training adaptations. This also means that if generalizations from a specific test are to be made to another activity, that test should be kinetically and kinematically similar to the activity.

Measurement of Strength (Force) and Related Factors

Reasonable assessment of training program results and potential for sport performance should include measures (or reasonable estimates) of strength and other factors such as peak force, RFD, and power. Strength can be expressed and measured in a number of different ways. Furthermore, as noted earlier, a high degree of mechanical specificity appears to be involved in appropriate measurement of strength (and other parameters such as power and endurance) (Stone, Plisk, and Collins 2002). This means that not just any test of maximum strength, speed, or power will suffice. One important aspect of specificity in testing is muscle action type. Typical tests of strength and related parameters, particularly 1RM tests, could include different types of muscle actions.

The following are different types of muscle actions:

- Isometric: Muscle gains tension but does not appreciably change length (although some shortening in the contractile elements does occur, there is no change in joint angle in intact muscle).
- Concentric: Muscle gains tension and shortens.
- Eccentric: Muscle gains tension and lengthens.
- Plyometric: Concentric action is immediately preceded by an eccentric action (i.e., a stretch–shortening cycle).

The latter three types of muscle action are dynamic and can be applied in a variety of movement patterns and at different speeds and power outputs. Isometric muscle action, on the other hand, is an expression of static strength that can be applied in a number of positional patterns and at different rates of force development. All of these factors can make strength testing a confusing issue. Proper selection of the correct strength measurements for sport is of paramount importance.

Strength was defined previously in this section as the ability to produce force. As can be inferred from Newton's second law, force (strength) can be associated with the acceleration of an object, and therefore force application will impart velocity to an object. Thus strength can have great impact on various types of sporting activities in which velocity is imparted to an object, including the athlete's body mass.

Maximum strength levels have been associated with superior sport performance or with variables linked to sport performance (Stone et al. 2003a). Because of this association, measurements of maximum strength are often used to assess adaptations to strength training programs, with the assumption that improved maximum strength will carry over to sport performance. However, several important aspects of measurement must be satisfied before proper strength assessment can be carried out (see the previous section in this chapter, "Principles of Testing, Measurement, and Evaluation").

Any form of testing for physical performance, including strength or any other variable, must have established validity and reliability, as already discussed. One method of enhancing reliability is the process of familiarization, or allowing the subjects or athletes to become accustomed to the measurement exercise. The familiarization process would involve several practice sessions before testing begins. During this process it is very important to make sure that the athletes understand all of the instructions and can carry them out. Provided that familiarization is not a problem and that specificity aspects have been considered, strength testing generally shows a high degree of internal validity and reliability.

It is important to address the characteristics (Siff 2001; Stone 1993; Stone, Plisk, and Collins 2002) relating to mechanical specificity in order to increase the validity and reliability of the measurement. Knowing how these characteristics can affect measurement validity and reliability is helpful for an understanding of appropriate strength measurement.

Muscle Action

Isometric testing has been used in scientific study and as a field test for well over 50 years. The reliability and internal validity are generally excellent provided that positional considerations are appropriate. However, the external and prediction validity of isometric testing has been questioned (Wilson and Murphy 1996). Low external and prediction validity results from neural, mechanical, and methodological factors, which can reduce or obviate the usefulness of isometric measures in assessing dynamic movement. Thus nonspecific isometric measurement generally has only limited value in assessing alterations in sport performance, as discussed later within the context of positional and movement pattern specificity.

Concentric-only testing can be used for a number of reasons. For example, many athletic movements start with no countermovement (e.g., sprinters' starts, American football linemen's movements); thus it may be useful to assess the strength attributes related to these static-start performances. Testing concentric muscle actions also can assist in assessment of the contractile apparatus independent of the effects of muscle stretch or a stretch–shortening cycle (SSC). Furthermore, concentric movements can have high correlations with specific aspects of plyometric (SSC) movements (Cronin, McNaira, and Marshall 2000) and certain sport performances that have plyometric aspects (Stone et al. 2003b). Additionally, in relatively untrained or frail individuals for whom the eccentric portion of an exercise may be difficult to control, concentric testing may allow a degree of experimental control not otherwise possible.

Eccentric muscle action testing can also be important, for a number of reasons. For example, maximum force applied during eccentric movements is generally higher than maximum force in either isometric or concentric movements. The difference between eccentric and isometric or concentric forces can be viewed as a deficit, which can be affected by the type of training an athlete has undertaken (Gohner 1994; Zatsiorsky 1995). Large deficits could indicate that the type of strength training program employed is not adequate for the sport in question. Many sports require achievement of high eccentric forces in certain elements of performance. Weightlifting, for example, requires the generation of very high peak eccentric forces during the downward phase of the jerk. The inability to generate high forces could compromise the corresponding concentric movement phase. Eccentric strength testing could indicate a problem with force-generating abilities during an eccentric portion of a movement.

Plyometric testing is the most common form of strength testing. Typically strength is measured both in the laboratory and in the field via plyometric movements such as a parallel squat. This type of testing takes advantage of a muscle connective tissue stretch (SSC), which is a characteristic of many types of performance in sport (Asmussen and Bonde-Petersen 1974; Bobbert et al. 1996; Komi and Bosco 1978; Newton et al. 1996, 1997). One-repetition maximum (1RM) testing is likely the most common type of maximum strength evaluation. The 1RM value is a reasonable measure of maximum dynamic strength in that it is directly proportional to the force required to overcome a given load. It is the 1RM type of test that most coaches and athletes use to evaluate strength training programs. Plyometric testing in the form of weightlifting movements, throws, and jumps is also valuable for evaluating explosive strength and power.

Positional and Movement Pattern Specificity

Positional specificity and movement pattern specificity are often overlooked aspects of strength testing. A high degree of intramuscular, and particularly intermuscular, task specificity exists. This means that during a particular movement, specific motor units are activated within a muscle in a specific time sequence, and that there is a specific activation pattern for prime movers, synergists, and stabiliz-

ers. These patterns can be altered by even slight changes in moment pattern and likely by changes in velocity (Stone, Plisk, and Collins 2002; Zajac and Gordon 1989). Thus, selection of strength testing procedures that have a greater similarity to a specific sporting performance allows one to make better inferences. Positional specificity and movement pattern specificity are important considerations when one is selecting testing modes and considering single-joint versus multijoint tests or isometric versus dynamic movements.

Single Versus Multiple-Joint Testing While single-joint testing is often used in some types of research necessitating a high degree of control, multijoint testing is more appropriate in most athletic and many injury rehabilitation settings. The need for multijoint assessment of strength (and other force-related characteristics) has to do with the fact that most athletic activity is multijoint in character. It is important to understand that the functional behavior of muscles during multijoint activities, particularly those with velocity changes, may be quite different from the behavior of those same muscles during single-joint movements (Zajac and Gordon 1989).

Isometric Testing Isometric peak forces change as a function of body position and joint angle; thus it is crucial to select positions that are related to a specific sport. Use of positional specificity can greatly strengthen the isometric-dynamic relationships (Haff et al. 1997; Stone et al. 2003b; Wilson and Murphy 1996). This means testing in a position specific to that used in the performance of interest and choosing joint angles that involve the highest force outputs in the performance. This in turn entails isometrically measuring a specific position within the range of motion of the exercise of interest. Evidence indicates that the most appropriate position for isometric maximum strength testing is one in which joint angles are likely to be those at which peak forces are developed (Murphy et al. 1995; Stone et al. 2003b). This specific position likely will allow the best inference to dynamic activity (Haff et al. 1997; Stone et al. 2003b; Wilson and Murphy 1996). For example, the greatest vertical forces in sprinting are produced at a knee angle of approximately 135° to 140° with the trunk upright. Thus, testing sprinters in this position likely will enhance the usefulness of the measurement. Figure 8.10 shows a force/power rack that can be used to test a variety of isometric movements such as squats, pulls, and pressing movements. Force–time characteristics for these movements are measured on a

Figure 8.10 A force/power rack. The athlete is standing on a large force plate; on command, the athlete (without a countermovement) pulls as hard and as fast as possible, generating an isometric force–time curve (figure 8.11*a*). The immovable bar can be adjusted to any height and locked into place using pins and clamps. Other lifts such as squatting and pressing movements can also be measured.

Courtesy of Mike Stone.

force plate. The bar (immovable) can be adjusted to any height using pulleys and hydraulic jacks. Thus an apparatus of this type can be used to enhance positional specificity.

A very important consideration is that maximum strength may not be the only factor or the best characteristic to test. In terms of enhancing external validity, one should take into account several other force-related characteristics. Among the most important are time and RFD.

Rate of Force Development   For many sports (perhaps most), being able to produce force quickly may be more important than maximum force production. Thus the rate of force production is an important aspect to consider for measurement. Rate of force development (RFD) is a change in force divided by change in time. The RFD is a function of the rate of increase in muscle activation by the nervous system (Komi and Viitasalo 1976; Sale 1992) and is associated with the ability to accelerate objects (Schmidtbleicher 1992). Measurement

of RFD requires special equipment; usually a force plate is used for RFD measures of athletic movements. For example, an athlete could perform isometric squats or static or dynamic jumps from a force plate, and one or more force–time curves could be generated (figure 8.11, *a* through *c*).

Figure 8.11*a* presents a typical isometric force–time curve (F-TC). The force generated in the first 30 ms has been termed "starting strength" and is related to the initial RFD (Schmidtbleicher 1992). The peak RFD (PRFD) has been termed "explosive strength" (Schmidtbleicher 1992; Stone 1993). Peak force (PF) is the greatest force that can be produced under the conditions of the measurement. It appears (Schmidtbleicher 1992) that a high starting strength and a high isometric and dynamic PRFD are necessary for optimal performance in sports in which light loads are moved very fast, for example fencing and boxing. The PRFD or explosive strength becomes increasingly important as the load increases (e.g., shot put); and as the load approaches maximum, maximum

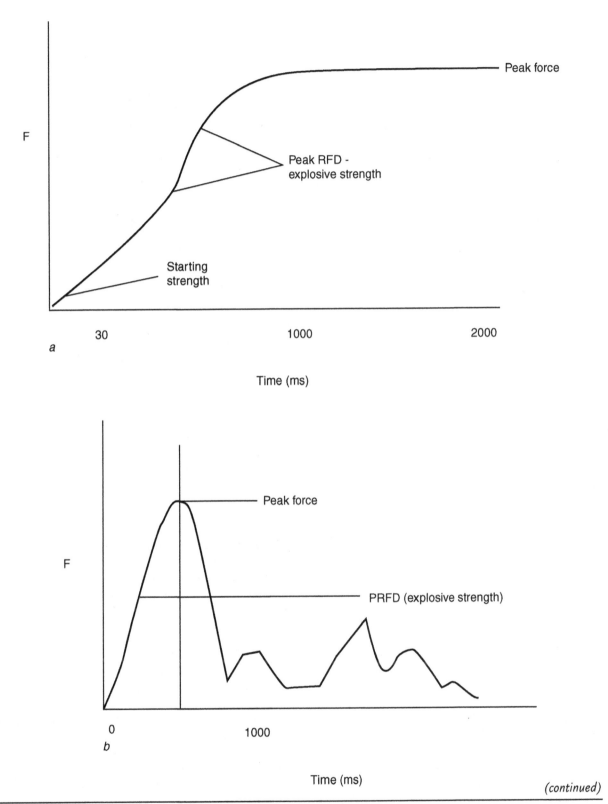

Figure 8.11 Explosive exercise measurement. *(a)* An isometric force-time curve. "Starting strength" is the force produced at 30 ms; "explosive strength" is peak rate of force development; "peak force" is the greatest force produced under a given set of conditions. *(b)* A concentric-only force-time curve. *(c)* A plyometric movement (countermovement vertical jump). UW = unweighting phase; ECC = eccentric braking phase; CON = concentric propulsion phase.

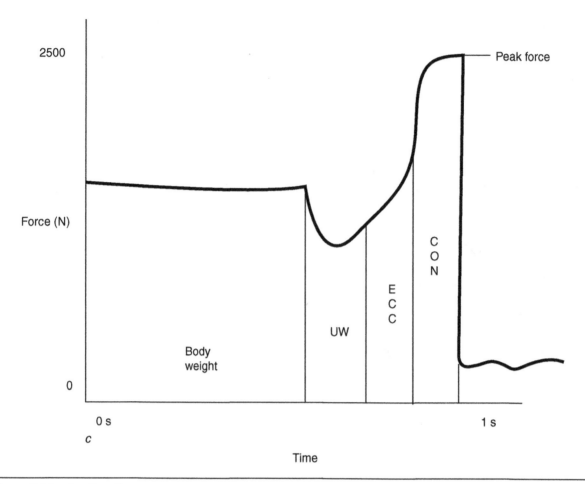

Figure 8.11   *(continued)*

strength predominates (e.g., in powerlifting). Using a force plate, isometric F-TCs can be generated for a number of positions including various pressing, squatting, and pulling positions.

Figure 8.11*b* presents a concentric dynamic force–time curve. As with the isometric force–time curve, starting strength, explosive strength, and peak force can be described dynamically. Note that peak force decreases as the load lifted decreases. Although not all studies agree (Muller 1987), evidence indicates that during dynamic exercise, PF and PRFD are inversely related, particularly in large muscle mass exercises (Haff et al. 1997; Stone et al. 2003b). Thus (at least to a point), lighter loads can produce a higher PRFD than heavier loads. However, there is also evidence that maximum strength, as estimated from 1RM data, is associated with PRFD in both isometric and dynamic movements and with peak power (Aagaard et al. 1994; Haff et al. 1997; Stone et al. 2003b). This observation is interesting in that it suggests that maximum strength and PRFD may be enhanced simultaneously with appropriate strength train-

ing. Indeed, appropriate strength training has been shown to enhance both maximum strength and PRFD in untrained subjects (Aagaard et al. 2002) as well as strength-trained athletes (Stone et al. 2003b). Given these relationships, testing in which these characteristics of strength can be simultaneously measured is very much worth consideration. Concentric force–time curves can be generated using pressing, pulling, squatting, and jumping movements. Furthermore, a variety of loads can be used, allowing a more complete picture of force-generating capabilities.

Figure 8.11*c* presents a plyometric force–time curve. Many movements involve a plyometric component, in which there is an SSC. The figure shows a typical force–time curve resulting from a jumping movement. During a typical countermovement jump, an unweighting phase initiates the SSC and produces a plyometric movement. The resulting upward force can be augmented by previous stretching of the muscle. The mechanism by which concentric force can be augmented by a previous stretch is not completely clear but involves several possibilities, including (a) muscle elastic properties, (b) a myotatic reflex, (c) return of the muscle to its optimal length, and (d) optimization of the muscle activation pattern. As with the concentric tests, a variety of movements and loadings can be measured.

Power

For most sports, power is the most important characteristic to develop (Garhammer 1993; Kauhanen, Garhammer, and Hakkinen 2000; McBride et al. 1999; Schmidtbleicher 1985, 1992; Thomas et al. 1994). A simple way to begin to understand the importance of power is to conceptualize power as a work rate: In most cases the athlete getting work accomplished at the fastest rate wins. Therefore, appropriate measurement of power is paramount. Power measurement exercises can be of two types:

- Maximal single-effort explosive moments such as a single vertical jump
- Overcoming a resistance with a series of maximum efforts for a given distance, as with a stair climbing test, or for a given time, as with Wingate power tests

Average and peak power can be measured using both exercise types. From a metabolic standpoint, power is directly related to the rate at which ATP is being used to fuel muscle contraction. As the intensity of the contraction increases, so does the rate requirement for ATP. Thus, the measurement of power is a reflection of the intensity of muscle contraction and the rate at which ATP is being used. Average power output reflects the average rate of ATP use, and peak power reflects the peak rate of ATP use. As with strength or endurance measures, the selection of an appropriate power test depends primarily on specificity considerations. For example, a vertical jump power test might be chosen for a volleyball player, a modified Wingate test for a sprint cyclist.

One can estimate power output with reasonable accuracy using very simple equipment. The following are two examples, one with a single maximum-effort test and one with a multiple maximum-effort test.

For a single maximum-effort test, using a jump and reach, or using a switch mat and deriving jump height from flight time, enables one to derive power from jump height and body mass. Average power can be estimated using a modified falling-body equation:

$$AP \text{ (W)} = SqR \text{ jump height (meters)} \times \text{body mass} \times 2.21 \times 9.8 \text{ m} \cdot \text{s}^{-2}$$

The equation of Sayers and colleagues (1999) for estimated peak power has good validity and reliability and is not affected by sex differences (Carlock et al. 2004; Hertogh and Hue 2002; Sayers et al. 1999):

$$PP \text{ (W)} = (60.7) \times \\ \text{(jump height in centimeters)} + \\ 45.3 \times \text{body mass} - 2055$$

Maximum single-effort tests like these can easily be performed at various loads or percentages of maximum so that a peak power curve can be produced (McBride et al. 1999; Stone et al. 2002).

For multiple maximum-effort tests, stair climbing can be used to produce an average power output (Margaria, Aghemo, and Rovelli 1966; Stone and O'Bryant 1987). For these tests the athlete performs a maximum-effort run up a flight of stairs (usually with a 5-6 m [5.5-6.6 yd] lead-in). The time of ascent can be measured with a stopwatch or switch mats. Using the equation for power (work rate), average power can be calculated:

$$AP = F \times D/T$$

where

F = force that is proportional to body mass,

D is the vertical rise of the stairs, and

T is the time taken to complete the stair climb.

The Margaria-Kalamen stair climb test has been standardized, and normative data are available for males and females at different ages (Stone and O'Bryant 1987).

Power can also be measured with more complex equipment. For example, interfacing (and synchronizing) of potentiometers with a force plate allows one to obtain simultaneous measures of position and force. As the change in position per unit of time can also be measured, velocity of movement can be determined. Power (F × V) can be calculated from the measurements of force and velocity. Figures 8.10 and 8.12 show a force/power rack in which a variety of pulling, jumping, or pressing movements can be measured. Potentiometers, located on top of the rack, are attached to each end of the bar at the collar. With use of two potentiometers, an average (of the two) will give a reasonable measure of the velocity of the middle of the bar. This is important because in many movements, especially jumps, one end of the bar may move at a faster rate than the other, which can reduce reliability. Thus reasonable measures of force, velocity, and power

Figure 8.12 A weighted countermovement vertical jump in a force/power rack. With use of a combination of potentiometers (not shown in this image) and a force plate, power exerted on the bar can be calculated.

Courtesy of Mike Stone.

can be derived and displayed from this type of instrumentation (figure 8.13). Besides measuring single maximum-effort movements, this type of device can measure a series of efforts in which the power (and force characteristics) can be determined for each individual effort. In this way the effects of fatigue and short-term high-intensity exercise endurance can be examined.

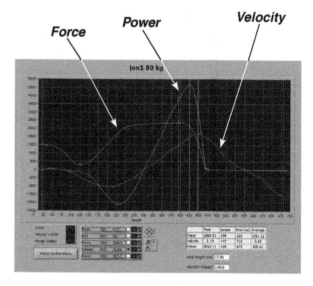

Figure 8.13 Computer graphic of a weighted countermovement jump displaying force, rate of force development, velocity, power, and jump height.

CHAPTER SUMMARY

Sport science (and good coaching) concerns the enhancement of sport performance through the application of scientific methods and principles. Sport scientists are engaged in a variety of endeavors, including research and service testing. If service and research are to be useful, then related measurements must be specific and must be valid and reliable.

The scientific literature clearly indicates that the magnitude of gains in endurance, strength, or other variables such as velocity or power resulting from a specific training program depends on the similarities between the testing exercises and those used in training (Stone, Plisk, and Collins 2002). For example, if an athlete trains using squats, then 1RM measurements of the squat are more likely to reflect training adaptations in maximum strength than leg extension measurement. This relates to the concept of movement pattern specificity.

Reliability deals with the repeatability or consistency of measurement scores, and validity deals with whether or not the testing instrument is actually measuring what it is supposed to be measuring. Reliability and validity of measurement are necessary because evaluation of performance and performance-related parameters is not possible otherwise.

Testing results and evaluation must be returned to the coach and athlete in a reasonable amount of time, usually within three days. This ensures that appropriate alterations in training can be made while there is still time to correct problems that may become obvious as a result of the tests and evaluation.

Therefore, in assessing the fitness level of an athlete or in order to appropriately track adaptations to a training program, it is paramount that tests be specific, valid, and reliable. Additionally, test results must be returned to the coach and athlete in comprehensible form in a reasonable time frame.

CHAPTER 9

Monitoring Resistance Training

Monitoring training is a spectrum of activities leading to an understanding of the training and performance process. Training monitoring can be as simple as mental notes of training produced from simple observation, or as complex as serial tests of electroencephalography combined with blood, endocrine, immunity, and other tests. Training monitoring can occur over relatively short durations, but is usually considered a long-term process of serial measurements used to track and characterize the tasks of training and the athlete's responses to these tasks. However, in order to understand training monitoring, it is helpful to define training.

Training has been defined in the following ways:

"Any organized instruction whose aim is to increase man's physical, psychological, intellectual, or mechanical performance rapidly" (Harre 1982, p. 10)

"Preparing sportsmen for the highest levels of performance" (Harre 1982, p. 10)

"The physical, technical, intellectual, psychological and moral preparation of an athlete by means of physical exercises" (Harre 1982, p. 10)

"The entire systematic process of preparation of athletes for the highest levels of athletic performance" (Harre 1982, p. 10)

These definitions singly and in sum indicate that training is a process that leads to enhanced or increased preparedness. By increasing preparedness, the athlete should increase performance. Training monitoring attempts to characterize the time-based status of and change in an athlete's preparedness. Preparedness can be classified by physical, psychological, intellectual, and mechanical means. An athlete enhances his or her preparedness by performing physical, technical, tactical, and psychological tasks that are slightly beyond the athlete's current capabilities. By taking on these tasks, collectively called stressors, the athlete attempts to train the body to adapt and thus increase his or her fitness so that future, more difficult, tasks can be performed and accomplished. The stressors applied to the athlete are called a training *dosage,* while the adaptations to these stressors are called *responses.* Training monitoring seeks to understand training by measuring, characterizing, comparing, and depicting the relationships of dosage to response.

Training dose involves the tasks of training. Training tasks can be broadly categorized as just described. These categories are the "loads" of training. Of course, athletes are also subjected to many other "loads" or stressors such as social, family, school, work, and other demands. All of these demands are the "inputs" to the athlete's adaptational resources. These demands act singly and in concert to cause the athlete's organism to react. Selye (1956) defined stress as anything that causes an organism to react. Selye further divided stress into eustress ("good" stress) and distress ("bad" stress). These subtypes of stress weigh on the adaptive resources of the athlete. *Adaptive resources,* as referred to here, are similar in concept to the cumulative adaptive reserves of Verkhoshansky (1985) and the concept of adaptation energy from Selye (1956).

Training dose involves all of the things an athlete does or all of the training tasks that cause the athlete to react. Training dosage is the input of tasks to the dose–response relationship that influences the athlete. Training factors are largely under the control of coaches and sport scientists, while life factors are subject to far less scrutiny and control. In spite of the little control over life factors or stresses, the athlete's preparedness can be overwhelmed by these nontraining factors due to their potential to accumulate and sum or interact with training tasks and stressors. The athlete's reaction to these stressors, tasks, and demands is the athlete's response.

The athlete's response to training tasks and life stresses is the output of the dose–response relationship. Athletes do not have an infinite capacity to respond to training and life stresses; thus training and life-stress dosage must be appropriate for the current condition of the athlete so that the athlete achieves an optimal response for any given tasks or loads. Failure to achieve this optimal balance often results in athletic performance failure when training dosage is too low and the athlete is defeated by opponents who prepare more thoroughly and intensely. Or the athlete's performance may fail because he or she receives training or has life demands that are too great, and the failure is due to injury or an overwhelming fatigue.

Training monitoring seeks to characterize dosage and response so that the athlete is given optimal training tasks in concert with appropriate life demands such that optimal adaptations are achieved. The athlete should progress optimally without threat of injury or overtraining. Since each athlete may have varying capacities for training demands, and these capacities are largely unknown, the only logical means of preventing injury and overtraining is careful monitoring of training dose and response so that response information is fed back to training demands. Information from monitoring can then be used to moderate training and life-stress inputs in order to achieve optimal performance outputs.

Importance of Monitoring Resistance Training

Only comprehensive monitoring offers a means of measuring and then controlling both the planned and unplanned aspects of training. It is difficult to imagine a systematically successful project or process without planning. The West has embraced planning via training theory and periodization (see chapters 1 and 13) as an important means of enhancing training and performance (Bompa 1984a, 1984b, 1990a, 1990b, 1993; Bondarchuk 1988; Charniga et al. 1986a, 1986b, 1987; Fry, Morton, and Keast 1992; Matveyev 1977; Stone, O'Bryant, and Garhammer 1981; Verhoshansky 2002; Verkhoshansky 1998). The tenets of periodization have found their way into virtually all modern coaching education, as well as the preparation of sport scientists, as a unifying scheme for delivering training programs over the long term. While periodized planning is clearly a crucial initial step, planning alone does not steer an athlete through a training program. Numerous unpredictable events can shift an athlete's performance and adaptation capabilities from an intended path to an unintended path. Illness, injury, overestimation of the athlete's adaptive resources, winning, losing, and changes in competition schedules are examples of things that can undermine even the best training plans.

Investigating training in the time domain, even with relatively simple and noninvasive measures, may provide considerable insight into qualitative dose–response relationships. For example, how do various training periods influence injury? Figures 9.1 and 9.2 show the number of injuries per exposure of a nationally ranked collegiate women's gymnastics team. Note that the patterns of injury are different. Total injuries includes the sum of new injuries (recorded for the first time) and old injuries (injuries still being recorded). The definition of an injury in this study was any damaged body part that would constrain or reduce training that day (Sands, Shultz, and Newman 1993). The data shown in figures 9.1 and 9.2 were obtained simply by recording injuries daily for all athletes. Figure 9.3 shows monitoring data of prepractice resting heart rate and prepractice scale mass for a single female collegiate gymnast. The data depicted in figure 9.3 were drawn from simple observations and assessments. However, the stories told by these data are profound with regard to what a coach might modify in order to reduce the likelihood of injury (since now he or she has an idea when injuries are likely), and the coach may have a new respect for the relationship of heart rate and scale mass in some athletes. Thus the coach may exercise more caution in training when confronted by a similar pattern in the future.

Purposes of Monitoring Resistance Training

There are two overall purposes to monitoring training: (1) general monitoring and (2) specific monitoring. General monitoring seeks to determine the dose–response relationship of overall training and life stresses that are imposed on an athlete. Specific monitoring seeks to determine the dose–response relationship, usually in a shorter term, of particular training loads and tasks. For example, training

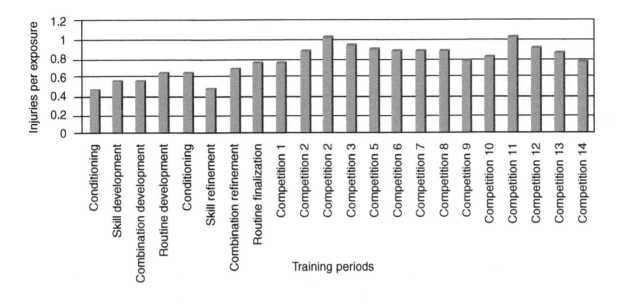

Figure 9.1 Total injuries per exposure during five years of training and competition with a nationally ranked women's gymnastics team. Data are collapsed across the five years and averaged for each training period.

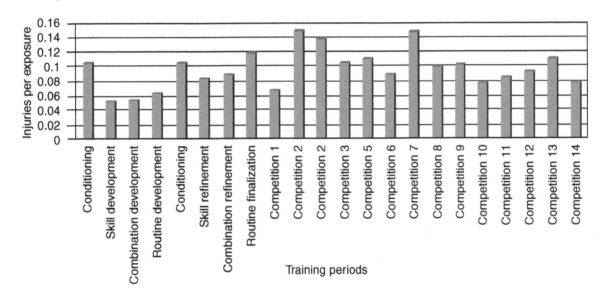

Figure 9.2 New injuries per exposure during five years of training and competition with a nationally ranked university women's gymnastics team. Data are collapsed across the five years and averaged for each training period.

diaries of morning heart rate, sleep disturbances, and psychological mood states are often used to determine an overall response to training, while 1RMs are used to determine specific adaptations to one aspect of a given resistance exercise. Of course, these purposes tend to overlap, and much of the distinction arises from the number of measurements and the duration in which the measurements are taken. Tests repeated only a few times are likely used to assess readiness, while tests used often and over a relatively longer duration are more likely

to serve as measures of a more global response to training. The function of these two levels of training monitoring is to assess the short- and long-term effects of training on the entire organism.

Aspects of Resistance Training Worth Monitoring

Due to the problem of finding reliable and valid markers of training status, Hopkins raised the

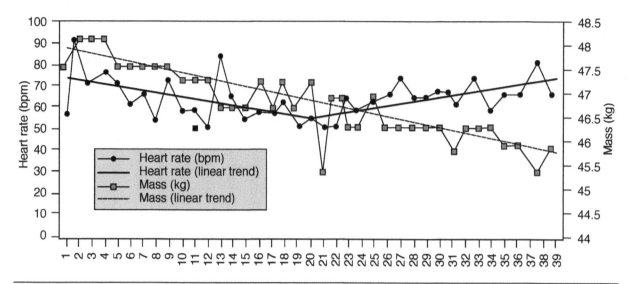

Figure 9.3 This graph shows a classic pattern of overtraining. The athlete shows a decreasing heart rate and decreasing weight until approximately day 20, when the athlete's prepractice resting heart rate begins to trend upward. Increasing resting heart rate and decreasing weight are considered classic symptoms of sympathetic overtraining. Sadly, day 39 was this athlete's last day as a collegiate gymnast because she suffered a career-ending injury on that day.

question of what is worth monitoring (Hopkins 1991, 1998b). Viru has also written that while many variables can be measured in the name of monitoring training, not all variables are suitable indicators of performance status or change in the athlete's adaptation capabilities over time (Viru and Viru 2001). However, before searching for a specific marker, one should clearly identify the purpose of monitoring.

Monitoring Dosage

Training dosage is perhaps the easiest, most logical, and simplest area of monitoring—both general and specific. Training dosage is divided into volume, intensity, density, and frequency. Volume is the quantity of training demands, usually measured as sets, repetitions, or how much the athlete does. Intensity is the force, rate of work, or how hard the athlete performs training. Density refers to the amount of training that is packed into a given time period. "Two-a-days" is a denser training dosage than "one-a-days." Frequency simply refers to the number of training sessions.

Resistance training provides many relatively easily measured dosage variables. The type of exercise, number of repetitions, resistance used, percentage of 1RM, speed of the movement, range of motion of the movement, number of sets, rest period between sets, body positions, order of exercise, time of day, preceding exercise characteristics,

activities during rest, and many other variables can be assessed and recorded. All of these variables have some impact on the character of the athlete's training and ultimately on the character of the athlete's response to training. Resistance training has traditionally monitored the number of sets, repetitions, weight lifted, percentage of 1RM, and duration of rest periods between sets. However, we now know that these variables, while important, are often not sufficient to fully characterize athlete training (Abernethy and Wilson 2000; Harman 1995; Logan et al. 2000 ; Sands 2000). Power monitoring, rate of force development, speed of movement, and even the shape of the force–time curve of an explosive effort can be used to characterize and monitor resistance training.

Monitoring Response

Compared to dosage variables, valid response variables are much more difficult to determine (Hopkins 1991). The difficulties come from three areas:

1. Specific training stressors may result in nonspecific physiological responses (Cannon 1928; Cohen and Williamson 1991; Hatfield and Landers 1983; Kellmann 2002c; Lacey, Bateman, and VanLehn 1953; Obrist 1968; O'Leary 1990; Steinacker and Lehmann 2002; Tucker 1990).

2. Training responses may not be linearly related to training dose (Viru 1995, 1994; Viru and Viru 2002).

3. Training responses may become manifest only after a variable duration delay (Verchoshanskij 1999; Verhoshansky et al. 1991; Verkhoshansky 1985).

Although the determination of one or a few reliable and valid markers of training response has been a highly prized and sought-after area of sport physiology, there is little consensus as to which marker variables work with all athletes in all circumstances.

Choosing a reliable and valid response variable or variables depends on the purpose of the response monitoring (i.e., what you want to know), level of invasiveness you can achieve (e.g., blood tests vs. a questionnaire), desired frequency of measurements (tests may be painful or difficult, or may result in problems with test sensitivity), financial resources available (some marker variables are quite expensive to measure), and ease of data analyses and reporting.

Response variables are generally used to determine two things—changes in fitness and changes in fatigue or recovery. Fitness variables, when they decline, may be attributed to fatigue. However, recent investigators have begun to address recovery as a separate aspect of response to training. For example, it may be that an athlete's overall fitness level is quite high but he or she doesn't show a high fitness level in a test due to a lack of local or short-term recovery. Measures of recovery, or the lack of it, have been addressed by Kellmann and others (Beckmann 2002; Davis, Botterill, and MacNeill 2002; Hanin 2002; Kallus 2002; Kellmann 2002a, 2002b, 2002c; Kenttä and Hassmén 2002; Steinacker and Lehmann 2002).

If monitoring is ongoing, continuous, and daily or nearly daily, then monitoring of fitness and recovery is likely to be accomplished as a matter of course. However, in the case of intermittent tests that may occur at regular intervals, but less frequently than daily (e.g., monthly, quarterly, semiannually), specialized tests may be needed to assess local or recent recovery so that they are conducted with the athlete in a rested state or at least a consistent state from test to test. In other words, administered tests should be detecting changes in fitness, not random states of recent or local fatigue. For example, athletes should be well hydrated; a simple urine specific-gravity test performed prior to a testing session can indicate those athletes who are dramatically dehydrated, and testing can be post-poned until they are sufficiently hydrated. Tests that are contaminated by dehydration are not as helpful in determining the athlete's current status as those performed in a euhydrated state. Other tests that have been used to determine current fatigue status or readiness for testing (or both) have included the Margaria test, lactate level in resting blood, and the Rusko heart rate response test. Of course, all of these tests are compared against baseline values.

However, we would like to argue that the traditional approaches to training monitoring are not just problematic, but largely doomed to failure in a practical training setting. The reason has to do with the typical reliance on group data (nomothetic investigations) rather than monitoring, studying, and analyzing individual athlete data (ideographic investigations). Responses to training appear to be characteristic, but idiosyncratic, which means that an individual athlete tends to respond similarly over time to a given training or life stress, but that these responses may differ from individual to individual (Barlow and Hersen 1984; Bates 1996; Bryan 1987; Cooper 1981; Dishman 1983; Jacobson 1967; Lacey, Bateman, and VanLehn 1953; Lacey and Lacey 1958; Newsham-West 2002; Nourbakhsh and Ottenbacher 1994; Ottenbacher and Hinderer 2001; Riddoch and Lennon 1994; Shephard 1998). The techniques for single-subject research designs have been well established for many years, but very few sport scientists are trained in these methods (Barlow and Hersen 1984; Bates 1996; Bithell 1994; Bryan 1987; Cicciarella 2000; Cooper 1981; Dunn 1994; Duquin 1984; Hrycaiko and Martin 1996; Kinugasa et al. 2002; Maas and Mester 1996; Mueser, Yarnold, and Foy 1991; Newsham-West 2002; Nourbakhsh and Ottenbacher 1994; Riddoch and Lennon 1994). Moreover, because training response variables may be idiosyncratic, traditional inferential statistics methods are problematic due to small samples, inability to find a sufficiently large and matched control group, and heterogeneity of the athletes, particularly elite athletes (Hopkins 2002; Hopkins, Hawley, and Burke 1999). Alternatives to traditional inferential statistics are well suited for monitoring resistance training. These analysis methods include single-subject experimental designs, graphical analysis, statistical process control, trend analyses, and time-series analysis.

How to Monitor Resistance Training

First and foremost, select and monitor the best variable(s) you can afford. (Note that the selection of specific variables is beyond the reach of this chapter and depends on the specific physical, physiological, psychological, or other information you want to know. Chapters 2 through 6 and chapters 10 through 11 in this book address those variables that are well established or promising for use in training monitoring.)

Once you have selected one or more variables, data acquisition must occur as frequently as the variable and the collection circumstances permit. Dosage and response data collected in the form of training diaries or questionnaires can be obtained daily. Dosage data that require a difficult, exhausting, or costly test may be acquired less often but should be acquired at regularly spaced intervals. Response data obtained from invasive tests such as blood tests, biopsies, and so forth must be limited because of their invasiveness and because they are sometimes painful. Tests that interrupt training too much should be avoided or assigned to specific and preplanned times in the training plan. If tests are envisioned that require extreme efforts or significant recovery times, the coach and athlete must plan for these types of tests by incorporating a special microcycle prior to each test, with the aim of ensuring that the athlete is in roughly the same state of rest for each test.

Problems may arise when one is planning to obtain long-term training and performance data from conventional human subjects approval committees in universities (Stone, Sands, and Stone 2004). Studies lasting longer than one year and requiring frequent testing may be difficult for conventional human subjects committees to fit into their more normal paradigm of pretest, posttest, control group designs. Moreover, because individual athletes may not respond the same way to training interventions, one cannot expect that univariate-type tests will yield sufficient fidelity when one is trying to ascertain how athletes are training and how they respond to training. Finally, the point of doing training monitoring is to give the coach sufficient evidence to modify training loads "on the fly," such that the athlete is always kept in an optimal response window of adaptation. This means that the coach will be constantly modifying training load based on monitoring results and then the scientist must take a "wait and see" approach to data analyses. This in turn means that typical hypothesis-testing approaches will not work well, and the investigator will need to present his or her case to the human subjects committee with a large number of unknowns. This usually flies in the face of human subjects committee mandates

and the committee's ability to closely control what investigators do with human subjects.

Monitoring has been accomplished largely in two forms: (1) training logs, questionnaires, or survey-type tools and (2) specific physiological, psychological, nutritional, or biomechanical tests (or some combination of these) performed at varying intervals, depending on the nature of the tests. Each form of monitoring has its strengths and weaknesses. Training logs are able to provide information on a more regular and immediate basis but may not specifically address aspects of training that require invasive or more ambitious tests. Specific physiological tests are more time-consuming, disruptive of training, expensive, and infrequent. However, specific physiological, psychological, and biomechanical tests usually result in higher-quality information due to their more targeted approach.

Training Logs

Training logs have been proposed and used by coaches and athletes for many years (Hopkins 1998a, 1998b; Kellmann 2002c; Kenttä and Hassmén 2002; Mackinnon and Hooper 1994; Sands 1990b, 1991b, 1991a; Sands, Henschen, and Shultz 1989). Training logs have been kept in books, on paper, and more recently via computer (figures 9.4, 9.5, and 9.6). Training logs are the simplest, cheapest, and easiest of the monitoring methods to use in practical training settings. Training logs can record almost any aspect of training and performance, and provide the highest-resolution and densest data acquisition of all training monitoring approaches. However, training logs require diligent recording of training data. The biggest problems with training logs are compliance among athletes (i.e., the "hassle" factor) and the difficulty of translating data into an easily analyzable form. The hassle and tedious data entry usually result in abandonment of training logs after a short period of implementation. However, there are new methods that have been shown to be effective in providing training monitoring via logs and that result in relatively easy analysis of training data (Sands, Henschen, and Schultz 1989; Sands 1990b, 1991b, 1991a, 1992).

Figure 9.4 shows a computer "dot" sheet that was used to record gymnastics training data for male gymnasts. Similar dot sheet forms were also used by the women's national gymnastics team and the University of Utah's women's gymnastics team. Notably, the University of Utah's gymnastics team accumulated more than 5000 training records over

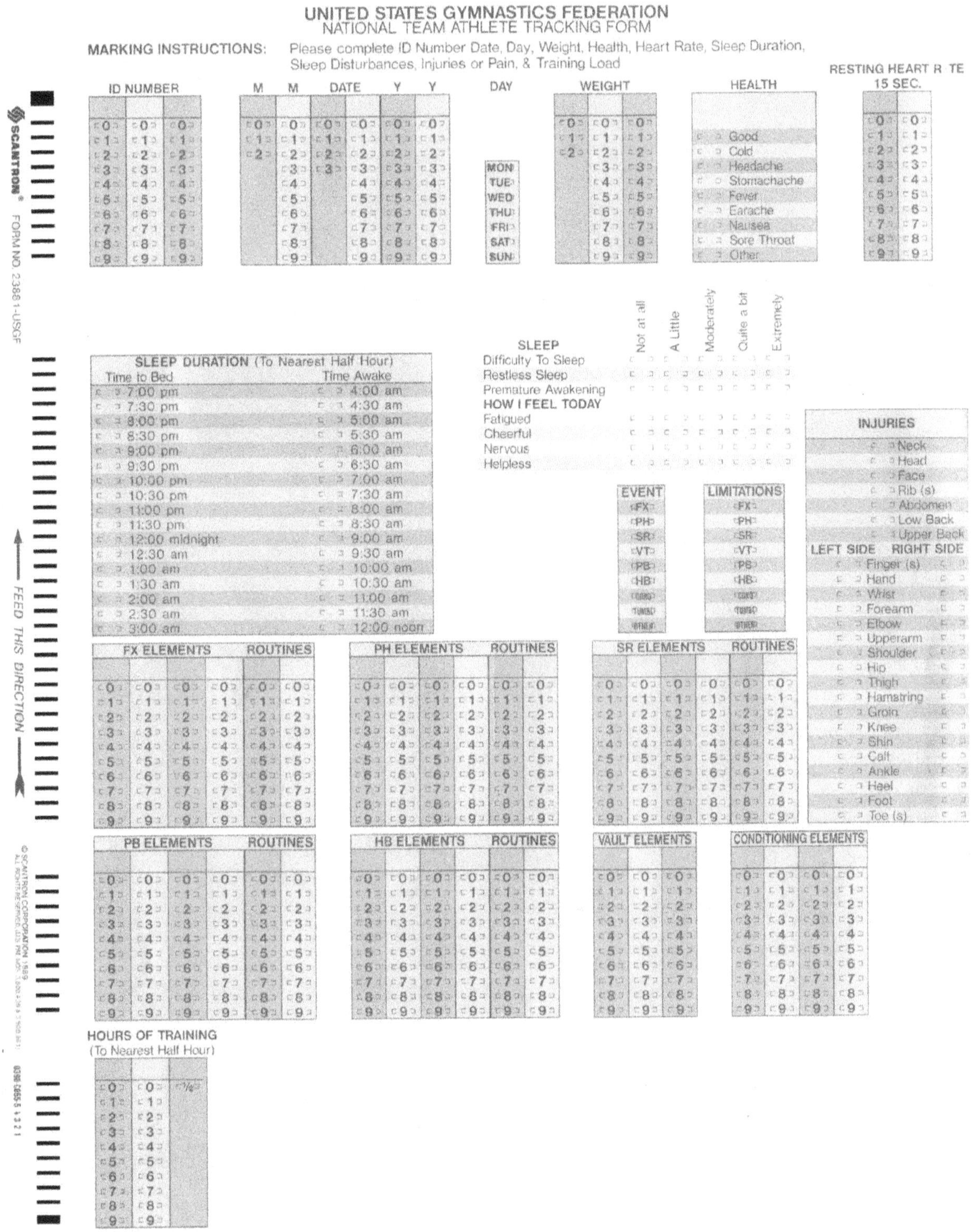

Figure 9.4 Monitoring form for U.S. men's national gymnastics team. Note that the form permitted the recording of numerous dosage (lower half of the form) and response (upper half of the form) variables. This form was disseminated to athletes via their coaches for daily training data recording.

Courtesy of Bill Sands.

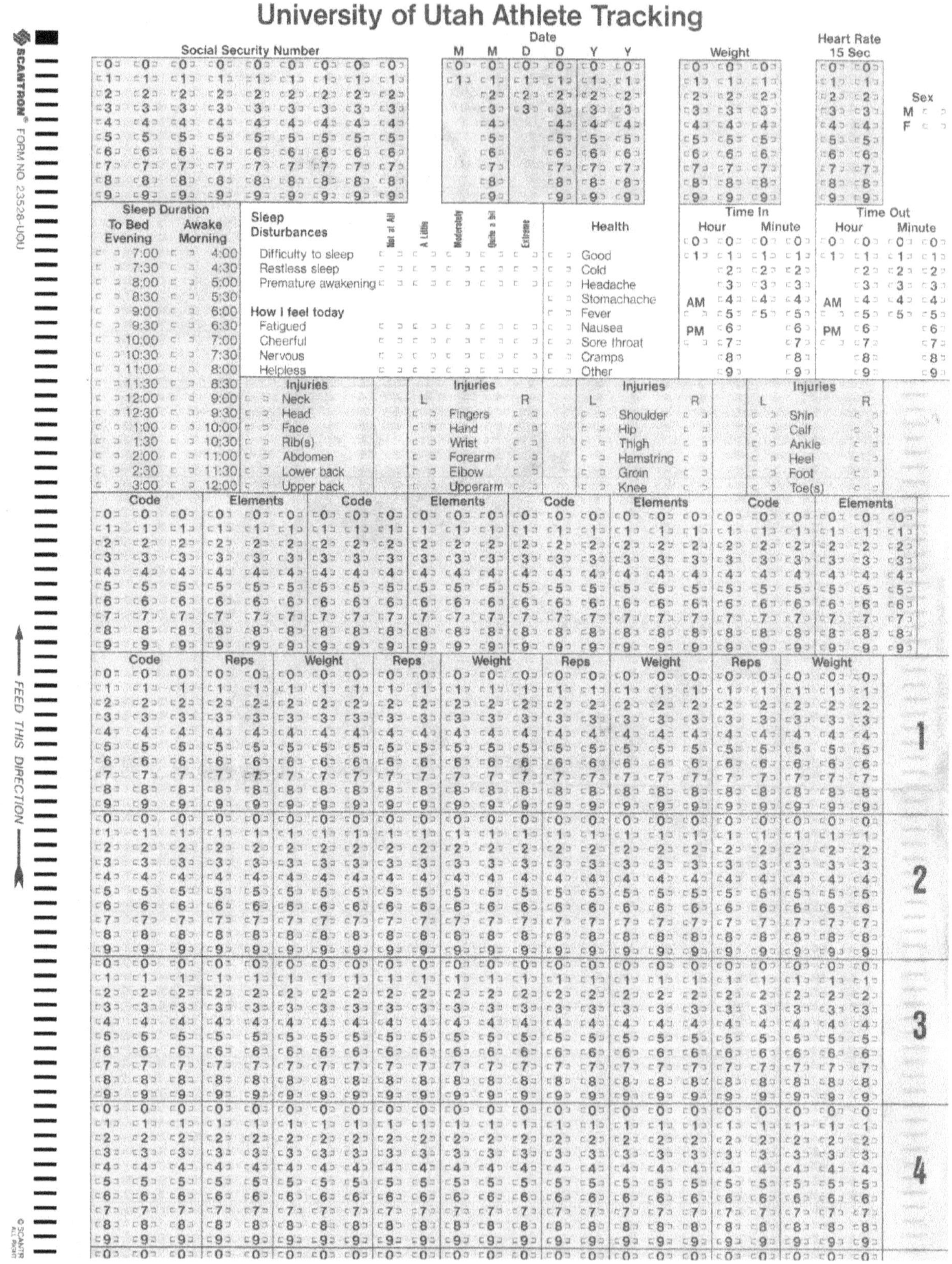

University of Utah Athlete Tracking

Figure 9.5 Monitoring form for resistance training. This was an 11 by 18 in., two-sided form. All lifts had a code number. The upper part of the form recorded response data, and the lower half and back side recorded dosage data.

Courtesy of Bill Sands.

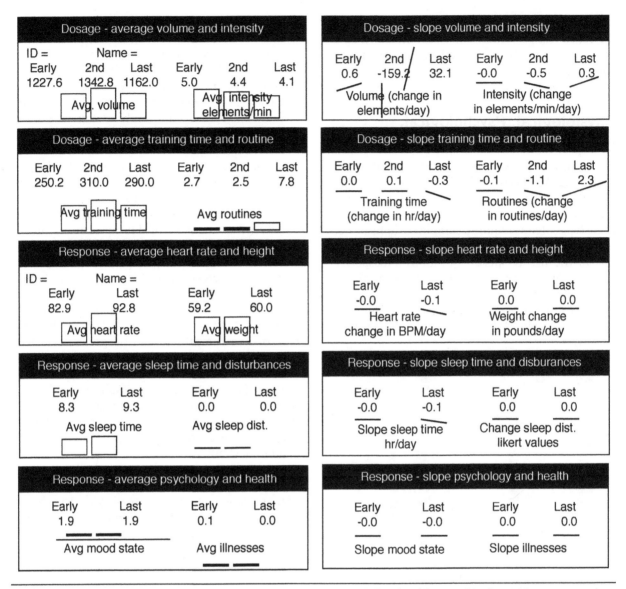

Figure 9.6   Graphic display of data returned to coaches. The top left side of the graphic shows the average values for dosage information. For example, under "volume," the three bars indicate the last seven training days (right-most bar), second-to-last seven training days (middle bar), and the average training volume (in total elements per day) preceding the last 14 training days and returning to the beginning of the training macrocycle. The bottom left side of the graphic shows response information. The response information is divided into the last 10 training days (rightmost bar) and the remainder of training back to training onset (leftmost bar). The right side of the graphic depicts slope (i.e., rates of change of each training variable indicated by a line showing a relative slope).

five years and demonstrated the value of training monitoring on many occasions (Hopkins 2002; Hopkins, Hawley, and Burke 1999; ; Sands 1990a, 1990b, 1991b, 1991a, 1992; Sands, Henschen, and Schultz 1989; Sands, Shultz, and Paine 1993). The dot sheets were designed specifically as a training log and could be completed by an athlete in less than 1 min. Each athlete completed the dot sheet at each practice. The sheets were collected and then

scanned on a full-page scanner. Custom software analyzed the collected data for trends and employed artificial intelligence techniques to mine the data for subtle or hidden relationships (Sands 1991a, 1992). Sheets were scanned weekly, and a complete multipage report was returned to each coach. The artificial intelligence-based software was used as an expert system that analyzed the data records and then responded with English sentences as to the current status of each individual athlete. Thus, the coach was presented with numeric data, graphs of raw data, graphs of distilled trends, and a text-based report of the athlete's data (figure 9.6) (Sands 1991b, 1991a, 1992).

Physiological, Psychological, Nutritional, and Biomechanical Tests

The nature of physiological, psychological, nutritional, and biomechanical tests ensures that they are highly targeted at a particular training or performance question. Often, the data acquired by these types of tests require a computer, sophisticated processing, and expert interpretation. Moreover, due to the highly specific questions and specialized instrumentation required, the turnaround time for getting analyses back to the coach and athlete can range from hours to weeks. Figure 9.7 shows a specialized testing apparatus for strength

and power. This versatile device can be used for a number of important strength and power measurements. However, it is expensive to construct and requires a force platform and bar tracking sensors. The data acquired can be analyzed and returned to a coach within approximately one day. More sophisticated analyses can take more time. A graphic of the output from such a test is shown in figure 9.8.

Vertical jumps can be used to assess jump height, peak force, power, and rate of force development. Figure 9.9 shows a portable force platform used to measure more than two dozen strength and power variables from static vertical jumps, countermovement vertical jumps, and drop jumps with and without additional weights. Although data can be returned quickly with this device, usually in a matter of hours, the apparatus costs a few thousand dollars and requires a computer and custom software (Major et al. 1998). However, the data returned to the athlete can be precise and rich (figure 9.10).

Interpretation of specialized tests is dependent on the specific test. The greater resolution and precision of these tests make them ideal for addressing specific performance problems and investigating deeper aspects of physiology, psychology, nutrition, and biomechanics.

Whether the training log type of data or specialized tests are used for monitoring, the analyses of these data in the time domain are basically the same. There are a number of commonsense, statistical, and graphical methods for analyzing long-term aspects of resistance training.

Figure 9.7   The power rack. The athlete is standing on a force platform; the ends of the bar are being tracked by potentiometers (tiny cables not visible in this image), and all data are being recorded via a computer (not shown).
Courtesy of Mike Stone.

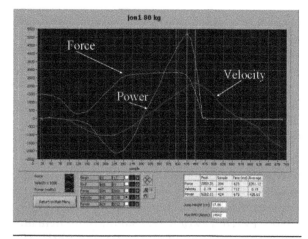

Figure 9.8   Force-, power-, and velocity–time curves for a weighted vertical jump using the apparatus shown in figure 9.7.

Figure 9.9 Vertical jump of a weightlifter being measured on a portable force platform.

Courtesy of Mike Stone.

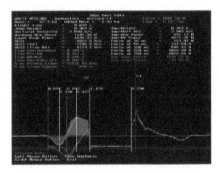

Figure 9.10 Screen image of the variables returned from a single countermovement jump from the portable force platform.

Analyzing Training Monitoring Data

Whenever athletes progress from one state to another with some type of training intervention in the middle, the data are analyzed in a time

domain. However, training monitoring results in multiple sequential measurements that bring with them a unique dimension of analysis—time-series analysis. Time-series analysis can be as common-sense as graphing the data and noting whether some variable appears to be increasing, decreasing, or staying about the same. Or time-series analysis can be as complex as determining the frequency characteristics of several cyclic variables to predict how these variables may behave in the future. A number of analysis tools have evolved, especially since the advent of the computer, that are designed to render time-series data in ways that make the data tell a story or serve as the raw material for predictive models of future performance.

Time-series data are arranged in arrays. Arrays are ordered lists of things. Training monitoring data are collected and sequenced in an array, with each array position representative of a specific (and usually uniform) time duration. Thus, each variable has both a value and a position within the array, with the position signifying a time. Both aspects of the variable are important. In contrast to what happens with the typical pretest, posttest, control group design that is commonly used in experimental settings, time-series data are analyzed as group data, individual data, and data sequences with respect to time. For example, if an athlete determines his or her resting heart rate upon rising each morning for 10 consecutive days, the data will result in a 10-position array of heart rate values. This array of data can be treated with numerous conventional statistical methods. The mean, median, mode, and standard deviation of the series can be calculated, along with least squares fit regression approaches that can identify simple linear trends. Figure 9.3 shows heart rate and mass data for a gymnast with linear trends included. Figure 9.11 shows heart rate data for an entire training year with mean and standard deviation information included.

Single-Subject Design Investigations and Monitoring

Resistance training is fundamentally a problem of improving the strength and power fitness of an individual. However, analysis of the individual has fallen into disrepute due to the modern emphasis on determination of "covering laws" applying to individuals generally rather than individually. Research on an individual is called ideographic research and is conducted via single-subject research designs.

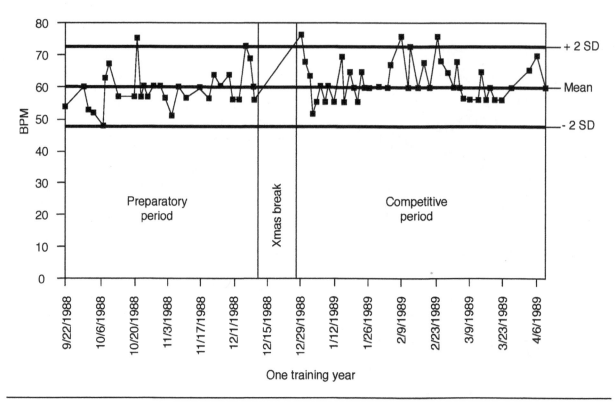

Figure 9.11 Time series of prepractice resting heart rate data for an entire training year in a female collegiate gymnast. Note that the mean and standard deviation (× 2) lines portray the control limit boundaries for these data.

Investigations conducted on groups of individuals, in search of covering laws, are called nomothetic research. Interestingly, much of science during the 19th century was conducted by ideographic methods. The rise of inferential statistics in the 20th century resulted in a shift in emphasis from the study of individuals to the study of groups of individuals (Barlow and Hersen 1984). However, it is noteworthy that some of our most prized scientific discoveries were based on investigations involving a single subject. For example, Broca's study of the speech area of the brain was based on one patient, and Pavlov reportedly studied one dog in developing the idea of stimulus–response conditioning (Barlow and Hersen 1984).

Ideographic research has been considered antithetical to nomothetic investigations largely due to poor understanding of the strengths and weaknesses of both types of investigation. Applied research investigating clinical interventions and outcomes may be better served by a combined approach involving nomothetic investigations to describe covering principles or laws, while ideographic research can represent a second stage of applied investigation used to determine if the findings of nomothetic investigations are effective in real-world clinical interventions with individuals

(Dunn 1994). The clinical research setting is analogous to the athletic training setting.

Single-subject investigations involve the systematic study of individuals. There is a common misconception that single-subject design investigations are "case studies." Case studies usually involve two phases: a baseline period, either measured or assumed, and a treatment period. The treatment may be either a coincidence of observation (the investigator is in the right place at the right time to see the results of some treatment, e.g., training) or the investigator caused the treatment (Hrycaiko and Martin 1996). The case study is a relatively weak design because any number of variables may have influenced the observed result besides the variables considered causative or simply under observation. Single-subject designs may involve the careful manipulation of one or more variables through the recording of a sufficiently long baseline period, the controlled introduction of a treatment variable, observation of the effects of the treatment, removal of the treatment variable, and then reintroduction of the treatment variable with commensurate observations. The case study can be generally classified as an A-B design. The A refers to a baseline condition; the B refers to a treatment condition. Single-subject designs can use a number of different approaches, but the approach just described is an A-B-A-B design (Barlow and Hersen 1984). "A" in this case refers to baseline or a period of no intervention, while "B" refers to implementing or imposing the intervention.

For those schooled in typical inferential statistics, single-subject designs may seem both foreign and antiscientific. Rejecting an alternative method without consideration is dogmatic and potentially harmful to both types of investigations. There are a number of misconceptions regarding single-subject designs that should be addressed. The primary issue advocating for single-subject designs is the fact that by using and relying on mean values, one may find that no single individual among a group of individuals under investigation actually matches the mean of the group (Dunn 1994). Moreover, it is not uncommon to find group investigations in which some individuals show no improvement as a result of the treatment, or even get worse, while the average of the group shows an improvement. Because means tend to the extreme scores, situations that result in significant differences between groups may be mainly due to large improvements shown by a few individuals while others show little, no, or negative improvement. Of course, the absence of improvement, or individuals actually getting worse, is not acceptable in a clinical or training setting. Training interventions must result in individual athlete improvement. As in clinical investigations in medicine, a physician has failed if his or her patient doesn't improve. Whether the average of a group of patients improves is certainly important, but the focus of the physician has to be the individual patient. Likewise, coaches and strength and conditioning specialists must demonstrate improvement in individual athletes, particularly their best athletes.

There are a number of additional misconceptions involving single-subject designs. Unlike nomothetic investigations, single-subject investigations are usually conducted over many practices or competitions or both. Single-subject designs rely on the logic of replication rather than the probability of sampling. As a result of a longitudinal approach and the repeated data collections, the athlete's natural variability in performance can be determined. Group investigations of this type do not consider the variability of individual athletes as important and often lose important information when calculating a mean. In order to use inferential statistics for analysis in group designs, the number of subjects or athletes has to be relatively large (Hopkins 2002; Hopkins, Hawley, and Burke

1999). Research and monitoring involving truly elite athletes (e.g., Olympic teams, Olympic medalists) are nearly impossible to conduct using group designs because elite athletes are rare by definition. Single-subject designs are often conducted on one to five subjects or athletes. The relatively small number of subjects required in single-subject designs permits assessment of nearly any level of athlete, at nearly any time, and for nearly any duration. Single-subject designs do not require a control group since each subject serves as his or her own control. Thus, single-subject approaches can involve a small number of athletes and the intervention can begin at any time; and coaches and athletes do not have to be concerned that some athletes are not receiving the treatment because they are in a control or nontreatment group (Hrycaiko and Martin 1996). While these ideas may be an asset in the study of athletes, the need for relatively long baseline periods of data collection cannot be overemphasized. The performance of an athlete on some variable of interest has to be studied long enough that the inherent variability of that variable is allowed to stabilize, permitting reliable recognition of excursions from normal behavior.

As an example, we can consider how single-subject investigations and monitoring in resistance training are conducted. Let's begin with a hypothetical study. We would like to know if serious stretching designed to enhance flexibility in the hip and lower back will serve to enhance strength and power among our top team of four Olympic weightlifters in the snatch. We decide to use an A-B-A-B design. We begin by collecting twice-weekly training information on the total amount and type of stretching being performed now with the athletes in question. We obtain a four-week baseline of stretching activity, current flexibility performance using the sit and reach test, Thomas test, and goniometric measurements of joint angles obtained from a side view of video of snatch performance, as well as 1RMs of supportive lifts such as the squat, power clean, and stiff-leg deadlift; this is the first "A." We collect this information once per week. Then we implement our stretching program and monitor these tests two times per week for eight weeks; this is the first "B." We record and graph all of the test values as a function of time. Then we remove the stretching program for four weeks while continuing to perform all of the tests listed; this is the second "A." Finally we reinstate the stretching program for eight weeks while continuing to monitor all test results; this is the final "B."

Figure 9.12 shows a hypothetical longitudinal graph of some of the results of our stretching intervention on all four of our athletes' bar speeds during the 24 weeks. In the name of simplification, only the sit and reach test and the bar speed data are shown for illustrative purposes. Note that three of the four athletes show trends of improvement. During the A or baseline periods, improvements seem to show little more than noise, while during the B or treatment periods, both flexibility and speed of bar movement tend to improve. The athlete who doesn't show the same trend, or doesn't seem to respond to the training like the others, may be unable to change his or her flexibility or may have been ill or injured; we cannot say from the information in this graph. However, we do know that our intervention appears to be effective for three of the athletes and not for the fourth.

The strength of this type of analysis is in its repeatability. When stretching is imposed, the ath-letes tend to improve in stretching and bar speed. When stretching is removed, the athletes tend to decay in both flexibility and bar speed. Moreover, subject 4 does not follow this trend. It would be well worth the scientist's and coach's time to find out why subject 4 does not respond in the same way. This may help the scientist and coach in further diagnosis of training-related problems and perhaps help identify other characteristics of subject 4 and why this athlete might not respond to training like the others. This may open an opportunity for better training and coaching of subject 4. Clearly, in a nomothetic approach to this type of question, the four athletes' variability would be lost in the calculation of a mean. If the sample size was sufficiently large, with this type of study we might be able to reach statistical significance indicating that stretching might benefit bar speed. However, such an analysis would mask the result that one or more athletes do not respond well to this type of intervention.

Monitoring resistance training can be served well by single-subject design methods. Ideographic

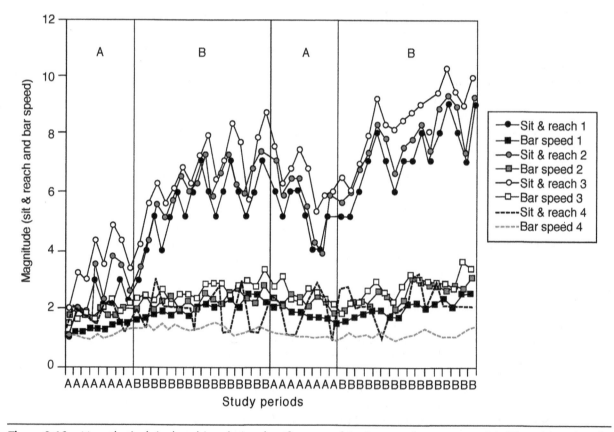

Figure 9.12 Hypothetical single-subject design data for a stretching intervention among weightlifters. Note that the A period is baseline, with no stretching imposed. The B period is the one in which stretching is imposed. Note also that subjects 1, 2, and 3 tend to show improving flexibility during the B periods, and this coincides with improving bar speed. Note also that subject 4 does not share this trend.

methods make some different assumptions than traditional nomothetic research approaches, but ideographic methods lend themselves well to individual athlete longitudinal assessments.

Graphing, Trend Analysis, and Autocorrelation

One of the simplest and a fundamental means of monitoring resistance training is to graph the data. Simply graphing data and reporting the observed trends may appear to be unsophisticated, but the simple calculation of a statistic can also be deceiving (Hrycaiko and Martin 1996). One need only view a range of scatter plots to see that a large correlation coefficient may simply be indicative of data from two populations that are clustered relatively far apart, resulting in an inflated correlation coefficient (Vincent 1995). Thus, a correlation coefficient alone may be deceptive while the accompanying scatter plot can show that the data pairs come from one or more populations. Typical spreadsheet and statistics

software packages provide a multitude of graphing options, and recent work has shown that graphing data alone can be more enlightening than any table or text (Tufte 1983, 1990).

As data are acquired from monitoring procedures, the data may reflect a trend. Trends are usually linear, curvilinear, or cyclic. Linear trends can be determined in a variety of ways. For example, a split-middle analysis comes from single-subject design methods. The split middle is used to calculate a median slope that is representative of a trend. To calculate a split middle, the data array is divided in half by array position, and the median of each half is calculated. Then the data array is divided into quarters. The median of the latter half of the data is plotted over the existing data at the point of 75% of the data array. The median of the earlier half of the data array is plotted at the point of 25% of the data array. Then a line is drawn from these two points and indicates the median slope or median trend of the data (figure 9.13) (Barlow and Hersen 1984). Linear trends can also be calculated from simple least squares regression procedures (Jackson 1989;

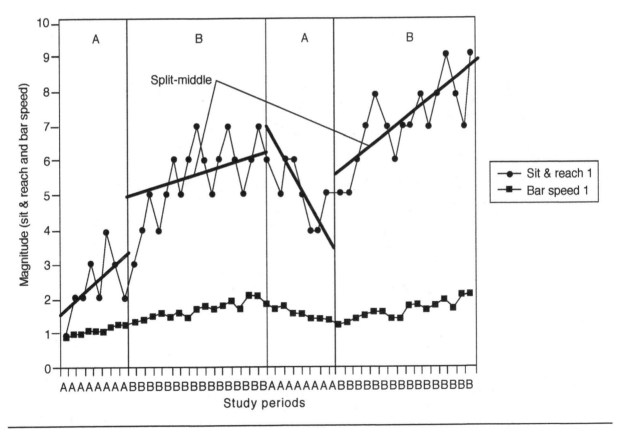

Figure 9.13 Single-subject design data showing split middle (median slopes) of hypothetical sit and reach data. Note that both the medians (centers of split-middle lines) of these data and the split middles indicate that stretching may be helpful, although the initial baseline A period should result in cautious interpretation for this one subject.

Vincent 1995). Curvilinear trends can be calculated similarly but require slightly more sophisticated mathematics. While the split-middle analysis may need to be done by hand, regression software is readily available to perform linear regression and curve-fitting. These methods are extremely helpful in designing computer software to automatically analyze time-series data; however, in monitoring athletes in resistance training in the field, simple graphing and linear methods are usually more than adequate to assist in regulating training (Sands 1991a, 1991b, 1992).

Autocorrelation is a special case of simple bivariate correlation used to detect and characterize cyclic behavior of data. The Pearson product-moment correlation coefficient is the statistic, but there is an added dimension. The Pearson product-moment correlation coefficient is also often described as a zero-order correlation coefficient, referring to the idea that the two variables being correlated are not displaced in time, or at least that the time of the measurements is not important. For example, a Pearson product-moment zero-order correlation

coefficient could be calculated between height and weight. Autocorrelation uses the same mathematics to calculate the correlation coefficient, but the data being correlated are for the same variable displaced in time. The time or array position displacement is called a lag. For example, calculating a correlation coefficient between data positions 1 and 2, between 2 and 3, between 3 and 4, and so forth is an autocorrelation with a lag of 1. One would calculate an autocorrelation with a lag of 2 by correlating array positions 1 and 3, positions 2 and 4, positions 3 and 5, and so forth (figure 9.14). This procedure is repeated iteratively through the entire data array using lags that make theoretical sense. An example of a correlogram is shown in figure 9.15. Note that the highest autocorrelations were achieved with lags of 2 and 10, indicating that the most covariance or predictability (or both) along the data array comes in predicting only two or 10 data points into the future. However, one is hard pressed to determine a good theoretical reason for these apparent but modest cyclic characteristics.

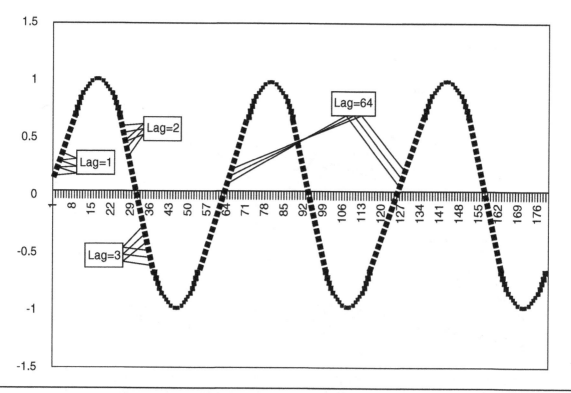

Figure 9.14 Correlation coefficient and lag. This graphic shows the overall approach to calculating an autocorrelation. The lag values indicate the array distances or positions that are used in calculation of a correlation coefficient. Note that as the lag values reach points in the array where values on corresponding parts of the cyclic curve are similar, this will result in larger correlation coefficients. Using this method, the investigator can determine whether cyclic behavior is present and the best lag or distance between array points, thus characterizing the time period of the cyclic behavior.

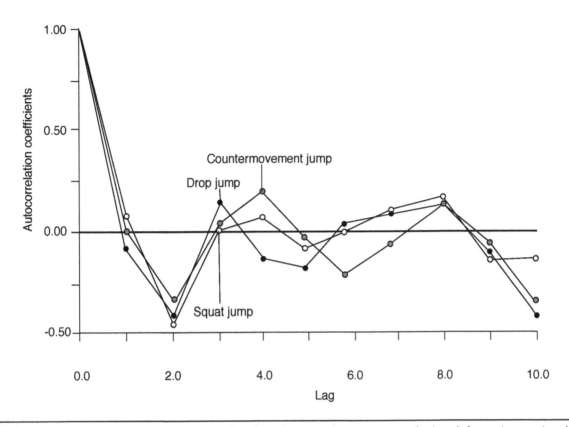

Figure 9.15 Correlogram of vertical jumps height. This correlogram was calculated from time-series data involving collegiate female track and field athletes. The intent was to determine if the vertical jump heights obtained from serial testing showed any cyclic behavior. As can be seen, modestly high autocorrelation coefficients were seen at lags of 2 and 10 test periods, which in this particular study were weeks. This would indicate that a possible cyclic component to the vertical jump performances could be present at periods of 2 to 10 weeks. However, the negative values indicate that when an athlete was high during a given week, that athlete was likely to be lower 2 and 10 weeks later.

Statistical Process Control

Statistical process control (SPC) is an entire field of study that has become ubiquitous in industrial manufacturing (Pitt 1994; Shewhart 1986). As manufacturing is a process, so is training. Statistical process control provides a powerful statistical toolset that can be used to analyze longitudinal data in resistance training monitoring. Although many tools are used in SPC, training monitoring can be served well by a few of the simplest.

The underlying premise of SPC is that longitudinal data, when examined in totality, are distributed in ways that permit standard statistical procedures. For example, if we were monitoring resting heart rate for a few months we would find that if the data were collapsed over time, the resulting distribution would be quite close to a normal distribution and thus we could use the properties of the normal distribution to determine the relative rarity of each data point. By using the mean and standard deviation to calculate Z-scores, we could apply an associated probability to each heart rate value. Figure 9.16 shows prepractice resting heart rate data. Statistical process control uses the mean and standard deviation to classify data relative to "control limits." One standard deviation above or below the mean represents the first control limit. Two standard deviations above or below the mean are the second control limit and so forth. The elegance of this information lies in the fact that we can determine what values are rare enough that they need explanation. When data values exceed two standard deviations, for example, we know that this should happen less than or equal to 5% of the time. Something this rare demands an explanation. If a resting heart rate value exceeds two standard deviations, this may be indicative of a problem. As shown in figure 9.16, all of the resting heart rate values that exceeded the second control limit (two standard deviations from the mean), except one, were coincident with illness symptoms.

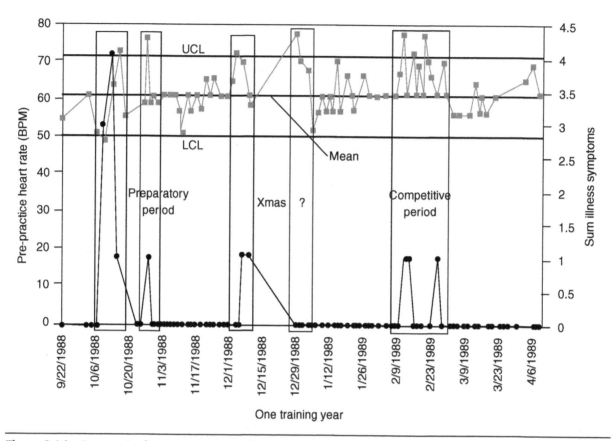

Figure 9.16 Prepractice heart rate and sum illness symptoms. Data are from a single female collegiate gymnast. The graph shows that in all cases but one (?), the athlete's prepractice resting heart rate exceeded the UCL (upper control limit, 2 × SD) whenever the athlete also reported significant illness symptoms. The range between the UCL and the LCL (lower control limit) represents where 95% of the data should fall based on a normal distribution of these data. Note that there is only a 5% likelihood that prepractice resting heart rate should exceed the UCL and LCL; thus values that exceed these levels are indeed rare and demand explanation.

A word of caution is warranted. Although the data shown in figure 9.16 are displayed relative to a normal distribution, there should be statistical justification for using a normal distribution, as opposed to one that may deviate considerably from normality assumptions, when one is making probability-based decisions. Clearly, in terms of prepractice resting heart rate, there may be more of a tendency for these values to increase rather than decrease and may alter the underlying assumptions of the data distribution.

When longitudinal data are analyzed relative to their mean and standard deviation, and the data are distributed normally, we can determine whether the data values are rare or common. When viewed as part of a process, rare data values are almost always indicative of something that demands explanation. If training methods have resulted in improvements that are greater than two standard deviations, you can be relatively assured that these are not chance

variations. If data are within one standard deviation, since we know that approximately 68% of all data values should fall within plus or minus one standard deviation, these data are probably not rare. For ranges in between, one can make arguments regarding what is rare enough to demand explanation. These types of decisions may require long-term analysis in order to warrant coupling training and performance observations and decisions with data that may be only modestly rare.

Expert Systems

When implementing a training monitoring program, one quickly encounters the most significant practical problem—too much data. Training logs, whether paper or computer based, suffer in practical implementation because of an inability to quickly see the obvious and the subtle aspects of training trends. Computerized analyses of training data are much more than just a simple database. Although all training monitoring software requires a database "front end" for acquisition and storage of training data, training monitoring cannot end with simply storing data. The optimal approach to training monitoring includes a computerized means of extracting all of the important relationships in the data without having to manually search for them.

Computer programs designed to analyze training data have been developed (Sands 1991a, 1991b, 1992, 2002; Sands, Shultz, and Paine 1993, 1994). These programs use an artificial intelligence paradigm called an *expert system*. Expert systems are created by computer scientists to get a computer to perform like a human expert. Expert systems are usually rule-based programs that apply a set of rules to data. The rules in this case would apply to training monitoring, overtraining detection, and other aspects of resistance training. For example, a common symptom of overtraining is increasing resting heart rate with simultaneously decreasing weight (Nye 1987; Rusko et al. 1989; Sands 1990b, 1991a, 1991b, 1992, 2002; Sands, Shultz, and Paine 1993, 1994; Uusitalo 2001; Yushkov, Repnevsky, and Serdyuk 1986). Therefore, the computer-based expert system used to analyze training data should have a rule embedded in the code in something like the following form:

overtraining = increasing heart rate
[and] decreasing weight

Expert systems can be programmed both to analyze the appropriate data (via rules derived from training literature, personal experience, and other sources) and to describe important aspects of the current status of training in understandable English sentences.

Many other means of data summaries and graphical displays can be achieved using modern computer graphics tools, statistical programs, and artificial intelligence methods. Artificial intelligence, while suffering from the initial overhyped idea of making a computer think, has reached a level of maturity such that the techniques have made their way into mainstream commercial products. Computer scientists found that making a computer think like a human was much more difficult than anticipated. By using the techniques learned in this quest on smaller problems, computer scientists have been able to arrive at many useful and previously unanticipated benefits. Training monitoring could profit enormously from these methods in providing coaches and scientists with "decision support" when data are available but interpretation is difficult and time consuming (Bahill, Harris, and Senn 1988; Bailey, Thompson, and Feinstein 1989; Graham and Jones 1988; Lane 1989; Menzies 1989; Parsaye and Chignell 1988; Sherald 1989).

CHAPTER SUMMARY

Resistance training monitoring can be a key to high-performance success. Characterizing the process of training for each individual athlete via a dose–response relationship, identifying trends, noting outliers, and invoking rules from training literature make it possible to better study and control training and performance. The strength coach, sport scientist, and coach can use the training monitoring paradigm to provide enhanced control of training for each individual athlete.

CHAPTER 10

Physical and Physiological Adaptations to Resistance Training

B efore a reasonable discussion of responses and adaptations to resistance training can occur, it is important to differentiate health fitness from sport fitness. Training for health and training for fitness are not the same things; in fact, training for sport performance can be antagonistic to good health. For example, a body mass of over 140 kg (309 lb) is likely not a healthy characteristic to develop; however, it may allow you to earn several million dollars playing in the National Football League or to become an Olympic shot-put gold medalist.

Definitions and Key Factors of Training Adaptation

Exercise is a single bout of physical activity. Acute physiological responses occur in the immediate postexercise period. For example, performing a set of 10 in the squat or running 2 miles (3.2 km) (exercises) will result in an increase in heart rate and blood pressure. *Training* is regular exercise that results in chronic physical and physiological alterations (adaptations).

An important aspect of sport science is the concept of *specificity*. Specific exercises result in specific responses, and specific types of training result in specific adaptations. For example, training as a shot-putter results in physical and physiological adaptations that are quite different from the adaptations of a 10,000 m runner. Furthermore, conceptually this means that the term *fitness* has specific meaning for each sport. Thus, fitness for shot-putting is not the same as fitness for distance running.

Figure 10.1 depicts an idealized adaptive process leading to improved performance. Whether the coach actually realizes it or not, various physiological factors contribute to the improvement in sport performance as a result of an appropriately designed training program. The desired outcome of the training program is to stimulate protein synthesis, resulting in greater enzyme concentrations, changes in isozyme ratios, and tissue remodeling. The stimulation of protein synthesis eventually leads to enhanced performance. To promote the coach's goal and enhance protein synthesis, it is necessary to consider the recovery and adaptation process.

Recovery is a process of getting back what was lost or simply bringing an athlete's performance back to where it was. *Adaptation* deals with the process of long-term adjustment or alterations related to a specific training program. Thus, the coach and athlete cannot simply be satisfied with recovery but must strive to enhance "recovery-adaptation." This concept is dealt with in detail in chapter 13, "The Concept of Periodization."

Adaptation to training can be affected by a number of different variables, including genetics, age, maturation level, sex, psychosocial aspects, nutrition, environment, and coach–athlete interaction characteristics (figure 10.2). Heredity plays the largest role in determining factors that may be linked to performance (Huygens et al. 2004; Rotter et al. 1985; Simoneau and Bouchard 1995). The exercise response and training adaptation are also influenced by the trained state (advanced vs. beginning), the volume and intensity factors associated with the training program, exercise selection, and the degree of fatigue.

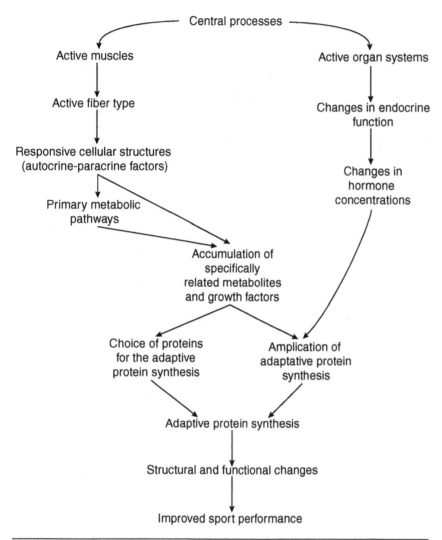

Figure 10.1 The training program is created to produce adaptations leading to improved sport performance. The training program engages various organ systems such as the central nervous system, cardiorespiratory system, neuroendocrine and paracrine-autocrine systems, and immune system. Metabolic parameters and these systems work together to alter protein synthesis such that enzymes are produced and tissues, particularly muscle, are remodeled. These adaptations are specific to the training program and can result in improved function, leading to improved skill and performance.

Adapted, by permission, from A. Viru and M. Viru, 2000, Nature of training effects. In *Exercise and Sport Science*, edited by J. Bangsbo (Baltimore, MD: Lippincott, Williams, and Wilkins), 68.

Genetics

Heredity plays the most important role in determining success in sport performance for two important reasons: (1) Genetically linked factors have been associated with specific performance abilities (Huygens 2004), and (2) genetics establish the boundaries for adaptation—some athletes have greater boundaries (i.e., greater adaptability) than others (Bouchard et al. 1992 ; Klissouras 1971).

For example, the high heritability of resting testosterone concentrations (Harris, Vernon, and Boomsma 1998), the protein alpha-actinin-3 (Yang et al. 2003), and enhanced motor control at fast movement speeds (Missitzi and Klissouras 2004) can be associated with strength-power athletes. Having a large number of type I muscle fibers (Jones 2002; Zhang et al. 2003) and a greater ability to produce cardiac adaptations (Hernandez et al. 2003) are highly heritable factors associated with a higher $\dot{V}O_2$max and success in long-term endurance sports. Indeed, the heritability of factors associated with success helps to explain why some individuals are "hard gainers" and others are not. For example, somatotype, which is a heritable factor, has a great effect on how much strength and hypertrophy gain occurs as a result of resistance training (Van Etten, Verstappen, and Westerterp 1994). While genetically linked physical and physiological factors are arguably the strongest determinant in someone's becoming an elite athlete, psychological factors may play a very important role in determining success among elite athletes (Klissouras et al. 2001) (see chapter 11).

Trained State

Studies dealing with various types of training programs clearly indicate that beginners progress at a faster rate than well-trained individuals (Sale 1988; Stone et al. 1998). Figure 10.3 depicts the theoretical gains in strength resulting from a resistance training program. Note that there are basically two mechanisms responsible for gains in performance, hypertrophy (muscle cross section) and neural factors. Neural factors account for most of the early gains in strength (and power), with hypertrophy accounting for most of the later gains (Sale 1988). This does not mean that neural factors cannot be altered in the later stages of strength development, or that some hypertrophy cannot occur in the early phases of training, but rather that neural factors predominate in the early stages. It may be argued that hypertrophy lags behind

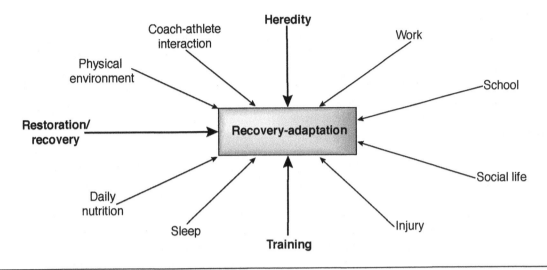

Figure 10.2   Factors (stressors) affecting sport performance.

neural factors because the ability to reach maximum or near maximum levels of exertion must be developed (learned) before sufficient intensity of training can be achieved. Being able to produce maximum or near maximum levels of exertion appears to be necessary to supply enough stress on the musculature to achieve marked levels of muscle growth. Regardless of the underlying mechanisms, the window for adaptation is large in beginners and novices but becomes markedly smaller as training progresses. Untrained individuals can make progress with almost any reasonable training program, but advanced athletes need greater levels of stimulation and variation in training.

Fatigue

Fatigue can be considered in two ways. Acute fatigue occurs during exercise and in the immediate postexercise phase, resulting in the inability to maintain or repeat an absolute force or power level. Acute fatigue displays a high degree of task specificity (Hunter, Duchateau, and Enoka 2004), so that even subtle variation in the task results in substantial differences in the fatigue rates (i.e., time to failure). Acute fatigue has been associated with a breakdown of excitation-coupling as a result of increased hydrogen ion concentrations (Stackhouse et al. 2001), alterations in the concentration of intra- and extracellular Ca^{++} (Allen, Kabbara, and Westerblad 2002; Carins et al. 1998; Stackhouse et al. 2001), and an increase in inorganic phosphates from the breakdown of phosphocreatine (PCr) (Westerland, Allen, and Lannergren 2002).

The degree to which the nervous system is involved in acute fatigue is unclear, as neuro-

muscular transmission failure has been difficult to demonstrate (Gardiner 2001). Some have speculated that heavy loading (i.e., lower repetitions and heavy weight) may result in nervous system fatigue; however, there is little evidence for this supposition.

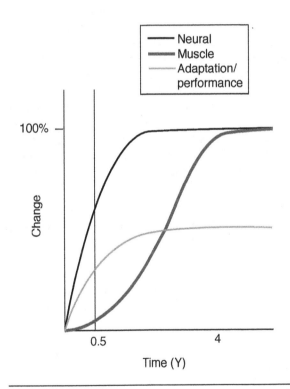

Figure 10.3   Theoretical time course for strength adaptation. Beginners adapt at a faster rate than well-trained individuals. The early stages of adaptation involve primarily neural mechanisms, and later stages primarily hypertrophic mechanisms.

Indeed, nervous system involvement in heavy resistance exercise loading protocols appears to be more a function of the work accomplished than of the absolute load (Behm et al. 2002). However, some evidence suggests that work resulting from high-intensity dynamic, explosive exercise such as repeated high-power jumps at 50% 1RM (Linnammo et al. 2000), or repeated drop jumps (Skurvydas et al. 2002), may fatigue the nervous system more than typical heavy weight training. Fatigue resulting from continuous prolonged exercise may also have a basis in the nervous system (Millet and Lepers 2004). Regardless of the mechanism, strength training can increase acute fatigue resistance (O'Bryant, Byrd, and Stone 1988; Robinson et al. 1995). However, the rate of recovery from fatigue produced by some types of high-intensity exercise with impact (drop jumps) may be dependent on training (endurance vs. sprint) or fiber type prevalence (Skurvydas et al. 2002).

Chronic fatigue results in chronic poor or diminished performance as a result of the inability to recover from the training load and the summation of physical and emotional stressors. Chronic fatigue can be a precursor to and a symptom of overtraining (see chapter 13, "The Concept of Periodization") and may be associated with depleted energy stores, hormonal alterations (Busso et al. 1992; Stone and Fry 1997), chronic dehydration (Bigard et al. 2001; Monnier et al. 2000), sarcoplasmic reticulum calcium regulation abilities (Li et al. 2002), and perhaps neural fatigue, particularly as a result of explosive exercise (Linnammo et al. 2000). Chronic fatigue can result in decreased force production, power production, rate of force development, motor control, and technical ability. At the same time, chronic fatigue can cause increased feelings of tiredness and increased recovery time.

As a result of chronic fatigue, the ability to respond to exercise is diminished and the ability to adapt to training can be diminished. Therefore great care must be taken to avoid chronic fatigue that would interfere with the adaptation process. This does not mean that training should never produce fatigue; it does mean that training (and the sum of stressors) should not be so great that recovery-adaptation becomes a negative characteristic and maladaptation occurs (see "Adaptations Associated With Strength-Power Performance" later in this chapter).

If the stressors encountered by the athlete are too great, then maladaptation (overtraining) can occur. Overtraining can be characterized by a performance plateau or a loss of performance that is not in keeping with the goals of the training phase and may not be explained by training load. It should be noted that *overtraining* is a misnomer in that training alone is unlikely to cause a problem; rather the cause is an accumulation of stressors. Overtraining has been divided into different types (figure 10.4) based on the type and degree of symptoms (Stone et al. 1991b). Briefly, overtraining can be divided into *monotonous training* and *overwork/overstress*. Monotonous training is not characterized by high levels of fatigue or any of the usual overt symptoms associated with overtraining; rather it is an overadaptation of the CNS to the same mechanics repeated over and over (see chapter 13, "The Concept of Periodization") in which performance plateaus and even falls off slightly. Overwork or overstress results from the summation of all of the daily stressors encountered (including training); when these stressors become too great, the recovery-adaptive process begins to fail.

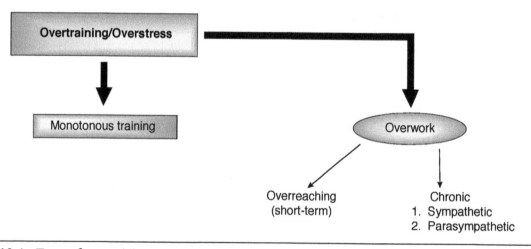

Figure 10.4   Types of overtraining.

Adapted from M.H. Stone et al., 1991, "Overtraining: A review of the signs and symptoms and possible causes of overtraining," *Journal of Applied Sports Science Research* 5(1): 35-50.

Overwork or overstress can further be divided into short-term (overreaching) and chronic. Overreaching can be defined as a condition resulting from a short-term increase in training volume or intensity (or both) that may lead to a short-term performance decrement. The signs and symptoms of overreaching are not typically as extensive or severe as those associated with overtraining. Importantly, restoration of performance can occur in a few days to a few weeks. Often there is a delayed increase in performance two to five weeks after the overreaching phase (Stone et al. 1991b). The signs and symptoms of chronic overwork/overstress are much more severe and can involve the CNS. Furthermore, these symptoms may mimic overstimulation of the sympathetic or parasympathetic nervous system, and these symptoms may be more or less prevalent in different types of sport. It is also possible that the sympathetic type of overstress is a preparasympathetic mechanism (figure 10.5).

Although the symptomatology associated with overwork or overstress is a function of the total stressors, the degree and severity of symptoms do appear to increase with increasing intensity and especially volume of training (Stone et al. 1991b). Figure 10.6 shows the theoretical changes in symptoms associated with the progression toward overwork or overstress. The progression among strength-power athletes appears to follow a pathway beginning with alterations in the nervous system (motor control and technique alterations leading to more overt hormonal changes, figure 10.7). The exact underlying mechanism of overtraining (figures 10.8 and 10.9) is unknown but may involve an intricate alteration of several physiological systems as a result of cytokine synthesis (Armstrong and VanHoost 2002; McKinnon 2000; Smith 2000).

Age and Maturation Level

The aging process eventually results in a loss of performance. Using cross-sectional isometric strength values in untrained subjects, Åstrand and Rodahl (1970) indicated that peak strength is reached at

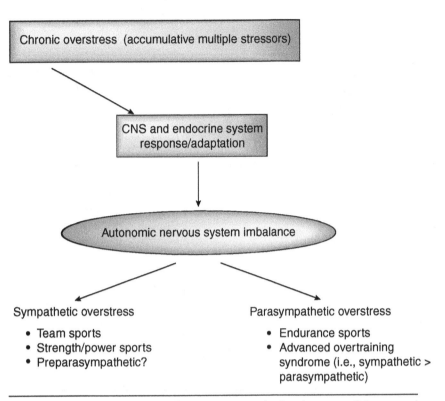

Figure 10.5 Chronic overwork or overstress—the involvement of the central nervous system and sport characterization.

Adapted from M.H. Stone et al., 1991, "Overtraining: A review of the signs and symptoms and possible causes of overtraining," *Journal of Applied Sports Science Research* 5(1): 35-50.

approximately 20 years in males and 18 years in females. Isometric strength levels decline until, at age 70, peak strength is about the same as at age 15. Aging appears to result in an approximately 11% loss in isometric and dynamic maximum strength per decade after 40 among both untrained men and women (Harries and Bassey 1990; Lindle, Metter, and Lynch 1977). However, individual muscles or groups of muscles do not necessarily decline in strength at the same rate (Amara et al. 2003).

Among previously trained athletes (powerlifters), basic strength in dynamic multijoint activities (squat, bench press, and deadlift) appears to decline at about 1% to 3% per year from 40 to 50 years old and at about 1% per year thereafter (Galloway, Kadoko, and Jokl 2002). Although the decline in dynamic explosive strength among male weightlifters is not constant, it appears to average approximately 1% to 1.5% per year after age 40 (The and Ploutz-Snyder 2003; Meltzer 1994) and is similar to the age-related decline in performance among master track and field athletes (Baker, Tang, and Turner 2003; Fung and Ha 1994). The age-related decline in explosive strength appears to be somewhat greater among women (Baker, Tang, and Turner 2003).

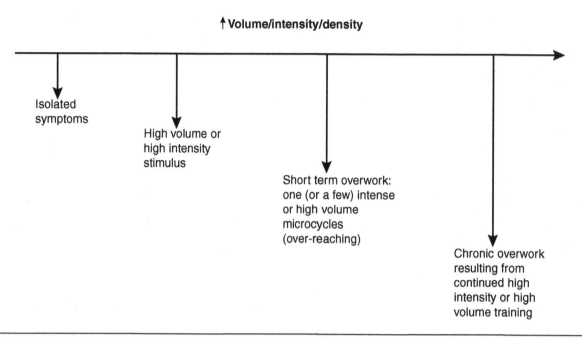

↑ **Volume/intensity/density**

Isolated
symptoms

High volume or
high intensity
stimulus

Short term overwork:
one (or a few) intense
or high volume
microcycles
(over-reaching)

Chronic overwork
resulting from
continued high
intensity or high
volume training

Figure 10.6   The continuum of overwork/overstress symptoms associated with training.

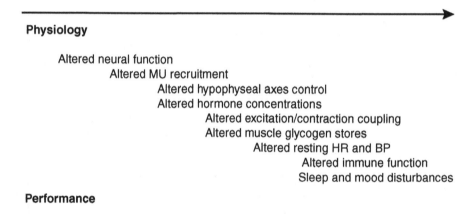

Physiology

Altered neural function
Altered MU recruitment
Altered hypophyseal axes control
Altered hormone concentrations
Altered excitation/contraction coupling
Altered muscle glycogen stores
Altered resting HR and BP
Altered immune function
Sleep and mood disturbances

Performance

Diminished coordination
Deteriorating technique
Decreased PRFD
Decreased maximum power
Decreased maximum strength

Figure 10.7   The progression of overtraining symptoms among strength-power athletes.

For example, in 1997 the women's world records for both the snatch and clean and jerk averaged about 68% of the men's records over five weight categories (Rozenek and Garhammer 1998). At ages 40 to 54 years this ratio had decreased to about 50%, and at ages 55 to 59 the ratio drops to about 30%. Because weightlifting movements have a large explosive component, this observation could indicate a loss of speed and power at a faster rate among women. However, because of the small numbers of women competing in the older age groups it is not possible to draw definitive conclusions.

Assuming that strength (and power) declines at the same rate in trained and untrained populations, being strength trained would offer health and performance advantages in that at any age the strength-trained individual would still be stronger

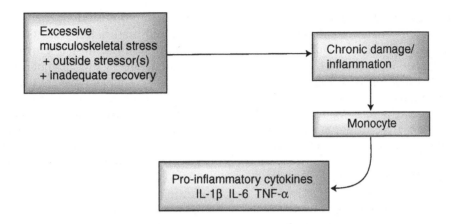

Figure 10.8 Theoretical overtraining mechanism: Excessive stress leads to the production of proinflammatory proteins (cytokines).

Adapted, by permission, from L. Smith, 2000, "Cytokine hypothesis of overtraining: a physiological adaptation to excessive stress?" *Medicine and Science in Sports and Exercise* 32(2): 317-331.

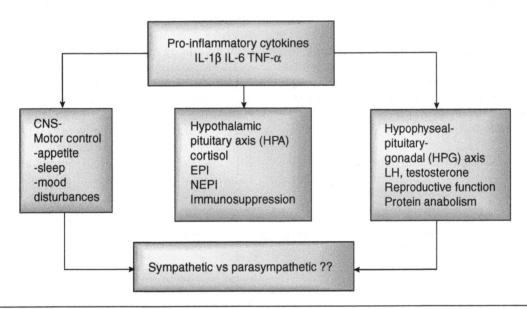

Figure 10.9 Cytokine production leads to the altered function of several different systems.

Adapted, by permission, from L. Smith, 2000, "Cytokine hypothesis of overtraining: a physiological adaptation to excessive stress?" *Medicine and Science in Sports and Exercise* 32(2): 317-331.

than a lesser-trained or sedentary individual. The age-related decline in strength and power appears to be associated with several factors, including a more sedentary lifestyle; sarcopenia and alterations in body composition; a preferential loss of type II motor units; a loss of maximum shortening velocity in specific muscle fiber types (Evans 1995; Krivickas et al. 2001; Larsson and Karlsson 1978; Proctor, Balagopal, and Nair 1998); neural degeneration (Ward and Frackowiak 2003); and alterations in hormones, particularly insulin-like growth factor 1 (IGF_1), testosterone, and dehydroepiandrosterone-

sulfate (Kamel, Maas, and Duthie 2002; Proctor, Balagopal, and Nair 1998). Endurance also declines, but at a slower rate compared to maximum strength (Baker, Tang, and Turner 2003; Galloway, Kadoko, and Jokl 2002), perhaps as a result of the retention of slower motor units during aging (Larsson and Karlsson 1978).

Resistance training appears to reduce the effect of age-related decline in endurance and perhaps in strength and power (Bemben 1998; Lemmer et al. 2000). Resistance training can promote retention of muscle mass and type II fibers, can enhance connective tissue strength, may enhance motor control, can enhance hormone concentrations, and can produce health and performance benefits (Johnson et al. 1983; Stone 1988; Stone et al. 1991a; Stone and Karatzeferi 2002). However, very young and very old individuals do not have the same adaptive levels as teenagers and young adults. Aging reduces the ability of the muscle to hypertrophy and reduces the rate of gain in the 1RM; however, specific tension (isometric maximum-to-cross-sectional area) is not affected by aging (Johnson et al. 1982, 1983; Welle, Totterman, and Thorton 1996).

Initiating resistance training programs with older adults requires a more gradual approach, often using much longer warm-ups before the training session. Loading should also be more gradual both in the training session and across time. Tests of maximum strength including 1RMs can be carried out safely and with excellent reliability given sufficient familiarization with the test exercises (Phillips et al. 2004).

Although in the past, resistance training for children was controversial, evidence indicates that preadolescents and adolescents can benefit from a resistance training program. Part of the controversy dealt with the degree to which children could gain strength or power, and part of it dealt with safety issues.

Critics of strength training for children (preadolescents) suggested that increased maximum strength beyond that occurring with normal growth and maturation was at best minimal; the reasoning was that muscle growth would not be stimulated due to low anabolic hormone levels (Katch 1983; Legwold 1982). At puberty, strength increases resulting from resistance training rise markedly along with lean body mass and increases in anabolic hormones (the "trigger hypothesis"). However, empirical data and even casual observation of children participating in a number of sports with a loading component, particularly gymnastics, indicated that these children were considerably stronger and more powerful than their untrained counterparts. Although peak hormonal stimulation and modulation for muscle growth or performance are low among children, adaptations in the nervous system are likely to occur.

Figure 10.10 depicts a model of physical and physiological maturation for children, adolescents, and adults. The model suggests that motor unit and nervous system maturation would be advanced enough among children, even as young as 7 or 8 years old, to support adaptations to strength training. Furthermore, recent data indicate that it may also be possible to increase resting hormone concentrations, including testosterone, in prepubertal (11-13 years) and pubertal boys (14-16 years) as a result of a strength training program (Tsolakis, Messinis, and Apostolos 2000). Studies and reviews of resistance training indicate that beneficial altera-

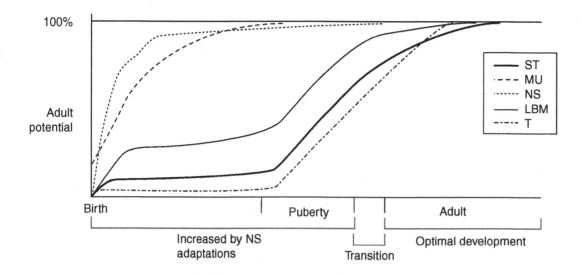

Figure 10.10 Theoretical development for strength factors for males. This is a theoretical model of physical and physiological maturation. Whereas maximum strength (ST) and lean body mass (LBM) are associated with hormonal changes (T), the nervous system (NS) and motor units and fiber type (MU) mature much earlier. Thus, the nervous system provides a means of adaptation to strength training among preadolescents.

Adapted, by permission, from W.J Kraemer et al., 1989, "Resistance training and youth," *Pediatric Exercise Science* 1: 336-350.

tions in strength, motor performance, cardiovascular variables, and body composition can occur in preadolescents (Blimkie 1993; Byrd et al. 2003; Faigenbaum 2000; Falk and Tenenbaum 1996; Lillegard et al. 1997; Payne et al. 1997; Sothern et al. 2000). Among postpubertal adolescents, alterations in both physiology and performance abilities can be quite marked (Falk and Tenenbaum 1996; Payne et al. 1997). Indeed, resistance training has been shown to enhance sport-related performance among adolescents (Byrd et al. 2003; Drozdov and Petrov 1983; Dvorkin and Medvedev 1983).

Safety concerns have arisen regarding whether children, particularly prepubertal children, should participate in resistance training and especially weightlifting and powerlifting (Blimkie 1993). While injuries as a result of resistance training, powerlifting, and weightlifting in children occur, the rate is relatively low, and severe injuries are rare (Byrd et al. 2003; Drozdov and Petrov 1983; Dvorkin and Medvedev 1983; Hamill 1994). There has been particular concern over epiphyseal injuries (growth plate injuries). Although epiphyseal injuries occur in children as a result of many high-intensity activities, particularly contact sports, they quite rarely result from resistance training, including weightlifting, especially in supervised programs (Hamill 1994). Furthermore, when growth plate injuries have occurred, with proper medical intervention they have not typically resulted in long-term problems (Maffulli 1990).

Some data indicate that children do not fatigue to the extent adults do during high-intensity exercise. During running and cycling sprints, children as well as adults showed a greater decline in both peak and mean power output during running than during cycling; but children showed less fatigue than adults in both the running and cycling sprints (Ratel et al. 2004). However, it is not known whether this occurred because the adults (compared to the children) were most likely performing closer to their true maximum.

Of particular importance to sport is the early development of motor skills and technique. Teaching children (or any beginner) proper technique for resistance training exercise, or any other exercise, will

- reduce potential injury,
- enhance the retention of a technique or skill,
- enhance the long-term progression of training,
- enhance the long-term adaptation to training, and

- enhance the transfer-of-training effect (i.e., increase transfer from training to a sport performance).

Additionally, evidence suggests that through teaching proper exercise technique to children, the motor skill task becomes engrained. Andren-Sandberg (1998, p. 4480) indicates that "prepubescent training of motor skills yield long lasting benefits whereas as with adults—the benefits derived from training of condition and strength rapidly disappear if not continually maintained." This concept is important in two respects. First, if technique is already at a high level, then constantly training technique in sport may be somewhat counterproductive, and training to improve or sustain sport-specific fitness may be more productive. Second, this concept also suggests that technique becomes highly engrained as a motor engram. Thus, after technique is learned it may be difficult to change; therefore, great pains should be taken to teach children (and other beginners) proper technique.

Before a child engages in a resistance training program, the following issues should be addressed. The child should be physically (e.g., Tanner staging) and emotionally mature enough to engage in the training program. Care should be taken in differentiating between chronological age and physical-physiological age. Some 11-year-olds are as physically mature as some 14-year-olds. Naim Suleymanoglu (60-64 kg [132-141 lb], Bulgaria, Turkey) began weightlifting training at 10 years of age; he set his first senior world records at age 15. He went on to win four world and three Olympic championships. Had he lived in most areas of the United States or Great Britain he would still have been waiting to get into the gym at 15 years old. Gauging emotional maturity is difficult at best. Although some instruments have been developed to aid in this measurement, such as Janus and Offord's Early Development Instrument (2000), these instruments are really aimed at determining a child's readiness for entering school and not necessarily for engaging in sport or resistance exercise. Although these instruments may be helpful, it is still the task and responsibility of the training supervisor to determine whether a child is emotionally ready for training.

The resistance training equipment should fit the child, although free weights fit all sizes whereas machines are usually sized for adults. The child and the supervisor must understand proper lifting technique for every exercise in the program. The child should not move on in training until he or she has mastered proper technique. The child and the supervisor must understand correct spotting techniques and when they should be used.

Although there is still some controversy concerning the type of program, the supervisor should have a reasonable idea of the type of resistance training program the child should follow. Generally, for prepubescent trainers, a multiset program of 10 to 15 repetitions per set, at least two days per week, would be appropriate at the initiation of the program (Byrd et al. 2003; Faigenbaum et al. 2002). Maximum strength testing (1RM) should be performed with caution but has not been shown to be detrimental or injury-producing in children (Byrd et al. 2003; Faigenbaum, Milliken, and Wescott 2003). The supervisor should also understand the potential results of the training program.

Sex

Strength-power performance differences between men and women are to an extent a result of differences in size (Van Den Tillaar and Ettema 2004), although size cannot completely explain all observed differences (Batterham and Birch 1996; Vanderburgh et al. 1997).

Maximum strength comparisons among untrained men and women (Lewis, Kamon, and Hodgson 1986; Miller et al. 1993; Sanborn and Jankowski 1994) indicate that average strength ratios of women:men are as follows: total body, 64%; upper body, 56%; lower body, 74%. It should be noted that these values are a summary of different methods and modes of testing, such as isometric versus freely moving, machines versus free weights, and eccentric versus concentric versus plyometric muscle action. Thus, it would be expected that some differences may be observed with different testing devices. These values are to an extent independent of body mass and muscle distribution differences.

When body mass and lean body mass are partially accounted for, the differences between men and women are not as great.

For the upper body, women's maximum strength per kilogram of body mass compared to men is approximately 60%, and maximum strength per kilogram of lean body mass (LBM) is approximately 70% to 75%. For the lower body, women's maximum strength per kilogram of body mass is approximately 80% to 85%, and maximum strength per kilogram of LBM is approximately 95% to 100%.

Although there are, as yet, relatively few data on highly strength-trained women, the strength ratio differences between untrained men and women appear to be similar among strength-power athletes, including elite weightlifters and powerlifters (Kraemer and Koziris 1994) and throwers (Stone, Triplett-McBride, and Stone 2001). Table 10.1a shows the relationship between elite U.S. men and women weightlifters on maximum isometric strength using a midthigh pull, and table 10.1b shows the relative weightlifting performance consisting of maximum dynamic explosive lifts (snatch and clean and jerk). Data are presented in absolute terms and with four methods of normalizing for body mass differences. The method of "normalizing" data was to divide by body mass (strength per kilogram), divide by LBM (strength per kilogram of LBM), use allometric scaling (strength/body mass $^{0.67}$), and use the Sinclair formula (polynomial regression = strength × coefficient). (See chapter 3, "Biomechanics of Resistance Training.")

These data indicate that in a test exercise (isometric midthigh pull) and for weightlifting movements, all of which are primarily lower body movements, trained men are stronger than women. Although attempting to obviate body mass or size using various methods reduces the difference between men and women, the differences are not accounted for

Table 10.1a   **Isometric Maximum Strength and Relative Maximum Strength (Midthigh Pull) of Female and Male Elite U.S. Weightlifters**

	IPF	IPF/kg	IPFa	IPFs	IPF/LBM
Women (n = 6)					
M	3424	47.0	193.5	3753	61.4
SD	593	6.6	28.7	587	7.6
Men (n = 9)					
M	5127	54.0	241.6	5746	63.4
SD	1056	5.1	25.8	774	6.5
W:M	67%	87%	80%	65%	97%

Numbers in cells are means with standard deviations in parentheses. IPF = isometric peak force (N); IPF/kg = IPF per kilogram of body mass (N/kg); IPFa = IPF scaled by body mass$^{0.67}$ (N/body mass$^{0.67}$); IPFs = IPF scaled by the Sinclair formula (N); LBM = lean body mass; W:M = ratio of women to men by percent.

Table 10.1b   **Weightlifting and Relative Strength Performance of Female and Male Elite U.S. Weightlifters**

					WEIGHTLIFTING MOVEMENTS					
	SN	SN/kg	SNa	SNs	SN/LBM	C&J	C&J/kg	C&Ja	C&Js	C&J/LBM
Women (n = 6)										
M	92.5	1.29	5.3	101.5	1.66	112.9	1.57	6.4	123.8	2.03
SD	6.8	0.11	0.4	6.3	0.10	8.9	0.14	0.4	7.7	0.10
Men (n = 9)										
M	146.9	1.57	7.0	165.8	1.84	176.9	1.86	8.3	198.1	2.19
SD	16.9	0.17	0.4	8.6	0.15	33.6	0.16	0.9	23.5	0.23
W:M	63%	82%	75%	61%	91%	64%	84%	77%	63%	93%

SN = snatch (kg); SN/kg = snatch per kilogram of body mass (kg/kg); SNa = snatch scaled by body mass$^{0.67}$ (kg/body mass$^{0.67}$); SNs = snatch scaled by the Sinclair formula (kg); LBM = lean body mass; C&J = clean and jerk (kg); C&J/kg = clean and jerk per kilogram of body mass (kg/kg); C&Ja = clean and jerk scaled by body mass$^{0.67}$ (kg/body mass$^{0.67}$); C&Js = clean and jerk scaled by the Sinclair formula (kg); W:M = ratio of women to men by percent.

completely. It should be noted that the ratio (W:M) of strength in the midthigh pull was 97% when LBM was considered, indicating that differences in body fat are a primary factor explaining isometric maximum strength differences (table 10.1a). However, the differences in load during measures of explosive strength (i.e., weightlifting movements), when normalized by LBM, are somewhat greater than the ratio of isometric maximum values (SN = 91%, C&J = 93% vs. IPF = 97%). This last observation indicates that several factors other than LBM likely contribute to differences in dynamic explosive strength.

Power is strongly related to performance in a number of sports and is a key characteristic separating winning from losing. Power is a measure associated with dynamic explosive strength; measurements of power also point to differences between men and women that are not completely explained by body size (Garhammer 1991). Peak power output for women is about 65% that of males during the snatch and clean (Garhammer 1991) and in various jumping tasks (Fleck and Kraemer 1997). Both untrained and trained women appear to generate lower power outputs per volume of muscle and to generate lower peak rates of force development compared to men (Komi and Karlsson 1978; Ryushi et al. 1988), a factor that may contribute to differences in absolute power.

Besides body fat and rate of force development, other factors influencing dynamic explosive strength differences may include hormonal differences, relative differences in upper body strength (force is transmitted through the upper body in these movements), greater anterior pelvic tilt in women, or other biomechanical factors such as wider hips among women, agreeing with previous observations among untrained men and women

(Batterham and Birch 1996; Vanderburgh et al. 1997).

Data on male and female collegiate and elite throwers, powerlifters, and weightlifters indicate the following:

- There is a strong relationship between maximum strength and power and between maximum strength and sport performance even at light loads (Stone, Triplett-McBride, and Stone 2001; Stone et al. 2003a, 2003b).

- Sex-related strength differences are greater in the upper body than the lower (Stone, Triplett-McBride, and Stone 2001).

- Lower-level athletes often show greater strength differences between genders than elite athletes (Stone, Triplett-McBride, and Stone 2001).

This information indicates that a major consideration for women in reaching the upper levels of strength-power sports is a marked increase in strength-power. The strength differences in upper and lower body between men and women are likely related to differences in total muscle distribution. Men have a greater relative distribution of muscle in the upper body (Janssen et al. 2000).

Several factors specific to women have implications for training, including injury, upper body and lower body strength levels, and menstrual cycle effects. Women athletes in some sports, particularly strength-power sports involving contact or sudden direction changes such as jumping and cutting, sustain up to six times as many anterior cruciate ligament (ACL) injuries as men (Zelisko, Noble, and Porter 1982; Zillmer, Powell, and Albright 1991). Reasons for this relatively high incidence of knee ligament injury are not completely clear but may include lack of strength (absolute and relative), which would affect the ability to control body movements; rate of force development (women take longer to develop the same relative force level) (Bell and Jacobs 1986), again affecting control of movement and control of balance; hamstring activation, which may be important because women tend to have a quadriceps-dominant knee upon landing, which results in greater anterior tibial translation (Huston and Wojtys 1996); and differences in the way women position themselves during single-leg squatting movements compared to men (greater ankle dorsiflexion, hip adduction, hip flexion, hip external rotation [Zeller et al. 2003]), indicating that movements during squatting and jumping may predispose women to more ACL injury than men.

As a result of the relatively lower strength values (both absolute and normalized) for the upper body in women compared to men, it has been suggested that increased emphasis should be placed on upper body training for women (Gotshalk et al. 1998). This additional emphasis in training may improve performance in tasks that depend in part or as a whole on upper body strength. Part of the reasoning for this greater emphasis on upper body strength training is the assumption that the weaker upper body musculature may limit strength gains in the lower body (i.e., squats, cleans, etc.).

The menstrual cycle is associated with relatively large variations in several hormones (e.g., progesterone, estradiol). These hormonal fluctuations, as well as menses, can be associated with mood swings, changes in cognition, and feelings of illness. It is interesting to note that untrained women (nonathletes) have reported more problems (e.g., inability to focus, cramps) due to menses than athletic groups of women (Golub 1992). Many of these problems could interfere with training and must be addressed. Athletic women either have fewer problems or have developed strategies to deal with problems.

Alterations in hormones can affect physiological parameters, which in turn can affect force production parameters (Kraemer 1992; McMillan et al. 1993). Indeed, strength gains in women have been correlated to serum concentrations of both total and free testosterone (Hakkinen et al. 1990). The menstrual cycle is characterized by large variations in several hormones on a regular (or nearly regular) basis. Because these hormones (estradiol, progesterone, etc.) have effects on metabolic and neuromuscular function, it is possible that training and performance can be affected during different phases of the cycle. Although most studies do not show profound effects of the menstrual cycle on various parameters of performance, some evidence (Reis, Frick, and Schmidtbleicher 1995) suggests that strength gains may be negatively affected during the early follicular phase and positively affected during the late follicular and early luteal phase. Increases in strength gains noted during the late follicular and early luteal phase were associated with increases in serum estradiol and testosterone. Additionally, Reis and colleagues (1995) suggest that altering the number of training sessions (reduced during the luteal phase) during various phases of the cycle may enhance the training effect (i.e., greater increases in maximum strength). Obviously more study is necessary; however, investigating the effect of the menstrual cycle on adaptation to training is difficult because not all women cycle at the same time and because the use of birth control drugs alters the normal cycle and the normal variation in hormones.

Neural, Biomechanical, and Anthropometric Factors Influencing Strength and Power

The underlying factors associated with strength (ability to produce force) are as follows:

Motor unit recruitment

Motor unit activation frequency (rate coding)

Synchronization (ballistic movements)

Motor unit activation pattern (intramuscular activation)

Muscle action pattern (intermuscular activation)

Use of elastic energy and reflexes (stretch–shortening cycle)

Neural inhibition

Motor unit type (muscle fiber type)

Biomechanical and anthropometric factors

Muscle cross-sectional area

These factors can be roughly divided into three areas: (1) neural, (2) hypertrophic, and (3) anthropometric. The relative time course of alteration of neural and hypertrophic factors due to training is depicted in figure 10.3. Note that neural factors predominate during the early phases of initial training, while hypertrophic alterations predominate in the later phases of training. One explanation for the later development of hypertrophy is that people must learn how to exert themselves (i.e., learning effect) before the muscle and connective tissue can be adequately stressed (stimulated) to adapt.

Neural Factors

Figure 10.11 depicts the basic interactions between the nervous system and muscle that are necessary for muscle contraction and force production. The intent to perform a movement is developed in the higher brain centers and transferred to the motor cortex. The motor cortex transmits signals by way of the brainstem and spinal cord to the appropriate motor neurons. This is the basic pattern of nervous system activity that describes *motor control*.

Although there is little doubt that resistance training has an effect on the nervous system, it is not always completely clear what or how neural components are affected. Most (not all) of the evidence for this neural effect is indirect and has been arrived at through elimination of other factors. For example, in the initial stages of training, strength, power, and other performance variables such as rate of force development increase at a much faster rate than muscle girth or measures

of LBM (Hakkinen et al. 1998; Ploutz et al. 1994); therefore the strength gains are assumed to be one or more neural components. At the other end of the spectrum, advanced and elite strength-power athletes have difficulty increasing LBM and muscle mass, particularly athletes in body weight classes such as weightlifters and powerlifters. However, these advanced athletes do still make strength gains (although relatively small) with little or no alteration in body composition or muscle size, again suggesting that neural component adaptation is taking place (Stone et al. 2000, 2003a).

Recruitment and Rate Coding

The force of muscle contraction is primarily altered as a result of the number and type of recruited motor units and the frequency of stimulation (rate coding). Figure 10.12 illustrates this relationship. The exact degree to which one mechanism is emphasized over the other during muscle activation depends on the amount of force required and the size and type of muscle being activated (Gardiner 2001). However, there is some doubt that an untrained muscle can be fully activated under normal voluntary conditions (Aagaard et al. 2000; Semmler and Enoka 2000). Furthermore, strength training can result in a greater activation of muscle, thus influencing strength production.

Motor Unit Recruitment Motor unit (MU) recruitment within a muscle normally takes place in a reasonably orderly fashion according to size (Henneman, Somjen, and Carpenter 1965; Henneman 1982). To an extent, the size of the MU dictates the activation threshold; larger MUs have higher thresholds. Motor unit size covaries with MU type (Gardiner 2001); thus, larger, more powerful MUs would be recruited last in a mixed muscle. However, even within muscles containing only or primarily one fiber type, the size principle is still evident (Blinder et al. 1983).

Rate Coding Rate coding deals with the frequency at which recruited MUs are activated. Typically, faster MUs are activated at higher frequencies. Rate coding strongly influences the rate of MU and whole-muscle activation and is a primary factor influencing the rate of force development (Komi and

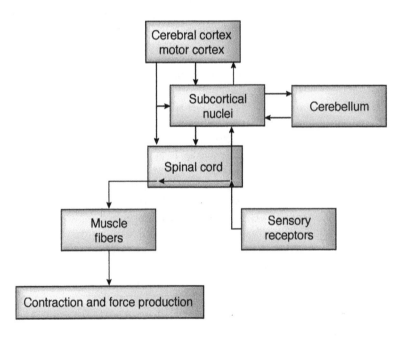

Figure 10.11 Theoretical nervous system mechanisms associated with voluntary movement. Muscle fiber contraction results in force production and is the stimulus for tissue remodeling and selective fiber hypertrophy, leading to improved function and performance.

Adapted from J. Noth, 1992, Cortical and peripheral control. In *Strength and power in sport*, edited by P.V. Komi (London: Blackwell Scientific), 9-20.

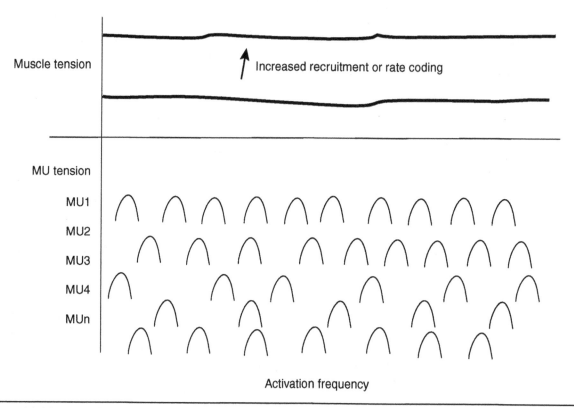

Figure 10.12   Recruitment and rate coding of whole-muscle tension (force) is directly related to the number of motor units activated and their frequency of activation. Larger MUs tend to be activated at a higher frequency.

Viitasalo 1976). A study by Viitasalo and Komi (1981) clearly pointed out that the rise in MU activation as measured by electromyography (EMG) is associated with a rise in muscle force. Evidence of this relationship can be observed in figure 10.13. Note that in tracing A, the initial rate of activation and force development is higher than in tracing B. Thus, the rate of force development is largely a function of the nervous system's ability to activate muscle. Typically, high rates of force development are necessary for success in explosive and high-power activities such as sprinting, throwing, and weightlifting. Interestingly, maximum strength has strong relationships with rate of force development; thus, building maximum strength may be a prime ingredient in producing high rates of force development and explosive strength for many sport activities (Andersen and Aagaard 2005).

Activation Frequency and Synchronization

Another mechanism that can affect the ability of a muscle to produce force is the synchronization of MUs. Motor units typically are activated as brief "dynamic" twitches. Figure 10.14 depicts the asyn-chronous activation patterns of several MUs. Note that during asynchronous activation, when one MU deactivates, another is being activated; this pattern creates a relatively smooth muscle tension production, which allows a relatively smooth movement to occur. Increased muscle activation through recruitment or rate coding can increase muscle force.

Under normal low-intensity muscle activation, MUs fire asynchronously. However, as the maximum level of strength is approached, some MUs are activated at exactly the same time as other MUs. As force output is increased, greater levels of synchronization can occur. The maximum frequency of activation can range from 30 to 50 Hz for low-threshold MUs and up to 100 Hz for high-threshold MUs, depending upon the type and the intensity of the muscle action. Furthermore, strength training can enhance the number of MUs synchronizing and can result in synchronization at lower force outputs (Semmler and Nordstrom 1998). The degree to which synchronization affects maximum strength, especially when measured iso-metrically, appears to be minimal (Yao, Fuglevand, and Enoka 2000). However, synchronization does appear to play an important role in ballistic move-ments.

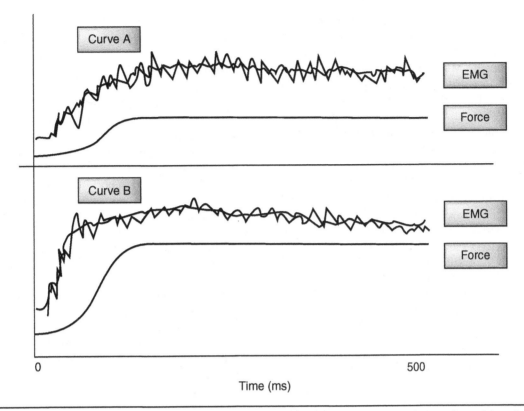

Figure 10.13 Effects of rate coding on rate of force development. The faster a muscle is activated (EMG, electromyography), the higher the rate of force development.

Adapted from P.V. Komi and J.H. Vitasalo, 1976, "Signal characteristics of EMG at different levels of muscle tension," *Acta Physiologica Scandinavica* 96: 267-276.

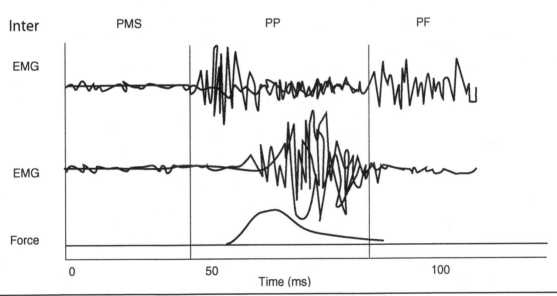

Figure 10.14 The triphasic response associated with ballistic movements. PMS = premotor silent period; PP = preprogrammed phase; PF = proprioceptive facilitatory phase.

Adapted from E.P. Zehr and D.G. Sale, 1994, "Ballistic movement: Muscle activation and neuromuscular adaptation," *Canadian Journal of Applied Physiology* 19(4): 363-378.

In figure 10.14, note the characteristic triphasic muscle activation pattern as recorded by EMG. In the first phase, there is a silent period (about 50 ms) in which the MUs have enough time to complete their refractory periods. This "premotor silent period" precedes activation of the prime mover or agonist. The premotor silent period allows for a large number of MUs to synchronize, which in turn produces a brief but very large force impulse during the second phase or preprogrammed period. After the burst of activity from the prime mover, the antagonistic muscle is activated and acts as a braking system, which slows movement and reduces injury potential. In the third and last phase, *proprioception*, the prime mover again becomes active in order to produce subtle adjustments in the final stages of movement. This basic triphasic response is activated in all ballistic movements and can be refined by appropriate training procedures.

Task Specificity

There is a great deal of evidence for the concepts of intra- and intermuscular task specificity. Intramuscular task specificity has to do with specific patterns of activation for MUs, while intermuscular task specificity relates to the interplay and pattern of activation among muscles during a specific task. Some muscles are compartmentalized anatomically, and these compartments may be more or less active during different tasks (Wickham and Brown 1998). Furthermore, neurons are compartmentalized functionally into task groups, such that specific groups of neurons are activated as a result of specific tasks being performed (Loeb 1987). The concept of intramuscular task specificity may help explain the phenomenon of regional hypertrophy (Abe et al. 2003; Antonio 2000; Daneels et al. 2001; Tan 1999), in which a specific exercise causes hypertrophy in one region of a muscle but not in others. Bodybuilders have intuitively recognized this aspect of training, arguing that to more completely develop a muscle, it is necessary to perform many different exercises for that muscle.

Both intra- and intermuscular activation patterns can change with very slight alterations in movement pattern, eccentric versus concentric actions, or changes in velocity (Semmler and Enoka 2000; Zajac and Gordon 1989). Because of these alterations in activation patterns, selection of exercises for strength-power training should be viewed as movement specific rather than simply a matter of training one or more muscles. Improvement in the efficiency of intra- and especially intermuscular activation implies an enhanced coordinative ability and is an important mechanism contributing to improved strength expression (Semmler and Enoka 2000).

Neural Inhibition

The degree of neural inhibition can also affect strength capabilities. Inhibition can take two different forms: conscious and somatic-reflexive. Conscious inhibition involves a perception (right or wrong) that a given weight may produce injury. For example, if you have never performed squats before and are asked to perform a 300 kg full squat, chances are (if you are remotely intelligent) that you will refuse. However, through proper training you may eventually squat 300 kg (660 lb).

Somatic-reflexive neural inhibition includes feedback from various muscle and joint receptors, and has been suggested to be part of a protective mechanism (figure 10.14). This protective mechanism can reduce muscle tension during maximum and near-maximum efforts. Strength training appears to reduce receptor sensitivity and diminish inhibition, and this diminished inhibition is partially responsible for the greater forces achieved (Aagaard et al. 2000).

Stretching–Shortening Cycles

The use of reflexes and stretch–shortening cycles (SSC) can also alter the production of force (Bobbert et al. 1996; Cronin et al. 2000). In essence an SSC consists of a plyometric muscle action in which an eccentric action immediately precedes a concentric action. The mechanisms involved in concentric enhancement may include use of elastic energy, a stretch reflex, optimization of muscle length, and optimization of muscle activation and muscle activation patterns (Bobbert et al. 1996; Bobbert and van Soest 2001). Learning to use an SSC more efficiently can markedly increase force production. Evidence indicates that improving maximum strength can augment both the eccentric and the concentric portion of the SSC (Aagaard et al. 2000; Cronin et al. 2000).

Motor Unit Types

Motor unit and fiber type also influence strength and particularly power. Studies and review of the literature have indicated that a greater percentage and a large cross-sectional area of type II muscle fibers may be advantageous in terms of dynamic force production (Hakkinen 1994; Powell et al. 1984), even when muscle architecture and other mechanical factors are taken into consideration. Strength-power athletes typically have both a somewhat higher percentage of type II fibers and a large total type IIX cross-sectional area compared to untrained subjects. Strength training, particularly explosive strength training, appears to increase the ratio of type II to type I muscle fiber cross-sectional area in a manner favoring strength and particularly power production (Hakkinen 1994). However, myosin heavy chain adaptation appears to be such that a reduction in the percentage of type IIX fibers and an increase in IIA fibers occur as the volume of resistance training increases (Adams et al. 1993; Kadi and Thornell 1999). Although this alteration (IIX to IIA) would slightly reduce the myosin ATPase activity of the fiber and therefore the potential power output, other adaptive mechanisms more than compensate. Changes in the nervous system and fiber or muscle hypertrophy could offset the potential reduction in power. As the nervous system effect and perhaps hypertrophy are longer lasting than the MU transformation effect, short-term reduction in training volume, as with a taper, appears to allow a transformation back toward the IIX MU type and slightly higher power outputs (Ross and Leveritt 2001).

Biomechanical and Anthropometric Factors

Factors such as gross muscle architecture, angle of pinnation, muscle insertion point, height, limb length, and moment arm may alter the mechanical advantage of the intact muscle lever system. For example, weightlifters possess a high ratio of body mass to height (Bm/h) compared to untrained subjects and other athletic groups. This Bm/h is advantageous because it can provide an increased force production (see chapter 3, "Biomechanics of Resistance Training"). This advantage is associated with the strong positive relationship between a muscle's physiological cross-sectional area and maximum muscle force-generating capabilities (Semmler and Enoka 2000). If two athletes of different heights and different limb lengths have the same muscle mass and volume, the shorter athlete will have the greater muscle cross section and therefore a greater muscle generating force.

Muscle responds to resistance training by enlarging its cross-sectional area (i.e., hypertrophy). In this manner additional contractile elements (myofibrils) are added to the muscle fiber. The underlying mechanisms are complex and still not completely understood. The primary stimulus for skeletal muscle hypertrophy appears to be a gain in tension and mechanical strain that results in muscle damage (Goldspink 1999; Nosaka et al. 2003). Secondarily, there may be metabolic factors as a result of repeated contractions that also stimulate

the hypertrophic adaptations (Armstrong, Warren, and Warren 1991; Nosaka et al. 2003). The stimulus causes a cascade of multilevel effects as illustrated in figure 10.15.

Differences in sarcomere length appear to be associated with disruption of the shorter sarcomeres and perhaps the plasma membrane as a result of forceful stretch, as occurs during eccentric muscle action (Proske and Morgan 2001). Indeed, some evidence indicates that as a result of eccentric actions, muscle damage, delayed muscle soreness (Gibala et al. 2000), and the subsequent hypertrophic adaptation are considerably greater than with concentric exercise (Higbie et al. 1996; Hortabagyi et al. 1996). There are also data to indicate that greater stretch or greater force during eccentric movement (i.e., greater ranges of motion) results in greater damage and therefore could result in greater hypertrophy (Nosaka and Newton 2002; Nosaka and Sakamoto 2001). These observations may help explain the very small effect of isometric exercise on hypertrophy adaptations (Ishii 1994; Conley et al. 1997). Furthermore, mixed methods (concentric + eccentric, i.e., SSC) appear to produce greater hypertrophy than concentric-only training (Hortabagyi et al. 2000). However, at equal power outputs, concentric exercise may result in as much or more hypertrophy compared to eccentric exercise (Mayhew et al. 1995); this suggests that it is the increased force and greater muscle damage that occur during eccentric actions with a heavy load, or during slow-speed semi-isokinetic motions, that produce a greater hypertrophy response than with concentric actions. Additionally, evidence indicates that type II fibers are more susceptible to damage than type I fibers (Friden and Leiber 1998), possibly explaining the greater hypertrophy response of type II fibers undergoing resistance training.

During repeated contractions, cytosolic Ca^{++} concentrations can exceed a threshold value (>0.1 mmol $\cdot$ L^{-1}), triggering a calcium-sensitive degradation pathway (Armstrong, Warren, and Warren 1991; Clarkson and Sayers 1999; Friden and Leiber 2001). As a result, secondary damage is produced, partially by activation of the nonlysomal calcium-activated protease *calpain*, which catabolizes cytoskeletal proteins and induces degradation of myofibrillar structure (Friden and Leiber 2001; Goldspink 1999). The secondary damage is followed by an inflammatory process that is apparently necessary for tissue remodeling (Armstrong 1991; Clarkson and Sayers 1999). This inflammatory process includes the infiltration of macrophages and neutrophils that degrade damaged proteins (Armstrong 1991; Pyne 1994; Stauber

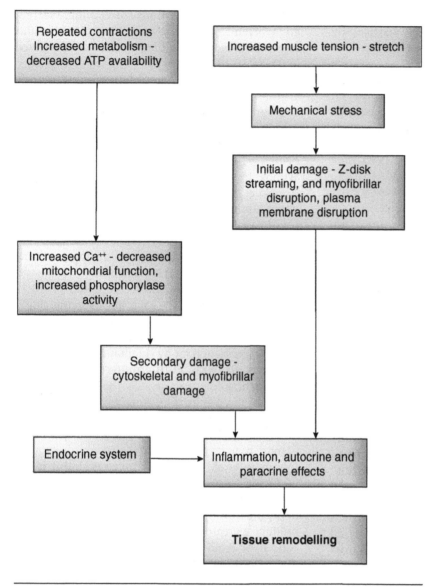

Figure 10.15 Potential mechanisms stimulating tissue remodeling and hypertrophy.

Adapted from K. Nosaka, A. Lavender, M. Newton, and P. Sacco, 2003, "Muscle damage in resistance training. Is muscle damage necessary for muscle hypertrophy?" *International Journal of Sport and Health Science* 1: 1-8.

appear to be the link between the mechanical stimulus (stretch or tension resulting in damage) and the activation of gene expression (Bickel et al. 2003; Goldspink 2002, 1999). Additionally, the endocrine system influences tissue remodeling (see chapter 5, "Neuroendocrine Factors"). Acute responses and particularly chronic adaptations of anabolic and catabolic hormones potentially alter the hypertrophy and hyperplasia adaptations to training (Ahtiainen et al. 2003).

Hyperplasia is in an increase in cell number. Hyperplasia may be stimulated through extensive long-term damage to the muscle cell and is associated with satellite cell activation (Gardiner 2001; Nosaka et al. 2003). There is reasonable evidence that overload-induced hyperplasia does occur in animals, although the increased fiber number is greater in avians compared to mammals (Kelly 1996). The occurrence of overload-induced hyperplasia in humans is controversial. Short-term studies (two to three months) of resistance training in humans have shown little evidence to support the occurrence of hyperplasia (McCall et al. 1996). However, cadaver data and studies of bodybuilders suggest that undergoing long-term resistance training may be a necessary stimulus (Abernethy et al. 1994; Larsson and Tesch 1986; MacDougall et

and Smith 1998). The inflammatory process can also result in cytokine release that can stimulate satellite cell activation and incorporation (Stauber and Smith 1998). Satellite cell activation and subsequent fusion with existing fibers and possibly hyperplasia appear to require considerable muscle damage in order to occur (Nosaka et al. 2003). The damage to muscle structure also stimulates autocrine and paracrine systems to release mitogens or muscle growth factors such as IGF_1 and mechano growth factor (MGF), enhancing the hypertrophy process (Goldspink 1999). These growth factors or mitogens

al. 1982). The possibility of hyperplasia occurring in humans is typically investigated by the use of tomographic scans, in which the method of estimating fiber number is to divide the average cross-sectional area (CSA) by the average fiber area (Gardiner 2001). Using this method, MacDougall and colleagues (1984) concluded that total muscle CSA area was more related to fiber area than to fiber number. However, the authors also noted that bodybuilders with the largest total CSA possessed the largest estimated fiber number. Larsson and Tesch (1986) indicated that bodybuilders with larger muscles had more fibers, and supported their claim with intramuscular EMG evidence suggesting that the bodybuilders had a greater fiber density (i.e., more fibers per MU) than expected. Assuming that hyperplasia does occur in humans, its effect on the total CSA of muscle is likely small (Abernethy et al. 1994).

Connective tissue is responsible for the transmission of forces created by skeletal muscle. Connective tissue remodeling also occurs with resistance training, and the underlying mechanisms appear to be somewhat similar to that for skeletal muscle (Nosaka et al. 2003; Stone and Karastzeferi 2002). However, as with satellite cell activation, connective tissue remodeling appears to require considerable exercise-induced muscle damage and may be more responsive to eccentric loading than to concentric-only muscle actions (Ishii 1994).

An important question is how much muscle damage is necessary for muscle hypertrophy or hyperplasia. Some evidence indicates that the protein synthesis-stimulatory effects of a single bout of eccentric exercise are reduced in trained subjects (Phillips et al. 1999). Trained subjects also experience less muscle damage and muscle soreness from the same relative exercise load; thus it is reasonable to expect that the hypertrophy adaptation would be smaller in trained subjects. Furthermore, it should be noted that among relatively untrained subjects during the initial stages of training, relatively little hypertrophy occurs; this may result simply from an inability to handle a great enough load to result in a stimulus sufficient to promote tissue remodeling and hypertrophy. Thus, among relatively untrained subjects, it is possible that substantial hypertrophy does not occur until they learn how to exert themselves sufficiently. However, as concentric muscle actions do not typically damage the muscle to the same extent as eccentric actions but can still produce hypertrophic adaptations (Housh et al. 1992), it would appear that extensive muscle damage may not be a prerequisite for muscle hypertrophy. This may not be the case, though, for connective tissue hypertrophy or muscle hyperplasia. The relative theoretical contributions of different contraction types to an enlarged CSA are shown in table 10.2.

The maximum CSA attainable for muscle fiber hypertrophy is unknown (Gardiner 2001); however, the range of adaptation appears to be on the order of 30% to 70% depending on the type and length of the training program (Alway, MacDougall, and Sale 1989; Staron et al. 1989; Thorstensson, Sjodin, and Karlsson 1975). The average fiber CSA of highly strength-trained athletes can be between two and three times as large as those of sedentary subjects (Alway et al. 1988; Fry et al. 2003; Hakkinen et al. 1987; Prince, Hikida, and Hagerman 1976; Tesch and Karlsson 1985). Generally type II fibers hypertrophy at a faster rate than type I fibers, so it is not surprising to find large total CSA of type II fibers among strength-power athletes (Fry et al. 2003; Hakkinen et al. 1987).

Of the various mechanisms relating to absolute maximum strength, the most important is the physiological CSA of a muscle and the total CSA of type II fibers (Thorstensson, Sjodin, and Karlsson 1975). (See chapter 3, "Biomechanics of Resistance Training.") From a practical standpoint, if CSA were not the most important factor affecting absolute muscular strength, there would not be body weight classes in sports such as boxing, judo, wrestling, or weightlifting. The relationship between strength and the physiological CSA of muscle stems from the number of sarcomeres in parallel. The more sarcomeres in parallel, the greater the maximum strength of a muscle. The process of hypertrophy resulting from strength training adds sarcomeres in parallel, thus raising the muscle's potential force production (Goldspink 1999). Furthermore, some evidence suggests that the packing density of myofibrils is slightly greater after resistance training-induced hypertrophy (Jones and Rutherford 1987).

Table 10.2 **The Relative Effects of Contraction Type on Hypertrophy and Hyperplasia**

Contraction type	Muscle cross-section	Muscle hyperplasia	Connective tissue cross-section
Isometric	NA, +	NA	NA
Concentric	++	NA, +	NA, +
Eccentric	+++	+	++
SSC (plyometric)	+++	+	+

NA = no apparent effect.

Adapted from K. Nosaka et al., 2003, "Muscle damage in resistance training. Is muscle damage necessary for muscle hypertrophy?" *International Journal of Sport and Health Science* 1: 1-8; and N. Ishii, 1994, Resistance training and muscle hypertrophy. In *Resistance training*, edited by Training Science Association (Tokyo: Asakura), 19-31.

Metabolic and Ultrastructural Alterations Associated With Resistance Training and Hypertrophy

Generally, anaerobic metabolic-related components of the fiber can be altered with resistance training, but there is less impact on aerobic-related components.

Enzyme Alterations

Few enzyme alterations have been shown to result from resistance training. Creatine kinase and myokinase have shown concentration increases as a result of isometric training in rats (Exner, Staudte, and Pette 1973). In humans, myokinase activity has been correlated with muscle force production (Borges and Essen-Gustavsson 1989) and has been demonstrated to increase somewhat with resistance training (Thorstensson 1977). Enzymes associated with aerobic metabolism, such as succinate dehydrogenase, have shown increased activity as a result of isometric training in both animals (Exner, Staudte, and Pette 1973) and humans (Grimby et al. 1973). However, typical resistance training protocols (e.g., heavy weight training) have not generally produced alterations in enzyme activities (Tesch 1992b). Conversely, high-volume (i.e., high repetitions per set), short-rest resistance training protocols may produce a number of anaerobic and aerobic enzyme alterations (Costill et al. 1979; Tesch 1992b); this observation indicates that the type of training protocol influences enzymatic alterations. Indeed, longer-lasting high-intensity contractions such as high-repetition strength training or sprint training may alter a number of enzyme activities, particularly those associated with anaerobic metabolism (MacDougall et al. 1998; Thorstensson, Sjodin, and Karlsson 1975).

One area in particular that is not well studied is isozyme alterations and long-term training. For example, some types of strength training and sprint training produce a lactate dehydrogenase (LDH) profile (LD1/LD5) such that the "muscle-type" isozyme (LD5) is favored (Karlsson et al. 1975), while endurance training enhances the heart-type isozyme (LD1) (Apple and Tesch 1989). Isozyme shifts with training may allow for superior performance even though total enzyme activity shows little adaptation to training.

Muscle Substrates

Phosphagen stores (ATP and PCr) are crucial for high-intensity exercise such as resistance training.

Although resistance training can increase peak power and increase fatigue resistance (factors partially dependent on phosphagen availability), there is little evidence that resistance training markedly alters phosphagen stores in animals (Hornberger and Farrar 2004) or humans (Tesch, Thorsson, and Colliander 1990).

Blood glucose uptake by muscle fiber increases during resistance exercise in both humans (McMillan et al. 1993) and animals (Yaspelkis et al. 2002). Resistance training has produced increases in glucose uptake, transport, and the concentration of transport proteins (GLUT-4) (Yaspelkis et al. 2002). Thus, resistance training may positively alter glucose uptake.

Blood glucose concentrations have not been shown to change appreciably during resistance training (Keul et al. 1978), indicating that increased uptake is matched by increased glucose availability. However, glycogen stores can be markedly reduced as a result of a resistance training session (Conley and Stone 1996; Haff et al. 2003). These observations indicate that blood glucose is not the limiting factor during resistance exercise, but rather that the exercise is more glycogen dependent. Thus training-induced increases in glycogen would have a positive benefit (Conley and Stone 1996). Glycogen stores have been shown to increase markedly after five months of heavy resistance training (MacDougall et al. 1977); a shorter training period (three months) did not result in appreciable glycogen concentration adaptations (Tesch, Thorsson, and Colliander 1990).

Although resistance exercise is supported by anaerobic mechanisms, considerable evidence indicates that fat oxidation increases markedly postexercise (Binzen, Swan, and Manore 2001; McMillan et al. 1993; Petitt, Arngrimsson, and Cureton 2003) and that resistance exercise can lower both postprandial and baseline measures of triglycerides (Petitt, Arngrimsson, and Cureton 2003). These observations suggest that resistance training (with enough volume) can be used to alter fat content. How much triglyceride is used during exercise is unknown, but the amount is likely small. Increases of muscle triglyceride stores were shown to occur with short-term resistance training but were not consistent among muscle groups (Tesch 1992a). It is likely that triglyceride stores are minimally affected by resistance training.

Two important factors related to resistance training and energy store alterations are nutrition and the type of training program. It is logical to assume that considerable variation in energy store adaptations can occur through the interaction of training protocol and nutritional strategies (see chapter 6, "Nutrition and Metabolic Factors," and chapter 7, "Ergogenic Aids").

Training Adaptations to Different Training Protocols

The first half of this chapter dealt with factors that may influence training adaptations. This section addresses specific training adaptations primarily associated with sport performance. One of the important issues facing the coach and athlete is the method of training. It is quite apparent that different methods of training effect different adaptations.

Adaptations Associated With Strength-Power Performance

Training adaptations can depend upon a number of factors, including training variables such as volume and intensity, mechanical specificity, and the trained state. Furthermore, different methods of training can result in markedly different long-term adaptations. For example, typical heavy strength training would be expected to produce increases in the high-force end of a force–time curve. Explosive training, particularly dynamic explosive training, would likely affect the initial rise in force rather than peak force. It should be noted that in order to effect reasonable long-term adaptations, coaches and athletes should consider appropriate volume and intensity characteristics in training.

Hakkinen and colleagues (1987, 1988) studied elite weightlifters over a two-year period, noting that maximum strength levels depended upon maximum muscle activation. Maximum muscle activation (EMG) was achieved only when the training intensity was 80% of the 1RM or greater. When the average relative training intensity dropped below 80%, maximum strength also decreased, as did maximum muscle activation. These data indicate that among elite weightlifters, the threshold for maintaining or increasing maximum strength is about 80% of 1RM. Data of this type support the adage, "If you want to be strong, you have to lift heavy weights."

However, Hakkinen and colleagues (1987, 1988) also noticed that if the weightlifters trained at high intensities (above 80%) for too long, maximum strength and power decreased regardless of the intensity of training. More recently, Fry and colleagues (1994) presented data indicating

that constant high-intensity training can diminish maximum strength and explosive strength performance in as little as two to four weeks. Interestingly, this phenomenon was observed even when high-intensity training was carried out only two days per week (Fry et al. 2000). This type of overtraining has been attributed to neural fatigue and points out the necessity of variation in training. Similar arguments can be made for volume considerations.

Specificity of Training

As discussed in chapters 1 and 8, specificity of training refers to the degree of similarity between regularly used training exercises and those making up performance. Transfer-of-training effect refers to the degree of performance adaptation that can result from a training exercise and is strongly related to the concept of training specificity. Mechanical specificity concerns the kinetic and kinematic associations between a training exercise and a physical performance. Thus, mechanical specificity includes movement patterns, peak force, rate of force development, acceleration, and velocity parameters. The more similar a training exercise is to the actual physical performance, the greater the probabilities of transfer (Behm 1995; Sale 1992; Schmidt 1991; Stone, Plisk, and Collins 2002).

Various strength-power training methods can be employed in an effort to improve performance. However, these training methods can result in markedly different effects on neuromuscular physiology and performance variables. Four types of training are discussed in this section: isometric, heavy weight, high-power or speed-strength, and intentionally slow training. Table 10.3 presents comparisons for the relative effects on the neuromuscular system resulting from these four types of training protocols (Hakkinen 1994; Hunter, Seelhorst, and Snyder 2003; Jones et al. 1999, 2001; Morrissey et al. 1998; Stone, Triplett-McBride, and Stone 2001).

Table 10.3 Specificity of Strength-Power Training: Relative Neuromuscular Adaptations

Type of training	Hypertrophy	II/I CSA	Neural
Isometric	+	+	+++
Heavy weight	++++	++	+
Speed-strength	+	+++	++++
Intentionally slow	++	+	++

Data from Hakkinen 1994; Hunter et al. 2003; Jones et al. 1999, 2001; Keeler et al. 2001; McBride et al. 2002; Morrissey et al. 1998; Olsen and Hopkins 2003; Stone 1993; Stone, Triplett-McBride, and Stone 2001.

Isometric training, which reached peak popularity in the 1960s, has not been shown to produce extensive hypertrophy. Heavy weight training is characterized by nonballistic exercises, loading that is typically 80% of 1RM or higher, and typically five to eight repetitions. The load lifted moves slowly, even if lifted explosively, because it is relatively close to maximum values. Heavy weight training can produce marked hypertrophy except during the initial stages of a beginning training program, during which nervous system alterations (learning) are emphasized. Speed-strength weight training with a high power output typically does not produce marked hypertrophy, except in sedentary individuals, but can result in profound alterations in the nervous system. Intentionally slow training has recently become popular among health clubs. Basically a relatively light weight is moved in an intentionally slow movement pattern both eccentrically and concentrically (Keeler et al. 2001). The intentionally slow movement can result in a high MU fatigue rate, which is believed to cause more MUs to be recruited. Many proponents of intentionally slow movements believe that the time during which a muscle is under tension enhances both hypertrophy and strength. Often this type of training is performed for only one set. Although currently there is little information concerning the effect of intentionally slow movement on hypertrophy, available evidence suggests that some hypertrophy can occur but is not as extensive as that resulting from heavy weight training (Keeler et al. 2001).

Differential effects have been noted for fiber type adaptations. As previously mentioned, type II fibers typically display a faster rate of hypertrophy than type I fibers, although the reason is not completely clear. Almost all forms of resistance training can produce fiber hypertrophy such that the II:I CSA ratio increases; however, the degree of increase appears to depend on the type of training. Evidence

indicates that speed-strength (high-power) training enhances the II:I ratio of muscle fiber CSA to a greater degree than other types of training (Fry et al. 2003; Hakkinen 1994). A high II:I ratio is potentially advantageous in producing explosiveness and high power outputs.

Table 10.4 shows relative comparisons of training methods based on potential performance outcomes. Although angle specificity is often observed, isometric training can enhance measures of maximum strength over a relatively wide range of angles, especially when maximum strength is measured isometrically. In relatively untrained subjects, isometric training may enhance speed of movement, provided that a conscious effort to move fast is made (Behm 1995). However, the effects on power and speed are relatively minor compared to those with speed-strength training (Hakkinen 1994; McBride et al. 2002), particularly in more highly skilled athletes (Olsen and Hopkins 2003). Heavy weight training has its greatest effect on maximum strength as measured by a 1RM. Among beginners and novices, relatively large gains in power, rate of force development, and speed can occur. Speed-strength training has its greatest effects on rate of force development and power output, with lesser effects on measures of maximum strength (Hakkinen 1994). Intentionally slow training appears to have its greatest effect on measures of maximum strength, with much smaller and perhaps negative effects (authors' personal observation) on rate of force development, power, and speed.

A comparison between heavy weight training and speed-strength training (figure 10.16), carried out in a series of studies by Hakkinen and Komi (1985a, 1985b), illustrates the concept of specificity of training. Two groups of physical education students, familiar with the exercises and testing procedures, either received training in the half squat using heavy weight training methods or

Table 10.4 Specificity of Strength-Power Training: Relative Performance Effects

Type of training	Isometric PF	1RM	IPRFD	DPRFD	PP	Max vel.
Isometric	++++	+++	++	+	+	+
Heavy weight	+++	++++	++	++	++	++
Speed-strength	+	++	+++	++++	++++	+++
Intentionally slow	+++	++	?	+	+	+, -

Note: Time course and trained state are paramount. IPRFD = isometric peak rate of force development; DPRFD = dynamic peak rate of force development; PP = peak power; max vel. = maximum velocity of movement.

Data from Aagard et al. 2000; Hakkinen 1994; Hunter et al. 2000; Jones et al. 1999; Jones et al. 2001; Keeler et al. 2001; McBride et al. 2002; Morrisey et al. 1998; Olsen and Hopkins 2003; Peterson et al. 2004; Rhea et al. 2003; Stone 1993; Stone et al. 2001.

used explosive jumping (speed-strength training) with weights of approximately 30% of their 1RM. Isometric force–time curves derived from pre-post training measurements indicated different adaptations. The heavy weight training group showed a 27% improvement in peak force but relatively little adaptation in peak rate of force development. Simultaneous EMG tracings showed alterations corresponding to changes in the force–time curve, with only a 3% increased activation in the peak force region and no apparent change in the peak rate of force development region. The gain in peak force shown by the heavy weight training group was attributed to muscle hypertrophy. On the other hand, the speed-strength group showed gains of 11% in the peak force region of the force–time curve and a 24% improvement in the peak rate of force development region. Simultaneous EMG tracings indicated that EMG enhancement generally corresponded to the relative gains in peak force and force development. It was apparent that the speed-

strength group showed the greatest adaptations in the nervous system, while the heavy weight training group showed greater gains in hypertrophy.

As previously discussed, another factor that affects the transfer of training to performance is movement pattern. Movement pattern has to do with applying forces in the most efficient manner and in the appropriate directions. Movement pattern specificity includes both intra- and intermuscular aspects.

Intramuscular Movement Pattern Specificity

Several studies have shown that there is a high degree of intramuscular task specificity (Sale 1992). These studies indicate that for a given movement, groups of motor neurons are activated in a specific manner for a specific task. If the task is changed, through alterations in movement pattern or perhaps velocity, then the neuronal task group will be changed. Data of this type lend support to the practice among bodybuilders of using many different

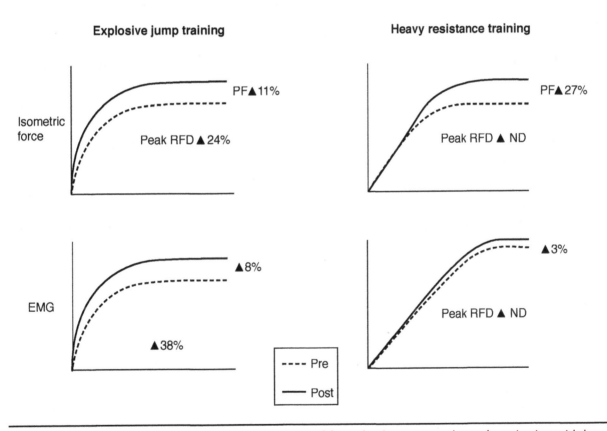

Figure 10.16 Alterations in isometric peak force, rate of force development, and muscle activation with heavy weight training and explosive strength training. PF = peak isometric force; RFD = rate of force development; ND = no difference.

Adapted from K. Hakkinen and P.V. Komi, 1985a, "Changes in electrical and mechanical behaviour of leg extensor muscle during heavy resistance strength training," *Acta Physiologica Scandinavica* 125: 573-585; K. Hakkinen and P.V. Komi, 1985b, "Effect of explosive type strength training on electromyographic and force production characteristics of leg extensor muscles during concentric and various stretch shortening cycle exercises," *Acta Physiologica Scandinavica* 125: 587-600.

exercises to more fully develop a muscle (Antonio 2000).

Intermuscular Movement Pattern Specificity

The pattern of activation of whole muscles, which includes the efficient use of reflexes and SSC, is also task specific. In this respect the functional role of muscles as agonists, antagonists, or stabilizers must be characterized with care, as these terms are actually anatomical rather than functional. These functional roles can change from single-joint to multiple-joint movements and with movement velocity alterations (Zajac and Gordon 1989). This means that in sport or daily living settings in which multiple-joint movements occur, especially those requiring high power or high velocity, transfer-of-training effect is more likely accomplished using complex multijoint movements that have similar kinetic and kinematic characteristics.

Because of the high degree of task specificity, gains in strength may be affected by several factors, including the number of joints involved, velocity of movement, and position (Rasch and Morehouse 1957; Stone, Triplett-McBride, and Stone 2001; Zajac and Gordon 1989). For example, Thorstensson (1977) trained university physical education students in the half squat for eight weeks. Measurements before and after the eight weeks included the half squat (the training mode), an isometric leg press, and leg extensions. Training produced an approximately 75% improvement in the 1RM half squat. However, the isometric leg press improved only about 40%, and essentially no improvement occurred in the seated leg extension. Although the half squat training affected muscles used in all three tests, it is clear that movement pattern differences altered the apparent strength gains. Data such as these (Rasch and Morehouse 1957; Thorstensson 1977) indicate that the greater the movement pattern similarities between training exercises and performance, the greater the transfer.

Speed-Strength Exercises

Many sports require the development of speed. In order to enhance speed development, a special category of exercise termed *speed-strength* can be used. Speed-strength exercises are performed with maximal effort and are characterized by high peak rates of force development and high power outputs. Typically these exercises are performed with submaximal weights selected to maximize power. Evidence indicates that for single-joint and small muscle mass exercises, power is at its peak at about 30% of peak isometric force. For multiple-joint

exercises in which the body weight is involved, as in a jump or in weightlifting movements, it appears that peak power may occur somewhere between 10% and 50% of peak isometric force. The exact load resulting in maximum peak power likely depends upon the trained state, the type of exercise, and whether or not body mass is included in the movement (Stone et al. 2003a).

An important consideration is whether or not exercises are ballistic. Ballistic exercises are not limited by end-point deceleration as are joint range-limited exercises such as typical bench presses or typical squats (Newton et al. 1996). Ballistic exercises include various types of throws, jumps, and weightlifting movements. It should be noted also that ballistic movements can be concentric or can be plyometric (SSC). Evidence indicates that if the sport performance is ballistic, much, if not most, of the training should also be ballistic (Newton, Kramer, and Hakkinen 1999).

Exercises for the development of power and speed can be characterized and classified based on their speed of movement and on whether they contain a plyometric (SSC) element. For example, jumping movements can be performed as heavy squats or heavy jump squats or can be performed as speed-strength exercise; however, in both cases they would typically have a preliminary eccentric phase (countermovement). In some sports the initial movement takes place without a countermovement, for example, when a sprinter comes out of the blocks. In concert with the concept of movement pattern specificity, some of the training exercises should attempt to duplicate this type of start. So, for example, depending on the emphasis of the training phase, people could perform heavy or light squats by descending and then stopping for several seconds before ascending, or could perform concentric squats from a pin set at a specific height in a power rack.

Successful Transfer-of-Training Effect

As previously noted, an exercise must meet several important criteria for a successful transfer-of-training effect. These include movement pattern, force production, and velocity considerations. There also must be an overload application for successful performance adaptation. If there is no overload, then sport performance will not improve beyond adaptation to simple practice of the sport. Necessary characteristics for successful application of an exercise include the following (Siff and Verkoshansky 1998; Stone, Triplett-McBride, and Stone 2001):

- Movement pattern specificity
  - Type of muscle action (eccentric vs. concentric vs. stretch–shortening)
  - Accentuated regions of force production
  - Complexity, amplitude, and direction of movement
  - Ballistic versus nonballistic movements
- Factors that can be overloaded
  - Force production
  - Rate of maximum force production
  - Power output
- The trained state

Figure 10.3 represents a qualitative expression of the potential chronological strength adaptations and underlying mechanisms. The underlying mechanisms have been grossly divided into neural and hypertrophic factors. Initial neural adaptation occurs quite rapidly compared to hypertrophic factors and represents the primary mechanism of strength gain during this early phase of training. Later adaptation is typically more dependent on increased muscle CSA. However, both of these factors have genetic limitations that make it difficult for advanced athletes to achieve additional strength or power gains.

Interestingly, almost any reasonable training program can enhance maximum strength, power, and speed among initially untrained subjects due to rapid neural adaptations (Peterson, Rhea, and Alvar 2004; Rhea et al. 2003). However, the training of advanced and elite athletes requires considerable variation, as well as creative approaches, in order to elicit gains in performance.

Specificity of Strength-Power Training in Untrained Subjects

Table 10.5 lists the expected primary performance adaptations of three different methods of training in initially untrained subjects. The current scientific literature, as well as experience, suggests that

heavy weight training should produce marked and substantial alterations in maximum strength, rate of force development, and power. Speed-strength training should have its greatest effects on rate of force development and power, and intentionally slow training should show gains in strength but much smaller effects on rate of force development and power (Hakkinen 1994).

Specificity of Strength-Power Training in Previously Trained Subjects

The training of advanced and elite athletes requires considerable variation as well as creative approaches in order to elicit gains in performance. For example, Wilson and colleagues (1993), in a study using males with previous heavy weight training, examined the effects of various types of training on leg and maximum strength and measures of explosiveness. The 55 subjects were divided into four groups. A control group continued with heavy weight training but did not attempt to overload; they simply trained with already established weights. A second group continued their training routines but overloaded by increasing the weights lifted over the experimental period. A third group switched from heavy weight training squats to depth jumps, beginning with boxes at 0.2 m (7.9 in.) and progressing to 0.8 m (31 in.). A fourth group switched to explosive jumping movements using a load equal to approximately 30% of their peak isometric force measured at 135° knee angle.

Pre- and postmeasurements included countermovement and static vertical jumps, isokinetic leg extension at $400° \cdot s^{-1}$, and a modified Wingate cycle maximum power test. After 10 weeks of training, the control group did not change on any measure. The traditional strength training group improved on the countermovement and static jumps and the cycle power test. The depth jump group improved only on the countermovement vertical jump. However, the group switching to speed-strength exercises improved on all measures. Furthermore, the percent improvement made by the speed-strength

Table 10.5 **Specificity of Strength and Power Training (Performance): Untrained**

Type of training	Primary adaptation
High force, low velocity (heavy explosive weight training	Increased strength, rate of force development (RFD), power (especially in weighted movements)
High-power training (speed-strength training)	Increased RFD and power; some gain in max strength
Intentionally slow movements	Increased strength; smaller gains in RFD and power

Data from Sale 1988, 1992; Hakkinen and Komi 1985a, b; Stone, Johnson, and Carter 1979; Stone et al. 1993; Hakkinen 1994.

group on these measures was as good as or better than that for any other group. These data indicate that speed-strength exercises can increase explosive performance in previously trained subjects. Additionally they suggest the possibility that previous strength training may enhance the optimization process for improving explosiveness and power output. Thus, it is possible that a sequenced approach to strength-power training could produce superior results (see chapter 13, "The Concept of Periodization").

Support for the concept that sequenced training potentiates subsequent phases of training can be found in observations of elite weightlifters training in different ways. Medvedev and colleagues (1981) divided several hundred elite Soviet weightlifters into three different training groups. Group 1 performed heavy training (>80% 1RM) throughout the entire experimental period lasting several months and emphasized heavy weight training and strength increases. Group 2 trained primarily for power using relatively light weights, approximately 70% to 80% of 1RM. Group 3 used a sequenced approach such that the initial training phase (about one month) was devoted to strength training with heavy weights and the remainder of the experimental period was used for speed-strength training. At the end of the experimental period (about three months), group 3 produced superior improvements in weightlifting total, primarily through an improved snatch. Furthermore, group 3 produced superior improvements in other explosive measurements, such as sprinting ability and medicine ball throws, compared to the other two groups. These data indicate that a sequenced training program, in which an initial emphasis on strength training is followed by power training, can produce superior results, particularly in measures of explosiveness.

To further investigate the concept of sequenced training, Harris and colleagues (2000) used a group of 42 American football players. This study was unique in that the athletes were very well trained

prior to the study. Training concentrated on leg and hip maximum strength and explosiveness. Initially (first four weeks), all of the athletes trained using a high-volume strength-endurance program (multiple sets of 10 repetitions). Following the initial four weeks of strength-endurance training, the athletes were divided into three groups equalized on the 1RM squat and body mass. Group 1 trained for an additional nine weeks using heavy weight training (>80% 1RM). Group 2 used speed-strength training methods with weights equivalent to 30% to 40% of their 1RM squat. Group 3 used a sequenced combination training program; for the first five weeks (after the four-week strength-endurance phase), group 3 trained in the same manner as group 1 except that they used heavy and light days. Light days consisted of the same lifts as on the heavy days except at 20% less weight. During the last four weeks, group 3 used a combination of heavy weight training and speed-strength exercises. For example, the squat incorporated a form of contrast exercise: After warm-up sets, one heavy set of 85% to 90% of 1RM was performed, followed by three sets of jumps at 30% of the 1RM. The athletes were all consistently admonished to perform each movement as explosively as possible.

Pre- and postmeasures included various measurements of maximum strength, a countermovement vertical jump, vertical jump power, a Margaria stair climb power test, a 30 m (33 yd) sprint, a 9.1 m (9.6 yd) agility test, and a standing long jump. The results indicated that the heavy weight training group (group 1) and the combination group (group 3) produced the greatest gains in maximum strength measures. However, in measures of power and explosiveness, the speed-strength group (group 2) and the combination group (group 3) produced the best gains. Furthermore, the percent gains for the combination group (group 3) in all tests were as good as or better than those of the other two groups. Again the data indicated that (1) combination training can produce superior gains across

Table 10.6 **Specificity of Strength and Power Training (Performance): Trained**

Type of training	Primary adaptation
High force, low velocity (heavy weight training)	Diminished or little gain in max strength, RFD, power
Speed-strength training	Increased RFD and power
Intentionally slow movements	Diminished or little gain in max strength, diminished RFD and power
Sequenced training	Increased potential for gains

Data from Sale 1988, 1992; Hakkinen and Komi 1985a, b; Stone, Johnson and Carter 1979; Stone et al. 1993; Wilson et al. 1993; Hakkinen 1994; Harris et al. 2000.

a wide spectrum of performance variables and (2) sequenced training consisting of strength-endurance, strength, and speed-strength phases can optimize these training responses.

Of concern to the coach is creating continued gains in trained athletes. Table 10.6 lists the potential strength-power adaptations in athletes who are already strength trained. For example, continued heavy weight training would likely result in diminished or little gain in maximum strength, rate of force development, or power; intentionally slow movements would most likely result in markedly diminished adaptations. Empirical evidence actually indicates that switching to intentionally slow movements may reduce maximum strength and especially rate of force development and power (authors' observations and personal communication from E. Harman). On the other hand, switching from heavy weight training to a speed-strength type of training program can elicit beneficial and quite marked alterations in rate of force development and power (Harris et al. 2000; Wilson et al. 1993).

Factors Affecting Strength and Power Gains

In addition to specific training protocols, several different factors can have a marked impact on the development of specific qualities in an athlete, particularly in relation to explosiveness. As discussed previously, these factors include maximum strength, fatigue levels, and cross-training.

The interaction of maximum strength and power and speed is of great importance to most athletes. Currently evidence indicates the following (Stone et al. 2002; Stone et al. 2003a, 2003b):

1a. Measures of maximum strength, explosive strength, and power can have strong to very strong correlations.

1b. Measures of maximum strength have moderate to very strong correlations with strength-power exercises.

2. The magnitude of the relationship between maximum strength and power, in part, depends on the mechanical similarity of the measures.

3. Although maximum strength has a significant influence on power at low resistances, its effect appears to increase with load (to a point).

4. Maximum power and speed are not achieved by heavy strength training alone.

Sequenced periodized training and its variations can offer advantages in achieving performance goals.

Thus, the development of power and explosiveness can be augmented through development of strength. However, it should be noted that strength alone will not maximize power output; a sequenced training protocol appears to have the greatest potential for producing high power outputs and explosiveness.

While factors such as maximum strength can have a positive effect on explosiveness, other factors such as fatigue and cross-training can have a negative impact. Two factors that must be considered in training programs are the degree of fatigue that occurs within a training session and the degree of residual fatigue that can accumulate between training sessions. Fatigue can result in reductions in maximum strength, rate of force development, and power output. Because of the fatigue-induced reduction in performance capability, increased fatigue levels can interfere with technique and with learning or stabilizing technique. Thus learning to be explosive, under fatigued conditions, can result in a compromise.

Additionally, evidence indicates that the combination of typical low-intensity aerobic training, such as distance running, and strength-power training can result in decreased muscle hypertrophy adaptations, maximum strength, and especially power and speed (Hakkinen et al. 2003; Izquierdo et al. 2004). Thus, if maximum levels of strength and especially power and speed are desired, typical aerobic training should be minimized or eliminated.

Injury Potential of Resistance Training

It is well known that the injury potential of weight training is low compared to that with other recreational (Powell et al. 1998) and sport activities (Hamill 1994). Although it is commonly believed that free weights produce a higher injury rate than machines, there is no evidence for this belief (Requa, DeAvilla, and Garrick 1993). This last statement is particularly important to understand because free weights can produce a superior transfer-of-training effect, especially for explosive strength, compared to machines (Stone, Triplett-McBride, and Stone 2001); thus the training of athletes should center on free weights (see chapter 12, "Modes of Resistance Training").

Another commonly held belief is that weightlifting and other ballistic explosive exercises produce high injury rates. As with overall injury rates from resistance training, there are few data to support the idea that injury rates resulting from ballistic training are excessive or that catastrophic injuries are common. Hamill (1994) studied the injury rates of several different sports in the United Kingdom and United States. Based on injury rates per 100 participation hours, both general resistance training and weightlifting training produced injury rates that were some of the lowest among the sporting activities studied. Thus, there is little evidence that weight training, explosive or not (including weightlifting), produces excessive amounts of injuries.

Potential Health Benefits of Resistance Training

Although this textbook primarily deals with strength-power training for sports, it is important for the coach and athlete to understand the potential health benefits that may be derived from resistance training. This section deals very briefly with those potential health alterations.

Resistance training is a general term used to refer to a number of different training goals, such as training for improved performance, hypertrophy (i.e., bodybuilding), increased fitness and health for a variety of populations, injury prevention, or rehabilitation (Stone et al. 1991). Health-associated changes resulting from resistance training can include improved cardiovascular parameters such as resting and especially exercise cardiac output and blood pressure (Stone et al. 1991a). Additionally, beneficial endocrine and serum lipid adaptations,

increased LBM and decreased fat, increased tissue tensile strength (including bone), and decreased physiological stress (Conroy et al. 1993; Johnson et al. 1983, 1982; McMillan et al. 1993; Poehlman et al. 1992; Stone et al. 1991a) can be derived. In addition to its potential disease-preventive aspects, resistance training may be an important tool in treating degenerative diseases such as metabolic syndrome and diabetes (Jurca et al. 2004, 2005). Resistance training has been shown to positively alter blood lipids; decrease hemoglobin A1c (HbA1c); and increase insulin-mediated glucose uptake, GLUT-4 content, and insulin signaling in persons with type 2 diabetes (Cauza et al. 2005; Holten et al. 2004). Furthermore, resistance exercise can have a large effect on many of these factors compared to aerobic training (Cauza et al. 2005). An important component associated with improvement in health-related factors is total energy expenditure. Currently, the evidence indicates that health benefits derived from resistance training are associated with training volume (Stone et al. 1991a). Thus, to a point, health benefits are likely to increase as the volume of training increases.

However, improved physical performance is the parameter most often associated with resistance training. Programs incorporating strength training as an integral part of physical conditioning have been shown to improve performance in ergonomic tasks such as lifting weighted boxes to different heights (Asfour et al. 1984; Genaidy et al. 1994) and have been associated with improved well-being.

CHAPTER SUMMARY

Thus we can conclude that resistance exercise, when properly integrated into a training program, can be a valuable part of overall training. It should be noted that different training programs can elicit very specific long-term adaptations; different trained states alter the adaptation to training; maximum-exercise effort is necessary for a maximum adaptation to training; and the training of advanced athletes requires creative planning. This planning should incorporate a periodized sequenced structure (see chapters 1 and 13).

CHAPTER 11

Psychological Aspects of Resistance Training

There is a temptation to focus entirely on an idea of humans as motors when one considers resistance training. However, athletic skills must be performed in the environment of human beings and their cultures, expectations, and predispositions, all of which can influence how well strength ability is expressed. Thus all skilled movement requires command and control. Athletes must select appropriate skills, perform skills in appropriate ways, and develop strength abilities over many years in order to ultimately show continual fitness progress or perform complex athletic skills in the decisive moments of competition. Clearly, resistance training requires more than simply being a powerful motor.

Sport psychology has been defined as "the subdiscipline of exercise science that seeks to understand the influence of behavioral processes on skilled movement" (Hatfield and Brody 1994, p. 188). This chapter covers psychology in resistance training in relation to two major areas: what the research literature says about psychological aspects of resistance training, and how psychological skills might be used to enhance resistance training and strength-oriented performance.

Literature on Psychology and Resistance Training

There is a paucity of specific information on psychology and resistance training. Existing psychological literature on aspects of resistance training provides some insight into areas of mental health and sport psychology, including psychological well-being; self-concept, self-esteem, self-efficacy, and self-worth; body image; and arousal and anxiety. Psychological skills that may serve athletes and others participating in resistance training include goal setting, relaxation, concentration, imagery, and ritualization (Ogilvie and Henschen 1995).

Psychological Well-Being

Although not specifically related to resistance training, school athletic participation has been shown to result in positive effects on school grades, coursework selection, homework, educational and occupational aspirations, self-esteem, applications for higher education, enrollment in higher education, and eventual educational attainment. The benefits of extramural sport participation are better than those of intramural participation, and the positive effects remain after a host of confounding variables are controlled for (Marsh and Kleitman 2003).

Resistance training is often an integral part of these same activities. These results indicate that athletic participation is beneficial for a large constellation of things that one would probably label as positive with regard to mental health, psychosocial health, and achievement.

In a position statement on resistance training in young people, the British Association of Exercise and Sport Sciences indicated that resistance training provides psychosocial benefits to youth participants (Stratton et al. 2004). The group suggested that resistance training offers psychological benefits because the incremental increases in strength provide an easy format for short- and long-term goal setting, the training can take place in partnerships and groups fostering social benefits, and this type of training can be used to educate young people on how the body works in movement. These benefits are particularly applicable to adolescents. The authors argued that children are motivated by the here and now, which would likely make the long-term lag of the training effect of resistance training a potential problem for motivation in young children. However, the authors also indicate that young children may be motivated by resistance-oriented activities such as rope climbing, games, and so forth. They suggest as well that the few studies on exercise and children have shown positive effects on psychological well-being. Additionally, they caution that resistance training programs should be based on sound educational and age-appropriate activities.

Psychological well-being includes aspects of basic mental health. For example, people with anorexia commonly use aerobic-oriented exercise compulsively due to an inappropriate fear of weight gain. Szabo and Green (2002) studied hospitalized anorexic patients and the impact of resistance training on psychological well-being and body composition. They noted that resistance training was associated with an improvement in body composition and psychological well-being. Although resistance training did not provide an outcome advantage, the authors noted that resistance training was a useful adjunct in the treatment of persons with anorexia. In a case study of two persons with anorexia, the investigator noted that weight training may benefit anorexic patients who have had the disorder less than two years and have an authentic desire to recover (Phillips 1988). The potential increase in lean body mass that accompanies resistance training may be feared by some persons with anorexia but benefit those who have reached a stage of desired recovery. Moreover, as the program continues, the individual with anorexia may come to fear the lean mass weight gain less and thus embrace further resistance training and the nutritional interventions needed to support such training.

Investigators of resistance training among elderly females (ages 75 to 80) indicated subjectively that these women showed increased self-confidence and felt that activities they had believed they could not do were newly accessible (Bracewell et al. 1999). The investigators also noted that the general activity level of these women increased over the duration of the study. Interestingly, the authors also reported that one of the primary issues they faced was that after the women felt comfortable with resistance training, some tended to push themselves too hard. Both general health and transitional health were shown to be improved in elderly women (75-80 years) participating in a weight training program lasting three months (Taunton et al. 2002).

In a study of the treatment of clinical depression, running was compared with resistance training (Doyne et al. 1987). The authors commented that the results were remarkably consistent across measures and exercise groups. Both the running group and the resistance group significantly reduced depression as measured by three depression scales. Although running or other aerobic exercise had been the exercise modality of choice in most investigations of the psychological effects of exercise (Tucker 1987), Doyne and colleagues showed that the resulting decrease in depression symptoms was not due to an aerobic effect. Thus resistance training could benefit men and women who are depressed but cannot run due to environment, body composition, or other restrictions. In a second publication on apparently the same subjects, the women demonstrated a similar pattern of enhanced self-concept through exercise (Ossip-Klein et al. 1989). Again, no differences were shown between exercise groups; however, both groups showed enhanced self-concept when compared to a delayed-treatment control group.

Using self-efficacy theory, Ewart (1989) examined the psychological effects of weight training on cardiac patients. Ewart emphasized the importance of self-perceptions in exercise selection and adherence, as well as in the individual's expectations of costs and benefits. However, self-efficacy theory also emphasizes the idea that a person's self-appraisal of his or her ability to perform requisite tasks has a major influence on whether the person will attempt the tasks. Although personal efficacy does not generalize from task to task, there are four important aspects through which personal efficacy arises: (a) prior successful performance of the tasks or similar tasks, (b) social modeling or being around others doing the tasks, (c) persuasion by a respected other, and (d) internal feedback from the person's current physical and mental state. These factors are significant in resistance training because they roughly translate to using progression to ensure that tasks are well within the person's developing performance envelope, that people train with partners or groups, that respected others provide supportive feedback, and that mood states and other environmental and internal cues are perceived as fun so as to maintain or increase arousal. Although Ewart (1989) noted that there were numerous subject-specific preferences and responses to exercise, he also noted that in his early work on circuit resistance training, psychological measures (i.e.,

Profile of Mood States) were related to strength measures but not to treadmill endurance or mood. The overall picture of resistance training effects on these subjects was not always clear-cut, however, as changes in mood or self-efficacy were not related to gains in endurance or strength.

In a paper on the compatibility of cardiac rehabilitation and resistance training (Vescovi and Fernhall 2000), the authors indicated that one of the major issues in returning a patient to full function following a cardiac incident is his or her self-efficacy. Thus, one of the goals of cardiac rehabilitation programs should be to present the patient with a wide variety of exercise tasks that are similar to the daily tasks encountered in normal activity. In so doing, the cardiac rehabilitation program will help build self-efficacy so that patients will pursue and not fear strength-oriented lifting, pushing, and pulling activities.

Another investigation of the psychological benefits of weight training involved state law enforcement personnel. The study used a circuit weight training protocol and a control group on a wait list for the exercise program (Norvell and Belles 1993). Forty-three officers who were not regularly exercising participated in the four-month study. Significant increases in both cardiovascular and strength variables were noted. The exercising subjects also demonstrated improved mood, including decreased somatization, anxiety, depression, hostility, and reports of physical symptoms. Job satisfaction improved as well. Officers who dropped out of the program had shown significantly greater hostility, depression, and anxiety during the pretest, suggesting that some self-selection may have occurred. However, the investigators concluded that circuit weight training could provide important psychological benefits to law enforcement officers.

A series of studies conducted by Tucker and colleagues (Tucker 1982b, 1982a; Tucker and Maxwell 1992; Tucker and Mortell 1993; Tucker 1983a, 1983b; Tucker 1987) showed that weight training has a positive influence on psychological well-being of a variety of subpopulations. These studies demonstrate that resistance training can be a powerful influence on participants' psychological states, although the effect is mitigated by a number of other variables.

Collins (1993-1994) described psychological issues among resistance-trained athletes in three categories: recreational lifters, those engaged in resistance training for sport, and competitive lifters. Recreational lifters may be served by resistance training if they place emphasis on upper body strength and attractiveness; however, novices who cannot measure up may feel threatened. The fact that early progress in resistance training among novices is usually rapid and obvious makes resistance training for this group particularly attractive. Thus, Collins recommends that instructors provide plenty of positive feedback and use incremental goal setting.

Athletes from other sports often use weight training as a means of enhancing their sport performance. This group is usually dominated by mesomorphic athletes because they tend to progress more rapidly than ectomorphic or endomorphic athletes. Collins argues that athletes tend to be drawn to those things they already do well, which may explain this tendency. Additionally, Collins cautions that because progress in weight training is so obvious and measurable, slumps and staleness are easily apparent and thus may lead to overtraining and feelings of failure and burnout. Some athletes may become overly obsessed about achieving personal bests in their lifts and may soon find that progress slows considerably. These athletes may be more susceptible to self-imposed frustration due to unrealistic expectations. In competitive lifting, the athletes' responses may be similar to those of weight trainers for sport, but even more dramatic. Collins recommends that since weightlifting may be somewhat boring and extremely fatiguing, athletes may need to learn concentration and imagery skills in order to maintain their focus during training and competition. Emphasis on specific technique areas may also help focus attention during training and competition.

Self-Concept, Self-Esteem, and Self-Efficacy

Self-concept denotes a set of thoughts held by oneself and about one's self in mental, emotional, and physical realms (Trujillo 1983). Self-esteem refers to the individual's evaluation of his or her self-concept. Self-efficacy is similar to self-confidence in that self-efficacy is a level of certainty that one can perform a task or behavior (Ewart 1989).

Trujillo (1983) compared running, weight training, and nonexercise groups on self-esteem using the Tennessee Self-Concept Scale. She showed a common pattern that did not differ statistically between running and weight training, and both exercise groups showed improved self-esteem relative to the nonexercising control group.

Changes in self-concept may be dependent on muscle group. Van Vorst and colleagues (2002) showed that while strength may increase in certain muscle groups, individuals may have a threshold above which these changes affect self-concept and below which no self-concept changes are evident. Moore and Bartholomew (2003) studied physical self-perception via self-esteem measures and noted that physical changes in terms of strength tended to outpace psychological changes.

Weight training experience was not related to physical self-efficacy among males in a comparison of various self-efficacy scales with the number of semesters of weight training experience in high school (Black, Gibbons, and Blassingame 1998). However, the use of semesters of weight training as a variable for comparison may have been too coarse a measure to evaluate this question in depth.

In a study of both body cathexis and self-esteem among college students in weight training classes, Melnick and Mookerjee (1991) showed that weight training resulted in significantly higher self-esteem and body cathexis as compared to values in a nonexercising control group. These changes were attributed in part to the increased strength fitness of the subjects. Moreover, according to the authors, their study supported the idea that self-esteem is a multidimensional construct that is at least somewhat reliant on alterations in the physical self. Tucker performed two similar studies on male weight trainers and nonexercising controls (1982a, 1983b). The weight trainers showed significantly higher scores on every self-esteem variable. However, many of the variables showed nonlinear relationships, and Tucker indicated that future studies of psychological effects of exercise must pursue higher-order models.

Body Image

In a study of males in beginning weight training classes and nonexercising controls, Tucker (1987) showed that males improve body image concepts significantly in conjunction with their participation in resistance training. This study also showed that preexisting characteristics of the subjects helped predict the psychological outcomes of resistance training. For example, those males who entered the study with low levels of strength fitness showed the greatest increase in body cathexis ratings. However, Tucker noted that males who came into the study in good physical condition began with higher levels of self-confidence and satisfaction with their existing body image status. Thus, those who are already strong and in good physical condition may show a ceiling effect with regard to body image enhance-

ments following resistance training. In a separate study, Tucker again demonstrated that body image characteristics are complex, with the athlete's pre-existing somatotype and fitness interacting with changes in body image as a result of training (Tucker 1983b). In a study of lifters versus walkers, Tucker and Mortell (1993) showed that walkers improved in endurance while lifters improved in strength, but lifters tended to improve more in body image than walkers. Tucker and Maxwell (1992) demonstrated that general well-being and body cathexis scores were significantly improved after a 15-week weight training course, along with strength values. Moreover, they showed that the best predictors of general well-being were lower parental income, greater loss of body weight, and lower posttest skinfolds. The best predictors of body cathexis were lower pretest body cathexis, greater body weight at pretest, shorter stature, less experience in weight training, and lower posttest skinfolds.

Body image dissatisfaction was studied by Bietz Hilton (1997) in an investigation of the influence of lectures and weight training versus weight training alone. Body image and body composition were assessed in a 14-week beginning weight training course. The results showed that five of the 10 components of body dissatisfaction were significantly improved over the course of the study only in the combined group. No significant differences in body dissatisfaction were observed in the weight training-only group. A similar finding of satisfaction with body image was observed among elite women weightlifters (Stoessel et al. 1991).

Arousal and Anxiety

Arousal is the level of intensity of behavior or physiology, while anxiety is defined in two dimensions, state and trait (Hatfield and Brody 1994). State anxiety is a subjective experience of dread or apprehension. Uncertainty usually accompanies state anxiety. Although state anxiety appears negative, its effects on performance can be negative, neutral, or positive. For example, a certain level of anxiety will accompany competitive performance, attacking a new weight, or performing a new skill. It is a common belief among athletes that they need a little anxiety to perform at their best. Trait anxiety is a more permanent psychological characteristic that is part of one's personality. Trait anxiety might be looked upon as the background anxiety against which state anxiety is expressed. Anxiety can also be classified as cognitive (e.g., psychological, as with apprehensive thoughts) and somatic (e.g., muscle tension, increased heart rate, restlessness, and the sensation of butterflies in the stomach).

Arousal and anxiety are thought to operate as an optimization problem relative to performance. In other words, arousal and anxiety need to be at optimal levels in order to optimally enhance performance—neither very high nor very low (Hatfield and Brody 1994). This has been codified in the inverted-U theory (Hatfield and Brody 1994; Yerkes and Dodson 1908) and in terms of Individual Zones of Optimal Functioning (IZOF) (Hanin 1995). The two models agree in the basic idea of optimal levels of arousal and anxiety, while the IZOF model goes further by embracing task difficulty, past experience, skill level, and so forth. However, the efficacy of these models remains controversial (Arent and Landers 2003). Resistance training appears to have a positive influence on arousal and anxiety.

Anxiety and arousal are coupled with the concept of stress. Stress can be defined as anything that causes a person to react (Selye 1956). Both state anxiety and arousal are responses to stress. Everyone needs to learn to cope with stress, and this occurs via state anxiety, through controlled arousal, against a background of trait anxiety. In a study of coping strategies used by athletes from different sports, weightlifters had a lower mean score on avoidance-coping than other groups of athletes (Antonini Philippe, Seiler, and Mengisen 2004). Gender differences in coping strategies were also demonstrated, with women using more emotion-focused strategies and men tending to use more problem-focused coping. Avoidance-oriented coping involves seeking out other people who may be able to help, or simply engaging in another task, or both. Sport psychologists have assumed that avoidance-oriented coping is less functional in a competitive setting and therefore that lower scores on this coping strategy indicate a better overall profile for competitive success. However, agreement on this idea is not total. For example, it is thought that being able to distract oneself from mistakes using an avoidance-oriented approach may help athletes such as tennis players quickly return attentional focus to the game. However, low avoidance-coping may also indicate the extent to which the athlete believes he or she has control over the competitive situation. Clearly, a weightlifter has considerable control over the competitive situation and therefore may not engage in avoidance-coping because it is simply less effective.

In a weight training study of prepubescent female gymnasts aged 8 to 13, using the Sport Competition Anxiety Inventory (SCAI), the participants showed an overall increase in all strength variables and an overall decrease in competitive trait anxiety (Henderson 1995). There was no change in competitive state anxiety. The decrease in competitive trait anxiety occurred mostly in the first 10 of the 20 weeks of the study. However, the investigators attempted to generalize to competitive situations and thus may have encountered uncontrolled confounding variables. A second study of prepubescent female gymnasts by O'Nan and colleagues (2000), involving weight training and competitive state and competitive trait anxiety, showed again that as strength increased, competitive anxieties decreased, although the findings did not reach statistical significance. Low trait anxiety was also demonstrated among elite male weightlifters (Hall, Church, and Stone 1980).

Several other investigations have focused on weight training in relation to anxiety and mood states. Lyon (1995) studied the effects of six weeks of aerobic conditioning, weight training, and a structured stress management program on fitness and psychophysiological responses to cognitive stress. Lyon found that all of the interventions were successful in reducing state anxiety and state anger. Interestingly, the nonexercise stress management program was similar to the two exercise programs in reducing state anxiety and state anger. Koltyn and colleagues (1995) investigated a single bout of weight training relative to state anxiety and body awareness. State anxiety was not reduced after a single weight training bout, but body awareness was significantly improved. Using the Profile of Mood States, Tharion and colleagues (1991) examined the influence of two types of weight training protocols among novice lifters. They found that a 5RM protocol with lower total work resulted in less attenuation of mood states than a higher total work protocol. Moreover, they found that males tended to respond better in terms of mood states than did females. Hale and Raglin (2002) examined the acute state anxiety responses to resistance training and step aerobic exercise. In this study, both resistance training and step aerobic exercise resulted in acutely reduced state anxiety. The state anxiety responses were stable across the eight weeks of the study.

Although psychological information on resistance training is not overwhelming, one can conclude that there are a number of potential benefits from resistance training in terms of mental health, self-concept and its derivations, and anxiety and arousal. Resistance training may be an important tool in assisting people in psychological development and maintaining mental health.

Psychological Skills

Sport psychology has a great deal to offer the athlete involved in resistance training. The goal of an athlete is an ideal performance state. This goal is achieved by both psychological and physiological efficiency, or a minimum of energy investment to accomplish the target tasks (Hatfield and Brody 1994). The ideal performance state is marked by an absence of fear, appropriate attentional focus, positive self-talk, powerful self-efficacy, and an automaticity of movement. In order to achieve the ideal performance state, the athlete should learn and excel at several psychological skills and in varying environments (Ives and Shelley 2003). These skills are goal setting, relaxation, concentration, imagery, and ritualization (Henschen 1990, 1995a, 1995b; Heil 1995).

Goal Setting

Goal setting involves a process of choosing and embracing progressively greater challenges. Goal setting has been shown to facilitate performance by establishing target behaviors and outcomes (Gould and Vory 1995). Goal setting helps direct and focus attention on the things that really matter. However, while goal setting might seem to be a somewhat obvious idea, goal-setting implementation is far from trivial. Resistance training lends itself particularly well to goal setting due to the inherently measurable nature of weight training—sets, repetitions, weight, rest interval, speed, and so forth.

Achieving goals has a lot to do with *setting* effective goals. One should bear in mind the following issues when setting strength training goals or helping athletes set such goals.

- *Realistic goals.* Goals should be challenging but realistic. Unrealistic goals can often be demotivators rather than motivators. Moreover, when realistic goals are achieved, this sets the stage for further goal setting that tends to continue to increase the likelihood of further achievement.

- *Short-term versus long-term goals.* It is wise to set only a small number of long-term goals (perhaps one to three), and long-term goals should be easily broken down into short-term goals. Short-term goals serve as the building blocks for long-term goals. The goals should be stated in measurable and behavioral terms, not vague generalities. At any given time, an athlete should be working on only three or fewer goals.

- *Performance versus outcome goals.* Performance goals are also called *process* goals. Outcome goals are sometimes called *results* goals. Performance goals

are basically improvement goals. Outcome goals might include winning a particular contest. The athlete should concentrate on performance goals as opposed to outcome goals, primarily because performance goals are considered to be under greater control of the athlete, while outcome goals are seldom under such control. Environment, cheating, bad officiating, and other factors can render an athlete's control of a competitive situation moot (Gould and Vory 1995).

- *Flexible goals.* Goals should be elastic so that the athlete has the options of moving faster or slower, pursuing slightly different goals, and undertaking targets of opportunity. Goal setting is not a foolproof endeavor. Athletes may have set goals without knowing how difficult they might be, or without knowing that resources may become more limited in the interim. Injury, illness, and other factors may also force a revision of goals.

- *Individual goals.* Goals should be applied to individuals as much as possible. Clearly, applying individual goals when members of a group are pursuing the same outcome may be redundant and unnecessary. However, individual goals are more common in resistance training because of individual differences in experience and abilities.

- *Goal assessments.* Goals should be measured at regular intervals. Setting goals without monitoring and measurement does not serve to establish when goals have been achieved. The process of goal setting and goal assessment should be cyclic, in that each time a goal is achieved a new goal should be set.

Goal setting is among the first steps in implementing principles of sport psychology in resistance training. Goal setting should be encouraged so that continual progress is both demanding and measurable.

Relaxation

Relaxation is considered one of the foundational skills in mental skills training. It may seem somewhat paradoxical to talk about relaxation in a book about resistance training, but coordinated movement requires that while some muscles contract, other muscles must relax. Moreover, the correct muscles must be summoned at the right time and in the right magnitude. Coordinated movement requires that the athlete be able to selectively recruit and inhibit muscles.

Relaxation techniques are generally used to reduce anxiety and arousal to a more controlled level so that the athlete can better attend to those crucial aspects of performance that lead to success (Dishman 1983; Drozdowski et al. 1990; Hardy and Jones 1994; Hatfield and Brody 1994; Henschen 1995b; Ogilvie and Henschen 1995; Orlick 1980; Weiss 1991). Relaxation techniques assume that relaxation and tension are opposites and cannot occur simultaneously, and that by learning relaxation techniques the athlete can summon the appropriate level of tension when needed (Henschen 1995c). Relaxation is perhaps the oldest of the mental training techniques, dating from ancient China as qi gong and from India as a component of yoga. Relaxation techniques include the following three:

- *Breathing.* One method of relaxation training is diaphragmatic breathing, also called *belly breathing* (Hatfield and Brody 1994). Breath control and deep breathing techniques, usually involving deep inhalation followed by slow exhalation, have been shown to reduce heart rate and muscle tension due to feedback pathways that link cardiorespiratory control centers to the brainstem (Hatfield and Brody 1994). Together, these lead to increased vagal tone and increased parasympathetic nervous activity, resulting in a lowering of arousal and anxiety and a more relaxed state (Henschen 1995c). Breathing awareness comes with practice. This method can be practiced at almost any time, and as the athlete becomes more aware of breathing patterns the method naturally moves into training and performance.

- *Progressive relaxation.* Contrasting relaxation with tension is the goal of progressive relaxation (Henschen 1995c). The athlete makes note of the feelings engendered by tension and relaxation so that the contrast between the two ultimately helps him or her to summon tension and relaxation in appropriate amounts for a given skill or task. The methods are quite straightforward. The athlete adopts a particular posture, usually lying supine, and then progressively and systematically tenses and relaxes each muscle group. One can begin with the feet, systematically tensing and then relaxing muscles of the feet and lower legs. The next step is to move upward along the body, shifting tension and relaxation cycles from one muscle group to the next. When the process has included the entire body, the final cycle should result in relaxation of the whole body. This method can be practiced multiple times each day and can be used as an adjunct to achieving sleep.

- *Autogenic training.* Autogenic training is a relatively new technique that originated in the 1930s in Germany; it is a method that involves self-hypnosis through use of a formulaic induction. One repeats a series of formulas to oneself while controlling diaphragmatic breathing. An autogenic formula might include, for example, repeating phrases such as the following: *comfortably heavy, comfortably warm, heartbeat calm, breathing calm, abdomen comfortably warm, forehead pleasantly cool.* The premise is that limbs and body are meant to feel warm and heavy due to simple suggestion (Henschen 1995c). This method may be more attractive to athletes who do not prefer the discomfort of high muscle tension that is developed during the tension phase of a tense–relax cycle in progressive relaxation (Hatfield and Brody 1994).

Of course, other methods may promote relaxation, such as massage, hydrotherapy, hypnosis, and meditation. Relaxation techniques can also be a powerful aid to recovery within and between training sessions (Drozdowski et al. 1990; Lidell 1984). Relaxation techniques can benefit an athlete's performance and may be a welcome life skill that can aid the athlete outside of athletics.

Concentration

Concentration is an ability to focus on appropriate cues and to act on those cues in an efficient and effective manner (Henschen 1995a). Concentration has become somewhat synonymous with attention. Attention can be defined as the processing of sensory cues that rise to awareness (Hatfield and Brody 1994). Concentration is the act of focusing attention appropriately. For example, in a study of several sports, the ability to focus on task-relevant cues or to use task-specific information to make important decisions differed between expert and novice athletes (Nougier, Ripoll, and Stein 1989).

Nideffer has been considered one of the preeminent investigators of attention and attentional styles (Hatfield and Brody 1994; Nideffer 1985, 1990). His work has led to characterizing attention along two intersecting continuums reflecting types of concentration: broad–narrow and internal–external. Broad attentional focus refers to the ability to take in a wide view of the environment and other cues. Narrow attentional focus refers to the ability of the athlete to confine or constrain his or her attention to a smaller view more intensely focused on a smaller aspect of the environment. External attentional focus refers to awareness of things other than one's self. Internal attentional focus refers to a personal awareness. The combinations of these attentional or concentration factors result in four primary quadrants of awareness: broad-external, broad-internal, narrow-external, and narrow-internal. Moreover, the athlete must be able to shift attentional focus in order to cope with the demands of performance environments. For example, a quarterback may need narrow-external focus in addressing the center prior to receiving the ball from the snap, then broad-external focus in sizing up the defense once he steps backward to pass, then narrow-internal focus as he prepares to throw and recalls specific technical issues he must remember in order to throw accurately, and finally narrow-external focus as he picks his receiver's hands and the spot to which he must throw to complete the pass.

Athletes in resistance training most commonly use internal attentional focus with broad or narrow dimensions depending on what is going on in the lift at any given moment. Moreover, one should realize that concentration or attentional control is a passive act, and that trying to consciously change or monitor this control usually results in a deterioration of concentration and attention relative to the target task (Henschen 1995a). Coaches and athletes can enhance their concentration by directing attention to specific aspects of technique, or the kinesthesis (feeling) of how a lift or movement is performed, or both.

Imagery

Imagery is one of the most commonly cited aspects of athletic performance and one that virtually all athletes experience at some time and in some form. Imagery or visualization is a psychological skill in which the athlete uses all of his or her senses to create a mental experience of a skill or performance (Hatfield and Brody 1994). Athletes using mental imagery involve all of their senses—including sight, hearing, smelling, and kinesthetic feeling—to rehearse a skill in their mind. Imagery, although a mental process, can result in physiological changes. For example, imagery has been shown to result in differences in electrical activity of muscle (Bakker, Boschker, and Chung 1996). In a study of electrical activity of the biceps muscle, Hale (1982) showed that imagining the feeling of a bicep curl resulted in greater muscle activation of the biceps than imagining an external image of the subject's bicep. Cornwall and colleagues (1991) showed that imagining contraction of the quadriceps resulted in a 12.6% gain in isometric strength over values in a control group. Of interest to the coach, instructor, and athlete is that demonstrations of skills should be done without error so that imagery using the demonstration is not flawed

and athletes vary in their ability to use imagery (Hall, Buckolz, and Fishburne 1992). Imagery may assist athletes, children, and others attempting to perform skills.

Imagery occurs in several dimensions or variations (Heil 1995). Imagery varies based on modality: visual, kinesthetic, auditory, olfactory, cutaneous, gustatory, visceral, and pain. These modalities can be used selectively by an athlete and may also represent modality preferences. The perspective of imagery can be classified as internal or external. Internal imagery is defined as imagery that occurs as if one is seeing or sensing through one's own eyes or senses and thus sees or feels the skill as if actually doing the task. External imagery is often characterized with reference to the visual modality; it is as if the athlete is watching him- or herself on a video screen. In other words, in external imagery the athlete imagines the skill or movement by viewing it the way another spectator would view it.

Imagery may also vary in speed. The athlete's mental image may occur at regular speed, in slow motion, or in faster than normal motion. Real-time imagery should portray the motion as it occurs in performance. Slower than real-time imagery may assist the athlete in seeing or feeling aspects of a skill more intensely. Faster than normal imagery may help athletes review choreography rapidly, quickly rehearse a race strategy over a long course, and so forth. Attentional focus may be associational or disassociational. Associational focus, considered the most common in sport, involves direct attention to the sport skill or movement. Disassociational focus may occur in some sports such as long distance running when an athlete purposely detaches from the running task and imagines him- or herself in a completely different place or in a completely different condition. Disassociation may be helpful to an athlete in an effort to reduce pain or fatigue sensations.

The following list is largely congruent with the findings from research on imagery. Imagery is more effective

- when many sensory modalities are used,
- with experienced athletes,
- among athletes who consider themselves already accomplished at imagery,
- in closed skills such as weightlifting compared to open skills such as soccer play (probably),
- when accompanied by physical practice, and

- in bouts longer than 1 min but shorter than 5 min.

Imagery appears to work with all ages (Howe 1991). There may be gender differences in the use of imagery and its effectiveness in learning skills, with males using imagery more effectively than females (Lovell and Collins 1997).

Ritualization

The final stage or culminating category of psychological skills for resistance training is ritualization or scripting. Performance scripts have been described previously (Ogilvie and Henschen 1995) and represent the culmination of psychological preparedness. According to Ogilvie and Henschen, "The ideal performance script will assume its final structure based on the identification of every thought and mental association that has actually contributed to the athlete's perception of her personal best. In essence, the script becomes the habitual internal dialogue that acts as a positive cue-specific verbal prompter"

(p. 47). The performance script permits the athlete to simply act out the script and thus control emotions, direct attention, and otherwise control tension such that the athlete can avoid unnecessary emotions and inappropriate attentional focus. Ritualization via a performance script also reduces the incidence of negative self-talk. Studies of flow in sport have also described the necessity of developing a preperformance and performance routine that evolves to automaticity as the athlete matures and reaches higher performance levels (Gordin and Reardon 1995).

Resistance training can provide an athlete with consistent, relatively simple, and clearly measurable opportunities to create, implement, and rehearse ritualization techniques and performance scripts. The resistance training environment is usually predictable, and the closed nature of the skills involved can make practicing performance scripts simpler than in other sport settings. Learning to set goals and control relaxation, concentration, and imagery behaviors and skills in a resistance training environment can serve the athlete in sport and in life.

CHAPTER SUMMARY

Athletes are more than motors. Sport psychology pursues the influence of mental skills and predisposition on the outcomes of sport performance. Resistance training can both benefit psychological skills and be benefited by them. The integration of psychological skills into the overall periodization plan should follow the format of goal setting, relaxation, concentration, imagery, and ritualization. These five stages should involve training and practice in the commensurate psychological skills in conjunction with the overall development of the athlete. The five stages should begin along with the general preparation phase of the typical periodization plan and should be largely completed when the athlete enters the competitive period. During preparation and competitive periods, the athlete should be able to call on these psychological skills as needed to enhance training and performance.

PART IV

Training Principles, Theory, and Practical Application

Part IV is the heart of this textbook. The first three parts of the textbook describe the underlying basic science, potential adaptations, and methods of measuring these adaptations. Part IV presents detailed discussions of how to meet the goals (specific adaptations leading to enhanced performance) of a training program. In meeting training goals, it is necessary to select appropriate modes of training (chapter 12), as well as to adhere to logical methods of training to achieve superior results (chapter 13). Finally, chapter 14 presents a culminating practical example of how to use the information previously presented in this textbook to build a training program.

CHAPTER 12

Modes of Resistance Training

Integrated program concepts are necessary in order to effectively improve performance. Integrating resistance training in an appropriate manner can increase the potential for performance alterations that can include improved maximum strength, power, and both low- and high-intensity exercise endurance (McGee et al. 1992; Paavolainen et al. 1999; Robinson et al. 1995). Adaptations in these variables (strength, power, endurance factors) resulting from resistance training can be related to improved measures of athletic performance such as the vertical jump, sprint times, distance running times, and measures of agility (Harris et al. 2000; Paavolainen et al. 1999; Wilson and Murphy 1996). These observations indicate that resistance training can have a transfer-of-training effect resulting in a change in specific abilities and capacities.

Appropriately choosing a training method (i.e., reps and sets, velocity of movement, periodization, etc.) can make a substantial difference in the outcome of a resistance training program (Fleck and Kraemer 1997; Garhammer 1981b; Harris et al. 2000; Stone and O'Bryant 1987; Stone et al. 1999a, 1999b; see chapter 13, "The Concept of Periodization"). For example, lower volume high-intensity programs influence maximum strength to a greater degree than high volume programs; however, high-volume resistance training programs potentially have a greater influence on body composition and endurance factors than low-volume programs (McGee et al. 1992). It is also very likely that the selection of training mode (type of equipment) can influence training adaptations.

In this discussion of the usefulness of various devices, the following definitions are used (Stone et al. 2002):

• Free weight: Resistance is created by use of a freely moving body. Free weights include barbells, dumbbells, associated benches and racks, medicine balls, throwing implements, body mass, and augmented body mass (e.g., weighted vests, limb weights). Free weights allow for force production application concomitant with the encountered resistance. The lifter is challenged to control, stabilize, and direct the movement.

• Machine: Resistance is created in a guided or restricted manner. Machines can include plate-loaded and selectorizer devices, electronically braked devices, springs, and rubber band devices. Using machines typically results in a smaller challenge for control, stabilization, and directed movement.

In the following discussion we examine the relative usefulness of various types of machines and free weights for sport performance enhancement in relation to training principles, comparison research, and practical aspects based on these principles and research.

Training Principles

The three training principles are overload, variation, and specificity (see chapter 13).

Overload concerns providing proper stimuli for eliciting specific physical, physiological, and performance adaptations. Overload consists of exercise and training that "force" the trainee beyond normal levels of physical performance. An overload stimulus has some level of intensity, frequency, and duration. Specifically with regard to resistance exercise and training, all stimuli have a level of intensity (absolute load), relative intensity (% of maximum), frequency, and duration (influence volume). The *training intensity* is associated with the rate of performing work and the rate at which energy is expended; the volume of training is a measure or estimate of how much total work is performed and the total amount of energy expended. The training volume is related to the number of repetitions and sets per exercise; the number and types of exercises used (large vs. small muscle mass); and the number of times per day, week, month, and so on that these exercises are repeated. Volume load (repetitions × the mass lifted) is the best estimate of the amount of work accomplished during training (Stone and O'Bryant 1987; Stone et al. 1999a, 1999b).

Training intensity and volume load can be related to competitive performance. For example, among elite weightlifters training for the 2003 world championships, both of these variables were strongly associated with lifting performance. Furthermore, it should be noted that while repetitions performed influence the volume load, repetitions were not correlated with performance. The poor association of repetitions with performance partly stems from the fact that repetitions alone are a poor estimate of work accomplished (table 12.1).

The application of training intensity and volume can be considered both in terms of all exercises performed during a specified period and in terms of individual exercises. Developing an understanding of overload factors can aid in the selection of exercises and equipment, particularly free weights versus machines. For example, changes in body composition, particularly decreases in body fat, are related to the total energy expenditure (during and after exercise) and therefore the total volume of training. With a few exceptions, such as leg press or elastic band devices, most machines are designed to use single-joint or small muscle mass exercises that do not require as much energy per repetition as large muscle mass exercises. Furthermore, training programs centered on machines are largely developed based on the use of several small muscle mass exercises; therefore, these types of programs result in a smaller energy expenditure than if several large muscle mass exercises were used. Thus, we make the argument that large muscle mass exercises and therefore larger energy expenditures are much more readily accomplished using free weights (see section "Advantages and Disadvantages Associated With Various Modes of Training"). Furthermore, large, multijoint exercises likely have greater carryover to both sport and daily activities compared to training with small muscle mass exercises (see section "Movement Pattern Specificity").

Variation deals with appropriate manipulation in training volume, exercise and training intensity factors, training density, speed of movement, and exercise selection (see chapter 1, "Introduction: Definitions, Objectives, Tasks, and Principles of Training" and chapter 13, "The Concept of Periodization"). Appropriate variation is a primary consideration for the prolongation of adaptations over a long term (Kramer et al. 1997; Kraemer 1997; Stone et al. 2000a, 2000b). Furthermore, appropriate sequencing of volume, intensity factors, and selection of exercises (including speed-strength exercises) in a periodized manner can lead to superior enhancement of a variety of performance abilities (Harris et al. 2000). Although changes in volume and intensity factors are pos-

Table 12.1 **Relationships of Training Volume and Intensity Among Elite U.S. Weightlifters**

	AREPS	TREPS	%-75	%PL-75	AVL	TVL	TI	TI-75
Men (n = 4)	339	3729	59.8	84	33,515	369,667	101	141
Women (n = 6)	338	3713	58.8	91	24,566	270,221	74	99
CORRELATIONS WITH AMERICAN CHAMPIONSHIPS TOTAL (N = 10)								
AREP	-0.19	AVL	0.72		TI	0.96		
TREP	-0.03	AVL-75	0.74					
AREP-75	0.13	TVL	0.73		TI-75	0.91		
TREP-75	0.19	TVL-75	0.70					

Exercises tracked: squats, pulls, snatch, clean and jerk. Ten weightlifters were tracked over 11 weeks before competing in the 2003 world championships. Correlations between repetitions (REPS) and performance were quite low. Correlations between average and total volume load (VL) and performance were quite high, indicating the relatively greater value of tracking VL compared to REPS. As might be expected, training intensity (TI) was very strongly correlated with final performance.

AREPS = average repetitions per week; TREPS = total repetitions over 11 weeks; %-75 = the percentage of the total repetitions made up of lifts above 75% of the 1RM; %PL-75 = the percentage of the total repetitions at 75% made compared to those planned; AVL = average volume load per week in kg; TVL = the total volume load over 11 weeks; TI = average load over 11 weeks; TI-75 = average load of the lifts above 75% over 11 weeks.

sible with machines, the ability to appropriately apply sequencing and variation of movement patterns, speed-strength exercises, and speed-oriented exercises is at best limited. Thus, limits on training variations are largely due to the limitations in the movement pattern and movement characteristics imposed by the mode of training.

Specificity, conceptually, includes both bioenergetics and mechanics of training (Stone and O'Bryant 1987; Wilmore and Costill 1994). This discussion concerns mechanical specificity; particularly, movements specific to the athlete's sport. Specificity of exercise and training is the most important consideration when one is selecting appropriate equipment for resistance training, particularly if performance enhancement is the primary goal. Mechanical specificity has been extensively studied as it affects strength training exercise.

Transfer-of-training effect deals with the degree of performance adaptation that potentially results from a training exercise and is strongly related to the concept of specificity. Mechanical specificity refers to the kinetic and kinematic associations between an exercise used in training and a physical or sport performance. This includes movement patterns, muscle action type, peak force, rate of force development, acceleration, and velocity parameters. The more similar a training exercise is to the actual physical performance, the greater the probabilities of transfer (Behm 1995; Sale 1992; Schmidt 1991).

Siff (2000), Siff and Verkoshansky (1998), and Stone and colleagues (2002) indicate that the degree of transfer-of-training effect depends on the degree of "dynamic correspondence." This means that the basic mechanics, but not necessarily the outward appearance, of training movements must be similar to those of performance in order to achieve maximum transfer. For example, sprinting appears to be largely dependent on horizontal forces; however, studies have clearly shown that upright sprinting performance is primarily limited by vertical forces (Weyand et al. 2000). As a result, vertical resistance training movements such as squats and pulling movements can have a large transfer-of-training effect. Based on this information it should become apparent that, in selecting training modes, a number of performance criteria can be used to maximize transfer-of-training effect.

Training exercises that optimize transfer-of-training effect include the appropriate application of

- type of muscular actions (eccentric vs. concentric vs. stretch–shortening actions),

- force magnitude—accentuated regions of force production,
- amplitude and direction of movement,
- dynamics of effort (i.e., static vs. dynamic characteristics of the movement and appropriate power output), and
- rate and time of maximum force production.

Additionally, if continued adaptations are to occur, these factors (particularly force magnitude, rates of force development, and power) must be overloaded.

Explosive Strength and Power

Understanding the components of dynamic explosive exercises is important in the selection of training modes. Strength is the ability to produce force (Stone 1993). "Explosive strength" refers to the ability to produce high peak rates of force development (PRFD) and is related to the ability to accelerate objects, including body mass (Schmidtbleicher 1992; Stone 1993). Explosive strength can therefore be produced both dynamically and isometrically (Stone 1993). Dynamic explosive strength exercises (speed-strength exercises) resulting in high PRFDs and in high power outputs are crucial in training athletes from a variety of sports (Schmidtbleicher 1992; Stone 1993).

Work is the product of force and the distance the object moves in the direction resulting from the force application. Power is the rate of doing work ($P = force \times distance/time$) and can be expressed as the product of force and velocity ($P = force \times velocity$). Power can be calculated as an average over a range of motion or as an instantaneous value occurring at a particular instant during the displacement of an object. Peak power (PP) is the highest instantaneous power value found over a range of motion. Maximum power (MP) is the highest peak power output one is capable of generating under a given set of conditions (i.e., state of training, type of exercise, etc.). Depending on the complexity of the exercise, typically the highest concentric power outputs occur at approximately 30% to 50% of maximum isometric force capabilities.

Clearly, a primary factor determining sport performances (i.e., who wins and who loses) is power output. While average power output is associated with performance in endurance events, for dynamic explosive activities such as jumping, sprinting, and weightlifting movements, PP is typically strongly related to success (Garhammer 1993; Kauhanen, Garhammer, and Hakkinen 2000; McBride et al. 1999; Thomas, Fiataron, and Fielding 1996).

Among previously untrained subjects, heavy weight training can produce a rightward shift across the entire or nearly the entire force–velocity curve (Hakkinen 1994; Stone and O'Bryant 1987). As a result of these force–velocity alterations, power output would be enhanced across a wide range of velocities among the previously untrained. However, evidence also indicates that among well-trained subjects, high-velocity training is necessary to make further alterations in the high-velocity end of the force–velocity curve (Hakkinen 1994; Harris et al. 2000; McBride et al. 2002; Stone and O'Bryant 1987).

Isometric Training

Among relatively untrained subjects, isometric training has been shown to result in an increased PRFD and velocity of movement (Behm 1995). This result was only observed provided that the intent to contract the muscles explosively was emphasized during the isometric actions. However, the overall effectiveness of isometric training on dynamic explosive force production is relatively minor, particularly among well-trained strength-power athletes (Hakkinen 1994). Indeed, examination of the relative PRFD of isometric movement compared to fast and fast ballistic movement supports the use of movements with high velocity and high rates of force development to enhance dynamic explosiveness (Haff et al. 1997; McBride et al. 2002).

Although there is some overlap, studies and reviews of the scientific literature indicate that the primary effect of ballistic training is an increased rate of force production and velocity of movement, while traditional heavy weight training primarily increases maximum strength (Hakkinen 1994; Harris et al. 2000; McBride et al. 1999, 2002; Sale 1988). Additionally, some evidence indicates that high-power training can beneficially alter a wider range of sport performance variables compared to traditional heavy weight training, especially in subjects with a reasonable initial level of maximum strength (Harris et al. 2000; Wilson et al. 1993). However, improvements in strength, power, and measures of athletic performance resulting from combination and sequenced training (strength >> power >> speed) may be superior to those with either heavy resistance training or high-speed

resistance training alone (Hakkinen 1994; Medvedev et al. 1981; Stone 1993). A longitudinal study using American collegiate football players (Harris et al. 2000) indicates that combination training (heavy training followed by combination training) produces superior results in that a greater number of variables encompassing a wide range of performance measures showed significant improvement. These variables included measures of maximum strength (1RMs) and other measures of athletic performance such as the vertical jump, standing long jump, and 10-yard shuttle run (Harris et al. 2000).

These data strongly indicate that, in order to optimally increase power and speed of movement, resistance training using exercises that emphasize power and speed of movement (as well as appropriate variation) are necessary considerations in the formulation of training programs. High-speed and high-power training is obviously limited during isometric work and also with the use of most machines, relative to that available through free weights, due to limitations on acceleration patterns (particularly in variable-resistance and semi-isokinetic devices), friction, inappropriate movement patterns, and limited ranges of motion (Cabell and Zebas 1999; Chow, Darling, and Hay 1997; Harman 1983). Thus, we argue that strength-power training employing dynamic explosive exercises can be more effectively performed using free weights and free body exercises.

Joint Angle Specificity

In very sedentary subjects, isometric training may improve strength at a variety of angles (Marks 1994). However, among physically active and trained populations, isometric strength training typically produces gains that are joint angle specific; that is, gains are greatest at and near the angle trained. Progressively smaller gains in isometric maximum strength are found as measurement of strength gained moves away from the training angle (Atha 1983; Logan 1960).

For maximum strength gains, ideally, during exercise, maximum contractions could be sustained throughout a range of motion via the maintenance of optimal length–tension and leverage characteristics. The aim in variable-resistance devices is to match the encountered resistance to the changes in muscle force production (human strength curves) by the use of various cams and lever systems. Nevertheless, there is little evidence that these devices succeed in matching resistance to human strength curves

(Cabell and Zebas 1999; Harman 1983, 1994). There are two possible reasons:

1. Humans show a relatively high degree of variability (e.g., differences in limb lengths, moment arms, etc.); thus machines in which resistance only matches average strength curves would not appropriately match every individual's strength curve (Cabell and Zebas 1999; Harman 1983, 1994). Furthermore, even if the resistance could be matched to the strength curve of an individual, a compounding factor is the force–velocity relationship. The velocity of movement would have to be constant in order for an individual to maximally load the involved muscles throughout the range of motion, an exercise pattern that is difficult to achieve and for which the neural control would be nonspecific to most real-life movements.

2. There is no evidence that variable-resistance devices match the average human strength curves (Cabell and Zebas 1999; Harman 1983, 1994). Additionally, for many movements, particularly complex movements, multiple joints and groups of muscles are actually involved rather than a single joint or muscle. Because each individual muscle has a different moment arm, there may be no common force–velocity (or length–tension) relationship; thus a constant velocity of movement would not necessarily fit every muscle involved. As a result, variable-resistance devices may apply resistance inappropriately or inconsistently with "naturally occurring movement," thus limiting adaptation.

In this context it has been noted that the use of variable-resistance devices typically produces strength gains that are the greatest at the joint angle at which the highest resistance is applied, and that gains may be considerably less at other angles (Atha 1983). Angle-specific training adaptation is not an apparent result with the use of free-swinging or freely moving devices (Kovaleski et al. 1995; Nosse and Hunter 1985).

Although it is not a new idea, varying resistance applied through the use of chains and elastic bands has recently become popular. The idea of resistance application is similar to that of variable-resistance machines except that the devices (i.e., chains and elastic bands) are attached to free weights. When chains are attached to each end of a bar during a squat, for example, as the lifter descends, the weight decreases, and during ascension, the load increases. Theoretically this might enhance the training effect, as greater external forces can be produced at greater knee angles, thus requiring a greater resistance to stimulate overload. Care must be taken in how the additional resistance is added. For example, addition of resistance before the "sticking region," during which mechanical advantage is relatively low, will limit the effectiveness of this arrangement, as the weight added will have to be reduced to get through the sticking region. Measures (EMG) of muscle activation using elastic bands or chains during the parallel squat have not shown any significant differences; however, there were significant differences in vertical ground reaction forces, indicating that the usefulness of these devices for strength enhancement was questionable (Ebben and Jensen 2002). It should be noted that Ebben and Jensen (2002) used only one type of chain or elastic band arrangement, and it is clear that further study is necessary.

Movement Pattern Specificity

Studies and reviews of the literature have consistently concluded that the magnitude of measured maximum strength gains depends on the degree of similarity between the strength test and the actual training exercise (Abernethy and Jurimae 1996; Behm 1995; Fry, Powell, and Kraemer 1992; Rasch and Morehouse 1957; Rutherford and Jones 1986; Sale 1988, 1992; Stone et al. 2000a; Stone, Plisk, and Collins 2002).

Observation of the great majority of athletes, particularly strength-power athletes, indicates that most of their resistance training is centered on free weights. Assuming that athletes and coaches are at least reasonably pragmatic, this observation would indicate that free weights may offer some advantages that machines do not. Furthermore, several investigations and reviews have indicated that specific movements with free weights can have strong kinetic and kinematic relationships to a number of specific activities such as the vertical jump (Canavan, Garret, and Armstrong 1996; Garhammer 1981a; Stone, Plisk, and Collins 2002; Stone et al. 2002). As a logical extension of these observations and relationships, a strong probability exists that training with free weights may have a greater transfer of training to sport (and ergonomic) tasks compared to machines (Nosse and Hunter 1985; Stone 1982; Stone and Borden 1997; Stone and Garhammer 1981). The primary basis for this possibility is the observation that movements with free weights can mechanically simulate sport performance tasks more effectively than machines. However, very few studies are available that actually compare alterations in performance using various devices for training.

As previously pointed out, the concept of training specificity dictates that a number of kinetic and kinematic parameters must be appropriately overloaded to adequately stimulate gains in performance. One of the most often studied and contemplated performance aspects of specificity deals with weightlifting and associated movements, the training practices of weightlifters, and the vertical jump (VJ). Improved weightlifting performance as a result of training has been associated with increased VJ height and associated power output among novices (Stone et al. 1980). Among national- and international-level weightlifters, performance in the snatch and clean and jerk has been associated with both countermovement VJ and static VJ power production (Carlock et al. 2004), and VJ height can be stratified by achievement level among weightlifters (i.e., better weightlifters jump higher) (Stone and Kirksey 2000). Furthermore, weightlifters have been shown to have superior weighted and unweighted VJ heights and power outputs compared to other athletes (McBride et al. 1999, Stone 1991; Stone et al. 2003). Part of the reason for these superior performance characteristics is likely related to the training mode and methods used by weightlifters. Although adaptations to training are always multifactorial, one potential contributing factor is the degree of associated mechanical specificity that has been observed between weightlifting movements (e.g., snatch, clean and jerk, and derivatives) and the VJ (Canavan, Garret, and Armstrong 1996; Garhammer 1981a, 1981b). These factors include a combination of high power output, high rates of force development, and movement patterns that cannot be easily duplicated by machine use.

Consideration of movement pattern specificity aspects is perhaps the most crucial if one is to be able to gain the most efficient transfer and maximize training transfer to performance. Movement pattern aspects include kinetic chain considerations, muscle action, and stable and unstable surfaces, as well as the potential effects of vibration.

Closed Versus Open Kinetic Chain Exercises

The concepts of open (OKCE) and closed kinetic chain exercises (CKCE) have received considerable attention in the scientific literature, especially concerning injury rehabilitation (Beynnon and Johnson 1996; Fitzgerald 1997; Palmitier et al. 1991). Although the exact definitions for various types and combinations of movements have been debated and gray areas exist (Blackard, Jensen, and Ebben 1999; Dillman, Murray, and Hintermeister 1994), exercises can *generally* be divided into movements in which the peripheral segment can move freely and those in which the peripheral segment is fixed. For the purposes of the present discussion, a CKCE consists of a movement in which the foot or hand is fixed and force (usually in a weight-bearing manner) is transmitted directly through the foot or hand as in a leg press, squat, or bench press. An OKCE movement occurs when the foot or hand is not fixed, as in a leg extension, and the peripheral segment can move freely (Palmitier et al. 1991; Steindler 1973).

Typically CKCE produce markedly different muscle recruitment and joint motions compared to OKCE (Stensdotter et al. 2003), for example, the isolated knee articulation of a leg extension versus the multiple articulations of the ankle, knee, and hip in a squatting movement. Although it is apparent that some human movements (such as walking and running) may contain a combination of open and closed kinetic chain aspects, it is the closed chain aspects of movement that are most important to performance and especially in improving performance (Palmitier et al. 1991; Steindler 1973). Because many machines are OKCE devices, it is unlikely that these devices will provide the same level of specificity for training or testing as gained through the use of CKCE (Abernethy and Jurimae 1996; Augustsson et al. 1998; Blackburn and Morrissey 1998; Palmitier et al. 1991).

It is possible that studies comparing various modes of training may result in some apparent differences because of movement pattern differences (i.e., OKCE vs. CKCE) rather than differences in muscle contraction type (e.g., semi-isokinetic vs. isoinertial). These specific adaptation differences as a result of different movement patterns would reflect different neural activation patterns during training (i.e., neural specificity). It is probable that monoarticular (single joint) or small muscle mass training programs (or testing) may not provide adequate movement pattern specificity. Indeed, muscle action has been shown to be task dependent, and muscle function during isolated movements is unlikely to be the same as during multijoint movements (Zajac and Gordon 1989). Therefore it is quite possible that differences noted between semi-isokinetic devices and free weights (Abernethy and Jurimae 1996) actually result from differences in the pattern of movement rather than differences in contraction type. If movement patterns for these modes could be made more similar, then results might be more readily comparable and many of the apparent differences would be obviated.

Machines Versus Free Weights

Short-term studies (Boyer 1990; Jesse et al. 1988; Stone, Johnson, and Carter 1979; Wathen and Shutes 1982) in which maximum strength gain was measured on the different types of apparatus used in training (i.e., specific strength tests) have consistently indicated that free weights produce superior results. These studies (Boyer 1990; Jesse et al. 1988; Stone, Johnson, and Carter 1979; Wathen and Shutes 1982) suggest that among young males, when maximum strength is measured as 1RMs, free weight training transfers to machine testing better than machine training transfers to free weight testing. In our laboratory (Brindell 1999, unpublished data), we have also shown that this effect occurs in women.

However, studies in which the strength testing has not been specific (strength was measured on an apparatus different from that used in training) have not shown strength gain differences between devices (Messier and Dill 1985; Saunders 1980; Silvester et al. 1982). For example, studies by Saunders (1980) and Silvester and colleagues (1982) used dynamic exercise for training; but strength testing was non-joint-angle-specific isometric testing, which potentially mutes or reduces maximum strength gains or differences between groups (Wilson and Murphy 1996).

Furthermore, even with use of dynamic tests of strength in which the testing device is supposedly nonspecific, either the use of free weight or machine training will be favored. The reason is that the dynamic testing device has to be either free weights or a machine, open or closed kinetic chain, and the testing device will be more like one training device or the other (i.e., biased data). For example, Messier and Dill (1985) compared Nautilus machine training to free weight training. In this study, tests of leg strength were performed on a Cybex II semi-isokinetic leg extension device, providing an "open kinetic chain exercise." The Nautilus group used leg extensions (open kinetic chain) as one of the training exercises. However, the free weight training was carried out using the squat, a "closed kinetic chain exercise," and no leg extensions were performed. Therefore, the Nautilus group potentially had an advantage in testing because part of their training was more biomechanically similar to exercise on the testing device. (See "Problems Associated With Training Mode Comparisons"; kinetic chain discussion later.) Interestingly, although training differences may be masked or muted with the use of a "nonspecific device" to measure strength, these studies do demonstrate a degree of transfer-of-training effect for strength gains in that strength gains were noted on all devices regardless of the training mode employed.

Isokinetic Devices

Many clinicians and some exercise scientists believe that "isokinetic" training and testing may offer advantages over other modes and methods. However, the scientific literature does not support this belief. Evidence demonstrating that isokinetic training and testing offer such an advantage is lacking, and in many instances the literature indicates that isokinetics may be inferior to other modes and methods (Augustsson et al. 1998; Hakkinen 1994; Kovaleski et al. 1995; Petsching, Baron, and Albrecht 1998).

Isokinetic literally means "same speed" and is used to refer to exercise in which a constant angular velocity is maintained by application of force on a machine level arm. Theoretically, an isokinetic device will accommodate force production and maintain a constant velocity, regardless of the amount of force application; thus a maximum-force effort can be made through the complete range of motion. However, currently there are no commercially available devices that can produce an isokinetic movement throughout a complete range of motion, especially at the faster available speeds (Chow, Darling, and Hay 1997; Tunstall, Mullineaux, and Vernon 2005). Acceleration at the beginning and deceleration at the end of a movement prevent the achievement of a completely isokinetic range of motion (Chow, Darling, and Hay 1997; Murray and Harrison 1986). Thus, these devices are more properly termed "semi-isokinetic." Semi-isokinetic testing results in fair-to-good reliability (Abernethy and Jurimae 1996). Proponents suggest that one advantage of semi-isokinetic testing (and other machine-based testing) is that movement is less technique dependent compared to that used in many free weight exercises (Augustsson et al. 1998) and therefore testing can be carried out on a variety of trained states with good validity and reliability. However, the external and prediction validity and reliability of semi-isokinetic devices are questionable (Abernethy and Jurimae 1996; Augustsson et al. 1998; Fry, Powell, and Kraemer 1992; Issifidou and Baltzopoulos 1998; Kovaleski et al. 1995; Tunstall, Mullineaux, and Vernon 2005).

This means that the degree of transfer-of-training effect for semi-isokinetic devices can be relatively poor. As a result, maximum strength and power gains from free weight training or variable-resistance training are not always demonstrable when measured on semi-isokinetic devices (Abernethy and Jurimae 1996; Augustsson et al. 1998; Fry, Powell, and Kraemer 1992).

Studies and reviews comparing semi-isokinetic and other resistance training modes indicate a high degree of strength specificity (Hakkinen 1994; Morrissey, Harman, and Johnson 1995). For example, moments (forces) produced during semi-isokinetic contractions of the same muscles at the same velocities can be different from those resulting from freely moving activities. Bobbert and van Ingen Schenau (1990) compared the moments produced during plantar flexion in a VJ to semi-isokinetic movement. The forces produced during the VJ were substantially higher, as well as creating differences in the timing of muscle activation (Bobbert and van Ingen Schenau 1990).

During sport and daily life, movement is rarely, if ever, performed at a constant velocity through a full range of motion, and it may be argued that a freely moving object or device will allow muscle activity to occur in a more natural manner (Stone and O'Bryant 1987). Indeed, a training comparison of "isotonic" (freely moving leg extension device) and semi-isokinetic leg extension training indicated that dynamic nonisokinetic training is superior in producing alterations in both maximum strength and power over a wide movement range (Kovaleski et al. 1995).

It has been further suggested that semi-isokinetic devices offer a degree of velocity specificity that cannot be achieved using other devices, including free weights, presumably as a result of the ability of the device to overload at fast speeds (Watkins and Harris 1983). However, use of most commercially available semi-isokinetic devices can result in maximum testing (or training) speeds of only 400° to 500° · s^{-1} or less, angular velocities that are typically far less than either some single or most multiple (summated) joint peak velocities occurring in many athletic activities (Colman, Benham, and Northcutt 1993). However, movements with free weights, particularly those with multiple-joint actions such as weightlifting movements (snatch, clean and jerk) and unweighted or weighted jumps, can result in much higher angular velocities than are possible with use of the currently available semi-isokinetic devices. Even in maximum attempts, angular velocities at the hip and knee during the snatch can exceed 500° · s^{-1} (Baumann et al. 1988); lifts with submaximal weights would potentially produce even higher values. An important consideration for training is whether or not overload forces can be sustained at high angular velocities. Baumann and colleagues (1988) carefully studied the forces and velocities produced. They noted that peak angular velocities can occur at joint angles at which force is still being exerted on the bar, clearly illustrating the potential for a force overload stimulus at angular velocities that can exceed the limits of semi-isokinetic devices.

As a result of the relatively poor transfer-of-training effect provided by semi-isokinetic devices, we would argue that it appears unlikely that these devices can adequately provide a force-velocity-specific stimulus comparable to that of free movements, particularly in relation to multijoint movements.

Vibration

One of the newer concepts that show promise in developing strength and power is vibration. Vibration is a mechanical stimulus that results from an oscillatory motion. Manipulating the intensity, frequency (Hz), and amplitude can result in changes in vibration oscillation states.

Effects from low-frequency vibration (<60 Hz) can have both acute and chronic aspects. Acutely, vibration exposure, depending on frequency and duration applied, results in neuromuscular potentiation. Acute vibration has been shown to increase measures of power and velocity while at the same time increasing neuromuscular efficiency (Gullich and Schmidtbleicher 1996; Torvinen et al. 2002, 2003). Additionally, acute effects of low frequency may include elevated testosterone, decreased cortisol, decreased antagonistic inhibition, and increased measures of strength and power (Bosco et al. 1998, 2000; Cardinale and Bosco 2003; De Ruiter et al. 2003; Issurin and Tenenbaum 1999). Thus, acute vibration may be useful as a warm-up device or (over the long term) as a recovery device.

Chronic exposure has also produced interesting results. Increases in human growth hormone and testosterone and decreased cortisol have been noted as a result of vibration exposure over several weeks (Bosco et al. 2000). Although not all studies agree, some have noted training effects, among them improved strength measures and improvements in some related variables including the VJ (Delecluse, Roelants, and Verschueren 2003; Roelants et al. 2004; Torvinen et al. 2002, 2003). Body composition appears to be largely unaffected (Roelants et al. 2004). These effects appear to be somewhat similar to those of moderate-load resistance training among previously untrained subjects (Bosco, Cardinale, and Tsarpela 1999; Delecluse, Roelants, and Verschueren 2003; Rittweger, Mutschelknauss, and Felsenberg 2003; Roelants et al. 2004).

The exact mechanism or mechanisms underlying the potential adaptations associated with vibration training are unknown but most likely include nervous system alterations. Increased muscle activation as a result of vibration as measured by EMG has been noted (Bosco, Cardinale, and Tsarpela 1999; Bosco et al. 2000; Cardinale and Bosco 2003). The increased muscle activation is likely a result of a myototic reflex. As a muscle is stretched, the muscle spindle contained within it is also stretched (see chapter 2, "Neuromuscular Physiology"). Within the stretched region of the intrafusal fiber (muscle fiber within the muscle spindle) is a central sensory area that can relay information concerning rapid changes in length and tension back to the spinal cord. This sensory area, referred to as nuclear chain fibers, is innervated by group 1a afferent nerve endings. The group 1a afferent nerve fibers also interact with α-motor neurons in a manner leading to facilitation (reduction in threshold) of the MUs within the stretched muscle and inhibition of muscles antagonistic to the stretched muscle. Therefore, activation of the α-motor neurons by rapid stretch can lead to increased neural drive, resulting in greater force-velocity production from increased motor unit activation. This type of reflexive activity is referred to as the stretch reflex, or myototic reflex (Bove, Nardone, and Schieppati 2003).

Electromyography can be used to assess the degree of motor unit activation. It is important to note that muscle activation can either increase or decrease depending on the frequency and the duration of vibration exposure (Bosco, Cardinale, and Tsarpela 1999; Cardinale and Bosco 2003). Some research indicates that a preferential increase in motor unit synchronization is a major contributing factor when an increase in EMG activity is observed (Bosco, Cardinale, and Tsarpela 1999). Furthermore, the frequency that results in the greatest muscle activation can change with the trained state (Cardinale, personal communication). These data indicate that the most effective method of vibration training would be to simultaneously record EMG values so that muscle activation is always optimized.

It is important to note that certain vibration frequencies can be deleterious; for example, vibration having very high amplitude and a low frequency (less than 1 Hz) can result in motion sickness (e.g.,

seasickness). Interestingly, the human body has its own natural resonance frequency, and individual tissues within the body show resonance at different frequencies. For instance, the retina within the eye has a resonance frequency of approximately 15 Hz. As a result, when vibration frequencies of around 15 Hz are applied directly to the retina, over a period of time tissue damage may occur. As vibration is encountered daily, especially within an occupational setting, this constant exposure raises long-term health concerns. For example, humans operating a chain saw or pneumatic drill are exposed to very high-frequency vibrations, especially in the upper body. Long-term exposure to such high-frequency vibrations has been linked to joint and musculoskeletal problems as well as internal organ damage (Mester et al. 1999). Considering this information, one must also use vibration devices associated with physical training with great care, as no long-term studies on the health effects of these devices are currently available.

Transfer-of-Training Effect

Few studies dealing with modes of training have addressed carryover to aspects of performance other than strength, such as sprinting or jumping, and none have investigated effects on ergonomic tasks. Only a few studies have compared free weights and resistance machines (Augustsson et al. 1998; Bauer, Thayer, and Baras 1990; Jesse et al. 1988; Silvester et al. 1982; Stone, Johnson, and Carter 1979; Wathen 1980; Wathen and Shutes 1982) as to their effects on performance other than maximum strength. All of these studies made training comparisons based on the VJ and VJ power indices. The VJ is typically chosen as an indicator of explosive performance because (1) the VJ is a primary component of many sports (e.g., basketball, volleyball), (2) there are reasonable associations or correlations between the VJ and the performance capabilities of athletes excelling at other "explosive" exercises (e.g., sprinters jump higher and sprint faster than distance runners or untrained individuals) (Hollings and Robson 1991), (3) the VJ (or its components, including velocity and power output) has been associated with performance ability in numerous specific sports (Anderson, Montgomery, and Turcotte 1990; Barker et al. 1993; Carlock et al. 2004; Stone et al. 1980; Thissen-Milder and Mayhew 1991), and (4) the VJ is relatively nonfatiguing and easy to measure.

Five studies (Augustsson et al. 1998; Bauer, Thayer, and Baras 1990; Silvester et al. 1982; Stone,

Johnson, and Carter 1979; Wathen 1980) showed that free weights produced superior VJ results compared to machines; two studies (Jesse et al. 1988; Wathen and Shutes 1982) yielded statistically equal results, although the percent gains in VJ favored the free weight groups. No studies could be located indicating that machine training produces superior results compared to free weights in gains in VJ (or any other performance variable). While these studies generally suggest the superiority of free weights in producing a transfer-of-training effect, they are not definitive. More investigation is needed for a full understanding of the training adaptations associated with both machines and free weights.

Other erroneous assumptions have been made concerning the use of free weights versus machines. For example, it is sometimes assumed that throwing motions requiring trunk rotation cannot be made and trained appropriately with free weights and that rotational machine exercises are necessary. However, this idea may be more related to lack of experience with free weight training than to the inherent characteristics of free weights or machines. First, most throwing movements are made in a standing or upright position, and most rotational machines are used in a sitting position. For many years athletes, particularly field event throwers, have simulated these upright throwing motions using weighted balls and implements; additionally, exercises including walking twists and weighted hammer throw exercises have been used successfully to overload upright trunk rotation and throwing motions. Second, in most throwing movements the motion is initiated by hip rotation and not by the trunk (i.e., leading with the shoulder). Inspection of most rotation machines indicates that the hips (and often the feet) are fixed and that rotation must be initiated by trunk rotation, a movement not particularly specific to throwing. Furthermore, with the aid of benches or pommel horses, a variety of appropriate positional exercises using both weights and balls can stress trunk rotation from a variety of angles that cannot be attained with most machines.

Unstable Training

Training in unstable conditions has also recently become popular, especially for "core training" (midsection). Most often, the exerciser brings about unstable conditions by performing exercises on physio balls. The idea behind unstable training is that additional musculature will be brought into play, enhancing the training effect. However, there are few studies comparing unstable to stable training modes. Research does indicate that when one performs peripheral movements such as leg extensions and plantar flexion in unstable conditions, stabilizer activation (ratio of antagonist to agonist) can be increased (Behm, Anderson, and Curnew 2002). However, the unstable conditions also reduced the muscle activation of the primary movers and reduced external force production (i.e., overload forces) by as much as 70% depending on the exercise (Behm, Anderson, and Curnew 2002).

While the primary use of unstable training has been to increase core strength (midsection strength), there is no clear definition of what exactly constitutes the core. Identification of the muscles making up the core has ranged from only the abdominal muscles to the abdominal muscles, paraspinals, and hip extensors (Leetun et al. 2004; Nadler et al. 2002). Thus, a more appropriate term would be midsection. It is clear that different exercises, including stable versus unstable, cause different specific activation patterns of midsection musculature (Hildenbrand and Noble 2004). While midsection strength is obviously related to performance, there is also some evidence that midsection strength is related to lower body injury, especially in women (Leetun et al. 2004; Nadler et al. 2002). Although there is an apparent relationship between midsection strength and lower body injury (especially lower back), there is surprisingly little evidence that specific midsection strengthening reduces injury (Nadler et al. 2002). Currently no evidence exists to suggest that unstable midsection training results in reduced injuries or superior performance. If one considers the concept of training specificity, one might argue that if performance is on a stable surface, then most of the training should be stable. If the performance is on an unstable surface (e.g., surfing, roller skating, gymnastics rings), then a good deal of the training probably should be unstable (W.A. Sands, unpublished data). However, it is important to remember that unstable training will decrease the ability to produce overload forces peripherally; thus even for unstable performances, much, perhaps most, of the training should be on stable surfaces.

While most physical activities can be simulated and appropriately trained using free weights, there are possible exceptions. For example, some aspects of swimming in which motion is generated in a supine or prone position largely through propulsion by the upper body may require specialized dryland training. In this case it may be advantageous to use a "swim bench" associated with pulley systems to simulate and overload stroke mechanics.

Problems Associated With Training Mode Comparisons

Training adaptation comparisons of various modes of resistance exercise can be quite difficult. Several confounding factors become apparent, including subject number, study length and trained state, work equalization, and mixed protocols.

Subject Number

The subject number in many of the comparative studies is relatively small. For example, in the study by Wathen and Shutes (1982), the authors concluded that there was no difference in VJ gains between free weights and a jumping device (n = 8 per group), although the absolute and percent gains favored the free weight group. The authors indicated that a potentially significant difference favoring the free weight group would have been reached if the subject number had been higher.

Study Length and Trained State

Regardless of the purpose, a significant problem with the majority of training studies is their length. In comparing training modes, studies to date have been quite short (<14 weeks). Study length (i.e., training time) is an important consideration as it affects the training status of the subjects. Marked increases in maximum strength-power can occur among initially untrained subjects using almost any reasonable training program or device. Obviously both neural and muscle adaptations affect long-term alterations in maximum strength. However, early strength improvements primarily involve neural changes associated with learning how to activate muscle and learning a new skill rather than muscle cross-sectional adaptations. In the initial stages of learning a new movement, performance gains are typically rapid, with subsequent improvements becoming asymptotic (Crossman 1964; Schmidt 1991). It is highly probable that initial gains in performance, in any exercise regime, will be primarily due to the improved central representation of the skill rather than to hypertrophic adaptations. Indeed, mental practice alone has resulted in substantial strength gains (i.e., no physical training, only imagining an execution of the movement). Therefore, it is likely that both central representation (learning the skill) and learning how to better activate muscle account for more variance in the early "strength" gains resulting from training (Smith et al. 1998; Yue and Cole 1992).

Thus we would argue that although some specificity has been demonstrated over a relatively short term (Abernethy and Jurimae 1996), comparisons between devices that last only a few weeks are likely measuring only initial changes in learning. Many of these initial alterations are more general in nature, particularly intramuscular adaptations. Furthermore, these initial changes are typically quite large compared to adaptations in the same variables occurring later in the training program. While these initial changes can lead to an increased ability to exert maximum force, many training-specific effects may be masked by the large initial changes in the nervous system and may require much longer periods to become evident. Consequently, longer observation periods (>0.5 year) are likely required to completely elucidate long-term intra- and intermuscular task specificity or specific alterations in hypertrophy and muscle physiology as a result of training with different modes. The initial phase in which people learn to more effectively activate muscle may partly explain why muscle cross-sectional alterations lag behind neural effects. It can be argued that there may be a "threshold" of hypertrophic stimulation; thus, part of the reason that cross-sectional adaptation lags behind neural adaptation is that beginners simply cannot exert themselves with enough intensity to reach this threshold.

Only three studies in the scientific literature were found that used previously strength-trained subjects (Stone, Johnson, and Carter 1979; Wathen 1980; Wathen and Shutes 1982). These studies generally suggest that free weights produce superior gains compared to machines. One might assume that skill acquisition would play a much smaller role in adaptations to training among previously trained subjects. However, there is still a high probability that skill acquisition effects could have confounded the results of these investigations. When individuals or groups skilled in one set of movements (e.g., squats, weightlifting movements, and so on) change to an exercise requiring another skilled movement (even though it may be related), the neural adaptations and skill acquisition gains previously described (i.e., initial learning)

(continued)

suggest that those switching to the novel skill would be expected to improve more rapidly than those still using the previous training mode. From a motor control perspective, differences in the complexity of the exercises used (e.g., squats vs. a leg extension) can also serve to confound effects in short-term studies, as learning simple movements is typically easier and progresses faster than learning complex movements. Furthermore, prior skill level can contaminate results through the test exercise itself; because of previous experience and practice levels, some subjects may have a performance advantage over others. Consequently, reasonable conclusions concerning the direct comparison of different training modes can be made only from investigations that use repeated-measures designs or use the preintervention performance on the test exercise as a covariate, and that allow for the differential impact of learning effects (Stone et al. 2002). Finally, to date, few studies have used women as subjects. Obviously, the only reasonable conclusion is that much more comprehensive study needs to be carried out over longer periods of time.

Work Equalization

When one is studying the effects of various training devices, it can be advantageous to obviate any potential differences between devices due to work differences. However, equalizing the amount of work accomplished is very difficult, if not impossible, even when set and repetition combinations are the same. Primarily this difficulty is due to the variety of methods employed by machines to produce resistance (e.g., semi-isokinetic, variable-resistance cams, friction, elastic bands, springs, etc.); thus, it is difficult to make accurate calculations of work (Augustsson et al. 1998; Cabell and Zebas 1999).

We must also question the logic of equalizing programs from a very practical standpoint. Often different set and repetition combinations must use vastly different loading schemes to equalize work. Thus, the load for one set and repetition scheme may not be optimal for that scheme. For example, let's consider an athlete that can squat 180 kg for 1RM. Using a squat and performing 3 sets of 10 repetitions (3 x 10) with 100 kg provides a relative intensity (%1RM) of 56%. This loading is reasonable to stimulate strength-endurance gains using 3 x 10 repetitions. This loading also provides the same work load (volume load) as performing the squat as 10 sets of 3 (10 x 3) with 100 kg. While the 3 x 10 at 100 kg is likely a reasonable stimulus for gains using 3 x 10 repetitions, it is not a good stimulus when using 10 x 3 repetitions and is likely an underload for strength stimulus.

Compounding this problem, from the standpoint of practical application, is the observation that outside of the laboratory, training protocols with equal workloads are rarely chosen. Training protocols are typically selected because they are believed to produce desired results. However, machine manufacturers or retailers often recommend training protocols that can be different from those commonly used, particularly protocols used by serious athletes interested in improving performance (e.g., one set to failure vs. multiple sets, nonballistic vs. ballistic movements). Consequently, many studies actually compared one device and protocol with a different device and protocol. For example, in studying methods and modes of training and comparing a manufacturer's recommendations, Stone and colleagues (1979) used one set to failure with the Nautilus group and compared this with multiple sets used by the free weight group. While this approach is quite pragmatic in that the studied devices were used in a "real-life" manner, the approach could preclude definitive conclusions as to the effectiveness of the mode of training independent from the training program.

Mixed Protocols

Some studies have compared protocols using various combinations (mixtures) of devices. For example Meadors and colleagues (1983) compared free weights and machines to machine-only training. This is a pragmatic and quite reasonable approach using real-life programs; however, it makes it difficult to separate out individual effects for the different devices. Additionally, it is important to take care in properly characterizing and describing the training devices being studied. For example, in the study by Boyer (1990), the leg sled used for the lower body training program was described as a "free weight." It is not actually a true free weight device because its movement is restricted to a single fixed plane that results in guided movements, and the guiding apparatus can produce considerable friction not encountered in a freely moving object.

Lag Time

For daily living and especially for athletes, maximizing transfer-of-training effect is the most important aspect of the training program; otherwise considerable effort is wasted in training. However, the exact degree of transfer is difficult to establish at best. Maximum strength, power, or specific performance variables have never been shown to change at exactly the same rate over time as a result of training. Furthermore, the increases in maximum strength may continue after the changes in power or sport performance become asymptotic (or vice versa). It is possible that the lack of direct correspondence between maximum strength gains and other performance variables is at least partly associated with a lag time (Abernethy and Jurimae 1996; Delecluse 1997; Verkhoshansky 1985). Lag time refers to the period of time in which a specific adaptation manifests itself or the period of time in which the athlete learns how to use the increased strength-power resulting from training; the lag time may extend many months in some cases and may be viewed as a type of aftereffect. It is possible that different devices may produce different lag times or produce qualitatively different aftereffects. It is also possible that lag time may be reduced by careful coaching strategies in which the potential link between strength and technique is carefully explained to the athlete. This may partly be accomplished if similarities between training exercises (i.e., mechanical specificity) and performance exercises are pointed out. Thus, exercises having a high degree of similarity to performance would be expected to have the greatest transfer.

Advantages and Disadvantages Associated With Various Modes of Training

The currently available scientific literature and logical arguments, as well as careful observation, indicate that different training modes can be associated with possible advantages or disadvantages, as discussed next (Nosse and Hunter 1985; Stone and Borden 1997; Stone et al. 1991, 2000b, 2002).

We would argue that for most physical activities, transfer-of-training effect is the most important aspect for consideration when one is developing a training program. The transfer-of-training effect is highly dependent on the concept of mechanical specificity. Thus, we would argue that the development of training protocols containing a high degree of mechanical specificity coupled with appropriate training variation is a major advantage of free weights. Use of free weights allows proprioceptive and kinesthetic feedback to occur in a manner more similar to that occurring in most athletic and daily movements. Therefore, free weights can be used to produce patterns of intra- and (especially) intermuscular activation (as a result of exercise selection) that can be more similar to the movement characteristics involved in performing a specific task, raising the potential for a superior transfer-of-training effect. Superior transfer is possible because, with free weights, movement can take place in all three planes and is not guided or otherwise restricted by the device. Machines can limit movement or exercise selection in various ways, such as the following (Stone, Plisk, and Collins 2002).

- Usually machines are limited to only one or two exercises; thus often many machines are necessary for a complete training session. The use of free weights can allow many different exercises to be performed with minimum equipment.

- Machines typically allow relatively little mechanical exercise variation (i.e., changes in hand or foot spacing); free weights allow unlimited variation.

- Most machines typically permit movement to occur only in a single plane. On the other hand, free weights require balance and therefore permit exercise to occur in multiple planes, as would usually occur in athletic and ergonomic tasks.

- Some machines (variable-resistance and semi-isokinetic devices) restrict normal acceleration and velocity patterns, which in turn can alter normal proprioceptive and kinesthetic feedback. For example, the aim in many variable-resistance machines is to match human strength curves with the resistance curve that results from the design of the machine. However, due both to human mechanical differences (e.g., moment arms, limb length, different muscle insertion points, etc.) and to limitations in machine design, matching individual strength curves to an exact resistance curve has not been accomplished by machine manufacturers.

From a very practical standpoint we would argue that a primary reason for the use of multijoint exercises such as jumps, presses, weightlifting movements, and their derivatives is that muscles act—and therefore must be targeted—as functional task groups rather than in isolation. For most sports, and perhaps for most daily tasks, power output is the most important characteristic for development. It can be further argued that for any resistance exercise, the greater the effort (i.e., force, power, rate of force development), the greater the subsequent training effect on neuromuscular activation and force, impulse, and power output development. Furthermore, in many sports the ability to transmit force or power "from the ground up" through the kinetic chain is a primary prerequisite for the development of neuromuscular synergy, stabilization, kinesthesis, and proprioception—in turn carrying over to athletic movements as well as daily tasks.

Compared to typical isolated or small muscle mass exercises, the use of multiple-joint, large muscle mass exercises requires a much more complex neurological organization. This complexity automatically confers a greater degree of neurogenic and skill acquisition; complex movements are more easily and effectively accomplished using free weights (i.e., free weights have greater degrees of freedom) compared to typical machines. Even if these complex exercises are not identically matched with the target movements (e.g., sports performance movements), some transfer is likely to occur (Thorstensson 1977). However, since free weight movements can be designed to more closely approximate sport skills in comparison to those with machines, greater transfer and consequently better motor performance can be expected.

In comparing modes of training, it is important also to consider metabolic factors. A wide variety of large muscle mass exercises can be performed using free weights, and these exercises are much more easily accomplished than with machines. The metabolic consequences of large muscle mass exercises include energy expenditure and organ system responses that potentially influence training adaptations to a greater degree than small muscle mass exercises do. For example, large muscle mass exercises require more energy than small muscle mass exercises (Scala et al. 1987; Stone et al. 1983). Because energy expenditure strongly influences body mass and body composition, large muscle mass exercises are likely to be more effective in causing body composition as well as metabolic adaptations (Stone et al. 1991).

Large muscle mass, multijoint exercises raise the potential for producing a more time-efficient training session. One large muscle mass exercise, such as a squat press or snatch, can exercise as many muscle groups as four to eight small muscle mass exer-

cises. The relative advantages of large muscle mass compared to smaller muscle mass exercises and single-joint exercises are associated with metabolic considerations (Scala et al. 1987, see point number 2), as well as EMG findings (Stuart et al. 1996; Wilk et al. 1996). For example, the power snatch or squat press involves both upper and lower body musculature; in order to activate the same muscle mass, several isolated upper and lower body exercises would be required. Movements that, based on outward appearance, stress some or all of the same muscles, such as squats versus a leg press or leg extension, clearly do not activate the musculature to the same extent (Wilk et al. 1996). Therefore, the use of a few large muscle mass exercises rather than many small or isolated muscle mass exercises can be time efficient.

Time may be a major factor in some training situations. If the rest period between sets is very short (<30 s), the ease of moving a pin into a weight stack can be a time advantage. However, it is an erroneous belief that machines can always save time. In most training situations, especially priority training, the rest time between sets is typically a function of the volume load (amount of work) per set and usually lasts about 2 to 3.5 min. The relatively long rest periods obviate the idea of changing a pin to save time.

Although moving a weight stack pin is usually easier and faster than changing weights on a bar, training progression may be quite difficult, as weight stack machines typically offer loading increments ranging from 7.5 to 12.5 kg (17 to 28 lb). Although some machine manufacturers offer lighter additional weights that can be added to the weight stack, many do not; and these smaller add-on weights are not always available. Additionally, devices that use springs and elastic bands to produce resistance do not typically provide for small loading increments (typically the increments are approximately 5-10 kg [11-22 lb]). With typical free weights, the incremental load changes can be made from approximately 0.5 kg to 50 kg (1-110 lb). This wider range of loading increments can allow more accurate resistance loading and more efficient progression, especially if percentages of maximum are used in planning training programs.

Learning the technique of some multijoint free weight movements may require some additional time and effort. However, we would argue that the cost-to-benefit ratio of learning a new skill can often be worth the effort. Paying attention to appropriate technique in the initial stages of training is a necessity. First, learning good technique will allow an athlete to progress in a given exercise to greater levels than would be possible with poorer technique. Secondly, poor technique increases the injury potential and also decreases the potential for transfer-of-training effect.

Spotters are necessary to catch the weight if a repetition is missed, to provide feedback concerning proper technique, and to provide encouragement. A few free weight exercises (e.g., heavy bench presses and squats), and occasionally some machine exercises, require the use of spotters.

Training isolated muscle groups or single joints can be important in specific aspects of health and bodybuilding programs, initial rehabilitation, or perhaps as a part of injury prevention programs. The isolation of specific small muscle groups and the use of single-joint exercises are quite easy using machines. Under some specific conditions, machines may isolate small muscle masses or stress specific parts of small muscle masses more efficiently or more easily than with free weights.

Space for training equipment is usually not a major limitation in most public gyms, nor is it typically a problem for dedicated gyms such as the sport weight rooms at major American universities and some national sport institutes (e.g., Australian Institute of Sport, Canberra). However, space can be a problem in some cases. For example, storage and training space in many private homes is limited. In the military, space is often at a premium, especially aboard boats and ships. Transportation and storage of equipment often dictate the type of equipment that can be used. In many cases machines, especially those using springs and elastic bands, can be advantageous as they take up less training and storage space.

The expense of a device is often a major determining factor in the selection of training equipment. Machines, particularly semi-isokinetic devices, are usually more expensive than free weights. In considering the cost of multistation machines and the total cost of purchasing several single-exercise machines, one should remember that free weight equipment can be used to train the same number of people for considerably less money. In a typical training facility, free weight equipment can also allow more people to be trained at the same time for the same (or less) monetary outlay and with the same space requirements.

Resistance training exercises, particularly movements with a ballistic component such as jumps and weightlifting movements, have been criticized as producing excessive injuries (Brzycki 1994). However, there is little objective evidence substantiating this claim (Byrd et al. 2003; Hamill 1994; Surakka et al. 2003). Reviews and studies of injury type and injury rates associated with weight training and weightlifting indicate the following:

- Rates of injury resulting from weight training and weightlifting are not excessive, and the incidence of injury is typically less than those associated with sports such as American football, basketball, gymnastics, soccer, or rugby (Hamill 1994; Stone et al. 1994; Zaricznyj et al. 1980).

- There is no evidence that the severity of injury or incidence of traumatic injury is excessive (Hamill 1994; Stone et al. 1994), even among previously untrained middle-aged men and women (Surakka et al. 2003).

Inappropriate and poorly designed training programs can increase the potential for injury. As with adults, resistance training programs for children and adolescents that follow appropriate guidelines have a low risk of injury (Faigenbaum et al. 1996). Indeed, supervised weightlifting programs have been shown to have an even lower rate of injury than other forms of resistive training (Byrd et al. 2003; Hamill 1994). This low injury rate is related to well-supervised programs constructed and implemented by a knowledgeable coach (Byrd et al. 2003; Faigenbaum et al. 1996).

Although resistance training is a relatively safe method and typically both the rate of injuries and the number of severe injuries are low (Hamill 1994; Stone et al. 1994), it is commonly believed that machines are safer than free weights. However, there is very little evidence to support this belief (Requa, DeAvilla, and Garrick 1993), particularly in supervised settings (Hamill 1994). The authors have a combined experience in the weight room and with resistance training of well over 60 years. During this experience we have observed no more injuries among free weight users than among those using machines.

While resistance training is safe and effective, supervision is a necessity. Supervisors must have knowledge of training room safety procedures, knowledge of technique for a variety of exercises, and a good knowledge of training principles and theory.

Free Weight Training With Nonathletic Populations

While this textbook primarily concerns training-induced strength-power adaptations for competitive athletes, coaches (and other fitness specialists) may be called on to supervise, advise, or assist with the training of recreational athletes or nonathletic groups. As a result, it is logical to reach some reasonable level of knowledge concerning the potential use of various modes of resistance training for these groups (Stone et al. 2002).

There is little doubt that resistance training can be of benefit for recreational athletes and for performing daily living tasks. This chapter has presented arguments for the primary use of free weights among athletes; the same arguments likely hold true for nonathletic populations. A commonly held assumption is that specific nonathletic populations, particularly groups comprising elderly persons or those with certain degenerative disease states, such as arthritis, should use machines as their primary mode of resistance training. Indeed, the belief holds that most individuals within these groups cannot use free weights due to physical or psychological limitations. This belief or assumption may be based on real or perceived limitations within these populations. Examples of such limitations include (1) the inability to undergo weight-bearing movements (either whole body or specific segments) as a result of pain, weakness, and balance problems; (2) psychological factors, as reflected in the idea that free weights can be perceived as "intimidating"; and (3) the requirement for more "technique training" and supervision with free weights (Stone et al. 2002).

We argue, however, that this assumption has not been adequately tested. In fact, evidence indicates that using free weights can be a safe and effective method of enhancing performance in nonathletic populations, including the elderly, in whom the frequency and severity of degenerative diseases would be increasing. For example, among previously sedentary men ranging in age from approximately 30 to 60 years, training programs that used primarily free weights have resulted in a number of beneficial alterations, including increased maximum strength and power, body composition changes, and beneficial alterations in blood lipids (Blessing et al. 1987; Johnson et al. 1982, 1983). Among the very elderly, Brill and colleagues (1998) successfully used a free weight program with a group 73 to 91 years of age to promote beneficial adaptations in several performance measures that affect daily living (such as balance and stair climbing). No adverse effects were noted in these investigations.

The important aspect to consider is "primary" exercises. Training exercises should be primarily carried out with free weights for the same reasons that athletic populations should use them. There is no reason to believe that the superior transfer-of-training effect that can be realized with free weights would not be effective in improving daily tasks such as lifting, carrying, and shoveling. In this context it should be noted that "free weights" do not necessarily have to take the traditional form of barbells and dumbbells; rather weighted vests and limb weights can be used to advantage among some groups, such as people who are frail or elderly. With use of this form of free weights, daily activities can be directly overloaded through augmented body or limb mass movements. For example, rising from a chair or stair climbing can be trained using a weighted vest. This type of free weight training may be less intimidating for some populations than traditional barbells and dumbbells (Stone et al. 2002).

While some machine exercises may be advantageous, most exercises should be performed with free weights for all populations. Exceptions are not usually population but rather situation related, for example, when space is at a premium (e.g., submarine crews have used elastic bands, which take up less space than either free weights or most machines). Indeed, the likelihood that someone will not be able to perform a particular exercise may be more a function of individual physical and psychological characteristics, which may be coupled with specific disease states or injuries, than of characteristics of a population. Competent strength training personnel can easily recognize these problems and make program adaptations accordingly to fit the individual. In this context, the authors have a background not only of training competitive athletes, but also of working with or supervising strength training programs that have included recreational athletes, athletes with disabilities, and middle-aged and elderly groups. Although some individuals have problems that would preclude the use of certain free weight exercises, it is our opinion that most people can safely and effectively take part in training programs based primarily on the use of free weights.

CHAPTER SUMMARY

It is obvious that a great deal of additional research is necessary to establish the exact effects of different modes of training on sport (and ergonomic) performance. However, current information and empirical evidence indicate that for most activities, training with complex, multijoint exercises using free weights can produce superior results compared to training with machines. There are a number of reasons why free weights should be used as the primary mode of resistance training; a major factor is mechanical specificity. Considering the evidence that specificity of exercise and training results in a greater transfer-of-training effect, free weights should produce a more effective training transfer. Future research should attempt to obviate several methodological problems associated with past comparison studies, particularly those associated with the trained state and length of study.

Given the information presented in this chapter, we would argue that free weights should make up the majority of resistance exercises composing a resistance training program. These exercises, particularly multijoint exercises, should emphasize mechanical specificity. Machines can be used as an adjunct to primary training, and in sport can be used to a greater or lesser extent during various phases of the training period (preparation, precompetition, competition) or if there is a need to isolate specific muscle groups.

CHAPTER 13

The Concept of Periodization

The intent of planning a training program is to enhance performance. From a physiological perspective, appropriate training increases the synthesis of specific proteins, eventually resulting in tissue remodeling, improved function, and improved sport skill and performance (figure 13.1). Therefore, whether the coach or athlete is aware of it or not, the aim of a training program is to increase protein synthesis in accordance with the specific demands of the training stimulus. Exactly how to best plan training to enhance protein synthesis and eventually performance is not always clear.

Currently, the concept of planning for sport training is largely based on practical knowledge and careful observation. Although there are some controlled studies, scientific evidence supporting sport planning concepts is scarce. The purpose of this discussion is to integrate scientific and practical knowledge in an effort to characterize sport

planning in a logical manner. Much of this discussion centers on concepts and ideas presented in "Periodization Strategies" (Plisk and Stone 2003) and the two-part paper "Periodization: Effects of Manipulating Volume and Intensity" (Stone et al. 1999a, 1999b).

Most coaches and athletes use many of the principles described in chapter 1, "Introduction: Definitions, Objectives, Tasks, and Principles of Training." Coaches and athletes attempt to manipulate variation in exercise selection, training volume, and intensity in an effort to enhance performance and decrease the chance of maladaptation. Often the use of these principles has been intuitive. However, in an effort to optimize the manipulation of volume, intensity, and exercise selection, many, perhaps most, coaches and practitioners have embraced periodization theory over the last 20 years.

Despite the apparent popularity of periodization, some coaches and athletes still seem to struggle

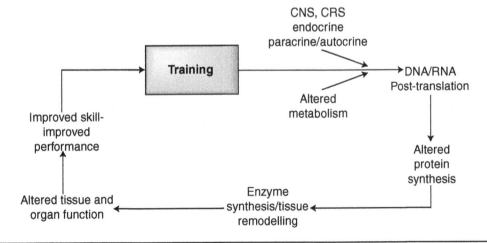

Figure 13.1 The intent of training. Appropriate training programs lead to enhanced protein synthesis, eventually resulting in altered tissue remodeling, improved function, and improved skill and sport performance.

with the concept. Indeed, the concept often seems disconnected from other knowledge and experiences. Different interpretations of the periodization concept are now commonly applied in practice and discussed in publications or meetings. The term periodization appears to have originated in Eastern Europe and is perceived by many Westerners as a foreign idea (Graham 2002; Pedemonte 1986a, 1986b; Siff 2000). Furthermore, in order to understand the concept of periodization, one must also understand a good deal of scientific theory and jargon. This has made some straightforward issues appear complicated and has alienated its share of coaches or athletes (Stone, Sands, and Stone 2004). The intent of this discussion is to

- explain the underlying mechanisms that form the basis for the concept of periodization,

- present periodized models of training based on the principle of variation, and

- present some examples of applied strategies.

As Plisk and Stone (2003) point out, there are definite gaps in our current knowledge. The gaps exist because periodization theory is based largely on hypothesis-generating studies, empirical evidence, related research (e.g., on overtraining), and a few mesocycle-length variation studies, most of which deal exclusively with resistance training. Furthermore, most of these studies involved experimental periods no longer than 5 to 16 weeks and often used subjects with limited training experience. To date, no actual multiple-mesocycle or integrated research studies (e.g., on combined strength-power and speed-endurance training) on advanced or elite athletes have been published in English. Neverthe-

less, the currently available evidence supports two conclusions (Stone et al. 1999a). First, periodization appears to be a superior approach to training, including strength-power training, even over a short term, especially in previously trained subjects. Second, one can achieve optimal results by manipulating training variables in appropriate sequence(s) and combination(s) rather than simply performing a given amount of work or reaching a given intensity. Our objective in this chapter is to discuss both the theoretical and practical issues involved in applying these conclusions, especially as these conclusions relate to strength-power training.

Recovery-Adaptation

Recovery deals with the process of getting back what was lost. However, in a sport context, this implies that (e.g., postexercise) the athlete merely returns to his or her previous state before the next training session. For the coach and athlete this is not very satisfying. Adaptation is the process of long-term adjustment to a specific stimulus or group of stimuli. A positive adjustment (adaptation) means that performance is enhanced; a negative adjustment would produce poorer results. Figure 13.2 represents the basic idea of metabolism. Metabolism is essentially made up of two types of reactions: *exergonic* (energy releasing) and *endergonic* (energy requiring). Exergonic reactions, which are catabolic, include the breakdown of protein, carbohydrates, and fats for energy supply. Endergonic reactions include anabolic reactions such as protein synthesis and muscle contraction. Indirectly, part of the energy released during an exergonic reaction can be used to drive the endergonic reactions. Conceptually, metabolism can be viewed as a seesaw. During exercise (and illness), the exergonic side prevails (i.e., an increase in catabolism); during recovery from exercise, the endergonic side increases in magnitude and anabolic effects can prevail, leading to adaptation to the exercise stimulus. Thus, during recovery, adaptations can be promoted. Therefore, the coach and athlete should be concerned with recovery-adaptation.

The coach and athlete have two avenues available to enhance recovery-adaptation:

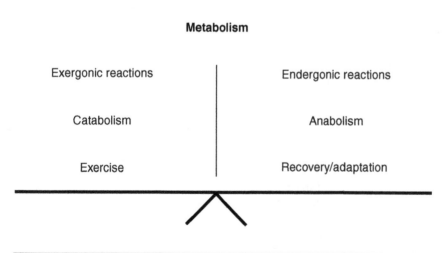

Figure 13.2 Metabolism: the basis of recovery-adaptation.

(1) planning the training program in a manner that promotes recovery-adaptation and (2) using means outside the training program to promote recovery-adaptation (see chapter 7, "Ergogenic Aids").

Observation of the training process (Edington and Edgerton 1976; Harre 1982) and some data (Fry et al. 2000b) indicate the following (figure 13.3):

- The average intensity of the training program is inversely related to the time a performance peak can be held.

- The average intensity of the training program is inversely related to the height of the performance peak.

Observational evidence also suggests that a true peak can be sustained only for very short periods (two to three weeks). This indicates that during a specific training program, there is only a rather narrow window of opportunity during which an athlete can perform at his or her highest level. This makes appropriate planning crucial, especially for sports with a climax to their season such as Olympic sports.

Three possible underlying mechanisms may explain the observations characterized in figure 13.3. These mechanisms are (1) Selye's general adaptation syndrome (GAS); (2) stimulus-fatigue-recovery-adaptation theory (SFRA), and (3) the fitness-fatigue theory (Fit-Fat).

General Adaptation Syndrome

Around 1928, Hans Selye began developing the concept of the general adaptation syndrome (GAS). It is generally believed that many of the original ideas concerning periodization of training stem from the concept of GAS (Zatsiorsky 1995). This concept describes an organism's changing ability to adapt to stress throughout its lifetime. Hans Selye characterized a stressor as any physical or emotional factor that produces a *stress response* and proposed that all stressors result in similar physiological responses (Selye 1956). While it is currently recognized that this concept does not explain all responses to stress, it can serve as a model in efforts to understand physiological responses to exercise and adaptation to training (Garhammer 1979).

The GAS implies that an athlete is subject to three distinct phases during a training period (figure 13.4). As with the SRFA and Fit-Fat, the GAS can be applied to a single exercise stimulus or multiple stimuli over several weeks or months. The *alarm phase* represents the initial aspect of training in which the training stimulus is recognized. During the alarm phase, there can be a negative response resulting in diminished performance because of soreness, stiffness, and fatigue. The alarm phase sets in motion adaptive mechanisms, giving rise to the *resistance phase*. During the resistance phase, positive adaptations can occur, returning the organism

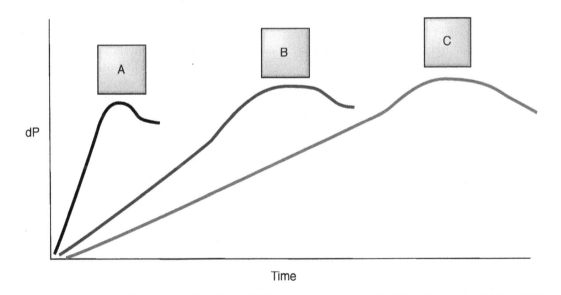

Figure 13.3 Theoretical rates of performance adaptation. Observational differences in training programs (A, B, C) based on average intensity. Average intensity increases from C to B to A. Note that (1) the height of the peak is inversely related to the average intensity and (2) the higher the intensity, the earlier the peak.

Based on D. Harre, 1982, *Principles of sports training* (Berlin, Germany Democratic Republic: Sportverlag), 73-94; and D.E. Edington and V.R. Edgerton, 1976, *The biology of physical activity* (Boston, MA: Houghton Mifflin).

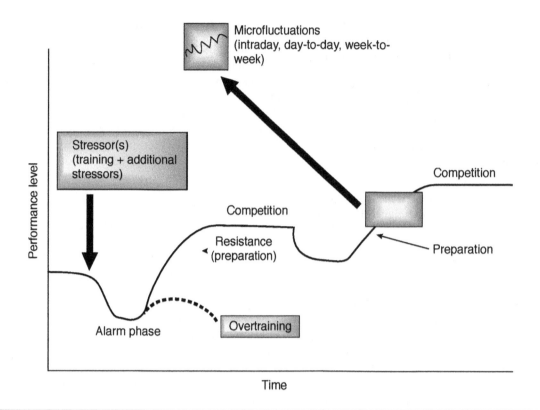

Figure 13.4 Factors (stressors) affecting performance. General adaptation syndrome, modified to describe potential training adaptations.

to baseline (i.e., recovery) and often to a higher state (i.e., supercompensation). One of the important and often overlooked features of GAS is that performance is viewed as a multifactorial problem in which performance alterations are subject to accumulative stress (i.e., stressors are additive). The various factors or stressors affecting recovery-adaptation and therefore performance are shown in figure 13.5. If the accumulation of stressors is too great, then the exhaustion stage (overtraining) can occur. The GAS lays the foundation for variation in training in suggesting that (1) the additive effect of multiple alarm-resistance phases may push the athlete's performance to higher levels and (2) periodically reducing the training volume or intensity may reduce the potential for reaching the exhaustion stage (overtraining).

Stimulus-Fatigue-Recovery-Adaptation (SFRA)

Figure 13.6 characterizes the basis of SFRA (Kipke 1985; Rowbottom 2000; Verkhoshansky 1979, 1981, 1988). The application of a stimulus activates

mechanisms leading to enhanced protein synthesis (Rowbottom 2000) but also creates fatigue. Fatigue accumulates in proportion to the stimulus strength and duration. Postexercise rest allows fatigue to dissipate and stimulates recovery-adaptation. The adaptation can be viewed as an effect of overcompensation or supercompensation. It is important to note that this concept is not limited to a single exercise response but may refer, over a longer period of time, to producing long-term training adaptations. For example, Verkhoshansky (1981, 1988) noted that a concentrated, primarily unidirectional, loading of strength or strength-endurance training for several weeks could result in a diminished power or speed capability among track and field athletes, at least partly as a result of fatigue. After the athlete returns to normal training, an increase in power and speed performance can often be observed, sometimes beyond initial values (i.e., supercompensation). Similar results have been observed among young weightlifters after a planned high-volume overreaching phase (Fry et al. 2000a; Stone and Fry 1998) and among collegiate throwers (Stone et al. 2003).

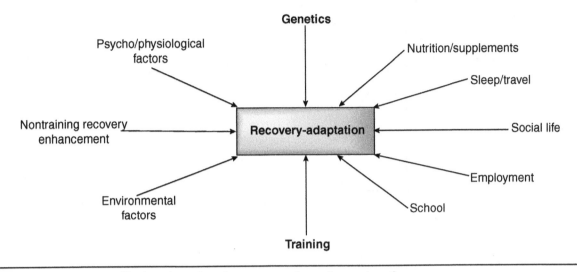

Figure 13.5   Factors affecting alterations in recovery-adaptation and performance.

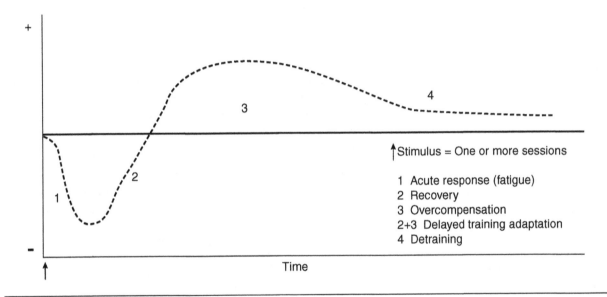

Figure 13.6   The stimulus-fatigue-recovery-adaptation model.

Adapted from Yakolev, 1965, *Exercise and sports science* (Philadelphia, PA: Lippincott, Williams, and Wilkins).

Some evidence indicates that these observations may be linked to alterations in anabolic and catabolic hormones (Fry et al. 2000a; Hakkinen et al. 1989; Stone and Fry 1998), alterations in motor unit subtypes (Ross and Leveritt 2001), or a learning lag-time effect associated with increased strength (Abernethy and Jurimae 1996; Delecluse 1997). Thus, a high-volume strength-endurance phase (concentrated loading) may potentiate gains in power when one moves to lower-volume phases. The observation of SFRA has a foundation and support in the concept of the GAS.

Fitness-Fatigue Paradigm (Fit-Fat)

The current prevailing theory of training adaptation is the *fitness-fatigue* paradigm (figure 13.7) (Bannister 1982; Zatsiorsky 1995). According to this theory, an athlete's preparedness is defined as the summation of two aftereffects of training: fatigue and fitness. In contrast to the supercompensation theory based on a cause-and-effect relationship between these factors, the fitness-fatigue model proposes that fitness and fatigue have opposing effects. This has a simple but profound implication for program

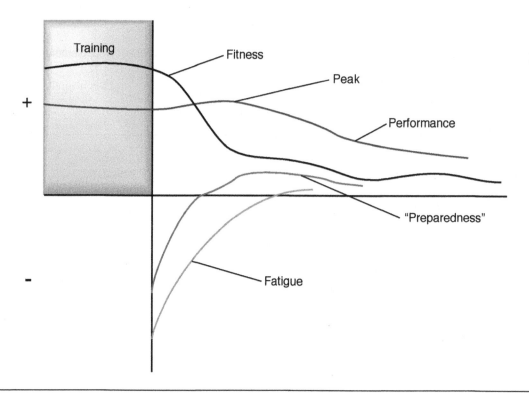

Figure 13.7 The fitness-fatigue relationship. The fitness-fatigue theory of preparedness and performance states that preparedness is determined by the summation of positive (fitness) and negative (fatigue) responses to a stimulus. Note that as training load decreases, fitness also decreases; however, fatigue falls off at a faster rate, allowing preparedness to manifest itself. An athlete's performance is (to a large extent) a reflection of how well he or she is prepared. In contrast to the stimulus-fatigue-recovery-adaptation theory, based on a cause-and-effect relationship between these two processes, this model proposes that immediate training effects are characterized by their opposing actions.

design and implementation: Preparedness can be optimized with strategies that maximize the fitness responses to training stimuli while attempting to minimize fatigue.

Readers should note that the generalized aftereffects of fitness and fatigue likely have specific subcomponents; this results from the observation that sports typically depend on more than one type of fitness component. Thus, there may be differences in the longevity of specific types of fitness or resulting fatigue depending on how they were derived as a product of training. The existence of multiple specific aftereffects likely explains why individual physiological and performance variables respond differently to variations in training (Chui and Barnes 2003; Plisk and Stone 2003). For example, high volume load strength-endurance training can produce a decrease in power but an increase in high-intensity exercise endurance. It is possible that different fitness-fatigue aftereffects exist for different training characteristics such as high-intensity exercise endurance, maximum absolute strength, or power. Thus, emphasizing one characteristic over

another may result in a diminishment of the aftereffects for the other nontrained characteristics.

While it is apparent that aftereffects are not completely independent, it is probable that various levels of interdependency of aftereffects occur. For example, heavy strength training can increase explosiveness in novices (Stone, Johnson, and Carter 1979). Although the specific aftereffects are to an extent independent of each other, there is also likely an accumulative or overall summated effect (figure 13.8) as a result of the interplay of the various aftereffects. The idea of summated effects is similar to GAS in that adaptation relates to the summation of multiple stressors. The concept of summated preparedness and performance peaking is a basic tenet of the use of a taper (Mujika and Padilla 2003).

Periodization: Conceptual Applications

Two important ideas are paramount in planning a training program: understanding the nature of

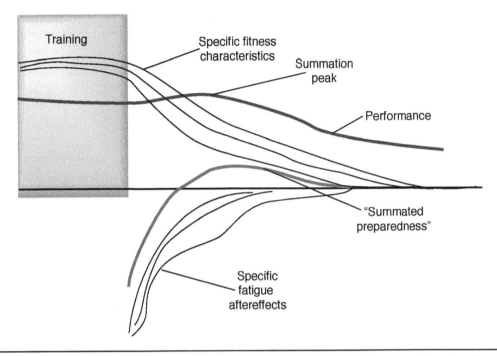

Figure 13.8 Fatigue-fitness relationship and the cumulative impact of different specific aftereffects. Although specific aftereffects can be semi-independent of each other, there is an overall cumulative effect; the summation of aftereffects results in a window of opportunity to produce a peak in preparedness.

variation and the fact that there are different levels of variation, and understanding that creativity is a necessity, as well as knowing how and when to be creative.

Coaching Strategy

Coaching is much like the practice of medicine; medical practice is an art with a scientific underpinning. The greater understanding coaches have of the scientific basis of training, the better choices they can make in carrying out the art of coaching. One of the most important aspects of coaching is how to organize the plan.

The essence of a well-planned program design is to skillfully combine different training modes and methods in order to yield better results than can be achieved through exclusive or long-term disproportionate use of any one of them. Coaches can use a "mixed-methods" strategy that exploits certain physiological responses and achieves specific objectives. The first step in the planning process is to classify one's training tactics into a logical system. Tables 13.1 and 13.2 outline reasonable taxonomies of strength, power, and endurance development methods that can be used as a menu. These methods reflect general agreement in the literature and thus are useful examples.

Periodization: Making Decisions and Assessing Cost

Periodization can be defined as a logical phasic method of manipulating training variables in order to increase the potential for achieving specific performance goals. Periodization is nonlinear training. These are the goals of periodization:

1. Reduction of overtraining potential
2. Peaking at an appropriate time or providing maintenance for sports with a specific season

Goals are met by appropriate multilevel variation of volume, intensity factors, and exercise selection.

Good periodized program design is a type of multilevel diversification. The coach can direct the adaptation process toward specific goals by varying the load (methods) and selection of exercises for training across, as well as between, levels of variation (i.e., macro-, meso-, and microcycles; daily and intratraining sessions). In fact, the available strategies are so numerous that the important issue really becomes one of avoiding haphazard strategies and too much variation.

However, there are several potential trade-offs in planning training for which the cost–benefit

Table 13.1   Continuum of Basic Training Methods for Specialized Development

Maximum Strength and Hypertrophy

- Brief maximal efforts [maximum strength, intra- and intermuscular coordination; rate of force development, especially in novices]*
  - Plyometric relative intensity: 75-100% of 1RM
  - Eccentric relative intensity: 105-120% of 1RM
  - Action speed: slow, as the relative load is heavy
  - Rate of force development: maximum to near maximum
  - Repetition volume: 15-25 reps/session @ 95-100%; 20-40 reps/session @ 90-95%; 35-85 reps/session @ 80-90%; 70-110 reps/session @ 75-80% (≤6 reps/set for low-skill movements; ≤3 reps/set for high-skill movements)
  - Set volume (not including warm-up): 3-5 sets per exercise
  - Session density: full (up to 8 min) recovery between sets
- Repeated submaximal efforts [hypertrophy]
  - Relative intensity: 80-90% of 1RM
  - Action speed: slow, as the relative load is heavy
  - Repetition volume: 5-12 reps/set
  - Set volume (not including warm-up): 5-10 sets per exercise
  - Session density: 1-4 min recovery between sets; 24-48 h between sessions
  - Combination methods: heavy clusters, contrasting sets, eccentric accentuated

Speed-Strength (High Power)

- Submaximal accelerative efforts [power; rate of force development]
  - Relative intensity: 30-85% of 1RM
  - Action speed: maximal and explosive
  - Repetition volume: 1-3 reps/set @ 70-85%; 3-5 reps/set @ 50-70%
  - Set volume (not including warm-up): 3-7 per exercise
  - Session density: 3-8 min recovery between sets; daily sessions
- Reactive-ballistic efforts [stretch–shortening cycle; stiffness regulation]
- Contrast methods [acute aftereffects; potentiation]

Strength-Power-Endurance

- Extensive interval [low-moderate-intensity endurance capacity; recoverability]
  - Relative intensity: 30-65% of 1RM—use lighter loads to emphasize power and heavier loads for strength emphasis
  - Action speed: brisk and continuous
  - Repetition volume: 8-20 reps/set
  - Set volume (not including warm-up): 3-5 per exercise
  - Session density: <5 min recovery between sets
- Intensive interval [high-intensity endurance capacity; recoverability]
  - Relative intensity: 40-60% of 1RM
  - Action speed: explosive
  - Volume: 3-6 sets per exercise; 20-45 s duration per set (rep count is irrelevant)
  - Session density: 1-3 min recovery between sets

*Objectives indicated in brackets.

Adapted from S. Plisk and M.H. Stone, 2003, "Periodization strategies," *Strength and Conditioning* 25: 19-37.

Table 13.2 Continuum of Training Methods for Speed, Agility, and Speed-Endurance Development

Competitive-Trial—Continuous Effort [Special Endurance]*

- Supramaximal training
  - Intensity: greater than competition
  - Duration/distance: less than competition
- Maximal training
  - Intensity: equal to or less than competition
  - Duration/distance: equal to competition
- Submaximal training
  - Intensity: less than competition
  - Duration/distance: greater than competition

Distance-Duration [Submaximal Endurance]

- Continuous training: 70-95% competitive speed and power
- Fartlek training: unstructured changes in intensity, duration, volume, and density
- Variable training: structured changes in intensity, duration, volume, and density

Interval [Speed-Endurance]

- Extensive training
  - Relative intensity: low-medium (60-80% competitive speed/power)
  - Duration/distance: short-medium (e.g., 14-180 s over 100-1000 m running distance for advanced athletes; 17-100 s over 100-400 m running distance for novices)
  - Volume: large (e.g., 8-40 reps for advanced athletes; 5-12 reps for novices)
  - Session density: high; short incomplete relief interval allowing heart rate to recover to 125-130 bpm for advanced athletes or 110-120 bpm for novices (i.e., <1/3 the time needed for complete recovery; e.g., 45-90 s or 60-120 s for advanced or novice athletes, respectively)
- Intensive training
  - Relative intensity: high (80-90% competitive speed/power)
  - Duration/distance: short (e.g., 13-180 s over 100-1000 m running distance for advanced athletes; 14-95 s over 100-400 m running distance for novices)
  - Volume: small (e.g., 4-12 reps for advanced athletes; 4-8 reps for novices)
  - Session density: medium; longer but still incomplete relief interval allowing heart to recover to 110-120 bpm (e.g., 90-180 s for advanced athletes; 120-240 s for novices)—advanced athletes can use "intermittent exercise" (e.g., 10 s maximum effort followed by 15 s of submaximal at 50% effort, performed in sets)

Repetition [Speed and Agility]

  - Relative intensity: very high (90-100% competitive speed/power)
  - Duration/distance: very short/medium (e.g., 2-3 s up to several minutes)
  - Volume: very small (e.g., 3-6 reps)
  - Density: low; long near-complete rest interval allowing heart rate to recover to ≤100 bpm (e.g., 3-45 min)

*Objectives indicated in brackets.

Adapted from S. Plisk and M.H. Stone, 2003, "Periodization strategies," *Strength and Conditioning* 25: 19-37.

must be understood. This section considers how the following paradoxes influence the decisions involved in program design: fitness versus fatigue, intensity versus volume, specificity versus variation, strength versus endurance, and periodization versus programming.

Fitness Versus Fatigue

Because fatigue is a primary aftereffect of training stress (especially with high volume loads), and adaptations are manifested during subsequent unloading periods, fatigue management strategies are integral to a sound program. These can be implemented at different levels (Chui and Barnes 2003; Dick 1997; Fry, Morton, and Keast 1992a, 1992b; Harre 1982; Rowbottom 2000; Siff 2000; Viru 1995; Viru and Viru 2001):

- *Quadrennium:* rest or extended active rest after the Olympics or four years of college athletics

- *Macrocycle:* active rest or transition periods, or both, after competitive periods

- *Mesocycle:* recovery microcycles after over-reaching microcycles, concentrated blocks, or stressful competitions

- *Microcycle:* maintenance or restitution workloads or recovery days; daily training routines distributed into modules separated by recovery breaks; and additional intrasession relief breaks (e.g., rather than using a "repetition maximum" approach in which each set is completed in continuous fashion, it can be advantageous to subdivide assigned workloads into clusters separated by rest pauses; note the consistency of this approach with the *brief maximal efforts, submaximal accelerative efforts,* and *reactive-ballistic efforts* methods described in table 13.1 [Haff et al. 2003; Siff 2000; Zatsiorsky 1995]).

Note that logical program design is only one aspect of a recovery-adaptation plan that should also address nutrition, sleep, and regenerative or therapeutic techniques or both (see chapter 7, "Ergogenic Aids").

Intensity Versus Volume

The idea of a trade-off between *intensity* and *volume* appears to be fundamental, but has important ramifications because the interaction of these variables drives many of the decisions one makes when designing training programs. Periodization involves emphasizing these variables in a fluctuating manner such that adaptation is steered toward specific objectives. However, it is rather meaningless to consider one independently of the other, hence the practical value of work accomplished as an indicator of training stress. In resistance training, *volume load* (repetitions × load) is a reasonable estimate of work and training stress (Stone and O'Bryant 1987; Stone et al. 1998, 1999a, 1999b).

Volume load prescription should be viewed in the context of productive workload ranges. At the lower end is the stimulus threshold required to trigger desired effects; at the upper end is a point of diminishing returns, beyond which further application yields no beneficial, or perhaps even detrimental, effects. The volume load prescription will be altered as an athlete's adaptivity and fitness improve with long-term development.

Among advanced athletes, primary emphasis is generally placed on training quality (i.e., some measure of intensity), which can be expressed in quantitative terms such as impulse or power output during task execution. In practice, such parameters are useful indicators of stimulus intensity and resulting training effect. A central issue regarding programming strategy is the method by which increased intensity is achieved. Variable rather than linear workload progressions tend to yield superior results (Dick 1997; Foster 1998; Fry, Morton, and Keast 1992a, 1992b; Harre 1982; Hartmann and Tünnemann 1989; Matveyev 1972, 1981; Rowbottom 2000; Siff 2000; Stone and O'Bryant 1987; Stone et al. 1998, 1999a, 1999b; Viru 1995; Zatsiorsky 1995). Furthermore, nonlinearity can be accomplished through a variety of strategies.

High work volumes are typically associated with the development of endurance qualities (tables 13.1 and 13.2). But work volume also fulfills several other important functions when logically applied with respect to intensity. In terms of general preparation, extensive volume loads establish a base of work capacity, influence the duration and stability of corresponding training effects, and are an important prerequisite for intensive efforts involved in special and technical preparation.

Two basic strategies are typically associated with extensive work volumes: (1) high-repetition sets with corresponding reductions in workload and (2) increased number of sets, exercises, or both. There are other tactics that should also be considered. For example, volume loads can also be adjusted through periodic manipulation of density variables (e.g., adjusting training session distribution and frequency) in order to achieve specific objectives. A more detailed discussion of this issue is found in the "Applied Strategies" section later in the chapter.

Specificity Versus Variation

Zatsiorsky (1995) suggests that a sound periodization plan is a trade-off between the conflicting demands for training variable fluctuation (according to the principle of *variability*) and stability (to satisfy the demand for *specificity*) (pp. 108-135). Optimal effects can be achieved through systematic variation in training content, workload, or both, whereas monotonous loads or tasks (e.g., entirely activity-specific movements) can predispose an athlete to accommodation or stagnation problems (figure 13.9). This stagnation likely occurs because the nervous system, as a result of mechanical monotony, is no longer challenged to adapt (Stone et al. 1991). This is the rationale for the regular application of novel and seminovel tasks. Figure 13.10 illustrates this type of seminovel task introduction and rein-

troduction. Note that before complete adaptation or accommodation can take place, the task is removed for a period of time and then reintroduced, theoretically producing a greater adaptation. In practice, the challenge is to structure the introduction and removal of specific exercises into appropriate variation periods so that no specific task or stressor is trained to the point of stagnation.

A basic principle of training is that adaptation becomes increasingly specific to the demands imposed on an athlete as his or her preparation level improves. Specificity exists in several areas, including metabolic, biomechanical, and motor control levels, each of which can be a useful criterion for selecting and prioritizing training tasks. In the planning of a training program, the relative emphasis placed on different means and methods should reflect the athlete's developmental status, especially with regard to potential critical or sensitive periods (Dick 1997; Harre 1982; Viru 1995; Viru et al. 1996, 1998, 1999). Preadolescence seems to be the optimal window for

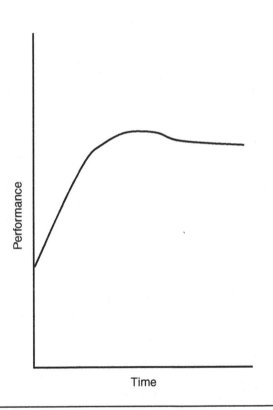

Figure 13.9 Stagnation as the result of a monotonous training routine. The athlete is not overly fatigued; rather, the nervous system is no longer challenged to adapt as a result of the lack of mechanical variation in the program (Stone et al. 1991; Zatsiorsky 1995).

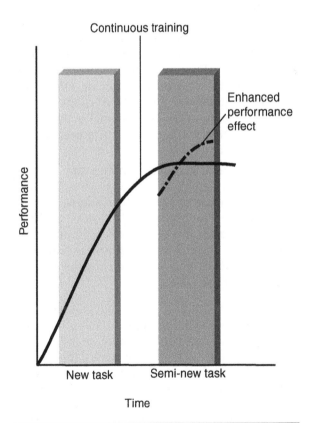

Figure 13.10 Theoretical performance response to exercise deletion-replacement. Introduction and reintroduction of a novel or seminovel task. The task is removed before accommodation takes place and then is reintroduced at a later time, theoretically producing a greater performance adaptation.

enhancing motor control aspects and characteristics, on which motor skills are based (Andren-Sandberg 1998). Although these characteristics are still trainable to an extent during and after adolescence, training should shift toward a greater emphasis on strength-power improvement as the athlete reaches puberty. This issue has intriguing and important implications in all aspects of program planning, but has received much less attention in the West than in other countries, particularly those in Northern and Eastern Europe.

Strength Versus Endurance

Review of the literature indicates that some types of endurance training can hinder strength, power, and particularly speed development when performed concurrently (Kraemer 2000; Leveritt et al. 1999; Siff 2000; Viru 1995). This creates at least two problems:

1. High levels of these qualities must be developed in specific combinations in order to optimize athletic performance. Even explosive-strength sports require that the athlete have special high-intensity endurance qualities in order to achieve the prescribed volume loads in training. Obviously, most transitional or "mixed" sports involve combinations of submaximal activity and repetitive, intense bursts of power output with limited relief allowance.

2. Although advanced athletes can tolerate greater training stress than novices, cumulative fatigue can be problematic when they are developing multiple fitness qualities simultaneously. Unfortunately, compatibility studies dealing with multifitness characteristic development in well-trained or elite athletes are lacking.

The challenge in practice is to integrate strength and endurance training effects (tables 13.1 and 13.2) such that they enhance rather than interfere with one another. In basic applications, this may be achievable with fairly simple training and recovery tactics. However, for athletes with sufficient developmental background, advanced variation strategies are valuable in minimizing cumulative fatigue and compatibility problems.

Periodization Versus Programming

If there is one self-limiting tendency among coaches, it is the focus on numerical or set models rather than on underlying principles and programming strategies in the design of training programs. This may be a remnant of the rep/set counting mentality that was prevalent before periodization became popular in the West. In any case, it creates an interesting problem: A given training stimulus (input) results in a response (output) that is not entirely predictable.

According to Siff (2000, p. 326), "The use of numerical computations as the sole descriptor of loading often overlooks the fact that apparently objective measures like this do not take into account the athlete's *subjective perception of the intensity and overall effects of the loading.*" Siff recommended a combined objective-subjective approach referred to as *cybernetic periodization* in which zones of workload intensity are planned in advance, but tactics can be adjusted as necessary based on technique/technical evaluation by the coach as well as performance feedback from the athlete (e.g., regarding perceived effort and fatigue). Although the athlete's subjective input is a necessity, the approach suggested by Siff (2000) assumes that the athlete's perceptions are always reasonably accurate, an assumption that is not necessarily true.

Siff's (2000) proposal is not meant to dissuade practitioners from carefully calculating a thoughtful training program. Rather, the important point is that intensity and volume load parameters, rep/set schemes, and so on are secondary to training goals and objectives. Furthermore, rather than applying training principles and theory rigidly, intuitive factors or, more importantly, monitored factors can be used to make prudent adjustments during implementation. Indeed, one must be careful of making training adjustments without good reason. This point emphasizes the need for close and appropriate monitoring of training (see chapter 8, "Testing, Measurement, and Evaluation").

Strategic decision making would be unnecessary if all the pieces of the program design puzzle fell together automatically. The art and science of periodization involves resolving some challenging paradoxes as part of a coherent plan.

Basis and Guidelines of Cyclic Program Structure

The cyclic structure of earlier periodization models was often based more on the competitive calendar than on recovery-adaptation processes because information regarding the latter was limited. As our knowledge base has expanded, it has become apparent that there are opportunities to augment and enhance training effects by exploiting certain biological phenomena. For example, with the use of appropriate sequencing or timing strategies, the aftereffect of one training stimulus can modulate the response to another. This is a fundamental objective of contemporary periodization: to systematically converge the cumulative or interactive effects of different means and methods—that is, to set up potentiation in one variable as a result of emphasis on a previous variable. Such strategies are particularly valuable when training time is restricted or an athlete is approaching the limits of his or her developmental potential.

Rate of involution (or decay of various training effects) is a central physiological consideration in cyclic program design (Viru 1995; Viru and Viru 2001; Zatsiorsky 1995). Theoretically, this is a function of the half-life of synthetic reactions or enzymes associated with those reactions during adaptive tissue remodeling. As might be expected, involution time courses vary. For example, variation in involution time potentially results from the half-life of glycolytic enzymes, which is relatively brief (ranging from ~1 1/2 h to a few days), whereas oxidative enzymes turn over less rapidly and myofibrillar proteins have a comparatively long life span. From a practical standpoint, involution is modulated by the length of the preparation period. Generally, the greater the duration of a training program, the more stable its residual training effect (Zatsiorsky 1995). As a result of this stability, fitness qualities acquired during one phase can be maintained with relatively less training of those qualities during the next, so that emphasis can be redirected and cumulative fatigue problems can be minimized. This is the rationale for using sequential training strategies with qualified athletes, as will be discussed in the "Applied Strategies" section.

The consensus arising from the literature (Plisk and Stone 2003; and the authors' observations) is to organize training programs into four-week (plus or minus two weeks) periods, which, as evidenced by the following findings, seem to be an optimal biological window for integrating responses.

• Matveyev (in Kukushkin 1983) cites the existence of natural monthly biocycles as a fundamental basis for constructing brief intense training periods that are approximately one month in duration, each consisting of three to six subcycles of approximately one-week duration, in order to exploit cumulative training effects (pp. 245-259).

• Viru (1995) cites the half-time of training effect involution as the rationale for a 24- to 28-day

cyclic training structure consisting of four to six subcycles, each four to seven days in duration, in order to summate their training effects (pp. 241-299).

• Zatsiorsky (1995) indicates a need to structure training cycles around a four-week (plus or minus two weeks) window in order to superimpose the delayed training effects of distinct targets distributed over that time (pp. 344-421).

Even with use of the most advanced training strategies—for example, the conjugate sequence system discussed in subsequent sections—there is general agreement with this four- to six-week cycle guideline. This period can be structured in at least two different ways: as a mesocycle to be subdivided into multiple microcycles and objectives (for basic and intermediate applications), or as a "block" with essentially one objective arranged as part of a series (for advanced applications).

Many coaches and sport scientists still perceive Matveyev's basic model (1972, 1977), which involves gradual, wavelike increases in volume and intensity over each phase, as the standard approach to periodization (see figure 13.11; also refer to Harre [1982], Kukushkin [1983], and Ozolin [1970, 1972]). From his discussions of microcycle variations and intermediate mesocycles during the competition period, it is evident that Matveyev did not intend for this model to be rigidly or universally applied (Matveyev 1972, 1977, 1981, 1992, 1994). Indeed, there have been varied interpretations throughout the international sport science community. Examples of different periodization schemes designed for specific applications are discussed next.

From the standpoint of manipulating volume and intensity, four basic periodization paradigms can be used:

1. Figure 13.11 represents a very basic traditional model of periodization that is highly applicable to beginners and novices. This type of variation scheme has been used in a variety of sports; this paradigm has potential advantages and disadvantages.

   • Advantages
   – Long-term experience: This basic concept is not new, and many coaches have a good deal of experience with it, with reasonable results.

   – General preparation and special preparation ensure that sport-specific fitness is enhanced.

   – The potential for phase potentiation is high (see "Applied Strategies" section).

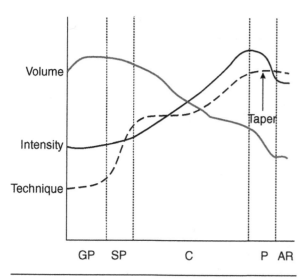

Figure 13.11 Generalized periodization model of strength-power training (basic application). The main premise is a wavelike shift from high-volume, low-intensity training to low-volume, high-intensity training over the mesocycle or macrocycle. GP = general preparation; SP = special preparation (first transition), during which emphasis shifts from extensive to intensive methods and technique training; C = competition; P = peaking; AR = active rest (second transition), consisting of unstructured or recreational activities in which both intensity and volume are reduced and restitution is the main objective.

- Disadvantages
  - A long competition phase can reduce the potential for maintaining sport-specific fitness.
  - It is difficult to hold peaks for more than three weeks, so this model will not work well for team sports or if there are many important competitions close together.

2. Figure 13.12 represents a periodized approach in which intensity is maintained at relatively high levels (with some variation) and volume is manipulated around it. This type of variation scheme has been used in sports such as gymnastics, and this paradigm has the following potential advantage and disadvantages.
   - Advantage
     - Although not necessarily peaked, performance can theoretically be maintained

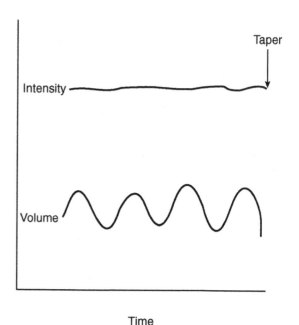

Time

Figure 13.12 Intensity-predominant plan. Intensity remains high throughout the macrocycle, and volume fluctuates markedly.

at fairly high levels because intensity remains high, which is good when competitions are close together, provided that some recovery (taper) occurs.

- Disadvantages
  - Sport-specific fitness may suffer.
  - One is never really sure if the highest level of sport performance has been achieved.
  - The potential for phase potentiation is low.
  - The potential for intensity-induced overtraining is high.

3. Figure 13.13 represents a periodized approach in which volume is maintained at relatively high levels (with some variation) and intensity is manipulated around it. This type of variation scheme has been used in sports such as distance running; the following are the potential advantage and disadvantages.
   - Advantage
     - High levels of sport-specific fitness can be maintained over long periods (provided some recovery variation is built in).
   - Disadvantages
     - The potential for volume-induced overtraining is high.

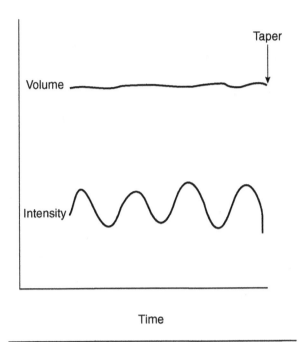

Figure 13.13 Volume-predominant plan. Volume remains high throughout the macrocycle, and intensity fluctuates markedly.

- The potential for phase potentiation is low.

4. A final approach is to combine the three preceding basic types.

Other specialized approaches are also possible, for example, abrupt steplike alterations in workload over weekly or monthly cycles (Ermakov and Atanosov 1975; Ermakov, Abramyan, and Kim 1980; Vorobyev 1978).

Balanced distribution of technical skill and strength workloads during preparation as well as competition phases (Bondarchuk 1994), or emphasizing technique during the preparatory period and strength during the competitive period (Komarova 1984; Topchiyan, Kadachkova, and Komarova 1984) can also be successful methods, provided they are applied appropriately. Generally balanced distributions of technical and strength workloads may not be as successful as other strategies due to accumulative fatigue from strength work interfering with technique training.

An interesting strategy for elite athletes that is addressed in more detail in the "Applied Strategies" section is the "conjugate sequence" system, in which concentrated workloads with one primary emphasis are arranged in a series of blocks (Verkhoshansky 1986, 1988; Werchoshanski 1978; also refer to Hartmann and Tünnemann 1989; Satori and

Tschiene 1988; Siff 2000; Tschiene 1990, 1992, 1995, 1997a, 1997b; Viru 1995; Zatsiorsky 1995). This approach emphasizes the potential role of delayed training effects in the adaptation process and rejects the idea that the development of different abilities should be simultaneously emphasized in training.

As is the case in any sport, there are likely as many interpretations of training strategy as there are practitioners applying them. It is interesting and educational to compare training philosophies of coaches throughout the former Eastern Bloc. Using the sport of weightlifting as an example, the training means and methods advocated by coaches Medvedev (Russia) and Abadzhiev (Bulgaria) involved very different approaches to training variable variation (Furnadzhiev and Abadzhiev 1982; Jones 1991; Medvedev et al. 1981; Medvedyev 1986; Zatsiorsky 1992, 1995). Although it is not completely clear, the Bulgarians *apparently* used much less variation, although athletes from the two countries achieved similar competitive success. Arguably the latter training method may have been more effective because Bulgaria's athlete population was smaller. Aján and Baroga (1988) offer a combined Hungarian-Romanian perspective that is similar in some ways to Abadzhiev's ideas. However, the exact nature of the training programs is partly speculation, as very little direct observation over a long term was made of these programs by Westerners. Additionally, the degree to which the success of these approaches has depended on ergogenic aids or drug use is unknown. Furthermore, it is possible that optimal training effects may be achieved by blending methods (tables 13.1 and 13.2). This includes combining methods that are sport or activity specific with some that are not, such that the response or adaptation to one amplifies the activity.

Applied Strategies

The following is a brief discussion of some basic, intermediate, and advanced approaches to periodization. This discussion is intended to illustrate how strategic thinking can be applied to training program design, but is not an exhaustive summary of tactics. Moreover, since content variations (e.g., technique variants, assistance movements) are inherent in skill-based programs, focus is directed toward workload and recovery issues. Several other points should also be kept in mind (Plisk and Stone 2003), as outlined next.

Many concepts proposed in this section originated in the former Eastern Bloc and are based on careful observation and empiricism more than on controlled trials. While potentially this information can be useful to coaches in the West, it is important to recognize and understand the societal and cultural differences in research, approach to ergogenic aid use, and training practices.

The "basic–intermediate–advanced" scheme discussed here is a continuum with no discrete divisions and is not intended as a rating system. All athletes should begin at a basic level and then progress through an intermediate developmental process; skipping or reducing the basic and intermediate stages in the development reduces the athletes' potential to achieve mastery in sport. It is a serious mistake to perceive basic and intermediate approaches as inferior, insignificant, or unnecessary and to move into advanced programming too early in an athlete's long-term preparation.

Stressors should be applied with regard to integration rather than isolation of responses to stimuli. While our understanding of training effect interaction and subsequent aftereffects may be in its infancy, there are important opportunities to enhance sport-specific fitness and manage fatigue, thereby optimizing an athlete's overall preparation by exploiting specific training characteristics.

A periodized plan should reflect an increasing level of variation and micromanagement as the athlete's development progresses. This does not necessarily mean that all decisions should be deferred to the coach, but instead that more sophisticated variation should be applied on multiple fronts—that is, training methods and means, as well as within and between cycles.

Basic Strategy

Generally, basic periodization strategy (figure 13.11) can be characterized by relatively limited variation in training methods and means. As mentioned earlier, a case can be made for this type of strategy as the most valuable of all because of its broad applicability. Obviously, there are many more beginning and novice athletes, in the early stages of development (for whom advanced tactics would be inappropriate), than there are elite athletes in later stages of development. As is the case with other stressors, the initial adaptive responses tend to be relatively general, and relatively simple training and recovery strategies can be very effective in these situations. However, with chronic application, adaptation becomes increasingly specific, difficult to achieve, and resistant to low-level or monotonous stimuli.

The traditional periodization model is a simple approach characterized by gradual, wavelike increases in workload (figure 13.11) (Matveyev 1972, 1977). Note that this diagram was originally intended to illustrate a basic concept, but sometimes has been simplistically and erroneously interpreted as a linear periodization model (Baker, Wilson, and Carlyon 1994; Bradley-Popovich and Haff 2001; Wathen, Baechle, and Earle 2000). The term *linear periodization* has been used to describe training cycles involving relatively gradual, progressive increases in intensity or workload. It was originally adopted by Baker and colleagues (1994) from Charles Poliquin's discussion of problems with linear intensification strategies (Poliquin 1988). Part of the misunderstanding surrounding this term likely stems from the erroneous use of repetitions to establish training volume, or the amount of work performed during a specific phase of the training process. Repetitions, while related to volume, are not the best estimate of how much work is performed or of the intensity of training (Stone et al. 1999a, 1999b). For further discussion, the reader should refer to the editorial letters by Stone and O'Bryant (1995) and Stone and Wathen (2001).

Furthermore, *linear periodization* is a contradiction in terms because, by definition, periodization implies nonlinear variation in training parameters. For example, figure 13.11 could represent a mesocycle that would produce an undulating long-term pattern if repeated over a macrocycle. Furthermore, these intensity and volume progressions typically fluctuate at the microcyclic level (Stone et al. 1999a, 1999b). Therefore, it would be more appropriate to refer to periodization models as traditional or nontraditional, as the terms *linear* and *nonlinear* are misleading.

A potential problem exists with steplike versions of this model in which relatively flat workloads are prescribed over a period of several weeks (e.g., three- to four-week *strength-endurance* phase, three- to four-week *maximum strength* phase, three- to four-week *speed-strength* phase). The intent of this approach is to increase the intensity of the workloads used at each step before proceeding to the next. But consecutive weeks spent within narrow workload ranges can effectively amount to one week of novel stimulus followed by up to three weeks of monotony, which may increase the likelihood of accommodation and stagnation problems. However, this strategy is appropriate and can be quite viable for beginner or novice athletes who are learning new movement techniques or using unaccustomed high volumes and intensities. For more advanced athletes, it is possible to alleviate the shortcomings of the model by using progressions in which volume loads are varied within reasonable ranges (e.g., a system that alternates between maximal efforts made with heavy and light loads) (Stone et al. 1999a, 1999b; table 13.1).

Intermediate Strategy

Intermediate periodization strategies can be characterized by increasing levels of variation within, as well as between, respective cycles. Whereas a beginner's program may consist of a simple progression on a macrocycle basis, tactical decisions are now directed more toward meso- and microcycle variables (e.g., the degree of workload contrast between monthly phases, weeks, or individual training sessions as well as within sessions, or some combination of these). Emphasis on intensive methods can be increased (e.g., *brief maximal efforts, reactive-ballistic efforts;* table 13.1), and a broader range of means can be applied as the athlete's repertoire of movement skills and abilities grows. While this is limited to some extent by practical considerations such as the coach-to-athlete ratio and time available for instruction and supervision, it can certainly be beneficial to expand training content to include additional exercises or variants (or both) up to a point and depending on the demands of the sport. In any case, the need for creative training and recovery tactics increases as athletes progress beyond the developmental stage.

Based on the training effect summation phenomenon discussed earlier, the concept of *summated microcycles* can be valuable as an intermediate strategy (figure 13.14, *a & b*). Summated microcycles are typically characterized by a series of four-week blocks with an extensive-to-intensive workload progression and a brief restitution period. This concept allows specific complementary stimuli to be introduced and reintroduced in a regular cyclic fashion such that their effects do not decay significantly. The method of workload distribution is the key difference from the basic approach described earlier. Several different applications are possible with this approach. For example, each summated microcycle (four weeks) rather than an entire mesocycle can be allocated for strength-endurance, maximum strength, and speed-strength peaking methods, respectively (table 13.3). This pattern of loading (figure 13.14a), in which three weeks of increasing volume, intensity, or both are followed

by an unloading week and the progression is then repeated at higher intensities, is typically used to enhance maximum strength. Coaches and athletes should be careful when using this type of 3:1 approach because the greatest workloads occur in week 3, by which time cumulative fatigue can hinder speed-strength expression and adaptation—thus the need for unloading week 4 to reduce fatigue, reduce the overtraining potential, and promote adaptation. A different pattern of loading can be used to promote power gains (figure 13.14b). In this paradigm, the largest volume of training (usually a strength emphasis) occurs during the first week; the volume load during this first week can be viewed as a planned overreaching phase. The first week (as a result of accumulated fatigue) decreases power performance; however, during subsequent weeks, a return to normal levels of power training coupled with an unload week (week 4) can increase power performance (see "Advanced Strategies" section).

The use of summated microcycles potentially offers dual benefits (Fry, Morton, and Keast 1992a; Matveyev 1977; Rowbottom 2000). (1) As an advanced form of intramesocycle variation, it increases the probability of converging training effects while minimizing the likelihood of overstress or accommodation or involution problems. (2) This approach also adds an aspect of intermesocycle contrast that may stimulate adaptation over the long term. Other strategies (e.g., planned overreaching) may be more effective for advanced athletes whose training goals are to maximize strength, power, and speed, as discussed in the next section.

Summated microcycles can be complemented with intramicrocycle variation tactics. For example, the progression just described can be enhanced simply and efficiently by using a "heavy/light day" system in which the emphasis alternates between *maximum strength* and *speed-strength* methods, respectively (table 13.1). Both animal (Bruin et al. 1994) and human (Foster 1998) data indicate that regular inclusion of submaximal workload days within a microcycle allows specific training loads to be accomplished with a much greater potential for positive adaptations and results in fewer problems. Likewise, *competitive-trial, interval,* and *repetition* methods can be distributed among speed and speed-endurance sessions or modules in the field or on the track (table 13.2). More research is needed to expand our understanding of this issue.

Intrasession variation is also useful and can be applied with both intermediate and advanced athletes. Many of these intrasession variation schemes are based on acute aftereffect phenomena such as postactivation potentiation (Sale 2002) and include tactics like combination or hybrid exercises (e.g., clean and front squat; snatch and overhead squat), complex training (e.g., alternating between *maximum strength* and *speed-strength* methods; table 13.1), and wave loading (e.g., alternating between *brief maximum* or *near-maximum efforts* and *submaximal accelerative efforts;* table 13.1). The underlying strategy is to use one type of stimulus to enhance acute power output or rate of force development (or both) in another. Advanced athletes can strategically use movements that are not necessarily mechanically specific to their sport to augment the effects of more specialized tasks.

The following examples are methods of training that can be applied to intermediate and especially advanced athletes. Although these examples involve resistance training, the basic concepts are useful for a variety of training activities.

Exercise Deletion and Re-Presentation

As previously discussed in the section "Specificity Versus Variation," continually performing an exercise in the same manner for long periods of time can lead to staleness and loss of performance even though fatigue or overtraining is not a problem (Stone et al. 1991). Although decreased motivation is probably part of the reason for the performance

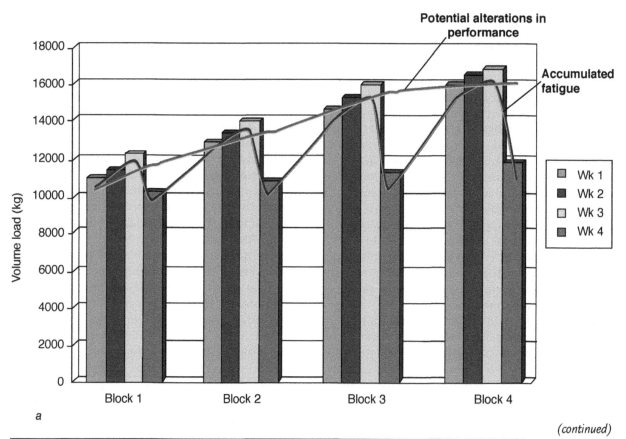

a

(continued)

Figure 13.14 *(a)* Mesocycles consisting of three to four blocks of summated microcycles at progressively higher workloads. Blocks are continuous over time, and each block consists of three weeks of increasing workload followed by a recovery-unloading week (intermediate application). Volume loads are highest in week 3, by which time cumulative fatigue may hinder certain adaptations (e.g., explosiveness and power), hence the need for unloading week 4 to reduce overtraining potential and promote adaptation. The same basic pattern can be used in each cycle to repeatedly introduce strength stimuli at progressively higher workloads. *(b)* Mesocycles consisting of three- to four-week blocks of summated microcycles at progressively higher workloads. Each block consists of one week of high workload followed by two weeks of "normal" training, then an unload week (intermediate and advanced application). Again, blocks are continuous over time. Volume loads (usually dedicated to strength) are very high in week 1 (planned overreaching); lowering the volume load in weeks 2 to 4 can promote power adaptations. The same basic pattern can be used in each cycle to repeatedly introduce power stimuli at progressively higher workloads.

Based on Plisk and Stone 2003.

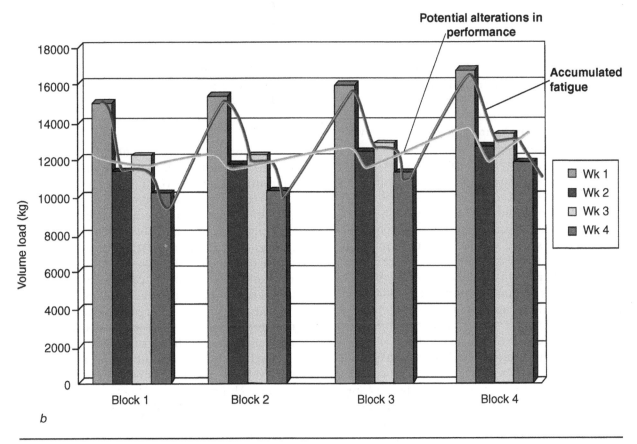

Figure 13.14 *(continued)*

Based on Plisk and Stone 2003.

Table 13.3 **Generalized Periodization Scheme of Strength-Power Training (Basic Application)**

Phase: objective variable	General preparation: strength-endurance	Special preparation: basic strength	Competition: strength and power	Peaking/Active rest: peaking/maintenance
Intensity	Low to moderate	High	High	Very high to low
Volume	High	Moderate to high	Low	Very low
Repetitions	8-20	4-6	2-3	1-3
Sets*	3-5	3-5	3-5	1-3
Sessions/day	1-3	1-3	1-2	1
Days/week	3-4	3-5	3-6	1-5
Intensity cycle†	2-3/1	2-4/1	2-3/1	—

"Strength-endurance" is a more accurate objective of the GP phase than "hypertrophy" because increased anaerobic work capacity is the primary objective; body composition changes, although important, are secondary. "Basic strength," "strength and power," and "peaking/maintenance" reflect a continuum of training objectives during subsequent periods (note that peaking applies to sports with climax; maintenance applies to sports with extended season).

*Sets: excludes warm-ups. †Intensity cycle: ratio of heavy to light training weeks. Heavy and light days should also be incorporated into the training protocol.

decline, the exact reasons are unknown but likely have to do with nervous system adaptations to monotony. This phenomenon is a common problem among advanced athletes. One possible solution is to remove the exercise from the training program for a few weeks and then re-present it several weeks later; this can be accomplished across several mesocycles as shown in figure 13.15 or across several summated microcycles (blocks).

Another theoretical possibility, which takes advantage of deletion and re-presentation, is that a new exercise or a new variation of an exercise can be presented to an advanced athlete (or a moderately trained athlete). When this relatively novel exercise is presented, adaptation occurs quite rapidly initially. If this task is withdrawn before adaptation begins to plateau and then is re-presented as a seminovel task several weeks later, it is possible that the accumulative adaptation may be greater than it would have been if training had been continuous. This concept is shown in figure 13.10.

Offset loading can be used to emphasize one exercise over another. During this process the volume load (VL) of one exercise can be decreased across a block while the VL of a second related exercise is increased. Offset loading may be very helpful for intermediate or advanced athletes using very heavy loading in structurally related exercises. For example, pulling movements and the squat activate similar muscle groups, and both have a relatively high metabolic cost per repetition; therefore simultaneous increases in VL can result in excessive fatigue that may interfere with optimum performance development in either or both exercises. To avoid interference, the VL could

be decreased in one exercise as it increases in the other. Figure 13.16 depicts an example in which the strength training emphasis is on development of leg and hip strength using the squat; to avoid interfering with squat gains, across each block the VL of pulls is decreased as the squat VL increases.

Clusters

Under normal conditions, weight training exercises are performed in a rather continuous fashion using a concentric-eccentric cycle (i.e., the weight moves up, the weight moves down) with no rest between repetitions. This training method produces reasonable gains in strength and power. One aspect of its effectiveness is that accumulative fatigue during the exercise can result in the recruitment of additional motor units, thus augmenting the potential training adaptation (Rooney et al. 1994). However, it should be noted that as a set proceeds, the accumulative fatigue can also reduce force and particularly power output and velocity. These reductions can be easily perceived by the trainee and are usually readily observed by the coach. Clusters are sets performed with very short rest periods between repetitions (15-45 s). Several potential advantages are possible as a result of using this method of exercise (Haff et al. 2003; Roll and Omer 1987):

- At the same weight, power and velocity can be maintained at higher values across a set.

- Short-term rest between repetitions can allow the use of a heavier load.

- The reduction of power may be a particularly critical factor in training ballistic movements

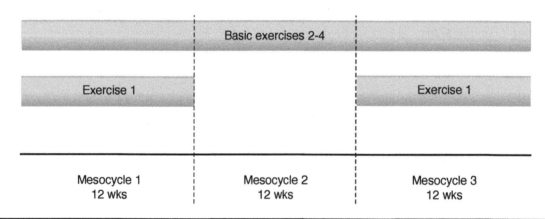

Figure 13.15 Exercise deletion and re-presentation. Exercise 4 was deleted for 12 weeks during the second mesocycle and then inserted (re-presented) in the third mesocycle.

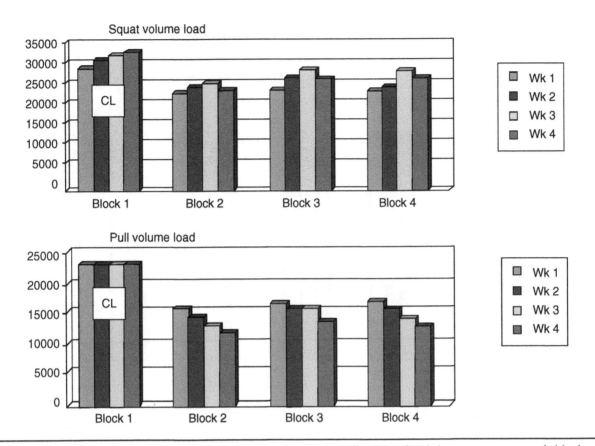

Figure 13.16 Offset loading emphasizing squat development. Pull volume load decreases across each block as squat VL increases. Blocks are continuous over time.

Adapted from S. Plisk and M.H. Stone, 2003, "Periodization strategies," *Strength and Conditioning* 25: 19-37.

(Haff et al. 2003). During the short-term rest the load can be altered in specific patterns, which can augment power and velocity (Haff et al. 2003). For example, in a set of five, the load could be undulated (i.e., 100, 105, 110, 105, 100 kg [220, 231, 243, 231, 220 lb]) such that as fatigue increased, the weight could be lowered to compensate, resulting in higher power outputs.

- Observation in athletic populations indicates that clusters may be particularly advantageous for intermediate and advanced trainees (Roll and Omer 1987). Figure 13.17 depicts the resultant velocity from traditional and cluster types of training (Haff et al. 2003).

Potentiation Complexes

Evidence indicates that force, power, and velocity can be potentiated by previous intense muscular contraction (Gullich and Schmidtbleicher 1996; Young et al. 1998). The underlying mechanisms for acute potentiation are not well understood but

likely include phosphorylation of myosin heavy chains or disinhibition of the nervous system. In a practical setting this method, for example, could involve a short series (one to three) of heavy squats (90+% of 1RM) followed by a high-power or high-velocity movement such as the vertical jump. Although the mechanism is not completely understood, the potentiation mechanism appears to cause an increased activation of motor units and during the subsequent high-power movement may increase the rate of force development. It is important that the initial heavy movements not create excessive fatigue, or potentiation will not occur. A special type of potentiation complex is eccentric accentuated loading (EAL), involving a stretch–shortening cycle in which heavy eccentric loading is followed by a high-power movement during the concentric portion.

With this method, a load near or above the concentric capabilities of the athlete is used for the eccentric portion (usually lowering the weight); a portion of the weight is quickly removed (causing the load to be well within concentric capabilities), and an explosive concentric phase is performed.

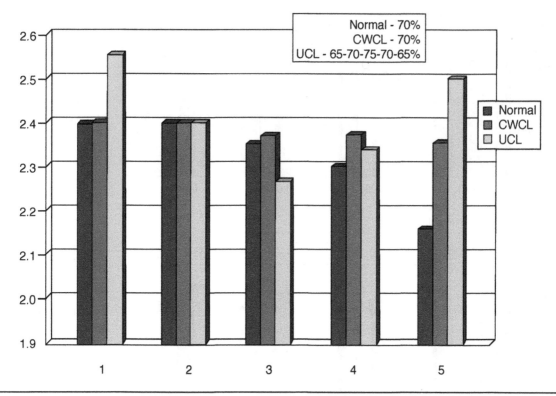

Figure 13.17 Peak velocity of three different set configurations. Cluster versus traditional methods: Clean pulls (70% 1RM) from the floor were performed in the normal manner (no rest between repetitions). Note that velocity decreases rapidly until at the fifth repetition it has decreased approximately 10.4%. Using a cluster (CWCL) at the same loading with 15 s rest between repetitions results in a velocity decrease of approximately 2.1%; thus there can be a velocity maintenance. A cluster could also be undulated (UCL) such that with heavier loads the velocity first decreases and then rises as the load decreases, adding variation to the set.

Adapted from G.G. Haff et al., 2003, "Effects of different set configurations on barbell velocity and displacement during a clean pull," *Journal of Strength and Conditioning Research* 17: 75-103.

This method has potential to stimulate adaptation beyond that of normal training procedures for two primary reasons (Brandenberg and Docherty 2002; Doan et al. 2002):

1. It has been well established that concentric performance is enhanced by a prior countermovement (Komi and Bosco 1978). Thus, placing an emphasis on the training of the eccentric portion of the stretch–shortening cycle could enhance concentric performance. Enhancement of the concentric portion of movement has been noted in studies of the effects of drop jumps on the vertical jump (Asmussen and Bonde-Petersen 1974; Komi and Bosco 1978). The mechanisms underlying the potentiation from a prior stretch are not completely understood but could include optimum length factors, optimization of muscle activation patterns, and imparting additional energy into the cross-bridge formations (Bobbert et al. 1996; Enoka 1979; Newton et al. 1997). Indeed, higher eccen-

tric loads (i.e., forces) could lead to greater force generation resulting from neural disinhibition in a manner similar to that occurring with potentiation complexes.

2. Maximum eccentric muscle forces can be higher than concentric forces; however, during typical training movements (plyometric), the training load is a function of the concentric action. As a result, the *relative* eccentric load during typical weight training movements is lower than the concentric load, which may diminish the training effect (Brandenberg and Docherty 2002). Using a heavy eccentric load during the EAL will not only be useful as a potentiation tool but also may train the eccentric portion of movements better than typical training movements during appropriate phases when strength gains are being emphasized.

Figure 13.18 depicts the resultant power output of an EAL potentiation complex. As a result of the heavy eccentric phase, power output at the lighter

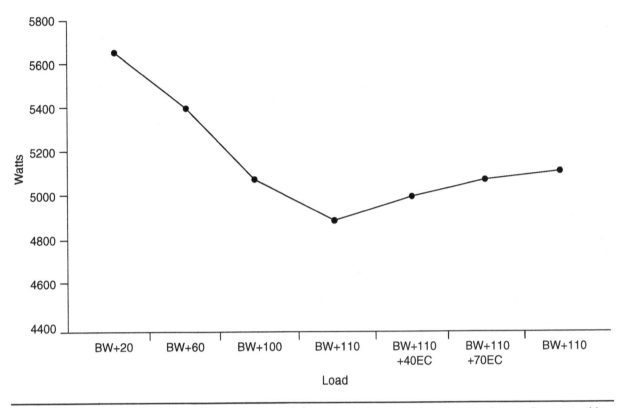

Figure 13.18 Eccentric-loaded squat jumps. Eccentric accentuated potentiation: Advanced strength-power athlete performed loaded jumps with 20, 60, 100, and 110 kg, then descended (eccentric phase) with 150 kg and 180 kg (twice), each time ascending (jumping) with 110 kg. The extra weight for the eccentric phase was immediately unloaded at the bottom of the descent. A final unloaded jump was performed with 110 kg. Approximately 2 min rest was given between jump trials. Note that the peak power output steadily increases as a result of the eccentric loading (final increase ∼ 6%). The athlete was well warmed up before the complex, having completed 2 to 3 min of calisthenics and parallel squats at 60 kg × 3, 100 kg × 2, and 140 kg × 2, plus several unloaded jumps. Thus, the observed increase in peak power was likely a potentiation effect.

weight (approximately 50% of 1RM) was increased markedly (6%). While potentiation complexes can be used to acutely enhance power performance, their efficacy as a training method has not been well studied. However, potentiation complexes do offer a unique form of exercise variation that may be advantageous for advanced athletes. One study indicates that potentiation complexes may offer a superior method of short-term training to enhance power-oriented movements (Harris et al. 2000). Based on the authors' experience and that of other coaches (Roll and Omer 1987), potentiation complexes can be among the more valuable variation methods for advanced athletes.

Collectively, these concepts should be viewed in a strategic context. If they are applied with discretion, there may be opportunities to include certain training and recovery tactics fairly early in an athlete's development. Likewise, intermediate approaches need not be abandoned when the ath-

lete reaches an advanced stage. The key in either case is systematic application of sound means and methods in order to enhance their effects. At present, however, the summated training concept is based largely on empiricism and intuition. Further research is needed to investigate the possibilities of this and other strategies.

Advanced Strategies

Highly qualified athletes require greater stimulus variation and novelty than intermediate or novice athletes, especially at the microcyclic level. As they approach their developmental limits, higher workload intensities and volumes are necessary to trigger further adaptation and achieve peak performance. Thus, advanced and elite athletes typically train with greater volume loads and may be closer than others to an overtraining threshold. The key is to avoid monotonous or too-frequent heavy loading, which can increase training strain and the potential for negative results (Foster 1998; Fry, Morton, and Keast 1992a, 1992b; Rowbottom 2000; Stone et al. 1991).

Advanced periodization strategies can therefore be characterized by relatively extensive, systematic variation in both content and workload at multiple levels of the program (i.e., between and within micro-, meso-, and macrocycles). While the training plans for advanced and elite athletes are extensions of the means and methods presented for basic and intermediate approaches, such training and recovery strategies can become quite sophisticated.

The conjugate sequence system is an intriguing approach for advanced athletes (figure 13.19, a & b) (Hartmann and Tünnemann 1989; Satori and Tschiene 1988; Siff 2000; Stone et al. 1998, 2000; Tschiene 1990, 1992, 1995, 1996; Tschiene 1997b, pp. 71-73; Werchoshanski 1978; Zatsiorsky

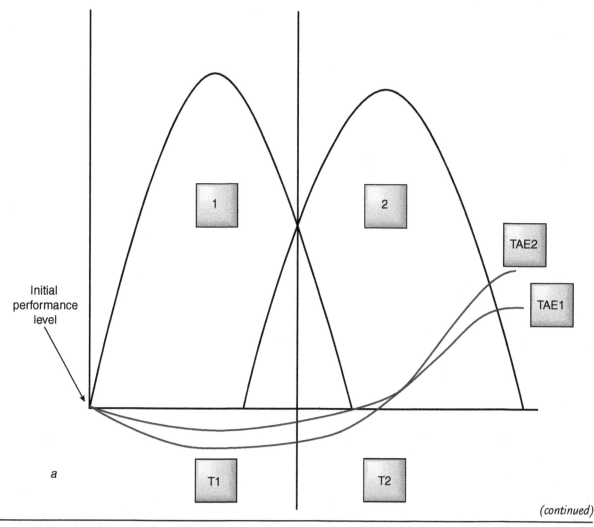

(continued)

Figure 13.19 *(a)* The general scheme of the long-term delayed training effect (LTDE) of concentrated strength loading associated with the conjugate sequence system (advanced application). The duration of the LTDE (T2) is approximately equal to that of the concentrated strength block (T1) and may last 4 to 8 weeks depending on volume load and individual recoverability. Within optimal ranges, the greater the decrement in speed-strength indices (TAE1, TAE2) during accumulation block A, the greater their recovery during the restitution block. *(b)* Increase in speed-strength by a systematic, overlapping sequence of concentrated and moderate volume loads associated with the conjugate sequence system (advanced application). Accumulation blocks 1, 3, and 5 represent periods of high-volume, relatively low-intensity strength training during which temporary performance decrements are expected. Restitution blocks 2, 4, and 6 represent moderate volumes of specialized, high-intensity speed-strength and technique training during which supernormal responses are exploited (and performance capabilities rebound by virtue of the LTDE phenomenon).

Adapted from M.C. Siff, 2000, *Supertraining*, 5th ed. (Denver, CO: Supertraining Institute), 362.

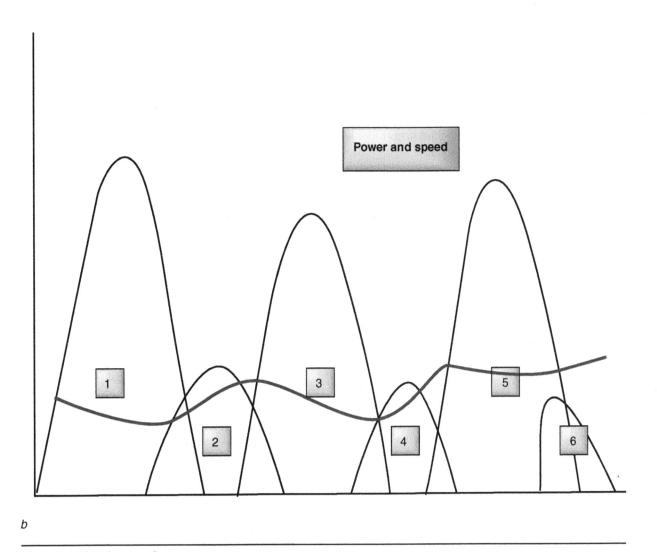

b

Figure 13.19 *(continued)*

1995). This concept was originally referred to as the *coupled successive* system and was pioneered by Yuri Verkhoshansky (Plisk and Stone 2003).

Basically, the conjugate sequence system is an intermesocycle variation strategy that involves periods of *accumulation* followed by *restitution* and recovery during which superior adaptations can be exploited. This is achieved through a series of concentrated blocks that are up to four weeks in duration. For example, during the first block, a strength-power athlete interested in maximizing power and speed would perform high volume loads of work with one primary emphasis (e.g., strength or strength-endurance, with minimal volume loads allocated to other abilities designed as maintenance work). The objective is to saturate the system with one type of stress over a period of several weeks, during which temporary decrements in certain performance capabilities can occur due to specific accu-mulative fatigue aftereffects. Emphasis is essentially reversed during the subsequent restitution block: Strength training volume load is markedly reduced while the volume load of work allocated to another quality (e.g., speed or technique) is increased. If this method is implemented skillfully and logically, the athlete's performance capabilities rebound to above baseline values by virtue of a delayed training effect phenomenon, allowing the achievement of new levels of movement speed and technical execution. The athlete can then proceed to the next sequence of blocks with progressively stronger specific stimuli.

Proponents of this strategy suggest several advantages (Hartmann and Tünnemann 1989; Satori and Tschiene 1988; Siff 2000, Stone et al. 1998, 2000; Tschiene 1990, 1992, 1995, 1996; Tschiene 1997b, pp. 71-73; Werchoshanski 1978; Zatsiorsky 1995): First, it provides the stimulus strength necessary to bring advanced athletes to a new functional state that cannot be achieved through traditional methods. Second, through emphasis on specified qualities during separate blocks, the cumulative fatigue problems associated with concurrent training can be reduced. Third, total work volumes can be reduced over the long term. This comes with a price over the short term, however. During each accumulation block, athletes must be able to tolerate high volume loads for several consecutive weeks. This can be particularly problematic without the systematic application of restorative and regenerative measures that enhance the recovery-adaptation process.

One line of evidence supporting the sequenced training concept is based on longitudinal and cross-sectional studies suggesting superior gains in athletic performance variables (particularly those involving power and speed) compared to those with heavy resistance or speed-strength training exclusively (Hakkinen 1994; Harris et al. 2000; Stone et al. 1998). More significantly, beneficial changes have been demonstrated in both a wider range and a greater extent of parameters (Hakkinen 1994; Harris et al. 2000; Medvedev et al. 1981). More research is needed to expand on these findings.

Additional supporting evidence can be found in studies of endocrine responses to planned overreaching strategies (i.e., periodic increases in volume load aimed at enhancing adaptation and performance two to five weeks after the return to normal training). For example, resting serum testosterone concentration [T] and the testosterone-to-cortisol ratio T:C have been associated with lean body mass, strength levels, and explosiveness and furthermore have been associated with accumulative fatigue and "training strain" (note that resting [T] and T:C can be useful markers for monitoring an athlete's response to *overreaching* protocols, but do not necessarily indicate an *overtraining* syndrome) (Keizer 1998; Urhausen and Kindermann 2000; Vorobeyev 1978). Resting or preexercise [T] and T:C have been shown to decrease significantly in response to severe, prolonged (three weeks or more) increases in volume load (Hakkinen et al. 1988, 1989; McMillan et al. 1993; Pendlay and Kilgore 2001) or very severe short-term loading (Stone et al. 1989). On the other hand, resting values above baseline and corresponding performance improvements have been documented on the return to normal volume loads with a subsequent taper (Hakkinen et al. 1988; Hakkinen 1989; Pendlay and Kilgore 2001).

However, it has also been demonstrated that increased T:C concentrations result from substantial increases in training volume over a short term (one week) among well-conditioned athletes (Fry et al. 1994; Stone and Fry 1998). Regardless of the initial change in [T] and T:C, it appears that prior exposure to short-term volume increases (i.e., planned overreaching) may enhance an athlete's T:C ratio and can increase tolerance for subsequent high volume load training and associated performance gains (Fry et al. 1994; Fry, Morton, and Keast 2000a; Stone and Fry 1998). Collectively, these findings explain some of the results of sequenced training and support its role as a useful periodization strategy for advanced athletes. Ongoing research is needed to enhance our understanding of sequenced training and other advanced periodization strategies.

In contrast to the concurrent approach used in many basic and intermediate programs, sequenced training is a significant departure—that is, developing various qualities over successive mesocycles such that one potentiates another while minimizing residual fatigue and compatibility problems. Unfortunately, most advocates of this strategy describe it in theoretical terms but offer limited practical guidelines for safe and effective implementation.

In any case, several things are clear. Sequenced training methods are intended for advanced (not novice) athletes. In sports with a clearly defined season, the duration of the off-season period must be long enough to allow deployment of a series of blocks; this deployment may not be possible in sports with long competitive seasons. Appropriate ordering can potentiate the effect of one block on the next block, whereas inappropriate ordering may have a negative effect. The coach/athlete needs to understand the basic principles concerned with mechanical specificity (Siff 2000; Stone, Plisk, and Collins 2002; Verkhoshansky 1986, 1988), as well as the nature of residual or delayed training effects (Siff 2000; Verkhoshansky 1986, 1988; Viru 1995; Zatsiorsky 1995), in order to increase the potential for success using sequenced programming. Intensive means and methods should be used with discretion during accumulation periods because of the high work volumes being performed. Likewise, practitioners should limit the duration of these blocks so that an overtraining syndrome does not develop and should be attentive to potential signs and symptoms with each passing week (Foster 1998; Keizer 1998; Kraemer 2000; Siff 2000; Stone et al. 1991; Urhausen and Kindermann 2000; Viru 1995; Viru and Viru 2001).

The sequenced training concept arose in an environment without external constraints on training time. The following are some practical suggestions for adapting this concept to situations in which athletes are bound by such restrictions. For example, a 14-week preseason program can be organized into a series of blocks such as these (Plisk and Stone 2003):

- *Accumulation I (four-week duration):* 16 strength-power sessions distributed over this period on a four day per week schedule; 8 speed-agility-conditioning sessions distributed on a two day per week schedule

- *Restitution-recovery I (three-week duration):* 9 strength-power sessions distributed over this period on a three day per week schedule; 9 speed-agility-conditioning sessions distributed on a three day per week schedule

- *Accumulation II (four-week duration):* 16 strength-power sessions distributed over this period on a four day per week schedule; 8 speed-agility-conditioning sessions distributed on a two day per week schedule

- *Restitution-recovery II (three-week duration):* 9 strength-power sessions distributed over this period on a three day per week schedule; 6 speed-agility-conditioning sessions distributed on a two day per week schedule

In this way, markedly different training volumes can be allocated to specific qualities through manipulation of the training density and duration of each phase without changing basic intensity and volume parameters. One can achieve even greater contrast by further reducing density (and volume) during the restitution blocks (e.g., distributing six strength-power sessions over these periods on a two day per week schedule).

Another way of achieving additional variation is to adjust the prescribed number of sets per exercise, exercises per session, or sessions (modules) per day (or some combination of these). These are simple but effective ways to alter the amount of work apportioned to the development of different abilities during particular phases. When evaluating the pros and cons of various options, it is important to consider their practical implications, for example, other stressors encountered such as school, work, and family.

Applied Strategy Summary

While relatively simple programming can be effective for novices, more sophisticated training and recovery methods are applicable in intermediate or advanced situations. The practical challenge is to direct adaptation toward specific targets by prescribing a range of stimuli appropriate for the athlete's sport and developmental status.

Long-term planning is a priority. Training tasks have to be distributed logically during the whole period of an athlete's training program, perhaps over as much as 10 to 20 years. *Training strategy* determines how to distribute the tasks, taking into account the athlete's development from adolescence. This means that the most favorable periods have to be found for inducing the necessary structural, metabolic, and functional changes. Training strategy entails planning the distribution of various tasks within macro-, meso-, and microcycles. Necessary variation is part of *training tactics and methodology* (Viru 1995).

CHAPTER SUMMARY

It is the authors' opinion that currently, planning for sport training is largely based on practical knowledge, observation, and at times intuition. Although intuitive strategies can sometimes produce optimal results, our actions are often guided—correctly or otherwise—by emotion and impulse instead of rational decision making. However, by understanding training principles and their application within a logical theoretical framework, one can optimize recovery-adaptation, leading to superior performance.

Although there have been some controlled studies, scientific evidence supporting sport planning concepts is scarce. However, the evidence to date does indicate that integration of scientifically backed knowledge and practices into a comprehensive training process can yield superior results. In an effort to optimize the manipulation of volume, intensity, and exercise selection, many coaches and practitioners have embraced periodization theory.

Periodization is a logical phasic method of manipulating training variables in order to increase the potential for achieving specific performance goals. Because of the training variable manipulation process, periodization is nonlinear training. The goals of periodization are a reduction of overtraining potential and the ability to peak at the appropriate time or the provision of maintenance for sports with a specific season. These goals can be met by appropriate multilevel variation of volume, intensity factors, and exercise selection. Thus, a good coach can direct the adaptation process toward specific goals by varying the load (methods) or exercise selection of training (or both) across, as well as between, levels of variation (i.e., macro-, meso-, microcycles; daily and intratraining sessions). The final outcome will be a superior performance.

CHAPTER 14

Developing Resistance Training Programs

One major purpose of this book has been to assist coaches and athletes in the development of strength-power training programs for sport. It is important to remember that an effective training program is not one in which the components are thrown together in relative isolation, but rather are molded in an integrated fashion. The integrated approach should be such that all of the components lead to the enhancement of a specific characteristic (e.g., explosiveness) and ultimately to a specific goal (e.g., improved sport performance). It is not the primary purpose of this chapter to offer specific programs for a variety of sports, but rather to provide a detailed example of how to develop training programs.

To begin the development of a training program, the first step should be the physiological and performance characterization of the sport. Tables 14.1, 14.2, and 14.3 give examples of three sports and a

Table 14.1 **Characterization of Advanced and Elite Shot-Putting**

Absolute strength	1-2
Relative strength (per kilogram)	2-3
Explosiveness	1
High-intensity endurance	2-3
Low-intensity endurance	5
Body mass	1-2
Height	2-3
Somatotype	2.5-3
Aggressiveness	1-2

1 = highest, 5 = lowest. Somatotype: 1 = endomorph, 3 = mesomorph, 4 = ectomorph.

Table 14.2 **Characterization of American Collegiate Football**

	LM	LB	DB/RB	WR/QB
Absolute strength	1-2	1-2	2-3	3-4
Relative strength (per kilogram)	2-3	2	1-2	1-3
Explosiveness	1-2	1-2	1	1-2
High-intensity endurance	1-2	1-2	1-2	1-2
Low-intensity endurance	4	3-4	3	3
Body mass	1-2	2-3	3	3-4
Height	1-2	2-3	2-3	2-3
Somatotype	2-3	3	3-3.5	3-4
Aggressiveness	1		1-2	1-2

1 = highest, 5 = lowest. Somatotype: 1 = endomorph, 3 = mesomorph, 4 = ectomorph. LM = linemen; LB = linebackers; DB = defensive backs; RB = running backs; WR = wide receivers; QB = quarterbacks.

Table 14.3 **Characterization of Distance Running (>5000 m)**

Absolute strength	4
Relative strength (per kilogram)	3-4
Explosiveness	4
High-intensity endurance	3-4
Low-intensity endurance	1
Body mass	4-5
Height	4-5
Somatotype	4
Aggressiveness	3-4

1 = highest, 5 = lowest; somatotype: 1 = endomorph, 3 = mesomorph, 4 = ectomorph.

method of characterization. Characterization of the sport is important, as this provides the goals for the training program. From the examples in the tables one can surmise that these three sports would not be trained in the same manner and that distance runners would be trained considerably differently from athletes in the two strength-power sports.

In this chapter we provide an example of a training program for an individual sport, the shot put, and also a brief discussion of training programs for team sports.

Program Design

Elite shot-putters are among the strongest and most powerful and explosive of all athletes. Here we describe the training program of a high-level (near elite) shot-putter across two mesocycles leading to a national championship competition.

A monitoring program was put in place so that training progress could be tracked. The initial tests showed that the athlete (19 years) was 186.5 cm (6 ft 1 in.) in height and had a body mass of 112 kg (247 lb). At the initiation of this training program (fall), the athlete's best performance values were as follows:

Throw = 17.32 m (7.26 kg), 18.20 m (6 kg), 16.10 m (8 kg)

Squat = 215 kg

Power snatch = 105 kg

Power clean = 137.5 kg

Bench press (10°) incline = 150 kg

Vertical jump (hands on hips) = 60 cm

Static vertical jump (hands on hips) = 50 cm

Additionally, blood work, including a complete blood count and measures of resting concentrations of testosterone and cortisol, was initiated. These tests indicated normal levels of blood constituents and testosterone in the high normal range.

Examination of these values indicated that the athlete's explosive strength and particularly basic strength levels were quite a bit lower than those of elite-level shot-putters (Gundlach et al. 1991, unpublished observations). Additionally, the distance drop-off between the 7.26 kg implement and the 8 kg shot and the difference between the countermovement and static vertical jumps indicated a potential basic strength deficit. Furthermore, the athlete performed in a relatively poor manner on 10 consecutive vertical jump tests with 60 kg (132 lb) load, showing considerable drop-off in jump height and power output over the 10 jumps.

On the basis of these values, the coach believed that neither the athlete's basic strength (especially lower body) nor body mass was great enough to reach the elite level; thus emphasis was placed initially on basic strength and body mass gain. Furthermore, the coach (in conjunction with a sport nutritionist) developed a sound dietary and dietary supplement plan designed to help the athlete gain body mass with a minimum fat gain (see chapter 6, "Nutrition and Metabolic Factors").

The coach developed a four-year training program leading up to the next Olympic trials. The first two years of the plan placed a greater emphasis on basic strength, and the next two years became more progressively oriented toward power and explosive strength.

Here we discuss in detail the first two mesocycles (40 weeks beginning in the fall) of this overall plan (figures 14.1 and 14.5). The first mesocycle (20 weeks) emphasizes strength-endurance and strength development (figure 14.1). Figure 14.2 shows the set, repetition, and relative intensity scheme created in accordance with the overall mesocycle plan. Day-to-day variation is accomplished using heavy and lighter days (figure 14.3). The basic resistance training exercises are shown in figures 14.4 and 14.5. Note that some intermediate and advanced methods are being used (see chapter 13) and that even though mesocycle 1 has a strength emphasis, a considerable number of power exercises are still included. Also note that the first block is devoted to a unidirectional concentrated load (i.e., strength-endurance exercises) and will

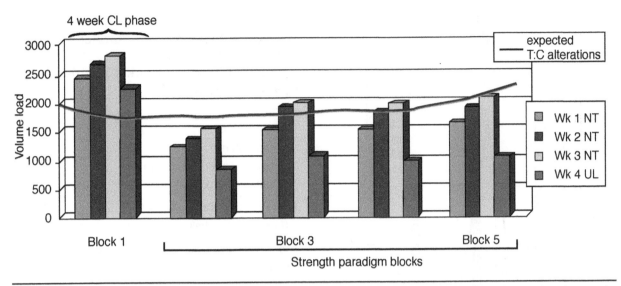

Figure 14.1 Twenty-week mesocycle for shot-putter: strength-endurance and strength emphasis. The first four weeks (block 1) represent a concentrated load of strength-endurance training. Each block uses a summated microcycle in which the stimulus is increased over the first three weeks (normal training increase) followed by an unload week (see chapter 13). Blocks are continuous over time. The expected alterations in the testosterone-to-cortisol (T:C) ratio are superimposed on the volume load changes. NT = normal training week; UL = unload week.

Based on S. Plisk and M.H. Stone, 2003, "Periodization Strategies," *Strength and Conditioning* 25: 19-37.

Example-sequencing: Advanced throwers preparation mesocycle (emphasis on strength gains)

Volume by repetitions

	Block 2	Block 3	Block 4	Block 5
Week 1	3 x 5 (1 x 5)	3 x 5 (1 x 5)	3 x 5 (1 x 5)	3 x 5 (1 x 5)
Week 2	3 x 5 (1 x 5)	3 x 5 (1 x 5)	3 x 5 (1 x 5)	3 x 5 (1 x 5)
Week 3	3 x 5 (1 x 5)	3 x 5 (1 x 5)	3 x 5 (1 x 5)	3 x 3 (1 x 5)
Week 4	3 x 3 (1 x 5)	3 x 3 (1 x 5)	3 x 3 (1 x 5)	3 x 3 (1 x 5)

Relative intensity—% of initial 1RM for major exercises on heavy day

This is a guideline

	Block 2	Block 3	Block 4	Block 5
Week 1	75	77.5	80	82.5
Week 2	77.5	80	82.5	85
Week 3	80	82.5	85	87.5
Week 4	77.5	85	87.5	80

H = M
L = TH

Figure 14.2 Set and repetition scheme for mesocycle 1: strength-endurance and strength emphasis. Note that the sets in parentheses are "down" sets at approximately 50% of 1RM; block 1 (not shown) uses sets of 10 throughout.

likely potentiate the subsequent phases. After completing mesocycle 1, this athlete (at the stated initial level) should expect increases in basic strength of approximately 5% to 10%, so (for example) this athlete's 1RM squat would be expected to increase by about 25 to 30 kg (55-66 lb). It would also be

reasonable to expect a 5 to 10 kg (11-22 lb) gain in body mass with little fat gain.

The athlete may or may not use an active rest week between mesocycles; if there were one or more competitions at the end of the first mesocycle, then an active rest phase could be used with good

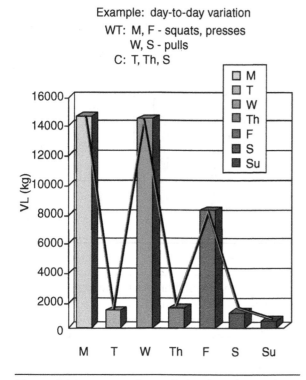

Example: day-to-day variation
WT: M, F - squats, presses
W, S - pulls
C: T, Th, S

Figure 14.3 Day-to-day variation based on volume load (VL). Note the relatively extreme variation; this represents heavy loading followed by relatively light loads to enhance recovery adaptation. WT = weight training; C = conditioning other than WT.

Mesocycle 1: Strength–endurance (concentrated load)
Example: Block 1: 4 weeks: 3 x 10 at target
Monday and Friday
- Squats
- Squat press
- Rest—30 min
- Push press (Fr-Sq 1st rep)
- Remedial work

Tuesday, Thursday, Saturday
(Power snatch, ball throws, midsection, candlesticks)

Wednesday (Purpose—raise sport specific fitness)
- CGSS
- CG pulls (thigh)
- Rest—30 min
- CG pulls (knee)
- Hyperextensions
- Rows

CGSS = clean grip shoulder shrugs
CG pulls = clean grip pulls

Figure 14.4 Exercises associated with block 1, mesocycle 1: strength-endurance and strength emphasis.

Mesocycle 1: Strength emphasis

Block 2	Block 3	Block 4	Block 5
Monday & Friday			
1. Squats*	1. Squats	1. ECL squats	1. 1/3 squats (rack)
2. Push jerk	2. Push jerks	2. Box jumps	2. Speed squats**
3. Bench press	3. Incline press	3. Bench press (10°)	3. Dumbbell bench press
Wednesday			
1. CGSS	1. CGSS	1. CGSS	1. SGSS
2. Clean pulls (floor)	2. Clean pulls***	2. Power clean (1 set)	2. Power snatch***
3. Stiff-legged deadlift	3. Power clean (1 set)	3. Stiff-legged deadlift	
	4. Stiff-legged deadlift		

Saturday
Power snatch

Split sessions if possible

* = off-set loading
** = alternating complex (contrast) with 1/3 squats
*** = complex with shoulder shrugs

ECL = eccentric accentuated squats; CGSS = clean grip shoulder shrugs; SGSS = snatch grip shoulder shrugs

Figure 14.5 Exercises associated with blocks 2 through 5, mesocycle 1: strength-endurance and strength emphasis.

effectiveness (see chapter 13). As the volume of work (i.e., volume load) is reduced toward the end of mesocycle 1, a reduction in sport specific fitness will also occur; this is especially apparent after an active rest period.

Figure 14.6 shows the basic plan for mesocycle 2 (20 weeks), which has a more power-oriented emphasis. The set and repetition scheme follows the basic characteristics for an advanced mesocycle emphasizing power development. The first block is a concentrated load of strength-endurance exercise designed to raise sport-specific fitness and potentiate subsequent phases; the next block returns to strength-oriented training, and the last three blocks are oriented more toward explosive strength and power. As with the first mesocycle, the set and repetition scheme reflects the overall plan (figure 14.7). Starting with block 3, an overreaching-power type of summated microcycle is introduced. Note that each overreaching week (first week of the blocks) consists of a marked increase in volume load and total repetitions (i.e., 5 3 5 reps). This overreaching week consists of heavier loading (note the higher relative intensity) and is more strength oriented. These overreaching weeks are designed to potentiate the subsequent higher-power movements (weeks 2-4 of blocks 3-5). As with all reasonable program design for advanced athletes, heavy and light days provide for a strong stimulus followed by recovery and adaptation days (figure 14.8). The

exercises (and loading) in block 1 are similar to those used in the same block during mesocycle 1; indeed, the purpose is similar (figure 14.9). Subsequent blocks (2 through 5) show a progressive move toward more explosive- and power-oriented characteristics with considerable use of potentiation complexes.

Obviously, throwing (shot-putting) is a necessity for shot-putters; however, relatively little shot throwing is performed during the first mesocycle so that concentration on strength development can be emphasized. Throwing is greatly increased during mesocycle 2, particularly from blocks 2 through 5.

Note also that across each mesocycle the volume drops both as a result of alterations in volume load and as a result of dropping exercises; this form of volume reduction adds to the potential for increased performance because of decreasing fatigue (Mujika and Padilla 2003). Furthermore, the types of exercises become more specific to the performance. For example, the bench pressing exercises move from a typical flat bench to a 10° dumbbell incline bench in which the hands are turned outward, simulating the release of the shot. The 10° incline also simulates the shot in that the shot is released at approximately a 10° angle from a line drawn from the shoulder joint to the hip joint. Here both weight training (figure 14.10) and the throwing (figure 14.11) become

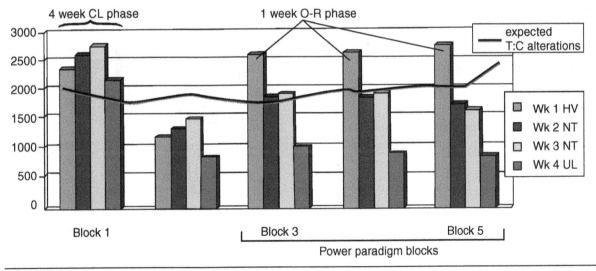

Figure 14.6 Mesocycle 2: greater power emphasis. Note that this mesocycle begins with a unidirectional concentrated load, moves to a block with a strength emphasis, and then to three blocks with an overreaching-power emphasis. Blocks are continuous over time. The expected alterations in the T:C ratio are superimposed on the volume load changes. CL = concentrated load; O-R = overreaching phase; HV = high-volume phase; NT = normal training; UL = unload week (because volume is low, explosive exercises and high-power exercise can be emphasized in this week).

Based on S. Plisk and M.H. Stone, 2003, "Periodization Strategies," *Strength and Conditioning* 25: 19-37.

Mesocycle 2: Set and repetition scheme

Volume by repetitions

	Block 2	Block 3	Block 4	Block 5
Week 1	3 x 5 (1 x 5)	5 x 5	5 x 5	5 x 5
Week 2	3 x 5 (1 x 5)	3 x 5 (1 x 5)	3 x 3 (1 x 5)	3 x 3 (1 x 5)
Week 3	3 x 5 (1 x 5)	3 x 5 (1 x 5)	3 x 3 (1 x 5)	3 x 3 (1 x 5)
Week 4	3 x 3 (1 x 5)	3 x 3 (1 x 5)	3 x 2 (1 x 5)	3 x 2 (1 x 5)

Relative intensity—% of initial 1RM for major exercises on heavy day

This is a guideline

	Block 2	Block 3	Block 4	Block 5
Week 1	75	82.5	87.5	90
Week 2	77.5	80	82.5	80
Week 3	80	82.5	80	77.5
Week 4	77.5	75	70	70

H = M
L = TH

Figure 14.7 Set and repetition scheme for mesocycle 1: strength-endurance and strength emphasis. Note that the sets in parentheses are "down" sets at approximately 50% of 1RM; block 1 (not shown) uses sets of 10 throughout.

Mesocycle 2: Strength–endurance (concentrated load)
Example: Block 1: 4 weeks: 3 x 10 at target

Monday and Friday

- Squats
- Squat press
- Rest—30 min
- Push press (Fr-Sq 1st rep)
- Remedial work

Tuesday, Thursday, Saturday

(Power snatch, ball throws, midsection, candlesticks)

Wednesday (*Purpose—raise sport-specific fitness*)

- CGSS
- CG pulls (thigh)
- Rest—30 min
- CG pulls (knee)
- Hypers
- Rows

Figure 14.9 Exercises associated with block 1, mesocycle 2. As with mesocycle 1 there is a strength-endurance emphasis during this block that aids in regaining sport-specific fitness and potentiates subsequent phases (see chapter 13).

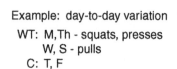

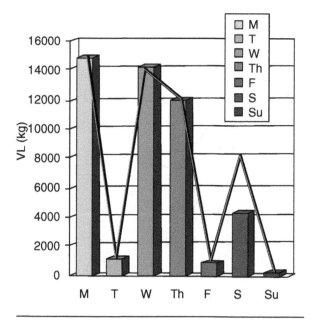

Figure 14.8 Day-to-day variation based on volume load. Note the relatively extreme variation; this represents heavy loading followed by relatively light loads to enhance recovery adaptation. The second day of squats has been moved to Thursday; this provides recovery on Friday and allows for somewhat greater loading on Saturday (throwing).

Mesocycle 2: Power emphasis

Block 2	Block 3	Block 4	Block 5
Monday & Friday			
1. Squats	1. Squats	1. ECL squats	1. 1/4 squats (rack)
2. 1/4 squats	2. SP-squats	2. SP-squats	2. Bounds/throws*
3. Bench press	3. Bench press (10°)	3. Dumbbell bench press (10°)	3. Dumbbell bench press (10°)
Wednesday			
1. CGSS	1. CGSS	1. CGSS	1. CGSS
2. Clean pulls (midthigh)	2. Clean pulls**	2. Power clean (1 set)	2. Power snatch**
3. Stiff-legged deadlift	3. Power clean (1 set)	3. Stiff-legged deadlift	
	4. Stiff-legged deadlift		

Split sessions if possible

* = alternating complex (contrast) with 1/3 squats

** = complex with shoulder shrugs

SP-squats = speed squats; CGSS = clean grip shoulder shrugs; SGSS = snatch grip shoulder shrugs

Figure 14.10 Exercises associated with blocks 2 through 5, mesocycle 2: increasing power emphasis.

Mesocycle 2: Throwing

Block 2: T, F, Sat*		**Block 4: T, F, Sat**	
Week 1:	Ball throws 5 x 5-fronts—overweight 5 x 5	**Week 1:**	Ball throws 5 x 5-fronts—overweight 5 x 5
Week 2:	Ball throws 3 x 5-fronts—overweight 3 x 5	**Week 2:**	Fronts—overweight 3 x 5—full 3 x 5
Week 3:	Fronts—overweight 3 x 5—full 3 x 5	**Week 3:**	Fronts 3 x 5—full 3 x 5
Week 4:	Fronts 3 x 5—full 3 x 5	**Week 4:**	Fronts 3 x 5—full 3 x 5
Block 3: T, F, Sat		**Block 5: T, F, Sat**	
Week 1:	Ball throws 5 x 5-fronts—overweight 5 x 5	**Week 1:**	Ball throws 5 x 5-fronts—overweight 5 x 5
Week 2:	Ball throws 3 x 5-fronts—overweight 3 x 5	**Week 2:**	Ball throws 3 x 5-fronts—overweight 3 x 5
Week 3:	Fronts 3 x 5—full 3 x 5	**Week 3:**	Fronts 3 x 3—full 3 x 5
Week 4:	Fronts 3 x 5—full 3 x 5	**Week 4:**	Fronts 3 x 3—full 3 x 5

*Only power snatch and ball throws.

Figure 14.11 Throwing schedule during mesocycle 2. Note that the throwing is treated as resistance training (sets and repetitions) and that the throwing method becomes more specific to the actual performance from block 2 to block 5.

steadily more specific, moving from primarily ball throws and partial movements with overweight implements to full movements with the competition implement. During this phase the athlete can expect another 2% to 5% increase in basic strength exercises, as well as a 2% to 5% increase in explosiveness (e.g., snatch and clean), along with considerable improvement in shot-put performance (2-5%) (Stone et al. 2003).

In the case of our shot-putter, blood work was monitored at regular intervals (every two weeks), and testosterone and cortisol were noted to respond to alterations in training stress (i.e., volume load) in an expected manner: At no time did the testosterone-to-cortisol ratio indicate that overtraining was an issue. The testosterone and the T:C ratio are important criteria for "preparedness." These measures reflect the potential to exert maximum strength and particularly explosive strength; thus their measurement added an important parameter to the monitoring aspect of the training program.

Program Design for Team Sports

Although many coaches believe that the training program for athletes in team sports is very different than for athletes in individual sports, this is to a great extent untrue. The principles of training are the same regardless of the type of sport. This means that emphasizing a training characteristic such as strength-endurance can be expected to produce the same results regardless of whether the athlete is in an individual or team sport. It also means that the training program can be divided up into phases of training, albeit with different names (e.g., off-season, in-season, postseason), each with slightly different characteristics and emphases. For example, the off-season can be treated like the preparation phases of a traditional periodization model, in-season treated much like the competition phase, and postseason treated as a transition phase (active rest). Monitoring the athlete and building into the training program a monitoring system are still a necessity.

It must be recognized that every team athlete may not respond to the team training program in the same manner and thus there may be some need for occasional individualization.

However, it is important to recognize that there can be some differences in the preparation of team athletes compared to those in individual sports. Most of these differences have to do with the psychology of producing a cohesive team and development of the team culture (i.e., belief in working together as a unit). Thus the coaching approach from a psychological standpoint may be different in some respects from the psychological approach used in individual sports (Jones, Armour, and Potrac 2004). One other important factor pointed out in chapter 13 is that one would rarely attempt to bring a team to a peak. The reason is that once a peak is reached, it is difficult to hold on to a high preparedness level, and performance can rapidly deteriorate (i.e., you may win some contests during the peak, but then you may lose some as performance deteriorates).

CHAPTER SUMMARY

Coaching is similar to the practice of medicine. Medical doctors gain a scientific background so that they can better practice the art of medicine. Good coaches gain a scientific background so that they can better practice the art of coaching. This textbook offers the coach and athlete basic and applied aspects of science that bridge the gap between science and sport. Gaining an understanding of scientific principles and methods enables better planning and therefore the achievement of superior sport performance.

1RM—1-repetition maximum

AA—amino acid

ACh—acetylcholine

AChE—acetylcholinesterase

AChR—acetylcholine receptor

ACL—anterior cruciate ligament

ACTH—adrenocorticotropic hormone

ADH—antidiuretic hormone

ADP—adenosine diphosphate

AI—adequate intake

AMDR—acceptable macronutrient distribution range

AMP—adenosine monophosphate

AMS—absolute maximum strength

ANCOVA—analysis of covariance

ANOVA—analysis of variance

AP—action potential

AS—anabolic steroid

AT—adaptive thermogenesis

ATP—adenosine triphosphate

ATPase—adenosine triphosphatase

ATP-CP—adenosine triphosphate-creatine phosphate

a-$\bar{v}O_2$ diff—arterial-venous oxygen difference

BCAA—branched chain amino acid

BMR—basal metabolic rate

BP—blood pressure

BV—biological value

Ca^{++}—calcium ion

cAMP—cyclic adenosine monophosphate

cGMP—cyclic guanosine monophosphate

C—cortisol

CK—creatine kinase

CKCE—closed kinetic chain exercise

CMJ—countermovement vertical jump

CNS—central nervous system

CoA—coenzyme A

CoQ—coenzyme Q

COMT—catechol-O-methyltransferase

CPK—creatine phosphokinase

Cr—creatine

CSA—cross-sectional area

CV—coefficient of variation

CVD—cardiovascular disease

CYT—cytochrome

DHEA—dehydroepiandrosterone

DHP—dihydropyridine

DHT—dihydrotestosterone

DNA—deoxyribonucleic acid

DRI—dietary reference intake

DSHEA—Dietary Supplement Health and Education Act

E_2—estradiol

EAA—essential amino acid

EAL—eccentric accentuated loading

EAR—estimated average requirement

EER—estimated energy requirement

EF—effect size

EFA—essential fatty acid

EKG—electrocardiogram

EMG—electromyogram, electromyography

EPI—epinephrine

EPO—erythropoietin

EPOC—excess postexercise oxygen consumption

EPP—end plate potential

E-TKAC—erythrocyte transketolase activation coefficient

ETS—electron transport system

FA—fatty acid

FAD—flavin adenine dinucleotide

FADH—reduced FAD

FDA—Food and Drug Administration

FF—fast-twitch fatigue sensitive (MU type)

FFA—free fatty acid

FG—fast-twitch glycolytic (MU type)

FOG—fast-twitch oxidative glycolytic (MU type)

FR—fast-twitch fatigue resistant (MU type)

FSH—follicle-stimulating hormone

F-TC—force–time curve

G×T—group by trials

GAS—general adaptation syndrome

GDP—guanosine diphosphate

GH—growth hormone

GH-RF—growth hormone-releasing factor

GIP—gastric inhibitory peptide

GLUT—glucose transporter

GRF—gonadotropin releasing factor

GTO—Golgi tendon organ

GTP—guanosine triphosphate

HDL—high-density lipoprotein

hGH—human growth hormone

HMM—heavy meromyosin

HSL—hormone-sensitive lipase

IAAF—International Association of Athletics Federations

ICC—intraclass correlation

IDL—intermediate-density lipoprotein

I:G—insulin:glucagon

IGF—insulin-like growth factor

IMP—inosine monophosphate

IOC—International Olympic Committee

IP$_3$—inositol triphosphate

IZOF—Individual Zones of Optimal Functioning

LBM—lean body mass

LCAT—lecithin cholesterol acetyl transferase

LDH—lactate dehydrogenase

LDL—low-density lipoprotein

LDL-C—low-density lipoprotein cholesterol

LH—luteinizing hormone

LLTE—long-term lag of training effect

LMM—light meromyosin

LT—lactate threshold

MANOVA—multivariate analysis of variance

MAO—mitochondrial monamine oxidase

MCT—monocarboxylate transport protein

MGF—mechano growth factor

MHC—myosin heavy chain

MI—primary motor cortex

MLC—myosin light chain

MP—maximum power

MRI—magnetic resonance imaging

MU—motor unit

MVS—maximum voluntary strength

NAD—nicotinic adenine dinucleotide

NADH—reduced NAD

NEPI—norepinephrine

NGB—national governing body

NIH—National Institutes of Health

NMJ—neuromuscular junction

OBLA—onset of blood lactate

OKCE—open kinetic chain exercise

PCA—phosphatidic acid core

PCr—creatine phosphate

PCSA—physiological cross-sectional area

PF—peak force

PFK—phosphofructokinase

PFV—physiological fuel value

pH—acidity and alkalinity

P$_i$—inorganic phosphate

PMC—premotor cortex

PNS—peripheral nervous system

PP—peak power

PRFD—peak rate of force development

PSE—pseudoephedrine

PVC—premature ventricular contraction

r^2—coefficient of determination

RDA—recommended dietary allowance

RER—respiratory exchange ratio

RFD—rate of force development

RLAA—radiolabeled amino acid

RMP—resting membrane potential

RMR—resting metabolic rate

RNI—recommended nutrient intake (Canada)

ROC—recovery oxygen consumption

ROS—reactive oxygen species

RQ—respiratory quotient

RYR—ryanodine

S—slow-twitch (MU type)

SA—sinoatrial; also specific activity

SAID—specific adaptations to imposed demands

SC—spinal cord

SD—standard deviation

SEM—standard error of the mean

SFRA—stimulus-fatigue-recovery-adaptation theory

SHBG—sex steroid hormone-binding globulin

SJ—static vertical jump

SMA—supplementary motor area

SO—slow-twitch oxidative (MU type)

SPC—statistical process control

SR—sarcoplasmic reticulum

SRIF—somatotropin releasing inhibitory factor

SSC—stretch–shortening cycle

T—testosterone

T:C—testosterone:cortisol

T:E—testosterone:epitestosterone

TEA—thermic effect of physical activity

TEF—thermic effect of food

TEM—thermic effect of a meal

TSH—thyroid-stimulating hormone

UL—tolerable upper intake level

USADA—United States Anti-Doping Agency

VJ—vertical jump

VL—volume load

VLDL—very low-density lipoprotein

Vmax—maximum velocity

$\dot{V}O_2max$—maximal oxygen consumption

WADA—World Anti-Doping Agency

REFERENCES

Chapter 1

Banister, E.W. 1982. Exercise physiology. In: J.J. Jackson and H.A. Wenger (Eds.), *The sport sciences* (pp. 29-42). Victoria, British Columbia, Canada: University of Victoria.

Banister, E.W. 1991. Modeling elite athletic performance. In: J.D. MacDougall, H.A. Wenger, and H.J. Green (Eds.), *Physiological testing of the high-performance athlete* (2nd ed., pp. 403-424). Champaign, IL: Human Kinetics.

Banister, E.W., and T.W. Calvert. 1980. Planning for future performance: Implications for long term training. *Canadian Journal of Applied Sport Sciences* 5(3): 170-176.

Banister, E.W., P. Good, G. Holman, and C.L. Hamilton. 1986. Modeling the training response in athletes. In: D.M. Landers (Ed.), *Sport and elite performers* (*The 1984 Olympic Scientific Congress proceedings*, Vol. 3, pp. 7-23). Champaign, IL: Human Kinetics.

Bloom, B.S. 1985. Generalizations about talent development. In: B.S. Bloom (Ed.), *Developing talent in young people* (pp. 507-549). New York: Ballantine Books.

Bompa, T.O. 1985, February. Talent identification. *Science Periodical on Research and Technology in Sport*, 1-11.

Bompa, T.O. 1990a. Periodization of strength: The most effective methodology of strength training. *National Strength and Conditioning Association Journal* 12(5): 49-52.

Bompa, T.O. 1990b. *Theory and methodology of training* (2nd ed.). Dubuque, IA: Kendall/Hunt.

Bompa, T.O. 1993. *Periodization of strength*. Toronto, Ontario, Canada: Veritas.

Bondarchuk, A. 1988, Winter. Constructing a training system. *Track Technique* 102: 3254-3259, 3268.

Calvert, T.W., E.W. Banister, M.V. Savage, and T. Bach. 1976. A systems model of the effects of training on physical performance. *IEEE Transactions on Systems, Man, and Cybernetics* 6(2): 94-102.

Campney, H.K., and R.W. Wehr. 1965. An interpretation of the strength differences associated with varying angles of pull. *Research Quarterly* 36(4): 403-412.

Cratty, B.J. 1971. Perception. In: L.A. Larson (Ed.), *Encyclopedia of sport sciences and medicine* (pp. 998-999). New York: Macmillan.

Drabik, J. 1996. *Children and sports training*. Island Pond, VT: Stadion.

Editors. 1985, September 30. A plan for cleaning up college sports. *Sports Illustrated* 63(15): 36-37.

Estes, W.K. 1957. Of models and men. *American Psychologist* 12: 609-617.

Fleck, S.J. 1994. Detraining: Its effects on endurance and strength. *Strength and Conditioning* 16(1): 22-28.

Francis, C., and P. Patterson. 1992. *The Charlie Francis training system*. Ottawa, Ontario, Canada: TBLI.

Garhammer, J., and B. Takano. 1992. Training for weightlifting. In: P.V. Komi (Ed.), *Strength and power in sport* (pp. 357-369). Oxford, England: Blackwell Scientific.

Gilbert, D. 1980. *The miracle machine*. New York: Coward, McCann and Geoghegan.

Graves, J.E., M.L. Pollock, A.E. Jones, A.B. Colvin, and S.H. Leggett. 1989. Specificity of limited range of motion variable resistance training. *Medicine and Science in Sports and Exercise* 21(1): 84-89.

Graves, J.E., M.L. Pollock, S.H. Leggett, R.W. Braith, D.M. Carpenter, and L.E. Bishop. 1988. Effect of reduced training frequency on muscular strength. *International Journal of Sports Medicine* 9: 316-319.

Greenspan, E. 1983. *Little winners*. Boston: Little, Brown.

Harre, D. 1982. *Principles of sports training*. Berlin, German Democratic Republic: Sportverlag.

Harre, D. 1986, August. Recovery: Part two—overtraining. *Science Periodical on Research and Technology in Sport*, 1-7.

Harre, D. 1990. The dynamics of the training load. In: J. Jarver (Ed.), *A collection of European sports science translations part II* (pp. 39-41). Kidman Park, Australia: South Australian Sports Institute.

Hill, C.R. 1996. *Olympic politics* (2nd ed.). Manchester, U.K.: Manchester University Press.

Hoberman, J. 1992. *Mortal engines*. New York: Free Press.

Hodge, K.P., and D.A. Tod. 1993. Ethics of childhood sport. *Sports Medicine* 15(5): 291-298.

Hugh Morton, R. 1991. The quantitative periodization of athletic training: A model study. *Sports Medicine, Training and Rehabilitation* 3: 19-28.

Johnson, W.O., and A. Verschoth. 1991. *Thrown free*. New York: Simon & Schuster.

Jones, L.A. 1988. Motor illusions: What do they reveal about proprioception? *Psychological Bulletin* 103(1): 72-86.

Kurz, T. 1991. *Science of sports training.* Island Pond, VT: Stadion.

Lutz, D.J. 1990. An overview of training models in sport psychology. *Sport Psychologist* 4: 63-71.

Masood, E. 1996. Bannister urges spreading the net. *Nature* 382(6586): 13.

Matsudo, V.K.R. 1996. Prediction of future athletic excellence. In: O. Bar-Or (Ed.), *The child and adolescent athlete* (pp. 92-109). Oxford, England: Blackwell Science.

Matveyev, L. 1977. *Fundamentals of sports training.* Moscow: Progress.

Miracle, A.W., and Rees, C.R. 1994. *Lessons of the locker room.* Amherst, NY: Prometheus Books.

Moffroid, M., and R.H. Whipple. 1970. Specificity of speed of exercise. *Physical Therapy* 50: 1693-1699.

Morrissey, M.C., E.A. Harman, and M.J. Johnson. 1995. Resistance training modes: Specificity and effectiveness. *Medicine and Science in Sports and Exercise* 27(5): 648-660.

Morton, R.H., J.R. Fitz-Clarke, and E.W. Banister. 1990. Modeling human performance in running. *Journal of Applied Physiology* 69(3): 1171-1177.

Murphy, A. 1991, July 1. Unsportsmanlike conduct. *Sports Illustrated* 75(1): 22-24.

Nilsson, S. 1987. Overtraining. In: S. Maehlum, S. Nilsson, and P. Renstrom (Eds.), *An update on sports medicine* (*Proceedings from the Second Scandinavian Conference in Sports Medicine,* Soria Moria, Oslo, March 9-15, 1986, pp. 97-104). Oslo: Danish and Norwegian Sports Medicine Associations and the Swedish Society of Sports Medicine.

O'Brien, R. 1993. Preliminary talent identification test development: Physical performance measures of junior Olympic divers. In: R. Malina and J.L. Gabriel (Eds.), *U.S. Diving Sport Science Seminar 1993 proceedings* (pp. 17-25). Indianapolis: U.S. Diving.

Oda, S., and T. Moritani. 1994. Maximal isometric force and neural activity during bilateral and unilateral elbow flexion in humans. *European Journal of Applied Physiology and Occupational Physiology* 69: 240-243.

Olbrecht, J. 2000. *The science of winning.* Lutton, England: Swimshop.

Ozolin, N.G. 1970. Do not simplify the training program. *Yessis Review of Soviet Physical Education and Sports* 5(4): 84-93.

Poliquin, C. 1988, August. Variety in strength training. *Science Periodical on Research and Technology in Sport* 8: 1-7.

Poliquin, C. 1991. Training for improving relative strength. *Science Periodical on Research and Technology in Sport* 11: 1-9.

Pope, H.G., D.L. Katz, and R. Champoux. 1988. Anabolic-androgenic steroid use among 1,010 college men. *Physician and Sportsmedicine* 16(7): 75-81.

Preising, W. 1989. Children in sport: A European perspective. *Sports Coach* 12(3): 27-31.

Press, A. 1992, August 10. Old too soon, wise too late? *Newsweek,* 22-24.

Rasch, P.J., and L.E. Morehouse. 1957. Effect of static and dynamic exercise on muscular strength and hypertrophy. *Journal of Applied Physiology* 11(1): 29-34.

Reeve, T.G., and R. Mainor. 1983. Effects of movement context on the encoding of kinesthetic spatial information. *Research Quarterly for Exercise and Sport* 54: 352-363.

Sale, D., and D. MacDougall. 1981. Specificity in strength training: A review for the coach and athlete. *Canadian Journal of Applied Sport Sciences* 6(2): 87-92.

Sands, W.A. 1991a. Monitoring the elite female gymnast. *National Strength and Conditioning Association Journal* 13(4): 66-71.

Sands, W.A. 1991b. Science puts the spin on somersaulting. *RIP* 2(2): 18-20.

Sands, W.A. 1993. *Talent opportunity program.* Indianapolis: United States Gymnastics Federation.

Shultz, B.B., and W.A. Sands. 1995. Understanding measurement concepts and statistical procedures. In: P.J. Maud and C. Foster (Eds.), *Physiological assessment of human fitness* (pp. 257-287). Champaign, IL: Human Kinetics.

Siff, M.C. 1996a. *Puzzle & Paradox,* 73.

Siff, M.C. 1996b. *Puzzle & Paradox,* 73.

Siff, M.C., and Y.V. Verkhoshansky. 1993. *Supertraining.* Johannesburg, South Africa: University of the Witwatersrand, School of Mechanical Engineering.

Simon, R.L. 1991. *Fair play.* Boulder, CO: Westview Press.

Tabachnik, B., and V. Mekhrikadze. 1986. The aim of training—the competitive model (sprint). *Soviet Sports Review* 21: 105-108.

Taranov, V., I. Mironenko, and V. Sergejev. 1995. A cyclic blocks system for jumping events. *Modern Athlete and Coach* 33(4): 28-30.

Telander, R., and R. Sullivan. 1989, February 27. You reap what you sow. *Sports Illustrated* 70(9): 20-26.

Todd, T., and D. Hoover. 1979. *Fitness for athletes.* Chicago: Contemporary Books.

Verhoshansky, U.V. 1985a. The long-lasting training effect of strength exercises. *Soviet Sports Review* 20: 1-3.

Verhoshansky, U.V. 1985b. The long-lasting training effect of strength exercises. *Soviet Sports Review* 20: 91-93.

Verkhoshansky, U. 1981. How to set up a training program in speed-strength events. *Soviet Sports Review* 16: 53-57.

Verkhoshansky, Y.V. 1977. *Fundamentals of special strength-training in sport.* Moscow: Fizkultura i Sport; Livonia, MI: Sportivny Press, 1986 [translated by A. Charniga].

Verkhoshansky, Y.V. 1981. Special strength training. *Soviet Sports Review* 16: 6-10.

Verkhoshansky, Y.V. 1985. *Programming and organization of training.* Moscow: Fizkultura i Sport; Livonia, MI: Sportivny Press, 1988 [translated by A. Charniga].

Viru, A. 1988. Planning of macrocycles. *Modern Athlete and Coach* 26: 7-10 [translated from *Kehakultuur* 47(19), 1986, Tallinin, Estonian U.S.S.R.].

Viru, A. 1990. Some facts about the construction of microcycles in training. In: J. Jarver (Ed.), *A collection of European sports science translations* (pp. 11-13). Kidman Park, Australia: South Australian Sports Institute.

Viru, A. 1995. *Adaptation in sports training.* Boca Raton, FL: CRC Press.

Yesalis, C.E. 1993. Introduction. In: C.E. Yesalis (Ed.), *Anabolic steroids in sport and exercise* (pp. xxiv-xxxiv). Champaign, IL: Human Kinetics.

Yesalis, C.E., S.P. Courson, and J. Wright. 1993. History of anabolic steroid use in sport and exercise. In: C.E. Yesalis (Ed.), *Anabolic steroids in sport and exercise* (pp. 35-47). Champaign, IL: Human Kinetics.

Zatsiorsky, V.M. 1995. *Science and practice of strength training.* Champaign, IL: Human Kinetics.

Chapter 2

Alexander, R.M., and A. Vernon. 1975. The dimensions of knee and ankle muscles and the forces they exert. *Journal of Human Movement Studies* 1: 115-123.

Anderson, D.C., S.C. King, and S.M. Parsons. 1982. Proton gradient linkage to active uptake of [³H] acetylcholine by Torpedo electric organ synaptic vesicles. *Biochemistry* 21: 3037-3043.

Baldwin, K.M. 1984. Muscle development: Neonatal to adult. In: R.L. Terjung (Ed.), *Exercise and sport science reviews* (Vol. 12, pp. 1-19). Lexington, MA: Collamore Press.

Barany, M. 1967. ATPase activity of myosin correlated with speed of muscle shortening. *Journal of General Physiology* 50: 197-218.

Barchi, R.L. 1988. Probing the molecular structure of the voltage-dependent sodium channel. *Annual Review of Neuroscience* 11: 455-495.

Barnard, R.J., V.R. Edgerton, and J.B. Peter. 1970. Effect of exercise on skeletal muscle: I. Biochemical and histochemical properties. *Journal of Applied Physiology* 28: 762-766.

Bennett, M.K., N. Callakos, and R.H. Scheller. 1992. Syntaxin: A synaptic protein implicated in docking of synaptic vesicles at presynaptic active zones. *Science* 257: 255-259.

Bergstrom, J. 1962. Muscle electrolytes in man. *Scandinavian Journal of Clinical Investigation* (Suppl.) 14: 1-110.

Billeter, R., C.W. Heizmann, H. Howald, and E. Jenny. 1981. Analysis of myosin light and heavy chain types in single human muscle fibers. *European Journal of Biochemistry* 116: 389-395.

Billeter, R., and H. Hoppler. 1992. Muscular basis of strength. In: P.V. Komi (Ed.), *Strength and power in sport* (pp. 39-63). Champaign, IL: Human Kinetics.

Binkhorst, R.A., and M.A. van't Hof. 1973. Force velocity relationship and contraction time of the rat fast plantaris muscle due to compensatory hypertrophy. *Pfluegers Archiv* 342: 145-158.

Brooke, M.H., and K.K. Kaiser. 1970. Three "myosin adenosine triphosphatase" systems: The nature of their pH lability and sulfhydryl dependence. *Journal of Histochemistry and Cytochemistry* 18: 670-672.

Brooks, G.A., T.D. Fahey, and T.P. White. 1996. *Exercise physiology* (2nd ed.). Mountain View, CA: Mayfield.

Burke, R.E. 1981. Motor units: Anatomy, physiology and functional organization. In: V.B. Brooks (Ed.), *Handbook of physiology,* Section I, *The nervous system II* (pp. 345-422). Washington, DC: American Physiological Society.

Burke, R.E., D.N. Levine, and F.E. Zajac. 1971. Mammalian motor units: Physiological histochemical correlation in three types in cat gastrocnemius. *Science* 174: 709-712.

Caldwell, P.C. 1968. Factors governing movement and distribution of inorganic ions in nerve and muscle. *Physiological Reviews* 48: 1-38.

Catterall, W.A. 1988. Structure and function of voltage sensitive channels. *Science* 242: 50-61.

Chalmers, G. 2002. Do Golgi tendon organs really inhibit muscle activity at high force levels to save muscles from injury and adapt with training? *Sports Biomechanics* 1(2): 239-249.

Dean, R.B. 1941. Theories of electrolyte equilibrium in muscle. *Biological Symposium* 3: 331-339.

Dulhunty, A.F., and C. Franzini-Armstrong. 1975. The relative contribution of the folds and caveolae to the surface membrane of the frog skeletal fibers at different sarcomere lengths. *Journal of Physiology* 250: 513-539.

Duysens, J., F. Clarac, and H. Cruse. 2000. Load-regulating mechanisms underlying the clasp-knife reflex in the cat. *Journal of Neurophysiology* 64: 1303-1318.

Ebashi, S., and M. Endo. 1968. Calcium ion and muscle contraction. *Progress in Biophysics and Molecular Biology* 18: 125-183.

Eccles, J., R. Eccles, and A. Lundberg. 1957. Synaptic actions on motoneurones caused by impulses in Golgi tendon organ afferents. *Journal of Physiology* 138: 227-252.

Edman, K.A.P., and C. Reggiani. 1987. The sarcomere length-tension relation determined in short segments of intact muscle fibres of the frog. *Journal of Physiology* 385: 709-732.

Edman, K.A.P., C. Reggiani, S. Schiaffino, and G. te Kronnie. 1988. Maximum velocity of shortening related to myosin isoform composition in frog skeletal muscle. *Journal of Physiology* 395: 679-694.

Eisenberg, B.R. 1983. Quantitative ultrastructure of mammalian skeletal muscle. In: L.D. Peachy, R.H. Adrian, and S.R. Geiger (Eds.), *Handbook of physiology. Skeletal muscle* (pp. 73-112). Baltimore: Williams & Wilkins.

Engel, A.G., T.J. Walls, A. Nagel, and O. Uchitel. 1990. Newly recognized congenital myasthenic syndromes: I. Quantal release. II. High conductance fast-channel syndrome. III. Abnormal acetylcholine receptor (AChR) interaction with acetylcholine. IV. AChR deficiency and short channel-open time. *Progress in Brain Research* 84: 125-137.

English, A.W. 1984. An electromyographic analysis of compartments in cat lateral gastrocnemius during unrestrained locomotion. *Journal of Neurophysiology* 52: 114-125.

English, A.W., and W.D. Ledbetter. 1982. Anatomy and innervation patterns of cat lateral gastrocnemius and plantaris muscles. *American Journal of Anatomy* 164: 67-77.

Ennion, S., J.S. Pereira, A.J. Sargent, A. Young, and G. Goldspink. 1995. Characterization of human skeletal muscle fibers according to the myosin heavy chains they express. *Journal of Muscle Research and Cell Motility* 16: 35-43.

Fambrough, D.M. 1979. Control of acetylcholine receptors in skeletal muscle. *Physiological Reviews* 59: 165-227.

Feinstein, B., B. Lindegard, E. Nyman, and G. Wohlfart. 1955. Morphologic studies of motor units in normal human muscles. *Acta Anatomica* 23: 127-142.

Fenn, W.O. 1923. The relation between the work performed and the energy liberated in muscle. *Journal of Physiology (London)* 180: 343-345.

Finer, J.T., R.M. Simmons, and J.A. Spudich. 1994. Single myosin molecules mechanics: Piconewton forces and nanometer steps. *Nature* 368: 113-119.

Fukunaga, T., Y. Ichinose, M. Ito, Y. Kawakami, and S. Fukashiro. 1997. Determination of fascicle length and pennation in contracting human muscle in vivo. *Journal of Applied Physiology* 82(1): 354-358.

Gage, P.W., and R.S. Eisenberg. 1969. Action potential, after potentials and excitation coupling in frog sartorius fibers without transverse tubules. *Journal of General Physiology* 53: 298-310.

Gans, C., and A.S. Gaunt. 1991. Muscle architecture in relation to function. *Journal of Biomechanics* 24(Suppl. 1): 53-65.

Gardiner, P.F. 2001. *Neuromuscular aspects of physical activity.* Champaign, IL: Human Kinetics.

Geren, B.B. 1954. The formation from the Schwann cell surface of myelin in the peripheral nerves of chick embryos. *Experimental Research* 7: 558-562.

Gordon, A.M., A.F. Huxley, and F.J. Julian. 1966. The variation in isometric twitch tension with sarcomere length in vertebrate muscle fibers. *Journal of Physiology* 184: 170-192.

Gordon, D.C., C.G.M. Hammond, J.T. Fisher, and F.J.R. Richmond. 1989. Muscle-fiber architecture, innervation, and histochemistry in the diaphragm of a cat. *Journal of Morphology* 201: 131-143.

Gowitzke, B.A., and M. Milner. 1988. *Scientific basis of human movement.* Baltimore: Williams & Wilkins.

Granit, R., J-O. Kellerth, and A. Szumski. 1966. Intracellular autogenic effects of muscular contraction on extensor motoneurones. The silent period. *Journal of Physiology* 182: 484-503.

Green, D., and J-O. Kellerth. 1967. Intracellular autogenic and synergistic effects of muscular contraction on flexor motoneurones. *Journal of Physiology* 193: 73-94.

Grill, S.E., and M. Hallet. 1995. Velocity sensitivity of human muscle spindle afferents and slowly adapting type II cutaneous mechanoreceptors. *Journal of Physiology (London)* 489(Part 2): 593-602.

Guyton, A.C. 1976. Organ physiology: *Structure and function of the nervous system.* Philadelphia: Saunders.

Hannerz, J. 1974. Discharge properties of motor units in relation to recruitment order in voluntary contraction. *Acta Physiologica Scandinavica* 91: 374-384.

Henneman, E.H., P. Clamann, J.D. Giles, and R.D. Skinner. 1974. Rank order of motoneurons within a pool, law of combination. *Journal of Neurophysiology* 37: 1338-1349.

Heuser, J.E., and T.S. Reese. 1973. Evidence for a recycling of synaptic vesicle membrane during transmitter release at frog neuromuscular junction. *Journal of Cell Biology* 57: 315-344.

Hubbard, J.I. 1973. Microphysiology of vertebrate neuromuscular transmission. *Physiological Reviews* 53: 674-692.

Huijing, P.A. 1992. Mechanical muscle models. In: P.V. Komi (Ed.), *Strength and power in sport* (pp. 130-150). Champaign, IL: Human Kinetics.

Hutton, R.S. 1992. The neuromuscular basis of stretching exercise. In: P.V. Komi (Ed.), *Strength and power in sport* (pp. 29-38) Champaign, IL: Human Kinetics.

Huxley, A.F., and R. Niedergerke. 1954. Structural changes in muscle during contraction. Interference microscopy of living muscle fibers. *Nature* 173: 971-973.

Huxley, H.E. 1958. The contraction of muscle. *Scientific American* 199: 67-82.

Huxley, H.E. 1969. The mechanism of muscular contraction. *Science* 164: 1356-1366.

Huxley, H.E., and J. Hanson. 1954. Changes in the cross striations of muscle during contraction and stretch and their structural interpretation. *Nature* 173: 973-976.

Kamb, A., L.E. Iverson, and M.A. Tanouye. 1987. Molecular characterization of *Shaker,* a Drosophila gene that encodes a potassium channel. *Cell* 50: 405-413.

Kimura, M. 1990. Behaviorally contingent property of movement related activity of the primate putamen. *Journal of Neurophysiology* 63: 1277-1296.

Knuttgen, H.G., and W.J. Kraemer. 1987. Terminology and measurement in exercise performance. *Journal of Applied Sport Science Research* 1(1): 1-10.

Kuffler, S.W., and D. Yoshikami. 1975. The number of transmitter molecules in a quantum: An estimate from iontophoretic applications of acetylcholine at the neuro-muscular synapse. *Journal of Physiology* 251: 465-482.

Kyrolainen, H., R. Kivela, S. Koskinen, J. McBride, J.L. Andersen, T. Takala, S. Sipila, and P.V. Komi. 2003. Interrelationships between muscle structure, muscle strength and running economy. *Medicine and Science in Sports and Exercise* 35: 45-49.

Lowey, S., G.S. Waller, and K.M. Trybus. 1993. Skeletal muscle myosin light chains are essential for physiological speeds of shortening. *Nature* 365: 454-456.

McBride, J.M., T.N. Triplett-McBride, A.J. Davies, P.J. Abernethy, and R.U. Newton. 2003. Characteristics of titin in strength and power athletes. *European Journal of Applied Physiology* 88: 553-557.

McComas, A.J. 1996. *Skeletal muscle.* Champaign, IL: Human Kinetics.

Nosek, T.M., N. Guo, J.M. Ginsberg, and R.C. Kobeck. 1990. Inositol (1,4,5) triphosphate (IP_3) within dia-phragm muscles increases upon depolarization. *Biophysical Journal* 57: 401a.

Noth, J. 1992a. Cortical and peripheral control. In: P.V. Komi (Ed.), *Strength and power in sport* (pp. 9-20). Champaign, IL: Human Kinetics.

Noth, J. 1992b. Motor units. In: P.V. Komi (Ed.), *Strength and power in sport* (pp. 21-28). Champaign, IL: Human Kinetics.

Otten, E. 1988. Concepts and models of functional archi-tecture in skeletal muscle. *Exercise and Sports Sciences Reviews* 26: 89-137.

Payne, M.R., and S.E. Rudnick. 1989. Regulation of ver-tebrate striated muscle contraction. *Trends in Biochemical Sciences* 14: 357-360.

Peter, J.B., R.J. Barnard, V.R. Edgerton, C.A. Gillespie, and K.E. Stempel. 1972. Metabolic profiles of three fiber types of skeletal muscle in guinea pigs and rabbits. *Biochemistry* 11: 2627-2633.

Pette, D., and R.S. Staron. 1990. Cellular and molecular diversities of mammalian skeletal muscle fibers. *Reviews in Physiology, Biochemistry and Pharmacology* 116: 1-76.

Pette, D., and R.S. Staron. 2000. Myosin isoforms, muscle fiber types and transitions. *Microscope Research Technology* 50(6): 500-509.

Rayment, I., H.M. Holden, M. Whitiker, C.B. Yohnn, M. Lorenz, K.C. Holmes, and R.A. Milligan. 1993. Structure of the actin-myosin complex and its implications for muscle contraction. *Science* 261: 58-65.

Reiser, P.J., R.L. Moss, G.G. Giulian, and M.L. Geaser. 1985. Shortening velocity of single fibers from adult rabbit soleus muscles is correlated with myosin chain composition. *Journal of Biochemistry* 260: 9077-9080.

Richmond, F.J.R., and J.B. Armstrong. 1988. Fiber architecture and histochemistry in the cat neck muscle, biventer cervicis. *Journal of Neurophysiology* 60: 46-59.

Romanes, G.J. 1941. The development and significance of the cell columns in the ventral horn of the cervical and upper thoracic spinal cord of the rabbit. *Journal of Anatomy* 76: 112-130.

Romanes, G.J. 1951. The motor-cell columns of the lumbo-sacral cord of the cat. *Journal of Comparative Neurology* 94: 313-364.

Roy, R.R., and V.R. Edgerton. 1992. Skeletal muscle architecture and performance. In: P.V. Komi (Ed.), *Strength and power in sport* (pp. 115-129). Champaign, IL: Human Kinetics.

Sacks, R.D., and R.R. Roy. 1982. Architecture of the hind limb muscles of cats: Functional significance. *Journal of Morphology* 173: 185-195.

Sant'Ana Pereira, J.A., A.J. Sargeant, A.C. Rademaker, A. de Haan, and M. van Mechelen. 1996. Myosin heavy chain isoform expression and high energy phosphate content in muscle fibres at rest and post-exercise. *Journal of Physiology (London)* 496(Part 2): 583-588.

Sato, K.C., and J. Tanji. 1989. Digit-muscle response evoked from multiple intracortical foci in monkey precentral motor cortex. *Journal of Neurophysiology* 62: 959-970.

Seidel, J.C. 1967. Studies on myosin from red and white skeletal muscles of the rabbit. II. Inactivation of myosin from red muscles under mild alkaline conditions. *Journal of Biological Chemistry* 242: 5623-5629.

Sherrington, C.S. 1906. *The integrative action of the nervous system.* New Haven, CT: Yale University Press.

Sherrington, C.S. 1929. Some functional problems attaching to convergence. *Proceedings of the Royal Society of London (Series B)* 105: 332-362.

Slater, C.R., P.R. Lyons, T.J. Walls, P.R.W. Fawcett, and C. Young. 1992. Structure and function of the neuro-muscular junction in the vastus lateralis in man. *Brain* 115: 451-478.

Soechting, J., and M. Flanders. 1991. Arm movements in three-dimensional space: Computation, theory and observation. *Exercise and Sport Sciences Reviews* 19: 389-418.

Spector, S.A., P.F. Gardiner, R.F. Zernicke, R.R. Roy, and V.R. Edgerton. 1980. Muscle architecture and force-velocity characteristics of cat soleus and medial gastrocnemius: Implications for motor control. *Journal of Neurophysiology* 44: 951-960.

Staron, R.S. 1997. The classification of human skeletal muscle fiber types. *Journal of Strength and Conditioning Research* 11(2): 67.

Staron, R.S., and R.S. Hikida. 1992. Histochemical, bio-chemical and ultrastructural analyses of single human muscle fibers with special reference to the C-fiber population. *Journal of Histochemistry and Cytochemistry* 40(4): 563-568.

Stone, M.H., and H. Lipner. 1978. Response to intensive training and methandrostenolone administration: I. Contractile and performance variables. *Pfluegers Archiv* 375: 141-146.

Tidball, J.G. 1983. The geometry of actin filament-membrane interactions can modify adhesive strength of the myotendinous junction. *Cell Motility* 3: 439-447.

Tihanyi, J., P. Apor, and G.Y. Fekete. 1982. Force-velocity-power characteristics and fiber composition in human knee extensor muscles. *European Journal of Applied Physiology* 48: 331-343.

Trinick, J. 1991. Elastic filaments and giant proteins in muscle. *Current Opinion in Cell Biology* 3: 112-119.

Usdin, T.B., and G.D. Fischbach. 1986. Purification and characterization of a polypeptide from chick brain that promotes accumulation of acetylcholine receptors in chick myotubes. *Journal of Cell Biology* 103: 493-507.

Wagenknecht, T., R. Grassucci, J. Frank, A. Saito, M. Inui, and S. Fleischer. 1989. Three-dimensional architecture of calcium channel/foot structure of sarcoplasmic reticulum. *Nature* 338: 167-170.

Wickiewicz, T.L., R.R. Roy, P.L. Powell, and V.R. Edgerton. 1983. Muscle architecture of the human lower limb. *Clinical Orthopaedics and Related Research* 179: 275-283.

Wickiewicz, T.L., R.R. Roy, P.L. Powell, J.J. Perrine, and V.R. Edgerton. 1984. Muscle architecture and force-velocity relationships in humans. *Journal of Applied Physiology* 57: 435-443.

Wise, S.P., and P.L. Strick. 1984. Anatomical and physiological organization of the non-primary motor cortex. *Trends in Neuroscience* 7: 442-446.

Chapter 3

Aagaard, P. 2003. Training-induced changes in neural function. *Exercise and Sport Sciences Reviews* 31: 61-67.

Adams, G.R., B.M. Hather, K.M. Baldwin et al. 1993. Skeletal muscle myosin heavy chain composition and resistance training. *Journal of Applied Physiology* 74: 911-915.

Alway, S.E., W.H. Grumbt, W.J. Gonyea et al. 1989. Contrast in muscle and myofibers of elite male and female bodybuilders. *Journal of Applied Physiology* 67: 24-31.

Asmussen, E., O. Hansen, and O. Lammert. 1965. The relation between isometric and dynamic muscle strength in man. *Communications from the Testing and Observation Institute of the Danish National Association for Infantile Paralysis,* No. 20.

Åstrand, P-O., and K. Rodahl. 1970. *Textbook of work physiology.* New York: McGraw-Hill.

Barham, J. 1978. *Mechanical kinesiology.* St. Louis: Mosby.

Bawa, P. 2002. Neural control of motor output: Can training change it? *Exercise and Sport Sciences Reviews* 30: 59-63.

Bernardi, M., M. Solomonov, G. Nguyen et al. 1996. Motor unit recruitment strategy changes with skill acquisition. *European Journal of Applied Physiology* 74: 52-59.

Bobbert, M.F. 2001. Dependence of human squat jump performance on the series elastic compliance of the triceps surae: A simulation study. *Journal of Experimental Biology* 204(Part 3): 533-542.

Bodine, S., R.R. Roy, E. Eldred et al. 1987. Maximal force as a function of anatomical features of motor units in the cat tibialis anterior. *Journal of Neurophysiology* 57: 1730-1745.

Bodine, S., R.R. Roy, D.A. Meadows et al. 1982. Architectural, histochemical and contractile characteristics of a unique biarticular muscle: The cat semitendinosus. *Journal of Neurophysiology* 48: 192-201.

Brooks, G.A., T.D. Fahey, and T.P. White. 1996. *Exercise physiology: Human bioenergetics and its applications.* Mountain View, CA: Mayfield.

Burke, E., F. Cerny, D. Costill et al. 1977. Characteristics of skeletal muscle in competitive cyclists. *Medicine and Science in Sports* 9: 109-112.

Chow, J.W., W.G. Darling, and J.G. Hay. 1997. Mechanical characteristics of knee extension exercises performed on an isokinetic dynamometer. *Medicine and Science in Sports and Exercise* 29: 794-803.

Clamann, H.P., and T.B. Schelhorn. 1988. Nonlinear force addition of the newly recruited motor units in the cat hindlimb. *Muscle and Nerve* 11: 1079-1089.

Conley, M., M.H. Stone, M.J. Nimmons, and G.A. Dudley. 1997. Resistance training specificity and neck muscle hypertrophy. *European Journal of Applied Physiology* 75: 443-448.

Cronin, J.B., P.J. McNaira, and R.N. Marshall. 2000. The role of maximum strength and load on initial power production. *Medicine and Science in Sports and Exercise* 32:1763-1769.

Cutts, A., and B.B. Seedhom. 1993. Validity of cadaveric data for muscle physiological cross-sectional area ratios: A comparative study of cadaveric and in-vivo data in human thigh muscles. *Clinical Biomechanics* 8: 156-162.

Desmedt, J.E., and E. Godaux. 1979. Voluntary motor commands in human ballistic movement. *Journal of Physiology* 264: 673-693.

Desmedt, J.E., and E. Godaux. 1981. Spinal motoneuron recruitment in man: Rank deordering with direction but not with speed of voluntary movement. *Science* 214: 933-936.

Duchateau, J., S. LeBozec, and K. Hainaut. 1986. Contribution of slow and fast muscles of triceps surae to a cyclic movement. *European Journal of Applied Physiology* 55: 476-481.

Edgerton, V.R., R.R. Roy, R.J. Gregor et al. 1986. Morphological basis of skeletal muscle power output. In:

N.L. Jones, N. McCartney, and A.J. McComas (Eds.), *Human muscle power* (pp. 43-64). Champaign, IL: Human Kinetics.

Edstrom, L., and B. Ekblom. 1972. Differences in sizes of red and white muscle fibers in vastus lateralis of musculus quadriceps femoris of normal individuals and athletes. Relation to physical performance. *Scandinavian Journal of Clinical Laboratory Investigation* 30: 175-181.

Faulkner, J.A., D.R. Claflin, and K.K. McCully. 1986. Power output of fast and slow fibers from human skeletal muscle. In: N.L. Jones, N. McCartney, and A.J. McComas (Eds.), *Human muscle power* (pp. 81-94). Champaign, IL: Human Kinetics.

Finni, T., S. Ikegewa, and P.V. Komi. 2001. Concentric force enhancement during human movement. *Acta Physiologica Scandinavica* 173: 369-377.

Fitts, R.H., and J.J. Widrick. 1997. Muscle mechanics: Adaptations with exercise-training. In: J.O. Holloszy (Ed.), *Exercise and sport sciences reviews* (pp. 427-473). Baltimore: Williams & Wilkins.

Fleckstein, J.L., D. Watumull, L.A. Betocci et al. 1992. Finger specific flexor recruitment in humans: Depiction by exercise-enhanced MRI. *Journal of Applied Physiology* 72: 1974-1977.

Friden, J., M. Sjostrom, and B. Ekblom. 1981. A morphological study of delayed muscle soreness. *Experientia* 37: 506-507.

Fukunaga, T., R.R. Roy, F.G. Shellock et al. 1996. Specific tension of human plantar flexors and dorsiflexors. *Journal of Applied Physiology* 80: 158-165.

Garhammer, J. 1989. Weightlifting and training. In: C. Vaughn (Ed.), *Biomechanics of sport*. Boca Raton, FL: CRC.

Gowitzke, B.A., and M. Milner. 1988. *Scientific bases of human movement* (3rd ed.). Baltimore: Williams & Wilkins.

Grimby, L., and J. Hannerz. 1977. Firing rates and recruitment order of toe extensor motor units in different modes of voluntary contraction. *Journal of Applied Physiology* 264: 865-879.

Hakkinen, K., K. Alen, and P.V. Komi. 1984. Neuromuscular, anaerobic and aerobic performance characteristics of elite power athletes. *European Journal of Applied Physiology* 53: 97-105.

Harman, E. 1994a. Biomechanical factors in human strength. *Strength and Conditioning* 16(1): 46-53.

Harman, E. 1994b. Resistance training modes: A biomechanical perspective. *Strength and Conditioning* 16(2): 59-65.

Hay, J.G. 1992. Mechanical basis for strength expression. In: P.V. Komi (Ed.), *Strength and power in sport*. Champaign, IL: Human Kinetics.

Henneman, E., G. Somjen, and D.O. Carpenter. 1965a. Functional significance of cell size in spinal motoneurons. *Journal of Neurophysiology* 28: 560-580.

Henneman, E., G. Somjen, and D.O. Carpenter. 1965b. Excitability and inhibitability of motoneurons of different sizes. *Journal of Neurophysiology* 28: 599-620.

Herzog, W. 1996. Force-sharing among synergistic muscles: Theoretical considerations and experimental approaches. In: J.O. Holloszy (Ed.), *Exercise and sport sciences reviews* (pp. 173-202). Baltimore: Williams & Wilkins.

Hester, D., G. Hunter, K. Shuleva et al. 1990. Review and evaluation of relative strength-handicapping models. *National Strength and Conditioning Association Journal* 12(1): 54-57.

Holloszy, J.O., and E.F. Coyle. 1984. Adaptations of skeletal muscle to endurance exercise and their metabolic consequences. *Journal of Applied Physiology* 56: 831-838.

Huijing, P.A. 1992. Mechanical muscle models. In: P.V. Komi (Ed.), *Strength and power in sport* (pp. 130-150). London: Blackwell Scientific.

Hunter, G., D. Hester, S. Snyder et al. 1990. Rationale and methods for evaluating relative strength-handicapping models. *National Strength and Conditioning Association Journal* 12: 47-57.

Huxley, A.F. 1957. Muscle structure and theories of contraction. *Progress in Biophysics and Biophysical Chemistry* 7: 255-318.

Jones, D.A., and J.M. Round. 1990. *Skeletal muscle in health and disease*. New York: Manchester University Press.

Kauhanen, H., J. Garhammer, and K. Hakkinen. 2000. Relationship between power output, body size and snatch performance in elite weightlifters. In: *Proceedings of the Fifth Annual Congress of the European College of Sports Science*, Jyvaskala, Finland (p. 383). Finland: University of Jyvaskala.

Kauhanen, H., P.V. Komi, and K. Hakkinen. 2002. Standardization and validation of the body weight adjustment regression equations in Olympic weightlifting. *Journal of Strength and Conditioning Research* 16: 58-74.

Komi, P.V., H. Rusko, J. Vos et al. 1977a. Anaerobic performance capacity in athletes. *Acta Physiologica Scandinavica* 100: 107-114.

Komi, P.V., J.T. Viitasalo, M. Havu et al. 1976. Physiological and performance capacity: Effect of heredity. *International series on biomechanics, biomechanics V-A* (Vol. 1A, pp. 118-123). Baltimore: University Park Press.

Komi, P.V., J.T. Viitasalo, M. Havu et al. 1977b. Skeletal muscle fibers and muscle enzyme activities in monozygous and dizygous twins of both sexes. *Acta Physiologica Scandinavica* 100: 385-392.

Lieber, R.L., T. McKee-Woodburn, and J. Friden. 1991. Muscle damage induced by eccentric contractions of 25% strain. *Journal of Applied Physiology* 70: 2498-2507.

Loeb, G. 1985. Motoneurone task groups: Coping with kinematic heterogeneity. *Journal of Experimental Biology* 115: 137-146.

Miller, A.E.J., J.D. MacDougall, M.A. Tarnopolsky et al. 1993. Gender differences in strength and muscle fiber characteristics. *European Journal of Applied Physiology* 66: 254-262.

Moritani, T., L. Oddsson, and A. Thorstensson. 1990. Differences in modulation of the gastrocnemius and soleus H-reflexes during hopping in man. *Acta Physiologica Scandinavica* 138: 575-576.

Morrow, M.A., and L.E. Miller. 2003. Prediction of muscle activity by populations of sequentially recorded primary motor cortex neurons. *Journal of Neurophysiology* 89: 2279-2288.

Nakazawa, K., Y. Kawakami, T. Fukunaga et al. 1993. Differences in activation patterns in elbow flexors during isometric, concentric and eccentric contractions. *European Journal of Applied Physiology* 66: 214-220.

Nardone, A., C. Romano, and M. Schieppati. 1989. Selective recruitment of high-threshold human motor units during voluntary isotonic lengthening of active muscles. *Journal of Physiology* 409: 451-471.

Nardone, A., and M. Schiepatti. 1988. Shift of activity from slow to fast muscle during voluntary lengthening contractions of the triceps surae muscle in humans. *Journal of Physiology* 395: 363-381.

Osternig, L.R. 1986. Isokinetic dynamometry: Implications for muscle testing and rehabilitation. In: K.B. Pandolf (Ed.), *Exercise and sport science reviews.* New York: Macmillan.

Ounjian, M., R.R. Roy, E. Eldred et al. 1991. Physiological and developmental implications of motor unit anatomy. *Journal of Neurobiology* 22: 547-559.

Patel, T.J., and R.L. Lieber. 1997. Force transmission in skeletal muscle: From actomyosin to external tendons. In: J.O. Holloszy (Ed.), *Exercise and sport sciences reviews* (pp. 321-363). Baltimore: Williams & Wilkins.

Powell, P.L., R.R. Roy, O. Kanim, M.A. Bello, and V.R. Edgerton. 1984. Predicability of skeletal muscle tension from architectural determinations in guinea pig hindlimbs. *Journal of Applied Physiology* 57: 1715-1721.

Roy, R.R., and V.R. Edgerton. 1992. Skeletal muscle architecture and performance. In: P.V. Komi (Ed.), *Strength and power in sport* (pp. 115-129). London: Blackwell Scientific.

Sale, D.G. 1992. Neural adaptations to resistance training. In: P.V. Komi (Ed.), *Strength and power in sport* (pp. 249-265). London: Blackwell Scientific.

Saltin, B., J. Henriksson, E. Nygaard et al. 1977. Fiber types and metabolic potentials of skeletal muscles in sedentary man and endurance runners. *Annals of the New York Academy of Science* 301: 3-29.

Schantz, P.G., and G.K. Dhoot. 1987. Coexistence of slow and fast isoforms of contractile and regulatory proteins in human skeletal muscle fibers induced by endurance training. *Acta Physiologica Scandinavica* 131: 147-154.

Schmidtbleicher, D., and A. Gollhofer. 1982. Neuromuskulare untersuchungen zur bestimmung individuellar belastungsgrossen fur ein teifsprung-training. *Leistungsport* 12: 298-307.

Siff, M.C. 1988. Biomathematical relationship between strength and body mass. *South African Journal of Research in Sport, Physical Education and Recreation* 11(1): 81-92.

Siff, M. 2001. Biomechanical foundations of strength and power training. In: V. Zatsiorsky (Ed.), *Biomechanics in sport* (pp. 103-139). London: Blackwell Scientific.

Simoneau, J-A., and C. Bouchard. 1989. Human variation in skeletal muscle fiber-type proportion and enzyme activities. *American Journal of Physiology* 257: E567-E572.

Sinclair, R.G. 1985. Normalizing the performance of athletes in Olympic weightlifting. *Canadian Journal of Applied Physiology* 10: 94-98.

Spector, S.A., P.F. Gardiner, R.F. Zernicke et al. 1980. Muscle architecture and force-velocity characteristics of the cat soleus and medial gastrocnemius: Implications for motor control. *Journal of Neurophysiology* 44: 951-960.

Staron, R., E.S. Malicky, M.J. Leonardi et al. 1989. Muscle hypertrophy and fast fiber type conversions in heavy resistance trained women. *European Journal of Applied Physiology* 60: 71-79.

Stone, M.H. 1993. Explosive exercise. *National Strength and Conditioning Association Journal* 15: 7-15.

Stone, M.H., W.A. Sands, K.C. Pierce et al. 2005. Relationship of maximum strength to weightlifting performance. *Medicine and Science in Sports and Exercise* 37: 1037-1043.

Street, S.F. 1983. Lateral transmission of tension in frog myofibers: A myofibrillar network and transverse cytoskeletal connections are possible transmitters. *Journal of Cell Physiology* 114: 346-364.

Tax, A.A.M., J.J. Denier van der Gon, C.C.A.M. Gielen et al. 1989. Differences in the activation of m. biceps brachii in the control of slow isotonic movements and isometric contractions. *Experimental Brain Research* 76: 55-63.

Tax, A.A.M., J.J. Denier van der Gon, C.C.A.M. Gielen et al. 1990. Differences in central control of m. biceps brachii in movement tasks and force tasks. *Experimental Brain Research* 79: 138-142.

Tesch, P.A., and L. Larsson. 1982. Muscle hypertrophy in body builders. *European Journal of Applied Physiology* 49: 301-306.

Tesch, P.A., A. Thorsson, and B. Essen-Gustavsson. 1989. Enzyme activities of FT and ST muscle fibers in heavy resistance trained athletes. *Journal of Applied Physiology* 67: 83-87.

Thorstensson, A., L. Larsson, P. Tesch et al. 1977. Muscle strength and fiber composition in athletes and sedentary men. *Medicine and Science in Sports* 9: 26-30.

Wathen, D. 1992. Muscle balance. In: T. Baechle (Ed.), *Essentials of strength training and conditioning* (pp. 424-430). Champaign, IL: Human Kinetics.

Wickiewicz, T.L., R.R. Roy, P.L. Powell et al. 1983. Muscle architecture of the human lower limb. *Clinical Orthopaedics and Related Research* 179: 275-283.

Wickiewicz, T.L., R.R. Roy, P.L. Powell et al. 1984. Muscle architecture and force-velocity relationships in humans. *Journal of Applied Physiology* 57: 435-443.

Wilson, G.J., and A.J. Murphy. 1996. The use of isometric tests of muscular function in athletic assessment. *Sports Medicine* 22(1): 19-37.

Yamashita, N. 1988. EMG activities in mono-and bi-articular thigh muscles in combined hip and knee extension. *European Journal of Applied Physiology* 58: 274-277.

Zahalak, F.E. 1986. A comparison of the mechanical behavior of the cat soleus muscle with a distribution moment model. *Journal of Biomechanical Engineering* 108: 131-140.

Zajac, F.E. 2002. Understanding muscle coordination of the human leg with dynamical situations. *Journal of Biomechanics* 35: 1011-1018.

Zajac, F.E., and M.E. Gordon. 1989. Determining muscle's force and action in multi-articular movement. *Exercise and Sport Sciences Reviews* 17: 187-230.

Chapter 4

Abernethy, P.J., R. Thayer, and A.W. Taylor. 1990. Acute and chronic responses of skeletal muscle to endurance and sprint exercise. *Sports Medicine* 10(6): 365-389.

Ahlborg, G., and P. Felig. 1967. Influence of glucose ingestion on the fuel-hormone response during prolonged exercise. *Journal of Applied Physiology* 41: 83-88.

Ahlborg, G., and P. Felig. 1982. Lactate and glucose exchange across the forearm, legs and splanchnic bed during and after prolonged leg exercise. *Journal of Clinical Investigation* 69: 45-54.

Asmussen, E., K. Klausen, L.E. Nielsen, O.A. Techow, and P.J. Ponder. 1974. Lactate production and anaerobic work capacity after prolonged exercise. *Acta Physiologica Scandinavica* 50: 731-742.

Åstrand, P.O., and K. Rodahl. 1970. *Textbook of work physiology* (2nd ed.). New York: McGraw-Hill.

Bahr, R., J. Ingnes, O. Vaage, O.M. Sejersted, and E.A. Newsholme. 1987. Effect of duration of exercise on excess postexercise oxygen consumption. *Journal of Applied Physiology* 62: 485-490.

Bahr, R., and O.M. Sejersted. 1991. Effect of intensity of exercise on excess postexercise oxygen consumption. *Metabolism* 40: 836-841.

Baily, M.L., N. Khodigiuian, and P.A. Farrar. 1996. Effects of resistance exercise on selected physiological parameters during subsequent aerobic exercise. *Journal of Strength and Conditioning Research* 10(2): 101-104.

Bangsbo, J., T. Graham, L. Johansen et al. 1992. Elevated muscle acidity and energy production during exhaustive exercise in humans. *American Journal of Physiology* 32: R891-R899.

Barnard, R.J., V.R. Edgerton, T. Furakawa et al. 1971. Histochemical, biochemical and contractile properties of red, white, and intermediate fibers. *American Journal of Physiology* 220: 410-441.

Bastiaans, J.J., A.B. van Diemen, T. Veneberg, and A.E. Jeukendrup. 2001. The effects of replacing a portion of endurance training by explosive strength training on performance in trained cyclists. *European Journal of Applied Physiology* 86: 79-84.

Behm, D.G., G. Reardon, J. Fitzgerald, and F. Drinkwater. 2002. The effect of 5, 10 and 20 repetition maximums on recovery of voluntary and evoked contractile properties. *Journal of Strength and Conditioning Research* 16: 209-218.

Bell, G.J., S. Peterson, J. Wessel et al. 1991. Physiological adaptations to concurrent endurance and low velocity resistance training. *International Journal of Sports Medicine* 4: 384-390.

Bell, G.J., G.D. Snydmiller, D.S. Davies, and H.A. Quinney. 1997. Relationship between aerobic fitness and metabolic recovery from intermittent exercise in endurance athletes. *Canadian Journal of Applied Physiology* 22: 78-85.

Bell, G., and H.A. Wenger. 1986. The effect of sprint training on intramuscular pH buffering capacity and lactates [Abstract]. *Canadian Journal of Applied Sport Sciences* 11(3).

Berg, W.E. 1947. Individual differences in respiratory gas exchange during recovery from moderate exercise. *American Journal of Physiology* 149: 507-530.

Billat, V., P. Sirvant, G. Py, J.P. Koralsztein, and J. Mercier. 2003. The concept of maximal lactate steady state: A bridge between biochemistry, physiology and sports science. *Sports Medicine* 33: 407-426.

Boger, A., B. Warren, M. Stone, and R. Johnson. 1992. Whole blood lactate and serum free fatty acid responses to supramaximal and submaximal cycling bouts. *Conference abstracts*, SEACSM.

Bond, V., R.G. Adams, R.J. Tearney et al. 1991. Effects of active and passive recovery on lactate removal and subsequent isokinetic muscle function. *Journal of Sports Medicine and Physical Fitness* 31(3): 357-361.

Boobis, I., C. Williams, and S.N. Wooten. 1983. Influence of sprint training on muscle metabolism during brief maximal exercise in man. *Journal of Physiology* 342: 36-37P.

Brehm, G.A., and B. Gutin. 1986. Recovery energy expenditure for steady state exercise in runners and nonexercisers. *Medicine and Science in Sports and Exercise* 18: 205-210.

Bridges, C.R., B.J. Clark III, R.L. Hammond et al. 1991. Skeletal muscle bioenergetics during frequency-dependent fatigue. *American Journal of Physiology* 29: C643-C651.

Brooks, G.A. 1986. The lactate shuttle during exercise and recovery. *Medicine and Science in Sports and Exercise* 18: 360-368.

Brooks, G.A., K.E. Brauner, and R.G. Cassens. 1973. Glycogen synthesis and metabolism of lactic acid after exercise. *American Journal of Physiology* 224: 1162-1186.

Brooks, G.A., T.D. Fahey, and T.P. White. 1996. *Exercise physiology* (2nd ed.). Mountain View, CA: Mayfield.

Brooks, G.A., K.J. Hittelman, J.A. Faulkner, and R.E. Beyer. 1971. Temperature, skeletal muscle mitochondrial functions and oxygen debt. *American Journal of Physiology* 220: 1053-1068.

Brouha, L., and E. Radford. 1960. The cardiovascular system in muscular activity. In: W. Johnson (Ed.), *Science and medicine of exercise and sports.* New York: McGraw-Hill.

Burke, R.E., and V.R. Edgerton. 1975. Motor unit properties and selective involvement in movement. In: J. Wilmore and J. Keough (Eds.), *Exercise and sport science reviews* (pp. 31-81). New York: Academic Press.

Burleson, M.A., H.S. O'Bryant, M.H. Stone, M. Collins, and T. Triplett-McBride. 1998. Effect of weight training exercise and treadmill exercise on post-exercise oxygen consumption. *Medicine and Science in Sports and Exercise* 30: 518-522.

Buskirk, E., and H. Taylor. 1957. Maximal oxygen intake and its relation to body composition, with special reference to chronic physical activity and obesity. *Journal of Applied Physiology* 11: 72-78.

Butler, T.C., W.J. Waddel, and D.T. Poole. 1967. Intracellular pH based on distribution of weak electrolytes. *Federation Proceedings* 26: 1327-1332.

Byrd, R., K. Pierce, R. Gentry, and M. Swisher. 1996. Prediction of caloric cost of the parallel back squat in women. *Journal of Strength and Conditioning Research* 10: 184-185.

Cain, D.F., and R.E. Davis. 1962. Breakdown of adenosine triphosphate during a single contraction of working muscle. *Biochemistry and Biophysics Research Communication* 8: 361-366.

Campos, G.E., T.J. Luecke, H.K. Wendein, K. Toma, F.C. Hagerman, T.F. Murray, K.E. Ragg, N.A. Ratamess, W.J. Kraemer, and R.S. Staron. 2002. Muscular adaptations in response to three different resistance-training regimens: Specificity of repletion maximum training zones. *European Journal of Applied Physiology* 88: 50-60.

Cerretelli, P., G. Ambrosoli, M. Fumagalli et al. 1975. Anaerobic recovery in man. *European Journal of Applied Physiology* 34: 141-148.

Cerretelli, P., D. Rennie, and D. Pendergast. 1980. Kinetics of metabolic transients during exercise. *International Journal of Sports Medicine* 55: 178-180.

Chappell, J.B. 1968. Systems used for the transport of substances into mitochondria. *British Medical Bulletin* 24: 150-157.

Coggan, A.R., and E.F. Coyle. 1987. Reversal of fatigue during prolonged exercise by carbohydrate infusion or ingestion. *Journal of Applied Physiology* 63: 2388-2395.

Conley, M.S., M.H. Stone, H.S. O'Bryant, R.L. Johnson, D.R. Honeycutt, and T.P. Hoke. 1993. Peak power versus power at maximal oxygen uptake. Presentation at the NSCA National Meeting, Las Vegas.

Constable, S.H., R.J. Favier, J.A. McLane et al. 1987. Energy metabolism in contracting rat skeletal muscle: Adaptation to exercise training. *American Journal of Physiology* 253: 316-322.

Cooke, S.R., S.R. Petersen, and H.A. Quinney. 1997. The influence of maximal aerobic power on recovery of skeletal muscle following anaerobic exercise. *European Journal of Applied Physiology* 75: 512-519.

Costill, D.L., D.D. Pascoe, W.J. Fink, R.A. Robergs, S.I. Barr, and D.R. Pearson. 1990. Impaired muscle glycogen resynthesis after eccentric exercise. *Journal of Applied Physiology* 69: 46-50.

Coyle, E.F., A.R. Coggan, M.K. Hemmart et al. 1984. Glycogen usage performance relative to lactate threshold [abstract]. *Medicine and Science in Sports and Exercise* 16: 120.

Coyle, E.F., J.M. Hagberg, B.F. Hurley et al. 1983. Carbohydrate feeding during prolonged strenuous exercise can delay fatigue. *Journal of Applied Physiology* 55: 230-235.

Craig, B.W., J. Lucas, R. Pohlmanet al. 1991. The effects of running, weightlifting and a combination of both on growth hormone release. *Journal of Applied Sport Science Research* 5(4): 198-203.

Crawford, W.W., S.F. Loy, A.G. Nelson, R.K. Conlee, A.G. Fisher, and P.E. Allsen. 1991. Effects of prior strength exercise on the heart rate oxygen uptake relationship during submaximal exercise. *Journal of Sports Medicine and Physical Fitness* 31: 501-505.

Davis, J.A., M.H. Frank, B.J. Whipp et al. 1979. Anaerobic threshold alterations caused by endurance training in middle-aged men. *Journal of Applied Physiology* 46: 1039-1046.

Dawson, B., M. Fitzsimmons, S. Green, C. Goodman, M. Carey, and K. Cole. 1998. Changes in performance, muscle metabolites, enzymes and fibre types after short sprint training. *European Journal of Applied Physiology* 78: 163-169.

diPrampero, P.E., L. Peeters, and R. Margaria. 1973. Alactic O_2 debt and lactic acid production after exhausting exercise in man. *Journal of Applied Physiology* 34: 628-632.

Doyle, J.A., W.M. Sherman, R.I. Strauss et al. 1993. Effects of eccentric and concentric exercise on muscle glycogen replenishment. *Journal of Applied Physiology* 74: 1848-1855.

Dudley, G.A., and R. Djamil. 1985. Incompatibility of endurance- and strength-training modes of exercise. *Journal of Applied Physiology* 59(5): 1446-1451.

Dudley, G., and T.F. Murray. 1982. Energy for sport. *National Strength and Conditioning Journal* 3(3): 14-15.

Dufaux, B., G. Assmann, and W. Hollman. 1982. Plasma lipoproteins and physical activity: A review. *International Journal of Sports Medicine* 3: 123-136.

Edington, D.E., and V.R. Edgerton. 1976. *The biology of physical activity.* Boston: Houghton Mifflin.

Elliot, D.L., L. Goldberg, and K.S. Kuel. 1992. Effect of resistance training on excess post-exercise oxygen consumption. *Journal of Applied Sport Science Research* 6(2): 77-81.

Ericksson, B.O., P.D. Gollnick, and B. Saltin. 1973. Muscle metabolism and enzyme activities after training in boys 11-13 years old. *Acta Physiologica Scandinavica* 87: 485-497.

Essen, B. 1978. Glycogen depletion of different fibre types in man during intermittent and continuous exercise. *Acta Physiological Scandinavica* 103: 446-455.

Fabiato, A., and F. Fabiato. 1978. Effects of pH on the myofilaments and sarcoplasmic reticulum of skinned cells from cardiac and skeletal muscle. *Journal of Physiology* 276: 233-255.

Farrel, P.A., J.H. Wilmore, E.F. Coyle et al. 1979. Plasma lactate accumulation and distance running performance. *Medicine and Science in Sports* 11(4): 338-344.

Freund, H., and P. Gendry. 1978. Lactate kinetics after short strenuous exercise in man. *European Journal of Applied Physiology* 39: 123-135.

Friedman, J.E., P.D. Neufer, and L.G. Dohm. 1991. Regulation of glycogen synthesis following exercise. *Sports Medicine* 11(4): 232-243.

Fuchs, F., Y. Reddy, and F.N. Briggs. 1970. The interaction of cations with calcium binding site of troponin. *Biochemistry Biophysics Acta* 221: 407-409.

Gladden, L.B., and H.G. Welch. 1978. Efficiency of anaerobic work. *Journal of Applied Physiology* 44: 564-570.

Gollnick, P.D., R.B. Armstrong, B. Saltin et al. 1973. Effect of training on enzyme activity and fibre composition of human muscle. *Journal of Applied Physiology* 34: 107-111.

Gollnick, P.D., R.B. Armstrong, W. Saubert et al. 1972. Enzyme activity and fibre composition in skeletal muscle of untrained and trained men. *Journal of Applied Physiology* 33: 312-319.

Gollnick, P.D., and W.M. Bayly. 1986. Biochemical training adaptations and maximal power. In: N.L. Jones, N. McCartney, and A.J. McComas (Eds.), *Human muscle power* (pp. 255-267). Champaign, IL: Human Kinetics.

Gollnick, P.D., W.M. Bayly, and D.R. Hodgson. 1986. Exercise intensity, training diet and lactate concentration in muscle and blood. *Medicine and Science in Sports and Exercise* 18: 334-340.

Gollnick, P.D., and L. Hermansen. 1975. Biochemical adaptations to exercise: Anaerobic metabolism. *Exercise and Sport Sciences Reviews* 1: 1-13.

Gollnick, P.D., and B. Saltin. 1982. Significance of skeletal muscle oxidative enzyme enhancement with endurance training. *Clinical Physiology* 2: 1-12.

Green, H.J., M.E. Houston, J.A. Thomson et al. 1979. Metabolic consequences of supra maximal arm work performed during prolonged submaximal leg work. *Journal of Applied Physiology* 46: 249-255.

Hadmann, R. 1957. The available glycogen in man and the connection between rate of oxygen intake and carbohydrate usage. *Acta Physiologica Scandinavica* 40: 305-330.

Hakkinen, K., M. Alen, W.J. Kraemer, E. Gorostiaga, M. Izquierdo, H. Rusko, J. Mikkola, H. Valkeinen, E. Kaarakainen, S. Romu, V. Erola, J. Ahtiainen, and L. Paavolainen. 2003. Neuromuscular adaptations during concurrent strength and endurance training versus strength training. *European Journal of Applied Physiology* 89: 42-52.

Harmer, A.R., M.J. McKenna, J.R. Sutton, R.J. Snow, P.A. Ruell, J. Booth, M.W. Thompson, N.A. Mackey, G.C. Stathis, R.M. Crameri, M.F. Carey, and D.M. Eager. 2000. Skeletal muscle metabolic and ionic adaptation during intense exercise following sprint training in humans. *Journal of Applied Physiology* 89: 1793-1803.

Harris, R.C., R.H.T. Edwards, E. Hultman et al. 1976. The time course of phosphocreatinine resynthesis during recovery of quadriceps muscle in man. *Pfluegers Archiv* 97: 392-397.

Hennessy, L., and W.S Watson. 1994. The interference effects of training for strength and endurance simultaneously. *Journal of Strength and Conditioning Research* 8: 12-19.

Henry, F.M. 1957. Aerobic oxygen consumption and alactic debt in muscular work. *Journal of Applied Physiology* 3: 427-450.

Hermansen, L. 1981. Effect of metabolic changes on force generation in skeletal muscle during maximal exercise. In: *Human muscle fatigue.* London: Pittman Medical.

Hermansen, L., and I. Stenvold. 1972. Production and removal of lactate in man. *Acta Physiologica Scandinavica* 86: 191-201.

Hermansen, L., and O. Vaage. 1977. Lactate disappearance and glycogen synthesis in human muscle after maximal exercise. *American Journal of Physiology* 233: E422-E429.

Hickson, R.C. 1980. Interference of strength development by simultaneously training for strength and endurance. *European Journal of Applied Physiology* 215: 255-263.

Hickson, R.C., B.A. Dvorak, E.M. Gorostiaga et al. 1988. Potential for strength and endurance training to amplify endurance performance. *Journal of Applied Physiology* 65(5): 2285-2290.

Hickson, R.C., M.A. Rosenkoetter, and M.M. Brown. 1980. Strength training effects on aerobic power and short-term endurance. *Medicine and Science in Sports and Exercise* 12: 336-339.

Hill, A.V. 1924. Muscular exercise, lactic acid and the supply and utilization of oxygen. *Proceedings of the Royal Society of London (Biology)* 96: 438.

Hirvonen, J., S. Ruhunen, H. Rusko et al. 1987. Breakdown of high-energy phosphate compounds and lactate accumulation during short submaximal exercise. *European Journal of Applied Physiology* 56: 253-259.

Hoffman, J.R. 1997. The relationship between aerobic fitness and recovery from high-intensity exercise in infantry soldiers. *Military Medicine* 162: 484-488.

Hogan, M.C., L.B. Gladden, S.S. Kurdak, and D.C. Poole. 1995. Increased [lactate] in working dog muscle reduces muscle tension development independent of pH. *Medicine and Science in Sports and Exercise* 27: 371-377.

Houston, M.E., and J.A. Thomson. 1977. The response of endurance-adapted adults to intense anaerobic training. *European Journal of Applied Physiology* 36: 207-213.

Hultman, E., and H. Sjoholm. 1986. Biochemical causes of fatigue. In: N.L. Jones, N. McCartney, and A.J. McComas (Eds.), *Human muscle power* (pp. 215-235). Champaign, IL: Human Kinetics.

Hultsmann, W.C. 1979. On the regulation of the supply of substrates for muscular activity. *Bibliotheca Nutrition Dictatica* 27: 11-15.

Hunter, G.R., C.J. Wetzstein, D.A. Fields, A. Brown, and M.M. Bamman. 2000. Resistance training increases total energy expenditure and free-living physical activity in older adults. *Journal of Applied Physiology* 89: 977-984.

Issekutz, B., H.I. Miller, P. Paul et al. 1965. Effect of lactic acid on fatty acids and glucose oxidation in dogs. *American Journal of Physiology* 209: 1137-1144.

Jacobs, I. 1981. Lactate, muscle glycogen and exercise performance in man. *Acta Physiologica Scandinavica* (Suppl.) 495: 1-35.

Jacobs, I. 1986. Blood lactate: Implications for training and sports performance. *Sports Medicine* 3: 10-25.

Jacobs, I., P. Kaiser, and P. Tesch. 1981. Muscle strength and fatigue after selective glycogen depletion in human skeletal muscle fibers. *European Journal of Applied Physiology* 36: 47-53.

Jacobs, I., P.A. Tesch, O. Bar-Or et al. 1983. Lactate in human skeletal muscle after 10 and 30 s of supramaximal exercise. *Journal of Applied Physiology* 55: 365-367.

Jones, N., and R. Ehrsam. 1982. The anaerobic threshold. *Exercise and Sport Sciences Reviews* 10: 49-83.

Jones, N.L., J.F. Heigenhauser, A. Kuksis et al. 1980. Fat metabolism in heavy exercise. *Clinical Science* 59: 469-478.

Juel, C. 1988. Intracellular pH recovery and lactate efflux in mouse soleus muscles stimulated in vitro: The involvement of sodium/proton exchange and a lactate carrier. *Acta Physiologica Scandinavica* 132: 363-371.

Karlsson, J. 1971. Lactate and phosphagen concentrations in working muscle of man. *Acta Physiologica Scandinavica* (Suppl.), 358-365.

Karlsson, J.L., O. Nordesco, L. Jorfeldt et al. 1972. Muscle lactate, ATP and CP levels during exercise and after physical training in man. *Journal of Applied Physiology* 33(2): 194-203.

Kindermann, W., G. Simon, and J. Jeul. 1979. The significance of the aerobic-anaerobic transition for the determination of work load intensities during endurance training. *European Journal of Applied Physiology* 42: 25-34.

Kleiber, M. 1950. Calorimetric measurements. In: F. Uber (Ed.), *Biophysical research methods.* New York: Interscience.

Klingerberg, M. 1970. Metabolite transport in mitochondria: An example for intracellular membrane function. *Essays in Biochemistry* 6: 119-159.

Komi, P.V., A. Ito, B. Sjodin et al. 1981. Lactate breaking point and biomechanics of running. [abstract]. *Medicine and Science in Sports and Exercise* 13: 114.

Koziris, L.P., W.J. Kraemer, J.F. Patton, N.T. Triplett, A.C. Fry, S.E. Gordon, and H.G. Knuttgen. 1996. Relationship of aerobic power to anaerobic performance indices. *Journal of Strength and Conditioning Research* 10(1): 35-39.

Kraemer, W.J., B.J. Nobel, M.J. Clark et al. 1987. Physiologic responses to heavy-resistance exercise with very short rest periods. *International Journal of Sports Medicine* 8: 247-252.

Kraemer, W.J., J. Patton, S.E. Gordon et al. 1995. Compatibility of high-intensity strength and endurance training on hormonal and skeletal muscle adaptations. *Journal of Applied Physiology* 78: 976-989.

Krebs, H.A. 1972. The Pasteur effect and the relation between respiration and fermentation. *Essays in Biochemistry* 8: 2-34.

Lambert, C.P., and M.G. Flynn. 2002. Fatigue during high-intensity exercise: Application to bodybuilding. *Sports Medicine* 32: 511-522.

Lambert, C.P., M.G. Flynn, J.B. Boone et al. 1991. Effects of carbohydrate feeding on multiple-bout resistance exercise. *Journal of Applied Sport Science Research* 5(4): 192-197.

Laritcheva, K.A., N.I. Valovarya, N.I. Shybin, and S.A. Smirnov. 1978. Study of energy expenditure and protein needs of top weightlifters. In: J. Parizkova and V. Rogozkin (Eds.), *Nutrition, physical fitness, and health. International series on sport sciences* (Vol. 7, pp. 53-68). Baltimore: University Park Press.

Lehninger, A.L. 2000. *Principles of biochemistry* (3rd ed). New York: Freeman.

Linossier, M.T., D. Dormois, C. Perier, J. Frey, A. Geyssant, and C. Dnis. 1997. Enzyme adaptations of human skeletal muscle during bicycle short-sprint training and detraining. *Acta Physiologica Scandinavica* 161: 439-445.

MacDougall, J.D. 1986. Morphological changes in human skeletal muscle following strength training and immobilization. In: N.L. Jones, N. McCartney, and A.J. McComas (Eds.), *Human muscle power* (pp. 269-288). Champaign, IL: Human Kinetics.

MacDougall, J.D., A.L. Hicks, J.R. MacDonald, R.S. McKelvie, H.J. Green, and K.M. Smith. 1998. Muscle performance and enzymatic adaptation to sprint interval training. *Journal of Applied Physiology* 84: 3138-3142.

MacDougall, J.D., S. Ray, N. McCartney et al. 1988. Substrate utilization during weight lifting [abstract]. *Medicine and Science in Sports and Exercise* 20: S66.

MacDougall, J.D., G.R. Ward, D.G. Sale et al. 1977. Biochemical adaptations of human skeletal muscle to heavy resistance training and immobilization. *Journal of Applied Physiology* 43: 700-703.

Marcinik, E.J., G. Potts, G. Schlabach et al. 1991. Effects of strength training on lactate threshold and endurance performance. *Medicine and Science in Sports and Exercise* 23: 739-743.

Margaria, R., H.T. Edwards, and D.B. Dill. 1933. The possible mechanism of contracting and paying the oxygen debt and the role of lactic acid in muscular contraction. *American Journal of Physiology* 106: 687-714.

Mazzeo, R.S., G.A. Brooks, D.A. Schoeller et al. 1986. Disposal of blood (1-^{13}C) lactate in humans during rest and exercise. *Journal of Applied Physiology* 60: 232-241.

McCann, D.J., P.A. Mole, and J.R. Caton. 1995. Phosphocreatine kinetics in humans during exercise and recovery. *Medicine and Science in Sports and Exercise* 27: 378-387.

McCarthy, J.P., J.C. Agre, B.K. Graf et al. 1995. Compatibility of adaptive responses with combining strength and endurance training. *Medicine and Science in Sports and Exercise* 27: 429-436.

McCartney, N., L.L. Spriet, G.J.F. Heigenhauser et al. 1986. Muscle power and metabolism in maximal intermittent exercise. *Journal of Applied Physiology* 60: 1164-1169.

McGilvery, R.W. 1975. *Biochemical concepts.* Philadelphia: Saunders.

McMillan, J.L., M.H. Stone, J. Sartain et al. 1993. 20-hour physiological responses to a single weight training session. *Journal of Strength and Conditioning Research* 7(1): 9-21.

Medbo, J.I., and S. Burgers. 1990. Effect of training on the anaerobic capacity. *Medicine and Science in Sports and Exercise* 22: 501-507.

Medbo, J.I., A-C. Mohn, I. Tabata et al. 1988. Anaerobic capacity determined by maximal accumulated O_2 deficit. *Journal of Applied Physiology* 64: 50-60.

Melby, C., C. Scholl, G. Edwards et al. 1993. Effect of acute resistance exercise on post-exercise energy expen-diture and resting metabolic rate. *Journal of Applied Physiology* 75(4): 1847-1853.

Melby, C.L., T. Ticknell, and W.D. Schmidt. 1992. Energy expenditure following a bout of non-steady state resistance exercise. *Journal of Sports Medicine and Physical Fitness* 32: 128-135.

Meyer, R.A., and R.L. Terjung. 1979. Differences in ammonia and adenylate metabolism in contracting fast and slow muscle. *American Journal of Physiology* 237: C111-C118.

Miller, H.I., B. Issekutz, P. Paul et al. 1964. Effect of lactic acid on plasma free fatty acids in pancreatechtomized dogs. *American Journal of Physiology* 207: 1226-1230.

Murphy, E., and R. Schwarzkopf. 1992. Effects of standard set and circuit weight training on excess post-exercise oxygen consumption. *Journal of Strength and Conditioning Research* 6: 88-91.

Nakamura, Y., and A. Schwartz. 1972. The influence of hydrogen ion concentration on calcium binding and release by skeletal muscle sarcoplasmic reticulum. *Journal of General Physiology* 59: 22-32.

Newsholme, E.A. 1986. Application of principles of metabolic control to the problem of metabolic limitations in sprinting, middle distance and marathon running. In: N.L. Jones, N. McCartney, and A.J. McComas (Eds.), *Human muscle power* (pp. 169-174). Champaign, IL: Human Kinetics.

Nielsen, J.J., M. Moher, C. Klarskov et al. 2004. Effects of high-intensity intermittent training on potassium kinetics and performance in humans. *Journal of Physiology* 554: 857-870.

Nummela, A., A. Mero, and H. Rusko. 1996. Effects of sprint training on anaerobic performance characteristics determined by the MART. *International Journal of Sports Medicine* 17(Suppl. 2): S114-119.

Olsen, H.L., E. Raabo, J. Bangsbo, and N.H. Secher. 1994. Maximal oxygen deficit of sprint and middle distance runners. *European Journal of Applied Physiology* 69: 140-146.

Opie, L.J., and E.A. Newsholme. 1967. The activities of fructose 1, 6-diphosphate, phosphofructokinase, and phosphoenolpyruvate carboxykinase in white and red muscle. *Biochemical Journal* 103: 391-399.

Parkhouse, W.S., D.C. McKenzie, P.W. Hochochka et al. 1983. The relationship between carnosine levels, buffering capacity, fiber type and anaerobic capacity in elite athletes. In: H.G. Knuttgen, J.A. Vogel, and J. Poortmans (Eds.), *Biochemistry of exercise* (pp. 590-594). Champaign, IL: Human Kinetics.

Pierce, K., R. Rozenek, M. Stone et al. 1987. The effects of weight training on plasma cortisol, lactate, heart rate, anxiety and perceived exertion [abstract]. *Journal of Applied Sport Science Research* 1(3): 58.

Pierce, K., R. Rozenek, M. Stone et al. 1993. Effect of weight training on lactate, heart rate, and perceived exertion. *Journal of Strength and Conditioning Research* 7(4): 211-215.

Pike, R.L., and M. Brown. 1975. *Nutrition: An integrated approach* (2nd ed.). New York: Wiley.

Plisk, S.S. 1991. Anaerobic metabolic conditioning: A brief review of theory, strategy and practical application. *Journal of Applied Sport Science Research* 5(1): 22-34.

Plisk, S.S., and V. Gambetta. 1997. Tactical metabolic training. *Strength and Conditioning* 19: 44-52.

Powers, S.K., and E.T. Howley. 1997. *Exercise physiology* (3rd ed.). Dubuque, IA: Brown and Benchmark.

Richter, E.A., H. Galbo, and N.J. Christensen. 1981. Control of exercise-induced muscular glycogenolysis by adrenal medullary hormones in rats. *Journal of Applied Physiology* 50: 21-26.

Robergs, R.A., D.R. Pearson, D.L. Costill et al. 1991. Muscle glycogenolysis during differing intensities of weight-resistance exercise. *Journal of Applied Physiology* 70(4): 1700-1706.

Roberts, A.D., R. Billeter, and H. Howald. 1982. Anaerobic muscle enzyme changes after interval training. *International Journal of Sports Medicine* 3: 18-21.

Rodas, G.J., L. Ventura, J.A. Cusso, and J. Parra. 2000. A short training programme for the rapid improvement of both aerobic and anaerobic metabolism. *European Journal of Applied Physiology* 82: 480-486.

Romijn, J.A., E.F. Coyle, J. Hibbert, and R.R. Wolfe. 1992. Comparisons of indirect calorimetry and a new breath 13C/12C ratio method during strenuous exercise. *American Journal of Physiology* 263: E64-E71.

Sahlin, K. 1978. Intracellular pH and energy metabolism in skeletal muscle of man, with special reference to exercise. *Acta Physiologica Scandinavica* (Suppl.) 455: 1-56.

Sahlin, K., R.C. Harris, B. Nylind et al. 1976. Lactate content and pH in muscle samples obtained after dynamic exercise. *Pfluegers Archiv* 367: 143-149.

Saltin, B., and P.D. Gollnick. 1983. Skeletal muscle adaptability: Significance for metabolism and performance. In: L.D. Peachey, R.H. Adrian, and S.R. Geiger (Eds.), *Handbook of physiology* (pp. 540-555). Baltimore: Williams & Wilkins.

Saltin, B., and J. Karlsson. 1971. Muscle glycogen utilization during work of different intensities. In: B. Pernow and B. Saltin (Eds.), *Muscle metabolism during exercise* (pp. 289-300). New York: Plenum Press.

Scala, D., J. McMillan, D. Blessing et al. 1987. Metabolic cost of a preparatory phase of training in weightlifting: A practical observation. *Journal of Applied Sport Science Research* 1(3): 48-52.

Scholl, C.G., R.C. Bullough, and C.L. Melby. 1993. Effect of different modes on postexercise energy expenditure and substrate utilization. *Medicine and Science in Sports and Exercise* 25(5): 532.

Schuenke, M.D., R.P. Mikat, and J.M. McBride. 2002. Effect of an acute period of resistance exercise on excess

post-exercise oxygen consumption: Implications for body mass management. *European Journal of Applied Physiology* 86: 411-417.

Sedlock, D.A., J.A. Fissinger, and C.L. Melby. 1989. Effect of exercise intensity and duration on postexercise energy expenditure. *Medicine and Science in Sports and Exercise* 21: 626-666.

Sherman, W.M., and G.S. Wimer. 1991. Insufficient carbohydrate during training: Does it impair performance? *Sport Nutrition* 1: 28-44.

Short, K.R., and D.A. Sedlock. 1997. Excess postexercise oxygen consumption and recovery rate in trained and untrained subjects. *Journal of Applied Physiology* 83: 153-159.

Sjodin, B., and I. Jacobs. 1981. Onset of blood lactate accumulation and marathon running performance. *International Journal of Applied Sports Medicine* 2: 23-26.

Sjodin, B., A. Thorstensson, K. Firth et al. 1976. Effect of physical training on LDH activity and LDH isozyme pattern in human skeletal muscle. *Acta Physiologica Scandinavica* 97: 150-157.

Sjogaard, G. 1984. Changes in skeletal muscle capillarity and enzyme activity with training and detraining. In: P. Marconnet, J. Poortmans, and L. Hermansen (Eds.), *Medicine and sport science* (Vol. 17, *Physiological chemistry of training and detraining*, pp. 202-214). Basel: Karger.

Spriet, L.L., M.L. Lindinger, and R.S. McKelvie. 1989. Muscle glycogenolysis and H^+ concentration during maximal intermittent cycling. *Journal of Applied Physiology* 66: 8-13.

Stainsby, W.M., and J.K. Barclay. 1970. Exercise metabolism: O_2 deficit, steady level O_2 uptake and O_2 uptake in recovery. *Medicine and Science in Sports* 2: 177-195.

Stone, M.H., and M.S. Conley. 1992. Bioenergetics. In: T. Baechle (Ed.), *Essentials of strength training and conditioning*. Champaign, IL: Human Kinetics.

Stone, M.H., S.J. Fleck, W.J. Kraemer et al. 1991a. Health and performance related adaptations to resistive training. *Sports Medicine* 11(4): 210-231.

Stone, M.H., and A.C. Fry. 1997. Increased training volume in strength/power athletes. In: R. Kreider, A. Fry, and M. O'Toole (Eds.), *Overtraining in sport* (chapter 5, pp. 87-106). Champaign, IL: Human Kinetics.

Stone, M.H., R.E. Keith, J.T. Kearney et al. 1991b. Overtraining: A review of the signs, symptoms and possible causes. *Journal of Applied Sport Science Research* 5(1): 55-60.

Stone, M.H., and H.S. O'Bryant. 1987. *Strength training: A scientific approach*. Minneapolis: Burgess.

Stone, M.H., K. Pierce, R. Godsen et al. 1987. Heart rate and lactate levels during weight-training in trained and untrained men. *Physician and Sportsmedicine* 15(5): 97-105.

Stone, M.H., B. Warren, J. Potteiger, and B. Bonner. 1988. Strength and vertical jump performance following varied recovery periods after high volume squatting. *Conference abstracts*, SEACSM. Presented at the SEACSM annual meeting, January.

Stone, M.H., G.D. Wilson, D. Blessing et al. 1983. Cardio-vascular responses to short-term Olympic style weight training in young men. *Canadian Journal of Applied Sport Sciences* 8: 134-139.

Sugden, P.H., and E.A. Newsholme. 1975. The effects of ammonium, inorganic phosphate and potassium ions on the activity of phosphofructokinase from muscle and nervous tissues of vertebrates and invertebrates. *Biochemical Journal* 150: 113-122.

Tabata, I., K. Irisawa, M. Kouzaki, K. Nishimura, F. Ogita, and M. Miyachi. 1997. Metabolic profile of high intensity intermittent exercise. *Medicine and Science in Sports and Exercise* 29(3): 390-395.

Tabata, I., K. Nishimura, M. Kouzaki, Y. Hirai, F. Ogita, M. Miyachi, and K. Yamamoto. 1996. Effects of moderate-intensity endurance and high-intensity intermittent training on anaerobic capacity and VO_2 max. *Medicine and Science in Sports and Exercise* 28: 1327-1330.

Tanaka, K., Y. Matsuura, S. Kumagai et al. 1983. Relationships of anaerobic threshold and onset of blood lactate accumulation with endurance performance. *European Journal of Applied Physiology* 52: 51-56.

Terjung, R. 1979. Endocrine response to exercise. In: R.S. Hutton and D.F. Miller (Eds.), *Exercise and sport sciences reviews* (Vol. 7, pp. 153-180). Philadelphia: Franklin Institute Press.

Tesch, P. 1980. Muscle fatigue in man, with special reference to lactate accumulation during short intense exercise. *Acta Physiologica Scandinavica* 480: 1-40.

Tesch, P.A., B. Colliander, and P. Kaiser. 1986. Muscle metabolism during intense, heavy resistance exercise. *European Journal of Applied Physiology* 55: 362-366.

Thorstensson, P. 1976. Muscle strength, fibre types and enzymes in man. *Acta Physiologica Scandinavica* (Suppl.), 443.

Thorstensson, P., B. Sjodin, and J. Karlsson. 1975. Actinomyosin ATPase, myokinase, CPK and LDH in human fast and slow twitch muscle fibres. *Acta Physiological Scandinavica* 99: 225-229.

Tomlin, D.L., and H.A. Wenger. 2001. The relationship between aerobic fitness and recovery from high intensity intermittent exercise. *Sports Medicine* 31: 1-11.

Triplett, N.T., M.H. Stone, C. Adams et al. 1990. Effects of aspartic acid salts on fatigue parameters during weight training exercise and recovery. *Journal of Applied Sport Science Research* 4(4): 141-147.

Vandewalle, H., G. Peres, and H. Monod. 1987. Standard anaerobic exercise tests. *Sports Medicine* 4: 268-289.

Vihko, V., A. Salmons, and J. Rontumaki. 1978. Oxidative and lysomal capacity in skeletal muscle. *Acta Physiologica Scandinavica* 104: 74-81.

Warren, B.J., M.H. Stone, J.T. Kearney et al. 1992. The effects of short-term overwork on performance measures and blood metabolites in elite junior weightlifters. *International Journal of Sports Medicine* 13: 372-376.

Welch, H.G., J.A. Faulkner, J.K. Barclay et al. 1970. Ventilatory responses during recovery from muscular work and its relation with O2 debt. *Medicine and Science in Sports* 2(1): 15-19.

Welch, H.G., and W.N. Stainsby. 1967. Oxygen debt in contracting dog skeletal muscle in situ. *Respiratory Physiology* 3: 229-242.

Wells, J., B. Balke, and D. Van Fossan. 1957. Lactic acid accumulation during work. A suggested standardization of work classification. *Journal of Applied Physiology* 10: 51-55.

Weltman, A., and U.L. Katch. 1977. Min-by-min respiratory exchange and oxygen uptake kinetics during steady-state exercise in subjects of high and low max VO2. *Research Quarterly* 47: 490-501.

Westerblad, H., D.G. Allen, and J. Lannegren. 2002. Muscle fatigue: Lactic acid or inorganic phosphate the major cause? *News in Physiological Science* 17: 17-21.

Whipp, B.J., C. Scard, and K. Wasserman. 1970. O_2 deficit-O_2 debt relationship and efficiency of aerobic work. *Journal of Applied Physiology* 28: 452-458.

Widrick, J.J., D.L. Costill, G.K. McConnell et al. 1992. Time course of glycogen accumulation after eccentric exercise. *Journal of Applied Physiology* 72: 1999-2004.

Withers, R.T., W.M. Sherman, D.G. Clark et al. 1991. Muscle metabolism during 30, 60 and 90 s of maximal cycling on an airbraked ergometer. *European Journal of Applied Physiology* 63: 354-362.

York, J., L.B. Oscai, and D.G. Penny. 1974. Alterations in skeletal muscle lactate dehydrogenase isozymes following exercise training. *Biochemistry and Biophysics Research Communication* 61: 1387-1393.

Yoshida, I. 1984. Effect of dietary modifications on lactate threshold and onset of blood lactate accumulation during incremental exercise. *European Journal of Applied Physiology* 53: 200-205.

Young, V.R., and B. Torun. 1981. Physical activity: Impact on protein and amino acid metabolism and implications for nutritional requirements. *Progress in Clinical and Biological Research* 77: 57-83.

Chapter 5

Adolphsson, S. 1973. Effects of insulin and testosterone on glycogen synthase activity in rat levator ani muscle. *Acta Physiologica Scandinavica* 88: 243-247.

Ahtiainen, J.P., A. Pakarinen, M. Alen, W.J. Kraemer, and K. Hakkinen. 2003. Muscle hypertrophy, hormonal adaptations and strength development during strength training in strength trained and untrained men. *European Journal of Applied Physiology* 89: 555-563.

Aizawa, K., T. Akimoto, H. Inoue, F. Kimura, M. Juo, F. Murai, and N. Mesaki. 2003. Resting serum dehydroepiandrosterone sulfate level increases after 8-week resistance training among young females. *European Journal of Applied Physiology* 90: 575-580.

Aldercruetz, H., M. Harkonen, K. Kuoppasalmi et al. 1986. Effect of training on plasma anabolic and catabolic steroid hormones and their response during physical exercise. *International Journal of Sports Medicine* (Suppl.) 7: 27-28.

Alen, M., and K. Hakkinen. 1987. Androgenic steroid effects on several hormones and on maximal force development in strength athletes. *Journal of Sports Medicine and Physical Fitness* 27: 38-46.

Alen, M., A. Pakarinen, K. Hakkinen et al. 1988. Responses of serum androgenic-anabolic and catabolic hormones to prolonged strength training. *International Journal of Sports Medicine* 9(3): 229-233.

Allenberg, K., N. Holmquist, S.G. Johnsen et al. 1983. Effects of exercise and testosterone on the active form of glycogen synthases in human skeletal muscle. In: H. Knuttgen, J. Vogel, and J. Poortmans (Eds.), *Biochemistry of exercise* (Vol. 13). Champaign, IL: Human Kinetics.

Arnold, A.P., and R.A. Gorski. 1984. Gonadla steroid induction of structural sex differences in the central nervous system. *Annual Review of Neuroscience* 7: 413-442.

Becker, A.B., and R.A. Roth. 1990. Insulin receptor structure and function in normal and pathological conditions. *Annual Review of Medicine* 41: 99-110.

Benfy, B.G., and D.R. Varma. 1967. Interactions of sympathomimetic drugs, propranalol and phentalamine, on a trial refractory period and contractility. *British Journal of Pharmacology and Chemotherapy* 30: 603-611.

Bjorntorp, P. 1981. The effects of exercise on plasma insulin. *International Journal of Sports Medicine* 2: 125-129.

Blessing, D., D. Wilson, R. Rozenek et al. 1986. Performance, body composition, heart rate, blood lipids and hormonal effects of short term jogging and weight training in middle age sedentary men. *Journal of Applied Sport Science Research* 1: 25-29.

Bloom, S.R., R.H. Johnson, D.M. Park et al. 1976. Differences in the metabolic and hormonal response to exercise between racing cyclists and untrained individuals. *Journal of Physiology* 258: 1-18.

Bonen, A. 1985. Glycogen loss is not an index of muscle activity. *Canadian Journal of Applied Sport Sciences* 10: 237.

Borst, S.E., D.V. DeHoyos, L. Garzarella, K. Vincent, B.H. Pollock, D.T. Lowenthal, and M.L. Pollock. 2001. Effects of resistance training on insulin-like growth factor-1 and IGF binding proteins. *Medicine and Science in Sports and Exercise* 4: 648-653.

Bosco, C., R. Colli, R. Bonomi, S.P. von Duvillard, and A. Viru. 2000. Monitoring strength training: Neuromuscular and hormonal profile. *Medicine and Science in Sports and Exercise* 32: 202-208.

Bosco, C., J. Tihanyi, and A. Viru. 1996. Relationship between field fitness test and basal serum testosterone and cortisol levels in soccer players. *Clinical Physiology* 16: 317-322.

Bourne, H.R., and J.M. Roberts. 1992. Drug receptors and pharmacodynamics. In: B.G. Katzung (Ed.), *Basic and clinical pharmacology* (5th ed., pp. 10-34). Englewood Cliffs, NJ: Appleton & Lange.

Brisson, G.R., M.A. Volle, M. Tanaka et al. 1977. A possible submaximal exercise induced hypothalamo-hypophyseal stress. *Hormone and Metabolism Research* 9: 520-524.

Brooks, R.V. 1984. Androgens: Physiology and pathology. In: H.L.J. Makin (Ed.), *Biochemistry of steroid hormones* (2nd ed., pp. 235-246). Oxford: Blackwell Scientific.

Bryan, R.M. 1990. Cerebral blood flow and energy metabolism during stress. *American Journal of Physiology* 259: H269-H280.

Bunt, J.C. 1986. Hormonal alterations due to exercise. *Sports Medicine* 3: 331-345.

Bunt, J.C. 1990. Metabolic actions of estradiol: Significance for acute and chronic exercise responses. *Medicine and Science in Sports and Exercise* 22: 286-290.

Busso, T., K. Hakkinen, A. Pakarinen et al. 1992. Hormonal adaptations and modeled responses in elite weightlifters during 6 weeks of training. *European Journal of Applied Physiology* 64: 381-386.

Clark, M.G., G.S. Patten, O.H. Filsell et al. 1983. Coordinated regulation of muscle glycolysis and hepatic glucose output in exercise by catecholamines acting via α receptors. *Federation of European Biochemical Societies Letters* 158: 1-5.

Craig, B., and H-Y. Yang. 1994. Growth hormone release following single versus multiple sets of back squats: Total work versus power. *Journal of Strength and Conditioning Research* 8: 270-275.

Cumming, D.C., G.D. Wheeler, E.M. McColl et al. 1989. The effect of exercise on reproductive function in men. *Sports Medicine* 7: 1-17.

Dessypris, K., K. Kuoppasalmi, and H. Aldercreutz. 1976. Plasma cortisol, testosterone, androstenedione and luteinizing hormone (LH) in a non-competitive marathon run. *Journal of Steroid Biochemistry* 7: 33-37.

Dodson, M.V., R.E. Allen, and K.L. Hossner. 1985. Ovine somatomedin, multiplication-stimulating activity and insulin promote skeletal muscle satellite cell proliferation in vitro. *Endocrinology* 117: 2357-2363.

Doerr, P., and K.M. Pirke. 1976. Cortisol-induced suppression of plasma testosterone in normal adult males. *Journal of Clinical Endocrinology and Metabolism* 43: 622-629.

Dohm, L., and T.M. Louis. 1978. Changes in androstenedione, testosterone and protein metabolism as a result of exercise. *Proceedings of the Society for Experimental Biology and Medicine* 158: 622-625.

Dresel, P.B., K.L. MacCannel, and M. Nickerson. 1960. Cardiac arrythmias induced by minimal doses of epinephrine in cyclopropane-anethetized dogs. *Circulation Research* 9: 948-955.

Dufaux, M.L., and K.J. Katt. 1978. Gonadotropin in receptors and regulation of steroidogenesis in testis and ovary. In: P.L. Manson (Ed.), *Vitamins and hormones* (pp. 462-492). New York: Academic Press.

Eik-Nes, K.M. 1969. An effect of isoproterenol on rates of synthesis and secretion of testosterone. *American Journal of Physiology* 217: 1764-1770.

Ellis, G.S., S. Lanza-Jacoby, A. Gow et al. 1994. Effects of estradiol on lipoprotein lipase activity and lipid availability in exercised male rats. *Journal of Applied Physiology* 77: 209-215.

Fellmann, N., J. Coudert, J.F. Jarrige, M. Bedu, C. Denis, D. Boucher, and J.R. Lacour. 1985. Effects of endurance training on the androgenic response to exercise in man. *International Journal of Sports Medicine* 6: 215-219.

Fleck, S.J., and W.J. Kraemer. 1987. *Designing resistance training programs.* Champaign, IL: Human Kinetics.

Florini, J.R. 1985. Hormonal control of muscle cell growth. *Journal of Animal Science* 61: 21-37.

Florini, J.R. 1987. Hormonal control of muscle growth. *Muscle and Nerve* 10: 577-598.

Freissmuth, M., P.J. Casey, and A.G. Gilman. 1989. G proteins control diverse pathways of transmembrane signaling. *FASEB Journal* 3: 2125-2128.

Frey, R., B.M. Doerr, L.S. Srivastava et al. 1983. Exercise training, sex hormones and lipoproteins in man. *Journal of Applied Physiology* 34: 757-762.

Friedman, J.E., P.D. Neufer, and L.G. Dohm. 1991. Regulation of glycogen synthesis following exercise. *Sports Medicine* 11: 232-243.

Fry, A.C., and W.J. Kraemer. 1997. Resistance exercise overtraining and overreaching: Neuroendocrine responses. *Sports Medicine* 23: 106-129.

Fry, A.C., W.J. Kraemer, M.H. Stone et al. 1990. Acute exercise responses in elite junior weightlifters. *Medicine and Science in Sports and Exercise* 22: S4.

Fry, A.C., W.J. Kraemer, M.H. Stone et al. 1994. Endocrine and performance responses to overreaching before and after 1 year of weightlifting. *Canadian Journal of Applied Physiology* 19(4): 400-410.

Fry, A.C., W.J. Kraemer, M.H. Stone, L.P. Koziris, J.T. Thrush, and S.J. Fleck. 2000. Relationships between serum testosterone, cortisol and weightlifting performance. *Journal of Strength and Conditioning Research* 14(3): 338-343.

Fry, A.C., B.K. Schilling, R.S. Staron, F.C. Hagerman, R.S. Hikida, and J.T. Thrush. 2003. Muscle fiber characteristics and performance correlates of male Olympic-style weightlifters. *Journal of Strength and Conditioning Research* 17(4): 746-754.

Galbo, H., and P.D. Gollnick. 1984. Hormonal changes during and after exercise. In: P. Marconnet, J. Poortmans, and L. Hermansen (Eds.), *Medicine and sport science* (Vol. 17, *Physiological chemistry of training and detraining,* pp. 97-110). Basel: Karger.

Galbo, H., L. Hamner, I.B. Petersen, N.J. Christensen, and W. Bie. 1977. Responses to graded and prolonged exercise in man. *European Journal of Applied Physiology* 36: 101-106.

Gotshalk, L.A., C.C. Loebel, B.C. Nindl, M. Putukian, W.J. Sebstianelli, R.U. Newton, K. Hakkinen, and W.J. Kraemer. 1997. Hormonal responses of multi-set versus single set heavy resistance exercise protocols. *Canadian Journal of Applied Physiology* 22: 244-255.

Gray, A.B., R.D. Telford, and M.J. Weidermann. 1993. Endocrine responses to intense interval exercise. *European Journal of Applied Physiology* 66: 366-371.

Guezennec, C.Y., P. Ferre, B. Serrurier et al. 1982. Effects of prolonged physical exercise and fasting upon plasma testosterone levels in rats. *European Journal of Applied Physiology* 49: 159-162.

Gyntelberg, F.M., M.J. Rennie, R.C. Hickson et al. 1977. Effect of training on the response of glucagon to exercise. *Journal of Applied Physiology* 43: 302-305.

Hakkinen, K., K.L. Keskinen, M. Alen et al. 1989. Serum hormone concentrations during prolonged training in elite endurance trained and strength trained athletes. *European Journal of Applied Physiology* 59: 233-238.

Hakkinen, K., and A. Pakarinen. 1991. Serum hormones in male strength athletes during intensive short-term strength training. *European Journal of Applied Physiology* 63: 194-199.

Hakkinen, K., and A. Pakarinen. 1993. Muscle strength and serum testosterone, cortisol and SHBG concentrations in middle-aged and elderly men and women. *Acta Physiologica Scandinavica* 148: 199-207.

Hakkinen, K., A. Pakarinen, M. Alen et al. 1985. Serum hormones during prolonged training of neuromuscular performance. *European Journal of Applied Physiology* 53: 287-293.

Hakkinen, K., A. Pakarinen, M. Alen et al. 1987. Relationship between training volume, physical performance capacity and serum hormone concentrations during prolonged training in elite weightlifters. *International Journal of Sports Medicine* (Suppl. 8): 61-65.

Hakkinen, K., A. Pakarinen, M. Alen et al. 1988a. Daily hormonal and neuromuscular responses to strength training in 1 week. *International Journal of Sports Medicine* 9: 422-428.

Hakkinen, K., A. Pakarinen, M. Alen et al. 1988b. Neuromuscular and hormonal adaptations in athletes to strength training in two years. *Journal of Applied Physiology* 65: 2406-2412.

Hakkinen, K., A. Pakarinen, and M. Kallinen. 1992. Neuromuscular adaptations and serum hormones in women during short-term strength training. *European Journal of Applied Physiology* 64: 106-111.

Hakkinen, K., A. Pakarinen, H. Kyrolainen et al. 1990. Neuromuscular adaptations and serum hormones in females during prolonged power training. *International Journal of Sports Medicine* 11: 91-98.

Hartley, L.H., J.W. Mason, R.P. Hogan et al. 1972. Multiple hormonal responses to graded exercise in relation to physical training. *Journal of Applied Physiology* 33: 602-606.

Haynes, R.C., and F. Murad. 1980. Adrenocorticotropic hormone, adrenocortical steroids and their synthetic analogs, inhibitors of adrenocortical steroid biosynthesis. In: A. Gilman, L. Goodman, and A. Gilman (Eds.), *The pharmacological basis of therapeutics* (pp. 1466-1496). New York: Macmillan.

Heikkinen, J., E. Kyllonen, E. Kurttila-Matero et al. 1997. HRT and exercise effects on bone density, muscle strength and lipid metabolism. *Maturitus* 26: 139-149.

Hepp, K.D. 1977. Studies on the mechanism of insulin action: Basic concepts and clinical implications. *Diabetologia* 13: 177-186.

Hickson, R.C., K. Hikida, C. Foster, M.T. Falduto, and R.T. Chatterton. 1994. Successive time courses of strength development and steroid hormone responses to heavy-resistance training. *Journal of Applied Physiology* 76: 663-670.

Highet, R. 1989. Athletic amenorrhea: An update on aetiology, complications and management. *Sports Medicine* 7: 82-108.

Himms-Hagen, J. 1967. Sympathetic regulation of metabolism. *Pharmacological Reviews* 19: 367-461.

Hodges, J.R., M.T. Jones, and M.A. Stockman. 1962. Effect of emotion and blood circulating corticotropin and cortisol concentration in man. *Nature* 193: 1187-1188.

Hoffman, B.B. 1992. Adrenoceptor-activating drugs. In: B.G. Katzung (Ed.), *Basic and clinical pharmacology* (5th ed., pp. 109-123). Englewood Cliffs, NJ: Appleton & Lange.

Jarholt, J., and J. Holst. 1979. The role of the adrenergic innervation to the pancreatic islets in the control of insulin release during exercise in man. *Pfluegers Archiv* 383: 41-45.

Jensen, J.H., H. Oftebro, B. Breigan et al. 1991. Comparison of changes in testosterone concentrations after strength and endurance exercise in well trained men. *European Journal of Applied Physiology* 63: 467-471.

Jezova, D., and M. Vigas. 1981. Testosterone response to exercise during blockade and stimulation of adrenergic receptors in man. *Hormone Research* 15: 141-147.

Jezova, D., M. Vigas, P. Tatar et al. 1985. Plasma testosterone and catecholamine response to physical exercise in man. *European Journal of Applied Physiology* 54: 62-66.

Johnson, C.C., M.H. Stone, R.J. Byrd et al. 1983. The response of serum lipids and plasma androgens to weight training exercise in sedentary males. *Journal of Sports Medicine and Physical Fitness* 23: 39-41.

Jones, M.T., and B. Gillham. 1988. Factors involved in the regulation of adrenocorticotropic hormone/β-lipotropic hormone. *Physiological Reviews* 68: 743-818.

Jovy, D., H. Bruner, K.E. Klein et al. 1965. Adaptive responses of adrenal cortex to some environmental stressors, exercise, and acceleration. In: *Hormonal steroids: Biochemistry, pharmacology, and therapeutics* (Vol. 2). New York: Academic Press.

Jurkowski, J.E., N.L. Jones, W.C. Walker et al. 1978. Ovarian hormonal responses to exercise. *Journal of Applied Physiology* 44: 109-114.

Keizer, H.A., and A.D. Rogol. 1990. Physical exercise and menstrual cycle alterations: What are the mechanisms? *Sports Medicine* 10(4): 218-235.

Kendrick, Z.V., C.A. Steffen, W.L. Rumsey et al. 1987. Effect of estradiol on tissue glycogen metabolism in exercised oophorectomized female rats. *Journal of Applied Physiology* 63: 492-496.

Kindermann, W., A. Schnabel, W.M. Schmitt et al. 1982. Catecholamines, growth hormone, cortisol, insulin and sex hormones in aerobic and anaerobic exercise. *European Journal of Applied Physiology* 49: 389-399.

Kjer, M. 1992. Regulation of hormonal and metabolic responses during exercise in humans. In: J.O. Holloszy (Ed.), *Exercise and sport science reviews* (Vol. 20, pp. 161-184). Baltimore: Williams & Wilkins.

Koziris, L.P., A.C. Fry, W.J. Kraemer et al. 1992. Hormonal and competitive performance responses to an overtraining stimulus in elite junior weightlifters. *Journal of Applied Sport Science Research* 6(3): 186.

Kraemer, W.J. 1992a. Endocrine responses and adaptations to strength training. In: P.V. Komi (Ed.), *Strength and power in sport* (pp. 291-304). Oxford: Blackwell Scientific.

Kraemer, W.J. 1992b. Hormonal mechanisms related to the expression of muscular strength and power. In: P.V. Komi (Ed.), *Strength and power in sport* (pp. 64-76). Oxford: Blackwell Scientific.

Kraemer, W.J. 1992c. Neuroendocrine responses to resistance exercise. In: T. Baechle (Ed.), *Essentials of strength training and conditioning* (pp. 86-107). Champaign, IL: Human Kinetics.

Kraemer, W.J., A.C. Fry, B.J. Warren et al. 1992. Acute hormonal responses in elite junior weightlifters. *International Journal of Sports Medicine* 13: 103-109.

Kraemer, W.J., L. Marchetelli, S.E. Gordon et al. 1990. Hormonal and growth factor responses to heavy resistance exercise protocols. *Journal of Applied Physiology* 69: 1442-1450.

Kraemer, W.J., B.J. Nobel, M. Clark et al. 1987. Physiological responses to heavy resistance training with very short rest periods. *International Journal of Sports Medicine* 8: 247-252.

Krnjevic, K. 1974. Chemical nature of synaptic transmission in vertebrates. *Physiological Reviews* 54: 418-540.

Kuoppasalmi, H., H. Nervi, K. Kousunen et al. 1981. Plasma steroid levels in muscular exercise. In: J. Poortmans and G. Niset (Eds.), *Biochemistry of exercise IV-B.* Baltimore: University Park Press.

Lamb, D. 1984. *Physiology of exercise.* New York: Macmillan.

Lamon-Fava, S.E., E.C. Fisher, M.E. Nelson et al. 1989. Effect of exercise and menstrual cycle status on plasma lipids, low density lipoprotein particle size and apolipoproteins. *Journal of Clinical Endocrinology and Metabolism* 68: 17-21.

Larner, J. 1980. Insulin and oral hypoglycemic drugs. In: A.G. Gilman, L. Goodman, and A. Gilman (Eds.), *The pharmacological basis for therapeutics* (pp. 1497-1523). New York: Macmillan.

Laron, Z. 1983. Deficiencies of growth hormone and somatostatin in man. *Special Topics in Endocrinology and Metabolism* 5: 149-199.

Lefkowitz, R.J., and M.G. Caron. 1988. Adrenergic receptors: Models for the study of receptors coupled to guanine nucleotide regulatory proteins. *Journal of Biological Chemistry* 263: 4993-4999.

Link, K., R.M. Blizzard, W.S. Evans et al. 1986. The effect of androgens on the pulsatile release and twenty-four hour mean concentration of growth hormone in peripubertal males. *Journal of Clinical Endocrinology and Metabolism* 62: 159-164.

Luger, A., B. Watschinger, P. Deuster, T. Svoboda, M. Clodi, and G.P. Chrousos. 1992. Plasma growth hormone and prolactin responses to graded levels of acute exercise and to a lactate infusion. *Neuroendocrinology* 56: 112-117.

Luyckx, A.S., F. Pirnay, D. Krzentowski et al. 1981. Insulin and glucagon during prolonged muscular exercise in normal man. In: J. Poortmans and G. Niset (Eds.), *Biochemistry of exercise IV-A* (pp. 131-148). Baltimore: University Park Press.

MacDougall, J.D. 1986. Adaptability of muscle to strength training: A cellular approach. In: B. Saltin (Ed.), *International series on sport sciences 16: Biochemistry of exercise VI* (pp. 501-503). Champaign, IL: Human Kinetics.

Mainwaring, W.I.P. 1979. The androgens. In: C.R. Austin (Ed.), *Mechanisms of hormonal action* (Vol. 7). London: Cambridge University Press.

Manchester, K.L. 1972. The effects of insulin on protein synthesis. *Diabetes* 21(Suppl. 2): 447-452.

Marx, J.O., N.A. Ratamess, B.C. Nindl, L.A. Gotshalk, J.S. Volek, K. Dohi, J.A. Bus, A.L. Gomez, S.A. Mazzetti, S.J. Fleck, K. Hakkinen, R.U. Newton, and W.J. Kraemer. 2001. Low-volume circuit versus high-volume periodized resistance training in women. *Medicine and Science in Sports and Exercise* 33: 635-643.

Mason, J.W., L.H. Hartley, T.A. Kotchen et al. 1973. Plasma cortisol and norepinephrine responses in anticipation of muscular exercise. *Psychosomatic Medicine* 35: 406-414.

Mayer, S.E. 1980. Drugs acting at synaptic and neuroeffector junctional sites. In: A. Gilman, L. Goodman, and A. Gilman (Eds.), *The pharmacological basis of therapeutics* (pp. 56-90). New York: Macmillan.

McCall, G.E., W.C. Byrnes, S.J. Fleck, A. Dickinson, and W.J. Kraemer. 1999. Acute and chronic hormonal responses to resistance training designed to promote muscle hypertrophy. *Canadian Journal of Applied Physiology* 24: 96-107.

McMillan, J., M.H. Stone, J. Sartain et al. 1993. The 20 h response to a single session of weight training. *Journal of Strength and Conditioning Research* 7(1): 9-21.

McMurray, R.G., T.K. Eubank, and A.C. Hackney. 1995. Nocturnal hormonal responses to resistance exercise. *European Journal of Applied Physiology* 72: 121-126.

Melby, C., C. Scholl, G. Edwards et al. 1993. Effect of acute resistance exercise on postexercise energy expenditure and resting metabolic rate. *Journal of Applied Physiology* 75: 847-853.

Meyer, M., and F. Rosen. 1975. Interaction of anabolic steroids with glucocorticoid steroid receptor sites in rat muscle control. *American Journal of Physiology* 229: 1381-1386.

Miller, W.J., W.M. Sherman, and J.L. Ivy. 1984. Effect of strength training on glucose tolerance and post-glucose insulin response. *Medicine and Science in Sports and Exercise* 16: 539-543.

Mulligan, S.E., S.J. Fleck, S.E. Gordon et al. 1997. Influence of resistance exercise volume on serum growth hormone and cortisol concentrations in women. *Journal of Strength and Conditioning Research* 10: 256-262.

Munck, A., P.M. Guyne, and N.J. Holbrook. 1984. Physiological functions of glucocorticoids in stress and their relation to pharmacological actions. *Endocrine Reviews* 5: 24-44.

Murad, F., and R.C. Haynes. 1980. Estrogens and progestins. In: A. Gilman, L. Goodman, and A. Gilman (Eds.), *The pharmacological basis of therapeutics* (pp. 1421-1447). New York: Macmillan.

Niklas, B.J., A.J. Ryan, M.M. Treuth, S.M. Harman, M.R. Blackman, B.F. Hurley, and M.A. Rogers. 1995. Testosterone, growth hormone and IGF-1 responses to acute and chronic resistive exercise in men aged 55-70 years. *International Journal of Sports Medicine* 16: 445-450.

Nimmons, M. 1995. High volume weight training with different rest periods and its effect on muscle hypertrophy. Master's thesis, Appalachian State University, Boone, NC.

O'Dowd, B.F., R.J. Lefkowitz, M.G. Caron et al. 1989. Structure of the adrenergic and related receptors. *Annual Review of Neurosciences* 12: 67-92.

Ostrowski, K.J., G.J. Wilson, R. Weatherby et al. 1997. The effect of weight training volume on hormonal output and muscular size and function. *Journal of Strength and Conditioning Research* 11: 148-154.

Phillips, G.B. 1977. Relationship between serum sex hormones and glucose, insulin and lipid abnormalities in men with myocardial infarction. *Proceedings of the National Academy of Science* 74: 1729-1733.

Pierce, K., R. Rozenek, M. Stone et al. 1987. The effects of weight training on plasma cortisol, lactate, heart rate, anxiety and perceived exertion [abstract]. *Journal of Applied Sport Science Research* 1(3): 58.

Porte, D., and R.P. Robertson. 1973. Control of insulin secretion by catecholamines, stress and the sympathetic nervous system. *Federation Proceedings* 32: 1729-1733.

Powers, S.K., and E.T. Howley. 1997. *Exercise physiology* (3rd ed.). Madison, WI: Brown and Benchmark.

Renold, A.E., D.H. Mintz, W.A. Muller et al. 1978. Diabetes mellitus. In: J.B. Stanbury, J.B. Wyngaarden, and D.S. Fredrickson (Eds.), *Metabolic basis of inherited disease* (4th ed.). New York: McGraw-Hill.

Rhea, M.R., B.A. Alvar, L.N. Burkett, and S.D. Ball. 2003. A meta-analysis to determine the dose response for strength development. *Medicine and Science in Sports and Exercise* 35: 456-464.

Robaire, B., and S.F. Bayly. 1989. Testicular signaling. Incoming and outgoing messages. *Annals of the New York Academy of Science* 264: 250-260.

Rowell, L.B. 1974. Human cardiovascular adjustments to exercise and thermal stress. *Physiological Reviews* 54: 74-159.

Sar, M., and W.E. Stumpf. 1977. Androgen concentration in motor neurons of cranial nerves and spinal cord. *Science* 19: 77-79.

Scheurink, A.J.W., A.B. Stephens, and R.P.A. Gaykema. 1990. Hypothalamic adrenoceptors mediate sympathoadrenal activity in exercising rats. *American Journal of Physiology* 259: H470-H477.

Schwab, R., G.O. Johnson, T.J. Housh et al. 1993. Acute effects of different intensities of weightlifting on serum testosterone. *Medicine and Science in Sports and Exercise* 25: 1381-1385.

Scow, R.O., and S.N. Hagen. 1965. Effect of testosterone proprionate and growth hormone on growth and chemical composition of muscle and other tissues in hypophysectomized male rats. *Endocrinology* 77: 852-858.

Shepard, R. 1982. Hormonal control systems. In: *Physiology and biochemistry of exercise*. New York: Praeger.

Shutz, G., L. Killewich, G. Chen et al. 1979. Control of the mRNA for the hepatic tryptophan oxygenase during hormonal and substrate induction. *Proceedings of the National Academy of Science* 72: 1017-1020.

Smilios, I., T. Pilianidis, M. Karamouzis, and S.P. Tokmakidis. 2003. Hormone responses after various resistance exercise protocols. *Medicine and Science in Sports and Exercise* 35: 644-654.

Spiegel, A., and J. Giese-Davis. 2003. Depression and cancer: Mechanisms and disease progression. *Biological Psychiatry* 54: 269-282.

Staron, R.S., D.L. Karapondo, W.J. Kraemer et al. 1994. Skeletal muscle adaptations during early phase of heavy

resistance training in men and women. *Journal of Applied Physiology* 76: 1247-1255.

Stoessel, L., M.H. Stone, R.E. Keith et al. 1991. Selected physiological, psychological and performance characteristics of national caliber United States women weightlifters. *Journal of Applied Sport Science Research* 5(2): 87-95.

Stone, M.H. 1992. Connective tissue and bone responses to strength training. In: P.V. Komi (Ed.), *Strength and power in sport* (pp. 279-290). Champaign, IL: Human Kinetics.

Stone, M.H. 1993. Anabolic steroids and athletics. *National Strength and Conditioning Association Journal* 15(2): 9-29.

Stone, M.H. 1995. Human growth hormone: Physiological functions and ergogenic efficacy. *Strength and Conditioning* 17(4): 72-74.

Stone, M.H., P. Borkowski, and S.L. Smith. 2003. The USOC symposium: The weightlifting project. Presented at the American College of Sports Medicine meeting, San Francisco, May 2003.

Stone, M.H., R. Byrd, and C. Johnson. 1984. Observations on serum androgen response to short-term resistive training in middle-aged sedentary males. *National Strength and Conditioning Association Journal* 5(6): 40-65.

Stone, M.H., T.J. Chandler, M.S. Conley et al. 1996. Training to muscular failure: Is it necessary? *Strength and Conditioning* 18(3): 44-48.

Stone, M.H., and A.C. Fry. 1997. Increased training volume in strength/power athletes. In: R. Kreider, A.C. Fry, and M. Fry (Eds.), *Overtraining in sport*. Champaign, IL: Human Kinetics.

Stone, M.H., R.E. Keith, J.T. Kearney et al. 1991. Overtraining: A review of the signs, symptoms and possible causes. *Journal of Applied Sport Science Research* 5(1): 35-50.

Stone, M.H., and H.S. O'Bryant. 1987. *Strength training: A scientific approach*. Minneapolis: Burgess.

Stone, M.H., S. Plisk, M.E. Stone, B. Schilling, H.S. O'Bryant, and K.C. Pierce. 1998. Athletic performance development: Volume load—1 set vs multiple sets, training velocity and training variation. *Strength and Conditioning* 20(6): 22-33.

Storer, T.W., L. Magliano, L. Woodhouse, M.L. Lee, C. Dzekov, J. Dzekov, R. Casaburi, and S. Bhasin. 2003. Testosterone dose-dependently increases maximal voluntary strength and leg power, but does not affect fatigueability. *Journal of Clinical Endocrinology and Metabolism* 88: 1478-1485.

Stromme, S.B., H.D. Meen, and A. Aakvaag. 1974. Effects of an androgenic-anabolic steroid on strength development and plasma testosterone levels in normal males. *Medicine and Science in Sports* 6: 203-208.

Sutton, J.R., and J.H. Casey. 1975. The adrenocortical response to competitive athletics in retired athletes.

Journal of Clinical Endocrinology and Metabolism 400: 135-138.

Sutton, J.R., P.A. Farrel, and V.J. Haber. 1990. Hormonal adaptation to physical activity. In: C. Bouchard, R.J. Shephard, T. Stephens, J.R. Sutton, and B. McPherson (Eds.), *Exercise, fitness, and health* (pp. 217-257). Champaign, IL: Human Kinetics.

Tabata, I., Y. Atomi, and M. Miyashita. 1984. Blood glucose concentration-dependent ACTH and blood glucose concentration and cortisol responses to prolonged exercise. *Clinical Physiology* 4: 299-307.

Tarnopolsky, L.J., J.D. MacDougall, S.A. Atkinson et al. 1990. Gender differences in substrate for endurance exercise. *Journal of Applied Physiology* 68: 302-308.

Terjung, R. 1979. Endocrine response to exercise. In: R.S. Hutton and D.I. Miller, *Exercise and sport sciences reviews* (Vol. 7, pp. 153-179). New York: Macmillan.

Tesch, P.A. 1992. Training for bodybuilding. In: P.V. Komi (Ed.), *Strength and power in sport* (pp. 370-380). Champaign, IL: Human Kinetics.

Tharp, G.D. 1975. The role of glucocorticoids in exercise. *Medicine and Science in Sports* 7: 6-11.

Tsolakis, C., D. Messinis, A. Stergioulas, and A. Dessypris. 2000. Hormonal responses after strength training and detraining in prepubertal and pubertal boys. *Journal of Strength and Conditioning Research* 14: 399-404.

Unger, R.H., and L. Orci. 1976. Physiology and pathophysiology of glucagon. *Physiological Reviews* 56: 778-826.

Vanhelder, W.P., M.W. Radomski, and R.C. Goode. 1984. Growth hormone during intermittent weight lifting exercise in men. *European Journal of Applied Physiology* 53: 31-34.

Vanhelder, W.P., M.W. Radomski, and R.C. Goode. 1985. Hormonal and metabolic responses to three types of exercise of equal duration and external work output. *European Journal of Applied Physiology* 54: 337-342.

Vernikos-Daniellis, J., and J. Heybach. 1980. Psychophysiologic mechanisms regulating the hypothalamic-pituitary-adrenal response to stress. In: H. Selye (Ed.), *Selye's guide to stress research* (Vol. 1). New York: Van Nostrand Reinhold.

Viru, A. 1992. Plasma hormones and physical exercise. *International Journal of Sports Medicine* 13: 201-209.

Von Euler, U.S. 1974. Sympatho-adrenal activity in physical exercise. *Medicine and Science in Sports* 6: 165-173.

Weicker, H., A. Rettenmeier, F. Ritthaler et al. 1981. Influence of anabolic and catabolic hormones on substrate concentrations during various running distances. In: J. Poortmans and G. Niset (Eds.), *Biochemistry of exercise IV-A* (pp. 208-218). Baltimore: University Park Press.

Weiner, N. 1980. Norepinephrine, epinephrine and the sympathomimetic amines. In: A. Gilman, L. Goodman, and A. Gilman (Eds.), *The pharmacological basis of therapeutics* (pp. 138-175). New York: Macmillan.

Weiss, L.W., K.J. Cureton, and F.N. Thompson. 1983. Comparison of serum testosterone and androstenedione responses to weight lifting in men and women. *European Journal of Applied Physiology* 50: 413-419.

White, T.P., and K.A. Esser. 1989. Satellite cell and growth factor involvement in skeletal muscle growth. *Medicine and Science in Sports and Exercise* 21(Suppl.): S158-S163.

Wilkerson, J.E., S. Horvath, and B. Gutin. 1980. Plasma testosterone during treadmill exercise. *Journal of Applied Physiology* 49: 249-253.

Wilkerson, J.G., L. Swain, and J.C. Howard. 1988. Endurance training, steroid interactions and skeletal interactions. *Medicine and Science in Sports and Exercise* 20: S59.

Williams, A.G., A.N. Ismail, A. Sharma, and D.A. Jones. 2002. Effects of resistance exercise volume and nutritional supplementation on anabolic and catabolic hormones. *European Journal of Applied Physiology* 86: 315-321.

Williams, R.H. 1981. *Textbook of endocrinology*. Philadelphia: Saunders.

Winder, W.W., J.M. Hagberg, R.C. Hickson et al. 1978. Time course of sympathoadrenal adaptation to endurance exercise in man. *Journal of Applied Physiology* 45: 370-374.

Wirth, A., C. Diehm, H. Mayer et al. 1981a. Plasma C-peptide and insulin in trained and untrained subjects. *Journal of Applied Physiology* 50: 71-77.

Wirth, A., U. Smith, B. Nilsson et al. 1981b. 125_I-insulin metabolism in exercised-trained rats. In: J. Poortmans and G. Niset (Eds.), *Biochemistry of exercise IV-B*. Baltimore: University Park Press.

Wolfe, R.R., E.R. Nadel, J. Shaw et al. 1986. Role of changes in insulin and glucagon in glucose homeostasis in exercise. *Journal of Clinical Investigation* 77: 900-907.

Yamada, S., N. Buffinger, J. Dimero et al. 1989. Fibroblast growth factor is stored in fiber extracellular matrix and plays a role in regulating muscle hypertrophy. *Medicine and Science in Sports and Exercise* 21(Suppl.): S173-S180.

Yki-Jarvinen, H., and V.A. Koivisto. 1983. Effects of body composition on insulin sensitivity. *Diabetes* 32: 965-969.

Yki-Jarvinen, H., V.A. Koivisto, M.R. Taskinen et al. 1984. Glucose tolerance, plasma lipoproteins and tissue lipoprotein lipase activities in body builders. *European Journal of Applied Physiology* 53: 253-259.

Young, R.J., and A.H. Ismail. 1978. Ability of biochemical and personality variables in discriminating between high and low fitness levels. *Journal of Psychomotor Research* 22: 193-199.

Zawadski, K.M., B.B. Yaspelkis, and J.L. Ivy. 1992. Carbohydrate complex increases the rate of muscle glycogen storage after exercise. *Journal of Applied Physiology* 72: 1854-1859.

Chapter 6

Acworth, I., J. Nicholass, B. Morgan et al. 1986. Effect of sustained exercise on concentrations of plasma aromatic and branched chain amino acids and brain amine. *Biochemistry and Biophysics Research Communication* 137(1): 149-153.

Afting, E.G., W. Bernhardt, R.W.C. Janzen et al. 1981. Quantitative importance of non-skeletal muscle N-methylhistidine and creatinine in human urine. *Biochemistry Journal* 220: 449-452.

Alborn, E.N., J.M. Davis, and S.P. Baily. 1992. Effects of ammonia on endurance performance in the rat. *Medicine and Science in Sports and Exercise* 24(5) (Suppl.): S50.

Alfin-Slater, R. 1973. *Nutrition for today.* Dubuque, IA: Brown.

American Alliance for Health, Physical Education, Recreation and Dance. 1971. *Nutrition for the athlete.* Washington, DC: AAPHERD.

American College of Sports Medicine, American Dietary Association, and Dieticians of Canada. 2000. Joint position statement: Nutrition and athletic performance. *Medicine and Science in Sports and Exercise* 32: 2130-2145.

Asha Devi, S., S. Prathima, and M.V. Subramanyam. 2003. Dietary vitamin E and physical exercise: I. Altered endurance capacity and plasma lipid profile in aging rats. *Experimental Gerontology* 38: 285-290.

Åstrand, P.O., and K. Rodahl. 1970. *Textbook of work physiology* (2nd ed.). New York: McGraw-Hill.

Avery, N.G., J.L. Kaiser, M.J. Sharman, T.P. Scheett, D.M. Barnes, A.L. Gomez, W.J. Kraemer, and J.S. Volek. 2003. Effects of vitamin E supplementation on recovery from repeated bouts of resistance exercise. *Journal of Strength and Conditioning Research* 17: 801-809.

Ayers, J.W.T., Y. Komesu, R.A. Romani et al. 1985. Anthropometric, hormonal and psychological correlates of semen quality in endurance-trained male athletes. *Fertility and Sterility* 43: 917-921.

Babij, P., S.M. Matthews, and M.J. Rennie. 1983. Changes in blood ammonia, lactate and amino acids in relation to workload during bicycle ergometer exercise in man. *European Journal of Applied Physiology* 50: 405-411.

Bahr, R., I. Ingnes, O. Vaage et al. 1987. Effect of duration of exercise on excess postexercise O_2 consumption. *Journal of Applied Physiology* 62: 485-490.

Bahr, R., P.K. Opstad, J.I. Medbo et al. 1991. Strenuous prolonged exercise elevates resting metabolic rate and causes reduced mechanical efficiency. *Acta Physiologica Scandinavica* 141: 555-563.

Ballor, D.L., V.L. Katch, M.D. Beque, and C.R. Marks. 1988. Resistance weight training during caloric restriction enhances lean body weight maintenance. *American Journal of Clinical Nutrition* 47: 19-25.

Banks, E.A., J.T. Brozinik, B.B. Yaspelkis et al. 1992. Muscle glucose transport, GLUT-4 content and degree of

exercise training in obese Zucker rats. *American Journal of Physiology* 263(5, Part 1): E1010-E1015.

Barnard, R.J., and J.F. Youngren. 1992. Regulation of glucose transport in skeletal muscle. *FASEB Journal* 6(14): 3238-3244.

Bergstrom, J., and E. Hultman. 1966. Muscle glycogen synthesis after exercise: An enhancing factor to the muscle cells in man. *Nature* 210: 309.

Bier, D.M. 1989. Intrinsically difficult problems: The kinetics of body proteins and amino acids in man. *Diabetes and Metabolic Reviews* 5: 111-132.

Birrer, R.B. 1984. *Sports medicine for the primary care physician.* Norfolk, CT: Appleton-Century-Crofts.

Blair, S.N. 1993. Exercise and chronic disease: Emerging evidence for a protective effect. Keynote address, Southeast ACSM meeting, Norfolk, VA.

Blair, S.N., H.W. Kohl, R.S. Paffenbarger et al. 1989. Physical fitness and all cause mortality. *Journal of the American Medical Association* 262: 2395-2401.

Bleich, H.L., E.S. Boro, M.H. Sleisenger et al. 1971. Protein digestion and absorption. *New England Journal of Medicine* 300: 659-663.

Bloomstrand, E., S. Andersson, P. Hassemen et al. 1995. Effect of branched-chain amino acid and carbohydrate supplementation on the exercise induced change in plasma and muscle concentration of amino acids in human subjects. *Acta Physiologica Scandinavica* 153: 87-96.

Bloomstrand, E., F. Celsing, and E.A. Newsholme. 1988. Changes in concentrations of aromatic and branched chain amino acids during sustained exercise in man and their possible role in fatigue. *Acta Physiologica Scandinavica* 133: 115-123.

Bloomstrand, E., P. Hassemen, B. Ekblom et al. 1991. Administration of branched-chain amino acids during sustained exercise—effects on performance and on plasma concentrations of some amino acids. *European Journal of Applied Physiology* 63: 83-88.

Bobb, A., D. Pringle, and A.J. Ryan. 1969. A brief study of the diet of athletes. *Journal of Sports Medicine* 9: 255-262.

Boissonneault, G.A., C.E. Elson, and M.W. Pariza. 1986. Net energy effects of dietary fat on chemically induced mammary carcinogenesis. *Journal of the National Cancer Institute* 76: 335-338.

Booth, F.W., W.F. Nicholson, and P.A. Watson. 1982. Influence of muscle use on protein synthesis and degradation. *Exercise and Sport Sciences Reviews* 10: 27-48.

Borgouts, L.B., G. Schaart, M.K. Hesselink, and H.A. Keizer. 2000. GLUT-4 expression is not consistently higher in type-1 than in type-2 fibres of rat and human vastus lateralis muscles; an immunohistochemical study. *Pfluegers Archiv* 441: 351-358.

Borsheim, E., K.D. Tipton, S.E. Wolfe, and R.R. Wolfe. 2002. Essential amino acids and muscle protein recovery from resistance exercise. *American Journal of Physiology, Endocrinology and Metabolism* 283: E648-657.

Bowers, R.W., and E.L. Fox. 1992. *Sports physiology* (3rd ed.). New York: Saunders.

Bray, G.A. 2003. Low-carbohydrate diets and realities of weight loss. *Journal of the American Medical Association* 289: 1853-1855.

Brehm, B.A., and B. Gutin. 1986. Recovery energy expenditure for steady state exercise in runners and nonrunners. *Medicine and Science in Sports and Exercise* 18: 205-210.

Brooks, G.A. 1987. Amino acid incorporation and protein metabolism during exercise and recovery. *Medicine and Science in Sports and Exercise* 19(Suppl.): S150-S156.

Brooks, G.A., T.D. Fahey, and T.P. White. 1996. *Exercise physiology* (2nd ed.). Mountain View, CA: Mayfield.

Brown, M.S., P.T. Kovanen, and J.J. Goldstein. 1981. Regulation of plasma cholesterol by lipoprotein receptors. *Science* 212: 628-635.

Brubacher, G.B. 1989. Scientific basis for the estimation of the daily requirements for vitamins. In: P. Walter, H. Stahelin, and G. Brubacher (Eds.), *Elevated dosages of vitamins* (pp. 3-11). Stuttgart: Hans Huber.

Burelson, M.A., H.S. O'Bryant, M.H. Stone et al. 1997. Effect of weight training exercise and treadmill exercise on post-exercise oxygen consumption. *Medicine and Science in Sports and Exercise* 30(4): 518-522.

Burhus, K.A., J.L. Lettunich, M.L. Casey et al. 1992. The effects of two different types of resistance training exercise on post-exercise oxygen consumption. *Medicine and Science in Sports and Exercise* 24: S76.

Burke, L.M., and J.A. Hawley. 2003. Effects of short-term fat adaptation on metabolism and performance of prolonged exercise. *Medicine and Science in Sports and Exercise* 34: 1492-1498.

Burke, L.M., J.A. Hawley, D.J. Angus, G.R. Cox, S.A. Clark, N.K. Cummings, B. Desbrow, and M. Hargreaves. 2002. Adaptations to short-term high-fat diet persist during exercise despite high carbohydrate availability. *Medicine and Science in Sports and Exercise* 34: 83-91.

Burke, L.M., and R.S. Read. 1993. Dietary supplements in sport. *Sports Medicine* 15: 43-65.

Butterfield, G.E. 1987. Whole-body protein utilization in humans. *Medicine and Science in Sports and Exercise* 19(Suppl.): S157-S165.

Bylund-Fellenius, A.C., K.M. Ojamaa, K.E. Flaim et al. 1984. Protein synthesis versus energy state in contracting muscles of perfused rat hindlimb. *American Journal of Physiology* 246: E297-E305.

Calders, P., J-L. Pannier, D.M. Matthys et al. 1997. Pre-exercise branched-chain amino acid administration increases endurance performance in rats. *Medicine and Science in Sports and Exercise* 29: 1182-1186.

Campbell, W.W., M.C. Crim, V.R. Young et al. 1994. Increased energy requirements and changes in body composition with resistance training in older adults. *American Journal of Clinical Nutrition* 60: 167-175.

Capurso, A. 1992. Lipid metabolism and cardiovascular risk: Should hypercholesterolemia be treated in the elderly? *Journal of Hypertension* (Suppl.) 110: S65-S68.

Casiglia, F., A. Mazza, V. Tikhonoff, R. Scarpa, L. Schiavon, and A.C. Paessina. 2003. Total cholesterol and mortality in the elderly. *Journal of Internal Medicine* 254: 353-362.

Celajowa, I., and M. Homa. 1970. Food intake, nitrogen, and energy balance in Polish weightlifters during training camp. *Nutrition and Metabolism* 12: 259-274.

Chandler, R.M., H.K. Byrne, J.G. Patterson et al. 1994. Dietary supplements affect the anabolic hormones after weight-training exercise. *Journal of Applied Physiology* 76: 839-845.

Christensen, E., and O. Hansen. 1939. Arbeits fahigheit und ernahrung. *Scandinavian Archives of Physiology* 81: 169.

Clement, D.B., and R.C. Admundsun. 1982. Nutritional intake and hematological parameters in endurance runners. *Physician and Sportsmedicine* 10: 37-43.

Conley, M.S., and M.H. Stone. 1996. Carbohydrate ingestion/supplementation for resistance exercise and training. *Sports Medicine* 21: 7-17.

Conley, M.S., M.H. Stone, J.L. Marsit et al. 1995. Effects of carbohydrate ingestion on resistance exercise. *Journal of Strength and Conditioning Research* 9: 201.

Conroy, B.P., W.J. Kraemer, C.M. Maresh, G.P. Dalskey, S.J. Fleck, M.H. Stone, A.C. Fry, and P. Cooper. 1993. Bone mineral density in weightlifters. *Medicine and Science in Sports and Exercise* 25: 1103-1109.

Dalqvist, A. 1962. The intestinal disaccharidases and disaccharide intolerance. *Gastroenterology* 43: 694-696.

Daugaard, J.R., and E.A. Richter. 2001. Relationship between muscle fibre composition, glucose transporter protein 4 and exercise training: Possible consequences in non-insulin-dependent diabetes mellitus. *Acta Physiologica Scandinavica* 171: 267-276.

Davies, K.J.A., C.M. Donavan, C.J. Refino, G.A. Brooks, L. Parker, and P.R. Dallman. 1984. Distinguishing effects of anemic and muscle iron deficiency on exercise bioenergetics in the rat. *American Journal of Physiology* 246: E535-E543.

Davies, K.J.A., J.J. Maguire, and G.A. Brooks. 1982. Muscle mitochondrial bioenergetics, oxygen supply and work capacity during iron deficiency and repletion. *American Journal of Physiology* 242: E418-E427.

Davis, J.M. 1995. Carbohydrates, branched-chain amino acids and endurance: The central fatigue hypothesis. *International Journal of Sports Medicine* 5(Suppl.): S25-S38.

Davis, J.M., and S.P. Baily. 1997. Possible mechanisms of central nervous system fatigue during exercise. *Medicine and Science in Sports and Exercise* 29: 45-57.

Deakin, V. 2000. Iron depletion in athletes. In: L. Burke and V. Deakin (Eds.), *Clinical sports nutrition* (pp. 270-310). Rossville, NSW: McGraw-Hill Australia.

De Feo, P. 1996. Hormonal regulation of human protein metabolism. *European Journal of Applied Physiology* 153: 7-18.

De Feo, P., and M.W. Haymond. 1994. Principles and calculations of the labeled leucine methodology to estimate protein kinetics in humans. *Diabetes, Metabolism and Nutrition* 7: 165-184.

Dibbern, V. 1981. *Nutrition research*—USSR(U) Dst-18105-144 [U.S Army document].

Dich, J., N. Grunnet, O. Lammert, P. Faber, K.S. Bjornsbo, L.O. Larsen, R.A. Neese, M.C. Hellerstein, and B. Quistorff. 2000. Effects of excessive isocaloric intake of either carbohydrate or fat on body composition, fat mass, de novo lipogenesis and energy expenditure in normal young men. *Ugeker Laeger* 162: 4794-4799.

Dietary Reference Intakes. 1997. DRI for calcium, phosphorus, magnesium, vitamin D and fluoride. www.nap.edu.

Dioguardi, F.S. 1997. Influence of the ingestion of branched chain amino acids on plasma concentrations of ammonia and free fatty acids. *Journal of Strength and Conditioning Research* 11(4): 242-245.

Dohm, G.L., A.L. Hecker, W.E. Brown et al. 1977. Adaptation of protein metabolism to endurance training. Increased amino acid oxidation in response to training. *Biochemistry Journal* 164: 705-708.

Dohm, G.L., G.J. Kasperek, E.B. Tapscott et al. 1985. Protein metabolism during endurance exercise. *Federation Proceedings* 44: 348-352.

Dohm, G.L., F.R. Puente, C.P. Smith et al. 1978. Changes in tissue protein levels as a result of endurance exercise. *Life Sciences* 28: 845-849.

Dohm, G.L., E.B. Tapscott, G.J. Kasperek et al. 1987. Protein degradation during endurance exercise and recovery. *Medicine and Science in Sports and Exercise* 19: S166-S171.

Dohm, G.L., R.T. Williams, G.J. Kasparek et al. 1982. Increased excretion of urea and N-methylhistidine by rats and humans after a bout of exercise. *Journal of Applied Physiology* 52: 27-33.

Donato, K., and D.M. Hegsted. 1985. Efficiency of utilization of various sources of energy for growth. *Proceedings of the National Academy of Science* 82: 4866-4870.

Dragon, G.I., A. Vasilu, and E. Georgescu. 1985. Effects of increased protein supply on elite weightlifters. In: T.E. Galesloot and B.J. Timbergen (Eds.), *Milk proteins* (pp. 99-103). Wageninen, The Netherlands: Poduc.

Drinkwater, B.L., K. Nilson, C.H. Chestnut, W.J. Bremer, S. Shainholtz, and M.B. Southworth. 1984. Bone mineral content of amenorrheic and eumenorrheic athletes. *New England Journal of Medicine* 311: 277-282.

Dufaux, B., G. Assmann, and W. Hollman. 1982. Plasma lipoproteins and physical activity: A review. *International Journal of Sports Medicine* 3: 123-136.

Durstine, J.L., P.W. Grandjean, C.A. Cox, and P. Thompson. 2002. Lipids, lipoproteins and exercise. *Journal of Cardiopulmonary Rehabilitation* 22: 385-398.

Ehn, L., B. Carlwark, and S. Hoglund. 1980. Iron status in athletes involved in intense physical activity. *Medicine and Science in Sports and Exercise* 11: 61-64.

Elliot, D.L., L. Goldberg, and K.S. Kuehl. 1992. Effect of resistance training on excess post-exercise oxygen consumption. *Journal of Applied Sport Science Research* 6(2): 77-81.

Engell, D.B., O. Maller, M.N. Sawka, R.P. Franseseconi, L. Drolet, and A.J. Young. 1987. Thirst and fluid intake following graded hypohydration in humans. *Physiological Behavior* 40: 226-236.

Evans, W.J., E.C. Fisher, R.A. Hoerr et al. 1983. Protein metabolism and endurance exercise. *Physician and Sportsmedicine* 11: 63-72.

Evans, W.J., C.N. Meredith, J.G. Cannon et al. 1986. Metabolic changes following eccentric exercise in trained and untrained men. *Journal of Applied Physiology* 61: 1864-1868.

Fahey, T.D., K. Hoffman, W. Colvin et al. 1993. The effects of intermittent liquid meal feeding on selected hormones and substrates during intense weight training. *International Journal of Sport Nutrition* 3: 67-75.

Felig, P., and J. Wahren. 1971. Amino acid metabolism in exercising man. *Journal of Clinical Investigation* 50: 2703-2714.

Fern, E.B., R.N. Belinski, and Y. Schutz. 1991. Effect of exaggerated amino acid and protein supply in man. *Experientia* 47: 168-172.

Fielding, R.A., and J. Parkington. 2002. What are the dietary protein requirements of physically active individuals? New evidence on the effects of exercise on protein utilization during post-exercise recovery. *Nutrition and Clinical Care* 5: 191-196.

Flatt, J.P. 1992. The biochemistry of energy expenditure. In: P. Bjorntop and B.N. Brodoff (Eds.), *Obesity* (pp. 100-116). New York: Lippincott.

Florini, J.R. 1987. Hormonal control of muscle growth. *Muscle and Nerve* 10: 577-598.

Fogelholm, G.M., R. Koskinen, J. Laakso, T. Rankinen, and I. Ruokonen. 1993. Gradual and rapid weight loss: Effects on nutrition and performance in male athletes. *Medicine and Science in Sports and Exercise* 25: 371-377.

Fogelholm, M. 2000. Vitamin, mineral and antioxidant needs of athletes. In: L. Burke and V. Deakin (Eds.), *Clinical sports nutrition* (pp. 312-340). Rossville, NSW: McGraw-Hill Australia.

Forbes, G.B. 1983. Some influences on lean body mass: Exercise, androgens, pregnancy and food. In: P.L. White and T. Mondieka (Eds.), *Diet and exercise: Synergism in health maintenance.* Chicago: American Medical Association.

Forbes, G.B. 1985. Body composition as affected by physical activity and nutrition. *Federation Proceedings* 4: 343-347.

Forsberg, A.P., P. Tesch, and J. Karlsson. 1978. Effects of prolonged exercise on muscle strength performance. In: E. Asmussen, and K. Jorgensen (Eds.), *Biomechanics VI-A*. Baltimore: University Park Press.

Foster, C., D.L. Costill, and W.J. Fink. 1979. Effect of preexercise feedings on endurance performance. *Journal of Applied Physiology* 11: 1-15.

Freidman, J.E., and P.W.R. Lemon. 1985. Effect of protein intake and endurance exercise on daily protein requirements. *Medicine and Science in Sports and Exercise* 17(Suppl.): S231.

Friedman, J.E., P.D. Neufer, and G.L. Dohm. 1991. Regulation of glycogen synthesis following exercise. *Sports Medicine* 11(4): 232-243.

Fry, A.C., W.J. Kraemer, and M.H. Stone. 1991. The effect of amino acid supplementation on testosterone, cortisol and growth hormone responses to one week of intensive training. Presented at the MAACSM annual meeting, New Brunswick, NJ.

Fry, A.C., W.J. Kraemer, M.H. Stone et al. 1993. Endocrine and performance responses to high volume training and amino acid supplementation in elite junior weightlifters. *International Journal of Sport Nutrition* 3: 303-322.

Galim, E.B., K. Hruska, and D.M. Bier. 1980. Branched chain amino acid nitrogen transfer to alanine in vivo in dogs: Direct isotopic demonstration with [^{15}N] leucine. *Journal of Clinical Investigation* 66: 1295-1304.

Gaster, M., W. Vach, H. Beck-Nielsen, and H.D. Schroder. 2002. GLUT 4 expression at the plasma membrane is related to fibre volume in human skeletal muscle fibres. *Acta Pathologica, Microbiologica et Immunologica Scandinavica* 110: 611-619.

Gastmann, U.A., and M.J. Lehmann. 1998. Overtraining and the BCAA hypothesis. *Medicine and Science in Sports and Exercise* 30: 1173-1178.

Geleijnse, J.M., F.J. Kok, and D.E. Grobbee. 2003. Blood pressure response to changes in sodium and potassium intake: A metaregression analysis of randomized trials. *Journal of Human Hypertension* 17: 471-480.

Gippini, A., A. Mato, R. Pazos, B. Suarez, B. Vila, P. Gayoso, M. Lage, and F.F. Casanueva. 2002. Effect of long-term strength training on glucose metabolism. Implications for individual impact of high lean mass and high fat mass on relationship between BMI and insulin sensitivity. *Journal of Endocrinological Investigation* 25: 520-525.

Gleeson, M., R.J. Maughn, and P.L. Greenhaff. 1986. Comparison of the effects of glucose, glycerol and placebo on endurance and fuel homeostasis in man. *European Journal of Applied Physiology* 55: 645-653.

Goldberg, R.L. 1980. Hormonal regulation of protein degradation and synthesis in skeletal muscle. *Federation Proceedings* 39: 31-36.

Goldstein, J., T. Kita, and M. Brown. 1983. Defective lipoprotein receptors and atherosclerosis. *New England Journal of Medicine* 309: 288-292.

Gontzea, I., P. Sutzscu, and S. Dumitrache. 1974. The influence of muscular activity on nitrogen balance and on the need for protein. *Nutrition Reports International* 10: 35-43.

Gontzea, I., P. Sutzscu, and S. Dumitrache. 1975. The influence of adaptation to physical effort on nitrogen balance in man. *Nutrition Reports International* 11: 231-236.

Graham, T.E., J.W.E. Rush, and D.A. MacLean. 1995. Skeletal muscle amino acid metabolism and ammonia production during exercise. In: M. Hargreaves (Ed.), *Exercise metabolism* (pp. 131-175). Champaign, IL: Human Kinetics.

Groussard, C., G. Machefer, F. Rannou, H. Faure, H. Zouhal, O. Sergent, M. Chevanne, J. Cillard, and A. Gratas-Delamarche. 2003. Physical fitness and plasma non-enzymatic antioxidant status at rest and after a Wingate test. *Canadian Journal of Applied Physiology* 28: 79-92.

Grunwald, K.K., and R.S. Baily. 1993. Commercially marketed supplements for bodybuilding athletes. *Sports Medicine* 15(2): 90-103.

Guillard, J.C., T. Penaranda, C. Gallet, W. Boggio, F. Fuchs, and J. Keppling. 1989. Vitamin status of young athletes including the effects of supplementation. *Medicine and Science in Sports and Exercise* 21: 441-449.

Hackney, A.C., R.L. Sharp, W.S. Runyan et al. 1989. Resting hormonal changes during intensive training: Effects of a dietary protein supplement. *Conference abstracts*, SEACSM.

Haff, G.G., M.J. Lehmkuhl, L.B. McCoy, and M.H. Stone. 2003. Carbohydrate supplementation and resistance training. *Journal of Strength and Conditioning Research* 17: 187-196.

Haff, G.G., C.A. Schroeder, A.J. Koch, K.E. Kuphal, M.J. Comeau, and J.A. Pottieger. 2001. The effects of supplemental carbohydrate ingestion on intermittent isokinetic leg exercise. *Journal of Sports Medicine and Physical Fitness* 41: 216-222.

Haff, G.G., M.H. Stone, B.J. Warren, R. Keith, R.L. Johnson, D.C. Nieman, F. Williams, and K.B. Kirksey. 1998. The effect of carbohydrate supplementation on multiple sessions and bouts of resistance exercise. *Journal of Strength and Conditioning Research* 13: 111-117.

Hakkinen, K., A. Pakarinen, M. Alen et al. 1985. Relationship between training volume, physical performance capacity and serum hormone concentrations during prolonged training in elite weightlifters. *International Journal of Sports Medicine* 8: 61-65.

Hamilton, E.M.H., E.N. Whitley, and F.S. Sizer. 1985. *Nutrition: Concepts and controversies.* St. Paul, MN: West.

Hamosh, M., and R.O. Scow. 1975. Lingual lipase and its role in the digestion of dietary lipid. *Journal of Clinical Investigation* 52: 88-95.

Hargreaves, B.J., D.L. Costill, W.J. Fink, D.S. King, and R.A. Fielding. 1987. Effects of preexercise carbohydrate feedings on endurance cycling performance. *Medicine and Science in Sports and Exercise* 19: 33-36.

Hargreaves, B.J., D.S. Kronfeld, J.N. Waldron, M.A. Lopes, L.S. Gay, K.E. Saker, W.L. Cooper, D.J. Sklan, and P.A. Harris. 2002. Antioxidant status and muscle cell leakage during endurance exercise. *Equine Veterinary Journal* (Suppl.) 34: 116-121.

Hauer, K., W. Hildebrandt, Y. Sehl, L. Elder, P. Oster, and W. Droge. 2003. Improvement in muscular performance and decrease in tumor necrosis factor level in old age after antioxidant treatment. *Journal of Molecular Medicine* 81: 118-125.

Hawley, J. 2000. Nutritional strategies to enhance fat oxidation during aerobic exercise. In: L. Burke and V. Deakin (Eds.), *Clinical sports nutrition* (pp. 428-454). Rossville, NSW: McGraw-Hill Australia.

Heaney, R.P. 1987. The role of calcium in prevention and treatment of osteoporosis. *Physician and Sportsmedicine* 15: 83-88.

Herbert, W.G. 1983. Water and electrolytes. In: M.H. Williams (Ed.), *Ergogenic aids in sport* (pp. 56-98). Champaign, IL: Human Kinetics.

Hetland, M.L., J. Haarbo, and C. Christiansen. 1993. Low bone mass and high bone turnover in male long distance runners. *Journal of Clinical Endocrinology and Metabolism* 77: 770-775.

Hickson, R.C., M.A. Roesenkoetter, and M.M. Brown. 1980. Strength training effects on aerobic power and short-term endurance. *Medicine and Science in Sports and Exercise* 12: 336-339.

Hollet, C.R., and J.V. Auditore. 1967. Localization and characterization of a lipase in rat adipose tissue. *Archives of Biochemistry and Biophysics* 9: 423-430.

Hood, D.A., and R.L. Terjung. 1990. Amino acid metabolism during exercise and following endurance training. *Sports Medicine* 9: 23-35.

Horton, E.S. 1982. Effects of low-energy diets on work performance. *American Journal of Clinical Nutrition* 35: 1228-1233.

Horton, T., H. Drougas, A. Brachey et al. 1995. Fat and carbohydrate overfeeding in humans: Different effects on energy stores. *American Journal of Clinical Nutrition* 62: 19-29.

Houmard, J.A., P.C. Eagen, P.D. Neufer et al. 1991. Elevated skeletal muscle glucose transport levels in exercise-trained middle-aged men. *American Journal of Physiology* 261(4, Part 1): E437-E443.

Hunter, G., L. Blackman, L. Dinnam et al. 1988. Bench press metabolic rate as a function of exercise intensity. *Journal of Applied Sport Science Research* 2(1): 1-6.

Hunter, G., D.R. Bryan, C.J. Wetstein, P.A. Zuckermann, and M.M. Baumann. 2002. Resistance training and intra-abdominal adipose tissue in older men and women. *Medicine and Science in Sports and Exercise* 34: 1023-1028.

Ivy, J.L. 2001. Dietary strategies to promote glycogen synthesis after exercise. *Canadian Journal of Applied Physiology* 26(Suppl.): S236-245.

Ivy, J., and R. Portman. 2004. *Nutrient timing.* North Bergen, NJ: Basic Health.

Jacobs, I., P. Kaiser, and P. Tesch. 1982. The effects of glycogen exhaustion on maximal short-term performance. In: P. Komi (Ed.), *Exercise and sport biology, International series on sport sciences* (pp. 103-108). Champaign, IL: Human Kinetics.

Jaquier, E. 1987. Energy, obesity and body weight standards. *American Journal of Clinical Nutrition* 45: 1035-1047.

Jenkins, D.G., J. Palmer, and D. Spillman. 1993. The influence of dietary carbohydrate on performance of supramaximal intermittent exercise. *European Journal of Applied Physiology* 67: 309-314.

Johnston, C.C., and C. Slemeda. 1987. Osteoporosis: An overview. *Physician and Sportsmedicine* 15: 65-68.

Kaplan, N.M. 1986. Dietary aspects of the treatment of hypertension. *Annual Reviews of Public Health* 7: 503-519.

Karlsson, J., and B. Saltin. 1971. Diet, muscle glycogen and endurance performance. *Journal of Applied Physiology* 31: 203-206.

Kennedy, E., S.A. Bowman, and J.T. Spence. 2001. Popular diets: Correlation to health, nutrition, and obesity. *Journal of the American Dietetic Association* 101: 411-420.

Kenny, A.M., C. Joseph, P. Taxel, and K.M. Prestwood. 2003. Osteoporosis in older men and women. *Connecticut Medicine* 67: 481-486.

Kiens, B., and J. Helge. 2000. Adaptations to a high-fat diet. In: R. Maughn (Ed.), *Nutrition in sport* (pp. 192-202). Oxford: Blackwell Science.

Kiens, B., A.B. Raben, A.K. Valeus, and E.A. Richter. 1990. Benefit of dietary simple carbohydrates on the early postexercise glycogen repletion in male athletes. *Medicine and Science in Sports and Exercise* 22(Suppl.): S88.

Kindermann, W., A. Schnabel, W.M. Schmitt et al. 1982. Catecholamines, growth hormone, cortisol, insulin and sex hormones in anaerobic and aerobic exercise. *European Journal of Applied Physiology* 49: 389-399.

Lamb, D.R., and G.R. Brodowicz. 1986. Optimal use of fluids of varying formulations to minimize exercise-induced disturbances in homeostasis. *Sports Medicine* 3: 247-274.

Lamb, D.G., K.F. Rinehardt, R.L. Bartels et al. 1990. Dietary carbohydrate and intensity of interval swimming. *American Journal of Clinical Nutrition* 52: 1058-1063.

Lambert, C.P., M.G. Flynn, J.B. Boone et al. 1991. Effects of carbohydrate feeding on multiple-bout resistance exercise. *Journal of Applied Sport Science* 5: 192-197.

Lane, N., W. Bevier, M. Bouxsein, R. Wiswell, R. Carter, and D.R. Marcus. 1988. The effect of intensity on bone mineral. *Medicine and Science in Sports and Exercise* 20(Suppl.): S51.

Laritcheva, K.A., N.I. Valovarya, V.I. Shybin et al. 1978. Study of energy expenditure and protein needs of top weightlifters. In: J. Parizkova and V.A. Rogozkin (Eds.), *Nutrition, physical fitness and health, International series on sport sciences* (Vol. 7, pp. 53-61). Baltimore: University Park Press.

Lehmann, M., H. Mann, U. Gastmann, J. Keul, D. Vetter, J.M. Steinacher, and D. Haussinger. 1996. Unaccustomed high-mileage vs intensity training-related changes in performance and serum amino acid levels. *International Journal of Sports Medicine* 17: 187-192.

Lemon, P.W.R. 1987. Protein and exercise. Update. *Medicine and Science in Sports and Exercise* 19(Suppl.): S179-S190.

Lemon, P.W.R. 1991. Effect of exercise on protein requirements. *Journal of Sports Sciences* 9: 53-70.

Lemon, P.W.R. 1995. Do athletes need more protein and amino acids? *International Journal of Sport Nutrition* 5(Suppl.): S39-S61.

Lemon, P.W.R. 1996. Is increased dietary protein necessary or beneficial for individuals with a physically active lifestyle? *Nutrition Reviews* 54: S169-S175.

Lemon, P.W., J.M. Berardi, and E.E. Noreen. 2002. The role of protein and amino acid supplements in the athlete's diet: Does type or timing of ingestion matter? *Current Sports Medicine Reports* 1: 214-221.

Lemon, P.W.R., and J.P. Mullin. 1980. Effect of initial muscle glycogen levels on protein catabolism during exercise. *Journal of Applied Physiology* 46: 624-629.

Lemon, P.W.R., and F.J. Nagle. 1981. Effects of exercise on protein and amino acid metabolism. *Medicine and Science in Sports and Exercise* 13: 141-149.

Lemon, P.W.R., M.A. Tarnopolsky, J.D. MacDougall et al. 1992. Protein requirements and muscle mass/strength changes during intensive training in novice bodybuilders. *Journal of Applied Physiology* 73: 767-775.

Leon, A.S. 1985. Physical activity levels and coronary heart disease. *Medical Clinics of North America* 69: 3-20.

Liberman, H.R., S. Corkin, and B.J. Spring. 1983. Mood, performance and pain sensitivity. *Journal of Psychiatric Research* 17: 135-146.

Lindsay, R. 1987. Estrogen and osteoporosis. *Physician and Sportsmedicine* 15: 105-108.

Lupton, J. 2005. The 2005 dietary guidelines advisory committee report: From molecules to dietary patterns. *Nutrition Today* 40: 215.

MaCance, R.A. 1936. Experimental sodium chloride deficiency in man. *Proceedings of the Royal Society of London* 119: 245-268.

MacLean, D.A., T.E. Graham, and B. Saltin. 1996. Stimulation of muscle ammonia production during exercise following branched-chain amino acid supplementation in humans. *Journal of Physiology* 493: 909-922.

Manore, M., and J. Thompson. 2000. Energy requirements of the athlete. In: L. Burke and V. Deakin (Eds.), *Clinical sports nutrition* (pp. 124-146). Rossville, NSW: McGraw-Hill Australia.

Maughn, R.J. 2000. Fluid and carbohydrate intake during exercise. In: L. Burke and V. Deakin (Eds.), *Clinical sports nutrition* (pp. 369-395). Rossville, NSW: McGraw-Hill Australia.

Maughn, R.J. 2003. Impact of mild dehydration on wellness and on exercise performance. *European Journal of Clinical Nutrition* 57(Suppl. 2): S19-S23.

Maughn, R.J., and D.C. Poole. 1981. The effects of a glycogen-loading regimen on the capacity to perform anaerobic exercise. *European Journal of Applied Physiology* 46: 211-219.

McMillan, J., R.E. Keith, and M.H. Stone. 1988. The effects of vitamin B6 and exercise on the contractile properties of rat muscle. *Nutrition Research* 8: 73-80.

McMillan, J., M.H. Stone, J. Sartain et al. 1993. The 20 h response to a single session of weight training. *Journal of Strength and Conditioning Research* 7(1): 9-21.

Melby, C., C. Scholl, G. Edwards et al. 1993. Effect of acute resistance exercise on postexercise energy expenditure and resting metabolic rate. *Journal of Applied Physiology* 75: 1847-1853.

Mero, A., H. Pitkanen, S.S. Oja et al. 1997. Leucine supplementation and serum amino acids, testosterone, cortisol and growth hormone in male power athletes during training. *Journal of Sports Medicine and Physical Fitness* 37: 137-145.

Mitchell, J.B., D.L. Costill, J.A. Houmard et al. 1990. Influence of carbohydrate ingestion on counter regulatory hormones during prolonged exercise. *International Journal of Sports Medicine* 11: 33-36.

Mitchell, R., R. Kreider, R. Miller et al. 1991. Effects of amino acid supplements on metabolic responses to ultraendurance triathlon performance. *Medicine and Science in Sports and Exercise* 23(4)(Suppl.): S15.

Montoye, H.J., H.C.G. Kemper, W.H.M. Saris, and R.A. Washburn. 1996. *Measuring physical activity and energy expenditure.* Champaign, IL: Human Kinetics.

Morris, J.N. 1987. Exercise and the incidence of coronary heart disease. In: *Exercise-heart-health.* London: Coronary Prevention Group.

Mosoni, L., and P.P. Mirand. 2003. Type and timing of protein feeding to optimize anabolism. *Current Opinion in Clinical Nutrition and Metabolic Care* 6: 301-306.

Moyad, M.A. 2003. The potential benefits of dietary and/or supplemental calcium and vitamin D. *Urology and Oncology* 21: 384-391.

National Academy of Sciences. 1989. *Recommended dietary allowances* (10th ed.). Washington, DC: National Academy of Sciences.

National Cholesterol Education Program, Expert Panel on Detection, Evaluation and Treatment of High Blood Cholesterol in Adults (Adult Treatment Panel III). 2001, May. *Journal of the American Medical Association* 16(285): 2486-2497.

Neaton, J.D., H. Blackburn, D. Jacobs, I. Kuller, D.J. Lee, R. Sherwin, J. Shih, J. Stamler, and D. Wentworth. 1992. Serum cholesterol level and mortality for men screened in the Multiple Risk Factor Intervention Trial. *Archives of Internal Medicine* 152: 1490-1500.

Newman, D.J., K.R. Mills, B.M. Quigley et al. 1983. Pain and fatigue after concentric and eccentric muscle contractions. *Clinical Science* 64: 55-62.

Newsholme, E. 1990. The metabolic causes of fatigue/overtraining. Keynote address, Southeast ACSM meeting, Charleston, SC.

Newsholme, E., I.N. Acworth, and E. Bloomstrand. 1985. Amino acids, brain neurotransmitters and a functional link between muscle and brain that is important in sustained exercise. *Advances in Biochemistry* 1: 127-133.

NHANES III (National Health and Nutrition Examination Survey). 1988-2004. Hyattsville, MD: U.S. Department of Health and Human Services, Centers for Disease Control.

Nicolette, R. 1993. Effect of two different resistance exercise bouts of equal work on post-exercise oxygen consumption. Master's thesis, Purdue University.

Nimmons, M.J., J.L. Marsit, M.H. Stone et al. 1995. Physiological and performance effects of two commercially marketed supplement systems. *Strength and Conditioning* 17(4): 52-58.

Nindl, B.C., K.E. Friedl, L.J. Marchitelli, R.L. Shippee, C.D. Thomas, and J.F. Patton. 1996. Regional fat placement in physically fit males and changes with weight loss. *Medicine and Science in Sports and Exercise* 28: 786-793.

O'Keefe, K., R.E. Keith, D.L. Blessing et al. 1987. Dietary carbohydrate and endurance performance. *Medicine and Science in Sports and Exercise* 19: S538.

Oppliger, R.A., and C. Bartok. 2002. Hydration in athletes. *Sports Medicine* 32: 959-971.

Petitt, D.S., S.A. Arngrimsson, and K.J. Cureton. 2003. Effect of resistance exercise on postprandial lipemia. *Journal of Applied Physiology* 94: 694-700.

Petruzzello, S.J., D.M. Landers, J. Pie et al. 1992. Effect of branched-chain amino acid supplements on exercise-related mood and performance. *Medicine and Science in Sports and Exercise* 24(5)(Suppl.): S2.

Philen, R.M., D.I. Ortiz, S.B. Auerbach et al. 1992. Survey of advertising for nutritional supplements in health and bodybuilding magazines. *Journal of the American Medical Association* 268(8): 1008-1011.

Piers, L.S., K.Z. Walker, R.M. Stoney, M.J. Soares, and K. O'Dea. 2002. The influence of the type of dietary fat on postprandial fat oxidation rates: Monounsaturated (olive oil) vs saturated fat (cream). *International Obesity Related Metabolic Disorders* 26: 814-821.

Pike, R.L., and M. Brown. 1984. *Nutrition: An integrated approach* (3rd ed.). New York: Macmillan.

Pitkanen, H.T., T. Nykanen, J. Knuutinen et al. 2003. Free amino acid and muscle protein balance after resistance exercise. *Medicine and Science in Sports and Exercise* 35: 784-792.

Pivarnik, J.M., J.F. Hickson, and I. Wolinsky. 1989. Urinary 3-methylhistidine excretion increases with repeated weight training exercise. *Medicine and Science in Sports and Exercise* 21: 283-287.

Powers, S.K., and K. Hamilton. 1999. Antioxidants and exercise. *Clinical Sports Medicine* 18: 525-536.

Rassmussen, B.B., and R.R. Wolfe. 1999. Regulation of fatty acid oxidation in skeletal muscle. *Annual Review of Nutrition* 19: 463-484.

Reeds, P.J., M.R. Fuller, and B.A. Nicholson. 1985. Metabolic basis of energy expenditure with a particular reference to protein. In: J.S. Garrow and D. Halliday (Eds.), *Substrate and energy metabolism* (pp. 102-107). London: Libbey.

Rennie, M.J., R.H.T. Edwards, S. Krywawych et al. 1981. Effect of exercise on protein turnover in man. *Clinical Sciences* 61: 627-639.

Risser, W.L., E. Lee, H.B.W. Poindexter, M.S. West, J.M. Pivarnik, J.M.H. Risser, and J.F. Hickson. 1988. Iron deficiency in female athletes: Its prevalence and impact on performance. *Medicine and Science in Sports and Exercise* 20: 116-121.

Rokitski, L., E. Logemann, G. Hunter, E. Keck, and J. Keul. 1994. Alpha-tocopherol supplementation in racing cyclists during extreme endurance training. *International Journal of Sport Nutrition* 4: 253-264.

Ronsen, O., J. Sundgot-Borgen, and S. Maehlum. 1999. Supplement use and nutritional habits of Norwegian elite athletes. *Scandinavian Journal of Medicine and Science in Sports* 9: 28-35.

Rontoyannis, G.P., T. Skoulis, and K.N. Pavlou. 1989. Energy balance in ultramarathon running. *American Journal of Clinical Nutrition* 49: 976-979.

Roy, S.R., and W. Irwin. 1983. *Sports medicine*. Englewood Cliffs, NJ: Prentice-Hall.

Rozenek, R., and M.H. Stone. 1984. Protein metabolism related to athletes. *National Strength and Conditioning Association Journal* 6(2): 42-62.

Ryan, G.B. 1977. Acute inflammation. *American Journal of Pathology* 86: 185-264.

Sacks, F.M., and M. Katan. 2002. Randomized clinical trials on the effects of dietary fat and carbohydrate on plasma lipoproteins and cardiovascular disease. *American Journal of Medicine* 113(Suppl. 9B): 13S-24S.

Saltin, B., and J. Stenberg. 1964. Circulatory response to prolonged severe exercise. *Journal of Applied Physiology* 19: 833-838.

Scala, D., J. McMillan, D. Blessing et al. 1987. Metabolic cost of a preparatory phase of training in weightlifting: A practical observation. *Journal of Applied Sport Science Research* 1(3): 48-52.

Schoffstall, J.E., J.D. Branch, B.C. Leutholtz, and D.E. Swain. 2001. Effects of dehydration and rehydration on the one-repetition maximum bench press of weight-trained males. *Journal of Strength and Conditioning Research* 15: 102-108.

Scholl, C.G., R.C. Bullough, and C.L. Melby. 1993. Effect of different modes on postexercise energy expenditure and substrate utilization. *Medicine and Science in Sports and Exercise* 25: 532.

Scott, K.C., R.C. Hill, D.D. Lewis, A.J. Boning, and D.A. Sunderstrom. 2001. Effect of alpha-tocopheryl acetate supplementation on vitamin E concentration in greyhounds before and after a race. *American Journal of Veterinary Research* 62: 1118-1120.

Sedlock, D.A., J.A. Fisinger, and C.L. Melby. 1989. Effect of exercise intensity and duration on postexercise energy expenditure. *Medicine and Science in Sports and Exercise* 21: 626-646.

Seguin, R., and M.E. Nelson. 2003. The benefits of strength training for older adults. *American Journal of Preventive Medicine* 25(3 Suppl. 2): 141-149.

Shahar, E., L.E. Chambless, W.D. Rosamond, L.L. Boland, C.M. Ballantyne, P.G. McGovern, and A.R. Sharrett. 2003. Plasma lipid profile and incident ischemic stroke: The Atherosclerosis Risk in Community (ARIC) study. *Stroke* 34: 623-631.

Sherman, W.M., and G.S. Wimer. 1991. Insufficient carbohydrate during training: Does it impair performance? *Sports Nutrition* 1: 28-44.

Shibata, Y., I. Ohsawa, T. Watanabe, T. Miura, and Y. Sato. 2003. Effects of physical training on bone mineral density and bone metabolism. *Journal of Anthropology and Applied Human Science* 22: 203-208.

Short, S.H., and W.R. Short. 1983. Four-year study of university athletes' dietary intake. *Journal of the American Dietary Association* 82: 632-645.

Simonses, J.C., W.M. Sherman, D.R. Lamb et al. 1991. Dietary carbohydrate, muscle glycogen and power output during rowing training. *Journal of Applied Physiology* 70: 1500-1505.

Slentz, C.A., E.A. Gulve, K.J. Rodnick et al. 1992. Glucose transporters and maximal transport are increased in endurance trained rat soleus. *Journal of Applied Physiology* 73(2): 486-492.

Smith, L.L. 1992. Causes of delayed onset muscle soreness and the impact on athletic performance. *Journal of Applied Sport Science Research* 6: 135-141.

Smith, N.J. 1976. Gaining and losing weight in athletics. *Journal of the American Medical Association* 236: 149-151.

Snyder, A.C., L.L. Dvorak, and J.B. Roepke. 1989. Influence of dietary iron source on measures of iron status among female runners. *Medicine and Science in Sports and Exercise* 21: 7-10.

Snyder, A.C., D.R. Lamb, T. Baur et al. 1983. Maltodextrin feeding immediately before prolonged cycling at 62% of VO_2 max increases time to exhaustion. *Medicine and Science in Sports and Exercise* 15: S126.

Sohar, E., and A. Adar. 1962. Sodium requirements in Israel under conditions of work in hot climate. In: *UNESCO/India Symposium on Environmental Physiology and Psychology*. Lucknow, India: UNESCO.

Sparge, E. 1979. Metabolic functions of man, mammals, birds and fishes: A review. *Journal of the Royal Society of Medicine* 72: 921-925.

Stone, M.H. 1990. Muscle conditioning and muscle injury. *Medicine and Science in Sports and Exercise* 22: 457-462.

Stone, M.H., S.J. Fleck, W.J. Kraemer, and N.T. Triplett. 1991a. Health- and performance-related potential of resistance training. *Sports Medicine* 11: 210-231.

Stone, M.H., and C. Karatzeferi. 2002. Connective tissue (and bone) response to strength training. In: P.V. Komi (Ed.), *Encyclopaedia of sports medicine: Strength and power in sport* (2nd ed.). London: Blackwell.

Stone, M.H., R.E. Keith, J.T. Kearney, G.D. Wilson, and S.J. Fleck. 1991b. Overtraining: A review of the signs, symptoms and possible causes. *Journal of Applied Sport Science Research* 5(1): 35-50.

Stone, M.H., R.E. Keith, D. Marple, S.J. Fleck, and J.T. Kearney. 1989. Physiological adaptations during a one-week junior elite weightlifting camp. *Conference abstracts, SEACSM annual meeting, January.*

Stone, M.H., G.D. Wilson, D. Blessing, and R. Rozenek. 1983. Cardiovascular responses to short-term Olympic style weight training in young men. *Canadian Journal of Applied Sport Sciences* 8: 134-139.

Strauss, R.H., R.R. Lanese, and W.B. Malarky. 1985. Weight loss in amateur wrestlers and its effect on serum testosterone levels. *Journal of the American Medical Association* 255: 3337-3338.

Strauzenberg, S.E., F. Schneider, R. Donath, H. Zerbes, and E. Kohler. 1979. The problem of dieting in training and athletic performance. *Bibliotheca Nutritio et Dieta* 27: 109-122.

Suominen, H. 1993. Bone mineral density and long-term exercise. An overview of cross-sectional athlete studies. *Sports Medicine* 16: 316-330.

Sutton, J.R., P.A. Farrell, and V.J. Harber. 1990. Hormonal adaptation to physical activity. In: C. Bouchard, R.J. Shepard, T. Stephens, J.R. Sutton, and B. McPherson (Eds.), *Exercise, fitness, and health* (pp. 217-257). Champaign, IL: Human Kinetics.

Takanami, Y., K. Iwane, Y. Kawai, and T. Shimomitsu. 2000. Vitamin E supplementation and endurance exercise: Are there benefits? *Sports Medicine* 29: 73-83.

Tanaka, H., K.A. West, G.E. Duncan, and D.R. Basset. 1997. Changes in plasma tryptophan/branched chain amino acid ratio in response to training volume variation. *International Journal of Sports Medicine* 18: 270-275.

Tarnoplosky, M. 2000. Protein and amino acid needs for training and bulking up. In: L. Burke and V. Deakin (Eds.), *Clinical sports nutrition* (pp. 90-123). Rossville, NSW: McGraw-Hill Australia.

Tarnopolsky, M.A., S.A. Atkinson, J.D. MacDougall et al. 1991. Whole body leucine metabolism during and after resistance exercise in fed humans. *Medicine and Science in Sports and Exercise* 23: 326-333.

Tarnopolsky, M.A., S.A. Atkinson, J.D. MacDougall et al. 1992. Evaluation of protein requirements for trained strength athletes. *Journal of Applied Physiology* 75: 1986-1995.

Tarnopolsky, M.A., J.D. MacDougall, and S.A. Atkinson. 1988. Influence of protein intake and training status on nitrogen balance and lean body mass. *Journal of Applied Physiology* 64: 187-193.

Thompson, J., M.M. Manore, and J.S. Skinner. 1993. Resting metabolic rate and thermic effect of a meal in low- and adequate intake male endurance athletes. *International Journal of Sport Nutrition* 3: 194-206.

Tipton, K.D., E. Borsheim, S.E. Wolfe, A.P. Sanford, and R.R. Wolfe. 2002. Acute response of net muscle protein balance reflects 24-h balance after exercise and amino acid ingestion. *American Journal of Physiology, Endocrinology and Metabolism* 28: E76-89.

Tischler, M.E. 1981. Hormonal regulation of protein degradation in skeletal and cardiac muscle. *Life Sciences* 28: 2569-2576.

Tsai, A.C., and T-W. Gong. 1987. Modulation of the exercise and retirement effects by dietary fat intake in hamsters. *Journal of Nutrition* 117: 1149-1153.

Van der Beck, E.J. 1991. Vitamin supplementation and physical exercise performance. *Journal of Sports Sciences* 9: 77-89.

Vandewalle, L., A.J.M. Wagenmakers, K. Smets et al. 1991. Effect of branched-chain amino acid supplementation on exercise performance in glycogen depleted subjects. *Medicine and Science in Sports and Exercise* 23(4)(Suppl.): S116.

van Hall, G., J.S.H. Raaymakerts, W.H.M. Saris et al. 1995. Ingestion of branched-chain amino acids and tryptophan during sustained exercise in man. *Journal of Physiology* 486: 789-794.

Verger, P., P. Aymard, L. Cynobert et al. 1994. Effect of administration of branched chain amino acids versus glucose during acute exercise in the rat. *Physiological Behavior* 55: 523-526.

Vincent, K.R., P.M. Clarkson, P.S. Freedson et al. 1993. Effect of a pre-exercise liquid, high carbohydrate feeding on resistance exercise performance. *Medicine and Science in Sports and Exercise* 25: S194.

Volek, J. 2003. Strength nutrition. *Current Sports Medicine Reports* 2: 189-193.

Vorobyev, A. 1978. *Weightlifting*. Budapest: International Weightlifting Federation, Medical Committee [translated by A.J. Brice].

Wagenmakers, A.J.M., K. Smets, L. Vandewalle et al. 1991. Deamination of branched-chain amino acids: A potential source of ammonia production during exercise. *Medicine and Science in Sports and Exercise* 23(4)(Suppl.): S116.

Walberg, J.L., M.K. Leidy, D.J. Sturgill et al. 1988. Macronutrient content of a hypocaloric diet affects nitrogen retention and muscle function. *International Journal of Sports Sciences* 4: 261-266.

Walberg-Rankin, J. 2000. Making weight in sports. In: L. Burke and V. Deakin (Eds.), *Clinical sports nutrition* (pp. 185-209). Rossville, NSW: McGraw-Hill Australia.

Walsh, R.M., T.D. Nokes, J.A. Hawley, and S.C. Dennis. 1994. Impaired high-intensity cycling performance time at low levels of dehydration. *International Journal of Sports Medicine* 15: 392-398.

Wang, S.C., B. Bednarski, S. Patel, A. Yan, C. Kohoyda-Inglis, T. Kennedy, E. Link, S. Rowe, M. Sochor, and S. Arbabi. 2003. Increased depth of subcutaneous fat is protective against injuries in motor vehicle collisions. *Annual Proceedings of the Advancement of Automotive Medicine* 47: 545-559.

Wee, S.L., C. Williams, and P. Garcia-Roves. 1999. Carbohydrate availability determines endurance running capacity in fasted subjects [abstract]. *Medicine and Science in Sports and Exercise* 31: S91.

Weideman, C.A., M.G. Flynn, F.X. Pizza et al. 1990. Effects of increased protein intake on muscle hypertrophy and strength following 13 weeks of resistance training [abstract]. *Medicine and Science in Sports and Exercise* 22:S37.

White, T.P., and K.A. Esser. 1989. Satellite cell and growth factor involvement in skeletal muscle growth. *Medicine and Science in Sports and Exercise* 21(Suppl.): S158-S163.

Whitley, H.A., S.M. Humphreys, I.T. Campbell et al. 1998. Metabolic and performance responses during endurance exercise after high-fat and high-carbohydrate meals. *Journal of Applied Physiology* 85: 418-424.

Williams, M.H. 1976. *Nutritional aspects of human physical and athletic performance*. Springfield, IL: Charles C Thomas.

Wilmore, J.H., and D.L. Costill. 1994. *Physiology of sport exercise.* Champaign, IL: Human Kinetics.

Wilmore, J.H., and B.J. Freund. 1984. Nutritional enhancement of athletic performance. *Nutritional Abstracts and Reviews* A54: 1-6.

Wilson, M.M., and J.E. Morley. 2003. Impaired cognitive function and mental performance in mild dehydration. *European Journal of Clinical Nutrition* 57(Suppl 2): S24-S29.

Wolfe, R.R. 1987. Does exercise stimulate protein breakdown in humans? Isotopic approaches to the problem. *Medicine and Science in Sports and Exercise* 19(Suppl.): S172-S178.

Wood, P.D., and M.L. Stefanic. 1990. Exercise, fitness and atherosclerosis. In: C. Bouchard, R.J. Shephard, T. Stephens, R. Sutton, and B.D. McPherson (Eds.), *Exercise, fitness, and health.* Champaign, IL: Human Kinetics.

Yamada, S., N. Buffinger, J. Dimero et al. 1989. Fibroblast growth factor is stored in fiber extracellular matrix and plays a role in regulating muscle hypertrophy. *Medicine and Science in Sports and Exercise* 21(Suppl.): S173-S180.

Yang, E.J., H.K. Chung, W.Y. Kim, J.M. Kerver, and W.O. Song. 2003. Carbohydrate intake is associated with diet quality and risk factors for cardiovascular disease in U.S. adults. NHANES III. *Journal of the American Medical Association* 22: 71-79.

Yates, A., K. Leechy, and C.M. Shisslak. 1983. Running: An analogue of anorexia? *New England Journal of Medicine* 308: 251-253.

Yokogoshi, H., T. Iwata, K. Ishida et al. 1987. Effect of amino acid supplementation to low-protein diet on brain and plasma levels of tryptophan and brain 5-hydroxyindoles in rats. *Journal of Nutrition* 117: 42-47.

Young, V.R., and H.N. Munroe. 1978 N+ - methylhistidine (3-methylhistidine) and muscle protein turnover: An overview. *Federation Proceedings* 37: 2291-2300.

Zelessky, M. 1977. Coaching: Medico-biological and psychological means of recovery. *Legkaya Atletica* 7: 20-22.

Chapter 7

Alen, M., K. Hakkinen, and P.V. Komi. 1984. Changes in neuromuscular performance and muscle fiber characteristics of elite power athletes self-administering androgenic and anabolic steroids. *Acta Physiologica Scandinavica* 122: 535-544.

Antonio, J., and J.R. Stout. 2001. *Sports supplements.* Baltimore: Lippincott, Williams & Wilkins.

Athlete Guilty. 1999, August 20. Gillon, D. *The Electronic Herald,* Glasgow, Scotland.

Ayoama, R., E. Hiruma, and H. Sasaki. 2003. Effects of creatine loading on muscular strength and endurance of female softball players. *Journal of Sports Medicine and Physical Fitness* 43: 481-487.

Balsom, P., K. Soderlund, and B. Ekblom. 1994. Creatine in humans with special reference to creatine supplementation. *Sports Medicine* 18: 268-280.

Beiner, J.M., P. Jokl, J. Cholewicki, and M.M. Panjabi. 1999. The effect of anabolic steroids and corticosteroids on healing of muscle contusion injury. *American Journal of Sports Medicine* 27: 2-9.

Besset, A., A. Bonardet, G. Rendouin, B. Decamps, and P. Passdouant. 1982. Increase in sleep related GH and Prl secretion after chronic arginine aspartate administration in man. *Acta Endocrinologica* 99: 18-23.

Bhasin, S. 2003a. Effects of testosterone administration on fat distribution, insulin sensitivity and atherosclerosis progression. *Clinical Infectious Disease* 37(Suppl. 2): S142-S149.

Bhasin, S. 2003b. Regulation of body composition by androgens. *Journal of Endocrinology Research* 26: 814-822.

Bhasin, S., T.W. Storer, N. Berman, C. Callegari, B. Clevenger, J. Phillips, T.J. Bunnell, R. Tricker, A. Shirazi, and R. Casaburi. 1996. The effects of supraphysiologic doses of testosterone on muscle size and strength in normal men. *New England Journal of Medicine* 335: 1-7.

Bhasin, S., L. Woodhouse, R. Casaburi, A.B. Singh, D. Bhasin, N. Berman, X. Chen, K.E. Yarasheski, L. Magliano, C. Dzekov, J. Dzekov, R. Boss, J. Phillips, I. Sinha-Hikim, R. Shen, and T.W. Storer. 2001. Testosterone dose-dependent relationship in healthy young men. *American Journal of Physiology, Endocrinology and Metabolism* 28: E1172-E1181.

Bigland, B., and B. Jehring. 1952. Muscle performance in rats: Normal and treated with growth hormone. *Journal of Physiology* 1167: 129-136.

Biolo, G., S.P. Maggi, B.D. Williams, K.D. Tipton, and R.R. Wolfe. 1995. Increased rates of muscle protein turnover and amino acid transport after resistance exercise in humans. *American Journal of Physiology* 268(3 Part 1): E514-520.

Biolo, G., K.D. Tipton, S. Klein, and R.R. Wolfe. 1997. An abundant supply of amino acids enhances the metabolic effects of exercise on muscle protein. *American Journal of Physiology* 273(1 Part 1): E122-129.

Bohn, A.M., M. Khodace, and T.L. Schwenk. 2003. Ephedrine and other stimulants as ergogenic aids. *Current Sports Medicine Reviews* 2: 220-225.

Boirie, Y., M. Dangin, P. Gachon, M.P. Vasson, J.L. Maubois, and B. Beaufrere. 1997. Slow and fast dietary proteins differently modulate postprandial protein accretion. *Proceedings of the National Academy of Science* 94: 1430-1435.

Bosco, C., M. Cardinale, and O. Tsarpela. 1999. Influence of vibration on mechanical power and electromyogram activity in human arm flexor muscles. *European Journal of Applied Physiology* 79: 306-311.

Bosco, C., M. Iacovelli, O. Tsarpela, M. Cardinale, M. Bonifazi, J. Tihanyi, M. Viru, A. De Lorenzo, and A. Viru.

2000. Hormonal responses to whole-body vibration in man. *European Journal of Applied Physiology* 81: 449-454.

Brilla, L.R., M.S. Giroux, A. Taylor, and K.M. Knutzen. 2003. Magnesium-creatine supplementation effects on body water. *Metabolism* 52: 1136-1140.

Brown, G.A., M.D. Vukovich, R.I. Sharp, T.A. Reifenrath, K.A. Parsons, and D.S. King. 1999. Effect of oral DHEA on serum testosterone and adaptations to resistance training in young men. *Journal of Applied Physiology* 87: 2274-2283.

Brown misses out. 1998, August 19. Sports, *BBC Online News.*

Burks, T.F. 1981. Drug use in athletics. *Federation Proceedings* 40: 2680-2681.

Call for fail safe drug tests. 1999, August 4. Sports, *BBC Online News.*

Cardinale, M., and J. Lim. 2003. Electromyography of vastus lateralis muscle during whole-body vibrations of different frequencies. *Journal of Strength and Conditioning Research* 17: 621-624.

Cardinale, M., and M.H. Pope. 2003. The effects of whole body vibration on humans: Dangerous or advantageous. *Acta Physiologica Hungaria* 90: 195-206.

Catlin, D.H., D.A. Cowan, R. de la Torre, M. Donike, D. Fraisse, H. Oftebro, C.K. Hatten, B. Starcevic, M. Becchi, X. de la Torre, H. Norli, H. Geyer, and C.J. Walker. 1996. Urinary testosterone (T) to epitestosterone (E) ratios by GC/MS. I. Initial comparison of uncorrected T/E in six international laboratories. *Journal of Mass Spectroscopy* 31: 397-402.

Catlin, D.H., and T.H. Murray. 1996. Performance enhancing drugs. Fair competition and Olympic sport. *Journal of the American Medical Association* 276: 231.

Chester, N., D.R. Mottram, T. Reilly, and M. Powell. 2004. Elimination of ephedrines in urine following multiple dosing: The consequences for athletes, in relation to doping control. *British Journal of Clinical Pharmacology* 57: 62-67.

Conley, M.S., and M.H. Stone. 1996. Carbohydrate ingestion/supplementation for resistance exercise and training. *Sports Medicine* 21: 7-17.

Conway, K.J., R. Orr, and S.R. Stannard. 2003. Effect of a divided dose on endurance cycling performance, postexercise urinary concentration and plasma paraxanthine. *Journal of Applied Physiology* 94: 1557-1562.

Corrigan, B. 2002. DHEA and sport. *Clinical Journal of Sports Medicine* 12: 236-241.

Crist, D.M., G.T. Peake, P.A. Eagen, and D.L. Waters. 1988. Body composition responses to exogenous GH during training in highly conditioned adults. *Journal of Applied Physiology* 65: 579-584.

Cuneo, R.C., F. Salomon, C.M. Wiles, R. Heep, and P.H. Sonksen. 1991. Growth hormone treatment in growth hormone-deficient adults. 1. Effects on muscle mass and strength. *Journal of Applied Physiology* 70: 688-694.

Dangin, M., Y. Boirie, C. Garcia-Rodenas, P. Gachon, J. Fauquant, P. Callier, O. Ballavre, and B. Beaufrere. 2001. The digestion rate of protein is an independent regulating factor of postprandial protein retention. *American Journal of Physiology* 280: E340-E348.

Dehennin, L., Y. Bonnaire, and P. Plou. 1999. Urinary excretion of 19-norandrosterone of endogenous origin in man: Quantitative analysis by gas chromatography-mass spectrometry. *Journal of Chromatography and Biomedical Application* 72: 301-307.

Dehennin, L., and G. Peres. 1996. Plasma and urinary markers of oral testosterone misuse by healthy men in presence of masking epitestosterone administration. *International Journal of Sports Medicine* 17: 315-319.

Dehennin, L., and R. Scholler. 1990. Detection of self-administration of testosterone as an anabolic by determination of the ratio of urinary testosterone to urinary epitestosterone in adolescents. *Pathological Biology* 38: 920-922.

Delecluse, C., M. Roelants, and S. Verschueren. 2003. Strength increase after whole-body vibration compared with resistance training. *Medicine and Science in Sports and Exercise* 335: 1033-1041.

Demands grow for drug test review. 1999, August 5. Sports, *BBC Online News.*

Demant, T.W., and E.C. Rhodes. 1999. Effects of creatine supplementation on exercise performance. *Sports Medicine* 28: 49-60.

DeMeersman, R., D. Getty, and D.C. Schaefer. 1987. Sympathomimetics and exercise enhancement: All in the mind? *Pharmacology, Biochemistry and Behaviour* 28: 361-365.

Derave, W., B.O. Eijnde, P. Verbessen, M. Ramaekers, M. Leemputte, E.A. Richter, and P. Hespel. 2003. Combined creatine and protein supplementation in conjunction with resistance training promotes muscle GLUT-4 content and glucose tolerance in humans. *Journal of Applied Physiology* 94: 1910-1916.

De Ruiter, C.J., S.M. Van Raak, J.V. Schilperoort, A.P. Hollander, and A. Haan. 2003. The effects of 11 weeks of whole body vibration training on jump height, contractile properties and activation of human knee extensors. *European Journal of Applied Physiology* 90: 595-600.

Dietary Supplement Health and Education Act (DSHEA). 1994. Food and Drug Administration. 1999. http://vm.cfsan.fda.gov/~dms/dietsupp.html.

Earnest, C.P., M.A. Olsen, C.E. Broeder, K.F. Breul, and S.L. Beckham. 2000. Oral 4-androstene-3,17-dione and 4-androstene-3,17-diol supplementation in young males. *European Journal of Applied Physiology* 81: 229-231.

Ebben, W.P., and R.L. Jensen. 2002. Electromyographic and kinetic analysis of traditional, chain and elastic band squats. *Journal of Strength and Conditioning Research* 16: 547-550.

Eckerson, J.M., J.R. Stout, G.A. Moore, N.J. Stone, K. Nishimura, and K. Tamura. 2004. Effect of two and five days of creatine loading on anaerobic capacity in women. *Journal of Strength and Conditioning Research* 18: 168-173.

Eichner, E.R. 1997. Ergogenic aids: What athletes are using—and why. *Physician and Sportsmedicine* 25: 70-77.

El Yacoubi, M., J. Costenin, and J.M. Vaugeois. 2003. Adenosine A2A receptors and depression. *Neurology* 61(11 Suppl. 6): S82-S87.

Evans, N.A. 2004. Current concepts in anabolic-androgenic steroids. *American Journal of Sports Medicine* 32: 534-542.

Fafournoux, P., A. Bruhat, and C. Jousse. 2000. Amino acid regulation of gene expression. *Biochemistry Journal* 351(Part 1): 1-12.

Farquhar, W.B., and E.J. Zambraski. 2002. Effects of creatine use on the athlete's kidney. *Current Sports Medicine Reports* 1: 103-106.

Finn, J.P., T.R. Ebert, R.T. Withers et al. 2001. Effect of creatine supplementation on metabolism and performance in humans during intermittent sprint cycling. *European Journal of Applied Physiology* 84: 238-243.

Fern, E.B., R.N. Bielinski, and Y. Schutz. 1991. Effects of exaggerated amino acid and protein supply in man. *Experientia* 47: 168-172.

Fogelholm, G.M., H.K. Naveri, K.T. Kiilavuori, and M.H. Harkonen. 1993. Low-dose amino acid supplementation: No effects on serum growth hormone and insulin in male weightlifters. *International Journal of Sports Medicine* 3: 290-297.

Forslund, A.H., A.E. El-Khoury, R.M. Olsson, A.M. Sjodin, L. Hambraeus, and Y.R. Young. 1999. Effect of protein intake and physical activity on 24-h pattern and rate of macronutrient utilization. *American Journal of Physiology* 276(Part 1): E974-E976.

Forslund, A.H., L. Hambraeus, R.M. Olsson, A.E. El-Khoury, Y.M. Yu, and V.R. Youn. 1998. The 24-h whole body leucine and urea kinetics at normal and high protein intakes with exercise in healthy adults. *American Journal of Physiology* 275(Part 2): E310-E320.

Frisch, H. 1999. Growth hormone and body composition in athletes. *Journal of Endocrinological Investigation* 22(5 Suppl.): 106-109.

Fruhbeck, G. 1998. Protein metabolism: Slow and fast dietary proteins. *Nature* 39: 843-845.

Fry, A.C., W.J. Kraemer, M.H. Stone, B.J. Warren, J.T. Kearney, C.M. Maresh, C.A. Weseman, and S.J. Fleck. 1993. Endocrine and performance responses to high volume training and amino acid supplementation in elite junior weightlifters. *International Journal of Sport Nutrition* 3: 306-322.

Fryberg, D.A., R.A. Gelfeld, and E.J. Barrett. 1991. Growth hormone acutely stimulates forearm muscle protein synthesis in normal adults. *American Journal of Physiology, Endocrinology and Metabolism* 23: E499-E504.

Garle, M., R. Ocka, E. Palonek, and I. Bjorkhem. 1996. Increased urinary testosterone:epitestosterone ratios found in Swedish athletes in connection with a national control program. Evaluation of 28 cases. *Journal of Chromatography and Biomedical Application* 687: 55-59.

Gater, D.R., D.A. Gater, J.M. Uribe, and J.C. Bunt. 1992. Impact of nutritional supplements and resistance training on body composition, strength and insulin-like growth factor-1. *Journal of Applied Sport Science Research* 6: 66-76.

Gleeson, M., G.I. Lancaster, and N.C. Bishop. 2001. Nutritional strategies to minimize exercise-induced immunosuppression in athletes. *Canadian Journal of Applied Physiology* 26(Suppl.): S23-S35.

Gosselink, K.L., R.R. Roy, H. Zhong, R.E. Grindeland, A.J. Bigbee, and V.R. Edgerton. 2004. Vibration-induced activation of muscle afferents modulates bioassayable growth hormone release. *Journal of Applied Physiology* 96: 2097-2102.

Greenwood, M., R.B. Kreider, L. Greenwood, and A. Byars. 2003. Cramping and injury incidence in collegiate football players are reduced by creatine supplementation. *Journal of Athletic Training* 38: 216-219.

Grivetti, L.E., and E.A. Applegate. 1997. From Olympia to Atlanta: A cultural-historical perspective on diet and athletic training. *Journal of Nutrition* 127: 8605-8685.

Haff, G.G., B. Kirksey, M.H. Stone, B.J. Warren, R.L. Johnson, M. Stone, H.S. O'Bryant, and C. Proulx. 2000. The effect of six weeks of creatine monohydrate supplementation on dynamic rate of force development. *Journal of Strength and Conditioning Research* 14: 426-433.

Haff, G., A. Whitley, L.B. McCoy, and M.H. Stone. 2003. Carbohydrate supplementation and resistance training. *Journal of Strength and Conditioning Research* 17: 187-196.

Hakkinen, K., A. Pakarinen, M. Alen, H. Kauhanen, and P.V. Komi. 1987. Relationships between training volume, physical performance capacity, and serum hormone concentrations during prolonged training in elite weightlifters. *International Journal of Sports Medicine* 1: 61-65.

Hanin, Y.L. 1989. Interpersonal and intragroup anxiety in sports. In: D. Hackford and C.D. Spielberger (Eds.), *Anxiety in sports: An international perspective*. New York: Hemisphere.

Hartgens, F., and H. Kuipers. 2004. Effects of androgenic-anabolic steroids in athletes. *Sports Medicine* 34: 513-554.

Haussinger, D., and F. Lang. 1991. Cell volume in the regulation of hepatic function: A mechanism for metabolic control. *Biophysica Acta* 1071: 331-350.

Haussinger, D., E. Roth, F. Lang, and W. Gerok. 1993. Cellular hydration state. An important determinant of catabolism in health and disease. *Lancet* 341: 1330-1332.

Hickson, R.C., S.M. Czerwinski, M.T. Falduto, and A.P. Young. 1990. Glucocorticoid antagonism by exercise and androgenic anabolic steroids. *Medicine and Science in Sports and Exercise* 22: 331-340.

Hile, A.M., J.M. Anderson, K.A. Fiala, J.H. Stevenson, D.J. Casa, and C.M. Maresh. 2006. Creatine supplementation and anterior compartment pressure during exercise in the heat in dehydrated men. *Journal of Athletic Training* 41: 30-35.

Hubbard, J.S., S. Rohrmann, P.K. Lnadia, E.J. Metter, D.C. Muller, B. Andres, H.B. Carter, and E.A. Platz. 2004. Association of prostate cancer risk with insulin, glucose and anthropometry in the Baltimore longitudinal study of aging. *Urology* 63: 253-258.

Isidori, A., A. Lo Monaco, and M. Cappa. 1981. A study of growth hormone release in man after oral ingestion of amino acids. *Current Medical Research Opinion* 7: 475-481.

Ivy, J.L. 2001. Dietary strategies to promote glycogen synthesis after exercise. *Canadian Journal of Applied Physiology* 26 (Suppl.): S236-245.

Ivy, J.L., A.L. Katz, C.L. Cutler, W.M. Sherman, and E.F. Coyle. 1988. Muscle glycogen synthesis after exercise: Effect of time of carbohydrate ingestion. *Journal of Applied Physiology* 64: 1480-1485.

Ivy, J., and R. Portman. 2004. *Nutrient timing*. North Bergen, NJ: Basic Health.

Jeffreys, M., P. McCarron, D. Gunnell, J. McEwen, and G.D. Smith. 2003. Body mass index in early and mid-adulthood, and subsequent mortality: A historical cohort study. *International Journal of Obesity Related Metabolism Disorders* 27: 1391-1397.

Juhn, M.S. 2000. Does creatine supplementation increase the risk of rhabdomylosis? *Journal of the American Board of Family Practice* 13: 150-151.

Kadi, F., A. Eriksson, S. Holmner, and L.E. Thornell. 1999. Effects of anabolic steroids on the muscle cells of strength-trained athletes. *Medicine and Science in Sports and Exercise* 31: 1528-1534.

Karila, T., V. Kosumen, A. Leinomen, R. Tahtela, and T. Seppala. 1996. High doses of alcohol increase urinary testosterone-to-epitestosterone ratio in females. *Journal of Chromatography Biological and Biomedical Application* 687(1): 109-116.

Kicman, A.T., and D.B. Gower. 2003. Anabolic steroids in sport: Clinical and analytical perspectives. *Annals of Clinical Biochemistry* 40(Part 4): 321-356.

Kilduff, L.P., Y.P. Pitsiladis, L. Tasker, J. Attwood, P. Hyslop, A. Dailly, I. Dickson, and S. Grant. 2003. Effects of creatine on body composition and strength gains after 4 weeks of resistance training in previously nonresistance-trained humans. *International Journal of Sport Nutrition and Exercise Metabolism* 13: 504-520.

King, D.S., R.L. Sharp, M.D. Vukovich, G.A. Brown, T.A. Reifenrath, N.L. Uhl, and K.A. Parsons. 1999. Effect of oral androstenedione on serum testosterone and adaptations to resistance training in young men. *Journal of the American Medical Association* 28(21): 2020-2028.

Kintz, P., V. Crimele, and B. Ludes. 1999. Nandrolone and noretiocholanolone: Metabolite markers. *Acta Clinica Belgica* (Suppl.) 1: 68-73.

Kirksey, B., M.H. Stone, B.J. Warren, R.L. Johnson, M.E. Stone, G.G. Haff, E.E. Williams, and C. Proulx. 1999. The effects of six weeks of creatine monohydrate supplementation on performance measures and body composition in collegiate track and field athletes. *Journal of Strength and Conditioning Research* 13: 1148-1156.

Kneiss, A., E. Ziegler, J. Kratzsch, D. Thieme, and B.K. Muller. 2003. Potential parameters for the detection of hGH doping. *Analytical and Bioanalytical Chemistry* 376: 696-700.

Koak, K.S. 2003. Effects of high dose oral creatine supplementation on anaerobic capacity of elite wrestlers. *Journal of Sports Medicine and Physical Fitness* 43: 488-492.

Kohler, R.M.N., and M.I. Lambert. 2002. Urine nandrolone metabolites: False positive doping test? *British Journal of Sports Medicine* 36: 325-329.

Kopera, H. 1993. Side effects of anabolic steroids and contraindications. *Wein Medicine Wochensch* 14: 399-400.

Krieder, R.B. 1999. Dietary supplements and the promotion of muscle growth with resistance exercise. *Sports Medicine* 27: 97-110.

Krieder, R.B., C. Melton, C.J. Rasmussen, M. Greenwood, S. Lancaster, E.C. Cantler, P. Milnor, and A.L. Almada. 2003. Long-term creatine supplementation does not affect clinical markers of health in athletes. *Molecular and Cellular Biochemistry* 244: 95-104.

Kuhn, C.M. 2002. Anabolic steroids. *Recent Progress in Hormone Research* 57: 411-434.

Kutz, M.R., and M.J. Gunter. 2003. Creatine monohydrate supplementation on body weight and percent body fat. *Journal of Strength and Conditioning* 17: 817-821.

Lambert, M.I., J.A. Hefer, R.P. Millar, and P.W. MacFarlane. 1993. Failure of commercial oral amino acid supplements to increase serum growth hormone in male body-builders. *International Journal of Sport Nutrition* 3: 298-305.

Lancaster, G.I., R.L. Jentjens, L. Mosely, A.E. Jeukendrup, and M. Gleeson. 2003. Effect of pre-exercise carbohydrate ingestion on plasma cytokine stress hormone and neutrophil degranulation responses to continuous high-intensity exercise. *International Journal of Sports Medicine* 13: 436-453.

Lange, K.H., J.L. Andersen, N. Beyer, F. Isaksson, B. Larsson, M.H. Rasmussen, A. Juul, J. Bulow, and M.

Kjaer. 2002. GH administration changes myosin heavy chain isoforms in skeletal muscle but does not augment muscle strength or hypertrophy, either alone or combined with resistance exercise training in healthy adults. *Journal of Clinical Endocrinology and Metabolism* 87: 513-523.

Lemon, P.W. 2000. Beyond the zone: Protein needs of active individuals. *Journal of the American College of Nutrition* 19(5 Suppl.): 513S-521S.

Lemon, P.W., J.M. Berardi, and E.E. Noreen. 2002. The role of protein and amino acid supplements in the athlete's diet: Does type or timing of ingestion matter? *Current Sports Medicine Reports* 1: 214-221.

Levenhagen, D.K, C. Carr, M.G. Carlson, D.J. Maron, M.J. Borel, and P.J. Falkol. 2002. Postexercise protein intake enhances whole-body and leg protein accretion in humans. *Medicine and Science in Sports and Exercise* 34: 828-837.

Levine, B.D., and J. Stray-Gundersen. 1997. Living high–training low: Effect of moderate altitude acclimatization with low-altitude training on performance. *Journal of Applied Physiology* 83: 102-112.

Loike, J.D., M. Somes, and S.C. Silverstein. 1986. Creatine uptake: Metabolism and efflux in human monocytes and macrophages. *American Journal of Physiology* 251(Part 1): C128-135.

Lombardo, J.A., R.C. Hickson, and D.R. Lamb. 1991. Anabolic/androgenic steroids and growth hormone. In: D.R. Lamb and M.H. Williams (Eds.), *Perspectives in exercise science and sports medicine* (pp. 249-284). Indianapolis: Brown and Benchmark.

Martens, R. 1975. *Social psychology and physical activity.* New York: Harper & Row.

McClelland, D.C., J.W. Atkinson, R.W. Clark, and E.L. Lowell. 1953. *The achievement motive.* New York: Appleton-Century-Crofts.

Mendes, R.R., and J. Tirapegui. 2002. Creatine: The nutritional supplement for exercise—current concepts. *Archives of Latin American Nutrition* 52: 117-127.

Nagulesparen, M., R. Trickey, M.J. Davies, and J.S. Jenkins. 1976. Muscle changes in acromegaly. *British Medical Journal* 2: 914-915.

Paluska, S.A. 2003. Caffeine and exercise. *Current Sports Medicine Reports* 2: 213-219.

Pepin, G., F. Vayssette, and Y. Gaillard. 2001. Urinary nandrolone metabolites in antidoping control. *Annales Pharmaceutiques Francaises* 59: 345-349.

Perry, P.J., J.H. MacIndoe, W.R. Yates, S.D. Scott, and T.L. Holman. 1997. Detection of anabolic steroid administration: Ratio of urinary testosterone:epitestosterone vs the ratio of urinary testosterone to luteinizing hormone. *Clinical Chemistry* 43: 731-735.

Poortmans, J.R., and M. Francaux. 2000. Adverse effects of creatine supplementation: Fact or fiction. *Sports Medicine* 30: 155-170.

Powers, M.E., B.L. Arnold, A.L. Weltman, D.H. Perrin, D. Mistry, D.M. Kahler, W. Kraemer, and J. Volek. 2003. Creatine supplementation increases total body water without altering fluid distribution. *Journal of Athletic Training* 38: 44-50.

Rae, C., A.L. Digney, S.R. McEwan, and T.C. Bates. 2003. Oral creatine monohydrate supplementation improves brain performance: A double blind, placebo-controlled, cross-over trial. *Proceedings of the Royal Society of London (Series B): Biological Sciences* 22: 2147-2150.

Rasmussen, B.B., K.D. Tipton, S.L. Miller, S.E. Wolf, and R.R. Wolfe. 2000. An oral essential amino acid-carbohydrate supplement enhances muscle protein anabolism after resistance exercise. *Journal of Applied Physiology* 88: 386-392.

Rawson, E.S., and J.S. Volek. 2003. Effects of creatine supplementation and resistance training on muscle strength and weightlifting performance. *Journal of Strength and Conditioning Research* 17: 822-831.

Reis, E., U. Frick, and D. Schmidtbleicher. 1995. Frequency variation of strength training sessions triggered by the phases of the menstrual cycle. *International Journal of Sports Medicine* 16: 545-550.

Rittweger, J., G. Beller, and D. Felsenberg. 2000. Acute physiological effects of exhaustive whole-body vibration in man. *Clinical Physiology* 20: 134-142.

Robinson, T.M., D.A. Sewell, A. Casey, G. Steenge, and P.L. Greenhaff. 2000. Dietary creatine supplementation does not affect some haematological indices or indices of muscle damage and hepatic and renal function. *British Journal of Sports Medicine* 34: 284-288.

Roelants, M., C. Delecluse, M. Goris, and S. Verschueren. 2004. Effects of 24 weeks of whole body vibration training on body composition and muscle strength in untrained females. *International Journal of Sports Medicine* 25: 1-5.

Rokitzki, L., E. Logemann, A.N. Sagredos, M. Murphy, W. Wetael-Roth, and J. Keul. 1994. Lipid peroxidation and antioxidative vitamins under extreme endurance stress. *Acta Physiologica Scandinavica* 151: 149-158.

Rozenek, R., C.H. Rahe, H.H. Kohl, D.N. Marple, G.D. Wilson, and M.H. Stone. 1990. Physiological responses to resistance-exercise in athletes self-administering anabolic steroids. *Journal of Sports Medicine and Physical Fitness* 30: 354-360.

Rudman, D., A.G. Feller, J.S. Nagraj, G.A. Goldberg, P.A. Schlenker, L. Cohn, I.W. Rudman, and D.E. Matson. 1990. Effects of human growth hormone in men over 60 years old. *New England Journal of Medicine* 323: 1-6.

Ryu, S., S.K. Choi, S.S. Joung, H. Suh, Y.S. Cha, S. Lee, and K. Lim. 2001. Caffeine as a lipolytic food component increases endurance performance in rats and athletes. *Journal of Nutrition Science and Vitaminology* 47: 139-146.

Saab, G., G.D. Marsh, M.A. Casselman, and R.T. Thompson. 2002. Changes in human muscle transverse relaxation following short-term creatine supplementation. *Experimental Physiology* 87: 383-389.

Salvadora, A., F. Suay, S. Martinnez-Sanchis, V.M. Simon, and P.F. Brain. 1999. Correlating testosterone and fighting in male participants in judo contests. *Physiological Behaviour* 68: 205-209.

Saunders, P.U., R.D. Telford, D.B. Pyne, R.B. Cunningham, C.J. Gore, A.G. Hahn, and J.A. Hawley. 2003. Improved running economy in elite runners after 20 days of moderate simulated altitude exposure. *Journal of Applied Physiology* 96: 931-937.

Schedel, J.M., P. Terrier, and Y. Schutz. 2000. The biomechanic origin of sprint performance enhancement after one-week creatine supplementation. *Japanese Journal of Physiology* 50: 273-276.

Schilling, B.K., M.H. Stone, A. Utter, J.T. Kearney, M. Johnson, R. Coglianese, L. Smith, H.S. O'Bryant, A.C. Fry, M. Starks, R. Keith, and M.E. Stone. 2001. Creatine supplementation and health: A retrospective study. *Medicine and Science in Sports and Exercise* 33: 183-188.

Schroeder, C., J. Potteiger, J. Randell, D. Jacobsen, L. Magee, S. Benedict, and M. Hulver. 2001. The effects of creatine dietary supplementation on anterior compartment pressure in the lower leg during rest and following exercise. *Clinical Journal of Sport Medicine* 11: 87-95.

Shakleton, C.H., A. Phillips, T. Chang, and Y. Li. 1997. Confirming testosterone administration by isotope ratio mass spectrometric analysis of urinary androstenediols. *Steroids* 62: 379-387.

Silver, M.D. 2001. Use of ergogenic aids by athletes. *Journal of the American Academy of Orthopedic Surgeons* 9: 61-70.

Sinclair, G.D., and D.A. Sinclair. 1994. Developing reflective performers by integrating mental management intervention. *Behavior Modification* 6: 443-463.

Sonksen, F.H. 2001. Insulin, growth hormone and sport. *Journal of Endocrinology* 170: 13-25.

Spriet, L.L., and M.J. Gibala. 2004. Nutritional strategies to influence adaptations to training. *Journal of Sports Sciences* 22: 127-141.

Starka, L., M. Hill, O. Lapcik, and R. Hampl. 1996. Epitestosterone as an endogenous antiandrogen in men. *Vnitrni Lekarstvi* 43(9): 620-623.

Stone, M.H. 1993. Position/policy statement and literature review for the National Strength and Conditioning Association on "explosive exercise." *National Strength and Conditioning Association Journal* 15: 7-15.

Stone, M.H. 1995. Human growth hormone: Physiological functions and ergogenic efficacy. Literature review for NSCA position stance. *Strength and Conditioning* 17: 72-74.

Stone, M.H., R. Keith, J.T. Kearney, G.D. Wilson, and S.J. Fleck. 1991. Overtraining: A review of the signs and symptoms of overtraining. *Journal of Applied Sport Science Research* 5(1): 35-50.

Stone, M.H., K. Sanborn, L. Smith, H.S. O'Bryant, T. Hoke, A. Utter, R.L. Johnson, R. Boros, K. Pierce, and M.E. Stone. 1999. Five week supplementation with creatine monohydrate, pyruvate and a combination in American football players. *International Journal of Sport Nutrition* 9: 146-165.

Storer, T.W., L. Magliano, L. Woodhouse, M.L. Lee, C. Dzekov, J. Dzekov, R. Casaburi, and S. Bhasin. 2003. Testosterone dose-dependently increases maximal voluntary strength and leg power, but does not affect fatigability or specific tension. *Journal of Clinical Endocrinology* 88: 1478-1485.

Street, C., J. Antonio, and D. Cudlipp. 1996. Androgen use by athletes: A reevaluation of the health risks. *Canadian Journal of Applied Physiology* 21: 421-440.

Svensson, J., K. Stibrant Suunerhagen, and G. Johannsson. 2003. Five years of growth hormone replacement therapy in adults: Age-and gender-related changes in isometric and isokinetic muscle strength. *Journal of Clinical Endocrinology and Metabolism* 88: 206-209.

Swain, R.A., D.M. Harsha, J. Baenzinger, and R.M. Saywell. 1997. Do pseudoephedrine or phenylpropanolamine improve maximum oxygen uptake and time to exhaustion? *Clinical Journal of Sports Medicine* 7: 168-173.

Sweeney, H.L. 2004. Gene doping. *Scientific American* 291: 62-69.

Taes, Y.E., J.R. Delanghe, A.S. De Vriese, R. Rombaut, J. Van Camp, and N.H. Lameire. 2003a. Creatine supplementation decreases homocysteine in an animal model of uremia. *Kidney International* 64: 1331-1337.

Taes, Y.E., J.R. Delanghe, B. Wuyts, J. van de Voorde, and N.H. Lameire. 2003b. Creatine supplementation does not affect kidney function in an animal model with pre-existing renal failure. *Nephrology, Dialysis, Transplantation* 18: 258-264.

Tarnopolsky, M.A. 1999. Protein and physical performance. *Current Opinion in Clinical Nutrition and Metabolic Care* 2: 533-537.

Thien, L.A., J.M. Thein, and G.L. Landry. 1995. Ergogenic aids. *Physical Therapy* 75: 426-439.

Torvinen, S., P. Kannu, H. Sievanen, T.A. Jarvinen, M. Pasanen, S. Kontulainen, T.L. Jarvinen, M. Jarvinen, P. Oja, and I. Vuori. 2002. Effect of a vibration exposure on muscular performance and body balance. Randomized cross-over study. *Clinical Physiology and Functional Imaging* 22: 145-152.

U.K. Sports Council. 2003. Nandrolone progress report to the UK Sports Council from the expert committee on nandrolone. *International Journal of Sports Medicine* 24: 620-626.

Urbanski, R.L., W.J. Vincent, and B.B. Yaspelkis. 1999. Creatine supplementation differentially affects maximal isometric strength and time to fatigue in large and small muscle groups. *International Journal of Sport Nutrition* 9: 136-145.

Ustunel, I., G. Akkoyunlu, and R. Demir. 2003. The effect of testosterone on gastrocnemius muscle fibres in growing and adult male and female rats: A histological, morphological and ultrastructural study. *Anatomy, Histology and Embryology* 32: 70-79.

Van Loon, L.J., M. Kruijshoop, H. Verhagen, W.H. Saris, and A.J. Wagenmakers. 2000a. Ingestion of protein hydrolysate and amino acid-carbohydrate mixtures increases postexercise plasma insulin responses in men. *Journal of Nutrition* 130: 2508-2513.

Van Loon, L.J., R. Murphy, A.M. Oosterlaar, D. Cameron-Smith, M. Hargreaves, A.J. Wagenmakers, and R. Snow. 2004. Creatine supplementation increases glycogen storage but not GLUT-4 expression in human skeletal muscle. *Clinical Science* 106: 99-106.

Van Loon, L.J., W.H. Saris, M. Kruijshoop, and A.J. Wagenmakers. 2000b. Maximizing postexercise muscle glycogen synthesis: Carbohydrate and the application of amino acid or protein hydrolysate mixtures. *American Journal of Clinical Nutrition* 72: 106-111.

Volek, J.S. 2004. Influence of nutrition on responses to resistance training. *Medicine and Science in Sports and Exercise* 36: 689-696.

Wagenmakers, A.J. 1999. Amino acid supplements to improve athletic performance. *Current Opinion in Clinical Nutritional and Metabolic Care* 2: 539-544.

Walberg-Rankin, J., C.E. Hawkins, D.S. Fild, and D.R. Sebolt. 1994. The effect of oral arginine during energy restriction in male weight trainers. *Journal of Strength and Conditioning Research* 8: 170-177.

Walker, J.B. 1979. Creatine: Biosynthesis, regulation and function. *Advances in Enzymology* 50: 177-242.

Warman, G., B. Humphries, and J. Purton. 2002. The effects of timing and application of vibration on muscular contractions. *Aviation, Space and Environmental Medicine* 73: 119-127.

Wilber, R.L., P.L. Holm, D.M. Morris, G.M. Dallam, and S.D. Callan. 2003. Effect of F(I)O on physiological responses and cycling performance at moderate altitude. *Medicine and Science in Sports and Exercise* 35: 1153-1159.

Wilder, N., R. Gilders, F. Hagerman, and R.G. Deivert. 2002. The effects of a 10-week, periodized, off-season resistance-training program and creatine supplementation among collegiate football players. *Journal of Strength and Conditioning Research* 16: 343-352.

Wilkes, R.L., and J.J. Summers. 1984. Cognition, mediating variables and strength performance. *Journal of Sport Psychology* 6: 351-359.

Williams, J.M. 1993. Psychological characteristics of peak performance. In: J.M. Williams (Ed.), *Applied sports psychology: Personal growth to peak performance*. Mountain View, CA: Mayfield.

Williams, M.H. 1984. Vitamin and mineral supplements to athletes: Do they help? *Clinical Sports Medicine* 3: 623-637.

Williams, M.H. 1996. Ergogenic aids: A means to Citius, Altius, Fortius and Olympic gold? *Research Quarterly for Exercise and Sport* 67(3 Suppl.): S58-64.

Williams, M.H. 2000. [Comment on Williams, M.H. 1994. The use of nutritional ergogenic aids in sports: Is it an ethical issue? *International Journal of Sport Nutrition* 4: 120-131.] *International Journal of Sport Nutrition and Exercise Metabolism* 10(2): vi-vii.

Whitmore, J. 1992. *Coaching for performance*. London: Nicholas Brealy.

Wu, F.C. 1997. Endocrine aspects of anabolic steroids. *Clinical Chemistry* 43: 1289-1292.

Wyss, M., and A. Schulze. 2002. Health implications of creatine: Can oral creatine supplementation protect against neurological and atherosclerotic diseases? *Neuroscience* 112: 243-260.

Yamaguchi, R., L.D. Johnston, and P.M. O'Malley. 2003. Relationship between student illicit drug use and school drug testing policies. *Journal of School Health* 73: 159-164.

Yarasheski, K.E., J.A. Campbell, K. Smith, M.J. Rennie, J.O. Holloszy, and D.M. Bier. 1992. Effects of growth hormone and resistance exercise on muscle growth in young men. *Endocrinology and Metabolism* 25: E261-E267.

Zawadzki, K.M., B.B. Yaspelkis, and J.L. Ivy. 1992. Carbohydrate-protein complex increases the rate of muscle glycogen storage after exercise. *Journal of Applied Physiology* 72: 1854-1859.

Chapter 8

Aagaard, P., E.B. Simonsen, J.L. Andersen, P. Magnusson, and P. Dyre-Poulsen. 2002. Increased rate of force development and neural drive of human skeletal muscle following resistance training. *Journal of Applied Physiology* 93: 1318-1326.

Aagaard, P., E.B. Simonsen, M. Trolle, J. Bangsbo, and K. Klausen. 1994. Effects of different strength training regimes on moment and power generation during dynamic knee extensions. *European Journal of Applied Physiology* 69: 382-386.

Andersen, L.L., and P. Aagaard. 2005. Influence of maximal muscle strength and intrinsic muscle contractile properties on contractile rate of force development. *European Journal of Applied Physiology* 96: 46-52.

Asmussen, E., and F. Bonde-Petersen. 1974. Storage of elastic energy in skeletal muscles in man. *Acta Physiologica Scandinavica* 91: 385-392.

Atha, J. 1981. Strengthening muscle. *Exercise and Sport Sciences Reviews* 9: 2-73.

Bastiaans, J.J., A.B. van Diemen, T. Veneberg, and A.E. Jeukendrup. 2001. The effects of replacing a portion of endurance training by explosive strength training on performance in trained cyclists. *European Journal of Applied Physiology* 86: 79-84.

Behm, D.G. 1995. Neuromuscular implications and applications of resistance training. *Journal of Strength and Conditioning Research* 9: 264-274.

Berger, R.A., and J.M. Henderson. 1966. Relationship of power to static and dynamic strength. *Research Quarterly* 37: 9-13.

Bobbert, M.F., K.G.M. Gerritsen, M.C.A. Litjens, and A.J. van Soest. 1996. Why is countermovement jump height greater than squat jump height? *Medicine and Science in Sports and Exercise* 28: 1402-1412.

Bosco, C. 1982. Physiological considerations of strength and explosive power and jumping drills (plyometric exercise). In: *Proceedings of Conference 82: Planning for elite performance* (pp. 27-37). Toronto: Canadian Track and Field Association.

Carlock, J., S.L. Smith, M. Hartman, R. Morris, D. Ciroslan, K.C. Pierce, R.U. Newton, E. Harman, W.A. Sands, and M.H. Stone. 2004. Relationship between vertical jump power estimates and weightlifting ability: A field-test approach. *Journal of Strength and Conditioning Research* 18: 534-539.

Cohen, J. 1988. *Statistical power analysis for the behavioral sciences* (2nd ed.). Hillsdale, NJ: Erlbaum.

Cronin, J.B., P.J. McNaira, and R.N. Marshall. 2000. The role of maximum strength and load on initial power production. *Medicine and Science in Sports and Exercise* 32: 1763-1769.

Garhammer, J.J. 1993. A review of the power output studies of Olympic and powerlifting: Methodology, performance prediction and evaluation tests. *Journal of Strength and Conditioning Research* 7: 76-89.

Gohner, U. 1994. Experimental results on force eccentric strength gains. *International Journal of Sports Medicine* 15(Suppl.): S43-49.

Haff, G.G., M.H. Stone, H.S. O'Bryant, E. Harman, C. Dinan, R. Johnson, and K.H. Han. 1997. Force-time dependent characteristics of dynamic and isometric muscle actions. *Journal of Strength and Conditioning Research* 11: 269-272.

Hertogh, C., and O. Hue. 2002. Jump evaluation of elite volleyball players using two methods: Jump power equations and force platform. *Journal of Sports Medicine and Physical Fitness* 42: 300-303.

Hopkins, W.G. 2000. A new view of statistics. Internet Society for Sport Science. www.sportsci.org/resource/stats/.

Kauhanen, H., J. Garhammer, and K. Hakkinen. 2000. Relationships between power output, body size and snatch performance in elite weightlifters. In: J. Avela, P.V. Komi, and J. Komulainen (Eds.), *Proceedings of the Fifth Annual Congress of the European College of Sports Science* (p. 383). Finland: University of Jyvaskala.

Komi, P.V., and C. Bosco. 1978. Utilization of stored elastic energy in leg extensor muscles by men and women. *Medicine and Science in Sports* 10: 261-265.

Komi, P.V., and J.H. Viitasalo. 1976. Signal characteristics of EMG at different levels of muscle tension. *Acta Physiologica Scandinavica* 96: 267-276.

Mann, R. 1994. *The mechanics of sprinting and hurdling.* Orlando, FL: Compusport.

Margaria, R., I. Aghemo, and E. Rovelli. 1966. Measurement of muscular power (anaerobic) in man. *Journal of Applied Physiology* 21: 1662-1664.

McBride, J.M., T.T. Triplett-McBride, A. Davie, and R.U. Newton. 1999. A comparison of strength and power characteristics between power lifters, Olympic lifters and sprinters. *Journal of Strength and Conditioning Research* 13: 58-66.

McCloy, C.H. 1934. The measurement of general capacity and general motor ability. *Research Quarterly* 5(1): 46-61.

Moss, B.M., P.E. Refsnes, A. Abildgaard, K. Nicolaysen, and J. Jensen. 1997. Effects of maximal effort strength training with different loads on dynamic strength, cross-sectional area, load-power, and load velocity relationships. *European Journal of Applied Physiology* 75: 193-199.

Muller, E.A. 1970. Influence of training and of inactivity on muscle strength. *Archives of Physical Medicine and Rehabilitation* 51(8): 449-462.

Muller, K. 1987. *Statische und Dynnamiche Muskelkraft.* Frankfort/M. Deutsch, Thun. Cited in Schmidtbleicher, D. 1992. Training for power events. In: P.V. Komi (Ed.), *Strength and power in sport* (pp. 381-395). London: Blackwell Scientific.

Murphy, A.J., G.J. Wilson, J.F. Pryor et al. 1995. Isometric assessment of muscular functions: The effect of joint angle. *Journal of Applied Biomechanics* 11: 205-215.

Nelson, R.C., and R.A. Fahrney. 1965. Relationship between strength, speed of elbow flexion. *Research Quarterly* 336(4): 455-463.

Nelson, R.C., and B.I. Jordan. 1969. Relationship between arm strength and speed in horizontal adductive arm movement. *American Corrective Therapy Journal* 23: 82-85.

Newton, R.U., W.J. Kraemer, K. Hakkinen, B.J. Humphries, and A.J. Murphy. 1996. Kinematics, kinetics and muscle activation during explosive upper body movements. *Journal of Applied Biomechanics* 12: 31-43.

Newton, R.U., A.J. Murphy, B.J. Humphries, G.J. Wilson, W.J. Kraemer, and K. Hakkinen. 1997. Influence of load and stretch shortening cycle on the kinematics, kinetics and muscle activation that occurs during explosive upper-body movements. *European Journal of Applied Physiology* 75: 333-342.

Paavolainen, L., K. Hakkinen, I. Hamalainen, A. Nummela, and H. Rusko. 1999. Explosive strength-training improves 5-km running time by improving running economy and muscle power. *Journal of Applied Physiology* 86(5): 1527-1533.

Plisk, S., and M.H. Stone. 2003. Periodization strategies. *Strength and Conditioning* 25:19-37.

Rhea, M.R. 2004. Determining the magnitude of treatment effects in strength training research through use of the effect size. *Journal of Strength and Conditioning Research* 18: 18-20.

Robinson, J.M., C.M. Penland, M.H. Stone, R.L. Johnson, B.J. Warren, and D.L. Lewis. 1995. Effects of different weight training exercise-rest intervals on strength, power and high intensity endurance. *Journal of Strength and Conditioning Research* 9(4): 216-221.

Sale, D.G. 1992. Neural adaptations to strength training. In: P.V. Komi (Ed.), *Strength and power in sport* (pp. 249-265). London: Blackwell Scientific.

Sands, W.A. 1991. Monitoring the elite female gymnast. *National Strength and Conditioning Association Journal* 13: 66-71.

Sayers, S.P., D.V. Harackiewicz, E.A. Harman, P.N. Frykman, and M.T. Rosenstein. 1999. Cross-validation of three jump power equations. *Medicine and Science in Sports and Exercise* 31: 572-577.

Schmidt, R.A. 1991. *Motor learning and performance*. Champaign, IL: Human Kinetics.

Schmidtbleicher, D. 1985. Strength training: Part 2: Structural analysis of motor strength qualities and its application to training. *Science Periodical on Research and Technology in Sport* 5: 1-10.

Schmidtbleicher, D. 1992. Training for power events. In: P.V. Komi (Ed.), *Strength and power in sport* (pp. 381-395). London: Blackwell Scientific.

Shewart, W.A. 1986. *Statistical method from the viewpoint of quality control*. New York: Dover.

Siff, M. 2001. Biomechanical foundations of strength and power training. In: V. Zatsiorsky (Ed.), *Biomechanics in sport* (pp. 103-139). London: Blackwell Scientific.

Steindler, A. 1935. *Mechanics of normal and pathological locomotion in man*. Baltimore: Thomas.

Stone, M.H. 1993. Explosive exercise. *National Strength and Conditioning Association Journal* 15(4): 7-15.

Stone, M.H., G. Moir, M. Glaister, and R. Sanders. 2002. How much strength is necessary? *Physical Therapy in Sport* 3: 88-96.

Stone, M.H., and H. O'Bryant. 1987. *Weight training: A scientific approach* (2nd ed.). Minneapolis: Burgess.

Stone, M.H., H.S. O'Bryant, L. McCoy, R. Coglianese, M. Lehmkuhl, and B. Schilling. 2003a. Power and maximum strength relationships during performance of dynamic and static weighted jumps. *Journal of Strength and Conditioning Research* 17: 140-147.

Stone, M.H., S. Plisk, and D. Collins. 2002. Training principle: Evaluation of modes and methods of resistance training—a coaching perspective. *Sport Biomechanics* 1(1): 79-104.

Stone, M.H., K. Sanborn, H.S. O'Bryant, M. Hartman, M.E. Stone, C. Proulx, B. Ward, and J. Hruby. 2003b. Maximum strength-power-performance relationships in collegiate throwers. *Journal of Strength and Conditioning Research* 17: 739-745.

Stone, M.H., W.A. Sands, and M.E. Stone. 2004. The downfall of sports science in the United States. *Strength and Conditioning* 26: 72-75.

Thomas, M., A. Fiataron, and R.A. Fielding. 1994. Leg power in young women: Relationship to body composition, strength and function. *Medicine and Science in Sports and Exercise* 28: 1321-1326.

Westing, S.H., J. Seger, and A. Thorstensson. 1990. Effects of electrical stimulation on eccentric and concentric torque-velocity relationships during knee extension. *Acta Physiologica Scandinavica* 140: 17-22.

Weyand, P.G., D.B. Sternlight, M.J. Bellizi, and S. Wright. 2000. Faster top running speeds are achieved with greater ground forces not more rapid leg movements. *Journal of Applied Physiology* 89: 1991-1999.

Wilmore, J.H., and D.L. Costill. 1994. *Physiology of sport and exercise*. Champaign, IL: Human Kinetics.

Wilson, G.J., and A.J. Murphy. 1996. The use of isometric tests of muscular function in athletic assessment. *Sports Medicine* 22(1): 19-37.

Zajac, F.E., and M.E. Gordon. 1989. Determining muscle's force and action in multi-articular movement. In: K. Pandolph (Ed.), *Exercise and sport science reviews* (Vol. 17, 187-230). Baltimore: Williams & Wilkins.

Zatsiorsky, V.M. 1995. *Science and practice of strength training*. Champaign, IL: Human Kinetics.

Chapter 9

Abernethy, P., and G. Wilson. 2000. Introduction to the assessment of strength and power. In: C.J. Gore (Ed.), *Physiological tests for elite athletes* (pp. 147-154). Champaign, IL: Human Kinetics.

Bahill, A.T., P.N. Harris, and E. Senn. 1988. Lessons learned building expert systems. *AI Expert* 3(9): 36-45.

Bailey, D., D. Thompson, and J. Feinstein. 1989. The practical side of neural networks. *PC AI* 3(2): 56-58.

Barlow, D.H., and M. Hersen. 1984. *Single case experimental designs: Strategies for studying behavior change*. New York: Pergamon Press.

Bates, B.T. 1996. Single-subject methodology: An alternative approach. *Medicine and Science in Sports and Exercise* 28(5): 631-638.

Beckmann, J. 2002. Interaction of volition and recovery. In: M. Kellmann (Ed.), *Enhancing recovery: Preventing underperformance in athletes* (pp. 269-282). Champaign, IL: Human Kinetics.

Bithell, C. 1994. Single subject experimental design: A case for concern? *Physiotherapy* 80(2): 85-87.

Bompa, T. 1984a. Peaking for the major competition(s) part one. *Science Periodical on Research and Technology in Sport*, 1-6.

Bompa, T. 1984b. Peaking for the major competition(s) part two. *Science Periodical on Research and Technology in Sport*, 1-6.

Bompa, T.O. 1990a. Periodization of strength: The most effective methodology of strength training. *National Strength and Conditioning Association Journal* 12(5): 49-52.

Bompa, T.O. 1990b. *Theory and methodology of training.* Dubuque, IA: Kendall/Hunt.

Bompa, T.O. 1993. *Periodization of strength.* Toronto, Ontario, Canada: Veritas.

Bondarchuk, A. 1988. Periodization of sports training. *Soviet Sports Review* 23(4): 164-166.

Bryan, A.J. 1987. Single-subject designs for evaluation of sport psychology interventions. *Sport Psychologist* 1: 283-292.

Cannon, W.B. 1928. The mechanism of emotional disturbance of bodily functions. *New England Journal of Medicine* 198(17): 877-884.

Charniga, A., V. Gambetta, W. Kraemer, H. Newton, H.S. O'Bryant, G. Palmieri, J. Pedemonte, D. Pfaff, and M.H. Stone. 1986a. Periodization part 1. *National Strength and Conditioning Association Journal* 8(5): 12-21.

Charniga, A., V. Gambetta, W. Kraemer, H. Newton, H.S. O'Bryant, G. Palmieri, J. Pedemonte, D. Pfaff, and M.H. Stone. 1986b. Periodization part 2. *National Strength and Conditioning Association Journal* 8(6): 17-24.

Charniga, A., V. Gambetta, W. Kraemer, H. Newton, H.S. O'Bryant, G. Palmieri, J. Pedemonte, D. Pfaff, and M.H. Stone. 1987. Periodization part 3. *National Strength and Conditioning Association Journal* 9(1): 16-26.

Cicciarella, C.F. 2000. Runs analysis—a tutorial with application to sport. *International Sports Journal* 4(1): 107-118.

Cohen, S., and G.M. Williamson. 1991. Stress and infectious disease in humans. *Psychological Bulletin* 109(1): 5-24.

Cooper, J.O. 1981. *Measuring behavior.* Columbus, OH: Charles E. Merrill.

Davis IV, H., C. Botterill, and K. MacNeill. 2002. Mood and self-regulation changes in underrecovery: An intervention model. In: M. Kellmann (Ed.), *Enhancing recovery: Preventing underperformance in athletes* (pp. 161-179). Champaign, IL: Human Kinetics.

Dishman, R.K. 1983. Stress management procedures. In: M.H. Williams (Ed.), *Ergogenic aids in sport* (pp. 275-320). Champaign, IL: Human Kinetics.

Dunn, J.G.H. 1994. Toward the combined use of nomothetic and idiographic methodologies in sport psychology: An empirical example. *Sport Psychologist* 8: 376-392.

Duquin, M.E. 1984. Perception of fairness in sport: Conflicts in psychological orientations. American Alliance for Health, Physical Education, Recreation and Dance. National Convention and Exhibition with Southwest

District and CAHPERD. University of Waterloo, Waterloo, Ontario, Canada: Author.

Fry, R.W., A.R. Morton, and D. Keast. 1992. Periodisation of training stress—a review. *Canadian Journal of Sport Sciences* 17(3): 234-240.

Graham, I., and P.L. Jones. 1988. *Expert systems knowledge, uncertainty, and decision.* London, England: Chapman and Hall.

Hanin, Y.L. 2002. Individually optimal recovery in sports: An application of the IZOF model. In: M. Kellmann (Ed.), *Enhancing recovery: Preventing underperformance in athletes* (pp. 199-217). Champaign, IL: Human Kinetics.

Harman, E.A. 1995. The measurement of human mechanical power. In: P.J. Maud and C. Foster (Eds.), *Physiological assessment of human fitness* (pp. 87-113). Champaign, IL: Human Kinetics.

Harre, D. 1982. *Principles of sports training.* Berlin, German Democratic Republic: Sportverlag.

Hatfield, B.D., and D.M. Landers. 1983. Psychophysiology—a new direction for sport psychology. *Journal of Sport Psychology* 5: 243-259.

Hopkins, W.G. 1991. Quantification of training in competitive sports. *Sports Medicine* 12(3): 161-183.

Hopkins, W.G. 1998a. Measurement of training in competitive sports. *Sportscience* 2(4). www.sportsci.org/jour/9804/wgh.html.

Hopkins, W.G. 1998b. Training: Quantification in competitive sports. *Sportscience* 2(4). www.sportsci.org/jour/9804/wgh.html.

Hopkins, W.G. 2002. Probabilities of clinical or practical significance [Web Page]. Available at: sportsci.org/jour/0201/wghprob.htm.

Hopkins, W.G., J.A. Hawley, and L.M. Burke. 1999. Design and analysis of research on sport performance enhancement. *Medicine and Science in Sports and Exercise* 31(3): 472-485.

Hrycaiko, D., and G.L. Martin. 1996. Applied research studies with single-subject designs: Why so few? *Journal of Applied Sport Psychology* 8: 183-199.

Jackson, A.S. 1989. Application of regression analysis to exercise science. In: M.J. Safrit and T.M. Wood (Eds.), *Measurement concepts in physical education and exercise science* (pp. 181-206). Champaign, IL: Human Kinetics.

Jacobson, E. 1967. *Biology of emotions.* Springfield, IL: Charles C Thomas.

Kallus, K.W. 2002. Impact of recovery in different areas of application. In: M. Kellmann (Ed.), *Enhancing recovery: Preventing underperformance in athletes* (pp. 283-300). Champaign, IL: Human Kinetics.

Kellmann, M. 2002a. Enhancing recovery: Preventing underperformance in athletes. In: D. Gould and K. Dieffenbach (Eds.), *Overtraining, underrecovery, and burnout in sport* (pp. 25-35). Champaign, IL: Human Kinetics.

Kellmann, M. 2002b. Planning, periodization, and sequencing of training and competition: The rationale for a competently planned, optimally executed training and competition program, supported by a multidisciplinary team. In: S.R. Norris and D.J. Smith (Eds.), *Enhancing recovery: Preventing underperformance in athletes* (pp. 121-141). Champaign, IL: Human Kinetics.

Kellmann, M. 2002c. Psychological assessment of underrecovery. In: M. Kellmann (Ed.), *Enhancing recovery: Preventing underperformance in athletes* (pp. 37-55). Champaign, IL: Human Kinetics.

Kenttä, G., and P. Hassmén. 2002. Underrecovery and overtraining: A conceptual model. In: M. Kellmann (Ed.), *Enhancing recovery: Preventing underperformance in athletes* (pp. 57-79). Champaign, IL: Human Kinetics.

Kinugasa, T., Y. Miyanaga, H. Shimojo, and T. Nishijima. 2002. Statistical evaluation of conditioning for an elite collegiate tennis player using a single-case design. *Journal of Strength and Conditioning Research* 16(3): 466-471.

Lacey, J.I., D.E. Bateman, and R. VanLehn. 1953. Autonomic response specificity: An experimental study. *Psychosomatic Medicine* 15(1): 8-21.

Lacey, J.I., and B.C. Lacey. 1958. Verification and extension of the principle of autonomic response-stereotypy. *American Journal of Psychology* 71: 50-73.

Lane, A. 1989. What is an expert system. *PC AI* 3(6): 20-23.

Logan, P., D. Fornasiero, P. Abernethy, and K. Lynch. 2000. Protocols for the assessment of isoinertial strength. In: C.J. Gore (Ed.), *Physiological tests for elite athletes* (pp. 200-221). Champaign, IL: Human Kinetics.

Maas, S., and J. Mester. 1996. Diagnosis of individual physiological responses in elite sport by means of time-series-analysis. In: P. Marconnet, J. Gaulard, I. Margaritio, and F. Tessier (Eds.), *Book of abstracts* (pp. 98-99). Nice, France: European College of Sport Science.

Mackinnon, L., and S. Hooper. 1994. Training logs: An effective method of monitoring overtraining and tapering. *Sports Coach* 17(3): 10-12.

Major, J.A., W.A. Sands, J.R. McNeal, D.D. Paine, and R. Kipp. 1998. Design, construction, and validation of a portable one-dimensional force platform. *Journal of Strength and Conditioning Research* 12(1): 37-41.

Matveyev, L. 1977. *Fundamentals of sports training*. Moscow: Progress.

Menzies, T. 1989. Domain-specific knowledge representation. *AI Expert* 4(6): 36-45.

Mueser, K.T., P.R. Yarnold, and D.W. Foy. 1991. Statistical analysis of single-case designs. *Behavior Modification* 15(2): 134-155.

Newsham-West, R. 2002. Why the need for the case report. *New Zealand Journal of Sports Medicine* 30(2): 44-46.

Nourbakhsh, M.R., and K.J. Ottenbacher. 1994. The statistical analysis of single-subject data: A comparative examination. *Physical Therapy* 74(8): 768-776.

Nye, S. 1987. Monitoring workouts with heart rate. *Swimming Technique* 24(2): 25-29.

Obrist, P.A. 1968. Heart rate and somatic-motor coupling during classical aversive conditioning in humans. *Journal of Experimental Psychology* 77(2): 180-193.

O'Leary, A. 1990. Stress, emotion, and human immune function. *Psychological Bulletin* 108(3): 363-382.

Ottenbacher, K.J., and S.R. Hinderer. 2001. Evidence-based practice methods to evaluate individual patient improvement. *American Journal of Physical Medicine and Rehabilitation* 80(10): 786-796.

Parsaye, K., and M. Chignell. 1988. *Expert systems for experts*. New York: Wiley.

Pitt, H. 1994. *SPC for the rest of us*. King of Prussia, PA: Tunnel Publishing Group.

Riddoch, J., and S. Lennon. 1994. Single subject experimental design: One way forward? *Physiotherapy* 80(4): 215-218.

Rusko, H.K., P. Rahkila, V. Vihko, and H. Holappa. 1989. Longitudinal changes in heart rate and blood pressure during overtraining period. *Proceedings 1st IOC World Congress on Sport Sciences* (October 28-November 3), 1, 45-46.

Sands, W.A. 1990a. Fragen zum training der nationalmannschaft der US-Junioren (Frauen) im kunstturnen. U. Gohner *Leistungsturnen im kindesalter* (pp. 81-96). Stuttgart, Germany: Internationaler Turnerbund (FIG) und das Organisationskomitee Weltmeisterschaften im Kunstturnen Stuttgart 1989.

Sands, W.A. 1990b. National women's tracking program, part 2: Response. *Technique* 10(1): 23-27.

Sands, W.A. 1991a. Monitoring elite gymnastics athletes via rule based computer systems. In: *Masters of innovation III* (p. 92). Northbrook, IL: Zenith Data Systems.

Sands, W.A. 1991b. Monitoring the elite female gymnast. *National Strength and Conditioning Association Journal* 13(4): 66-71.

Sands, W.A. 1992. AI and athletics. *PC AI* 6(1): 52-54.

Sands, W.A. 2000. Monitoring power. In: B.G. Bardy, T. Pozzo, P. Nouillot, N. Tordi, P. Delemarche, C. Ferrand, Y. Léziart, D. Hauw, J. Aubert, M. Loquet, A. Durny, and J.F. Robin (Eds.), *Actes des 2èmes Journées Internationales d'Etude de l'A.F.R.A.G.A.* (p. 102). Univeristé de Rennes, Rennes, France: L'Association Française de Recherche en Activités Gymniques et Acrobatiques (AFRAGA).

Sands, W.A. 2002. Monitoring gymnastics training. *3èmes Journées Internationales d'Etude de l'AFRAGA*. Lille, France: AFRAGA.

Sands, W.A., K.P. Henschen, and B.B. Shultz. 1989. National women's tracking program. *Technique* 9(4): 14-19.

Sands, W.A., B.B. Shultz, and A.P. Newman. 1993. Women's gymnastics injuries. *American Journal of Sports Medicine* 21(2): 271-276.

Sands, W.A., B.B. Shultz, and D.D. Paine. 1993. Gymnastics performance characterization by piezoelectric sensors and neural networks. *Technique* 13(2): 33-38.

Sands, W.A., B.B. Shultz, and D.D. Paine. 1994. Neural nets and gymnastics: Recognizing errors in athletic performance. *PC AI* 8(1): 42-43.

Selye, H. 1956. *The stress of life.* New York: McGraw-Hill.

Shephard, R.J. 1998. Assumptions inherent in biological research. *Adapted Physical Activity Quarterly* 15: 222-235.

Sherald, M. 1989. Neural nets versus expert systems. *PC AI* 3(4): 10-15.

Shewhart, W.A. 1986. *Statistical method from the viewpoint of quality control.* New York: Dover.

Steinacker, J.M., and M. Lehmann. 2002. Clinical findings and mechanisms of stress and recovery in athletes. In: M. Kellmann (Ed.), *Enhancing recovery: Preventing underperformance in athletes* (pp. 103-118). Champaign, IL: Human Kinetics.

Stone, M.H., H. O'Bryant, and J. Garhammer. 1981. A hypothetical model for strength training. *Journal of Sports Medicine* 21: 342-351.

Stone, M.H., W.A. Sands, and M.E. Stone. 2004. The downfall of sports science in the United States. *Strength and Conditioning Journal* 26(2): 72-75.

Tucker, L.A. 1990. Physical fitness and psychological distress. *International Journal of Sport Psychology* 21: 185-201.

Tufte, E.R. 1983. *The visual display of quantitative information.* Cheshire, CT: Graphics Press.

Tufte, E.R. 1990. *Envisioning information.* Cheshire, CT: Graphics Press.

Uusitalo, A.L.T. 2001. Overtraining. *Physician and Sportsmedicine* 29(5): 35-40, 43-44, 49-50.

Verchoshanskij, J.V. 1999. The end of "periodisation" of training in top-class sport. *New Studies in Athletics* 14(1): 47-55.

Verhohshansky, Y. 2002. Some principles of the construction of the yearly training cycles in speed strength events. *Modern Athlete and Coach* 40(2): 3-9.

Verhoshansky, Y.V., I.N. Mironenko, T.M. Antonova, and O.V. Hachatarian. 1991. Some principles of constructing the yearly training cycle in speed-strength sports. *Soviet Sports Review* 26(4): 189-193.

Verkhoshansky, Y.V. 1985. *Programming and organization of training.* Moscow: Fizkultura i Sport.

Verkhoshansky, Y. 1998. Organization of the training process. *New Studies in Athletics* 13(3): 21-31.

Vincent, W.J. 1995. *Statistics in kinesiology.* Champaign, IL: Human Kinetics.

Viru, A. 1994. Molecular cellular mechanisms of training effects. *Journal of Sports Medicine and Physical Fitness* 34: 309-322.

Viru, A. 1995. *Adaptation in sports training.* Boca Raton, FL: CRC Press.

Viru, A., and M. Viru. 2001. *Biochemical monitoring of sport training.* Champaign, IL: Human Kinetics.

Viru, M., and A. Viru. 2002, Fall. Monitoring of training. *Track Coach* 161: 5154-5155.

Yushkov, O.P., S.M. Repnevsky, and V.P. Serdyuk. 1986. Use of heart rate for control over training loads. *Soviet Sports Review* 21(3): 151-152.

Chapter 10

Aagaard, P., E.B. Simonsen, J.L. Andersen, S.P. Magnusson, J. Halkjaer-Kristensen, and P. Dyhre-Poulsen. 2000. Neural inhibition during maximal eccentric and concentric quadriceps contraction: Effects of resistance training. *Journal of Applied Physiology* 89: 2249-2257.

Abe, T., K. Kojima, C.F. Kearns, H. Yohena, and J. Fukuda. 2003. Whole body muscle hypertrophy from resistance training: Distribution and total mass. *British Journal of Sports Medicine* 37: 543-545.

Abernethy, P.J., J. Jurimae, P.A. Logan, A.W. Taylor, and R.E. Thayer. 1994. Acute and chronic response of skeletal muscle to resistance exercise. *Sports Medicine* 17: 22-38.

Adams, G.R., B.M. Hather, K.M. Baldwin, and G.A. Dudley. 1993. Skeletal muscle myosin heavy chain composition and resistance training. *Journal of Applied Physiology* 74: 911-915.

Ahtiainen, J.P., A. Pakarinen, M. Alen, W.J. Kraemer, and K. Hakkinen. 2003. Muscle hypertrophy, hormonal adaptations and strength development during strength training in strength-trained and untrained men. *European Journal of Applied Physiology* 89: 555-563.

Allen, D.G., A.A. Kabbara, and H. Westerblad. 2002. Muscle fatigue: The role of intracellular calcium stores. *Canadian Journal of Applied Physiology* 27: 83-96.

Alway, S.E., J.D. MacDougall, and D.G. Sale. 1989. Contractile adaptations in the human triceps surae after isometric exercise. *Journal of Applied Physiology* 66: 2725-2732.

Alway, S.E., J.D. MacDougall, D.G. Sale, J.R. Sutton, and A.J. McComas. 1988. Functional and structural adaptations in skeletal muscle of trained athletes. *Journal of Applied Physiology* 64: 1114-1120.

Amara, C.E., C.L. Rice, J.J. Koval, D.H. Paterson, E.M. Winter, and D.A. Cunningham. 2003. Allometric scaling of strength in an independently living population age 55-86 years. *American Journal of Biology* 15: 48-60.

Andersen, L.L., and P. Aagaard. 2005. Influence of maximal muscle strength and intrinsic muscle contractile properties on contractile rate of force development. *European Journal of Applied Physiology* 96: 46-52.

Andren-Sandberg, A. 1998. Athletic training of children and adolescents. *Lakartidningen* 95(41): 4480-4484.

Antonio, J. 2000. Nonuniform response of skeletal muscle to heavy resistance training: Can bodybuilders induce regional muscle hypertrophy? *Journal of Strength and Conditioning Research* 14: 102-113.

Apple, F.S., and P.A. Tesch. 1989. CK and LD isozymes in human single muscle fibers in trained athletes. *Journal of Applied Physiology* 66: 2717-2720.

Armstrong, L.E., and J.L. VanHoost. 2002. The unknown mechanism of the overtraining syndrome. *Sports Medicine* 32: 185-209.

Armstrong, R.B., G.L. Warren, and J.A. Warren. 1991. Mechanisms of exercise induced muscle fiber injury. *Sports Medicine* 12: 184-207.

Asfour, S.S., M.M. Ayoub, and A. Mital. 1984. Effects of an endurance and strength training programme on lifting capability of males. *Ergonomics* 27(4): 435-442.

Åstrand, P.O., and K. Rodahl. 1970. *Textbook of work physiology.* New York: McGraw-Hill.

Baker, A.B., Y.Q. Tang, and M.J. Turner. 2003. Percentage decline in masters superathlete track and field performance with ageing. *Experimental Aging Research* 29: 47-65.

Batterham, A.M., and K.M. Birch. 1996. Allometry of anaerobic performance: A gender comparison. *Canadian Journal of Applied Physiology* 21: 48-62.

Behm, D.G. 1995. Neuromuscular implications and applications of resistance training. *Journal of Strength and Conditioning Research* 9: 264-274.

Behm, D., G. Reardon, J. Fitzgerald, and E. Drinkwater. 2002. The effect of 5, 10, and 20 repetition maximums on the recovery of voluntary and evoked contractile properties. *Journal of Strength and Conditioning Research* 16: 209-218.

Bell, D.G., and I. Jacobs. 1986. Electro-mechanical response times and rate of force development in males and females. *Medicine and Science in Sports and Exercise* 18: 31-36.

Bemben, M.G. 1998. Age-related alterations in muscular endurance. *Sports Medicine* 25: 259-269.

Bickel, C.S., J.M. Slade, F. Haddad, G.R. Adams, and G.A. Dudley. 2003. Acute molecular responses of skeletal muscle to resistance exercise in able-bodied and spinal cord-injured subjects. *Journal of Applied Physiology* 94: 2255-2262.

Bigard, A.X., H. Sanchez, G. Claveyrolas, S. Martin, B. Thimonier, and M.J. Arnaud. 2001. Effects of dehydration and rehydration on EMG changes during fatiguing contractions. *Medicine and Science in Sports and Exercise* 33: 1694-1700.

Binzen, C.A., P.D. Swan, and M.M. Manore. 2001. Postexercise oxygen consumption and substrate use after resistance exercise in women. *Medicine and Science in Sports and Exercise* 33: 932-938.

Blimkie, C.J. 1993. Resistance training during preadolescence: Issues and controversies. *Sports Medicine* 15: 389-407.

Blinder, M.D., P. Bawa, P. Ruenzel, and E. Henneman. 1983. Does orderly recruitment of motoneurons depend upon the existence of different types of motor units? *Neuroscience Letters* 36: 55-58.

Bobbert, M.F., K.G. Gerritsen, M.C.A. Litjens and A.J. Van Soest. 1996. Why is countermovement jump height greater than squat jump height? *Medicine and Science in Sports and Exercise* 28: 1402-1412.

Bobbert, M.F., and A.J. Knoek van Soest. 2001. Why do people jump the way they do? *Exercise and Sports Sciences Reviews* 29: 95-102.

Borges, O., and B. Essen-Gustavsson. 1989. Enzyme activities in type I and type II muscles of human skeletal muscle in relation to age and torque development. *Acta Physiologica Scandinavica* 136: 29-36.

Bouchard, C., F.T. Dionne, J.A. Simoneau, and M.R. Boulay. 1992. Genetics of aerobic and anaerobic performance. *Exercise and Sport Sciences Reviews* 20: 27-58.

Busso, T., K. Hakkinen, A. Pakarinen, H. Kauhanen, P.V. Komi, and J.R. Lacour. 1992. Hormonal adaptations and modeled responses in elite weightlifters during 6 weeks of training. *European Journal of Applied Physiology* 64: 381-386.

Byrd, R., K. Pierce, L. Reilly, and L. Brady. 2003. Young weightlifters' performance across time. *Sports Biomechanics* 2: 133-140.

Carins, S.P., W.A. Wang, S.R. Slack, R.G. Mills, and S.S. Loiselle. 1998. Role of extracellular [Ca2+] in fatigue of isolated mammalian skeletal muscle. *Journal of Applied Physiology* 84: 1395-1406.

Cauza, E., U. Hanusch-Enserer, B. Strasser et al. 2005. The relative benefits of endurance and strength training in the metabolic factors and muscle function of people with type 2 diabetes mellitus. *Archives of Physical Medicine and Rehabilitation* 86: 1527-1533.

Clarkson, P.M., and S.P. Sayers. 1999. Etiology of exercise-induced muscle damage. *Canadian Journal of Applied Physiology* 24: 234-248.

Conley, M.S., and M.H. Stone. 1996. Carbohydrate ingestion/supplementation for resistance exercise and training. *Sports Medicine* 21: 7-17.

Conley, M.S., M.H. Stone, M.J. Nimmons, and G.A. Dudley. 1997. Specificity of resistance training response in neck muscle size and strength. *European Journal of Applied Physiology* 75: 443-448.

Conroy, B.P., W.J. Kraemer, C.M. Maresh, G.P. Dalsky, S.J. Fleck, M.H. Stone, A.C. Fry, and P. Cooper. 1993. Bone mineral density in weightlifters. *Medicine and Science in Sports and Exercise* 25(10): 1103-1109.

Costill, D.L., E.F. Coyle, W.F. Fink, G.R. Lesmes, and F.A. Witzmann. 1979. Adaptations in skeletal muscle following strength training. *Journal of Applied Physiology* 46: 96-99.

Cronin, J.B., P.J. McNair, and R.N. Marshall. 2000. Magnitude and decay of stretch-induced enhancement of power output. *European Journal of Applied Physiology* 84: 575-581.

Daneels, L.A., A.M. Cools, G.G. Vanderstraeten, D.C. Cambier, E.E. Witrouw, J. Bourgois, and H.J. de Cuyper. 2001. The effects of three different training modalities on the cross-sectional area of the paravertebral muscles. *Scandinavian Journal of Medicine and Science in Sports* 11: 335-341.

Drozdov, V.F., and N.Y. Petrov. 1983. Physical development and health of weightlifting students. *1983 Soviet weightlifting yearbook* (pp. 51-54). Moscow: Fizkultura Sport [translated by A. Charniga].

Dvorkin, L.S., and A.S. Medvedev. 1983. Age changes in muscular strength and speed-strength qualities. *Soviet weightlifting yearbook* (pp. 43-51). Moscow: Fizkultura Sport [translated by A. Charniga].

Evans, W.J. 1995. What is sarcopenia? *Journal of Gerontology (Series A): Biological Sciences and Medical Sciences* 50 (Spec. No.): 5-8.

Exner, G.U., H.W. Staudte, and D. Pette. 1973. Isometric training of rats: Effects upon fast and slow muscle and modification by an anabolic hormone in female rats. *Pfluegers Archiv* 345: 1-4.

Faigenbaum, A.D. 2000. Strength training for children and adolescents. *Clinical Sports Medicine* 19: 593-619.

Faigenbaum, A.D., L.A. Milliken, R.L. Loud, B.T. Burak, C.L. Doherty, and W.L. Wescott. 2002. Comparison of 1 and 2 days per week of strength training in children. *Research Quarterly for Exercise and Sport* 73: 416-424.

Faigenbaum, A.D., L.A. Milliken, and W.L. Wescott. 2003. Maximal strength testing in healthy children. *Journal of Strength and Conditioning Research* 17: 162-166.

Falk, B., and G. Tenenbaum. 1996. The effectiveness of resistance training in children. A meta-analysis. *Sports Medicine* 22: 176-186.

Fleck, S.J., and W.J. Kraemer. 1997. *Designing resistance training programs* (2nd ed.). Champaign, IL: Human Kinetics.

Friden, J., and R.L. Leiber. 1998. Segmental muscle fiber lesions after repetitive eccentric contractions. *Cell and Tissue Research* 293: 165-171.

Friden, J., and R.L. Leiber. 2001. Eccentric exercise-induced injuries to contractile and cytoskeletal muscle fibre components. *Acta Physiologica Scandinavica* 171: 321-326.

Fry, A.C., W.J. Kraemer, M. Lynch, T. Triplett, and L.P. Koziris. 1994. Does short-term near-maximal intensity machine resistance training induce overtraining? *Journal of Strength and Conditioning Research* 8: 188-191.

Fry, A.C., B.K. Schilling, R.S. Staron, F.C. Hagerman, R.S. Hikida, and J.T. Thrush. 2003. Muscle fiber characteristics and performance correlates of male Olympic-style weightlifters. *Journal of Strength and Conditioning Research* 17: 746-754.

Fry, A.C., J.M. Webber, L.W. Weiss, M.D. Fry, and Y. Li. 2000. Impaired performances with excessive high-intensity free-weight training. *Journal of Strength and Conditioning Research* 14: 34-61.

Fung, L., and H. Ha. 1994. Changes in track and field performance with chronological aging. *International Journal of Aging and Human Development* 38: 171-180.

Galloway, M.T., R. Kadoko, and P. Jokl. 2002. Effect of aging on male and female master athletes' performance in strength versus endurance athletes. *American Journal of Orthopedics* 31: 93-98.

Gardiner, P.F. 2001. *Neuromuscular aspects of physical activity.* Champaign, IL: Human Kinetics.

Garhammer, J.J. 1991. A comparison of maximal power outputs between elite male and female weightlifters in competition. *International Journal of Sport Biomechanics* 7: 3-11.

Genaidy, A., N. Davis, E. Delgado, S. Garcia, and E. Al-Herzalla. 1994. Effects of a job-simulated exercise programme on employees performing manual handling operations. *Ergonomics* 37(1): 95-106.

Gibala, M.J., S.A. Interisano, M.A. Tarnopolsky, B.D. Roy, J.R. Macdonald, K.E. Yaresheski, and J.D. MacDougall. 2000. Myofibrillar disruption following concentric and eccentric resistance exercise in strength trained men. *Canadian Journal of Physiology and Pharmacology* 78: 656-661.

Goldspink, G. 1999. Changes in muscle mass and phenotype and the expression of autocrine and systemic growth factors by muscle in response to stretch and overload. *Journal of Anatomy* 194(Part 3): 323-334.

Goldspink, G. 2002. Gene expression in skeletal muscle. *Biochemical Society Transactions* 30: 285-290.

Golub, S. 1992. *Periods: From menarche to menopause.* Newbury Park, CA: Sage.

Gotshalk, L., W.J. Kraemer, B.C. Nindl, S. Toeshi, J. Volek, J.A. Bush, W.J. Sebastianelli, and M. Putukian. 1998. Contribution of upper body training on total body strength and power in young women. *Medicine and Science in Sports and Exercise* 30(5): S162.

Grimby, G., P. Bjorntorp, M. Fahlen, T.A. Hoskins, O. Hook, H. Oxhof, and B. Saltin. 1973. Metabolic effects of isometric training. *Scandinavian Journal of Clinical Laboratory Investigation* 31: 301-305.

Haff, G., A. Whitley, L.B. McCoy, and M.H. Stone. 2003. Carbohydrate supplementation and resistance training. *Journal of Strength and Conditioning Research* 17: 187-196.

Hakkinen, K. 1994. Neuromuscular adaptation during strength training, aging, detraining and immobilization. *Critical Reviews in Physical and Rehabilitation Medicine* 6: 161-198.

Hakkinen, K., M. Alen, W.J. Kraemer, E. Gorostiaga, M. Izquierdo, J. Rusko, J. Mikkola, A. Hakkinen, H. Valkeinen, E. Kaarakainen, S. Romu, V. Erola, J. Ahtianen, and L. Paavolainen. 2003. Neuromuscular adaptations during concurrent strength and endurance training versus strength training. *European Journal of Applied Physiology* 89: 42-52.

Hakkinen, K., and P.V. Komi. 1985a. Changes in electrical and mechanical behaviour of leg extensor muscle during heavy resistance strength training. *Acta Physiologica Scandinavica* 125: 573-585.

Hakkinen, K., and P.V. Komi. 1985b. Effect of explosive type strength training on electromyographic and force production characteristics of leg extensor muscles during concentric and various stretch shortening cycle exercises. *Acta Physiologica Scandinavica* 125: 587-600.

Hakkinen, K., P.V. Komi, M. Alen, and H. Kauhanen. 1987. EMG, muscle fibre and force production characteristics during a 1 year training period in elite weightlifters. *European Journal of Applied Physiology* 56: 419-427.

Hakkinen, K., R.U. Newton, S.E. Gordon, M. McCormick, J.S. Volek, B.C. Nindl, L.A. Gotshalk, W.W. Campbell, W.J. Evans, A. Hakkinen, B.J. Humphries, and W.J. Kraemer. 1998. Changes in muscle morphology, electromyographic activity and force production characteristics during progressive strength training in young and older men. *Journal of Gerontology (Series A)* 53: B415-B423.

Hakkinen, K., A. Pakarinen, M. Alen, H. Kauhanen, and P.V. Komi. 1988. Neuromuscular and hormonal adaptations in athletes to strength training in two years. *Journal of Applied Physiology* 65: 2406-2412.

Hakkinen, K., A. Pakarinen, H. Kyrolainen, S. Cheng, D.H. Kim, and P.V. Komi. 1990. Neuromuscular adaptations and serum hormones in females during prolonged training. *International Journal of Sports Medicine* 11: 91-98.

Hamill, B.P. 1994. Relative safety of weightlifting and weight training. *Journal of Strength and Conditioning Research* 8: 53-57.

Harries, U.J., and B.M. Bassey. 1990. Torque-velocity relationships for the knee extensors in women in their 3rd and 7th decades. *European Journal of Applied Physiology* 60: 186-190.

Harris, G.R., M.H. Stone, H. O'Bryant, C.M. Proulx, and R. Johnson. 2000. Short term performance effects of high speed, high force and combined weight training. *Journal of Strength and Conditioning Research* 14(1): 14-20.

Harris, J.A., P.A. Vernon, and D.I. Boomsma. 1998. The heritability of testosterone: A study of Dutch adolescent twins and their parents. *Behavior Genetics* 28: 165-171.

Henneman, E. 1982. Recruitment of motor units: The size principle. In: J. R. Desmedt (Ed.), *Motor unit types, recruitment and plasticity in health and disease.* New York: Karger.

Henneman, E., G. Somjen, and D.O. Carpenter. 1965. Excitability and inhibitability of motoneurons of different sizes. *Journal of Neurophysiology* 28: 599-620.

Hernandez, D., A. de la Rosa, A. Barragan, A. Barrios, E. Salido, A. Torres, B. Martin, I. Laynez, A. Duque, A. De Vera, V. Lorenzo, and A. Gonzalez. 2003. The ACE/DD genotype is associated with the extent of exercise-induced left ventricular growth in endurance athletes. *Journal of the American College of Cardiology* 6(42): 527-532.

Higbie, E.J., K.J. Cureton, G.L. Warren III, and B.M. Prior. 1996. Effects of concentric and eccentric training on muscle strength, cross-sectional area and neural activation. *Journal of Applied Physiology* 81: 2173-2181.

Holten, M.K., M. Zacho, M. Gaster et al. 2004. Strength training increases insulin-mediated glucose uptake, GLUT4 content and insulin signaling in skeletal muscle in patients with type 2 diabetes. *Diabetes* 53: 294-305.

Hornberger, T.A., and R.P. Farrar. 2004. Physiological hypertrophy of the FHL muscle following 8 weeks of progressive resistance exercise in the rat. *Canadian Journal of Applied Physiology* 29: 16-31.

Hortabagyi, T., J. Barrier, D. Beard, J. Brapennincx, P. Koens, P. de Vita, L. Dempsey, and J. Lambert. 1996. Greater initial adaptation to submaximal muscle lengthening than maximal shortening. *Journal of Applied Physiology* 81: 1677-1682.

Hortabagyi, T., L. Dempsey, D. Fraser, D. Zheng, G. Hamilton, J. Lambert, and L. Dohm. 2000. Changes in muscle strength, muscle fibre size and myofibrillar gene expression after immobilization and retraining in humans. *Journal of Physiology* 524: 293-304.

Housh, D.J., T.J. Housh, G.O. Johnson, and W.K. Chu. 1992. Hypertrophy response to unilateral concentric isokinetic resistance training. *Journal of Applied Physiology* 73: 65-70.

Hunter, G.R., D. Seelhorst, and S. Snyder. 2003. Comparison of metabolic and heart rate responses to super slow vs. traditional resistance training. *Journal of Strength and Conditioning Research* 17: 76-81.

Hunter, S.K., J. Duchateau, and R.M. Enoka. 2004. Muscle fatigue and the mechanisms of task failure. *Exercise and Sport Sciences Reviews* 32: 44-49.

Huston, L.J., and E.M. Wojtys. 1996. Neuromuscular performance characteristics in the elite female athlete. *American Journal of Sports Medicine* 24: 427-435.

Huygens, W., M.A. Thomis, M.W. Peeters, R.F. Vlietinck, and G.P. Beunen. 2004. Determinants and upper-limit heritability of skeletal muscle mass and strength. *Canadian Journal of Applied Physiology* 29: 186-200.

Ishii, N. 1994. Resistance training and muscle hypertrophy. In: Training Science Association (Eds.), *Resistance training* (pp. 19-31). Tokyo: Asakura.

Izquierdo, M., J. Ibanez, K. Hakkinen, W.J. Kraemer, M. Ruesta, and E.M. Gorostiago. 2004. Maximal strength and power, muscle mass, endurance and serum hormones in weightlifters and road cyclists. *Journal of Sports Medicine* 22: 465-478.

Janssen, I., S.B. Heymsfield, Z.M. Wang, and R. Ross. 2000. Skeletal muscle mass and distribution in 468 men and women age 18-88 yr. *Journal of Applied Physiology* 89: 81-88.

Janus, M., and D.R. Offord. 2000. Readiness to learn at school. *Isuma: Canadian Journal of Policy Research* 1: 71-75.

Johnson, C.C., M.H. Stone, R.J. Byrd, and A. Lopez-S. 1983. The response of serum lipids and plasma androgens to weight training exercise in sedentary males. *Journal of Sports Medicine and Physical Fitness* 23: 39-41.

Johnson, C.C., M.H. Stone, A. Lopez-S, J.A. Herbert, L.T. Kilgore, and R. Byrd. 1982. Diet and exercise in middle-aged men. *Journal of the American Dietary Association* 81: 695-701.

Jones, A. 2002. Human performance: A role for the ACE genotype? *Exercise and Sport Sciences Reviews* 30(4): 184-190.

Jones, D.A., and O.M. Rutherford. 1987. Human muscle strength training: The effects of three different regimes on the nature of the resultant changes. *Journal of Physiology* 391: 1-11.

Jones, K., P. Bishop, G. Hunter, and G. Fleisig. 2001. The effects of varying resistance-training loads on intermediate- and high-velocity-specific adaptations. *Journal of Strength and Conditioning Research* 15: 349-356.

Jones, K., G. Hunter, G. Fleisig, R. Escamilla, and L. Lemak. 1999. The effects of compensatory acceleration on the development of strength and power. *Journal of Strength and Conditioning Research* 13: 99-105.

Jurca, R., M.J. Lamonte, T.S. Church et al. 2004. Associations of muscle strength and fitness with metabolic syndrome in men. *Medicine and Science in Sports and Exercise* 36: 1301-1307.

Jurca, R., M.J. Lamonte, C.E. Kampert et al. 2005. Association of muscular strength with incidence of metabolic syndrome in men. *Medicine and Science in Sports and Exercise* 37: 1849-1855.

Kadi, F., and L. Thornell. 1999. Training affects myosin heavy chain phenotype in the trapezius muscle of women. *Histochemistry and Cell Biology* 112: 73-78.

Kamel, H.K., D. Maas, and E.H. Duthie. 2002. Role of hormones in the pathogenesis and management of sarcopenia. *Drugs and Aging* 19: 865-877.

Karlsson, J., B. Sjodin, A. Thorstensson, B. Hulten, and K. Firth. 1975. LDH isozymes in skeletal muscles of endurance and strength trained athletes. *Acta Physiologica Scandinavica* 93: 150-156.

Katch, V. 1983. Physical conditioning of children. *Journal of Adolescent Health Care* 3: 241-246.

Keeler, L.K., L.H. Finkelstein, W. Miller, and B. Fernhall. 2001. Early-phase adaptations of traditional-speed vs. superslow resistance training on strength and aerobic capacity in sedentary individuals. *Journal of Strength and Conditioning Research* 15: 309-314.

Kelly, G. 1996. Mechanical overload and skeletal muscle fiber hyperplasia: A meta-analysis. *Journal of Applied Physiology* 81: 1584-1588.

Keul, J., G. Haralambie, M. Bruder, and H.J. Gottstein. 1978. The effect of weight lifting exercise on heart rate and metabolism in experienced lifters. *Medicine and Science in Sports and Exercise* 10: 13-15.

Klissouras, V. 1971. Adaptability of genetic variation. *Journal of Applied Physiology* 31: 338-344.

Klissouras, V., B. Casini, V. De Salvo, M. Faina, C. Marini, F. Pigozzi, M. Pittaluga, A. Spataro, F. Taddei, and P. Parisi. 2001. Genes and Olympic performance: A co-twin study. *International Journal of Sports Medicine* 22: 250-255.

Komi, P.V., and J. Karlsson. 1978. Skeletal muscle fiber types, enzyme activities and physical performance in young males and females. *Acta Physiologica Scandinavica* 103: 210-218.

Komi, P.V., and J.H. Viitasalo. 1976. Signal characteristics of EMG at different levels of muscle tension. *Acta Physiologica Scandinavica* 96: 267-276.

Kraemer, W.J. 1992. Endocrine responses and adaptations to strength training. In: P.V. Komi (Ed.), *Strength and power in sport* (pp. 291-304). London: Blackwell Scientific.

Kraemer, W.J., A.C. Fry, F.N. Frykman, B. Conroy, and J. Hoffman. 1989. Resistance training and youth. *Pediatric Exercise Science* 1: 336-350.

Kraemer, W.J., and L.P. Koziris. 1994. Olympic weightlifting and powerlifting. In: D.R. Lamb, H.G. Knuttgen, and R. Murray (Eds.), *Physiology and nutrition for competitive sports* (pp. 1-54). Carmel, IN: Cooper.

Krivickas, L.S., D. Suh, J. Wilkins, V.A. Houghes, R. Roubenoff, and W.R. Frontera. 2001. Age- and gender-related differences in maximum shortening velocity of skeletal muscle fibers. *American Journal of Physical Medicine and Rehabilitation* 80: 447-455.

Larsson, L., and J. Karlsson. 1978. Isometric and dynamic endurance as a function of age and skeletal muscle characteristics. *Acta Physiologica Scandinavica* 104: 129-136.

Larsson, L., and P.A. Tesch. 1986. Motor unit fibre density in extremely hypertrophied skeletal muscles in man. Electrophysiological signs of muscle fibre hyperplasia. *European Journal of Applied Physiology* 55: 130-136.

Legwold, G. 1982. Does lifting weights harm a prepubescent adolescent athlete? *Physician and Sportsmedicine* 10: 141-144.

Lemmer, J.T., D.E. Hurlbut, G.F. Martel, B.L. Tracy, F.M. Ey, E.J. Metter, J.L. Fozard, J.L. Fleg, and B.F. Hurley. 2000. Age and gender responses to strength training and detraining. *Medicine and Science in Sports and Exercise* 32: 1505-1512.

Lewis, D.A., E. Kamon, and J.L. Hodgson. 1986. Physiological differences between genders. Implications for sports conditioning. *Sports Medicine* 3: 357-369.

Li, J.L., X.N. Wang, S.F. Fraser, M.F. Crey, T.V. Wrigley, and M.J. McKenna. 2002. Effects of fatigue and training on sarcoplasmic reticulum Ca (2+) regulation in human skeletal muscle. *Journal of Applied Physiology* 94: 912-922.

Lillegard, W.A., E.W. Brown, D.J. Wilson, R. Henderson, and E. Lewis. 1997. Efficacy of strength training in prepubescent to early postpubescent males and females: Effects of gender and maturation. *Pediatric Rehabilitation* 1: 147-157.

Lindle, R., E. Metter, N. Lynch et al. 1997. Age and gender comparisons of muscle strength in 654 women and men aged 20-93. *Journal of Applied Physiology* 83: 1581-1587.

Linnammo, V., R.U. Newton, K. Hakkinen, P.V. Komi, A. Davie, M. McGuigan, and T. Triplett-McBride. 2000. Neuromuscular responses to explosive and heavy resistance loading. *Journal of Electromyography and Kinesiology* 10: 417-424.

Loeb, G.E. 1987. Hard lessons in motor control from the mammalian spinal cord. *Trends in Neuroscience* 10: 108-113.

MacDougall, J.D., A.L. Hicks, J.R. MacDonald, R.S. Mckelvie, H.J. Green, and K.M. Smith. 1998. Muscle performance and enzyme adaptations to sprint interval training. *Journal of Applied Physiology* 84: 2138-2142.

MacDougall, J.D., D.G. Sale, S.E. Alway, and J.R. Sutton. 1984. Muscle fiber number in biceps brachii in bodybuilders and control subjects. *Journal of Applied Physiology* 57: 1399-1403.

MacDougall, J.D., D.G. Sale, G.C.B. Elder, and J.R. Sutton. 1982. Muscle ultrastructural characteristics of elite power lifters and body builders. *European Journal of Applied Physiology* 48: 117-126.

MacDougall, J.D., G.R. Ward, D.G. Sale, and J.R. Sutton. 1977. Biochemical adaptation of human skeletal muscle to heavy resistance training and immobilization. *Journal of Applied Physiology* 43: 700-703.

Maffulli, N. 1990. Intensive training in young athletes. The orthopaedic surgeon's viewpoint. *Sports Medicine* 9: 229-243.

Mayhew, T.P., J.M. Rothstein, S.D. Finucane, and R.L. Lamb. 1995. Muscular adaptation to concentric and eccentric exercise at equivalent power levels. *Medicine and Science in Sports and Exercise* 27: 868-873.

McBride, J.M., T. Triplett-McBride, A. Davie, and R.U. Newton. 2002. The effect of heavy versus light load jump squats on the development of strength, power and speed. *Journal of Strength and Conditioning Research* 16: 75-82.

McCall, G.E., W.Q.C. Byrnes, A. Dickinson, P.M. Pattany, and S.J. Fleck. 1996. Muscle fiber hypertrophy, hyperplasia, and capillary density in college men after resistance training. *Journal of Applied Physiology* 81: 2004-2012.

McKinnon, L.T. 2000. Special feature for the Olympics: Effects of exercise on the immune system: Overtraining effects on immunity and performance in athletes. *Immunology and Cell Biology* 78: 502-509.

McMillan, J., M.H. Stone, J. Sartain, D. Marple, R. Keith, D. Lewis, and W. Brown. 1993. The 20-h hormonal response to a single session of weight training. *Journal of Strength and Conditioning Research* 7: 51-54.

Medvedev, A.S., V.F. Rodionov, V. Rogozkin, and A.E. Gulyants. 1981. Training content of weightlifters in preparation period. *Teoriya i Praktika Fizicheskoi Kultury* 12: 5-7 [translation by M. Yessis].

Meltzer, D.E. 1994. Age dependence of Olympic weightlifting ability. *Medicine and Science in Sports and Exercise* 26: 1053-1067.

Miller, A.E., J.D. MacDougall, M.A. Tarnopolsky, and D.G. Sale. 1993. Gender differences in strength and muscle fiber characteristics. *European Journal of Applied Physiology* 66(3): 254-262.

Millet, G.Y., and R. Lepers. 2004. Alterations in neuromuscular function after prolonged running, cycling and skiing exercises. *Sports Medicine* 34: 105-116.

Missitzi, J., and V. Klissouras. 2004. Heritability of neuromuscular coordination: Implications for control strategies. *Medicine and Science in Sports and Exercise* 36: 233-240.

Monnier, J.F., A.A. Benhaddad, J.P. Micallef, J. Mercier, and J.F. Bruin. 2000. Relationships between blood viscosity and insulin-like growth factor I status in athletes. *Clinical Hemorheology and Microcirculation* 22: 277-286.

Morrissey, M.C., E.A. Harman, P.N. Frykman, and K.H. Han. 1998. Early phase differential effects of slow and fast barbell squat training. *American Journal of Sports Medicine* 26: 221-230.

Newton, R.U., W.J. Kraemer, and K. Hakkinen. 1999. Effects of ballistic training on preseason preparation of the elite volleyball players. *Medicine and Science in Sports and Exercise* 31: 323-330.

Newton, R.U., W.J. Kraemer, K. Hakkinen, B.J. Humphries, and A.J. Murphy. 1996. Kinematics, kinetics and muscle activation during explosive upper body movements. *Journal of Applied Biomechanics* 12: 31-43.

Nosaka, K., A. Lavender, M. Newton, and P. Sacco. 2003. Muscle damage in resistance training. Is muscle damage necessary for muscle hypertrophy? *International Journal of Sport and Health Science* 1: 1-8.

Nosaka, K.A., and M. Newton. 2002. Differences in the magnitude of muscle damage between maximal and submaximal eccentric loading. *Journal of Strength and Conditioning Research* 16: 202-208.

Nosaka, K., and K. Sakamoto. 2001. Effect of elbow joint angle on the magnitude of muscle damage to the elbow flexors. *Medicine and Science in Sports and Exercise* 33: 22-29.

O'Bryant, H.S., R. Byrd, and M.H. Stone. 1988. Cycle ergometer and maximum leg and hip strength adaptations to two different methods of weight training. *Journal of Applied Sport Science Research* 2: 27-30.

Olsen, P.D., and W.G. Hopkins. 2003. The effect of attempted ballistic training on the force and speed of movement. *Journal of Strength and Conditioning Research* 17: 291-298.

Payne, V.G., J.R. Morrow, L. Johnson, and S.N. Dalton. 1997. Resistance training in children and youth: A meta-analysis. *Research Quarterly for Exercise and Sport* 68: 80-88.

Peterson, M.D., M.R. Rhea, and B.A. Alvar. 2004. Maximizing strength development in athletes: A meta-analysis to determine the dose-response relationship. *Journal of Strength and Conditioning Research* 18: 377-382.

Petitt, D.S., S.A. Arngrimsson, and K.J. Cureton. 2003. Effect of resistance exercise on postprandial lipemia. *Journal of Applied Physiology* 94: 694-700.

Phillips, S.M., K.D. Tipton, A. Aarsland, and S.E. Wolfe. 1999. Resistance training induces the acute exercise-induced increase in muscle protein turnover. *American Journal of Physiology, Endocrinology and Metabolism* 273: E99-E107.

Phillips, W.T., A.M. Batterham, J.E. Valenzuela, and L.N. Burkett. 2004. Reliability of maximal strength testing in older adults. *Archives of Physical Medicine and Rehabilitation* 85: 329-334.

Ploutz, L.L., P.A. Tesch, R.L. Biro, and G.A. Dudley. 1994. Effect of resistance training on muscle use during exercise. *Journal of Applied Physiology* 76: 1675-1681.

Poehlman, E.T., A.W. Gardner, P.A. Ades, and S.M. Katzman-Rooks. 1992. Resting energy metabolism and cardiovascular disease risk in resistance-trained and aerobically trained males. *Metabolism: Clinical and Experimental* 41(12): 1351-1360.

Powell, K.E., G.W. Heath, M.J. Kresnow, J.J. Sacks, and C.M. Branche. 1998. Injury rates from walking, gardening, weightlifting, outdoor bicycling and aerobics. *Medicine and Science in Sports and Exercise* 30: 1246-1449.

Powell, P.L., R.R. Roy, P. Kanim, M.A. Bello, and V.R. Edgerton. 1984. Predictability of skeletal muscle tension from architectural determinations in guinea pig hindlimbs. *Journal of Applied Physiology* 57: 1715-1721.

Prince, P.P., R.S. Hikida, and F.C. Hagerman. 1976. Human muscle fiber type in powerlifters, distance runners and untrained subjects. *Pfluegers Archiv* 363: 19-26.

Proctor, D.N., P. Balagopal, and K.S. Nair. 1998. Age-related sarcopenia in humans is associated with reduced synthetic rates of specific proteins. *Journal of Nutrition* 128(2 Suppl.): 351S-355S.

Proske, U., and D.L. Morgan. 2001. Muscle damage from eccentric exercise: Mechanical signs and adaptations and clinical applications. *Journal of Physiology* 537: 333-345.

Pyne, D.B. 1994. Exercise-induced muscle damage and inflammation: A review. *Australian Journal of Science and Medicine in Sport* 26: 49-58.

Rasch, P.J., and L.E. Morehouse. 1957. Effect of static and dynamic exercises on muscular strength and hypertrophy. *Journal of Applied Physiology* 11: 29-34.

Ratel, S., C.A. Williams, J. Oliver, and N. Armstrong. 2004. Effects of age and mode of exercise on power output profiles during repeated sprints. *European Journal of Applied Physiology* 92: 204-210.

Reis, E., U. Frick, and D. Schmidtbleicher. 1995. Frequency variations of strength training sessions triggered by the phases of the menstrual cycle. *International Journal of Sports Medicine* 16: 545-550.

Requa, R.K., L.N. DeAvilla, and J.G. Garrick. 1993. Injuries in recreational adult fitness activities. *American Journal of Sports Medicine* 21: 461-467.

Rhea, M.R., B.A. Alvar, L.N. Burkett, and S.D. Ball. 2003. A meta-analysis to determine the dose response for strength development. *Medicine and Science in Sports and Exercise* 35: 456-464.

Robinson, J.M., C.M. Penland, M.H. Stone, R.L. Johnson, B.J. Warren, and D.L. Lewis. 1995. Effects of different weight training exercise-rest intervals on strength, power and high intensity endurance. *Journal of Strength and Conditioning Research* 9: 216-221.

Ross, A., and M. Leveritt. 2001. Long-term metabolic and skeletal muscle adaptations to short-term sprint training: Implications for sprint training and tapering. *Sports Medicine* 31: 1063-1082.

Rotter, J.I., F.I. Wong, E.T. Lifrak, and L.N. Parker. 1985. A genetic component to the variation of dehydroepiandrosterone. *Metabolism* 34: 731-736.

Rozenek, R., and J.J. Garhammer. 1998. Male-female strength comparisons and rate of strength decline with age in weightlifting and powerlifting. *Conference: International Symposium on weightlifting and weight training* (pp. 287-288). Lahti, Finland.

Ryushi, T., K. Hakkinen, H. Kauhanen, and P.V. Komi. 1988. Muscle fiber characteristics, muscle cross-sectional area and force production in strength athletes and physically active males and females. *Scandinavian Journal Sport Science* 10: 7-15.

Sale, D.G. 1988. Neural adaptation to resistance training. *Medicine and Science in Sports and Exercise* 20(5) (Suppl.): S135-S145.

Sale, D.G. 1992. Neural adaptation to strength training. In: P.V. Komi (Ed.), *Strength and power in sport.* Oxford: Blackwell Scientific (pp. 249-265).

Sanborn, C.F., and C.M. Jankowski. 1994. Physiologic considerations for women in sport. *Clinical Sports Medicine* 13: 315-327.

Schmidt, R.A. 1991. *Motor learning and performance.* Champaign, IL: Human Kinetics.

Semmler, J.G., and R.M. Enoka. 2000. Neural contributions to changes in muscle strength. In V. Zatsiorsky (Ed.) *Biomechanics in sport.* Oxford, Blackwell Science, (pp. 3-20).

Semmler, J.G., and M.A. Nordstrom. 1998. Motor unit discharge and force tremor in skill- and strength-trained individuals. *Experimental Brain Research* 119: 27-38.

Siff, M.C., and Y. Verkhoshanski. 1998. *Supertraining: Strength training for sporting excellence* (3rd ed.). Johannesburg: University of the Witwatersrand.

Simoneau, J.A., and C. Bouchard. 1995. Genetic determinism of fiber type proportion in human skeletal muscle. *Federation of American Societies for Experimental Biology Journal* 9: 1091-1095.

Skurvydas, A., V. Dudoniene, A. Kalvenas, and A. Zuoza. 2002. Skeletal muscle fatigue in long-distance runners, sprinters and untrained men after repeated drop jumps performed at maximum intensity. *Scandinavian Journal of Applied Physiology* 12: 34-39.

Smith, L. 2000. Cytokine hypothesis of overtraining: A physiological adaptation to excessive stress? *Medicine and Science in Sports and Exercise* 32: 317-331.

Sothern, M.S., J.M. Loftin, J.N. Udall, R.M. Suskind, T.L. Ewing, and S.C. Blecker. 2000. Safety, feasibility and efficacy of a resistance training program in preadolescent obese children. *American Journal of Medical Science* 19: 370-375.

Stackhouse, S.K., D.S. Reisman, and S.A. Binder-Macleod. 2001. Challenging the role of pH in skeletal muscle fatigue. *Physical Therapy* 81: 1897-1903.

Staron, R.S., E.S. Malicky, M.J. Leonard, J.E. Falkel, F.C. Hagerman, and G.A. Dudley. 1989. Muscle hypertrophy and fast fiber type conversion in heavy-resistance trained women. *European Journal of Applied Physiology* 60: 871-879.

Stauber, W.T., and C.A. Smith. 1998. Cellular responses in exertion-induced muscular injury. *Molecular and Cellular Biochemistry* 179: 189-196.

Stone, M.H. 1988. Implications for connective tissue and bone alterations resulting from resistive exercise training. *Medicine and Science in Sports and Exercise* 20(5 Suppl.): S162-S168.

Stone, M.H. 1993. Revision and update: Position/policy statement and literature review for the National Strength and Conditioning Association on "anabolic steroids and athletics." *National Strength and Conditioning Association Journal* 15: 9-29.

Stone, M.H., S.J. Fleck, W.J. Kraemer, and N.T. Triplett. 1991a. Health and performance related adaptations to resistive training. *Sports Medicine* 11: 210-231.

Stone, M.H., and A.C. Fry. 1997. Increased training volume in strength/power athletes. In: *Overtraining in sport* (chapter 5, pp. 87-106). Champaign, IL: Human Kinetics.

Stone, M.H., R. Johnson, and D. Carter. 1979. A short term comparison of two different methods of resistive training on leg strength and power. *Athletic Training* 14: 158-160.

Stone, M.H., and C. Karatzeferi. 2002. Connective tissue (and bone) response to strength training. In: P.V. Komi (Ed.), *Encyclopaedia of sports medicine: Strength and power in sport* (2nd ed.). London: Blackwell Scientific.

Stone, M.H., R. Keith, J.T. Kearney, S.J. Fleck, G.D. Wilson, and N.T. Triplett. 1991b. Overtraining: A review of the signs and symptoms and possible causes of overtraining. *Journal of Applied Sport Science Research* 5: 35-50.

Stone, M.H., G. Moir, M. Glaister, and R. Sanders. 2002. How much strength is necessary? *Physical Therapy in Sport* 3: 88-96.

Stone, M.H., H.S. O'Bryant, L. McCoy, R. Coglianese, M. Lehmkuhl, and B. Schilling. 2003a. Power and maximum strength relationships during performance of dynamic and static weighted jumps. *Journal of Strength and Conditioning Research* 17: 140-147.

Stone, M.H., S. Plisk, and D. Collins. 2002. Training principles: Evaluation of modes and methods of resistance training—a coaching perspective. *Sport Biomechanics* 1: 79-104.

Stone, M.H., S. Plisk, M.E. Stone, B. Schilling, H.S. O'Bryant, and K.C. Pierce. 1998. Athletic performance development: Volume load—1 set vs multiple sets, training velocity and training variation. *Strength and Conditioning* 20(6): 22-33.

Stone, M.H., J. Potteiger, K. Pierce, C.M. Proulx, H.S. O'Bryant, R.L. Johnson, and M.E. Stone. 2000. Comparison of the effects of three different weight training programs on the 1 RM squat. *Journal of Strength Conditioning Research* 14: 332-337.

Stone, M.H., K. Sanborn, H.S. O'Bryant, M.E. Hartman, M.E. Stone, C. Proulx, B. Ward, and J. Hruby. 2003b. Maximum strength-power-performance relationships in collegiate throwers. *Journal of Strength and Conditioning Research* 17: 739-745.

Stone, M.H., N.T. Triplett-McBride, and M.E. Stone. 2001. Strength training for women: Intensity, volume and exercise factors: Impact on performance and health. In: W.E. Garret and D.T. Kirkendall (Eds.) *Women in sports and exercise* (pp. 309-328). Rosemont, IL: American Academy of Orthopaedic Surgeons.

Tan, B. 1999. Manipulating resistance training program variables to optimize strength in men: A review. *Journal of Strength and Conditioning Research* 13: 3289-3304.

Tesch, P.A. 1992a. Short- and long-term histochemical and biochemical adaptations in muscle. In: P.V. Komi (Ed.), *Strength and power in sport* (pp. 239-248). Oxford: Blackwell Scientific.

Tesch, P.A. 1992b. Training for bodybuilding. In: P.V. Komi (Ed.), *Strength and power in sport* (pp. 370-380). Oxford: Blackwell Scientific.

Tesch, P.A., and J. Karlsson. 1985. Muscle fiber types and size in trained and untrained muscles of elite athletes. *Journal of Applied Physiology* 59: 1716-1720.

Tesch, P.A., A. Thorsson, and E.B. Colliander. 1990. Effects of eccentric and concentric resistance training on skeletal muscle substrates, enzyme activities and capillary supply. *Acta Physiologica Scandinavica* 140: 575-580.

The, D.J., and L. Ploutz-Snyder. 2003. Age, body mass and gender as predictors of masters Olympic weightlifting performance. *Medicine and Science in Sports and Exercise* 35: 1216-1224.

Thorstensson, A. 1977. Muscle strength, fibre types and enzyme activities in man. *Acta Physiologica Scandinavica* (Suppl.): 443.

Thorstensson, A., B. Sjodin, and J. Karlsson. 1975. Enzyme activities and muscle strength after sprint training in man. *Acta Physiologica Scandinavica* 94: 313-318.

Tsolakis, C., D. Messinis, and S. Apostolos. 2000. Hormonal responses after strength training and detraining in prepubertal and postpubertal boys. *Journal of Strength and Conditioning Research* 14: 399-404.

Van Den Tillaar, R., and G. Ettema. 2004. Effect of body size and gender in overarm throwing performance. *European Journal of Applied Physiology* 91: 413-418.

Vanderburgh, P.M., M. Kusano, M. Sharp, and B. Nindl. 1997. Gender differences in muscular strength: An allometric model approach. *Biomedical Sciences Instrumentation* 33: 100-105.

Van Etten, L.M., F.T. Verstappen, and K.R. Westerterp. 1994. Effect of body build on weight-training-induced adaptations in body composition and muscular strength. *Medicine and Science in Sports and Exercise* 26: 515-521.

Viitasalo, J.T., and P.V. Komi. 1981. Interrelationships between electromyographic, mechanical, muscle structure and reflex time measurements in man. *Acta Physiologica Scandinavica* 111: 97-103.

Ward, N.S., and R.S. Frackowiak. 2003. Age-related changes in the neural correlates of motor performance. *Brain* 126: 873-888.

Welle, S., S. Totterman, and C. Thorton. 1996. Effect of age on muscle hypertrophy induced by resistance training. *Journal of Gerontology (Series A): Biological Sciences and Medical Sciences* 51: M270-275.

Westerland, H., D.G. Allen, and J. Lannergren. 2002. Muscle fatigue: Lactic acid or inorganic phosphate the major cause? *News in Physiological Sciences* 17: 17-21.

Wickham, J.B., and J.M.M. Brown. 1998. Muscles within muscles: The neuromotor control of intra-muscular segments. *European Journal of Applied Physiology* 78: 219-225.

Wilson, G.J., R.U. Newton, A.J. Murphy, and B.J. Humphries. 1993. The optimal training load for the development of dynamic athletic performance. *Medicine and Science in Sports and Exercise* 25: 1279-1286.

Yang, N., D.G. MacArthur, J.P. Gulbin, A.G. Hahn, A.H. Beggs, S. Easteal, and K. North. 2003. ACTN3 genotype is associated with elite athletic performance. *American Journal of Human Genetics* 73: 627-631.

Yao, W.X., A.J. Fuglevand, and R.M. Enoka. 2000. Motor unit synchronization increases EMG amplitude and decreases force steadiness of simulated contractions. *Journal of Neurophysiology* 83: 441-452.

Yaspelkis, B.B, M.K. Singh, B. Trevino, A.D. Krisan and D.E. Collins. 2002. Resistance training increases glucose uptake and transport in rat skeletal muscle. *Acta Physiologica Scandinavica* 175: 315-323.

Zajac, F.E., and M.E. Gordon. 1989. Determining muscle's force and action in multi-articular movement. *Exercise and Sport Sciences Reviews* 17: 187-230.

Zelisko, J.A., H.B. Noble, and M. Porter. 1982. A comparison of men's and women's professional basketball injuries. *American Journal of Sports Medicine* 10: 297-299.

Zeller, B.L., J.L. McCrory, W.B. Kibler, and T.L. Uhl. 2003. Differences in kinematics and electromyographic activity between men and women during the single-legged squat. *American Journal of Sports Medicine* 31: 449-456.

Zhang, B., H. Tanaka, N. Shono, S. Miura, A. Kiyonaga, A. Shindo, and K. Saku. 2003. The I allele of the angiotensin-converting enzyme gene is associated with an increased percentage of slow-twitch type I fibers in human skeletal muscle. *Clinical Genetics* 63: 139-144.

Zillmer, D.A., J.W. Powell, and J.P. Albright. 1991. Gender-specific injury patterns in high-school varsity basketball. *Journal of Women's Health* 1: 69-76.

Chapter 11

Antonini Philippe, R., R. Seiler, and W. Mengisen. 2004. Relationships of coping styles with type of sport. *Perceptual and Motor Skills* 98: 479-486.

Arent, S.M., and D.M. Landers. 2003. Arousal, anxiety, and performance: A reexamination of the inverted-U hypothesis. *Research Quarterly for Exercise and Sport* 74(4): 436-444.

Bakker, F.C., S.J. Boschker, and T. Chung. 1996. Changes in muscular activity while imagining weight lifting using stimulus or response propositions. *Journal of Sport and Exercise Psychology* 18: 313-324.

Bietz Hilton, W.L. 1997. The impact of lectures and weight training on body image dissatisfaction in a women's university conditioning course. Unpublished doctoral dissertation, University of South Dakota.

Black, G.M., E.S. Gibbons, and C. Blassingame. 1998. The relationship between weight training experience in high school athletics and physical self-efficacy in males. *1998 research abstracts.* Texas Association for Health, Physical Education, Recreation and Dance.

Bracewell, D.D., A. Dalton, M. Donnelly, T. Rhodes, J. Elliot, A.D. Martin, and R. Rhodes. 1999. Muscular strength changes in women ages 75-80 after 6 weeks of resistance training. *New Zealand Journal of Sports Medicine* 27(4): 51-54.

Collins, D. 1993-1994. Mental muscle: Psychological aspects of weight training and weight lifting. *Coaching Focus* 24: 6-7.

Cornwall, M.W., M.P. Bruscato, and S. Barry. 1991. Effect of mental practice on isometric muscular strength. *Journal of Orthopaedic and Sports Physical Therapy* 13(5): 231-234.

Dishman, R.K. 1983. Stress management procedures. In: M.H. Williams (Ed.), *Ergogenic aids in sport* (pp. 275-320). Champaign, IL: Human Kinetics.

Doyne, E.J., D.J. Ossip-Klein, E.D. Bowman, K.M. Osborn, I.B. McDougall-Wilson, and R.A. Neimeyer. 1987. Running versus weight lifting in the treatment of depression. *Journal of Consulting and Clinical Psychology* 55(5): 748-754.

Drozdowski, T., F. Feigin, I. Javorek, I. Pyka, G. Shankman, and D. Wathen. 1990. Restoration, part I. *National Strength and Conditioning Association Journal* 12(5): 20-29.

Ewart, C.K. 1989. Psychological effects of resistive weight training: Implications for cardiac patients. *Medicine and Science in Sports and Exercise* 21(6): 683-688.

Gordin, R.D., and J.P. Reardon. 1995. Achieving the zone: The study of flow in sport. In: K.P. Henschen and W.F. Straub (Eds.), *Sport psychology: An analysis of athlete behavior* (3rd ed., pp. 223-230). Longmeadow, MA: Mouvement.

Gould, D., and E. Vory. 1995. Goal setting and performance: A practitioner's guide. In: K.P. Henschen and W.F. Straub (Eds.), *Sport psychology: An analysis of athlete behavior* (pp. 213-222). Longmeadow, MA: Mouvement.

Hale, B.D. 1982. The effects of internal and external imagery on muscular and ocular concomitants. *Journal of Sport Psychology* 4: 379-387.

Hale, B.S., and J.S. Raglin. 2002. State anxiety responses to acute resistance training and step aerobic exercise across 8-weeks of training. *Journal of Sports Medicine and Physical Fitness* 42: 108-112.

Hall, C., E. Buckolz, and G.J. Fishburne. 1992. Imagery and the acquisition of motor skills. *Canadian Journal of Sports Sciences* 17(1): 19-27.

Hall, E.G., G.E. Church, and M. Stone. 1980. Relationship of birth order to selected personality characteristics of nationally ranked Olympic weightlifters. *Perceptual and Motor Skills* 51(3 Part 1): 971-976.

Hanin, Y.L. 1995. Individual zones of optimal functioning (IZOF model: an idiographic approach to performance anxiety). In: K.P. Henschen and W.F. Straub (Eds.), *Sport psychology: An analysis of athlete behavior* (3rd ed., pp. 103-119). Longmeadow, MA: Mouvement.

Hardy, L., and G. Jones. 1994. Current issues and future directions for performance-related research in sport psychology. *Journal of Sports Sciences* 12: 61-92.

Hatfield, B.D., and E.B. Brody. 1994. The psychology of athletic preparation and performance: The mental management of physical resources. In: T.R. Baechle (Ed.), *Essentials of strength training and conditioning* (pp. 163-187). Champaign, IL: Human Kinetics.

Heil, J. 1995. Imagery. In: K.P. Henschen and W.F. Straub (Eds.), *Sport psychology: An analysis of athlete behavior* (pp. 183-192). Longmeadow, MA: Mouvement.

Henderson, L.E. 1995. Effects of a weight training program on selected strength variables competitive trait anxiety and competitive state anxiety. Unpublished doctoral dissertation, Mississippi State University.

Henschen, K. 1990. Psychological readiness. In G.S. George (Ed.), *USGF gymnastics safety manual* (pp. 69-70). Indianapolis: U.S. Gymnastics Federation.

Henschen, K.P. 1995a. Attention and concentration skills for performance. In: K.P. Henschen and W.F. Straub (Eds.), *Sport psychology: An analysis of athlete behavior* (pp. 177-182). Longmeadow, MA: Mouvement.

Henschen, K.P. 1995b. Relaxation and performance. In: K.P. Henschen and W.F. Straub (Eds.), *Sport psychology: An analysis of athlete behavior* (3rd ed., pp. 163-167). Longmeadow, MA: Mouvement.

Howe, B.L. 1991. Imagery and sport performance. *Sports Medicine* 11(1): 1-5.

Ives, J.C., and G.A. Shelley. 2003. Psychophysics in functional strength and power training: Review and implementation framework. *Journal of Strength and Conditioning Research* 17(1): 177-186.

Koltyn, K.F., J.S. Raglin, P.J. O'Connor, and W.P. Morgan. 1995. Influence of weight training on state anxiety, body awareness and blood pressure. *International Journal of Sports Medicine* 16(4): 266-269.

Lidell, L. 1984. *The book of massage.* New York: Simon & Schuster.

Lovell, G., and D. Collins. 1997. The relationship between mental imagery ability and skill acquisition rate. *Journal of Sports Sciences* 15: 94.

Lyon, L.A. 1995. A comparative analysis of aerobic conditioning, resistance training and a structured stress management program in the attenuation of the adult psychophysiological response to cognitive stress. Unpublished doctoral dissertation, University of Maryland.

Marsh, H.W., and S. Kleitman. 2003. School athletic participation: Mostly gain with little pain. *Journal of Sport and Exercise Psychology* 25: 205-228.

Melnick, M.J., and S. Mookerjee. 1991. Effects of advanced weight training on body-cathexis and self-esteem. *Perceptual and Motor Skills* 72: 1335-1345.

Moore, J.B., and J.B. Bartholomew. 2003. The effect of a 10-week resistance training program on self-esteem and physical self-worth. *Journal of the Legal Aspects of Sport* 13(3): S97.

Nideffer, R.M. 1985. *Athlete's guide to mental training.* Champaign, IL: Human Kinetics.

Nideffer, R.M. 1990. Use of the Test of Attentional and Interpersonal Style (TAIS) in sport. *Sport Psychologist* 4: 285-300.

Norvell, N., and D. Belles. 1993. Psychological and physical benefits of circuit weight training in law enforcement personnel. *Journal of Consulting and Clinical Psychology* 61(3): 520-527.

Nougier, V., H. Ripoll, and J. Stein. 1989. Orienting of attention with highly skilled athletes. *International Journal of Sport Psychology* 20(3): 205-223.

Ogilvie, B.C., and K.P. Henschen. 1995. The art of application of psychological enhancing principles. In: K.P. Henschen and W.F. Straub (Eds.), *Sport psychology: An analysis of athlete behavior* (3rd ed., pp. 45-54). Longmeadow, MA: Mouvement.

O'Nan, D.A., R. Foxworth, R.B. Boling, and L.E. Henderson. 2000. Effects of weight training on selected strength and anxiety of prepubescent female gymnasts. *International Sports Journal* 4(1): 131-144.

Orlick, T. 1980. *In pursuit of excellence.* Champaign, IL: Human Kinetics.

Ossip-Klein, D.J., E.J. Doyne, E.D. Bowman, K.M. Osborn, I.B. McDougall-Wilson, and R.A. Neimeyer. 1989. Effects of running or weight lifting on self-concept in clinically depressed women. *Journal of Consulting and Clinical Psychology* 57(1): 158-161.

Phillips, E. 1988. The physiological and psychological effects of a weight training program on female adolescent anorexia nervosa sufferers. *Sport Health* 6(2): 6-12.

Selye, H. 1956. *The stress of life.* New York: McGraw-Hill.

Stoessel, L., M.H. Stone, R. Keith, D. Marple, and R. Johnson. 1991. Selected physiological, psychological and performance characteristics of national-caliber United States women weightlifters. *Journal of Applied Sport Science Research* 5(2): 87-95.

Stratton, G., M. Jones, K.R. Fox, K. Tolfrey, J. Harris, N. Mafulli, M. Lee, and S.P. Frostick. 2004. BASES position statement on guidelines for resistance exercise in young people. *Journal of Sports Sciences* 22: 383-390.

Szabo, C.P., and K. Green. 2002. Hospitalized anorexics and resistance training: Impact on body composition and psychological well-being. A preliminary study. *Eating Weight Disorders* 7: 293-297.

Taunton, J.E., M. Donnelly, E.C. Rhodes, J. Elliott, A.D. Martin, and J. Hetyei. 2002. Weight training in elderly women. *New Zealand Journal of Sports Medicine* 30(4): 106-113.

Tharion, W.J., E.A. Harman, W.J. Kraemer, and T.M. Rauch. 1991. Effects of different weight training routines on mood states. *Journal of Applied Sport Science Research* 5(2): 60-65.

Trujillo, C.M. 1983. The effect of weight training and running exercise intervention programs on the self-esteem of college women. *International Journal of Sport Psychology* 14: 162-173.

Tucker, L.A. 1982a. Effect of weight-training program on the self-concepts of college males. *Perceptual and Motor Skills* 54: 1055-1061.

Tucker, L.A. 1982b. Weight training experience and psychological well-being. *Perceptual and Motor Skills* 55: 553-554.

Tucker, L.A. 1983a. Effect of weight training on self-concept: A profile of those influenced most. *Research Quarterly for Exercise and Sport* 54(4): 389-397.

Tucker, L.A. 1983b. Weight training: A tool for the improvement of self and body concepts of males. *Journal of Human Movement Studies* 9: 31-37.

Tucker, L.A. 1987. Effect of weight training on body attitudes: Who benefits most? *Journal of Sports Medicine* 27: 70-78.

Tucker, L.A., and K. Maxwell. 1992. Effects of weight training on the emotional well-being and body image of females: Predictors of greatest benefits. *American Journal of Health Promotion* 6(5): 338-344.

Tucker, L.A., and R. Mortell. 1993. Comparison of the effects of walking and weight training programs on body image in middle-aged women: An experimental study. *American Journal of Health Promotion* 8(1): 34-42.

Van Vorst, J.G., J. Buckworth, and C. Mattern. 2002. Physical self-concept and strength changes in college weight training classes. *Research Quarterly for Exercise and Sport* 73(1): 113-117.

Vescovi, J., and B. Fernhall. 2000. Cardiac rehabilitation and resistance training: Are they compatible? *Journal of Strength and Conditioning Research* 14(3): 250-258.

Weiss, M.R. 1991. Psychological skill development in children and adolescents. *Sport Psychologist* 5(4): 335-354.

Yerkes, R.M., and J.D. Dodson. 1908. The relationship of strength of stimulus to rapidity of habit formation. *Journal of Comparative Neurology and Psychology* 18: 459-482.

Chapter 12

Abernethy, P.J., and J. Jurimae. 1996. Cross-sectional and longitudinal uses of isoinertial, isometric and isokinetic dynamometry. *Medicine and Science in Sports and Exercise* 28: 1180-1187.

Anderson, R.E., D.L. Montgomery, and R.A. Turcotte. 1990. An on-site battery to evaluate giant slalom skiing performance. *Journal of Sports Medicine and Physical Fitness* 30(3): 276-282.

Atha, J. 1983. Strengthening muscle. In: A.I. Miller (Ed.), *Exercise and sport sciences reviews* (Vol. 9, pp. 1-73). Philadelphia: Franklin Institute Press.

Augustsson, J., A. Esko, R. Thomes, and U. Svantesson. 1998. Weight training the thigh muscles using closed vs. open kinetic chain exercises: A comparison of performance enhancement. *Journal of Orthopaedic Sports Medicine and Physical Therapy* 27(1): 3-8.

Barker, M., T. Wyatt, R.L. Johnson, M.H. Stone, H.S. O'Bryant, C. Poe, and M. Kent. 1993. Performance factors, psychological factors, physical characteristics and football playing ability. *Journal of Strength and Conditioning Research* 7(4): 224-233.

Bauer, T., R.E. Thayer, and G. Baras. 1990. Comparison of training modalities for power development in the lower extremity. *Journal of Applied Sport Science Research* 4(4): 115-121.

Baumann, W., V. Gross, K. Quade, P. Galbierz, and A. Schwirtz. 1988. The snatch technique of world class weightlifters at the 1985 world championships. *International Journal of Sport Biomechanics* 4: 68-89.

Behm, D.G. 1995. Neuromuscular implications and applications of resistance training. *Journal of Strength and Conditioning Research* 9(4): 264-274.

Behm, D.G., K. Anderson, and R. Curnew. 2002. Muscle force and activation under stable and unstable conditions. *Journal of Strength and Conditioning Research* 16: 416-422.

Beynnon, D., and R.J. Johnson. 1996. Anterior cruciate ligament injury rehabilitation in athletics. *Sports Medicine* 22: 54-64.

Blackard, D.O., R.L. Jensen, and W.P. Ebben. 1999. Use of EMG in analysis in challenging kinetic terminology. *Medicine and Science in Sports and Exercise* 31(3): 443-448.

Blackburn, J.R., and M.C. Morrissey. 1998. The relationship between open and closed kinetic chain strength of the lower limb and jumping performance. *Journal of Orthopedic Sports and Physical Therapy* 27: 430-435.

Blessing, D., M.H. Stone, R. Byrd, D. Wilson, R. Rozenek, D. Pushparani, and H. Lipner. 1987. Blood lipid and hormonal changes from jogging and weight training of middle-aged men. *Journal of Applied Sport Science Research* 1(2): 25-29.

Bobbert, M.F., and G.J. van Ingen Schenau. 1990. Mechanical output about the ankle joint in isokinetic flexion and jumping. *Medicine and Science in Sports and Exercise* 22(5): 660-668.

Bosco, C., M. Cardinale, R. Colli, J. Thanyi, S.P. von Duvillard, and A. Viru. 1998. The influence of whole body vibration on jumping performance. *Biology of Sport* 15: 157-164.

Bosco, C., M. Cardinale, and O. Tsarpela. 1999. Influence of vibration on mechanical power and electromyogram activity in human arm flexor muscles. *European Journal of Applied Physiology* 79: 306-311.

Bosco, C., R. Colli, E. Introini, M. Cardinale, O. Tsarpela, O. Madella, J. Tihanyi, and A. Viru. 1999. Adaptive responses of human skeletal muscle to vibration exposure. *Clinical Physiology* 19: 183-187.

Bosco, C., M. Iacovelli, O. Tsarpela, M. Cardinale, M. Boifazi, J. Tihanyi, M. Viru, A. De Lorenzo, and A. Viru. 2000. Hormonal responses to whole-body vibration in men. *European Journal of Applied Physiology* 81: 449-454.

Bove, M., A. Nardone, and M. Schieppati. 2003. Effects of leg muscle tendon vibration on group 1a group 11 reflex responses to stance perturbation in humans. *Journal of Physiology* 550: 617-630.

Boyer, B.T. 1990. A comparison of three strength training programs on women. *Journal of Applied Sport Science Research* 4(5): 88-94.

Brill, P.A., J.C. Probst, D.L. Greenhouse, B. Schell, and C.A. Macera. 1998. Clinical feasibility of a free-weight strength-training program for older adults. *Journal of the American Board of Family Practice* 11(6): 445-451.

Brindell, G. 1999. Efficacy of three different resistance training modes on performance and physical characteristics in young women. Master's thesis, Appalachian State University.

Brzycki, M. 1994, Spring. Speed of movement an explosive issue. *Nautilus*, 8-11.

Byrd, R., K. Pierce, L. Reilly, and L. Brady. 2003. Young weightlifters' performance across time. *Sports Biomechanics* 2: 133-140.

Cabell, L., and C.J. Zebas. 1999. Resistive torque validation of the Nautilus multi-biceps machine. *Journal of Strength and Conditioning Research* 13: 20-23.

Canavan, P.K., G.E. Garret, and L.E. Armstrong. 1996. Kinematic and kinetic relationships between an Olympic-style lift and the vertical jump. *Journal of Strength and Conditioning Research* 10(2): 127-130.

Cardinale, M., and C. Bosco. 2003. The use of vibration as an exercise intervention. *Exercise and Sport Sciences Reviews* 31: 3-7.

Carlock, J., S.L. Smith, M. Hartman, R. Morris, D. Ciroslan, K.C. Pierce, R.U. Newton, E. Harman, W.A. Sands, and M.H. Stone. 2004. Relationship between vertical jump power estimates and weightlifting ability: A field-test approach. *Journal of Strength and Conditioning Research* 18: 534-539.

Chow, J.W., W.G. Darling, and J.G. Hay. 1997. Mechanical characteristics of knee extension exercises performed on an isokinetic dynamometer. *Medicine and Science in Sports and Exercise* 29(6): 794-803.

Colman, S.G.S., A.S. Benham, and S.R. Northcutt. 1993. A three-dimensional cinematographical analysis of the volleyball spike. *Journal of Sports Sciences* 11: 295-302.

Crossman, E.R.F.W. 1964. Information processes in human skill. *British Medical Bulletin* 20: 32-37.

Delecluse, C. 1997. Influence of strength training on sprint running performance. *Sports Medicine* 24: 147-156.

Delecluse, C., M. Roelants, and S. Verschueren. 2003. Strength increase after whole-body vibration compared with resistance training. *Medicine and Science in Sports and Exercise* 35: 1033-1041.

De Ruiter, C.J., R.M. Van der Linden, M.J.A. Van der Zijden, A.P. Hollander, and A. De Hann. 2003. Short term effects of whole body vibration on maximal voluntary isometric knee extensor force and rate of force rise. *European Journal of Applied Physiology* 88: 472-475.

Dillman, C.J., T.A. Murray, and R.A. Hintermeister. 1994. Biomechanical differences of open and closed chain exercises of the shoulder. *Journal of Sport Rehabilitation* 3: 228-238.

Ebben, W.P., and R.L. Jensen. 2002. Electromyographic and kinetic analysis of traditional, chain and elastic band squats. *Journal of Strength and Conditioning Research* 16: 547-550.

Faigenbaum, A., W. Kraemer, B. Cahill, J. Chandler, J. Dziados, L. Elfrink, E. Forman, M. Gaudiose, L. Micheli, M. Nitka, and S. Roberts. 1996. Youth resistance training: Position statement paper and literature review. *Strength and Conditioning* 18: 62-75.

Fitzgerald, G.K. 1997. Open versus closed kinetic chain exercise: Issues in rehabilitation after anterior cruciate ligament reconstructive surgery. *Physical Therapy* 77: 1747-1754.

Fleck, S.J., and W.J. Kraemer. 1997. *Designing resistance training programs* (2nd ed.). Champaign, IL: Human Kinetics.

Fry, A.C., D.R. Powell, and W.J. Kraemer. 1992. Validity of isometric testing modalities for assessing short-term resistance exercise strength gains. *Journal of Sport Rehabilitation* 1: 275-283.

Garhammer, J. 1981a. Equipment for the development of athletic strength and power. *National Strength and Conditioning Association Journal* 3(6): 24-26.

Garhammer, J. 1981b. *Sports Illustrated strength training.* New York: Time.

Garhammer, J.J. 1993. A review of the power output studies of Olympic and powerlifting: Methodology, performance prediction and evaluation tests. *Journal of Strength and Conditioning Research* 7: 76-89.

Gullich, A., and D. Schmidtbleicher. 1996. MVC-induced short-term potentiation of explosive force. *New Studies in Athletics* 11: 67-81.

Haff, G.G., M.H. Stone, H.S. O'Bryant, E. Harman, C. Dinan, R. Johnson, and K.H. Han. 1997. Force-time dependent characteristics of dynamic and isometric muscle actions. *Journal of Strength and Conditioning Research* 11: 269-272.

Hakkinen, K. 1994. Neuromuscular adaptation during strength training, aging, detraining and immobilization. *Critical Reviews in Physical and Rehabilitation Medicine* 6: 161-198.

Hamill, B.P. 1994. Relative safety of weightlifting and weight training. *Journal of Strength and Conditioning Research* 8: 53-57.

Harman, E. 1983. Resistive torque of 5 Nautilus exercise machines. *Medicine and Science in Sports and Exercise* 15(Suppl.): 113.

Harman, E. 1994. Resistance training modes: A biomechanical perspective. *Strength and Conditioning* 16(2): 59-65.

Harris, G.R., M.H. Stone, H. O'Bryant, C.M. Proulx, and R. Johnson. 2000. Short term performance effects of high speed, high force and combined weight training. *Journal of Strength and Conditioning Research* 14(1): 14-20.

Hildenbrand, K., and L. Noble. 2004. Abdominal muscle activity while performing trunk-flexion exercises using Ab Roller, ABslide, FitBall, and conventionally performed trunk curls. *Journal of Athletic Training* 39: 37-43.

Hollings, S.C., and G.J. Robson. 1991. Body build and performance characteristics of male adolescent track and field athletes. *Journal of Sports Medicine and Physical Fitness* 31(2): 178-182.

Issifidou, A.N., and V. Baltzopoulos. 1998. Inertial effects on the assessment of performance in isokinetic dynamometry. *International Journal of Sports Medicine* 19:567-573.

Issurin, V.B., and G. Tenenbaum. 1999. Acute and residual effects of vibratory stimulation on explosive strength in elite and amateur athletes. *Journal of Sports Sciences* 17: 177-182.

Jesse, C., D. McGee, J. Gibson, M. Stone, and J. Williams. 1988. A comparison of Nautilus and free weight training. *Journal of Applied Sport Science Research* 3(2): 59.

Johnson, C.C., M.H. Stone, R.J. Byrd, and A. Lopez-S, 1983. The response of serum lipids and plasma androgens to weight training exercise in sedentary males. *Journal of Sports Medicine and Physical Fitness*, 23: 39-41.

Johnson, C.C., M.K. Stone, A. Lopez-S, J.A. Herbert, L.T. Kilgore, and R. Byrd. 1982. Diet and exercise in middle-aged men. *Journal of the American Dietary Association*, 81: 695-701.

Kauhanen, H., J. Garhammer, and K. Hakkinen. 2000. Relationships between power output, body size and snatch performance in elite weightlifters. In: J. Avela, P.V. Komi, and J. Komulainen (Eds.), *Proceedings of the Fifth Annual Congress of the European College of Sports Science* (p. 383). Finland: University of Jyvaskala.

Kovaleski, J.E., R.H. Heitman, T.L. Trundle, and W.F. Gilley. 1995. Isotonic preload versus isokinetic knee extension resistance training. *Medicine and Science in Sports and Exercise* 27(6): 895-899.

Kraemer, W.J. 1997. A series of studies: The physiological basis for strength training in American football: Fact over philosophy. *Journal of Strength and Conditioning Research* 11(3): 131-142.

Kramer, J.B., M.H. Stone, H.S. O'Bryant, M.S. Conley, R.L. Johnson, D.C. Nieman, D.R. Honeycutt, and T.P. Hoke. 1997. Effects of single versus multiple sets of weight training: Impact of volume, intensity and variation. *Journal of Strength and Conditioning Research* 11(3): 143-147.

Leetun, D.T., M.L. Ireland, J.D. Wilson, B.T. Ballantyne, and I.M. Davis. 2004. Core stability measures as risk factors for lower extremity injury in athletes. *Medicine and Science in Sports and Exercise* 36: 926-934.

Logan, G.A. 1960. Differential applications of resistance and resulting strength measured at varying degrees of knee flexion. Doctoral dissertation, University of Southern California.

Marks, R. 1994. The effects of 16 months of angle specific isometric strengthening exercises in midrange on torque of the knee extensor muscles in osteoarthritis of the knee: A case history. *Journal of Orthopaedics and Sport Physical Therapy* 20: 103-109.

McBride, J., T. Triplett-McBride, A. Davie, and R.U. Newton. 1999. A comparison of strength and power characteristics between power lifters, Olympic lifters and sprinters. *Journal of Strength and Conditioning Research* 13: 58-66.

McBride, J.M., T. Triplett-McBride, A. Davie, and R.U. Newton. 2002. The effect of heavy versus light load jump squats on the development of strength, power and speed. *Journal of Strength and Conditioning Research* 16: 75-82.

McGee, D., T.C. Jesse, M.H. Stone, and D. Blessing. 1992. Leg and hip endurance adaptations to three different weight training programs. *Journal of Applied Sport Science Research* 6(2): 92-95.

Meadors, W.J., T.R. Crews, and K. Adeyonju. 1983, Fall. A comparison of three conditioning protocols and muscular strength and endurance of sedentary college women. *Athletic Training*, 240-242.

Medvedev, A.S., V.F. Rodionov, V. Rogozkin, and A.E. Gulyants. 1981. Training content of weightlifters in the preparation period. *Teoriya i Praktika Fizicheskoi Kultury* 12: 5-7 [translated by M. Yessis].

Messier, S.P., and M.E. Dill. 1985. Alterations in strength and maximal oxygen uptake consequent to Nautilus circuit weight training. *Research Quarterly* 56(4): 345-351.

Mester, J., P. Spitzenfeil, J. Schwarzer, and F. Seifriz. 1999. Biological reaction to vibration—implications for sport. *Journal of Science and Medicine in Sport* 2: 211-226.

Morrissey, M.C., E.A. Harman, and M.J. Johnson. 1995. Resistance training modes: Specificity and effectiveness. *Medicine and Science in Sports and Exercise* 27(5): 648-660.

Murray, D.A., and E. Harrison. 1986. Constant velocity dynamometer: An appraisal using mechanical loading. *Medicine and Science in Sports and Exercise* 18: 612-624.

Nadler, S.F., G.A. Malanga, L.A. Bartoli, J.H. Feinberg, M. Prybicien, and M. Deprin. 2002. Hip muscle imbalances and low back pain in athletes: Influence of core strengthening. *Medicine and Science in Sports and Exercise* 34: 9-16.

Nosse, L.J., and G.R. Hunter. 1985, Fall. Free weights: A review supporting their use in rehabilitation. *Athletic Training*, 206-209.

Paavolainen, L., K. Hakkinen, I. Hamalainen, A. Nummela, and H. Rusko. 1999. Explosive strength-training improves 5-km running time by improving running economy and muscle power. *Journal of Applied Physiology* 86(5): 1527-1533.

Palmitier, R.A., A. Kai-Nan, S.G. Scott, and E.Y.S. Chao. 1991. Kinetic chain exercise in knee rehabilitation. *Sports Medicine* 11(6): 402-413.

Petsching, R., R. Baron, and M. Albrecht. 1998. The relationship between isokinetic quadriceps strength test and hop test for distance and one-legged vertical jump test following anterior cruciate ligament reconstruction. *Journal of Orthopedic Sports Physical Therapy* 28(1): 23-31.

Rasch, P.J., and L.E. Morehouse. 1957. Effect of static and dynamic exercises on muscular strength and hypertrophy. *Journal of Applied Physiology* 11: 29-34.

Requa, R.K., L.N. DeAvilla, and J.G. Garrick. 1993. Injuries in recreational adult fitness activities. *American Journal of Sports Medicine* 21: 461-467.

Rittweger, J., A. Mutschelknauss, and D. Felsenberg. 2003. Acute changes in neuromuscular excitability after exhaustive whole body vibration exercise as compared to exhaustion by squatting exercise. *Clinical Physiology and Functional Immunology* 23: 81-86.

Robinson, J.M., M.H. Stone, R.L. Johnson, C.N. Penland, B.J. Warren, and R.D. Lewis. 1995. Effects of different weight training intervals on strength, power and high intensity exercise endurance. *Journal of Strength and Conditioning Research* 9: 216-221.

Roelants, M., C. Delecluse, M. Goris, and S. Verschueren. 2004. Effects of 24 weeks of whole body vibration training on body composition and muscle strength in untrained females. *International Journal of Sports Medicine* 25: 1-5.

Rutherford, O.M., and D.A. Jones. 1986. The role of learning and coordination in strength training. *European Journal of Applied Physiology* 55: 100-105.

Sale, D.G. 1988. Neural adaptations to resistance training. *Medicine and Science in Sports and Exercise* 20: S135-S245.

Sale, D.G. 1992. Neural adaptation to strength training. In: P.V. Komi (Ed.), *Strength and power in sport* (pp. 249-265). London: Blackwell Scientific.

Saunders, M.T. 1980, Spring. A comparison of two methods of training on the development of muscular strength and endurance. *Journal of Orthopaedic and Sports Physical Therapy*, 210-213.

Scala, D., J. McMillan, D. Blessing, R. Rozenek, and M.H. Stone. 1987. Metabolic cost of a preparatory phase of training in weightlifting: A practical observation. *Journal of Applied Sport Science Research* 1: 48-52.

Schmidt, R.A. 1991. *Motor learning and performance.* Champaign, IL: Human Kinetics.

Schmidtbleicher, D. 1992. Training for power events. In: P.V. Komi (Ed.), *Strength and power in sport* (pp. 381-395). London: Blackwell Scientific.

Siff, M.C. 2000. *Supertraining* (5th ed.). Denver: Supertraining Institute.

Siff, M.C., and Y.V. Verkhoshanski. 1998. Supertraining. In: *Strength training for sporting excellence* (3rd ed.). Johannesburg: University of the Witwatersrand.

Silvester, L.J., C. Stiggins, C. McGowen, and G.R. Bryce. 1982. The effect of variable resistance and free weight training programs on strength and vertical jump. *National Strength and Conditioning Association Journal* 3(6): 30-33.

Smith, D., P. Holmes, D. Collins, and K. Layland. 1998. The effect of mental practice on muscle strength and EMG activity. *Proceedings of the 1998 Annual Conference of the British Psychological Society* 22 BPS, Leicester, U.K.

Steindler, A. 1973. *Kinesiology of the human under normal and pathological conditions*. Springfield, IL: Charles C Thomas.

Stensdotter, A.K., P.W. Hodges, R. Mellor, G. Sundelin, and C. Hager-Ross. 2003. Quadriceps activation in closed and in open kinetic chain exercise. *Medicine and Science in Sports and Exercise* 35: 2043-2047.

Stone, M. 1982. Considerations in gaining a strength-power training effect. *National Strength and Conditioning Association Journal* 4(1): 22-24.

Stone, M.H. 1991. Physiological aspects of safety and conditioning. In: J. Chandler and M.H. Stone (Eds.), *United States Weightlifting Federation safety and conditioning manual*. Colorado Springs, CO: USWF.

Stone, M.H. 1993. NSCA position stance literature review: "Explosive exercise." *National Strength and Conditioning Association Journal* 15(4): 7-15.

Stone, M.H., and R.A. Borden. 1997. Modes and methods of resistance training. *Strength and Conditioning* 19: 18-24.

Stone, M.H., R. Byrd, J. Tew, and M. Wood. 1980. Relationship of anaerobic power and Olympic weightlifting performance. *Journal of Sports Medicine and Physical Fitness* 20: 99-102.

Stone, M.H., D. Collins, S. Plisk, G. Haff, and M.E. Stone. 2000a. Training principles: Evaluation of modes and methods of resistance training. *Strength and Conditioning* 22: 65-76.

Stone, M.H., S.J. Fleck, W.J. Kraemer, and N.T. Triplett. 1991. Health and performance related adaptations to resistive training. *Sports Medicine* 11: 210-231.

Stone, M.H., A.C. Fry, M. Ritchie, L. Stoessel-Ross, and J.L. Marsit. 1994. Injury potential and safety aspects of weightlifting movements. *Strength and Conditioning* 16: 15-24.

Stone, M.H., and J. Garhammer, J. 1981. Some thoughts on strength and power: The Nautilus controversy. *National Strength and Conditioning Association Journal* 3: 24-40.

Stone, M.H., R.L. Johnson, and D.R. Carter. 1979. A short term comparison of two different methods of resistance training on leg strength and power. *Athletic Training* 14: 158-160.

Stone, M.H., and K.B. Kirksey. 2000. Weightlifting. In: W.E. Garret and D.T. Kirkendall (Eds.), *Exercise and sport science* (pp. 955-964). Media, PA: Lippincott Williams & Wilkins.

Stone, M.H., and H.S. O'Bryant. 1987. *Weight training: A scientific approach*. Minneapolis: Burgess International.

Stone, M.H., H.S. O'Bryant, L. McCoy, R. Coglianese, M. Lehmkuhl, and B. Schilling. 2003. Power and maximum strength relationships during performance of dynamic and static weighted jumps. *Journal of Strength and Conditioning Research* 17: 140-147.

Stone, M.H., H.S. O'Bryant, K.C. Pierce, G.G. Haff, A.J. Koch, B.K. Schilling, and R.L. Johnson. 1999a. Periodization: Effects of manipulating volume and intensity. Part 1. *Strength and Conditioning* 21(2): 56-62.

Stone, M.H., H.S. O'Bryant, K.C. Pierce, G.G. Haff, A.J. Koch, B.K. Schilling, and R.L. Johnson. 1999b. Periodization: Effects of manipulating volume and intensity. Part 2. *Strength and Conditioning* 21(3): 54-60.

Stone, M.H., S. Plisk, and D. Collins. 2002. Training principles: Evaluation of modes and methods of resistance training—a coaching perspective. *Sport Biomechanics* 1: 79-104.

Stone, M.H., S. Plisk, M.E. Stone, B. Schilling, H.S. O'Bryant, and K.C. Pierce. 1998. Athletic performance development: Volume load—1 set vs multiple sets, training velocity and training variation. *Strength and Conditioning* 20: 22-31.

Stone, M.H., J. Potteiger, C.M. Proulx, H.S. O'Bryant, R.L. Johnson, and M.E. Stone. 2000b. Comparison of the effects of three different weight training programs on the 1 RM squat. *Journal of Strength and Conditioning Research* 14: 332-337.

Stone, M.H., M.E. Stone, M. Gattone, B. Schilling, K.C. Pierce, and R. Byrd. 2002. The use of weightlifting pulling movements in sport: International Society of Biomechanics, Coaches Information Service. www.coachesinfo.com/category/strength_and_conditioning/.

Stone, M.H., G.D. Wilson, D. Blessing, and R. Rozenek. 1983. Cardiovascular responses to short-term Olympic style weight-training in young men. *Canadian Journal of Applied Sport Science Research* 8: 134-139.

Stuart, M.J., D.A. Meglan, G.E. Lutz, G.S. Growney, and K. An. 1996. Comparison of intersegmental tibiofemoral joint forces and muscle activity during various closed kinetic chain exercises. *American Journal of Sports Medicine* 24: 792-799.

Surakka, J., S. Aunola, T. Nordblad, S. Karppi, and E. Alanen. 2003. Feasibility of power-type strength training for middle aged men and women: Self perception, musculoskeletal symptoms and injury rates. *British Journal of Sports Medicine* 37: 131-136.

Thissen-Milder, M., and J.L. Mayhew. 1991. Selection and classification of high school volleyball players from performance tests. *Journal of Sports Medicine and Physical Fitness* 31(3): 380-384.

Thomas, M., A. Fiataron, and R.A. Fielding. 1996. Leg power in young women: Relationship to body composition, strength and function. *Medicine and Science in Sports and Exercise* 28: 1321-1326.

Thorstensson, A. 1977. Observations on strength training and detraining. *Acta Physiologica Scandinavica* 100: 491-493.

Torvinen, S., P. Kannus, H. Sievanen, T.A. Jarvinen, M. Pasanen, S. Kontulainen, A. Nenonen, T.L. Jarvinen, T. Paakkala, M. Jarvinen, and I. Vuori. 2002. Effect of four-month vertical whole body vibration on performance and balance. *Medicine and Science in Sports and Exercise* 34: 1523-1528.

Torvinen, S., P. Kannus, H. Sievanen, T.A. Jarvinen, M. Pasanen, S. Kontulainen, A. Nenonen, T.L. Jarvinen, T. Paakkala, M. Jarvinen, and I. Vuori. 2003. Effect of 8-month vertical whole body vibration on bone, muscle performance and body balance: A randomized controlled study. *Journal of Bone Mineral Research* 18: 876-884.

Tunstall, H., D.R. Mullineaux, and T. Vernon. 2005. Criterion validity of an isokinetic dynamometer to assess shoulder function in tennis players. *Sports Biomechanics* 4: 101-111.

Verkhoshansky, Y.V. 1985. *Programming and organization of training.* Moscow: Fizkultura i Spovt; English: Livonia, MI: Sportivny Press, 1988 [translated by A. Charniga].

Wathen, D. 1980. A comparison of the effects of selected isotonic and isokinetic exercises, modalities and programs on the vertical jump in college football players. *National Strength and Conditioning Association Journal* 2: 47-48.

Wathen, D., and M. Shutes. 1982. A comparison of the effects of selected isotonic and isokinetic exercises, modalities and programs on the acquisition of strength and power in collegiate football players. *National Strength and Conditioning Association Journal* 41: 40-42.

Watkins, M., and B. Harris. 1983. Evaluation of isokinetic muscle performance. *Clinical Sports Medicine* 2: 37-53.

Weyand, P.G., D. Sternlight, M.J. Bellizzi et al. 2000. Faster top running speeds are achieved with greater ground forces not more rapid leg movements. *Journal of Applied Physiology* 89: 1991-1999.

Wilk, K.E., R.F. Escamilla, G.A. Fleisig, S.W. Barrentine, J.R. Andrews, and M.L. Boyd. 1996. A comparison of tibiofemoral joint forces and electromyographic activity during open and closed kinetic chain exercises. *American Journal of Sports Medicine* 24: 518-527.

Wilmore, J.H., and D.L. Costill. 1994. *Physiology of sport and exercise.* Champaign, IL: Human Kinetics.

Wilson, G.J., and A.J. Murphy. 1996. The use of isometric test of muscular function in athletic assessment. *Sports Medicine* 22: 19-37.

Wilson, G.J., R.U. Newton, A.J. Murphy, and B.J. Humphries. 1993. The optimal training load for the development of dynamic athletic performance. *Medicine and Science in Sports and Exercise* 25: 1279-1286.

Yue, G., and K.J. Cole. 1992. Strength increases from the motor program: Comparison of training with maximal voluntary and imagined muscle contractions. *Journal of Neurophysiology* 67: 1114-1123.

Zajac, F.E., and M.E. Gordon. 1989. Determining muscle's force and action in multi-articular movement. In: K. Pandolph (Ed.), *Exercise and sport science reviews* (Vol. 17, pp. 187-230). Baltimore: Williams & Wilkins.

Zaricznyj, B., L. Shattuck, T. Mast, R. Robertson, and G. D'Elia. 1980. Sports-related injuries in school-aged children. *American Journal of Sports Medicine* 8: 318-324.

Chapter 13

Abernethy, P.J., and J. Jurimae. 1996. Cross-sectional and longitudinal uses of isoinertial, isometric and isokinetic dynamometry. *Medicine and Science in Sports and Exercise* 28: 1180-1187.

Aján, T., and L. Baroga. 1988. *Weightlifting* (pp. 183-395). Budapest: International Weightlifting Federation/Medicina Publishing House.

Andren-Sandberg, A. 1998. Athletic training of children and adolescents. *Lakartidningen* 95: 4480-4484.

Asmussen, E., and F. Bonde-Petersen. 1974. Storage of elastic energy in skeletal muscles in man. *Acta Physiologica Scandinavica* 91: 385-392.

Baker, D., G. Wilson, and R. Carlyon. 1994. Periodization: The effect on strength of manipulating volume and intensity. *Journal of Strength and Conditioning Research* 8: 235-242.

Bannister, E.W. 1982. Modelling elite athletic performance. In: J.D. MacDougall, H.A. Wenger, and H.J. Green (Eds.), *Physiological testing of the high performance athlete* (pp. 403-424). Champaign, IL: Human Kinetics.

Bobbert, M.F., K.G.M. Gerritsen, M.C.A. Litjens, and A.J. van Soest. 1996. Why is countermovement jump height greater than squat jump height? *Medicine and Science in Sports and Exercise* 28: 1402-1412.

Bondarchuk, A. 1994. *Long term training for throwers* (pp. 12-20). Brisbane/Sydney: Australian Track and Field Coaches Association/Rothmans Foundation.

Bradley-Popovich, G.E., and G.G. Haff. 2001. Nonlinear versus linear periodization models [point/counterpoint]. *Strength and Conditioning Journal* 23: 42-43.

Brandenberg, J.P., and D. Docherty. 2002. The effects of accentuated eccentric loading on strength, muscle hypertrophy and neural adaptations in trained individuals. *Journal of Strength and Conditioning Research* 16: 25-32.

Bruin, G., H. Kuipers, H.A. Keizer, and G.J. VanderVusse. 1994. Adaptation and overtraining in horses subjected to increasing training loads. *Journal of Applied Physiology* 76: 1908-1913.

Chui, L.Z.F., and J.L. Barnes. 2003. The fitness-fatigue model revisited: Implications for planning short- and long-term training. *Journal of Strength and Conditioning* 25: 42-51.

Delecluse, C. 1997. Influence of strength training on sprint running performance. *Sports Medicine* 24: 147-156.

Dick, F.W. 1997. *Sports training principles* (3rd ed, pp. 253-304). London: A&C Black.

Doan, B.K., R.U. Newton, J.L. Marsit, N.T. Triplett-McBride, L.P. Koziris, D.C. Fry, and W.J. Kraemer. 2002. Effects of increased eccentric loading on the bench press. *Journal of Strength and Conditioning Research* 16: 9-13.

Edington, D.W., and V.R. Edgerton. 1976. *The biology of physical activity.* Boston: Houghton Mifflin.

Enoka, R.M. 1979. The pull in Olympic weightlifting. *Medicine and Science in Sports* 11: 131-137.

Ermakov, A.D., M.S. Abramyan, and V.F. Kim. 1980. Training load of weightlifters in pulls and squats. *Soviet Sports Review* 18(1): 33-35, 1983 [translated from *Tyazhelaya Atletika* 9: 20-22, 1980].

Ermakov, A.D., and N.S. Atanasov. 1975. The amount of resistance used in the training of high level weightlifters. *Soviet Sports Review* 18(3): 115-117, 1983 [translated from *Teoriya i Praktika Fizicheskoi Kultury* 2: 23-25, 1975].

Foster, C. 1998. Monitoring training in athletes with reference to overtraining syndrome. *Medicine and Science in Sports and Exercise* 30: 1164-1168.

Furnadzhiev, V., and I. Abadzhiev. 1982. The preparation of Bulgarian weightlifters for the 1980 Olympics. In: S.I. Lelikov et al. (Eds.), *1982 weightlifting yearbook* (pp. 83-89). Moscow: Fizkultura i Sport; English: Livonia, MI: Sportivny Press, 1984 [translated by A. Charniga, Jr.].

Fry, A.C., W.J. Kraemer, M.H. Stone, L.P. Koziris, J.T. Thrush, and S.J. Fleck. 2000a. Relationships between serum testosterone, cortisol, and weightlifting performance. *Journal of Strength and Conditioning Research* 14: 338-343.

Fry, A.C., W.J. Kraemer, M.H. Stone, B.J. Warren, S.J. Fleck, J.T. Kearney, and S.E. Gordon. 1994. Endocrine responses to overreaching before and after 1 year of weightlifting. *Canadian Journal of Applied Physiology* 19: 400-410.

Fry, A.C., J.M. Webber, L.W. Weiss, M.D. Fry, and Y. Li. 2000b. Impaired performances with excessive high-intensity free-weight training. *Journal of Strength and Conditioning Research* 14: 34-61.

Fry, R.W., A.R. Morton, and D. Keast. 1992a. Periodisation of training stress: A review. *Canadian Journal of Sport Sciences* 17: 234-240.

Fry, R.W., A.R. Morton, and D. Keast. 1992b. Periodisation and the prevention of overtraining. *Canadian Journal of Sport Sciences* 17: 241-248.

Garhammer, J.J. 1979. Periodization of strength training for athletes. *Track Technique* 73: 2398-2399.

Graham, J. 2002. Periodization research and an example application. *Strength and Conditioning Journal* 24(6): 62-70.

Gullich, A., and D. Schmidtbleicher. 1996. MVC-induced short-term potentiation of explosive force. *New Studies in Athletics* 11: 67-81.

Haff, G.G., A. Whitley, L.B. McCoy, H.S. O'Bryant, J.L. Kilgore, E.E. Haff, K. Pierce, and M.H. Stone. 2003. Effects of different set configurations on barbell velocity and displacement during a clean pull. *Journal of Strength and Conditioning Research* 17: 95-103.

Hakkinen, K. 1989. Neuromuscular and hormonal adaptations during strength and power training: A review. *Journal of Sports Medicine and Physical Fitness* 29: 9-26.

Hakkinen, K. 1994. Neuromuscular adaptation during strength training, aging, detraining and immobilization. *Critical Reviews in Physical and Rehabilitation Medicine* 6: 161-198.

Hakkinen, K., K.L. Keskinen, M. Alen, P.V. Komi, and H. Kauhanen. 1989. Serum hormone concentrations during prolonged training in elite endurance-trained and strength-trained athletes. *European Journal of Applied Physiology* 59: 233-238.

Hakkinen, K., A. Pakarinen, M. Alen, H. Kauhanen, and P.V. Komi. 1988. Neuromuscular and hormonal adaptations in athletes to strength training in two years. *Journal of Applied Physiology* 65: 2406-2412.

Harre, D., Ed. 1982. *Principles of sports training* (pp. 73-94). Berlin: Sportverlag.

Harris, G., M.H. Stone, H.S. O'Bryant, C.M. Proulx, and R.L. Johnson. 2000. Short-term performance effects of high power, high force, or combined weight-training methods. *Journal of Strength and Conditioning Research* 14: 14-20.

Hartmann, J., and H. Tünnemann. 1989. *Fitness and strength training.* Berlin: Sportverlag.

Jones, L. 1991. Do Bulgarian methods lead the way for USA? *Weightlifting USA* 9(1): 10-11.

Keizer, H.A. 1998. Neuroendocrine aspects of overtraining. In: R.B. Kreider, A.C. Fry, and M.L. O'Toole (Eds.), *Overtraining in sport* (pp. 145-167). Champaign IL: Human Kinetics.

Kipke, L. 1985. The importance of recovery after training and competitive efforts. *NZL Sports Medicine* 13: 120-128.

Komarova, A. 1984. The training loads of young throwers. *Soviet Sports Review* 20(2): 79-83 [translated from *Legkaya Atletika* 12: 3-4, 1984].

Komi, P.V., and C. Bosco. 1978. Utilization of stored elastic energy in leg extensor muscles by men and women. *Medicine and Science in Sports* 10: 261-265.

Kraemer, W.J. 2000. Physiological adaptations to anaerobic and aerobic endurance training programs. In: T.R. Baechle and R.W. Earle (Eds.)/National Strength and Conditioning Association, *Essentials of strength training* and conditioning (2nd ed., pp. 137-168). Champaign IL: Human Kinetics.

Kukushkin, G.I. 1983. The system of physical education in the USSR (pp. 128-174). Moscow: Raduga [translated by A. Zdornykh].

Leveritt, M., P.J. Abernethy, B.K. Barry, and P.A. Logan. 1999. Concurrent strength and endurance training: A review. Sports Medicine 28: 413-427.

Matveyev, L.P. 1972. Periodisierung Des Sportlichen Trainings. Moscow: Fizkultura i Sport; Berlin: Verlag Bartels and Wernitz [translated into German by P. Tschiene].

Matveyev, L. 1981. Fundamentals of sports training. Moscow: Fizkultura i Sport, 1977; Moscow: Progress [translated by A.P. Zdornykh].

Matveyev, L.P. 1992. Modern procedures for the construction of macrocycles. Modern Athlete and Coach 30(1): 32-34.

Matveyev, L.P. 1994. About the construction of training. Modern Athlete and Coach 32(3): 12-16.

McMillan, J.L., M.H. Stone, J. Sartin, R. Keith, D. Marple, C. Brown, and R.D. Lewis. 1993. 20-hour physiological responses to a single weight-training session. Journal of Strength and Conditioning Research 7(1): 9-21.

Medvedyev, A.S. 1986. A system of multi-year training in weightlifting. Moscow: Fizkultura i Sport; Livonia, MI: Sportivny Press, 1989 [translated by A. Charniga, Jr.].

Medvedev, A.S., V.I. Rodionov, V.N. Rogazyzn, and A.E. Gulyants. 1981. Training content of weightlifters in the preparatory period. Soviet Sports Review 17(2): 90-93, 1982 [translated from Teoriya i Praktika Fizicheskoi Kultury 12: 5-7, 1981].

Mujika, I., and S. Padilla. 2003. Scientific basis for precompetition tapering strategies. Medicine and Science in Sports and Exercise 35: 1182-1187.

Newton, R.U., A.J. Murphy, B.J. Humphries, G.J. Wilson, W.J. Kraemer, and K. Hakkinen. 1997. Influence of load and stretch shortening cycle on the kinematics, kinetics and muscle activation that occurs during explosive upper-body movements. European Journal of Applied Physiology 75: 333-342.

Ozolin, N.G. 1970. Souvremennaya Sistema Sportivnoy Trenirovki. Moscow: Fizkultura i Sport [cited in N.N. Schneidman, The soviet road to Olympus (pp. 110-124). Toronto, Ontario, Canada: Ontario Institute for Studies in Education, 1978].

Ozolin, N.G., and D.P. Markov. 1972. Legkaya Atletika. Moscow: Fizkultura i Sport [cited in N.N. Schneidman, The soviet road to Olympus (pp. 110-124). Toronto, Ontario, Canada: Ontario Institute for Studies in Education, 1978].

Pedemonte, J. 1986a. Foundations of training periodization. Part 1: Historical outline. National Strength and Conditioning Association Journal 8(3): 62-65.

Pedemonte, J. 1986b. Foundations of training periodization. Part 2: The objective of periodization. National Strength and Conditioning Association Journal 8(4): 26-28.

Pendlay, G., and L. Kilgore. 2001. Hormonal fluctuation: A new method for the programming of training. Weightlifting USA 19(2): 15.

Plisk, S.S. 2000a. Muscular strength and stamina. In: B. Foran (Ed.), High-performance sports conditioning (pp. 63-82). Champaign IL: Human Kinetics.

Plisk, S.S. 2000b. Speed, agility, and speed-endurance development. In: T.R. Baechle and R.W. Earle (Eds.)/ National Strength and Conditioning Association, Essentials of strength training and conditioning (2nd ed., pp. 471-491). Champaign IL: Human Kinetics.

Plisk, S., and M.H. Stone. 2003. Periodization strategies. Strength and Conditioning 25: 19-37.

Poliquin, C. 1988. Football: Five steps to improving the effectiveness of your strength training program. National Strength and Conditioning Association Journal 10(3): 34-39.

Roll, F., and J. Omer. 1987. Tulane football winter program. National Strength and Conditioning Association Journal 9: 34-38.

Rooney, K.J., R.D. Herbert, and R.J. Balnave. 1994. Fatigue contributes to the strength training stimulus. Medicine and Science in Sports and Exercise 26:1160-1164.

Ross, A., and M. Leveritt. 2001. Long-term metabolic and skeletal muscle adaptations to short-sprint training: Implications for sprint training and tapering. Sports Medicine 31: 1063-1082.

Rowbottom, D. 2000. Periodization of training. In: W.E. Garrett and D.T. Kirkendall (Eds.), Exercise and sport science (pp. 499-512). Philadelphia: Lippincott Williams & Wilkins.

Sale, D.G. 2002. Postactivation potentiation: Role in human performance. Exercise and Sport Sciences Reviews 30(3): 138-143.

Satori, J., and P. Tschiene. 1988. The further development of training theory: New elements and tendencies. Science Periodical on Research and Technology in Sport 8(4): (Physical Training W1).

Schmidtbleicher, D. 1985a, August. Strength training, part 1: Classification of methods. Science Periodical on Research and Technology in Sport (Physical Training/ Strength) W4: 1-12.

Schmidtbleicher, D. 1985b, September. Strength training, part 2: Structural analysis of motor strength qualities and its application to training. Science Periodical on Research and Technology in Sport (Physical Training/ Strength) W4: 1-10.

Schmolinsky, G. (Ed.). 1993. Track and field. Toronto: Sport Books.

Selye, H. 1956. The stress of life. New York: McGraw-Hill.

Siff, M.C. 2000. Supertraining (5th ed.). Denver: Supertraining Institute.

Stone, M.H., and A.C. Fry. 1998. Increased training volume in strength/power athletes. In: R.B. Kreider, A.C. Fry, and M.L. O'Toole (Eds.), *Overtraining in sport* (pp. 87-105). Champaign IL: Human Kinetics.

Stone, M.H., R. Johnson, and D. Carter. 1979. A short term comparison of two different methods of resistive training on leg strength and power. *Athletic Training* 14: 158-160.

Stone, M.H., R.E. Keith, J.T. Kearney, S.J. Fleck, G.D. Wilson, and N.T. Triplett. 1991. Overtraining: A review of the signs, symptoms and possible causes. *Journal of Applied Sport Science Research* 5: 35-50.

Stone, M.H., R. Keith, D. Marple, S. Fleck, and J.T. Kearney. 1989. Physiological adaptations during a one week junior elite weightlifting training camp. Presented at SEACSM meeting, Atlanta, January.

Stone, M.H., and H.S. O'Bryant. 1987. *Weight training.* Minneapolis: Bellwether Press/Burgess International Group.

Stone, M.H., and H.S. O'Bryant. 1995. Letter to the editor. *Journal of Strength and Conditioning Research* 9(2): 125-127.

Stone, M.H., H. O'Bryant, and J. Garhammer. 1981. A hypothetical model for strength training. *Journal of Sports Medicine and Physical Fitness,* 21: 342-351

Stone, M.H., H. O'Bryant, J. Garhammer, J. McMillan, and R. Rozenek. 1982. A theoretical model of strength training. *National Strength and Conditioning Association Journal,* 4(4): 36-39.

Stone, M.H., H.S. O'Bryant, B.K. Schilling, R.L. Johnson, K.C. Pierce, G.G. Haff, A.J. Koch, and M.E. Stone. 1999a. Periodization: Effects of manipulating volume and intensity. Part 1. *Strength and Conditioning Journal* 21(2): 56-62.

Stone, M.H., H.S. O'Bryant, B.K. Schilling, R.L. Johnson, K.C. Pierce, G.G. Haff, A.J. Koch, and M.E. Stone. 1999b. Periodization: Effects of manipulating volume and intensity. Part 2. *Strength and Conditioning Journal* 21(3): 54-60.

Stone, M.H., S. Plisk, and D. Collins. 2002. Training principles: Evaluation of modes and methods of resistance training—a coaching perspective. *Sport Biomechanics* 1: 79-104.

Stone, M.H., S.S. Plisk, M.E. Stone, B.K. Schilling, H.S. O'Bryant, and K.C. Pierce. 1998. Athletic performance development: Volume load—1 set vs. multiple sets, training velocity and training variation. *Strength and Conditioning* 20: 22-31.

Stone, M.H., J.A. Potteiger, K.P. Pierce, C.M. Proulx, H.S. O'Bryant, R.L. Johnson, and M.E. Stone. 2000. Comparison of the effects of three different weight-training programs on the one repetition maximum squat. *Journal of Strength and Conditioning Research* 14: 332-337.

Stone, M.H., K. Sanborn, H.S. O'Bryant, M.E. Hartman, M.E. Stone, C. Proulx, B. Ward, and J. Hruby. 2003.

Maximum strength-power-performance relationships in collegiate throwers. *Journal of Strength and Conditioning Research* 17: 739-745.

Stone, M.H., W.A. Sands, and M.E. Stone. 2004. The downfall of sports science in the United States [opinion paper]. *Strength and Conditioning Journal* 26(2): 72-75.

Stone, M.H., and D. Wathen. 2001. Letter to the editor. *Strength and Conditioning Journal* 23(5): 7-9.

Topchiyan, V.S., P.I. Kadachkova, and A.D. Komarova. 1984. Training young athletes in the yearly cycle in speed-strength and cyclical type sports. *Soviet Sports Review* 19: 157-160 [translated from *Teoriya i Praktika Fizicheskoi Kultury* 11: 47-50, 1983].

Tschiene, P. 1990. The current state of the theory of training. Adelaide: South Australian Sports Institute [translated from *Leistungssport* 20(3): 5-9, 1990].

Tschiene, P. 1992. The priority of the biological aspect in the "theory of training." Adelaide: South Australian Sports Institute [translated from *Leistungssport* 21(6): 5-11, 1992].

Tschiene, P. 1995. A necessary direction in training: The integration of biological adaptation in the training program. *Coaching and Sport Science Journal* 1: 2-14.

Tschiene, P. 1997a. Conditioning training: Formation of theory based only on adaptation models. Adelaide: South Australian Sports Institute, 1997 [translated from *Leistungssport* 26: 13-17, 1997].

Tschiene, P. 1997b. Theory of conditioning training: Classification of loads and modelling of methods from adaptation aspects. Adelaide: South Australian Sports Institute, 1998 [translated from *Leistungssport* 27(4): 21-25, 1997].

Urhausen, A., and W. Kindermann. 2000. The endocrine system in overtraining. In: M.P. Warren and N.W. Constantini (Eds.), *Sports endocrinology* (pp. 347-370). Totowa, NJ: Humana Press.

Verkhoshansky, Y.V. 1979. Principles of planning speed/strength training program in track athletes. *Legaya Athleticka* 8: 8-10.

Verkhoshansky, Y. 1981. How to set up a training program in speed-strength events. *Soviet Sports Review* 16: 123-126 [translated by M. Yessis].

Verkhoshansky, Y.V. 1986. *Fundamentals of special strength-training in sport.* Moscow: Fizkultura i Sport, 1977; Livonia, MI: Sportivny Press [translated by A. Charniga, Jr.].

Verkhoshansky, Y.V. 1988. *Programming and organization of training.* Moscow: Fizkultura i Sport, 1985; Livonia, MI: Sportivny Press [translated by A. Charniga, Jr.].

Viru, A. 1995. *Adaptation in sports training.* Boca Raton FL: CRC Press.

Viru, A., J. Loko, A. Volver, L. Laaneots, K. Karelson, and M. Viru. 1998. Age periods of accelerated improvement of muscle strength, power, speed and endurance in the age interval 6-18 years. *Biology of Sport* 15: 211-227.

Viru, A., J. Loko, A. Volver, L. Laaneots, K. Karelson, and M. Viru. 1999. Critical periods in the development of performance capacity during childhood and adolescence. *European Journal of Physical Education* 4: 75-119.

Viru, A., J. Loko, A. Volver, L. Laaneots, M. Sallo, T. Smirnova, and K. Karelson. 1996. Alterations in foundations for motor development in children and adolescents. *Coaching and Sport Science Journal* 1: 11-19.

Viru, A., and M. Viru. 2001. *Biochemical monitoring of sport training.* Champaign IL: Human Kinetics.

Vorobyev, A.N. 1978. *A textbook on weightlifting* (pp. 172-242). Budapest: International Weightlifting Federation [translated by W.J. Brice].

Wathen, D., T.R. Baechle, and R.W. Earle. 2000. Training variation: Periodization. In: T.R. Baechle and R.W. Earle (Eds.)/National Strength and Conditioning Association, *Essentials of strength training and conditioning* (2nd ed., pp. 513-527). Champaign IL: Human Kinetics.

Werchoshanski, J. 1978. Specific training principles for power. *Modern Athlete and Coach* 17(3): 11-13, 1979 [translated from *Legkaya Atletika* 1: 6-7, 1978].

Young, W.B., A. Jenner, and K. Griffiths. 1998. Acute enhancement of power performance from heavy load squats. *Journal of Strength and Conditioning Research* 12: 82-84.

Zatsiorsky, V.M. 1992. Intensity of strength training facts and theory: Russian and Eastern European approach. *National Strength and Conditioning Association Journal* 14: 46-57.

Zatsiorsky, V.M. 1995. *Science and practice of strength training.* Champaign IL: Human Kinetics.

Chapter 14

Gundlach, H., L. Hinz, K. Bartoneitz, M. Losch, J. Doit, F. Hamann, S. Hoffmann, and K-H. Schotte. 1991. Specific tests for selected distances thrown. *Leichtahletik—Wurf and Stoss.* Berlin: Sportverlag [translation in *The Thrower* (U.K.), April, pp. 24-25, 1994].

Jones, R., K. Armour, and P. Potrac. 2004. *Sports coaching cultures.* London: Routledge.

Mujika, I., and S. Padilla. 2003. Scientific basis for precompetition tapering strategies. *Medicine and Science in Sports and Exercise* 35: 1182-1187.

Stone, M.H., K. Sanborn, H.S. O'Bryant, M.E. Hartman, M.E. Stone, C. Proulx, B. Ward, and J. Hruby. 2003. Maximum strength-power-performance relationships in collegiate throwers. *Journal of Strength and Conditioning Research* 17: 739-745.

INDEX

Note: The italicized *f* and *t* following page numbers refer to figures and tables, respectively.

Michael H. Stone, PhD, is currently the director of the exercise and sports science laboratory in the department of kinesiology, leisure, and sport sciences at East Tennessee State University. Prior to this, Dr. Stone was the head of sport physiology for the United States Olympic Committee (USOC) and the chair of sport at Edinburgh University in Edinburgh, Scotland. He is also an adjunct professor at Edinburgh University; Edith Cowan University in Perth, Australia; and Louisiana State University in Shreveport.

Dr. Stone's service and research interests are primarily concerned with physiological and performance adaptations to strength and power training. He has more than 135 publications in peer-reviewed journals and has contributed chapters to several texts in the areas of bioenergetics, nutrition, and strength and power training. He helped form the National Strength and Conditioning Association (NSCA) as well as the British Strength and Conditioning Association. Dr. Stone was the 1991 NSCA Sport Scientist of the Year and was awarded the NSCA Lifetime Achievement Award in 2000. He has coached several international- and national-level weightlifters and throwers in both the United States and Great Britain.

Michael H. Stone

Meg Ritchie Stone, MS, is the director of the Sports Performance Enhancement Consortium and assistant track coach at East Tennessee State University. Stone holds the NCAA collegiate records in shot and discus and was a two-time Olympian in the discus for Great Britain. She also won a gold medal in the 1982 Commonwealth Games.

Stone was the first female to hold the position of head strength and conditioning coach at a Division I football playing institution, and she fulfilled that role at both the University of Arizona and Texas Tech. She also coached track and field at Appalachian State University, and in 1999 she returned to her native Scotland to become the national track and field coach—the first woman in Europe to hold a national coaching position. Stone has coached several international-level athletes, including four Olympians, in both the United States and Great Britain. She has also coached many athletes who later played in the NBA, MLB, and NFL. In addition, Stone has worked extensively with road cyclists and Paralympic groups through Carmichael Training Systems and the USOTC in Colorado Springs.

Meg Ritchie Stone

William A. Sands, PhD, is head of sport biomechanics and engineering for the United States Olympic Committee. He has served as senior sport physiologist at the Lake Placid Olympic Training Center as well as the physiologist for USA Track and Field and USA Diving. He has coached Olympic and world championship gymnasts and served as chair for the United States Elite Coaches Association for Women's Gymnastics. Dr. Sands is on the board of directors for the International Society of Biomechanics in Sports and is a member of the American College of Sports Medicine.

William A. Sands